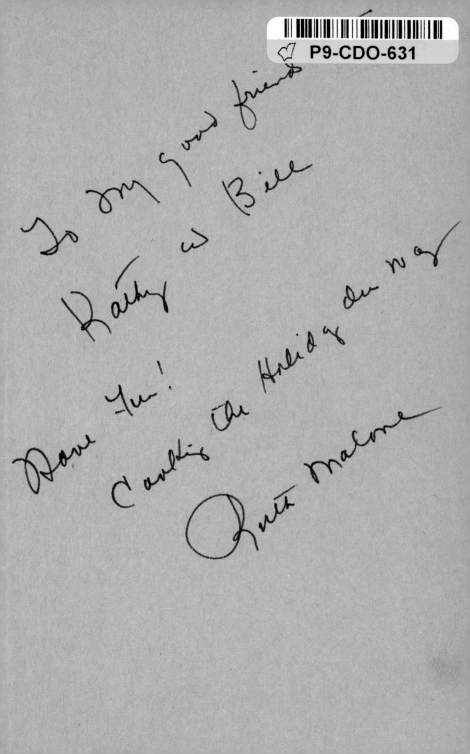

To My good friend
Kathy & Bill

Have Fun!
Reading the Holiday du now
Ruth Malone

HOLIDAY INN
INTERNATIONAL
COOK and Travel BOOK

Ruth Moore Malone

Editor

Bess Malone Lankford

Associate Editor

SEVENTH EDITION

To the memory of
Ruby "Doll" Wilson
Inspiration to the Innkeepers of the World

Have Fun! Cooking The Holiday Inn Way

Seviche from Mexico . . . Dutch Bitterballen . . . Puffed Mushrooms . . . Chicken Hors d'oeuvres from Arkansas are just starters.

You are about to embark on a gourmet trip around the world. This exciting new 7th edition includes over 1400 recipes from Holiday Inns in every state and from more than 60 foreign Inns.

For exotic meals, try recipes from Morocco or Swaziland. Serve corn bread as it is enjoyed in Virginia, Mississippi and Tennessee. Ground meat takes a gourmet step in French Meat Pie, Keeshi Yena and Canadian Tourtiere. It will take you years to try all the interesting chicken recipes. Meat Balls get in the variety act as Baked, Cocktail size, Lamb, Rice, Swedish and Italian.

Find out which Holiday Inns have revolving rooftop dining rooms or luxurious sixteen sided architecture. There's more to this book than recipes — it's a travel guide too. You can tell at a glance which Inns have a dock (should you want to arrive by boat) . . . where you can see rare white rhino in natural habitat . . . if you'll be staying near a golf course or historic sites.

You'll wonder how you ever cooked or traveled any other way.

Ruth M. Malone

Ruth M. Malone, better known as the "Cook Book Lady", is also Food Editor of The Holiday Inn Magazine. Before editing the first Holiday Inn Cook Book in 1962, Mrs. Malone was a syndicated newspaper writer, feature writer for national magazines and already had several cook books to her credit. Now 10 years, 7 editions and 4 printings later, over 120,000 copies have been sold. Holiday Inn Conferences, television and radio appearances, speaking engagements and visiting as many Holiday Inns as possible each year keep our popular "Cook Book Lady" busy. But not too busy to be a creative cook in her own kitchen — always delicious proof that she can really cook as well as write cook books.

INDEX OF
HOLIDAY INNS

INDEX OF
HOLIDAY INNS

xiii

xv

Maseru, Lesotho

Orpen Road

This Holiday Inn is actually pictured on a colorful postage stamp issued by the Lesotho government — a kingdom in southern Africa. It's an ideal vacation spot with trout fishing, snow skiing, horseback riding and beautiful scenery — even a casino at the Inn. Any drink is a favorite at the unique poolside bar in the form of a traditional thatched-roof hut. You'll enjoy shopping and seeing pottery and weaving exhibits.

TROUT MEUNIERE

    6 fresh brook trout
    ½ cup milk
       Salt and pepper
    ½ cup flour
    ½ cup butter
    2 tablespoons lemon juice
    2 tablespoons chopped parsley

Clean trout but leave heads and tails on (fins removed). Dip each fish in seasoned milk, then in flour. Shake off excess. Heat ¼ cup butter in frying pan and fry trout until they are delicately brown on each side, 6 to 8 minutes. Arrange on hot serving platter. Add rest of butter to a frying pan and brown until golden. Pour over fish. Squeeze lemon juice on top and add parsley. Serves 6.

BANANA SOUFFLE

Grease souffle dish with butter and chill. Remove and grease again, then coat with sugar. Invert pan to remove excess and chill. Cream bananas adding 3 tablespoons sugar gradually, then ½ cup whipped cream. Add 2 well beaten egg yolks. Add grated rind of 1 lemon and 2 teaspoons lemon juice. Fold in 2 stiffly beaten egg whites. Fill chilled souffle dish and set on sheet pan in 350 degree oven and cook until firm, 20 to 25 minutes. Serve with a thin custard sauce. Serves 4 to 5.

Casablanca, Morocco

Place Mohammed V

You'll be in the middle of everything in Casablanca when you stay at this Inn. It's located in the center of the city's business and shopping square — just between the ancient core formed by the old Medina and the vast modern city, with its beautiful boulevards, parks and edifices. Yet you'll be staying near enough to enjoy Casablanca's beautiful beaches and golfing facilities. Find out why the Inn's gourmet dining is becoming known throughout North Africa. Relax and listen to live entertainment in the Inn's lounge.

TAJINE
WITH PRUNES AND HONEY

    4½ pounds mutton
       Pinch ginger
       Pinch saffron
       Pinch salt
       Pepper to taste
    2 tablespoons olive oil
       Bunch coriander
    1 cinnamon stick
    1 onion
    2 pounds prunes, pitted
    2 tablespoons honey
    2 teaspoons orange flower water

In a taoua (or a large pot) boil the meat covered in water. Add ginger, saffron, salt, pepper, olive oil, coriander, cinnamon and onion. When meat is well cooked and liquid reduced to a thick sauce, remove coriander, cinnamon stick and onion. Add prunes and a few crushed sesame seeds. Simmer for 15 minutes. Then pour in honey and cook for another 15 minutes over low heat. Add orange flower water (or orange flavoring) last. Serves 8 to 10.

Fez, Morocco

Av des Far & Allal Ben Abdellah

The superb craftmanship of local artisans makes this a truly Moroccan Holiday Inn throughout. It's near the Roman Ruins at Volubilis. You'll meet people from all over the world in the Inn's popular dining room. Later, enjoy live native entertainment in the lounge. Plan to stay long enough to take advantage of the nearby hunting, fishing and skiing facilities. You'll enjoy shopping in Fez for silks, woolens, leather goods and of course, fezzes!

KAB EL GHZAL

    1 pound blanched almonds
    1 pound sugar
    1 cup water
       Orange flower water
    ¼ pound butter, unsalted
    ¾ cup sifted flour

Pound almonds in mortar until like powder. Using a saucepan, cook sugar and water to soft ball stage. Add almonds and a few drops of orange flower water (or orange flavoring). Stir until creamy and make a long sausage shape of the almond paste. Chill.

Cut stick of butter into 3 slices lengthwise. Chill in foil. Sprinkle flour and ¼ teaspoon salt over ¼ cup ice water. Blend, adding more water, if needed, to make dough into a ball. Put on lightly floured board, cover and let rest 5 minutes. Then knead at least 5 to 10 minutes, until smooth and elastic. Roll out oblong. Place pieces of butter on dough crosswise and fold dough over to cover butter. Press edges firmly together. Chill 30 minutes in foil wrapper. Take out and roll oblong shape 18x6 inches with light strokes. Fold 3 times, chill and roll out again. Chill and roll again as thin as possible. Roll dough around almond paste and make into crescent shape. Lay on baking sheet and bake in a 500 degree oven, reducing heat 50 degrees every 5 minutes, and bake until brown — about 15 to 25 minutes.

Marrakech, Morocco

Avenue de France

When the Kasbah and a world famous open air market place beckon, come to this beautiful Holiday Inn. Discover a wonderful way to vacation in French Morocco, nestled in the northern foothills of the Grand Atlas. Arrive by plane, boat or car. The Inn is only ½ mile from downtown, 1½ miles from the airport. Native dishes as well as American fare are offered in the dining room. There's live entertainment in the Golf and Ski Lounge.

DJAJ BILOUZ

    1 3- to 4-pound roasting chicken
    2 tablespoons butter (or oil)
    ½ cup Marinade
    1 to 1½ cups water
    5 to 6 onions, sliced
    1 tablespoon saffron
    1½ cups blanched almonds, slivered
    1 to 2 tablespoons flour

Cut up chicken in serving pieces. Marinate for 20 to 30 minutes in Marinade (below). Remove and place in a heavy heatproof casserole. Sauté in 2 tablespoons butter. Add leftover marinade and cook over low heat for 10 minutes. Add water and simmer over low heat until tender. Use more water if needed. Stir to keep chicken from sticking. Add sliced onions, saffron and almonds. Simmer 20 minutes. Dissolve 1 tablespoon flour in ¼ cup water and add to juices after chicken has been removed. Cook until thickened. Place chicken on serving platter and arrange vegetable on platter. Pour sauce over all. Serves 6.

Marinade

    ⅓ cup cooking oil
    ½ teaspoon pepper
    1 teaspoon salt
    4 tablespoons coriander
    ½ teaspoon ginger
    ⅓ cup minced parsley
    1 finely minced onion

Mix all ingredients.

Tangier, Morocco

Bay of Tangier at Malabata

A private beach and yacht club plus tennis, golf and horseback riding facilities make this Holiday Inn a perfect resort spot on the bay. You're sure to enjoy the native dishes in the dining room. And there's live entertainment in the lounge. Downtown Tangier is only 5 miles away. Take time to wander along the narrow native streets. Tangier has all the charm of an old Moorish town with the beauty of a modern port. From the sea, it resembles a huge amphitheater, with rows of white houses lining the hillsides.

MILK OF ALMONDS

3½ cups blanched almonds
1¼ cups sugar
2 quarts water
Orange flower water (or orange flavoring)

Pound the almonds into a smooth paste. Dilute the sugar with the water and blend with almond paste. Pass through a firm sieve. Flavor with orange flower water to tartness desired. Serve iced and cool. 2½ quarts.
On feast days, this is the drink of the rich bourgeois.

HARIRA

1 pound mutton
1 quart boiling water
2 tablespoons butter
¾ cup cooked rice
¾ cup cooked chick peas
1 sprig parsley, chopped
Pinch saffron
Salt and pepper

Cut mutton in small pieces and roll into balls. Place in pot of boiling water. Add butter and simmer 2 hours. Add remaining ingredients. Cook and stir often until the mixture boils again. Then cook 10 minutes. Serve very hot in rice bowls. Serves 6 to 8.

Ermelo, South Africa

Kerk Street

Ermelo, a typical South African town, is a convenient stopover on route to some of South Africa's finest game reserves. It's near the Swaziland border. Residents are predominately Afrikaans-speaking. Be sure to order "Melktert" with your coffee at this Holiday Inn. No cup of coffee is complete in South Africa without this tasty tart, literally translated as "Milk Tart".

MELKTERT
(Milk Tart)

1 cup butter
2 cups flour
Pinch salt
1 cup sour cream

Chop butter into flour and salt. Add sour cream and roll out on a floured board. Place in pie pan and bake at 450 degrees until brown. Makes 2 regular pies or 1 large pie.

Filling

1½ tablespoons flour
1½ tablespoons corn flour
Pinch salt
3 cups milk
1 tablespoon butter
4 eggs
6 tablespoons sugar

Mix flour, corn flour (cornstarch) and salt to a smooth paste with a little cold milk. Boil milk and add butter. Keep boiling and add flour mixture, stirring continuously to avoid lumps. Separate egg yolks from whites. Blend well beaten yolks, sugar and add vanilla flavoring to mixture. Add to milk mixture. Cook until **quite thick,** adding more sugar if sweeter custard is desired. Cool well. Fold in stiffly beaten egg whites, pour mixture into pie case, cover with cinnamon and cool until set. Filling for 2 pies.

Hluhluwe, South Africa

Outskirts of Hluhluwe Village

Wild animals live unhindered in their natural habitats all around this quaint Inn. On nearby False Bay, giant crocodiles bask in the sun. Rare white rhinoceros live in the Hluhluwe Game Reserve only 7 miles away. You're in luck if you're here for a "Braaiveis" . . . the South African version of a barbecue. Hluhluwe, pronounced "Shloo-shloo-wee", means "sweet waters" in the Zulu language. Legend has it that the word was originally the Zulu interpretation of the sound made when a hippopotamus lifts its feet out of the mud.

SOSATIES

1 leg of mutton
1 pound pork
4 large onions
2 tablespoons curry powder
½ teaspoon tumeric
2 tablespoons flour
2 tablespoons sugar
1 tablespoon coconut
1 tablespoon black pepper
   Salt
2 cups vinegar
2 cups water
½ cup stewed dried apricots
½ cup raisins
4 bay leaves

Cut the meat from the bones into small cubes. Cut onions in slices and fry in 2 tablespoons oil. Mix curry, tumeric, flour, sugar, coconut, pepper, salt, vinegar and water with onions. Add apricots and raisins and cook for 5 minutes. Add bay leaves last. Pour sauce over meat to cover all cubes. Leave for 3 days, stirring mixture a few times each day. Put pieces on skewers alternating lamb and pork and apricots. Cook over coals and grill slowly. 10-pound leg serves 12.

Mbabane, Swaziland

Main Rd. betw. Mbabane & Manzini

The Swaziland Holiday Inn is part of a complex which includes the Royal Swazi Casino, a championship 18-hole golf course and a natural health spa with hot mineral springs — even a health and beauty club! The thatch-roofed circular outdoor bar by the swimming pool is just one unique feature of this Inn. Zulu dancing and an adjoining game reserve are other exciting extras. Visit the Swazi market.

IMPALA
(African Antelope)

1 leg impala (or venison)
4 cloves garlic, slivers
½ pound bacon, slivers
1 jar olives, stuffed with anchovies
2 tablespoons cooking oil
3 potatoes, diced
3 carrots, diced
4 onions, minced
8 prunes, pitted

Wash meat and wipe dry. Remove lower shank bone and cook in pan with a little water for broth. Using a sharp knife, cut slits in meat and insert garlic, bacon and halves of olives. Season meat with salt and pepper, adding a pinch of spices. Place in pan with oil and cook at 325 degrees (25 to 35 minutes a pound). When done, remove to warm platter. Sauté vegetables in butter, add prunes and cook until done. Strain and add to juices left in pan. Add broth to make gravy. Pour warm brandy over meat and flame when serving. 10 to 16 servings.

BANANA AND CORN CASSEROLE

Wrap 4 peeled bananas in 4 slices bacon. Grill until tender. Pour off extra fat and place in a casserole. Season and heat 2 cups whole grain cooked corn. Thicken with 2 teaspoons maizena (cornmeal) mixed with a little cold water. Pour over bananas and sprinkle with bread crumbs. Bake 15 minutes in 350 degree oven. 4 servings.

Brussels, Belgium Airport

Hwy. Brussels-Brussels Airpt.

"Goedendag"! A Flemish hello is a familiar word around this friendly Holiday Inn. The 9 Provinces Restaurant derives its name from the nine provinces of Belgium. Besides American cuisine, it features some excellent Belgian dishes. The Waterloo Lounge is a great place to meet local people — everyone enjoys the live entertainment here. Downtown Brussels is only 10 minutes away.

BRAISED BELGIAN ENDIVE

Heat 4 tablespoons butter in casserole. Place 12 endives in casserole in 2 layers, depending on size of casserole. Sprinkle with salt and pepper, lemon juice and enough water to barely cover. Place buttered paper on top of endives and cover casserole. Cook in a slow oven until moisture evaporates and butter begins to brown. Add ½ cup demi-glace (thin brown sauce). Then brown endives briefly under broiler, adding a little more butter to make them golden. Serves 6.

FLEMISH CARBONADES

2½ pounds round steak
2 onions, sliced thin
12 ounces beer
½ teaspoon thyme
2 bay leaves
1 cup demi-glace

Cut meat into 6 steaks and dredge in seasoned flour. Add 3 tablespoons shortening to a heavy skillet and sauté steaks until brown on both sides. Remove meat and add onions to skillet. Sauté until light brown. Place layer of onions, then meat, then onion in a heat proof casserole. Add beer and bring to a boil. Add thyme, bay leaves, salt, pepper and demi-glace (thin brown sauce). Simmer about 1½ hours. Thicken, if sauce is thin. 6 servings.

Leicester, England

Applegate & St. Nicholas Sts.

Where else could you stay in the heart of downtown, atop Roman ruins nearly two thousand years old? You can look out your bedroom window on the gardens where the actual layout of the Roman settlement of Ratae Coritanorum is still plainly visible. Enjoy the best of English and Scottish ales in the traditional English pub. The Tail O' the Fox restaurant offers an international menu fit for a gourmet.

OLD RENNY'S FAVORITE

1 poussin (1-pound chicken)
4 tablespoons minced shallots
2 tablespoons minced green pepper
⅛ teaspoon fennel
½ cup uncooked rice
1 cup chicken stock

Prepare a risotto (rice cooked in broth) using the shallots, green pepper, fennel, rice and chicken stock. When cooked, use as a stuffing in the chicken. Place the stuffed chicken on a bed of chopped carrot (4 tablespoons), chopped onion (4 tablespoons) and ⅛ teaspoon fennel. Season with salt and pepper. Cook in a moderately hot oven for about 20 minutes. When cooked, remove chicken from pan.
Add 1 cup chicken stock to the extract left in the pan chicken was cooked. Reduce liquid to one-half over heat. Pour over chicken. Flame with a dash of warm brandy. Serves 1 to 2.

NOODLES ST. NICHOLAS

Prepare 1 pound noodles and keep warm. Melt ¼ cup butter in pan and sauté ¼ cup minced onion, ¼ crushed garlic clove, 1 diced green pepper and 1 cup chopped pork. Add ¾ cup veloute sauce (seasoned butter, flour and veal stock). Then add 1 or 2 ground peppercorns, a little minced parsley and salt. Simmer for about 5 minutes. Add ¼ cup cream and blend until smooth. Pour over noodles and serve. Serves 8.

Plymouth, England

Armada Way

This beautiful Holiday Inn is a reality of the present, located on soil of a famous past. Plymouth has been known as a harbor of hospitality since the pilgrims sought refuge here in 1620, enroute from the Netherlands to America. Overlooking the harbor, the Inn preserves England's fine old Innkeeping tradition. Historical sights are within walking distance. Rooftop dining offers a view of the Sound.

ENGLISH PLUM PUDDING

    2   cups suet
    2   cups sugar
    4   cups stale bread crumbs
    1   teaspoon cloves
    1   teaspoon cinnamon
    2   teaspoons cream of tartar
    1   cup flour
    2   cups currants
    1   pound raisins, cut fine
    ¼   pound citron, cut fine
    ½   pound figs, cut fine
    7   eggs, beaten
    1   cup milk
    1   teaspoon soda
    1   cup whiskey or wine

Grind or grate suet. Mix sugar, bread crumbs, spices, cream of tartar and flour. Combine with suet and fruit. Add eggs, one at a time, and mix thoroughly. Let stand overnight. In the morning, combine milk and soda and stir into mixture. Add whiskey and mix thoroughly.
Grease molds, then sprinkle with sugar. Fill each ⅔ full. Place in steamer over boiling water. Cover and use high heat first. Then lower heat and steam 6 to 8 hours, adding more boiling water, as needed. Serve with Wine Sauce. Serves 18 to 24.

Wine Sauce

Beat 2 eggs until light and gradually add 1 cup sugar. Add 2 tablespoons wine. Fold in 1 cup whipped cream and serve.

Hannover, Germany Airport

On airport grounds

The airport terminal is within walking distance, but the Inn offers free transportation too. Downtown Hannover is only 5 minutes away. Guests coming for the annual Hannover Industrial Fair (the biggest of its kind in the world) find this Inn a most convenient place to stay. An indoor swimming pool and live entertainment are enjoyable extras. And on the menu, you can expect specialties of Germany as well as traditional American favorites.

HERRING IN SOUR CREAM

    12 herring fillets
    1   pint sour cream
    2   teaspoons chopped chives
    3   tablespoons vinegar
    2   onions, sliced
    1   teaspoon freshly ground pepper
    1   bay leaf
    1   tablespoon lemon juice
    1   tablespoon olive oil

Wash fillets and drain. Cut into squares. Combine remaining ingredients for a marinade. Place fillets in a heavy bowl with a top. Place marinade over them, cover and refrigerate for 8 to 10 hours. Serve as hors d'oeuvres with Melba toast. Serves 8 to 12.

GERMAN POTATO SALAD

Wash 1½ pounds small new potatoes and drop in boiling water to cover. Cook until tender, from 15 to 20 minutes. Drain and cool thoroughly before peeling and slicing. Slice thin. Season with salt and pepper. Slice 3 green onions and add to potatoes. Then add 2 tablespoons sugar. Cut 3 slices of bacon in small pieces and fry until crisp. Pour hot bacon and grease from bacon over potatoes. Add 2 tablespoons vinegar last (use apple cider vinegar). Mix gently and sprinkle with minced parsley. Before serving, warm just enough so grease is not hard in salad. Serves 5 to 6.

Munich, Germany

It's worth a trip to Germany just to visit this Inn's "Yellow Submarine" . . . the sensation of Munich's night life. It's a gigantic salt water tank with 30 live sharks — you enter the lounge through an underwater tunnel and eye the sharks through large plate glass windows and portholes. The luxurious Inn is near just about everything too — including Schwabing (the "Left Bank" in Munich). Gourmet food (even shark steaks) and English speaking employees make Munich's Inn a must.

BAVARIAN CARAWAY ROAST
(Bayerischer Kümmelbraten)

1 2½-pound pork shoulder
1 onion, chopped
1 carrot, chopped
1 stalk celery, chopped

Remove meat from bone and saw bone in pieces. Rub meat with caraway seeds, salt, pepper and add to the bones in a roasting pan. Cook in a little fat over high heat until brown, then roast in oven at 350 degrees (45 minutes per pound). Baste regularly with its own juice and turn. About ½ hour before roast is done, add vegetables and brown. After roast is done, remove from pan and make a brown sauce from vegetables and bones by passing through a cheesecloth. Add a bit of cornstarch and cook again with 1 tablespoon caraway seeds. Serve with Bread Dumplings. Serves 4.

Bread Dumplings
(Semmelknödel)

Pour 2½ cups milk over 2 pounds thinly cut stale hard bread (rolls). Brown ½ cup chopped onion in 1 tablespoon butter until golden. Mix with 2 tablespoons finely chopped parsley, salt, pepper, nutmeg and grated lemon peel. Combine bread mixture with 4 beaten egg yolks and add to seasonings. Form round dumplings. Simmer for 20 minutes in boiling salted water.

Walldorf-Heidelberg Germany

Heidelberg is only minutes away from this Inn. Take time to visit its lovely old castle and of course, the picturesque University of Heidelberg. Back at the Inn you'll almost expect to hear the voices of the Student Prince and his friends as you lift your mug of German beer. Do try the excellent sausages too. When in Germany, dip them into mustard before every bite! Why not make this Inn your headquarters while in Germany — Frankfurt and Stuttgart are only 45 minutes away.

WIENER SCHNITZEL

4 6-ounce veal cutlets
  Flour
1 egg, beaten
1 teaspoon minced parsley
2 tablespoons Parmesan cheese
¼ teaspoon grated nutmeg
½ cup milk
2 tablespoons butter
1 tablespoon vegetable oil
1 tablespoon lemon juice
1 cup hot water
4 lemon slices

Wipe cutlets with damp cloth and pound until very thin. Dip in seasoned flour. Blend 2 tablespoons flour with egg, parsley, cheese, nutmeg and milk. Coat cutlets with this mixture.

Heat butter and vegetable oil in a heavy frying pan. Brown cutlets about 3 minutes on each side. Remove to hot serving plate. Make sauce by adding lemon juice and hot water to particles left in pan. Thicken with flour-water paste, if too thin. Serve cutlets with a slice of lemon atop each and sauce separately. Serves 4.

Luxembourg

Luxembourg-Kirchberg

Stay a stone's throw from the European Common Market Administrative Center. Take a historical trip into the past right in this Inn. For gourmet fare, step into Trois Glands — named for the acorn-shaped roofs of the fortress Thüngen. Order the Inn's drink of the month in the Kiem (meaning Roman Road from Reims to Tier). The Bock is the coffee shop. There's an indoor pool for year'round swimming, a golf course only minutes away.

NEPTUNE'S MUSTACHE

Take a champagne glass (flute). Put a cherry on the bottom and fill with crushed ice. Then add 2 bar spoons of creme de menthe (green) and a short jigger of cognac (or brandy). Serve with a straw and stirrer for a drink as refreshing as ocean diving.

TOURNEDOS "NOCTAMBULE"

    2 7-ounce tenderloin steaks
    1 ounce cognac (brandy)
    3 tablespoons butter
    6 minced shallots
   12 sliced mushrooms
    1 ounce porto
    1 cup cream
    2 slices goose liver pie (with truffles)

Season steak with salt, pepper and paprika. Sauté on each side and flame, using the brandy. Remove steak from pan. Then add the butter, shallots and mushrooms, one at a time. When a nice brown color, add the porto, a pinch of salt and the cream. Garnish steaks with goose liver pie, and cover the whole with the mushroom cream sauce.
Serve with croquette potatoes, French fries, rice or buttered noodles and green beans or a fresh salad. 2 servings.

Leiden, Holland

On Expressway nr. 4 between The Hague and Amsterdam

Holland's tulip fields are all around and the North Sea with its fine sand beaches is not far. A menu in four languages (Dutch, German, French and English) is used in the Dutch Mill Restaurant. Lively Dutch songs prevail in the Pirate Ship Bar overlooking the Inn's indoor swimming pool. Don't forget to ask for the famous "Bitterballen" with your Dutch Beer. The center of The Hague is only 15 minutes away.

BITTERBALLEN

    4 tablespoons butter
    1 medium onion, minced
    3 tablespoons flour
    1 cup beef stock
    2 cups cooked beef, chopped
    1 egg, beaten

Melt butter in small frying pan and sauté onion. Mix in flour until smooth. Add beef stock and thicken. Set aside until roux is cold. Add beef and season. Shape into 1-inch balls. Roll in fine dry bread crumbs, then in beaten egg. (Add a small amount of water to thin egg if necessary). Dip balls in bread crumbs again. Fry in deep fryer at about 400 degrees for 1 to 2 minutes. Drain on paper towels and serve piping hot. Place a toothpick in the middle of each ball and serve with mustard in a small side dish.

SOLE "NORTH SEA"

Prepare 1 sole of 6-8 ounces for each person. Wash fish fillets and season with salt. Shake in flour. Fry soles in butter in medium thick frying pan. Turn once while cooking so each side will be firm and golden. For sauce, combine in second frying pan: 1 minced onion, ½ cup minced celery, ½ cup thinly sliced mushrooms, ½ cup freshly cooked oysters and ½ cup small cooked shrimp. Sauté in 4 tablespoons butter until tender, adding 4 slices of tomato last. Season and pour over fish when serving. Sauce for 6 servings.

Utrecht, Holland

Jaarbeursplein 24

Come aboard! Slip into an authentic old train seat from the thirties in the Inn's "Railroad" cocktail lounge. A miniature train makes the rounds on the counter. (Utrecht is the headquarters of the Dutch Railroad Company). You'll be glad you made this Inn your headquarters. Go Dutch — in the "Utrecht House" restaurant. Enjoy a dip in any weather — there's an indoor pool. You'll be staying adjacent to the convention and exhibition center.

CHARLOTTE "UTRECHT HOUSE"

Using a 2-quart mold or a high straight pudding or gelatin mold, chill and line with a round of buttered waxed paper. Then line bottom with a spoke design of lady fingers (rounded side out). Place 1 row of lady fingers standing up around mold. Pour Semolina Pudding into mold to height of lady fingers. Let congeal in refrigerator. When chilled, repeat row of lady fingers around mold and add rest of pudding to cover lady fingers. Cover with foil and refrigerate overnight. When serving, loosen pudding and turn out on a chilled platter. Pour Orange Cream over pudding and decorate with candied cherries. 8 to 10 servings.

Semolina Pudding

Boil 2 quarts milk and 2 teaspoons vanilla. Combine 1⅓ cups farina, 4 tablespoons cornstarch, ½ cup sugar and pinch of salt. Add to milk mixture and stir vigorously until thickened. Lower heat and add 3 tablespoons butter and 3 egg yolks, one at a time. Cool. Fold in 3 stiffly beaten egg whites and 2 tablespoons grated orange peel.

Orange Cream

Combine 1 cup orange juice and 1 cup sugar. Cook over low heat until syrupy. Add ½ cup orange liqueur. Cool. Fold in 1 pint half whipped cream.

Calgary, Alberta, Can.

8th Ave. at 6th St. S.W.

Most of the stories told in the Smugglers Den lounge here are true. This is the heart of North America's finest hunting area. The Iron Gate dining room's gourmet delight is the Black Forest Platter . . . roast duck, chicken, filet mignon, pork tenderloin, bacon, mushrooms, rice and potatoes served on a flaming platter. There's underground heated parking too.

CHUCK WAGON STEW
(Calgary's Official Dish)

2 tablespoons cooking oil
2½ pounds rump of beef
2 large onions, chopped
    Salt and pepper to taste
½ teaspoon M.S.G.
⅓ teaspoon paprika
2 tablespoons flour
⅔ cup plum tomatoes
    Bouquet garni
1 quart good brown stock
1 teaspoon Worcestershire sauce
½ cup or more beer (optional)
1 cup medium-size mushrooms

Heat oil in the pan until slightly smoking. Cube meat. Arrange meat cubes and put in a preheated 400 degree oven for 15 minutes, shaking pan occasionally so meat can brown on all sides. Add onions, salt, pepper, M.S.G., paprika and sprinkle with flour. Continue cooking another 20 minutes, stirring occasionally. Add tomatoes, bouquet garni, stock, Worcestershire sauce, beer and mushrooms. Cover pan, reduce heat to 300 degrees and continue cooking until meat is tender. Then arrange stew in casseroles. Place biscuit dough crust over stew and seal tightly in order to keep all flavor in. Brush the tops with milk and bake 15 minutes in a hot oven. Serves 6.

Corner Brook Nfld., Can.

West St. at Tod St.

The world's finest salmon fishing streams are only a few miles away. This distinguished Inn is located in downtown Corner Brook and offers an unrivaled view of the city, the Humber River and the entire valley. You can expect seafood from the ocean's depths in the Humber Room. The Viking Lounge decor revives Newfoundland's history.

POACHED SALMON

4 salmon steaks
1 lemon, thinly sliced
1 onion, chopped
3 tablespoons salt

Place salmon steaks into boiling water with other ingredients and simmer for 20 minutes. Serves 4.

LOBSTER SALAD

2 lobsters, cooked and diced
¼ cup diced celery
1 chopped onion
½ cup mayonnaise
Pinch salt & pepper

Combine ingredients in a bowl and place salad in empty lobster shells. Serves 6.

HOT SPONGE CAKE

3 eggs
1 cup sugar
1 cup all purpose flour
1 teaspoon baking powder
6 tablespoons hot milk

Beat eggs, add sugar and beat thoroughly. Combine with sifted flour and baking powder. Add hot milk. Line a jelly roll pan with wax paper. Pour in batter and bake in a 350 degree oven for 25 minutes. Turn out on a cooling rack. Remove wax paper. Fill as desired and roll or cut in squares and top with fruit.

Gander, Nfld., Can.

Trans-Canada Hwy.

Meet people from all over the world at the "Crossroads of the World". The Gander International Airport is known all over the world for its importance to transatlantic air travel. This Inn is only 5 minutes from the airport. Visitors and local people meet in the Inn's congenial cocktail lounge. The Newfoundland Fish Chowder is a favorite on the menu in the adjoining dining room. Salmon is king in the Gander River. Moose, caribou and bear roam the surrounding forrest.

NEWFOUNDLAND FISH CHOWDER

1 pound fresh or frozen fillet of Newfoundland cod
½ cup chopped onion
½ cup diced celery
2 tablespoons butter or oil
1½ cups raw potatoes, diced
½ cup raw carrots, sliced
1½ cups boiling water
1 heaping teaspoon salt
1½ cups milk, scalded

Cut cod into bite-size pieces. Sauté onion and celery in butter or oil. Add potatoes, carrots, water and salt. Simmer until vegetables are tender. Add fish and cook 10 minutes longer. Add scalded milk and stir until well blended. Serves 6 to 8.

St. John's, Nfld., Can.

Portugal Cove Rd.

Stay at the very beginning of the Trans-Canada Highway. Your views from the Inn include the Provincial Government Offices, Kenny's Pond and the Atlantic Ocean. Sightseeing tours, big game hunting and tuna fishing may be arranged at the Inn. A ship's deck with all its rigging fascinates guests in the Matthew Room while they enjoy delicacies from the sea. There's a lot of talk under old guns and skins in the Sealers Lounge.

FRESH FLIPPER PIE

6 flippers
1 pound salt pork, sliced
6 large onions, diced
1 large turnip, diced
6 carrots, diced
1 stalk celery, diced

Skin seal flipper of all excess fat and parboil in salted water for 30 minutes. Remove seal flipper from salt water, make ready a roasting pan with salt pork and 1 sliced onion and roast at 350 degrees until golden brown. Remove the flipper from the pan and add stock. Place the vegetables in the pan (onions, turnip, carrots and celery). Let simmer until partly cooked, then add ½-¾ cup brown sauce. Add flippers and cook until tender. Make a baking powder pastry (fluffy pastry) and put on top. Keep in oven until pastry is baked (450 degrees for 15 to 20 minutes). Serves 8-10.

FISH CHOWDER

Poach 1 pound of halibut and 1 pound of cod in frying pan 1 inch deep with water. Heat water to just below boiling point, add fish and cook gently until fish flakes when tried with a fork. Strain fish bouillon in another pot, add flaked fish, 1 pound of clams and 1 pound of scallops. Simmer 15 minutes more, adding more water. Add 6 diced carrots, 8 diced onions and a few leeks. Simmer until tender. Season. Serves 8 to 10.

Barrie, Ont., Can.

Hwys. 400 & 27, Essa Rd. Exit

If you have reservations about fun where it's freezing, make reservations at this Inn. It's in one of the most popular winter sports areas. Skiing, curling, snowmobile races, ice skating and ice fishing are at their best here. And it's fun during the summer months too. Sightseers enjoy the nearby Historical Museum and Fort St. Marie. Sauna baths, excellent food and service, and a lounge featuring top entertainment complete the picture here.

BEEF PEPPER POT

8 slices cold roast beef
2 medium onions, sliced
8 cold boiled potatoes, sliced
   Salt and pepper to taste
2 quarts beef stock
   (or beef bouillon)

Place in buttered casserole or baking dish a layer of beef slices, then add a layer of sliced onions. Cover them with a layer of potatoes. Season with salt and pepper. Cover with beef stock and cook at 350 degrees for 1½ hours. If gravy needs thickening, add flour and water paste (2 tablespoons flour and ¼ cup water). Stir in casserole the last half hour of baking. Serves 8.

HOT BUTTERED RUM
(An After Skiing Favorite)

2 ounces dark rum
1 twist lemon peel
1 stick cinnamon
1 to 2 cloves
   Boiling cider
   Butter

Place rum, lemon peel, cloves and cinnamon in a pewter tankard or heavy mug. Fill with boiling cider. Float a pat of butter on top and stir well.

Brantford, Ont., Can.

Hwy. 403 and Park Road

Brantford is near Tutela Heights, where Alexander Graham Bell lived, invented the telephone and made the first long distance call to Paris (5 miles away) in 1876. His house is now a museum and open to the public. Visitors to Brantford also enjoy the Scottish Highland Games each autumn and the Six Nations Indian Reserve. Back at the Inn there's live entertainment in the lounge and superb food in the dining room.

POTTED STEAK

4 6-ounce Swiss steaks
  Salt
  Pepper
1 tablespoon butter
⅓ cup baby carrots, diced
⅓ cup little round potatoes
⅓ cup turnips, sliced
⅓ cup cherry tomatoes
2 cups beef stock

Season steaks with salt and pepper. Sauté in heavy frying pan with butter. After steaks have browned, place in casserole (top of stove type) with tight fitting lid. Before closing, add vegetables, then pour in beef stock. Cover and simmer for 30 minutes. Serves 4.

INDIAN PUDDING

1 quart scalded milk
½ teaspoon salt
¾ cup Indian corn meal (yellow)
1½ teaspoons ginger
½ cup molasses
1 egg, beaten
1 tablespoon butter

Combine scalded milk and salt. Add corn meal and ginger. Let stand 20 minutes. Add remaining ingredients and pour in a buttered baking dish. Bake 2 hours at 250 degrees. Let stand ½ hour. Serve with cream or ice cream, if desired. Serves 6.

Chatham, Ont., Can.

25 Keil Fr. N. & Grand Ave.

Just 3 minutes from downtown and on the shores of the Thames River, this Inn boasts a large outdoor recreational area. There's a pool, stone barbecue and dance area by the river. Yachtsmen enjoy the Inn's 400-foot dock with complete facilities. Everyone enjoys dining in the Kent Dining Room. The Inn is also handy to Lake Erie.

QUICK PINEAPPLE CHICKEN

1 2-pound frying chicken
1 cup flour
2 cups milk

Put chicken in pot. Cover with a good chicken stock and blanch for 5 to 10 minutes. Remove from pot and allow to cool. Then cut into small bite-size pieces. Season flour with salt, pepper and Accent. Dredge chicken in flour, then in milk with 1 egg beaten in. Then roll gently in cracker crumbs. Deep fry until golden brown at 300 degrees. Place in large casserole and add Pineapple Sauce.

Pineapple Sauce

2 14-oz. cans sliced pineapple
1 cup brown sugar
1 pinch dry mustard
1 dash soya sauce
2 tablespoons cornstarch
1 green pepper, cubed
½ cup maraschino cherries, quartered

Drain juice off pineapple in a saucepan. Add brown sugar, dry mustard, soya sauce and bring to a boil. Glaze with cornstarch mixed with water. Then add green pepper and maraschino cherries. Add the pineapple rings cut in cubes ½-inch square. Pour sauce over chicken while hot and serve on a bed of fluffy rice. Serves 2 to 4.

Hamilton, Ont., Can.

150 King St. E. at Catherine

Hamilton Harbor plays host to ships from all over the world. A world within walls awaits you at this Holiday Inn. Spain comes to life in the lush El Toro Dorado dining room. There's the freshness of Holland in the Dutch Coffee House. The Wunderbar Lounge is a German Beer Garden, featuring Barbecued Spareribs and Hot Beef Sandwiches (served from the Inn's famous butcher block) during the luncheon buffets.

BAKED FRENCH ONION SOUP

    ¼ cup butter or margarine
    4 large onions, thinly sliced
    1 tablespoon flour
    1½ quarts beef stock

Heat butter in saucepan. Add onions and cook over medium heat, stirring frequently. Onions should be tender and an even golden brown. Sprinkle with flour and stir until well blended. Pour beef stock over onions and stir. Boil for 5 to 10 minutes over low heat. Season with salt and pour into crockery dishes. Top with slices of toast cut to cover surface of the soup. Sprinkle grated Parmesan cheese on the toast and brown under broiler. Serves 6 to 8.

BAKED LAMB

    1 4- to 5-pound leg of lamb

Cut lamb leg into 7- to 8-ounce portions. Place each portion into enough foil to cover. Combine: ½ pound butter, 1½ teaspoons fresh garlic (chopped), 1 tablespoon oregano, 1 tablespoon parsley (chopped), 1½ teaspoons salt, 1½ teaspoons pepper, and juice of 2 lemons. Place 2 tablespoons of mixture over each portion and place 1 slice casino cheese on top. Wrap each portion and fold ends tightly together. Place lamb in baking pan and bake for 1-1½ hours in 350 degree oven. Remove portions from foil. Serves 8 to 10.

Hespeler-Galt Ont., Can.

At Hwy. 24 on Hwy. 401

Visitors to this area can never resist a shopping spree. The hand woven woolens are irresistible. The famous Kitchener farmers' market is a must for every visitor. It's just a 10 minute drive from the Inn. Enjoy year round swimming in a heated indoor pool. Sightseers always make it a point to be back at the Inn in time for dinner.

APPLE STRUDEL

    1 cup butter, melted and cooled
    3-4 apples, peeled, cored & diced
    1½ teaspoons cinnamon
    ½ teaspoon allspice

Beat 1 egg, add 2 tablespoons softened butter and gradually beat in 2 cups flour and a pinch salt. Add 1 cup lukewarm water gradually. Mix until dough is formed. Turn out on a lightly floured pastry board and knead, hitting dough hard against board. Cover and allow to rest 15 minutes. Place cloth on table, letting it go down sides. Lightly flour. Roll dough into a square on table. Reach under dough to center and pull and stretch, being careful not to tear—do not attempt to patch a tear. Pull first on one side, then other. Continue until dough is transparent and thin and hangs over all sides of the table. (About 2 yards square). Let dry a few minutes but not long enough to become brittle. Spread with melted butter; adding apples, spices and sugar to taste. Drizzle more butter on top. Fold the dough over one side. Pull cloth up and start rolling dough into a big roll. Place in large greased pan or cut in 2 pieces. Bake at 400 degrees for 30 minutes. Reduce heat to 350 degrees and bake until golden brown and crisp. Cool slightly on rack. Sift powdered sugar over all. Cut in 2-inch slices. Serve warm. Serves 6 to 8.

Huntsville-Hidden Valley Ont., Can.

Hwy. 60. On Peninsula Lake

You're in one of North America's truly great winter resorts. Skiing pleasure is guaranteed with full snowmaking for the longest skiing season in Ontario. For a change of pace, take off in one of the Inn's snowmobiles. After dark relax in the apres-ski surroundings of the cocktail lounge. After a gourmet dinner, join a sleigh ride group.

PARTRIDGE

  1 partridge
    Giblets of partridge
  4 ounces truffles
  1 cup croutons
  ¼ cup brandy, warmed

Avoid tearing the skin of the partridge; remove the breast bone from the bird. Mix giblets and a small quantity of meat from the bird with finely chopped truffles and bread crumbs. Stuff this mixture into the chest cavity of the bird. Make sure the stuffing is well seasoned with salt and pepper.

Cut small slits into the bird behind the wings and insert slices of truffles into these slits. Wrap the bird tightly in a piece of muslin cloth and poach the bird for approximately 25 minutes in salted water. Remove the bird from the water and let cool. Reduce liquor and keep hot. When ready to serve, reheat the bird in a 400 degree oven until heated thoroughly. Prepare the bird on a bed of croutons on a platter and pour mixture of reduced braising liquor and brandy over the bird and flambé. Serve immediately while flaming. Serves 2.

Kenora, Ont., Can.

Dwtn. on Trans. Can. Hwy. 17

This Holiday Inn is located right on Lake of the Woods and has its own boat docking facilities. You'll be staying near some of Canada's finest big game hunting country. Trophy fishing is at its best. Swimming, skiing, boating, ice boating and snowmobile races mean there's something fun to do for everyone. Superb cuisine and a congenial cocktail lounge await you after fun filled days.

BEAR STEW

  3 pounds bear meat
  ½ cup cooking oil
  1 cup water
    Bouquet garni
  2 cups red wine
  6 carrots, scraped
  6 onions, peeled
  6 turnips, peeled
  6 potatoes, peeled

Remove all fat from bear meat. Cut in good size chunks, season and dredge with flour. Sear in hot oil in heavy kettle until browned on all sides. Add water and bouquet garni. Heat to boiling point, reduce heat, add wine and simmer 2 to 4 hours, or until meat is tender. Add vegetables last half hour of cooking. Add more water and wine as needed to keep from sticking. Thicken gravy after taking up meat and vegetables if necessary. Serves 6 to 8.

FRESH BERRY TARTLETS CHANTILLY

Fill 8 baked tart shells with 2 cups thick and chilled custard. Top with fresh berries. With pastry brush glaze berries with ½ cup diluted berry jam and give shine. Whip 2 cups whipping cream, adding 4 teaspoons sugar while whipping. Decorate with cream in piping bag. Serve chilled. Serves 8.

Kingston, Ont., Can.

Princess St. on Lake Ont.

Each room at this Inn has a sweeping view of Lake Ontario. It's located in the business area of Kingston, yet situated where the Cataraqui River empties into the lake. The Panoramic Lounge affords a beautiful view. You can expect impeccable service and gourmet food in the dining room. Visitors enjoy an 1812 military ritual during the summer months at Old Ft. Henry, opposite the Inn. Kingston is also the home of Queen's University and the Royal Military College.

ROCK CORNISH HEN

    4 Rock Cornish hens
    2 ounces sherry
    1 cup good Brown Gravy
    ½ pound fresh mushrooms
    ¼ cup butter
    2 ounces cognac
    ½ cup cream
      Dash cayenne
      Salt and pepper

Season and tie game hens. Place in roasting pan and put in a 325 degree oven. Roast until browned, about 30 to 35 minutes. When done, remove game hens and the oil in the bottom of pan. Add sherry to pan drippings, then Brown Gravy. Strain and keep warm until ready to use. Sauté mushrooms in butter in separate dish. When ready to flame, put butter in flaming or chafing dish. Remove backbones of game hens and place hens in chafing dish. Let pan get hot and tilt to one side, add cognac. Flame and baste hens. Add cream, mushrooms, cayenne, seasonings and brown sauce. Blend and serve. Serves 4.

Brown Gravy

Brown 2 tablespoons flour lightly in a frying pan, adding 1 tablespoon chicken fat or butter. Stir and add 1 cup chicken broth. Simmer until it thickens, stirring continuously. Season. Makes 1 cup.

Kitchener-Waterloo Ont., Can.

30 Fairway Ave. at Hwy. 8

A huge 12-foot wide fireplace makes guests linger longer over the delicious food served at this twin cities Inn. The Five Swords Lounge is a popular gathering place before and after dinner. Stratford, where the world renowned Shakespearean Festival is held annually from June through October, is only 30 miles west on the River Avon. Antique hunters are delighted with the many shops nearby. Everyone enjoys the farmers' market in Kitchener.

SAUERBRATEN

    8 pounds bottom butt sirloin
    2 large carrots, cut coarse
    1 large onion, cut coarse
    2 celery stalks, cut coarse
      Red wine vinegar

Select a deep crock. Place meat and vegetables together in crock. Add a solution of half vinegar and half water, completely covering the meat. Add salt, pepper, pickling spice and bay leaves. Marinate for 48 to 72 hours. Remove from marinade. Put in a hot pan of oil and brown on all sides. Place meat in pan of marinade and bring to a boil. Then simmer until tender. Remove meat from marinade, strain and make sauce.

Gingersnap Sauce

Using excess fat from browning, add 3 teaspoons sugar and 12 crumbled gingersnaps and cook 10 minutes longer. Thicken with flour and water paste. Bring to a boil. Boil for 1 minute, then season and serve. Serves 12.

London, Ont., Can. Downtown

299 King Street

French pastries are compliments of the Inn in the Squire's Dining Room. Sip into something relaxing in the Squire's Tap Lounge. It overlooks the beautifully landscaped courtyard and swimming pool in the heart of downtown London. The University of Western Ontario is only 5 minutes away. Visit the nearby Storybook Gardens . . . a 7-acre children's paradise on the Thames River.

SEMMEL KNODEL

```
10  dinner rolls,
    sliced ¼ inch thick
½   cup bacon bits
    Chopped parsley to taste
¼   cup chopped onions
½   cup unsalted butter
½   cup flour (scant)
 2  whole eggs
⅔   cup milk
```

Dry rolls in oven. Sauté bacon, parsley, and onions in butter. Dice rolls, mix with flour, salt, eggs and milk and bacon mixture. Let rest 2 hours. Shape dumplings. Place in boiling salted water and simmer 15-20 minutes. Top with bread crumbs fried in butter and serve extra butter on the side. Serves 4-6. (For main dish or accompaniment).

ARCTIC CHAR FILLET SAUTÉ GRENOBLOISE

Season char fillet with salt and pepper. Dredge in flour and pan fry in oil. Place on dinner plate. Sprinkle with 1 tablespoon lemon cut in small cubes and ½ tablespoon capers. Pour 1 tablespoon hot brown gravy over top. Brown 2 tablespoons butter in frying pan and pour over fillet. Garnish with parsley. 1 serving. To cube lemon—cut off skin to bare lemon meat. Slice ¼ inch thick and cut cubes from slices.

London, Ont., Can. South

1210 Wellington Rd.

London has many landmarks following the tradition of its parent city in England — Victoria Park, Chelsea Green, Oxford Street, Piccadilly Street. This Inn offers old world hospitality in a country club setting on the outskirts of town. Find out why Roast Beef and Duck are the most ordered in the dining room overlooking the courtyard and pool. There's an outdoor cafe too.

VEAL SCALOPPINE

```
1   pound veal, thinly cut
¼   pound mushrooms
1   green pepper, thinly sliced
```

Pound veal between 2 pieces of waxed paper. Cut meat into 2 even squares. Dip in seasoned flour and shake off excess. Melt 2 tablespoons butter in frying pan and when bubbling add veal and cook until it is browned on both sides. Reduce heat, add mushrooms and green peppers. Last, add 4 ounces Marsala wine. Simmer 4 minutes. Serve veal on noodles. Serves 4.

RICE PUDDING

```
¾   cup raisins
1   quart milk
3   cups cooked rice
3   beaten egg yolks
```

Cook raisins in 1 cup hot water for 5 minutes. Drain and rinse in cold water. Boil milk, add rice and raisins. Bring to second boil. Mix 3 teaspoons cornstarch in ½ cup water and add to egg yolks. Combine with first mixture, adding ½ teaspoon salt. Place split piece of vanilla bean in a bowl and add same amount of sugar. Pound to extract vanilla powder. Then add ½ cup sugar. Remove rice mixture from heat and add vanilla-sugar blend. Place in a dish, sprinkle with cinnamon and add whipped cream. Serves 8.

Oakville, Ont., Can.

Queen Elizabeth Hwy.

Chateau type architecture (complete with shingles) makes this Holiday Inn unique. It's halfway between Hamilton and Toronto. This once peaceful boat building community today boasts Canada's largest research and development center. A favorite spot at the Inn is the Red Horse Tavern. There's the Coffee House for snacks or lunch and every dish is a masterpiece in the dining room.

CHICKEN A LA KING SUPERB

    1 pint white sauce
    ½ pint cream
    ¼ pound sliced mushrooms
    1 green pepper, minced
    ⅓ cup butter
    1 pimento, thinly sliced
    2 cups diced cooked chicken
    1 wine glass sherry
    1 teaspoon lemon juice
    2 egg yolks, slightly beaten
    ½ cup chopped almonds

Prepare white sauce using ½ pint milk and ½ pint chicken stock. Heat and thicken with roux (4 tablespoons butter + 4 tablespoons flour blended). Stir until smooth and right thickness. Add cream and bring to boil.

Peel mushrooms and sauté with green pepper in butter for 10 minutes, stirring frequently. Add pimento, chicken, sherry and lemon juice. Season to taste. Simmer 5 minutes. Stir in egg yolks and cook 1 minute, stirring constantly. Serve in vol-au-vent case (patty shells) or on toast. Garnish with chopped almonds. Serves 6.

Oshawa, Ont., Can.

On Hwy. 401 at Exit 72

You can unwind with a soothing sauna and an invigorating dip in the heated swimming pool at this Inn. The Auto-Pub is the right place for "happy hour" — rightly named since General Motors of Canada is located nearby. Gourmet fare in the dining room is lavish with its beautiful dessert table. Be sure to visit the nearby Canadian Automotive Museum. If you enjoy car racing, there's plenty of action at nearby Mosport.

CREME CARAMEL

Heat 6 cups milk, 1 cup sugar and ¼ teaspoon salt until boiling. Add 7 slightly beaten eggs and mix thoroughly. Pour Caramel Syrup into a 1½-quart mold, covering bottom and sides. Strain custard mixture into mold. Place mold over a pan containing a little hot water and bake at 350 degrees for 1 hour, or until set. Allow to cool completely before turning custard onto a deep platter. Serves 10 to 12.

Caramel Syrup

Place ⅔ cup sugar and ⅓ cup water in a saucepan and shake over moderate heat until sugar dissolves. Let boil until sugar is golden. Pour ⅓ cup water into caramel and simmer until all is liquid.

BAKED ALASKA

    4 egg whites
    ⅛ teaspoon cream of tartar
    ½ cup sugar
    1 quart ice cream
    1 layer sponge cake, 1 inch thick

Beat egg whites until stiff, adding cream of tartar while beating. Gradually add sugar and beat until very stiff. Shape cake to fit serving platter or board. Place ice cream on cake. Cover with meringue and seal sides. Bake in a preheated 450 to 500 degree oven for 3 to 5 minutes, until meringue browns a little. Serves 8.

Ottawa, Ont., Can.

350 Dalhousie Street

The Parliament Buildings and all of downtown are within easy walking distance of this Inn. You can watch the "changing of the guards" daily during the summer months. In mid-May a sea of tulips greets you at every turn along The Driveway. Ottawa's winter playground lies less than 15 miles north. You'll be especially glad you decided to stay at this Inn once you've tasted the French-Canadian cuisine.

TOURTIERE

Famous French Canadian Pie associated with early Christmas morning

- 1 pound minced fresh pork
- ½ pound minced beef
- 1 pound cooked potatoes, mashed
- 2 small onions, diced
- ¾ teaspoon salt
- ½ teaspoon savory
- ½ teaspoon celery pepper
- 1 garlic clove
- ¼ teaspoon cloves

Combine ingredients with ¾ cup water in a heavy pot and bring to a boil. Cook uncovered slowly for 20 minutes. Mixture should be damp—not watery! Cool and pour into pie shell. Cover with pastry and prick. Bake at 450 degrees for 10 minutes, then at 350 degrees until crust is light brown. Serve hot. Enough filling for 2 pies.

Pastry for Tourtiere

Sift 2 cups flour and 1 teaspoon salt into a bowl. Blend ¾ cup shortening into flour until crumbly. Mix 5½ tablespoons cold water with ¼ cup of the sifted flour. Mix until smooth and stir in shortening mixture. Stir with fork until particles stick together. Form pastry into a ball. Chill before rolling on a floured board. For 1 2-crust pie. (Double for 2 pies above).

Peterborough Ont., Can.

George St. at Towsend-Hwy. 7B

Come by boat if you like. This picturesque Inn is on the Otonabee River and Little Lake. The Inn overlooks the Centennial Fountain, the 2nd highest fountain in the world. Pickerel, trout, bass and muskie abound in Little Lake. Of course fish is king on the menu here, but the continental cuisine is superb. The Jolly Rodger Bar features entertainment nightly. The famous Peterborough Lift Lock is nearby. Downtown is only 2 blocks away.

OTONABEE RIVER DUCKLING A L'ANGLAISE

- 4- to 5-pound duckling
- Salt
- Pepper
- 3 cups bread crumbs
- 1 tablespoon onion, minced
- ¼ cup celery, chopped fine
- Thyme
- Hot water to moisten

Prepare duck for roasting and rub with salt. Use remaining ingredients for dressing. Stuff the duckling with dressing and sew securely. Rub outside with soft butter and place in a shallow pan. Place in a cold oven. Set temperature at 375 degrees and cook 30-35 minutes per pound. Serves 4.

Serve with carrots, turnips, cauliflower and boiled potatoes, all cooked in salt water. Applesauce and cranberry sauce make good accompaniments.

St. Catharines Ont., Can.

Queen Elizabeth Hwy. & Lake St.

St. Catharines, The Garden City, is in the midst of the beautiful Niagara fruit belt. Visitors enjoy watching ships from all over the world climb the 326-foot mountain through the Welland Canal. This popular Inn is only 8 miles from Niagara Falls. Seafood from Canadian waters and Roast Prime Ribs of Beef with Yorkshire Pudding vie for popularity in the gracious dining room.

NIAGARA RIVER PERCH

4 medium-size perch fillets
4 fresh peaches
2 tablespoons lemon juice
½ cup white wine
½ cup cream
1 egg yolk, beaten until light

Remove the fillets of perch. (Boil rest of fish in water and salt and pepper to season. Strain for fumet). Roll fillets to make paupiettes and hold together with toothpicks. Cut peaches in half and poach them in ¼ cup water, lemon juice and ¼ cup of the wine. Bring to a boil. Remove from heat. Poach fillets in ¼ cup of the wine and ¾ cup fish fumet until fish fillets are tender. Remove paupiettes and place in baking dish with peaches and sauce. Reduce fish stock by ⅔ (boil until reduced). Add ¼ cup cream and reduce more. Season with salt and white pepper. Add egg yolk and ¼ cup cream. Top fish and peaches with this sauce and glaze under broiler. Serves 4.

THE PENINSULA BARREL

Cut 1 cake (butter or sponge) in barrel shape, leaving hole in center. Cook 1 cup grapes (seeded or seedless) in sugar syrup (½ cup water, ½ cup sugar boiled 5 minutes). Chill. Combine pint vanilla ice cream and grapes in hole in cake. Top with ½ pint whipped cream. Serves 4 to 6.

Sarnia, Ont., Can.

Hwy. 40, Point Edward

A picturesque vacation awaits you here — at the foot of the Blue Water Bridge, overlooking the St. Clair River, in the charming village of Point Edward. There's something for everyone to enjoy — marina, golf course, saunas, health club, indoor and outdoor swimming pools. And you can expect excellent regional specialties in the dining room. After dinner, let them entertain you in the popular lounge.

ROAST LOIN OF PORK

5 to 6-pound center cut pork loin
1 cup light brown sugar
2 tablespoons dark rum
2 teaspoons finely chopped garlic
2 teaspoons ground ginger
2 teaspoons ground cloves
1 medium sized bay leaf, crumbled
1 teaspoon salt
¼ teaspoon black pepper
2 chicken bouillon cubes
2 cups hot water
2 teaspoons cornstarch
2 tablespoons cold water

Score fatty side of loin diagonally in 1-inch squares. Place in a baking pan, bone side down, and roast at 350 degrees for one hour. Meanwhile, put the brown sugar, rum, garlic, ginger, cloves, bay leaf, salt and pepper in a blender to make a smooth paste. Remove loin from the oven and pour out juices from the roasting pan. Spread paste over fatty side of loin and place in oven for another 30 minutes, until crusty and brown. Skim fat from juice and add bouillon cubes and hot water. Bring to a boil. Dissolve cornstarch in cold water and add to juices, stirring briskly. Serve loin with sauce on the side. Serves 6.

Sudbury, Ont., Can.

Ring Rd. at Notre Dame Ave.

Moose and bear abound in this area. And the fishing is just as good. If you're just hunting for a fun place to visit, you'll enjoy being in the center of the Nickle Capital of the World. Visit the nearby Numismatic Park and Model Mine. No matter why you visit Sudbury, you'll enjoy your stay at this Inn with its indoor pool and saunas. There's live entertainment in the lounge and excellent food. The theatre and shops are just a walk away.

MINESTRONE SOUP

    2 carrots
    2 stalks celery
    1 onion
    1 potato
    2 tablespoons olive oil
    1 can small tomato purée
    2 cups beef stock
    1 cup dry white beans
    1 cup shredded cabbage
    ¼ cup diced bacon
    ½ clove garlic, minced
    ¼ cup chopped parsley
    1 cup spaghetti
       Parmesan cheese

Dice vegetables in ½-inch squares. Put oil in pot and add carrots, celery and onion. Cook a little, then add tomato purée and stock.
Add white beans, which have been soaked overnight. Let cook 1 hour. Then add potatoes and cabbage. Cook another 1½ hours.
Fry bacon bits with garlic in fry pan until golden. Add chopped parsley and mix with minestrone.
Break spaghetti (or elbow macaroni) and add about 20 minutes before soup is to be served. Heat well. Soup should be thick. Sprinkle each serving with Parmesan cheese. Serves 6 to 8.

Thunder Bay, Ont. Canada

Donald & Brodie Streets

Take the spectacular north shore route along Lake Superior to this Inn in the heart of the area's business and shopping district. Nearby Mt. McKay chair lift presents the summer visitor with a dazzling view, and the winter skier the prospect of downhill thrills. It's hunting, fishing and camping country too. The Inn's Confederation dining room offers an exciting variety of gourmet dishes.

LAKE SUPERIOR TROUT

    4 6-ounce portions trout
       (leave skin on)
       Flour
    1 egg, beaten
    1 tablespoon water
    1 tablespoon butter
       Parsley Butter
    1 lemon, cut in 4 wedges

Wash fish well and pat dry with paper towel. Dust fresh trout in flour, then dip in egg-water mixture. Place butter in a heavy skillet and heat. Add fish being careful not to overlap. Cook until golden. Turn with wide pancake turner or spatula. Brown other side, then place in 350 degree oven for 15 minutes (no turning). Serve with Parsley Butter and lemon wedges. Serves 4.

Parsley Butter

    ½ cup softened butter
    1 tablespoon lemon juice
       Salt and pepper
    1 tablespoon finely chopped parsley

Season butter with lemon juice, salt and pepper. Add parsley and blend well.

Toronto, Ont., Can.
Don Valley

Don Valley Pkwy.

Check into a world of luxury and excitement overlooking a wooded parkland. This Inn has two beautiful pools—one under a plexiglass dome for year round swimming. You'll call the African bar (called "Dr. Livingstone") great. Step into the Savoir Fare for exquisite dining. Relax in Flanagan's, an Irish pub. Enjoy Ontario's Queen City, capital of the province.

SCAMPI BUON GUSTO

    16 scampi or large shrimp,
       shelled and deveined
    ½ cup flour
    1 egg, lightly beaten
    ¼ teaspoon salt
    ¼ teaspoon pepper
    1½ cups white bread crumbs
    1 sprig parsley, minced
    1 tablespoon grated Parmesan cheese
    1 cup oil
    2 tablespoons butter

Split scampi or shrimp into butterfly, and wash in cold water. Dry and roll in flour. Add salt and pepper to egg. Dip scampi into egg and cover with bread crumbs, parsley and Parmesan cheese. Fry in hot oil until golden brown on both sides. Place in serving dish. Heat butter in frying pan, add Worcestershire sauce, cayenne pepper and 1 tablespoon lemon juice. Pour this sauce over scampi. Serve hot with lemon wedges. Serves 2.

ZABAGLIONE

    6 egg yolks
    6 teaspoons sugar
    5 ounces Marsala wine, add gradually

Mix ingredients well and beat in double boiler until mixture gets foamy and stiff. Chill. Serve in champagne glasses with lady finger biscuit on the side. Serves 4 to 5.

Toronto, Ont., Can.
East

Warden Ave. Scarborough

Sing along in Le Bistro, the Inn's cocktail lounge with a nightclub atmosphere. Men enjoy the Boar's Head pub (it's for men only). Be sure to try the Coq Au Vin and Baked Alaska in the dining room or terrace cafe. Downtown Toronto is only 15 minutes from this Inn. A ferry ride to the parks and lagoons of the Toronto islands will give you the best views of the busy waterfront.

YORKSHIRE PUDDING

    2 cups flour
    ½ teaspoon salt
    1 cup milk
    3 eggs
    1 cup cold water

Sift flour and salt. Make well in center and pour in milk. Stir and beat vigorously. Add eggs, one at a time, beating with rotary beater. Add the cold water and beat until bubbles form on top. Leave 1 hour in cold place. Heat 8 large muffin tins. Put a teaspoon of hot fat from roast of beef in each. Pour in batter. Bake at 400 degrees for 30 minutes. Serves 8.

VEAL CUTLETS, TARRAGON

    4 veal cutlets (2½ ounces each)
    ¼ cup sweet butter
    1 tablespoon fresh tarragon
      White wine (dry)
    1 tablespoon demi-glace
      (thin brown sauce)

Season cutlets and dredge in flour. Brown on both sides in butter, using skillet. Add tarragon and just enough wine to cover meat. Cook for few minutes until meat is tender. Remove meat from pan. Reduce liquid then add demi-glace and let boil for a minute. Pour over cutlets and serve with rice. Serves 4.

Toronto, Ont., Can.
Etobicoke

Hwy. 27 & Burnhamthorpe Rd.

The Toronto International Airport is only 5 minutes from this Inn. Downtown Toronto is just 15 expressway minutes away. An ultramodern rotunda contains the Coffee House, Lounge and exquisite circular dining room. Be sure to order Sour Dough Flapjacks with a jug of honey in the Dutch Coffee House for breakfast.

SOLE HERMITAGE
WITH BONNE FEMME SAUCE

Remove black skin and spine from 12 Dover sole fillets by using sharp knife through centers. Melt 2 tablespoons butter in a skillet and add finely chopped chives (or green tops of young onions), parsley, tarragon, salt and pepper. Combine 6 beaten egg yolks with 1 cup bread crumbs and add to mixture. Make a soft stuffing. Stuff fillets and close incisions with skewers or string. Place in a single layer in a buttered baking dish. Pour some Bonne Femme Sauce over all. Cover and bake 15 minutes in a 350 degree oven. Baste with sauce and glaze under broiler. Serve in same casserole, adding additional sauce when serving. Serves 10 to 12.

Bonne Femme Sauce

    2 tablespoons butter
    1 cup sliced mushrooms
    2 tablespoons flour
    ½ cup milk
    ½ cup cream
    ½ cup dry white wine

Melt butter in saucepan, add mushrooms and saute gently. Add flour and blend, stirring in milk and cream gradually. Season. Cook until thickened. Add wine last. Do not boil.

Toronto, Ont., Can.
Malton International

917 Dixon Rd., Rexdale, Ont.

Enjoy a fascinating view without the sounds of the airport (only 9/10 of a mile away). International and provincial specialties, dancing and entertainment are yours at the rooftop Supper Club. There are also spectacular views from the plush Top-of-the Inn VIP suites. The Inn has Exec-Aide offices for rent by day or half-day. Heated indoor and outdoor swimming pools, sauna baths and exercise rooms make travelers welcome a layover here.

ROAST DUCKLING

    1 5½-pound duckling
      Salt and pepper
    1 celery stalk
    1 onion, sliced
    1 apple, quartered
    2 tablespoons vinegar
    2 tablespoons sugar
    1 tablespoon julienned orange rind
    ½ cup hot orange juice
    1 teaspoon lemon juice
    2 tablespoons curacao
      Orange sections

Prepare duck for cooking and season with salt and pepper. Stuff with pieces of celery, onion and apple. Place breast up on rack in roasting pan. Cook 15 minutes at 425 degrees. Then lower heat to 350 degrees, allowing about 20 minutes to the pound, or until tender. When done, remove celery, onion and apple. Place duck in a warm place.

Pour off fat in pan and deglaze with 1 cup stock. Thicken with 1 teaspoon cornstarch mixed with a little of the stock. In another pan, cook vinegar and sugar until light brown. Add sauce from roasting pan and cook 4 to 5 minutes. Then add orange rind, orange juice, lemon juice and curacao. Season. Serve sauce over duck and garnish with orange sections. 4 to 6 servings.

Toronto, Ont., Can.
Yorkdale

Dufferin St. at Hwy. 401

As you sweep across the top of Toronto on the fabulous 8-lane, toll-free Highway 401, the world famous enclosed Yorkdale Shopping Center comes into view. This Holiday Inn is right opposite. Plan to stay awhile. You'll need time to spend in a sauna, swim in the heated indoor pool, and dine luxuriously. Go to the Inn's Gypsy-Gypsy Lounge for fun. A gypsy singer leads the pubbers through familiar songs, dancers from middle Europe go through a variety of wild folk dances and everybody claps along.

SHRIMP ALLA DIAVOLO

    24 large fresh shrimp
    ½ cup butter
    ½ cup demi-glace (or thin brown sauce)
     1 teaspoon Worcestershire sauce
       Dash lemon juice
       Dash Tabasco sauce
     1 teaspoon chopped parsley

Without removing shells, butterfly shrimp (split down the back) and wash in cold water. Let shrimp drip dry, season with salt and pepper, and then place them on a buttered aluminum tray. The outside (shell) should be on the bottom and the inside of the shrimp should be facing up.

Add some chicken or beef broth, just enough to cover the bottom of the tray, then cover with foil. The liquid on the tray will turn into steam and prevent the shrimp from becoming too dry. Place the tray in a hot oven at 380 degrees and bake until shrimp are tender and cooked, about 10 to 15 minutes. Place shrimp on serving dish. Put butter in a medium-sized frying pan. When butter is golden brown, add demiglace, Worcestershire, lemon juice, Tabasco and chopped parsley. Pour over the shrimp. Garnish with lemon wedges and parsley sprigs. 4 servings.

Windsor, Ont., Can.

480 Riverside Drive West

Immediately at the edge of the Detroit River, this beautiful Inn gives a startling panorama of the Detroit skyline. Gourmet food vies with the view for attention in the dining room. Diners can see thousands of light reflections on the river and watch the ocean shipping. The lounge and coffee house also have panoramic views. There's a Movie Theatre on the premises. The Windsor-Detroit tunnel and bridge are only a few short blocks away.

COQUILLE OF SEAFOOD

    2 small spring onions, minced
    ½ cup fresh mushrooms
    ½ cup cooked shrimp
    ½ cup blanched scallops
    ⅓ cup fresh cooked lobster meat
    1½ cups cream
    ½ cup tuna fish (canned)
    ½ cup crab meat (canned)

Sauté onions in 4 tablespoons butter using saucepan. Add diced mushrooms and let simmer until mushrooms are cooked. Add shrimp, scallops and lobster, all cut in large dices. Sauté, then sprinkle with ½ teaspoon paprika and a little salt and pepper. Add 2 ounces sherry and reduce well. Then add 1¼ cups cream. Let simmer. Make paste of ¼ cup butter and 2 tablespoons flour. Add a little at a time to mixture, stirring well. Let cook a few minutes.

Add tuna and crab meat and juice of ¼ lemon. Mix yolk of 1 egg with ¼ cup of cream left and add to seafood mixture but do not boil. (Seafood should be thick enough to hold in a coquille).

Fill 4 large coquilles (shells) with seafood. Add 1 beaten egg yolk to 3 cups mashed potatoes and place in piping tube. Make border around each shell. Top with grated cheese or hollandaise. Put under broiler to brown. Serves 4.

Montreal, Que., Can.
Chateaubriand

6500 Cote de Liesse

French waiters in fancy dress, a wandering accordion player, and French culinary creations await you! It happens each week in the Inn's French cuisine restaurant, "Le Chateaubriand". There's a "real" wine cellar (looks like it's been here 2000 years). Montreal is named for Mount Royal . . . a high mountain which overlooks the city.

TOURNEDOS CHATEAUBRIAND

    6 tournedos
    6 baked tartlet cases
    4 mushrooms, minced
    1 slice ham, minced
    2 carrots, minced
    6 artichoke bottoms
    1 large wine glass old Port wine
    1 cup veal stock (or bouillon)

(The tournedo is a piece of filet of beef cut from the heart of the filet).

Cook meat in a buttered frying pan to doneness desired. Fill tartlets with a ragout (stew) made up of mushrooms, ham and carrots, all mixed and cooked. Arrange each tournedo on a tartlet and on every piece of meat add a nice bottom of artichoke cooked in butter. Pour old Port wine in the pan used to cook the tournedos, add veal stock and reduce the sauce. Arrange tournedos on a platter and garnish with watercress. Serve the sauce in a sauce boat. Serves 6.

GIGOT ST. ARROMAN

Soak a 2½- to 3½-pound leg of lamb in a good white wine, seasoned with ½ teaspoon thyme, 1 clove minced garlic, ¼ cup minced parsley, bay laurel, 1 clove and cognac. Leave it for 2 days. Roast at 325° for 45-50 min. taking care to baste it very often with the sauce. When the leg of lamb is done, add the leftover sauce and reduce it. Strain and thicken with butter. Season to taste and serve very hot. Serves 4 to 5.

Montreal, Que., Can.
Downtown

420 Sherbrooke W. (Hwy. 2)

All of Montreal is at the doorstep of this luxurious high-rise (23 floors) in the heart of the city. "Terre des Hommes" (formerly Expo '67) is not far away. Take an escalator to the Inn's health club for a sauna bath, or a dip in the year round pool. There's entertainment nightly in the plush Club Bar. Homemade French pastries delight guests in the El Castillo dining room with its sumptuous Spanish decor.

CANADIAN MEAT PIE

    1½ pounds ground pork meat
    ½ pound ground veal meat
    1 medium onion
    ¼ teaspoon cinnamon
    ¼ teaspoon clove, ground
    1 garlic clove
    1 pound cooked potatoes
    2 cups bouillon

Sauté the meat in butter or oil with onion, cinnamon, clove and garlic. When the meat is a nice brown, add the potatoes and bouillon. Let simmer until done.

Line a pie pan with pastry and pour in the above mixture. Cover with top crust. Bake in a 350 degree oven about 30 minutes, or until pastry is browned. Serves 8.

FARLOUCHE PIE

A favorite Canadian dessert

    2 cups water
    1½ cups molasses
    1 cup brown sugar
    ½ teaspoon cinnamon
    ¼ teaspoon clove
    ⅓ cup (heaping) cornstarch

Combine all ingredients and cook for 8 minutes. Line pie pan with pastry and put in filling. Bake in a moderate 350 degree oven for 30 minutes. Garnish with nuts. Serves 8.

Quebec, Que., Can.

Rond Point, Pont de Quebec

Enjoy dancing to the music of a friar accordionist in Les Caves de l'Abbaye . . . a unique wine cellar where your favorite specialties and refreshments are served by monk garbed waiters. Fabulous French cuisine is served in the old world atmosphere of Le Chateaubriand. There's an orchestra in the adjoining cocktail lounge. Quebec's annual Winter Carnival features sensational canoe races across the ice-strewn St. Lawrence River. The famous Quebec Bridge is not far from this Inn.

FILET OF BEEF, GASTRONOMY

Lard a 4- to 6-pound filet of beef with truffle and marinate in Madeira 4 to 5 hours. Then draw strips of fat pork through beef with larder.

Braise in Madeira (left from marinade) until desired doneness. Remove pork. Serve on platter garnished with chestnuts, chicken livers and mushrooms cooked in consomme and glazed (simmered in butter until shiny). Baste with champagne when serving. Serves 12 to 16.

QUAIL A LA RICHELIEU

Pluck and draw 4 fresh quail. Season each with salt and a little cognac. Insert raw truffle in each and truss securely—placing them side by side. Sprinkle with fine salt.

Cover with 2 tablespoons carrots, 2 tablespoons onions, and 2 tablespoons celery, all julienne, and which have been sautéed in butter. Cover birds with veal stock. Bring to a boil, then poach for 12 minutes. Add about ⅓ more vegetables as prepared before and poach 2 more minutes. Arrange in timbales, pouring off excess fat. Save juice from vegetables and pour over quail. Serve with pilaff. Serves 4.

Regina, Sask., Can.

777 Albert St.

Enjoy French table side cookery in the "1882 Room". Soft chandelier light adds royal charm to dining in the room honoring the year Regina was made the first capital of the NW Territory. "The Hunters" lounge is a favorite meeting place and the "777 Room" offers dancing and entertainment. Visit the historic barracks, training depot and museum of the Royal Canadian Mounted Police.

STEAK DIANE

    14-ounce beef tenderloin, trimmed
     3 tablespoons butter
     2 tablespoons parsley
     ½ cup walnuts
     2 ounces red wine
     1 ounce brandy to flambé

Salt and pepper steak. Place in a hot frying pan along with clarified butter. Cook until steak is almost to the degree of doneness desired. Then add chopped parsley and walnuts, and cook until tender. Add red wine. Tilt the pan so all the juice will run to one side, heat this bare side until good and hot. Add brandy and flambé. Serve as Chateaubriand, slicing the filet in two pieces, keeping sauce for each portion of steak. Serves 2.

VEAL CUTLETS CORDON BLEU

     4 4-ounce veal cutlets
     4 slices Swiss cheese
     4 slices ham (1 oz. each)
       Salt and pepper
       Egg wash (egg beaten slightly with 1
              tablespoon water)
       Bread crumbs

Pound veal cutlets very thin. On one half of each cutlet place a slice of Swiss cheese and a slice of ham. Fold over the other side of cutlet to cover. Pound together to seal edges. Season with salt and pepper, then dip in egg wash and crumbs. Pan-fry in clarified butter until done, about 20 minutes. Serves 4.

Acapulco, Mexico

Costera Miguel Aleman 1260

Fish for sailfish. Watch the daring Mexican boys dive from the cliffs into the bay. Sun, shop and sight-see. This luxurious and well-rounded Inn (it really is round) is located next to the beach and the main avenue of Acapulco. An adventure in Mexican and Yucatan dining awaits you in "El Banneret", the Inn's restaurant and bar. You can also enjoy dining under the stars, your favorite beverage under the palm roof of the "El Bergantin".

POLLO PIBIL

(Chicken Pibil)

Clean and cut 2 2½-pound chickens into serving pieces. Rub with clove of garlic and fry in heavy frying pan with hot cooking oil until golden.

Toast 5 cloves of garlic, add 12 black peppercorns, 8 cumin seeds, ½ teaspoon oregano and grind with 1½ teaspoons "Achiote" (saffron or paprika may be substituted). Add salt and combine with juice of 4 sour oranges. Rub chicken with mixture. Wrap in banana leaves.

Place in steamer on rack over boiling water and steam until tender. Serves 6-8.

CEVICHE SAN BLAS

Cut 1 pound corbina or Spanish mackerel into bite-size pieces and place in earthern bowl. Cover with lime juice and marinate 4 hours. No heat is applied but citrus juice cooks fish chemically.

Place in same bowl:
1 sliced onion
2 cubed tomatoes
1 cubed green pepper

Mix 1 tablespoon vinegar and 3 table-spoons olive oil and add to mixture. Season with oregano, salt and pepper. Place in covered bowl in refrigerator and chill well. Serve with cocktails. For 6-8 persons.

Guadalajara, Mexico

Lopez Mateos and M. Otero

Say "Salud" in "El Jaguar" with a welcome drink prepared especially for you. Enjoy Mexican style Holiday Inn hospitality. Superb native cuisine awaits you in "La Ceiba", the Inn's popular restaurant. There's live entertainment too. Guadalajara is a beautiful old city. Buildings, public squares and parks date back from the time when Mexico was a Spanish colony. Guadalajara is especially famous for its pottery. Watch it being made before you take some home.

GUACAMOLE

2 fresh tomatoes
3 very ripe avocados
½ onion, minced
1 clove garlic, minced
1 tablespoon lemon juice
1 3-ounce package cream cheese
Salt and pepper
1 tablespoon white wine

Place tomatoes in hot water and skin. Cut avocados in half, remove seeds and spoon out pulp. Mash and whip with a fork. Add tomatoes, mash and blend well. Stir in onion, garlic and lemon juice. Soften cheese and add to avocado mixture. Season to taste and add wine, if desired. Serves 4 to 6 as a salad. (Serves more as dip).

CHILI CON QUESO

½ onion, chopped
1 clove garlic, minced
2 tablespoons butter
3 tomatoes
6 green chili peppers
1 pound Cheddar cheese, grated
½ to 1 cup hot water

Sauté onion and garlic in butter until onion is limp. Add tomatoes (peeled and diced) and chili peppers (peeled and minced). Stir in grated cheese and season with salt, pepper, and paprika. Simmer for 20 minutes, adding enough water for consistency to serve as a dip. Makes approximately 2 cups.

Matamoros, Mexico

Cinco & Miguel Aleman Ave.

All the color and romance of Old Mexico awaits you at this Holiday Inn — just across the border from Brownsville, Texas. The Inn is right downtown, with sights and shops at your doorstep. There's an Arts & Crafts Center on the premises. After a fancy drink in the Jaguar Bar and a dinner to remember (order something flaming at your table), enjoy a night at the Inn — in the Conquistador Night Club. And if you're a fishing fan, ask for tips at the Inn.

RED SNAPPER
A LA VERACRUZANA
(Huachinango à la Veracruzana)

    1 2½-pound red snapper
    2½ cups chopped tomatoes
    2 .onions, chopped
    3 green peppers, chopped
    3 cloves garlic, crushed
    1 bunch parsley, chopped fine
    2 chile peppers, chopped fine
       (small elongated green chile)
    ⅓ cup finely chopped green olives
    ⅓ cup capers
    4 tablespoons vinegar
    8 jalapeño peppers (cut in half,
       fried and cut in strips)
    1 pint oil
    1 teaspoon oregano
       Salt and pepper
    ¼ pint dry sherry

Cut red snapper into 6-ounce fillets. Sauté the tomatoes in a skillet, adding onions, then green peppers, garlic, parsley and chile peppers. Then add chopped olives, capers, vinegar and jalapeño strips. Blend in oil. Season with oregano, salt and pepper. Simmer slowly until all is tender and thickened. Add sherry during last part of cooking.
In a separate skillet, heat a little oil and add well washed red snapper fillets. Cover fish with sauce. Cover and cook over low heat 20 minutes. Keep fish from sticking with a wide spatula. Serve with rice. Serves 4 to 6.

Mexico City, Mexico Airport

Blvd. Pto. Aereo No. 502

Get your Mexican vacation off to a flying start — just one mile from the airport. This is a most convenient place to stay in Mexico City. You're within minutes of the Chapultepec Castle and Park, and the Palace of Fine Arts. Pyramids and the Archaelogical Museum are only a few miles away. The heart of downtown is only 6 miles. You'll be glad you landed here, once you get a taste of the extraordinary Mexican cuisine in "La Ceiba". There's live entertainment in the Inn's popular lounge.

CAESAR SALAD

    1 large head romaine lettuce
    2 slices French bread
    1 garlic clove, split
    1 egg
    1½ teaspoons salt
       Freshly ground pepper
       Juice of ½ lemon
    1½ teaspoons Worcestershire sauce
    4 tablespoons olive oil
    2 tablespoons Parmesan cheese

Wash romaine well. Dry and wrap in paper towel. Refrigerate until time to serve. Toast bread, rub with garlic and butter. Cut into cubes and place in warm oven to crisp. Rub salad bowl with garlic clove. Boil an egg 1½ minutes. While it's boiling, remove romaine from refrigerator and tear into small pieces. Add egg to lettuce and toss, adding salt, pepper, lemon juice, Worcestershire sauce and olive oil. Then top with croutons and Parmesan cheese. Serves 4.

Monterrey, Mexico

Avenida Universidad 101

Mucho gusto! That's the way you'll feel the minute you arrive at this magnificent Inn. Dine elegantly in the Inn's "La Fuente", the gourmet's choice. Dance to the romantic South of the Border music in the showbar "El Jaguar". For fun away from the Inn, visit nearby Horsetail Falls and the famous Garcia Caves. Yell "Ole" at a bullfight. Shopping is unique at the leather, blown-glass and wrought iron factories.

SEVICHE*
(Seafood Cocktail)

1¼ pounds sierra fish
   (or Spanish mackerel)
  6 lemons (juice of)
  6 tablespoons oil
  1 tablespoon vinegar
  1 onion, chopped
1½ cups tomatoes, cut up
  ⅓ cup chopped green olives
  2 teaspoons chopped parsley
  3 jalapeños
    Salt
    Pepper
    Oregano
  1 avocado, sliced

Peel skin off fish and cut into squares (no bones). Place in earthen bowl. Cover with lemon juice and marinate 6 hours. Add oil, vinegar, onion, tomatoes, green olives, parsley and jalapeños (chile peppers which have been rinsed well and cut up). Season with salt, pepper and oregano. Serve in shells or seafood cocktail containers with crackers. Decorate with avocado slices. Serves 8.

*In some regions seviche is spelled ceviche.

Marmora Bay
Antigua, West Indies

On a peninsula

There are tennis courts for the energetic. Plenty of sea and sun for all. The Caricabana Dining Room is open to the moonlight on all sides. Enjoy exotic delicacies, continental cuisine and native desserts. Steel drums, limbo dancers and island drinks beckon you to the Night Club after dinner. A unique Reef Casino is on the premises. Lord Nelson's Dockyard (4 mi.) is a must for every visitor.

SHRIMP AND BANANA CURRY

  2 ripe bananas
1½ teaspoons butter
  3 cups Curry Sauce
  ½ cup shrimp
  1 stalk scallions, chopped
  1 green pepper chopped
  ½ cup diced tomatoes

Peel bananas. Place in baking dish and brush with butter. Pour half of Curry Sauce over bananas and bake in 350 degree oven 10-15 minutes. Cook shrimp in remaining Curry Sauce, add rest of ingredients. Season and serve over hot steamed rice. Serves 2.

Curry Sauce

  3 cups chicken broth
  ⅔ cup Coconut Milk
1½ tablespoons curry powder

Combine broth, Coconut Milk and curry powder. Heat while stirring until sauce bubbles. Thicken with cornstarch as needed. 3 cups.

Coconut Milk

  ½ cup boiling water
  1 coconut (grated meat, with or without brown skin)

Pour boiling water over grated coconut meat. Stir and press down with a spoon. Let stand 20 minutes. Strain through cheesecloth (double layer) squeezing until all juice is extracted. Makes 1 cup.

Freeport
Grand Bahama, Bahamas

On Lucayan Beach

Everything under the Bahamian sun awaits you only 35 air minutes from Florida. A mile long white sand beach and the ocean invite sunning, sailing, fishing, water skiing, skin and scuba diving. Dine elegantly in the Emerald Room—informally in the colorful Troubadour Room. Dance to the native music. Casinos and golf courses are nearby. Enjoy sauna baths and tennis at the Inn. Visit the International Bazaar for imports from all over the world.

COQUILLES ST. JACQUES

3¾ cups scallops
¾ cup butter
    Juice of 3 lemons
1½ teaspoons shallots, chopped
¾ cup mushrooms, sliced
6 ounces dry white wine
¾ cup heavy cream
6 egg yolks
⅓ cup grated cheese

Sauté scallops in ⅓ cup butter for 1 minute. Add lemon juice. Remove scallops and place in coquilles. Sauté shallots and sliced mushrooms in remaining butter, add wine and liquor from scallops. Reduce ⅓. Add hot Cream Sauce. Blend with cream and egg yolks mixed and seasoned to taste. Do not boil. Pour sauce over scallops. Sprinkle with cheese. Brown under broiler. Sprinkle with finely chopped parsley. Serve hot. Serves 8.

Cream Sauce

⅓ cup butter
⅓ cup flour
1½ teaspoons salt
3 cups milk

Melt butter in saucepan, add flour and blend. When well mixed, add salt and milk. Cook until thickened. Stir continuously. Makes 3 cups.

Bridgetown
Barbados, West Indies

Aquatic Gap

If you like the sea, you'll love Barbados. Water sports are endless. This ultra luxurious Inn has a magnificent expanse of white sand beach, sheltered by lush tropical plants and palms. The West Indian sun sets for festive evenings . . . barbeques, cocktails and buffets of Bajan cuisine. Dance to the calypso beat of steel bands. Watch a fiery limbo. Wind through the streets of Bridgetown for shopping and sightseeing by day.

BARBADOS FILLETS

6 fillets

Prepare firm fish fillets for cooking over grill outdoors or inside on broiling rack. Sprinkle with lime juice, salt and pepper. Brush with melted butter and grill on both sides until done.

While fish are cooking prepare sauce.
Mince: 1 onion, 1 clove garlic and 1 small green pepper. Sauté in 2 tablespoons cooking oil until golden. Add 2 tablespoons vinegar, juice of 1 lime and ⅓ cup tomato juice. Simmer 10 minutes. Serve with fish. Serves 6 persons.

COCONUT CUSTARD

1 quart milk
6 eggs
½ cup sugar
¼ teaspoon salt
½ teaspoon vanilla
1 cup shredded coconut

Scald milk. Beat eggs slightly. Add sugar and salt. Slowly add hot milk to eggs and sugar. Add vanilla and 1 cup shredded fresh coconut. Pour into custard cups. Set cups in pan of hot water. Bake at 300 degrees until firm. Test by running silver knife through custard. When done it will come out clean. Remove from pan of water. Cool and chill. Makes 12 custard cups.

St. George, Bermuda

Off Barry Rd. on Bates Bay

Bermuda is beautiful! The softest pink sand is surrounded by the bluest of seas. Pastel-hued houses dot the British colony in the mid-Atlantic. Motor bikes are the way to go — shopping, sightseeing and to the beaches. Over water courses challenge golfers. Bermuda's luxurious Holiday Inn blends into the island beautifully — it's pink. Dining is an international experience in the Inn's many dining areas.

CASSAVA PIE

The cassava root was brought to Bermuda in 1616 and Cassava Pie originated on the island.

    12 pounds cassava*, grated
    1½ pounds butter
     2 to 4 cups sugar
    1½ dozen eggs, beaten
    3½ tablespoons salt
     2 nutmegs, grated

Cream butter and sugar, adding eggs last. Add to cassava and seasonings. Mix ⅓ at a time, then combine as crust is heavy mixture. Use enamel pan 13x9x4 and grease well. Press cassava crust gently in bottom and around sides 2 inches thick. Meanwhile have ready 2 cut up chickens and 3 pounds pork loin, which have been stewed until done, using water to cover and seasoned with thyme, salt and pepper. Dice chicken and pork.

Place meat mixture on top of crust and cover with cassava mixture. Make a steam hole in center of crust so filling is visible. Press top with fork to make a pattern. Cook for 1 hour in a 300 degree oven, then lower heat to 250 degrees and cook for 4 hours. Use stock drained from meat mixture to baste crust while cooking.

*Farina can be used in place of cassava. Use only ½ amount and add water and evaporated milk (4 cups liquid per pound farina). Let set 1 hour.

Santo Domingo, Dominican Republic

Independencia Ave. #60

The oldest city in the new world awaits you. Its Holiday Inn is a vacation paradise in the Caribbean. Feast on native (and American) fare. Join in or just enjoy native entertainment. Free port shops, offering bargains galore, are nearby. Native shops feature pottery, hammocks, baskets and tortoise shell articles. The Inn is also near the race track, casinos and winter baseball. Be sure to visit Columbus Palace and Old Santo Domingo.

DOMINICAN RICE AND CHICKEN
(Arroz con Pollo Dominicano)

     2 pounds chicken
     2 teaspoons salt
    ¼ teaspoon pepper
    ¼ teaspoon oregano
     1 garlic clove, crushed
    ½ cup cooking oil
     2 tablespoons vinegar
     4 tablespoons tomato paste
     2 tomatoes, diced
     1 onion, diced
     1 green pepper, diced
     2 cups rice, uncooked
    3½ to 4 cups water

Cut chicken into serving pieces. Rub with seasonings. Sauté in 2 tablespoons of the oil, until cooked (10 to 15 minutes). To chicken add vinegar, tomato paste, tomatoes, onion, green pepper and rest of cooking oil. Add rice and water. Cover and cook slowly for 30 to 45 minutes, until dry. With large spoon turn rice from bottom to top while cooking. Add a little oil and stir. Serves 6.

Grenada, West Indies

On Grand Anse Beach

The Grenada air is filled with aromatic fragrance — this is the "Spice Island of the West". When you visit the isle's Holiday Inn you can expect wonderful spicy foods — fresh cinnamon, vanilla, ginger and nutmeg grow here in abundance. The colorful pastel buildings make nearby St. George's look like a toy town. You'll enjoy the leisurely life here. Good food, dancing, entertainment, sailing and tennis are at your ocean side doorstep.

WEST INDIAN SHRIMP

    2   pounds large shrimp
    1½ teaspoons cumin seeds
    1½ teaspoons whole black peppercorns
    ½   teaspoon crushed hot red pepper
    2   teaspoons curry powder
    1   cup finely chopped onions
    1   teaspoon finely chopped garlic
    2   cups canned tomatoes, chopped
    1   teaspoon salt
    2   tablespoons lime juice

Combine cumin, peppercorns, red pepper and curry powder. Place in blender until pulverized. Heat 3 tablespoons vegetable oil in a heavy iron skillet. Saute onions and garlic until transparent. Add spices, tomatoes (drained), salt, lime juice and 1 cup water. Bring to a boil, stirring constantly. Boil until liquid thickens. Add shrimp (cleaned and deveined) and simmer 10 to 15 minutes. Serve with rice and mango chutney. Serves 6.

BANANA FRITTERS

Peel 6 bananas and cut in halves lengthwise. Sprinkle with rum. Beat 2 egg yolks, adding ¼ cup water and ¼ cup rich milk. Then beat in 1 tablespoon rum and 1 tablespoon melted butter. Sift 1 cup flour with dash salt and 2 tablespoons sugar. Combine mixtures and fold in 2 beaten egg whites. Dip bananas in batter and fry in deep fat at 350 degrees until golden. Sprinkle freshly grated nutmeg over them and serve. Serves 6 to 8.

Montego Bay, Jamaica

Rose Hall Plantation

It's hard to tell summer from winter here. Swimming, deep sea fishing, skin diving, horseback riding and golf fill fun days. The evenings come alive at the Inn with calypso entertainment. And palm trees are everywhere — even inside the Inn's dining room. This Holiday Inn has Montego Bay's first convention facilities. You can buy imported products at unbelievable low duty-free prices in nearby Kingston.

ACKEE BREAKFAST RECIPE

Ackee is the national fruit of the island. When ripe it is completely open and looks like a gold star. (Caution: Do not use when unopened). Ackee is now being canned.

Boil ackee fruit and peel gently. Drain off the water. Melt 2 tablespoons butter in a frying pan. Add 2 tablespoons chopped onion and 2 tablespoons chopped bacon. Add freshly ground pepper and some salt. Fry onion and bacon until onion is glazed and bacon is crisp. Add ackee and simmer for 5 minutes. (Ackee fried looks like scrambled eggs). Presoak salted cod for 24 hours and serve portion with ackee.

COCONUT ICE CREAM

Crack coconut, saving coconut milk. Make syrup with ¾ cup sugar and coconut milk, adding enough water to make ¼ cup. Grate coconut, combine with 1 cup cream and squeeze through cheesecloth to make coconut creme. Chill thoroughly. Beat 4 egg yolks lightly and add 1 cup cream. Add hot syrup slowly and cook over low heat until custard consistency. Pour into bowl. Chill. Whip 1 cup cream. Whip coconut creme. Combine. Add to chilled egg yolk mixture, which has been beaten stiff after chilling. Add ¼ cup dark rum last and mix well. Place in paper cups or molds and freeze. Serves 8 to 10.

Aruba
Netherlands Antilles

On Palm Beach, Oranjestad

Aruba is just off the Venezuelan coast. This Holiday Inn is on the leeward side of the Dutch Island, where the sea is serene and the beaches rank among the world's finest. Native dishes as well as continental cuisine are served in the Supper Club. There's a Casino on the premises. Visitors enjoy free port shopping and touring the interior of the 69-square mile island.

STUFFED CHEESE

    1 Edam cheese
    2 pounds boiled fish, cut up
    1 onion, minced
    2 tablespoons butter
    2 tomatoes, cut up
   12 olives, cut up
    1 pickle, cut up
   ¼ hot pepper, minced
    3 raisins
    2 eggs, well beaten
   ½ cup bread crumbs

Scoop out inside of a Holland Edam cheese. Avoid breaking rind by leaving ¼ inch of cheese on inside. Cut out hole about 3 inches across to scoop out inside and reserve piece of rind for casserole cover. Place scooped out cheese in double boiler over hot water to soften. Soften outside shell by placing in hot water for 1 hour. Mix fish and onion. Simmer in butter. Add cheese, then rest of ingredients, eggs and bread crumbs last. Fill cheese shell with mixture and place in buttered casserole as near size of cheese shell as possible. Cook in a 350 degree oven for 1½ hours. Serves 6.

Curacao
Netherlands, Antilles

Pater Euwensweg Willemstad

A tropical Dutch treat awaits you at this unique Holiday Inn. It's located at Willemstad, the capital, with its toy town houses in candy colored hues. The imported bargains (duty-free) at rock bottom prices will astound you. Musicians from Venezuela, Colombia, Peru, Panama and the Dominican Republic compose the band in the Inn's beautiful Night Watch Night Club and Casino.

KEESHI YENA

    4 pounds ground beef
    3 whole dill pickles, minced
   10 stuffed olives, chopped fine
    8 pieces pimento, chopped fine
    1 pound dry raisins
    2 tablespoons tomato paste
    1 tablespoon catsup
   1½ pounds Gouda cheese, chopped
    4 ⅛-inch slices Gouda cheese.

Fry beef in pan with a little cooking oil. (Not too dry). Add pickles, olives, pimento, raisins, tomato paste, catsup and a little salt and pepper. Add a little cumin, ground cloves, nutmeg and soya sauce to taste. Simmer 15 minutes. Add chopped cheese and stir until it melts. Take from heat.

To Stuff:

Grease a small soup bowl with butter. Put slice of cheese on bottom then press slices on sides of bowl covering all of surface. Fill with meat mixture. Fold cheese over top. Put in a bain-marie (water-bath: warming anything in a vessel immersed in boiling water) until hot. Then turn bowl over a hot 12-inch platter so that cheese pie will be in middle of a piece of lettuce. Garnish with fried plantain (a kind of banana less sweet but more starchy than ordinary banana). 10 to 12 servings.

San Juan, Puerto Rico

Isla Verde Section

The Puerto Rican sun shines warmly on the Inn's 9 acres of tropical grounds and beautiful beach. Bullfights, races, cockfights and casinos are only minutes away. Guests are offered golf and tennis privileges nearby. Steak cook outs, beach parties, pig roasts, native steel bands and combos all add to the fun here. Be sure to visit historic Old San Juan, the walled in city.

CABRO EN FRICASSEE
(Kid Fricassee)

3 pounds tender goat meat
2 ounces diced cured ham
1 pound onions, peeled & sliced
2 bay leaves
2 green peppers, sliced
½ cup tomato sauce
2 tomatos, diced
12 green stuffed olives
2 tablespoons capers
2½ pounds cooked green peas
1 pound small potatoes, peeled
1 5-ounce glass Burgundy wine

Wash and cut meat (preferably kid) in 2-inch pieces. Sprinkle with sour orange juice and let marinate 2 hours. Drain and rinse in cold water. Mash in a mortar: 2 large cloves garlic, 2 teaspoons oregano, ½ tablespoon pepper, 1½ tablespoons salt and 1 tablespoon vinegar. Rub kid meat in this mixture, then sauté in saucepan over high heat. Brown ham in a large kettle. Add onions, bay leaves, green peppers, tomato sauce, tomatos, olives, capers and 2 cups water (or more if necessary). Add kid meat and bring to a boil. Cook covered for 30 minutes. Add peas, including liquid, and cook 30 minutes more covered. Add potatoes and cook uncovered for 1 hour or more. Add wine and let simmer until sauce thickens. Serves 6 to 8.

St. Lucia, West Indies

On Reduit Beach

Each Room has an ocean view. You can listen to native singers while enjoying gourmet cuisine . . . continental, American and many West Indian specialties. The Inn is near the charming town of Castries, a favorite port for international yachtsmen. Native women in colorful 17th century garments are always as happy as at carnival time. Fabulous deep sea fishing, bargain shopping, swimming, sailing and skin diving fill fun days. Wild orchids, hibiscus and tropical fruit trees add to the island paradise.

FISH AU GRATIN

1½-pound fresh fish, boned
½ pint water
1 pint rich milk
1 onion, sliced
2 lemon wedges
1 bunch herbs
4 tomatoes, skinned
¼ cup melted butter
¼ cup flour
4 to 6 ounces grated Cheddar cheese
    Mustard
    Juice of 1 lemon

Place the fish in a pan with water, milk, onion, 2 lemon wedges, herbs (tied in cheesecloth), salt and pepper. Simmer for 10 to 15 minutes. Lift fish out and place in large flakes in a fireproof casserole. Slice tomatoes and place on fish. Sprinkle with salt and pepper.
Blend butter and flour to make a roux. Add to strained liquid in which fish was cooked. Bring to boil and stir continuously. Boil 4 to 5 minutes. Add half of grated cheese and season with salt, pepper, mustard and lemon juice. Pour over fish. Sprinkle with remaining cheese and place in a 350 degree oven to heat through. Brown top and sprinkle with chopped parsley. (4 individual casseroles may be used, if desired). 4 servings.

Anniston-Oxford, Ala.

U.S. 78, 431 & Ala. 21

For a spectacular panorama, take a drive on the crest of the nearby Talladega Mountains. Then be off to Cheaha State Park. It's at the foot of Cheaha Mountain, the highest point in Alabama. Birds and animals now extinct are displayed in the Regar Museum of Natural History in Anniston. This Holiday Inn is only 4 miles from Anniston. It's easily accessible to Oxford too, and near both airports. Food is served in the true Southern tradition.

COLE SLAW

1 firm young cabbage
1 carrot
    Crisp outer leaves of lettuce

Remove outside leaves of cabbage. Cut the rest in quarters. With sharp knife cut cabbage in very thin slices, then chop coarse. Wash, peel and shred carrot fine. Add to cabbage. Soak in ice water for 1 hour. Just before serving, add Dressing and mix. Serve on crisp lettuce leaves. Serves 4 to 6.

Dressing

2 tablespoons sugar
¾ teaspon salt
¼ teaspoon white ground pepper
2 tablespoons vinegar
¼ cup mayonnaise

Mix sugar, salt, pepper, vinegar and mayonnaise. Add ½ teaspoon celery seeds or 1 tablespoon minced onion or green pepper, if desired. Makes approximately ½ cup.

Birmingham, Ala.
Civic Center

2230 10th Ave. N.

The heart of the city is only six blocks away. This Holiday Inn is a hub of activity since it is so near Birmingham's beautiful new Civic Center. There's a wading pool for tots and a big outdoor pool too. Each year the Festival of Art Show, Camellia Show and several concerts are held at the nearby Municipal Auditorium. Birmingham Southern College is only about 8 miles away.

CHICKEN LIVERS
IN SOUR CREAM SAUCE

1 pound chicken livers
¼ cup butter or margarine
1 green pepper, minced
2 tablespoons flour
½ pint commercial sour cream
¼ cup chicken stock
1 4-ounce can mushrooms, drained
2 tablespoons chopped parsley
1 tablespoon grated onion
    Salt and pepper to taste
½ teaspoon MSG

Cut livers in halves. Heat butter and sauté livers in it gently about 5 minutes. Remove livers. In the same pan sauté green pepper for 5 minutes. Sprinkle flour over green pepper and stir well. Add sour cream and chicken stock. Cook, stirring constantly, until mixture boils and thickens. Add all remaining ingredients but livers. Just before serving, add livers to sauce and heat gradually and thoroughly. Makes 6 servings.

Birmingham, Ala. Downtown

U.S. 11, 1313 3rd Ave. North

You'll enjoy your stay at this Holiday Inn in the heart of downtown Birmingham. It's so convenient for conventions, also for shoppers, travelers and business executives. Both hospitality and food are southern style. Be sure to see the Vulcan Monument, a mighty cast iron statue, atop Red Mountain. The Vulcan's torch burns green on days of no fatality in the steel mills. Birmingham is a famous steel, iron and coal center.

SHRIMP AU GRATIN

4 tablespoons butter
4 tablespoons flour
1 teaspoon salt
⅛ teaspoon pepper
1¾ cups milk
½ cup light cream
1 teaspoon Worcestershire sauce
1 tablespoon lemon juice
1 pound cooked, peeled shrimp
1 cup soft bread crumbs
2 tablespoons melted butter

Melt 4 tablespoons butter in saute´ pot. Stir in flour, salt and pepper. When the above ingredients are well blended, add milk and cream slowly. Stir constantly over low heat until mixture thickens and boils. Stir in Worcestershire sauce, lemon juice and shrimp. Pour in greased baking dish. Top with bread crumbs rolled in 2 tablespoons butter. Bake in moderately hot (375 degree) oven for about 15 minutes or until golden brown. Serves 6 to 8.

Birmingham, Ala.-South

U.S. 31 & I-65

The dining rooms at this Inn afford beautiful views of the mountains, as well as delicious food. Visitors enjoy journeys to the top of Red Mountain to see the 53-foot tall statue of Vulcan, god of fire and forge, that overlooks the greatest steel-making center south of Pittsburgh. The Arlington Historical Shrine is furnished with authentic antiques. Downtown Birmingham is 8 miles away.

SALMON LOAF

2 cups flaked cooked salmon
½ cup fine bread crumbs
4 tablespoons butter
2 eggs, slightly beaten
1 tablespoon chopped parsley
   Salt, pepper and Worcestershire

Mix all ingredients and place in a buttered baking dish. Set in a pan of hot water 1 inch deep. Bake at 350 degrees until firm, about 30 minutes. Serve hot with Mustard Sauce. Serves 6.

Mustard Sauce

2 tablespoons dry mustard
1 teaspoon flour
¼ teaspoon salt
1 cup evaporated milk or cream
¼ cup sugar
1 beaten egg yolk
½ cup vinegar

Mix mustard, flour, salt and ¼ cup evaporated milk or cream. Put ¾ cup evaporated milk or cream and sugar into a heavy saucepan or double boiler top and heat. Stir in mustard mixture. Then add egg yolk which has been beaten until thick. Add vinegar which has been heated. Makes 1½ or 2 cups.

Birmingham, Ala.-West

Bessemer, U.S. 11 S.

Resort to five acres in Jones Valley. This resort Inn offers gourmet fare at Michael's Restaurant. There's everything from a putting green and shuffleboard to bowling for fun. Only a few minutes away is Holiday Beach . . . a complete lake resort, free for the Inn's guests. The Birmingham-Bessemer area is sometimes called the Pittsburgh of the south with its T.C.I. Division of U.S. Steel.

PINEAPPLE CHEESE PIE

- 1 pound Philadelphia cream cheese
- 3 ounces butter
- ½ cup sugar
  Pinch of salt
- 1 tablespoon vanilla
- ¼ cup whole sweet milk
- 2 eggs, beaten
- 2 cups pineapple pie filling
- 1 9-inch unbaked pie shell
- ½ cup chopped almonds

Cream together cream cheese, butter and sugar. Add salt, vanilla, milk and eggs. Put pineapple pie filling about 1-inch thick into unbaked pie shell. Top with cheese mixture. Sprinkle top of pie with almonds and bake in 350 degree oven about 40 minutes, until filling is firm and crust is brown. Let cool before serving. Serves 6 to 8.

Pie Crust

Sift flour before measuring 1½ cups. Sift again with ½ teaspoon salt and 1 teaspoon baking powder. Cut ¼ cup shortening in with 2 knives or pastry blender. Sprinkle a little water over and toss with fork. Repeat until ¼ cup water is used. Make into a ball and chill if time permits. Roll out larger than pie pan and place in pan loosely. Cut and crimp edges.

Boaz, Ala.

U.S. 431 at Bethsaida Rd.

Boaz was the National Beautification Winner in 1967 and 1968. This Boaz Holiday Inn is famous for its fresh Strawberry Pie (served year round), Loin Club Steaks, Salad Bar and miniature homemade bread loaves. The chef will prepare wild game for sportsmen guests—if they bring it in. Excellent fishing, boating, swimming and picnicking facilities are only 16 miles away at Lake Guntersville.

CHICKEN BREAST SUPREME

- 4 chicken breasts, split
- ¼ teaspoon white pepper
- ½ teaspoon salt
- ½ cup softened margarine
  Dash of paprika
- 1 small can Cream of Mushroom Soup

Place chicken breasts in a buttered casserole and season. Baste with margarine. Bake in a preheated 375 degree oven for 20 minutes. Remove from oven and sprinkle with paprika. Dilute soup with ½ can of water or milk and spoon over chicken. Return to a 400 degree oven for 15 minutes. Serves 4.

SHRIMP BOAZ SPECIAL

Line an individual salad dish with an outer green leaf of lettuce and fill with tossed green garden salad. Arrange 6 salad shrimp, tomato wedges, egg slices and a scoop of potato salad on top of the lettuce. Top with Shrimp Sauce.

Shrimp Sauce

- 1 cup mayonnaise
- 1 tablespoon chives, chopped
- 1 tablespoon parsley, chopped
- 1 tablespoon tarragon, chopped
- 1 tablespoon spinach, chopped
- 1 tablespoon capers, chopped

Place all ingredients in blender and run on high speed for a few seconds, until smooth in texture. Makes 1¼ cups sauce.

Clanton, Ala.

Interstate 65 & U.S. 31

This is peach country and you'll know it at this Holiday Inn. Try peach preserves for breakfast and peach cobbler for dessert. Clanton is especially beautiful during peach blossom time. Anytime is a good time to try fishing for trout in the Coosa River. Both Coosa River and Mitchell Lake offer fishing, boating and water sports. Guides are available. Clanton hosts an annual Peach Festival.

CHEESE STEW

1 cup cooked beef
1 tablespoon chopped green pepper
3 tablespoons chopped carrots
3 tablespoons chopped cabbage
3 tablespoons chopped parsley
1 tablespoon finely chopped onion
1 cup diced potatoes
3 cups beef stock
2 teaspoons salt
½ cup grated cheese

Dice cooked beef. Add vegetables to beef and combine with beef stock. Season to taste. Cook until vegetables are tender. Serve piping hot on toast. Garnish with grated cheese and paprika. 8 servings.

HUNGARIAN GOULASH

2 pounds chuck roast, cubed
2 cups tomatoes
½ cup diced celery
1 green pepper, chopped
2 cups diced carrots
½ cup diced onion
2 tablespoons minced parsley

Flour beef and combine with 1 cup diced salt pork. Sauté in cooking oil until brown. Add water to prevent sticking. Cover and simmer until meat is done. Add vegetables and 4 cloves with water to cover. Season. Simmer until vegetables are tender. Serve with cooked noodles. 6 servings.

Cullman, Ala.

Ala. 69 & Interstate 65

Cullman is in the heart of Dixie. It's within minutes of Smith Lake (where the world's record spotted bass was caught), Natural Bridge, Bankhead National Forest and Ave Maria Grotto. Cullman Holiday Inn guests are delighted with homemade bread and pastries from the Inn's own bakery. The dining rooms and lobby overlook a beautiful glass enclosed swimming pool. Name bands are featured semiannually.

CHERRY CHEESECAKE

12 ounces cream cheese
½ cup sugar
2 tablespoons lemon juice
1 teaspoon vanilla
⅛ teaspoon salt
3 eggs
½ cup dairy sour cream
1 tablespoon sugar
½ teaspoon vanilla

Beat softened cream cheese until fluffy. Gradually blend in the ½ cup sugar, lemon juice, 1 teaspoon vanilla and salt. Add eggs, one at a time, beating well after each addition. Pour filling into a cooked zwieback crumb crust in an 8-inch spring form pan. Bake at 325 degrees for 35 minutes. Combine sour cream with remaining sugar and vanilla. Spread over top of cake and return to oven to bake another 5 minutes. Cool. Top with Sweet Cherry Glaze and chill for several hours. Makes 10 to 12 servings.

Sweet Cherry Glaze

Drain 1 (1 lb. 14 oz.) can pitted light sweet cherries and arrange over top of cheesecake. Heat ¾ cup red cherry jelly slightly to soften, stirring until smooth. Spoon softened jelly over cherries. Chill well.

Dauphin Island, Ala.

St. Hwy. 163

Come to Dauphin Island—it's surrounded by the Gulf of Mexico. Day after day charter boats bring Holiday Inn guests home with deep sea dinners and trophies. The Inn's restaurant is famous for preparing the catch of the day. An immense "Free Fishing Pier" extends 300 feet into the Gulf. The Alabama Deep Sea Fishing Rodeo is in late July or early August.

RED SNAPPER
WITH CREOLE SAUCE

    6 8-ounce red snapper steaks
    ½ cup chopped onion
    1½ cups chopped celery
    ¼ cup chopped green pepper
    6 tablespoons butter
    1 bay leaf
    1 teaspoon salt
    3 cups canned tomatoes

Sauté onion, celery and pepper in butter until tender. Add bay leaf, salt and tomatoes. Place red snapper steaks in a greased baking dish. Season with a dash red pepper and Worcestershire sauce. Add sauce. Bake in 350 degree oven for about 45 minutes. Serve with sauce over fish. Serves 6.

CREOLE SEAFOOD GUMBO

Sauté 4 ribs chopped celery (with leaves), 1 chopped green pepper, 1 chopped onion and 3 to 4 cups thinly sliced okra in 2 tablespoons butter or bacon drippings until tender. Add 1½ to 2 cups canned tomatoes. Then add salt and pepper to taste. Place ingredients in a large heavy pot and add 4 cups chicken stock, ½ pound raw white crab meat, 12 to 18 oysters and ½ pound raw shrimp. Cook slowly for 1 hour. Makes approximately 8 to 10 cupfuls.

Decatur, Ala.
Downtown

U.S. 31 and 20

Fishing, water skiing and swimming are at your doorstep here. Decatur's downtown Holiday Inn is on the shores of Lake Wheeler and the Tennessee River, with its busy colorful harbor. Hot muffins greet guests when they are seated in the Royal Hunt Restaurant. Be sure to save room for the Coconut Crunch Pie. Take time to visit Mooresville—the first incorporated town in Alabama has remained almost unchanged for a century.

TENNESSEE RIVER FISH

    4 small whole fish
      or fillets of larger fish

Clean fish and wash well. Dry with paper towel. Salt inside cavity and on outside too. Roll fish in corn meal until well coated. Place fish one layer deep in deep kettle of hot cooking oil. Fry until golden brown—time depends on thickness of fish—usually about 8 to 10 minutes. Serves 4.

HOT MUFFINS

    1 egg
    ¼ cup sugar
    1 cup milk
    1 teaspoon salt
    2 cups flour
    3 teaspoons baking powder
    ¼ cup melted butter

Beat egg, add sugar, milk and salt. Mix thoroughly. Measure and sift flour. Add baking powder and sift together. Add to liquid mixture. Mix well. Add melted butter. Do not over mix. Pour into greased muffin pans and bake at 425 degrees for 20 to 30 minutes. Makes 8 muffins.

Decatur, Ala.-South

U.S. 31 South

Everyone looks forward to breakfast at this southern Inn—Country Ham and Grits. The Inn is nestled in a wooded area on the edge of town, in the heart of Alabama's Tennessee River Valley. Fish are plentiful around here. There's duck and geese hunting in nearby Wheeler Basin Wildlife Refuge. Bankhead National Forest has annual hunts for wild turkey and deer.

APPLE SALAD

    6 medium-size apples, diced
    5 stalks celery, diced
    1 cup chopped pecans
    1 tablespoon vinegar
    1 tablespoon water
    ¼ cup sugar
    1 cup milk
    1 egg
    1½ tablespoons flour

Put diced apples and celery into a large bowl and mix. Add chopped pecans. For the apple dressing, dissolve the vinegar and water with the sugar on the stove. Have mixed together the milk, egg and flour. Beat until smooth and then add to the vinegar mixture and cook until thick. Mix with apples, celery and pecans. Serves 6.

SWISS STEAK

    1 pound round steak, 1½ inches thick
    1 medium-size onion, diced
    1 can tomato soup
    1 tablespoon cooking oil

Grease skillet, flour the steak and let brown on both sides. Then add the onion, tomato soup and a can or more of water. Add salt and pepper to taste. Simmer for about 2 hours, or until tender. Serves 3 to 4.

Dothan, Ala.

Ross Clark Circle, U.S. 84 W.

Drifts of delightful charcoal aroma lure people into The Charcoal Steak House at this Holiday Inn. Delicious food prepared with culinary know-how is graciously served. As an extra service at the Inn, there's free transportation to the Municipal Airport a mile away. There's an unusual monument nearby erected to the Boll Weevil. Dothan hosts the National Peanut Festival each October.

SIRLOIN TIPS WITH MUSHROOMS

    2½ pounds sirloin of beef, cubed
    ¼ cup cooking oil
    1 cup chopped onions
    2 cups green peppers, finely chopped
    1 tablespoon oregano
    1 teaspoon salt
    ⅛ teaspoon black pepper
    1¼ cups canned tomatoes
    1¼ cups tomato purée
    1 pint water
    ¼ cup flour
    1 8-ounce can mushrooms
    ½ pound egg noodles
    ¼ stick butter

Pan fry beef in oil until brown. Put in the onions, green peppers, oregano, salt, pepper, tomatoes, tomato purée and water. Cook until tender. Thicken with flour and pour in mushrooms. Cook slowly 10 minutes longer. Boil noodles in salted water and drain well when done. Butter the noodles and divide into 8 individual casseroles. Serve the sirloin tips over the noodles. Serves 8.

Eufaula, Ala.

U.S. 82 at Riverside Dr.

Eufaula is noted for its ante-bellum homes and "Old Fashioned Inn-keeping" at this Holiday Inn. Located high on a bluff overlooking Lake Eufaula, the Inn offers fishing from the bank of the lake for its guests. The region rewards hunters with every wild game, from deer to wiley wild turkey. Guests are especially pleased to find regional favorites and at least 8 fresh picked garden vegetables on the menu everyday.

EGG DUMPLING SOUP

Dumplings

2 cups plain flour
  Pinch of salt
2 teaspoons baking powder
1 cup ice water

Sift flour, salt and baking powder. Add ice water. Add more water if dough is too stiff. Roll out on floured board and cut into small round dumplings with a biscuit cutter. Drop into boiling chicken stock. When done, remove from heat and set aside.

Soup Base

2 quarts well-seasoned chicken stock
½ cup cornstarch
2 hard boiled eggs
¼ cup chopped parsley

Blend cornstarch in 1 cup of stock. Add to remaining stock and cook until medium thick. Add chopped eggs and parsley, after removing from heat. When ready to serve, add several dumplings to each soup bowl. Serves 8.

Florence, Ala.

504 S. Court, Hwys. 72 & 43

Fresh Tennessee River Catfish, Hush Puppies and Cole Slaw are delicious reasons to stop at this Holiday Inn. Excellent fishing awaits guests less than a mile away in the Tennessee River. Just a few blocks away you'll find an Indian Mound built before Columbus discovered America. The homes of Helen Keller and W. C. Handy are nearby.

ORANGE CHIFFON CAKE

Mix and sift together: 2¼ cups sifted cake flour, 1½ cups sugar, 3 teaspoons baking powder and 1 teaspoon salt. Make a well in mixture and add in order: ½ cup cooking oil, 5 unbeaten egg yolks, ¾ cup fresh orange juice and 3 tablespoons grated orange rind. Beat with spoon until smooth.

Measure into a large mixing bowl: 1 cup egg whites and ½ teaspoon cream of tartar. Whip until whites form stiff peaks. Pour egg yolk mixture gradually over whites, gently folding until blended. Do not stir! Pour into ungreased tube pan and bake at 325 degrees for 55 minutes. Immediately turn pan upside down on rack. Let stand until cold. Slice in 3 layers and put together with chilled Orange Filling. Stack cake on **heat resistant plate.**

Orange Filling

Mix 1½ cups sugar, 4 tablespoons cornstarch, ½ teaspoon salt, 1½ cups orange juice, 2 tablespoons lemon juice and 3 tablespoons butter in a saucepan and bring to a rolling boil. Boil 1 minute, stirring constantly. Slowly beat half of mixture into 4 slightly beaten egg yolks. Blend into remaining mixture in saucepan. Cook 1 minute, stirring all the time. Remove from heat. Blend 3 tablespoons orange rind into mixture. Chill. Cover with meringue and bake at 350 degrees until meringue is golden.

Greenville, Ala.

Ala. 185 & I-65 Interchange

Greenville's early settlers made their way on a "plant and pray" economy. Today King Cotton has been dethroned in the county by the broiler-fryer industry. The Camellia City, once in the heart of the Creek Indian Nation, offers travelers a nice easy pace only 45 miles from Montgomery. Southern Fried Chicken, Roast Beef and Homemade Rolls are favorites on the menu at this Inn.

CONGEALED CUCUMBER SALAD

1½ cups boiling water
1 box lime gelatin
1 cup grated cucumber
½ cup sour cream
1 tablespoon grated onion
    Salt to taste

Pour water over gelatin. Stir and let stand until it begins to set. Add other ingredienth and mix well. Pour into molds and chill until set. Serve on lettuce. Top with mayonnaise. Serves about 4.

FRESH APPLE CAKE

3 cups sugar
1 ⅓ cups cooking oil
2 eggs, beaten
3 cups flour
1 teaspoon baking soda
1 teaspoon cinnamon
1 teaspoon vanilla
3 cups fresh apples, pared and diced
1 cup pecans, chopped fine

Cream sugar and oil. Add eggs and flour which has been sifted with soda and cinnamon. Add vanilla, apples and pecans. Mix thoroughly. Batter will be very stiff. Bake in a tube pan for 1 hour at 325 degrees. Grate rind of one orange and mix with juice of two oranges and two cups sugar. Heat only to dissolve sugar. Pour over hot cake as soon as taken from oven.

Jasper, Ala.

1400 U.S. 78 Bypass

Here's a Holiday Inn right in the heart of scenic northwest Alabama. Smith Lake is less than 15 minutes away with some of the finest fishing in the southeast. Passes are available for golfers at the beautiful Musgrove Country Club. Delicious southern food awaits you at this Inn. You can't order Stuffed Peppers and Short Ribs everywhere! Homemade sweet rolls are a daily delight.

LEG OF LAMB

1 5- to 6-pound leg of lamb

Season lamb with salt and pepper. Use skewer or slim blade knife to make several holes and insert garlic slivers. Place in 400 degree oven for 1 hour. Drain off fat, add water to make natural gravy to surround lamb. Add 1 cup tomato juice for color. Sprinkle oregano over lamb, cover and steam 1½ hours at 375 degrees. Remove lamb and place on platter. Thicken juices with 1 tablespoon flour which has been blended with a little water. Bring to boiling point and season. Strain, if desired, for gravy. Serves 6 to 8.

CREOLE SAUCE

1 tablespoon onion, chopped
½ green pepper, chopped
2 tablespoons butter
1½ cups tomatoes, finely mashed
1 tablespoon chicken base
    Salt and pepper
1 teaspoon lemon juice
1 tablespoon flour
1 tablespoon water

Saute' onion and green pepper in butter. Add tomatoes, chicken base, seasonings and lemon juice. When vegetables are done, add flour which has been blended with water. Add more seasoning to make sauce hotter, if desired. Makes 2 cups.

Lanett, Ala.

(West Point, Ga.)

U.S. 29, next to I-85

Lanett is known as the "Textile City". Guests may tour through all of the mills daily, at no charge. It is best to be back at this Holiday Inn in time for King Crab Au Gratin. On Sunday guests look forward to the Inn's buffet. Wild game and fish abound nearby. Tour information for Georgia's nearby Callaway Gardens may be obtained at the Inn.

KING CRAB AU GRATIN

4 tablespoons melted margarine
2 tablespoons flour
2 cups milk, scalded
1 tablespoon chicken base or chicken bouillon cube
2 cups king crab meat
½ cup Cheddar cheese, grated

Blend margarine and flour. Slowly add scalded milk and stir well. Add chicken base and salt. Cook 5 minutes, until thickened. Add crab meat. Place in a baking dish and sprinkle top with cheese and paprika. Bake at 350 degrees only until cheese is melted. Serve immediately. Serves 6 to 8.

BLUE CHEESE DRESSING

4 tablespoons blue cheese, creamed
1 pint mayonnaise
1 cup milk
2 tablespoons onion, grated
4 tablespoons blue cheese

Cream cheese with spoon or in electric mixer. Add mayonnaise and milk alternately. Crumble remainder of blue cheese. Add to mixture. Add onion. Mix well with spoon. Chill and use with green salads. Serves 8.

Mobile, Ala.-West

3939 Hwy. 90 West

This port and industrial city reflects French and Spanish heritage. It's the bounteous days of the Old South that are reflected on the menus at this Holiday Inn. Culinary lore has been passed down through generations and some of the most prized recipes are prepared here. The Inn is 5 miles from downtown Mobile. The great battleship U.S.S. Alabama is permanently berthed just off U.S. 90. You're near enough to visit Bellingrath Gardens and Home.

SEAFOOD GUMBO

½ stalk celery, diced
2 large onions, diced (not thin)
1 clove garlic, chopped
1 bell pepper, cut up
½ cup cooking oil
1 No. 2 can tomatoes
1 quart water
1 pound raw shrimp
½ pint oysters
½ pound crab meat
1 pound okra
1 tablespoon gumbo filé
Cooked rice
Seasonings

Sauté celery, onions, garlic and bell pepper in cooking oil. Add tomatoes and water. Then add shrimp, oysters, and crab meat. Cook until done (about 10 to 12 minutes). Add okra, gumbo filé and let simmer until okra is done. Season to taste and serve with cooked rice. Makes 10 to 12 cupfuls.

Montgomery, Ala.-East

E. Bypass U.S. 231 & I-85

Historic Montgomery, Cradle of the Confederacy, has long been famous. This Holiday Inn specializes in South of the Border food in its Golden Touch Restaurant. The "Steak for Two" is always a popular order. For a real thirst quencher be sure to try the "Golden Touch Special" in the lounge. You'll enjoy seeing the plantations, ante-bellum homes, churches and museums in and around Montgomery.

UPSIDE-DOWN PINEAPPLE SQUARES

Melt ½ cup butter in a heavy skillet and add 1 cup brown sugar. Stir until sugar melts. Remove from heat and add 8 slices of well drained pineapple and 1 cup pecans.

Batter

1 cup cake flour
1 teaspoon baking powder
4 egg yolks
1 tablespoon melted butter
1 teaspoon vanilla
1 cup sugar
4 egg whites
¼ teaspoon salt

Sift flour, add baking powder and sift again. Beat egg yolks and add melted butter and vanilla. Sift sugar. Whip egg whites with salt. Fold sugar, a little at a time, into egg white mixture. Then fold in yolks and butter. Gradually add sifted flour and baking powder. Pour all in skillet with sugar/pineapple mixture and bake at 325 degrees for ½ hour. This may be baked in a long pan and cut in squares, but pan must be heavy. Turn out upside down when ready to serve. Serves 6 to 8.

Montgomery, Ala. Midtown

U.S. 80 & 231

In the heart of historic Montgomery, this modern Inn welcomes guests with casual informality. Statesmen and historians enjoy the Inn's convenient location — it's within walking distance of the State Capitol Building and the First White House of the Confederacy. The Top of the Star Restaurant serves flaming entrees and desserts. Enjoy live entertainment in the Little Foxes Rooftop Night Club.

BRAISED TENDERLOIN TIPS, MUSHROOM SAUCE

2 pounds tenderloin beef tips
2 tablespoons butter
2 cups Mushroom Sauce
8 ounces yellow noodles

Dice beef tips in 1-inch cubes and sauté in butter in a heavy frying pan. Add salt and pepper and cook to desired doneness. Add Mushroom Sauce and simmer for 10 minutes. Serve in a casserole over yellow noodles. Serves 6.

Mushroom Sauce

¼ pound mushrooms
2 tablespoons butter
3 tablespoons cornstarch
2 cups water or brown sauce

Sauté mushrooms in 1 tablespoon butter in heavy iron frying pan. Blend cornstarch in remaining butter and make a roux. Add brown sauce or water gradually and thicken. Add mushrooms and seasonings. Heat well. Makes approximately 2 cupfuls.

Montgomery, Ala.-SW

4231 Mobile Hwy., U.S. 31

A recreation room, well equipped playground and shuffleboard make this Inn a popular place to stay with families. Everyone enjoys the culinary treats served in the dining room. Many old-fashioned dishes served make one recall the days when Alabama's capital city was the first capital of the Confederacy. The Inn is near Dannley Field and Maxwell Air Force Base.

THE MILLIONAIRE

(A very rich pie)

- 2 cups powdered sugar
- ½ cup margarine
- 2 eggs
- 1 teaspoon vanilla
- 1 cup whipping cream
- 3 tablespoons powdered sugar
- 1½ teaspoons gelatin
- 2 tablespoons pineapple juice
- 1 8¼-ounce can pineapple (drained)
- 3 tablespoons chopped pecans
- 1 baked pie shell (thoroughly cooled)

Cream 2 cups powdered sugar, margarine, eggs and vanilla. Chill thoroughly. Whip cream, adding rest of sugar. Soak gelatin in pineapple juice and dissolve over hot water. Fold in crushed pineapple. Combine with whipped cream. Chill in a bowl. Spread first mixture (sugar, margarine, eggs and vanilla) on bottom of pie shell. Add pineapple/cream mixture for second layer. Sprinkle pecans over top. Chill well before serving. Serves 6 to 8.

Opelika-Auburn, Ala.

U.S. 280 & Ala. 147

In the mood for a candlelight dinner? The Holiday Room at this Inn is famous for serving them every night. That's just one reason guests enjoy their stay at this Holiday Inn down near the state line, 5 miles north of Auburn. Sightseeing visitors enjoy a trip to nearby Chewacla, an area of wild scenic beauty with an artificial lake, streams, cascades and rock palisades.

TURKEY-HAM AU GRATIN

- 4 slices cooked turkey
- 4 slices cooked ham
- 4 tablespoons butter
- 3 tablespoons flour
- 1½ cups chicken broth, hot
- ½ cup cream
- 1 cup soft bread crumbs
- 2 tablespoons melted butter
- ½ cup grated Cheddar cheese
- 4 slices toast

Place slices of toast, turkey and ham in 4 well buttered individual casseroles. Melt 4 tablespoons butter and blend in the flour, adding broth gradually. Cook until it thickens, stirring continuously. Add cream and seasonings. Cook until right consistency and pour into casseroles. Roll bread crumbs in remainder of melted butter and combine with cheese. Sprinkle on each casserole. Run under broiler for 8 to 10 minutes and cheese-crumbs mixture is bubbly and hot. Serves 4.

Ozark, Ala.

U.S. Highway 231

This is an Inn where people, who stop for a meal, usually decide to stay a day or two. The food is delicious! Be sure to order the Whole Fresh Flounder with the Chef's Special Sauce and the Broiled Chicken with Athenian Sauce. The Inn is only 1½ miles southeast of downtown Ozark and 6 miles from Ft. Rucker, an Army Aviation Center. Ozark is not far from Lake Tholocco and Blue Springs State Park.

BROILED FILET MIGNON EN CASSEROLE

Broil filet mignon until desired doneness, allowing 1 filet for each serving. Place in casseroles.

Mushroom Sauce

2 to 3 tablespoons butter
3 onions, diced
1 red pepper, diced
2 green peppers, diced
½ pound mushrooms
4 fresh tomatoes, cubed
2 tablespoons tomato purée
1 cup meat stock or bouillon
1 tablespoon parsley, chopped fine
1 ounce sherry (or more)
Dash Worcestershire sauce
Salt and pepper to taste
Dash garlic

Melt butter in a heavy skillet. Blend and sauté onions and peppers in butter. Add mushrooms and sauté. Add tomatoes and cook a few minutes, stirring frequently. Add remaining ingredients and cover. Put in a warm place. When ready to serve, cover steaks with sauce and place in a hot oven for 2 to 3 minutes. Garnish and serve. Makes approximately 4 cups sauce.

Tuscaloosa, Ala.-North

U.S. 82 Bypass

Downtown Tuscaloosa and the University of Alabama are just 10 minutes away. The Inn adjoins the beautiful Indian Hills Golf and Country Club. Hot homemade rolls, "real" southern fried chicken, and southern hospitality will make you want to stay longer than you planned. Take time to enjoy one of the oldest cities in Alabama, the state capital from 1826 to 1846. Mound State Park is only 30 minutes from the Inn.

DINNER ROLLS

1 yeast cake
9 tablespoons sugar
1 cup milk
7 tablespoons shortening
3 eggs, well beaten
1 teaspoon salt
4½ cups flour

Dissolve yeast in ¼ cup warm water and 2 tablespoons sugar. Scald milk, add shortening and stir until dissolved. Cool and combine with rest of sugar, eggs and salt which have been beaten together. Stir in yeast mixture. Add flour and beat until dough blisters. Let rise until double in bulk. Punch down.

Roll dough on floured board. Cut off strips and round like a rope. Cut into ½ inch strips. Lightly dip strips in oil or melted butter. Drop 2 pieces in each hole of 12-hole muffin tin. Place in warm place. Let rise double in size. Bake in 400 degree oven for 18 to 20 minutes. Makes 3 dozen. Leftover dough may be placed in greased bowl. Grease top, cover and refrigerate.

Anchorage, Alaska

239 West 4th Ave. Dwtn.

For an unusual vacation plan one at this Holiday Inn where natural beauty is displayed 21 hours a day during mid-summer. Or come in winter for excellent skiing. The Inn, with its striking Alpine decor, provides guests with a superb view of the harbor and Mt. McKinley. A "Top O' the Inn" supper club with the finest entertainment and the best Alaska king crab are reasons this Inn is the choice of oil company executives and military personnel.

ALASKA KING CRAB COCKTAIL

Place container with fresh crab meat, which has been boiled and chilled, over ice in large bowl. Serve with a choice of sauces.

Cocktail Sauce

¼ cup mayonnaise
¾ cup catsup or chili sauce
2 tablespoons lemon juice
1 tablespoon horseradish
1 teaspoon salt
2 drops Tabasco sauce
2 teaspoons Worcestershire sauce

Mix ingredients and chill. 1¼ cups.

Caviar Cocktail Sauce

¾ cup mayonnaise
1 tablespoon horseradish
3 tablespoons caviar

Mix ingredients and chill. 1 cup.

MOUSSELINE SAUCE
(Excellent for poached salmon)

Place 3 egg yolks in top of double boiler and beat smooth. Add 2 tablespoons lemon juice gradually, then add ½ cup melted butter and 2 tablespoons hot water, dash salt and cayenne. Beat over low heat until sauce thickens. Cool and add ½ cup cream which has been whipped just before serving. Serve hot or cold. 1½ to 2 cups.

Phoenix, Ariz. - Airport

2201 S. 24th Street

Expect the unusual at this Inn. When in the Lounge guests may listen to conversations between the control tower and the arriving airplanes. It's a new type of entertainment and has proven to be most interesting to guests. Many star attractions are among the entrée specialties in the dining room. This is a wonderful place for travelers, who have only a few hours between planes in the largest of the desert cities.

COLE SLAW

Remove the outside leaves of a firm young cabbage. Cut in quarters and with a very sharp knife cut off very thin slices. Let stand in cold water for ½ hour. Drain and mix with enough Sour Cream Dressing to moisten well. Serves 8.

Sour Cream Dressing

1 teaspoon dry mustard
1 teaspoon salt
1 tablespoon sugar
1 tablespoon flour
2 eggs
¾ cup milk
¼ cup vinegar and lemon juice mixed

Mix all dry ingredients together. Add well beaten eggs. Add milk and vinegar mixture. Cook until thickened while stirring continuously. Remove from heat. Add 1 tablespoon butter and cool. 1 cup.

WALDORF SALAD

2 cups diced apples
3 tablespoons lemon juice
1 cup diced celery
1 cup diced oranges
¼ cup sliced dates or raisins
½ cup chopped nuts
¼ teaspoon salt
¼ cup sugar

Marinate apples in lemon juice. Add celery, oranges, dates, nuts, salt and sugar. Moisten with mayonnaise. Mix lightly with 2 forks. Serve on crisp lettuce. Serves 8.

Phoenix, Ariz.-Central

U.S. 60, 70, 80 & 89

Start your desert days with piping hot sour dough biscuits for breakfast. Visit the Heard Museum, Desert Botanical Gardens and Pueblo Grande (inhabited 800 years ago by Hohokom Indians). Phoenix has 32 golf courses. When the Arizona sun sets there's live entertainment in the Villa Lounge. Authentic Mexican food and Prime Rib make dinner decisions difficult in the Villa Restaurant.

CHEESE ENCHILADAS

8 soft tortillas
½ cup peanut oil
2 cups cheese (mixture of longhorn, Cheddar and Mexican white cheese)
4 green onions, chopped
1 can enchilada sauce

Dip tortillas in hot oil for a few seconds to soften. Fill with grated cheese and chopped green onion. Roll up tortillas, place in shallow baking pan and cover with sauce. Sprinkle additional cheese on top. Bake 20 to 30 minutes at 350 degrees. Serve with grated lettuce and ripe olives. 4 servings.

RED INDIAN PEACHES AU COINTREAU

8 Indian peach halves
8 tablespoons peach juice
2 ounces Cointreau

Serve 2 peach halves in a stem glass with juice. Place on an underliner and top with Cointreau and serve. Serves 4.

The Indian peach is a native of India, and was brought to the region of Southern California several years ago where the tree grows quite well. The fruit is dark reddish color and very unusual in flavor—the color resembling the skin color of the people of India.

Tucson, Ariz.-North

I-10 at Grant Rd. Exit

This is the land of warm, sunny, dry days and crisp, clear nights. Make this Holiday Inn your headquarters in the western gateway to Mexico. It's near the University of Arizona. Old Tucson, an 1860 version of the present city built by Columbia Pictures, is only 12 miles away. See the Mission San Xavier Del Bac. Delicious food awaits you back at the Inn in the Catalina Restaurant. Whet your appetite in the Ocotillo Lounge.

RANCH STYLE BEANS

2 cups pinto beans
6 cups water
½ pound salt pork, cut in 1-inch pieces
2 onions, finely diced
1 green pepper, finely diced
2 teaspoons chili powder
1 clove garlic, mashed
2 cups canned tomatoes
Salt
Dash Worcestershire sauce

Wash beans and pick over. Drain. Place in a heavy kettle and pour in water to cover beans above about 1 inch. Simmer gently for 2 hours. Add salt pork, onion, green pepper, chili powder and garlic. Add tomatoes and salt to taste. Add Worcestershire sauce, if desired. Simmer 2 more hours, adding water if needed. If bean juice seems a little thin, blend 2 tablespoons flour with ¼ cup water and add to thicken. Serves 4 to 5.

Tucson, Ariz.-South

1010 S. Freeway at 22nd St.

Plan to stay awhile at this friendly Inn, located at the base of the scenic Tucson Mountains. The University of Arizona campus is only minutes away. Take a thrilling tour through the colorful chambers of the Colossal Cave. Visit the Saquaro National Monument with its forest of giant cacti. When you return to the Inn you can expect superb food in the Copper Hearth Restaurant. People from every state meet in the King's Den Lounge.

CHICKEN OF THE GODS

    4 whole breasts of chicken
    4 ounces ham, cut in thin strips
    2 eggs, beaten
    1 cup soft bread crumbs
    4 tablespoons melted butter

Wash chicken breasts and dry thoroughly. Place strip of ham in each one. Roll up tightly and fasten with toothpicks. Dip in eggs, then roll in bread crumbs. Sprinkle with butter. Place in baking pan and cover with foil. Bake at 325 degrees for 1¼ hours. Serve with Chicken Fricassee Sauce. Serves 4.

Chicken Fricassee Sauce

    3 tablespoons butter
    4 tablespoons flour
    1½ cups chicken broth
       Salt and pepper

Melt butter, add flour and stir until smooth. Add chicken broth gradually. Stir until thickened. Season with salt and pepper.

Arkadelphia, Ark.

I-30, Jct. Hwys. 67 & 7 N.

No wonder the dining room at this Holiday Inn is always crowded — the food is outstanding. Local residents and visitors go back again and again for exciting adventures in eating. And Arkadelphia has plenty of visitors. It's the home of Henderson State Teachers College and Ouachita Baptist College. There are many historic homes worth seeing and Caddo Indian relics in a museum.

BRAISED BEEF TIPS WITH MUSHROOMS

    2½ quarts prime rib trimmings
        (cut in 1-inch cubes)
    1¾ tablespoons cooking oil
    1½ cups sliced mushrooms
     ¾ cup flour
    1½ teaspoons Spanish paprika
    1¼ teaspoons white pepper
     3 tablespoons tomato paste
     6 cups French onion soup
    2½ tablespoons Burgundy
    1½ tablespoons Kitchen Quick
     6 tablespoons dried green and red
        pepper

Saute' meat in oil in heavy skillet but do not brown. If fresh mushrooms are used, saute' in same pan. Drain fat from pan and add remaining ingredients and stir until well blended and all drippings are combined with mixture. Place in buttered casserole and cover. Bake in 375 degree oven for 1 hour. Stir occasionally during baking time. 12 servings.

Benton, Arkansas

I-30 at Hwy. 5 Exit

Bring your family when you plan a business trip in the area. This Holiday Inn is near Little Rock's industrial center, yet Hot Springs with its lakes is only a few miles away. It's a scenic region and antique shops abound. The Inn's food is excellent — the best of regional dishes plus the little extras like home cooked vegetables and pastries. Join the after church crowd for Sunday dinner.

CHICKEN BREAST HOLIDAY

Bone 6 whole chicken breasts and flatten, leaving skin intact. Dip each in melted butter, then seasoned flour to coat completely. Sauté in melted butter over medium heat, until a light crust forms. Remove to baking dish and cover with can of mushroom soup. Mix 2 tablespoons melted butter and 2 tablespoons sherry. Pour on top. Place ½ cup of mushrooms on top of chickens and more sherry if desired. Breasts may be split for servings (do this before cooking). Serves 6 or more.

TOMATO CHEESE SALAD

    1 can tomato soup
    ½ cup cold water
    4 tablespoons gelatin
    3 3-ounce packages cream cheese
    1 cup mayonnaise
    ½ cup chopped celery
    ¼ cup chopped bell pepper
    ¼ cup sweet pickle relish
    ¼ cup chopped stuffed olives
    ¼ cup chopped onion

Bring soup to a boil. Dissolve gelatin in cold water. Add to soup. Cool, then add cheese which has been softened. Stir until smooth. Add mayonnaise and rest of ingredients. Pour into mold and chill thoroughly. Serve on lettuce. Serves 8 to 10.

Blytheville, Ark.

Exit I-55 at Ark. Hwy. 18

This is the land of rain grown cotton in the Mississippi Valley. The National Cotton Picking Contest is in October. Blytheville is near a large SAC Missile Base. Sportsmen and water enthusiasts enjoy nearby Big Lake Game Refuge and Herman Davis State Park. Reelfoot Lake and Crowley's Ridge State Park are only a short drive away. Many specialties of the area are served in this Inn's restaurant.

STEAK SPECIALTY

Dip T-Bone or Sirloin steak generously in Continental Sauce before charbroiling to doneness desired.

Continental Sauce a la Haab

    1 bottle soy sauce (5 ounces)
    1 bottle Dr. Pepper
    1½ ounces Worcestershire sauce

Combine thoroughly. Makes approximately 1⅔ cups sauce.

COCONUT CHESS PIE

    ½ cup butter
    1½ cups sugar
    1 teaspoon flour
    4 eggs
    ½ cup cream
    ½ teaspoon vanilla
    ½ teaspoon nutmeg
    ½ cup coconut (fresh or frozen)
    9-inch unbaked pie shell

Cream butter. Add sugar and flour and cream thoroughly. Add eggs which have been well beaten. Add cream, vanilla and nutmeg. Fold in coconut. Place in unbaked pie shell and bake at 300 degrees for 35 minutes.

Conway, Arkansas

I-40 and U.S. 65 N.

Bring your fishing rod — you'll be staying near Lake Conway, Lake Beaverfork and Greers Ferry Lake. And colleges abound in Conway. Many a college function is held at the Inn. Graduation parties and wedding receptions are personally planned. It's a great place for class reunions. Even waiting in the buffet line is fun here — you're sure to see friends and you know you'll find your favorite foods along the way.

SHRIMP SALAD SUPREME

1 pound shrimp
½ cup celery, chopped
2 hard-boiled eggs, diced
¼ cup Durkee's dressing
½ cup mayonnaise

Cook shrimp, peel and clean. Chill thoroughly. Combine with celery, eggs, dressing and mayonnaise. Serve in lettuce cups, garnished with sliced stuffed olives. Serves 4.

ROQUEFORT DRESSING

½ cup Roquefort cheese
   (blue cheese may be substituted)
½ cup light cream
1 cup mayonnaise
¼ teaspoon salt
1 tablespoon onion, grated with juice

Beat cheese until creamy, leaving some lumps of cheese. Add cream and mayonnaise alternately. Add salt and onion. 2 cups.

El Dorado, Ark.

U.S. 82, 167B & Ark. 7, 15

On Wednesday nights guests are greeted with a huge Roast Prime Rib of Beef cooking on a rotisserie at the entrance of the Golden Key Restaurant. There's a Smorgasbord on Friday nights from September through May—a favorite with football fans. Sundays are buffet days. People come from out of town, especially for the Mexican dinners. All this and fun too await guests in El Dorado, the Oil Capital of Arkansas.

GUACAMOLE SALAD

Peel 2 soft avocados. Add 2 chopped onions and 1 stalk chopped celery. Then add salt and pepper to taste, 1 teaspoon lemon juice, Jalapeno pepper (juice and minced pepper). Add 2½ cups mayonnaise last. Blend well. Avocado seed may be added to keep salad from turning dark, until ready to serve. Use for dip or salad. Makes approximately 3 cups.

RICE JAMBALAYA

⅓ cup chicken giblets, diced
⅓ cup green pepper, chopped
½ cup onion, chopped
1¾ cups converted long grain rice
2 tablespoons chicken base condensed
1 quart hot chicken stock
2 cups diced cooked chicken
1 tablespoon Worcestershire sauce
   Trace minced garlic
   Salt and pepper to taste
   Dash cayenne pepper
1 bay leaf
   Minced parsley

Sauté giblets in cooking oil. Add green pepper and onion. Cook until tender. Add rice and cook until coated with oil. Add diced chicken with hot stock and bring to a boil. Add seasonings and simmer until rice is done and liquid is absorbed, about 30 minutes. Serves 6 to 8.

Fayetteville, Ark.

U.S. 71 N., 2402 N. College

No doubt you'll hear someone "Call the Hogs" during your stay in Fayetteville. It's the home of the Razorbacks, the football team of the University of Arkansas. The buffet breakfasts served at this Inn during football season are gala occasions. You'll like the Inn's Ozark way of cooking Blueberry Hotcakes, Fried Chicken, Country Ham and Trout. A National Park where the Battle of Pea Ridge was fought is within a few miles.

LOBSTER IMPERIAL

1½ pounds boiled lobster meat
½ pound grated cheese
1 quart Cream Sauce
½ cup mushrooms
¼ cup champagne
Salt and pepper
¼ cup chopped pimento
¼ cup chopped green onion tops
4 egg yolks, beaten

Melt grated cheese in Cream Sauce. Add and mix in mushrooms, champagne, salt, pepper, pimento and onion tops. Then add lobster meat and fold in egg yolks. This may be served in a casserole or as stuffed lobster in shell. Top with more grated cheese. Serves 8 to 10.

Cream Sauce

Melt 4 tablespoons butter in a saucepan. Gradually add 4 tablespoons flour and 2 teaspoons salt. When well mixed, add 4 cups milk. Cook and stir until thickened. Makes approximately 1 quart.

Forrest City, Ark.

Jct. I-40 & St. Hwy. 1 North

Forrest City is in the rich delta country of cotton and agricultural empires. It's in peach country too—you can expect the best peach cobbler you've ever tasted at this Holiday Inn. The Inn is only 3 minutes from the heart of downtown and 4 miles from the airport. For sports enthusiasts there's the St. Francis River. Bear Creek Lake and its resort attractions are not far away.

FRESH PEACH COBBLER

3 cups fresh ripe peaches
2 tablespoons lemon juice
1 cup sugar
2 tablespoons flour
1 egg white (optional)
¼ pound melted butter
½ cup water (or more)
Pastry for 2 crust pie, rolled out in 1 large piece

Peel peaches and sprinkle with lemon juice to keep them from darkening. Mix ½ of the sugar and flour with peaches. Line an oblong baking pan with pastry, leaving enough to fold over and across top. Brush bottom with egg white to keep juice from soaking through.

Place peaches in pan, sprinkle with remaining sugar and dot with half of butter. Add water and fold pastry over. (If peaches are juicy ½ cup of water is enough, but cobbler must be juicy so add more if necessary). Add rest of butter and sugar on top. Bake in a 425 degree oven for 35 to 40 minutes and pastry is golden. 6 to 8 servings.

Fort Smith, Ark. Downtown

U.S. 64 & 71 N.

Ice carvings by the chef and special Sunday and holiday buffets featuring Chicken Isabello and Shrimp Louis are just a few reasons this Inn is so popular. Historic Old Fort and Hanging Judge Parker's Courtroom are only minutes away. Rodeo time in late May attracts thousands. "Western dress" is the order of the day and a jail plus a huge tank of water discourages anyone from breaking the law — an age old custom.

ROAST ROUND OF BEEF

5-8 pounds choice steer round
    (boned and rolled)
    Salt and pepper
    Seasoning salt
    Garlic powder
    MSG
¼ cup onions, diced
¼ cup carrots diced
¼ cup celery, diced

Leave roast at room temperature 1 hour before roasting. Place on rack in roasting pan with fat side up. Season. Cover with foil. Insert meat thermometer. Place in 220 degree oven and cook 2 hours. Remove foil and add enough water to wash seasonings to bottom of pan, to which is added onions, carrots and celery. Replace foil. Cook until 140 degrees shows on thermometer. Allow approximately 40 minutes per pound for entire time. Use drippings and vegetables for gravy. Add water to make right consistency and stir well to get all residue from bottom of pan for rich juice. Boned roast yields 3 to 4 servings per pound.

Fort Smith, Ark.-South

Hwys. 71 & 271 S.

Razorback fans enroute to the University for football games enjoy making this Inn their headquarters coming and going. Guests especially look forward to the Inn's delicious Kansas City Steaks and Ozark Broasted Chicken. Oklahoma is just across the river, so Fort Smith is at the Gateway to the West. Take time to visit the Old Fort site, museum and Judge Parker's famous courtroom.

DIRTY RICE

2 chicken livers
2 chicken gizzards
2 chicken hearts
1 green pepper (seeds removed)
4 fresh young onions
2 pieces of celery stalk
1 clove garlic
2 tablespoons margarine
2 tablespoons flour
½ cup chicken broth (or more)
3 cups cooked rice
1 tablespoon chopped parsley

Grind in food chopper: chicken livers, gizzards, hearts, green pepper, onions, celery and garlic. Make a roux of margarine and flour, cooking until dark brown. (Use a heavy iron skillet and cook over low heat, stirring constantly). Add to first mixture and thin with hot chicken broth. Mix with fluffy cooked rice. Just before serving add chopped parsley and chopped onion tops (leftover from onions ground). All liquid must be absorbed. Serves 6 to 8.

Harrison, Ark.

U.S. 62-65 N.

Comic characters come to life only 3 miles away in Dogpatch U.S.A. Ozark mountain trails, float trips, fishing, scenic caves and waterfalls are at the doorstep of Harrison. And it's just off Highway 7 South, chosen as one of the 10 most scenic drives in America. The Holiday Inn is the place to come home to — home baked breads and pastries. Be sure to try Batter Fried Fatback here!

EGGPLANT CASSEROLE

1 medium onion, chopped
2 tablespoons butter
1 eggplant peeled & sliced
1 #2 can tomatoes, drained
4 eggs, slightly beaten
½ cup grated cheese
1 cup bread crumbs

Sauté onion in butter (or bacon grease). Add parboiled eggplant and tomatoes. (Mash these slightly). Add eggs and stir until mixture looks like scrambled eggs. Stir in cheese. Add ¾ cup crumbs and pour into a buttered baking dish. Top with remaining crumbs. Bake at 350 degrees for 20 to 25 minutes. 6 servings.

FRUIT COCKTAIL CAKE

2 cups flour
1½ cups sugar
2 teaspoons baking soda
1 large can fruit cocktail
½ cup light brown sugar
½ cup coconut
½ cup chopped pecans

Mix flour, sugar, baking soda and fruit cocktail with a spoon and pour into a 9x13 greased pan. Combine brown sugar, coconut and pecans. Sprinkle on top of un-baked cake. Bake 45 minutes or until cake springs back at touch using 350 degree oven. Cook the following until thick and spread on warm cake: 1 cup sugar, 1 small can evaporated milk, ½ cup butter and 1 teaspoon vanilla.

Helena, Ark.

U.S. 49 at Bridge Road

The only thing this Holiday Inn overlooks is the Mississippi River. The red carpet is always rolled out. Step into the Red Coals Restaurant for unforgettable Catfish and Hush Puppies. The Inn will even prepare your own catch for your dinner. (Excellent fishing is less than a mile away). One of the many historical places in Helena is the Confederate Memorial to the seven Generals the city contributed to the Confederate Army.

CATFISH FILLETS

3 pounds catfish fillets
Salt
Pepper
Corn meal
Cooking oil

Wash fish and dry well. Rub with seasonings. Dip in corn meal. Fry in kettle of hot oil until done. (Use fresh cooking oil for golden brown fish). 4 to 6 servings.

HUSH PUPPIES

1 cup milk
2 cups corn meal
2 teaspoons baking powder
1 teaspoon salt
2 tablespoons onion, grated
1 egg

Scald milk. Sift dry ingredients. Add onion and hot milk. Last, add egg which has been well beaten. Shape in finger length rolls or balls. Drop in hot cooking oil where fish was fried. Drain on paper towel. 6 servings.

Hot Springs, Ark.

U.S. Hwy. 70 E.

Nestled at the base of famous Hot Springs Mountain, this Holiday Inn is only 3 minutes from exciting downtown Hot Springs and the world famous bathhouse row . . . 15 minutes away from the 100 mile chain of lakes . . . 8 minutes from Oaklawn Race Track. Hot Springs is the only city that surrounds a National Park. Enjoy delicious food served with a continental flair on this Inn's patio overlooking Tower Mountain.

PIONEER BEEF STEW

- 1 pound diced salt pork
- 2 pounds diced choice beef
- 1 teaspoon paprika
- 1 teaspoon Worcestershire sauce
- 1 bay leaf
- 1 teaspoon salt
- ½ teaspoon pepper
- 3 onions, sliced
- 3 carrots, scraped & halved
- 3 potatoes, peeled & diced
- 1 stalk celery, short lengths
- 3 whole fresh tomatoes

Use a heavy kettle and heat salt pork. Add beef and sauté with paprika until brown on all sides. Keep sizzling hot, then pour in 4 cups boiling water. Shift meat so it will not stick. Lower heat and add Worcestershire sauce, bay leaf, salt and pepper. Cook with lid on low heat for 2 hours. Add vegetables and cook for last 30 minutes. Blend 4 tablespoons flour with about ¼ cup cold water and make a smooth paste. Add a little more water. Remove meat and vegetables from pan. Add flour mixture to juices. Cook and stir until thickened. Add more water if necessary. Add meat and vegetables for quick warm up and serve. Serves 8 to 10.

Jacksonville, Ark.

Gregory St. at U.S. 67

You'll be accorded a warm welcome and good service, whether you choose just a quick sandwich or a leisurely meal at this Inn. Luncheon buffets feature the dishes that businessmen enjoy. The noon day crowds from nearby Jacksonville prove this. It's a fun place to meet friends from Little Rock A.F.B. as it's only a mile away and Arkansas' capital city just 10 miles.

TWICE-BAKED POTATOES

Scrub 6 Idaho baking potatoes and place in shallow pan. Bake potatoes in 350 degree oven for 1 hour or until they feel soft. Cut each potato in half lengthwise. Scoop out insides and mash thoroughly. Beat well, adding ¼ cup hot cream until mixture is fluffy. Season with melted butter, salt and pepper. Refill shells and sprinkle with grated cheese. Bake at 450 degrees until brown on top. Serves 6.

VEGETABLE SOUP

- 4-pound meaty soup bone
- 3 large onions, chopped
- 4 tablespoons butter
- 4 stalks celery, chopped
- 6 carrots, pared and sliced
- 2 turnips, peeled and sliced
- 2 cups tomatoes, stewed
- 4 potatoes, peeled and diced
- ¼ cup tomato purée
- ½ cup fresh green peas
- ½ cup fresh lima beans
- ½ cup shredded cabbage

Place soup bone in a large pot, add 1 of the onions and cover with water. Cook slowly 3 hours, until meat is done. Put butter in a heavy frying pan and sauté rest of onions, celery, carrots and turnips for a few minutes.

Skim fat from top of stock. Remove soup bone and cut meat into small pieces. Season stock with salt and pepper. Add pieces of meat and all of ingredients including sautéed vegetables. Cook for 1 to 1½ hours. Serves 12.

Jonesboro, Ark.

Dwtn. at Union & Matthews

Since this Inn is only minutes away from major industries and right downtown too, it's a favorite with travelers and local residents. Everyone enjoys the fine food and excellent service in the Red Carpet Restaurant. Arkansas State College is only 2 miles from the Inn. There's excellent fishing and hunting within a 60 mile radius of Jonesboro and a no closed fishing season. Crowley Ridge State Park is very near.

STRAWBERRY BANANA PIE

    2 cups frozen strawberries
    ½ cup strawberry juice
    ½ cup sugar
    1 teaspoon red food coloring
    3 tablespoons unflavored gelatin
    ½ cup cold water
    4 egg whites
    ¾ cup sugar
    3 large bananas

Completely thaw strawberries. Bring berry juice to a boil and add ½ cup sugar and food coloring. While still hot, add gelatin which has been dissolved in the cold water. Then add strawberries. Chill until thick. Beat egg whites until stiff but not dry and add ¾ cup sugar gradually. Fold strawberry mixture into egg whites. Peel and slice bananas in half lengthwise and place in a cooled pie shell. Pour strawberry mixture over bananas and chill until set. Top with Whipped Cream Topping. Serves 8 to 10.

Whipped Cream Topping

Whip 1½ cups heavy cream until stiff. Then add ½ cup powdered sugar and ½ teaspoon vanilla. Pile on pie and garnish with fresh strawberries.

Little Rock, Ark.-South

2600 W. 65th St., I-30 Exit

Business and pleasure are mixed at this Inn in the heart of an industrial area. The Red Fox Tavern and Red Coals Dining Room have live music and excellent food. The Inn's Pancake Parade is enjoyed any time of day. Downtown Little Rock is just a few Interstate minutes away. Visitors enjoy touring the Arkansas Arts Center. It's in MacArthur Park, birthplace of General Douglas MacArthur.

HOLIDAY INN PANCAKES

    1¼ cups all purpose flour
    ½ teaspoon salt
    3 teaspoons baking powder
    1 tablespoon sugar
    1 beaten egg
    1 cup milk
    2 tablespoons shortening

Heat an ungreased griddle slowly. Sift before measuring flour and sift again with salt, baking powder and sugar. Combine egg, milk and shortening, then add to flour mixture. Beat the batter until the flour is dampened—do not over beat. Place a few drops of cold water on griddle—if they jump about it is ready for pancakes. Pour about ¼ cup of batter quickly onto the griddle. Repeat until griddle is full. When some of the bubbles break on the pancakes, turn them. Serve with plenty of melted butter and syrup or honey. Makes 6 to 8 pancakes.

PANCAKE SANDWICH

    6 pancakes
    2 eggs
    6 strips bacon

Fry bacon and eggs. Cook pancakes and stack one pancake, bacon, another pancake, egg, and top with third pancake. Serves 2.

Little Rock, Ark.-SW

8001 New Benton Hwy.

Steamboats chugging along the Arkansas River no longer unload their passengers at "Petit Roche" . . . Little Rock, as it is now known. Today travelers pull in this Inn just off Interstate 30. Dining is an adventure in good eating in the Iron Gate Restaurant. There's also the colorful Stein Room to enjoy. Little Rock is the only city in the nation with 3 capitols . . . Arkansas Territorial Restoration, Old State House, and the present Capitol.

CHICKEN CACCIATORA

    2 2-pound fryers
    3 tablespoons olive oil
       Salt to taste
       Pepper to taste
       Pinch crumbled oregano
    2 leaves basil, crumbled
    1 tablespoon minced parsley
    4 cloves garlic, minced
    1 green pepper, diced
    1 medium onion, diced
    1 #2 can (2½ cups) whole tomatoes
    ¼ cup sherry

Disjoint fryers. Heat olive oil in a deep frying pan and fry chicken until golden. Add seasonings and chopped vegetables and let cook a little. Add tomatoes, cover and cook 20 minutes. Remove cover and add sherry. Cook uncovered for 10 more minutes. Sprinkle with chopped parsley. If thicker sauce is required, mix 2 teaspoons cornstarch with ¼ cup cold water and add to pan. When sauce thickens place all on a serving platter, garnish and serve. Serves 6.

Mountain Home, Ark.

U.S. 62 South. Downtown.

Lake Norfork, Bull Shoals Lake and the White River are only minutes away. You're in the land of famous Rainbow Trout fishing and float trips, in the heart of the Ozarks. Trout is a specialty at the Inn too. You catch them, the Inn will prepare them. A Smorgasbord featuring country style food is served daily at noon. There's courtesy car service for fly-in guests. Dogpatch U.S.A. is an easy drive away.

BAR-B-QUE PORK RIBS

    16 ribs (allow 2 ribs per portion)
        Salt and pepper
        Liquid smoke
     1 cup Bar-B-Que Sauce

Cut ribs in individual portions. Season with salt and pepper. Brush with liquid smoke. Place on cookie sheet or large shallow pan in 400 degree oven for 1½ hours. Brush generously with Bar-B-Que Sauce and place back in oven for 30 minutes or until sauce begins to brown. Serves 8.

Bar-B-Que Sauce

    2 tablespoons honey
    ¼ pound butter, melted
    ½ cup catsup
    3 tablespoons Worcestershire sauce
       Juice of ½ lemon
    1 teaspoon onion salt
    1 teaspoon garlic salt
    1 tablespoon mustard

Mix all ingredients and cook slowly in a saucepan for 15 to 20 minutes. Makes approximately 1 cup.

North Little Rock, Ark.

I-40, U.S. 67 & St. 5

Here's casual country club living right in the city. Fashion shows, parties, luncheons and conventions make this luxury Inn a very popular place. People have learned to expect outstanding food in the Red Carpet Restaurant and they are never disappointed. The Old English Pub is a great place to relax. North Little Rock is just across the river from Arkansas' capital city. The Little Rock Air Force Base is nearby.

PINEAPPLE AND BEAN SALAD

1 small can pineapple chunks
1 small can red kidney beans
1 package frozen baby limas
1 package frozen cut green beans
1 cup chopped celery
1 green pepper, cut in chunks

Drain pineapple and save syrup. Drain kidney beans. Cook limas and green beans until tender, drain and then combine with remaining ingredients. Cover and chill. Serve with Dressing below. Serves 10 to 12.

Salad Dressing

1 teaspoon cornstarch
1 teaspoon dry mustard
½ teaspoon black pepper
1 pinch dill weed
1 teaspoon sugar
1 teaspoon salt
¼ cup white vinegar
4 teaspoons olive oil

Mix cornstarch and seasonings. Then blend in vinegar. Add pineapple syrup and cook, stirring over moderate heat until thickened. Remove from heat and beat in olive oil. Chill until ready to serve with salad.

Pine Bluff, Ark.

U.S. 65 at City Rt. 65

Pine Bluff is a noted cotton market. During the Civil War soldiers used cotton bales piled high on the levee for barricades. Today Pine Bluff has a 10 million dollar Civic Center, which houses an Arts and Science Museum. The only thing old-fashioned about this Holiday Inn is the food. Just try the Chicken and Dumplings, Homemade Biscuits and Homemade Corn Bread in the Hurricane Room.

HEAVENLY CHICKEN

18 chicken wings
1 pint milk
½ teaspoon ground pepper
1 teaspoon salt
¾ cup all purpose flour

At the joint of wing closest to the breast, cut through the skin and notch the bone just below the joint. In a downward motion, break the joint and pull the meat down over the end of the joint. Separate the two joints. On the second joint pull the wing tip away from the joint in a downward motion until bones come through the skin. Place your thumb between the two bones and pull the meat down over the end of the joint, as above. Twist the small bone until it comes out. Cut off wing tip. Add salt and pepper to the milk. Dip chicken. Then roll in flour and fry at 300 degrees until done. For cocktail fare serves 8 to 9.

Fruit Sauce
(For Heavenly Chicken)

1½ teaspoons cornstarch
1 pint fruit juice
¼ cup lemon juice
¼ cup sugar
½ cup fruit cocktail
1 drop red food coloring

Mix cornstarch, fruit juice and lemon juice. Bring to a boil, then cook until thick. Add sugar, fruit cocktail and food coloring. Keep warm.

Rogers, Ark.

Highway 71 South

No wonder Rogers attracts so many visitors. Trout fishing is great. Deer and quail hunting are at their best. The Pea Ridge National Military Park offers historic attractions. There's a Grape Festival in nearby Tontitown each August. Rogers is also in the heart of the Ozark poultry industry. Be sure to order trout and chicken at this Inn. Both are deliciously prepared the Ozark way.

DANISH PASTRY

- 1 pint milk, scalded
- 2 yeast cakes
- 6 tablespoons sugar
- 6 tablespoons butter
- 3 eggs, beaten
- 8 cups flour
- 1 teaspoon salt
- ¾ pound sweet butter

Scald milk and allow to cool to lukewarm. Add yeast, sugar, 6 tablespoons butter and eggs. Sift flour and salt and add. Mix into a dough and knead about 5 minutes. Roll dough into an oblong piece. Cut sweet butter in small pieces and arrange on ⅓ of the dough (in center). Take the portion of dough without butter and fold over buttered dough. Dot with butter and fold remaining ⅓ of dough over the butter. This will make 3 thicknesses of dough. Press down edges and roll out again, about ¼-inch thick. Fold 3 times and roll out again. Fold again and allow to rise. Roll and shape into crescents, squares or any other shape desired and allow to rise. Then bake for 15 to 20 minutes at 375 degrees. Makes approx. 6 to 8 dozen.

For Danish Almond Roll: Roll dough thin and spread with a mixture of ground almonds and sugar moistened with a beaten egg. Roll up and shape into a roll. Let rise and bake until golden brown.

Russellville, Ark.

State 7 & Interstate 40

You're minutes away from Mt. Nebo State Park, Mt. Magazine National Park, Petit Jean State Park, and Winrock Farms. Wiederkehr Wineries are in nearby Altus. Dardanelle Lake may be seen from the Inn. Naturally picnics are fun for all—even more fun when the Holiday Inn chef fills your hamper with everything from luscious home grown strawberries in icy containers to Ozark fried chicken.

BAKED BASS, CREOLE

- 1 3-pound bass
- 6 tablespoons butter
- ½ cup celery, chopped
- ½ cup onion, chopped
- ¼ cup green pepper, chopped
- 2½ cups tomatoes (No. 2 can)
- 2 teaspoons Worcestershire sauce
- 1 tablespoon chili sauce
- ¼ cup lemon juice
- 1 bay leaf
- 1 clove garlic, minced
- 1 teaspoon salt
- ½ teaspoon pepper

Clean fish and season. Roll lightly in flour. Sauté in butter: celery, onion and green pepper, using heavy saucepan. Add tomatoes and rest of ingredients. Simmer until tender and thickened. Place fish in roasting pan. Pour sauce over it and bake in 325 degree oven for 45 minutes to 1 hour. 4 servings.

(To help prevent baked fish from breaking when moving to serving platter, place two thicknesses of greased foil in bottom of baking dish leaving ends long for handles. Fish can then be gently moved when done).

West Memphis, Ark.

210 I-40, U.S. 61, 63 & 64

Tennessee is just a river away. This Inn is only a few minutes from downtown Memphis and on the edge of the bustling city of West Memphis. You can enjoy the best of both Arkansas and Tennessee. The striking decor in the Viking Restaurant makes the food look as good as it tastes. There's the Valhalla Lounge too. For sports fans the Southland Greyhound Race Track is a sure bet for fun (June through October).

VIKING CASSEROLE

    3 #2 cans asparagus
    1 #2 can chestnuts
    1 #2 can mushroom soup
    1 teaspoon salt
    ½ teaspoon white pepper
    ½ cup American cheese

Grease pan with butter or margarine. Place a layer of asparagus in pan, then a layer of chestnuts, and next a layer of mushroom soup. Repeat until all are used. Add seasonings, then cover with cheese and cook at 350 degrees for 15 to 20 minutes. Serve in casserole. Serves 12.

OKRA AND HAM CREOLE

    1 onion
    1 green pepper
    1 tablespoon butter
    6 medium tomatoes
    10 to 12 okra pods, cut
    2 cups diced ham (boiled or baked)
    1 cup water
    3 cups hot steamed rice

Peel and chop onion. Remove seeds from pepper and slice. Sauté onion and pepper in butter. Add tomatoes and okra. Then add ham and water and simmer for 20 minutes. Serve over hot steamed rice. Serves 6.

Bakersfield, Calif.

White Lane Exit off U.S. 99

Bakersfield is located on the Kern River, at the southern end of San Joaquin Valley. In just two hours you can be skiing in the mountains or bathing on a beach. So it's no wonder this Inn hosts so many people coming and going. The delicious food is one reason it's a favorite spot to stop. A large herd of Tule Elk may be seen in the nearby zoological park by that same name.

ANGEL DESSERT

    3 eggs, separated
    ½ cup granulated sugar
    1 ounce brandy
    1 ounce rum
    ½ pint whipping cream
    1 teaspoon vanilla
    1 envelope unflavored Knox gelatin

Beat egg yolks until light and lemon colored. Add sugar gradually and continue beating until creamy. Add brandy and rum. Beat egg whites until stiff but not dry. Whip cream until stiff enough to stand in firm shiny peaks, then add vanilla. Fold in egg whites. Soak gelatin in ¼ cup cold water for 5 minutes, then stir over hot water until gelatin dissolves completely. Stir thoroughly into egg yolk mixture. Then fold in the egg white and whipped cream mixture. Pour into 4-ounce parfait glasses and let set in refrigerator for about 2 hours. Angel Desserts may be decorated with nuts, fresh berries or a liqueur like Creme de Menthe or Creme de Cacao. Makes approximately 8 to 10 servings.

Carmel, Calif.

Pacific Coast Hwy.

Slow down in Carmel—cars must drive around trees growing in the narrow winding roads. Carmel By-the-Sea lies on the oak and pine covered sand dunes of Carmel Bay on the Pacific Sea Coast. Carmel's Holiday Inn offers luxurious accommodations . . . extra-length beds, sauna baths, a heated pool, and the kind of gourmet food that makes guests write for the recipes.

CURRIED PRAWNS "MAHARADSHA"

    1½ pounds fresh prawns
    4 tablespoons butter
    2 tablespoons curry powder
    2 cups chicken stock
    2 tablespoons cornstarch
    ½ cup Major Grey's Chutney
    ½ teaspoon salt
    ¼ cup cream, whipped
    2 bananas
    4 slices pineapple
    1 egg, beaten
    ½ cup bread crumbs
      Shortening
    2 cups rice, steamed

Peel prawns. Saute' in 2 tablespoons butter for 3 minutes. Use heavy pan or casserole that can be used on top of stove. Add curry powder. Stir well and add chicken stock. Cook 5 minutes. Blend cornstarch in mixture. Add chutney and salt. Simmer 4 minutes. Gently stir in cream at serving time. Meanwhile have bananas peeled and cut in half. Dip pineapple slices and banana pieces in egg, then in bread crumbs. Fry in deep hot shortening. Season rice with rest of butter and pack in greased ring mold. Turn onto serving platter. Fill with curried prawns and garnish with pineapple and bananas. 4-6 servings.

Concord-Walnut Creek Calif.

Interstate 680 at Concord Ave.

It's worth going out of your way for the delicious food at this Inn. There's a Champagne Brunch each Sunday. Tempting seafood dishes are on the menu everyday. The Inn was awarded the best design award in 1968. Its adobe brick buildings, redwood trim and mansard roofs are in the tempo of early California. Famous Lake Berryessa and several championship golf courses are within minutes.

FILLET OF SOLE JEAN LAFFITE

    6 6-ounce fillets of sole
      Lobster Filling
    1 cup dry white wine
    ½ cup water
    1 cup Mornay Sauce

Prepare fillets for stuffing. Put 1 to 2 tablespoons Lobster Filling in each cavity and make secure with toothpicks. Place in pan with wine and water. Poach until tender and liquid is gone. Remove from pan carefully and place on heat-proof serving platter. Pour Mornay Sauce over tops of fillets. Glaze under broiler. Serve with lemon and garnish. Serves 6.

Lobster Filling

Heat ½ cup cream. Add ¼ cup bread crumbs and 1 cup chopped cooked lobster. Season with salt, cayenne and lemon juice.

Mornay Sauce

Blend 2 tablespoons butter and 2 tablespoons flour. Add 1 cup milk gradually and stir over low heat. Cook until thickened. Season. Add ¼ cup Parmesan and grated Swiss cheese. Just before serving, add 1 beaten egg yolk and 2 tablespoons butter, bit by bit.

El Centro, Calif.

I-8 at Imperial Ave. Exit

El Centro is a winter vegetable center so you can expect fresh vegetables year round at this Inn. Mexico is just the border away. Visit historic Mexicalli in Mexico. Salton Sea (208 feet below sea level) and Land of the Sun are nearby. You're on the route to Yuma Desert. You're in the land of giant sand dunes. After a day of sightseeing, return to the Inn for delicious food and live entertainment in the lounge.

STEAMED VEGETABLES

1 cauliflower
6 carrots
6 onions, medium-size
6 beets
6 turnips
6 potatoes (small)
1 cup green beans
3 sprigs parsley
3 sprigs mint
½ cup butter

Select fresh vegetables, peel and scrape and cut in uniform pieces. Place in saucepan and add ½ to ⅔ cup water, salt to season. Cover. (Cook strong vegetables separately). Cook 8 to 10 minutes after vegetables start steaming. Cook 10 minutes on medium heat. Total cooking time is 20 to 45 minutes, depending upon vegetables being cooked. (Do not let vegetables become dry, add more water if necessary). Place cauliflower in center of platter, surround with other vegetables. Pour melted butter on top. Add minced mint leaves to carrots and parsley over potatoes. Serves 6.

Fresno, Calif.

Ashlan Ave. at 99 Freeway

Take time to take tours. The Underground Gardens (65 rooms of trees, flowers and shrubs underground) is only a mile away. Roma Winery and Sun Maid Raisins tours are fun. There's an excellent zoo in Roeding Park. Children enjoy Storyland Park, a fairy tale village adjacent to the zoo. This Holiday Inn offers golf privileges at a private Country Club nearby. Take time to enjoy the superb food in the Inn's Country Squire Restaurant.

SARMA
(Armenian Lamb in Grape Leaves)

½ cup raw converted rice
½ pound lean ground lamb
¼ cup onions, chopped
2 teaspoons dry mint leaves, crushed
1 tablespoon lemon peel, grated
1 tablespoon parsley, chopped
2 tablespoons lemon juice
1 jar (15 ounce) grape leaves
2 lemons, unpeeled, thinly sliced
1½ cups tomato purée

Steam rice and 1½ cups water in covered pan 25 minutes, or until done. Heat oil in small skillet; add lamb, onions, mint, lemon peel, salt and pepper. Sauté, stirring constantly, until crumbly and done. Add parsley and lemon juice. Combine with cooked rice. Drain grape leaves.

For each sarma, spread a leaf, wrong side up and stem end towards you. Put 1 to 2 tablespoons filling near the stem end. Fold and cover the sides, then start rolling up from the stem end like a jelly roll. Cover bottom of 10 by 6-inch baking pan with extra leaves. Add layer of slices of lemon and pour over ½ cup tomato purée. Place sarma, side by side and smooth side up in pan. Pour over remaining purée and add remaining lemon slices. Top with layer of leaves, then cover and seal tightly with foil. Bake at 300 degrees for 1 hour. Makes 16 to 18 sarma. Allow 2 for each serving.

Livermore, Calif.

LaFlores Rd. and I-580

A huge wheel of aged Cheddar cheese is on a wine barrel in the Inn's Pub — ready to be sliced for hors d'oeuvres. This is wine country. The region is famous for dry, white wines. Guided tours through the nearby wineries may be arranged at the Inn. There's a floor-to-ceiling wine display in the Inn's lobby. The Inn's beautiful Regency Room offers gourmet dining, featuring native products. And the Inn offers a lot of extras . . . large size family rooms are available, even special conveniences for handicapped guests.

CHICKEN PAPRIKA

- 1 large frying-size chicken
- 1 large onion
- 2 tablespoons butter
- 1 tablespoon paprika
  Pinch cayenne
  Salt and pepper
- 1 ounce dry white wine
- 1 cup sour cream

Clean and cut chicken in serving size pieces. Thinly slice onion. Using a heavy skillet, sauté onion in butter. Remove from heat when transparent. Add paprika, cayenne, salt and pepper. Lay chicken pieces on mixture and sprinkle 1 tablespoon of the wine over all, adding a few drops of water as needed. Cover and simmer for ¾ hour, but do not brown chicken too much. Turn chicken and cook another ¾ hour.

Remove chicken to platter and keep warm. To juices in pan, add sour cream and rest of wine. Blend well and season, if needed. Heat and pour over chicken when serving. Serves 4.

Long Beach, Calif.

Lakewood Blvd. at I-405

Marineland, Disneyland and the Long Beach Arena are all near this Holiday Inn. The beautiful Pacific Coast beaches are just some sand away. Long Beach stretches for 8 miles and you can see U.S. Naval vessels at anchor from Rainbow Pier. It's easy to arrange harbor tours and deep sea fishing expeditions. Everything is easy-going at this Inn. Let them entertain you in the lounge.

STUFFED FRENCH CRÊPES

Stuff 8 to 12 French Crêpes with 1 cup Veronique Sauce to which 1 cup bite-size pieces turkey and 1 cup drained mushrooms have been added. After rolling crêpes, cover with 1 cup Veronique Sauce to which 1 cup tiny white seedless grapes has been added. Sprinkle with Parmesan cheese and glaze under broiler before serving. Allow 2 crêpes for each portion, using approximately 1 good spoonful of stuffing in each.

French Crêpes

Add 1 cup milk and 1 cup flour to 2 beaten eggs. Stir until smooth and blended. Use a small frying pan (6-inch) and allow butter to coat pan while heating. Pour in batter to cover pan (thin layer). Cook over medium heat until done on one side. Turn carefully and brown other side. (Grease after cooking each crêpe, using a piece of paper towel with oil on it). Makes 18 to 24 crêpes.

Veronique Sauce

Blend 4 tablespoons butter and 3 tablespoons flour, adding 2 cups chicken stock. Cook until thickened. Add 1 cup cream and 3 tablespoons sherry. Season to taste. Makes 2 to 2½ cups.

Los Angeles, Calif.
Central

S. Figueroa & Olympic Blvd.

If you want to stay in the middle of things, stay at Holiday Inn Central in L.A.—Disneyland, Knott's Berry Farm and movie studios are only minutes away. Hollywood tours can be easily arranged. People have a good reason for being back at the Holiday Inn in time for lunch . . . the Holiday Sandwich Buffet. There's a choice of five breads, not to mention the in betweens.

VEAL OSCAR

    4 6-ounce slices veal steak
    16 fresh asparagus spears (cooked)
    1⅓ cups Alaskan king crab
    1 shredded pimento

Sauté veal steaks. Place 4 asparagus spears on each slice. Place king crab on top and cover with Hollandaise Sauce. Garnish with parsley. Serves 4.

Hollandaise Sauce

    ½ cup butter
    3 egg yolks, slightly beaten
    1½ tablespoons lemon juice
    Cayenne pepper

Place half of butter and egg yolks in top part of double boiler (do not let water boil). Add lemon juice and stir until butter melts. Add rest of butter and stir until thick. Add cayenne. 1 cup.

SHRIMP SALAD SANDWICH

    1 pound cooked shrimp, cut
    2 cups medium chopped celery
    1 cup mayonnaise
    1 tablespoon diced pimentos

Mix all ingredients thoroughly. Place in refrigerator to chill. When ready to serve, spread shrimp salad generously on white bread, then put another slice of bread on top. Cover entire sandwich with hot Cheddar cheese sauce. Serves 6 to 8.

Los Angeles, Calif.
Hollywood

1755 N. Highland at Hollywood Blvd.

Oscar's, the revolving gourmet restaurant and night club high atop this high-rise Inn, has all that its name suggests . . . enchantment, glamour and exciting dining. Savor a dazzling first course — Camarones con Salsa Remoulade, then have Oscar's Spinach Salad for Two. It's not easy to choose a main course as each is enticing. The menu is full of surprises — in two languages so Japanese guests are pleased.

MEDALLION OF VEAL OSCAR

    3 2-ounce slices tender veal
    2 tablespoons butter
    2 spears cooked asparagus
    1 ounce crab meat
    ¼ cup Béarnaise sauce*

Preheat oven to 350 degrees. Lightly dredge veal with flour. Melt butter in sauté pan. Brown veal on both sides. Place asparagus spears on heat proof plate. Arrange veal slices over asparagus, leaving asparagus tips exposed. Top veal with crab meat. Coat veal with Béarnaise sauce. Place in 350 degree oven and bake for 10 minutes. Serve with rice. 1 serving.

*Béarnaise sauce may be prepared by making basic hollandaise sauce and adding 1 teaspoon tarragon wine vinegar to each half cup of sauce.

ABALONE STEAKS AMANDINE

Brown sliced blanched almonds in butter. Keep hot. Pound 4 center slices of abalone with a mallet. Dredge lightly in flour, then dip in an egg wash. Sauté in butter until lightly browned; about 2 minutes per side. Do not overcook. Just before removing from pan, squeeze juice from half a lemon over abalone. Remove abalone to heated serving platter and cover with browned almonds and butter. 2 servings.

Montebello, Calif.

Santa Ana Frwy. S.

This Inn is in the Greater Los Angeles area—close to all the glamour spread over miles of valleys and hills. Helicopter service is available to guests going to and from the Los Angeles International Airport. Guests spend much of the time saved enjoying live entertainment in the Inn's Dynasty Lounge. Gourmets are delighted in the dining room. The San Gabriel Mission, founded in 1771, is nearby.

CHIFFONADE SALAD

    1 head lettuce, torn in bits
    2 tomatoes, cut in wedges
    4 asparagus spears, cut
    2 tablespoons capers
    2 hard boiled eggs, sliced

Toss all ingredients with Chiffonade Salad Dressing. Serves 4.

Chiffonade Dressing

    1 egg white
    1 teaspoon mustard
    1 teaspoon paprika
    ¼ cup vinegar
    ¼ cup lemon juice
    1 clove garlic
    1½ cups salad oil
    1½ teaspoons salt
    1 shredded pimento
    1 tablespoon parsley, minced
    1 hard boiled egg, chopped

Place egg white, mustard, paprika in a bowl and beat. Pour all ingredients in a jar and shake. Makes 2½ cups.

Monterey, Calif.

2600 Sand Dunes Drive

If you choose, step outside and roam for miles on the beautiful white sand of Del Monte Beach. Ocean front relaxation awaits guests at this new Holiday Inn on the Monterey Peninsula with its great golf courses and scenic atmosphere. Guests are provided golfing privileges at some of the world's finest courses. Superb cuisine includes delicacies of the sea from Monterey Bay.

STUFFED PORK CHOPS

    6 6-ounce pork chops
    ½ pound pork sausage
    ½ cup bread crumbs
    ½ bell pepper, chopped
    ½ onion, chopped
    ¼ cup chopped celery
      Salt
      Pepper
      Thyme

Split pork chops on open side. Blend rest of ingredients for stuffing and fill cavity of each chop. Brown chops in hot oil, then place in casserole and bake 20 to 25 minutes. Serves 6.

BLEU CHEESE DRESSING

    ½ cup crumbled Bleu cheese
    2 cups mayonnaise
    1 cup sour cream
    ½ cup buttermilk
    2 to 4 green onions, chopped fine
    1 teaspoon salt
    ½ teaspoon each: basil, thyme, tarragon
    1 teaspoon Worcestershire sauce
      Dash garlic

Mix all ingredients and chill before serving. Approximately 1 quart.

Mt. View-Palo Alto Calif.

Calif. 82

Fresh brewed coffee is delivered to your room as a wake-up service! From then on you'll find pleasure unlimited at this Holiday Inn in Mountain View on El Camino Real (the "King's Highway"). It's the road early missionaries travelled when setting up the missions in California. The Inn is near Stanford University. You'll never want to be far away when it's time to eat. Every meal is a special treat here.

SWEDISH HOT CAKES

1 cup sifted flour
2 tablespoons sugar
Pinch salt
3 eggs, beaten
3 cups milk (half cream-half milk)
Butter
Powdered sugar, sifted

Sift flour, sugar and salt together. Then add eggs and milk gradually. Stir until thoroughly mixed, then let stand at least 1 hour or 2. Heat an ordinary griddle, skillet or pancake pan and brush well with butter. If cakes have tendency to stick, brush pan again with butter. Spread hot cake batter thin and turn hot cakes once so they will be brown on each side. When done, brush with butter and sift powdered sugar on them. Roll hot cakes, sprinkle again with powdered sugar. Serve with a favorite berry syrup. Makes 2 to 3 dozen, depending on size.

Syrup

Crush 2½ cups fresh fruit or berries. Add 1 cup sugar and 2 tablespoons white corn syrup. Let stand 1 hour. Strain juice and cook over low heat adding water to make a thin syrup.

Oakland, Calif.

Nimitz Freeway

Sports fans flock to this Holiday Inn. No wonder. It adjoins the parking area of the new Coliseum Complex. Whether guests are in Oakland for sports or visiting the University of California only 4 miles away, they all enjoy the delicious dishes prepared by the Inn's chef in the Den of the Red Lion. And all of this is only a twenty minute drive from San Francisco.

BEEF TERIYAKI

4 3-ounce steaks
    (top sirloin ¾" thick, no fat)
    Soy sauce
1 onion, ¼" wide strips
4 stalks celery, sliced on bias
1 green pepper, julienne
2 tablespoons cooking oil
½ cup pineapple juice, more if needed
1 cup pineapple chunks

Brush steaks with soy sauce and broil to mark on each side. Arrange down center of service platter. Saute vegetables in cooking oil over medium heat until lightly colored. Add soy sauce, pineapple juice and pineapple chunks. Bring to a boil and then simmer for 8 minutes. Spoon over steaks at serving time. Serves 4.

BARBECUED TUNA

½ cup margarine
1½ cups chopped celery
1 cup sliced onions
1 pint barbecue sauce
1 pound tuna, drained and flaked

Saute celery and onions in margarine. Add remaining ingredients to vegetables and simmer 10 minutes. Portion on buns or serve over rice. Serves 6 to 8.

Redding, Calif.

Interstate 5 and Hilltop Dr.

Where the Sacramento Valley ends and the mountains begin on a bend in the Sacramento River lies Redding. The Redding Holiday Inn is fashioned from the natural rock of Mt. Lassen. Decorated in the style of early western pioneer history, the Inn's restaurant is a popular place. Homemade biscuits are one reason for its popularity.

HOMEMADE BREAD

    2 packages or 2 cakes yeast
    2 cups tepid water
    1 tablespoon sugar
    4 cups sifted flour
    ½ teaspoon salt

Add yeast to water and dissolve. Add sugar and mix well. Add flour and salt. Mix thoroughly until mixture becomes very sticky. Sprinkle flour over mixture and let stand until double in size. When dough is double in size, place on board and knead. While kneading, sprinkle flour until mixture is no longer sticky. Pound on dough until it becomes rubbery. Then cut mixture in half and shape into loaf forms. Place in 2 well-greased bread pans and let rise to double in size. After dough has risen, place melted butter on top of dough by dripping. Bake in 400 degree oven for 25 to 35 minutes or until very brown on top. Makes 2 loaves.

ROQUEFORT DRESSING

Mix 4 tablespoons grated onion with ½ cup Roquefort cheese. Heat in saucepan slowly until cheese melts. Add ½ cup buttermilk and leave on heat until mixture forms semi-paste. Cool. Add ⅓ cup salad dressing (not mayonnaise), 1 tablespoon sauterne, 2 tablespoons beer, pinch of thyme, garlic salt and white pepper. Add 1 cup sour cream. Whip with hand whip. Chill. Whip again. Serve cold. 2 cups.

San Francisco, Calif. Airport

245 S. Airport Blvd.

Free transportation from the airport to this beautiful Inn 3 minutes away is the first bit of pampering you can expect. You'll be in the heart of the San Francisco Bay area, only minutes away from downtown, Candlestick Park, the Golden Gate Bridge, Tanforan Race Course and Chinatown. Choice dishes from Germany and Indonesia are served in the Inn's Royal Hall dining room. The Lancer's Lounge has live entertainment.

CRAB LEGS IN ASPIC

    1 cup cooked crab legs
      (cut in 1-in. pieces)
    2 to 3 peppercorns
    1 bay leaf
      Seasonings
    1½ cups broth or stock
    1 tablespoon gelatin
    ½ cup water

Place crab leg pieces in pan. Boil peppercorns, bay leaf and seasonings in broth. Soak gelatin in cold water and dissolve in broth. Pour over crab legs. Cut into rounds and serve on toast rounds. Will serve 10 to 12 at a party.

STUFFED CHERRY TOMATOES

    24 cherry tomatoes
    6 ounces Roquefort cheese
    2 tablespoons mayonnaise (or more)
      Seasonings
    ½ teaspoon lemon juice

Cut narrow top from each tomato and scoop out pulp from center of each tomato. Blend Roquefort cheese and mayonnaise with seasonings and lemon juice. Fill cavity of each tomato with cheese mixture. Chill. 24 stuffed tomatoes.

San Francisco, Calif.
Civic Center

50 Eighth Street, Downtown

Climb aboard a cable car (near the Inn) and discover this famous old city. King Arthur and Sir Lancelot vie for the best steaks in the Inn's red carpeted Victorian Dining Room. And one almost expects to find financial greats of the old west enjoying a lavish meal here — a clever designer used huge cartoons of the Gibson Girl era. Old pewter service plates and goblets add to the luxurious decor.

MUSHROOMS MAGNIFICENT

    8 large mushrooms
    1 to 1½ cups finely chopped sirloin
    2 tablespoons finely minced onion
    2 tablespoons finely minced celery
    1 to 2 eggs, slightly beaten
    1 tablespoon olive oil
      Salt and pepper
    1 carton sour cream
      Dash Worcestershire sauce
    2 teaspoons finely chopped chives
    ½ cup diced Cheddar cheese

Make scallop design on mushrooms. Pull out stems and mince fine. Add sirloin, onion, celery, eggs, olive oil and season. Stuff mushrooms and round filling. Make a sauce with sour cream, Worcestershire sauce, chives and cheese. Put in skillet and add mushrooms, tops up. Cover and simmer until cheese melts and mushrooms and meat are cooked to doneness desired. Do not turn mushrooms. Serve as an entrée. Number of servings depends on size of mushrooms.

CAROTTES A LA VINCHY

Peel and slice 1 bunch carrots. Put them in a saucepan with enough water to cover well. Add ½ teaspoon salt, 3 tablespoons sugar and 4 tablespoons butter. Cook until the water has almost entirely evaporated. Sauté the carrots until glazed. Sprinkle with fresh chopped parsley. 4 servings.

San Francisco, Calif.
Financial District

750 Kearny Street

A luxurious A-frame, 27-story Holiday Inn in the heart of the Wall Street of the west and adjacent to Chinatown is truly the "Inn of great happiness". Expect the unusual . . . an authentic Tea House in the lobby, escalators to The Eight Immortals dining room and China Cup Coffee Shop on the second floor. A Chinese Cultural Center covers the entire third floor.

WESTLAKE DUCK

    1 dressed duckling
    2 stalks celery
    2 pieces fresh ginger root, sliced
    1 bunch Chinese parsley roots
    7 Chinese black mushrooms, soaked
   10 bamboo shoots, sliced
    3 star anise
    2 teaspoons salt
    ½ teaspoon sugar

Rub duckling with soy sauce several hours before cooking. Fry in 2 to 3 tablespoons oil in pan until brown. Slash back of duckling, but do not cut through bone. Place in heavy casserole, add other ingredients and ½ cup water. Cover. Simmer about 1½ hours, until tender. Remove bones. Leave duckling in warm place. Thicken stock with 1 teaspoon cornstarch, adding water if needed. Serve duckling on large platter with loose lettuce underneath. Pour vegetables and gravy over duckling and garnish with Chinese parsley. Serves 4.

CHINESE BARBECUED SPARERIBS

Place 2½ pounds pork spareribs on baking sheet and crisscross down center with sharp knife. Blend: 1 tablespoon red bean curd, ½ teaspoon salt, 2 tablespoons sugar, ½ cup catsup, 1 crushed clove garlic, and 2 tablespoons soy sauce. Spread on both sides of ribs. Marinate overnight. Place in 350 degree oven and cook for 45 minutes. Turn ribs while cooking. Serves 4 to 5.

San Francisco, Calif.
Fisherman's Wharf

1300 Columbus Avenue

Bouillabaisse Marseillaise with its fragrances of fresh Pacific seafood blended harmoniously, is a Frenchman's adaptation to this area. When served at this Inn in a big brown fish shaped tureen with tableside service, it's elegant — not just a fish soup. The menu here is cosmopolitan but dominantly French. This beautiful Inn overlooks Fisherman's Wharf — it's easy walking to famous Ghirardelli Square and the Cannery Shopping Center.

BOUILLABAISSE MARSEILLAISE

    2 cups thinly sliced onions
    1 cup thinly sliced leeks
    2 cups dry white wine
    6 cups water
    4 cloves garlic, crushed
    6 fresh tomatoes, peeled and diced
    ¼ teaspoon saffron
    ½ teaspoon crushed fennel seeds
    2 sprigs parsley
    1 bay leaf
    1 sprig thyme
    1 pound scallops
    1 pound halibut, sliced
    ½ pound prawns, peeled and deveined
    ½ pound crab legs

Pour ¾ cup olive oil in a heavy pot, add onions and leeks, and cook over low heat 6 to 7 minutes, stirring frequently. Add remaining ingredients, season and bring to a fast boil for 15 minutes. 10 servings.

GOLDEN GATE CRAB

Combine 1 cup minced green onions, 4 tablespoons melted butter, 3 cups cream sauce, ½ cup heavy cream, 4 teaspoons curry, salt and pepper. Fold into 2 pounds Dungeness crab meat. Fill 6 abalone shells ¾ full of rice pilaf. Fill each shell to the top with crab filling. Sprinkle a mixture of bread crumbs and Parmesan on tops and brown in a hot oven. 6 servings.

San Rafael, Calif.

U.S. 101 at Terra Linda Exit

In this Inn's delightful restaurant you'll be transported to France via colorful, expertly prepared food — truly "haute cuisine". Discover sole in an exquisite sauce, luscious "boeuf" elegantly prepared and served flaming. Glamorous vegetables and unusual flambées cannot be bypassed. There's a connoisseur's wine list too. You'll enjoy your stay at this Inn, nestled in the foothills of Mt. Tamalpais.

FILLET OF SOLE

    4 fresh fillets of sole
    ½ teaspoon finely chopped shallots
    4 pats unsalted butter

Put sole and shallots in melted butter in a chafing dish. Season with dash cayenne pepper, dash nutmeg, dash M.S.G., salt to taste, juice of 1 lemon and simmer for 5 minutes. Add ½ ounce cognac, 1 ounce dry vermouth, 2 ounces white wine. Remove fillets to plate. Add to the chafing dish: 2 tablespoons sauce béchamel, ½ cup cooked bay shrimp, 1 tablespoon chopped parsley, 1 teaspoon Escoffier sauce, dash Angostura bitters, 1 teaspoon Worcestershire sauce, 1 tablespoon hollandaise sauce and simmer for 2 minutes, stirring constantly. Remove from heat and top sole with sauce. Serve with rice pilaf. Serves 4.

GRAND MARNIER SOUFFLÉ

    5 egg yolks, beaten
      Juice of 2 oranges
    1 tablespoon water
    1 tablespoon sugar
    1 ounce Grand Marnier

Combine above ingredients and beat over heat until thick. Remove from heat and beat until cold. Beat 6 egg whites, gradually add ¼ teaspoon cream of tartar, 1 tablespoon sugar and 1 drop vanilla extract. Fold into egg yolk mixture. Pour in well buttered form, which has been sprinkled with sugar. Place in preheated 375 degree oven for 35 minutes. Serves 4.

Santa Cruz, Calif.

611 Ocean Street

Step across a charming bow bridge behind this Inn — you'll be in the heart of the downtown shopping mall. The famous boardwalk and beach are only half a mile away. Just to read the menu here is a delight. Among the starters, perhaps the most exciting are Stuffed Mushrooms. Enjoy sampling the many unusual dishes with the beautiful Santa Cruz Mountains for scenery. Be sure to take the children on the Roaring Camp Narrow Gauge Railroad through the magnificent Redwood Forest.

STUFFED MUSHROOMS

12 mushrooms
1 medium onion
3 stalks celery
½ cup butter
1 teaspoon sage
6 to 8 slices dried bread (sour dough is best)
1 pound boneless turkey or chicken (light and dark)
3 eggs
Salt and pepper
2 cups sauterne wine

Wash mushrooms in cold water, remove stems and set aside. Chop onion, stems of mushrooms and celery fine and saute in ¼ cup butter about 5 to 6 minutes. Add sage and cook 1 minute. Soak bread in water and when soft, squeeze out all excess water. Chop or grind turkey meat fine. Mix all, add slightly beaten eggs, salt and pepper to taste. Stuff mushrooms with mixture. Place in buttered pan with sauterne or chicken stock and bake. These may be served for lunch or dinner with vegetables and potatoes of your choice. Juice in the bottom of the pan may be used for a base for sauce or to baste the mushrooms. 4 to 6 servings.

Santa Monica, Calif.

Colorado & Ocean Blvd. I-10

This Inn overlooks nothing—except the Pacific Ocean. Fishing is fun from the pier in the same block. Bring your catch back and the Inn will prepare it for your dinner. Wednesday night is Italian Night in the dining room. Hot muffins are delicious daily. There's live entertainment in the Esquire Lounge— often drop-in surprise entertainers. The Inn is only 5 minutes from the Civic Auditorium of Academy Award fame.

VEAL SCALOPPINE

1½ pounds veal cutlets
¼ cup flour
2 tablespoons olive oil
1 tablespoon butter
¼ cup onions, diced
1 clove garlic, minced fine
1 tomato, diced small
1 medium green pepper, diced
½ teaspoon salt
    Dash pepper
¼ cup red wine

Choose cutlets from leg of young beef and have them cut ½-inch thick. Wipe meat dry. Pound with edge of saucer until thin and tender. Sprinkle with flour. Heat olive oil and butter in skillet, add onion and brown lightly. Add veal cutlets and brown on each side. Add garlic, tomato, green pepper and cook slowly. Add seasonings and wine last. Simmer slowly for 25-30 minutes. Season more if needed, adding more wine if desired. Serves 4.

Sunnyvale, Calif.

U.S. 101 at Lawrence Expwy.

The menu is as delightful as the beautifully landscaped courtyard and view of the mountains at this Holiday Inn. The Beef Brochette marinated in wine, charbroiled and brought to the table right off the skewer is a must on the menu. The Inn is only minutes away from Lockheed, United Technology, Western Electric, General Electric, Westinghouse, N.A.S.A. and Moffett Field.

FILET OF BEEF STROGANOFF

1½ pounds filet of beef
1 teaspoon salt
¼ teaspoon pepper
1 or 2 small onions
⅓ cup butter
½ cup mushrooms
½ pint sour cream
1 dessert spoon flour
   Pinch mustard
1 tablespoon tomato purée

Cut beef into thin strips, about 2 inches long, and sprinkle with salt and pepper. Chop the onions very fine and fry in hot butter until golden brown. Wash, peel and slice the mushrooms and add to the onions. Make room in the pan for the meat and sauté for 5 minutes. Blend ½ of the sour cream with the flour, mustard and tomato purée. Mix well and pour into the pan. Stir the contents of the pan, cover and simmer gently for about 10 minutes or until the meat is tender. Add the rest of the sour cream before cooking is completed. Serve with steamed rice. Serves 4 to 6.

Van Nuys, Calif.

8244 Orion Ave. Downtown

In the heart of the famous San Fernando Valley stands this modern high-rise with its Lock Lomond and Scottish decor. Busch Gardens are directly across from the Inn. Guided tours through the brewery on a monorail, an exotic tropical bird show and samples of all beer brewed there are free to the public. Only about 3 miles away is the quaint San Fernando Mission with guided tours. There's night golfing nearby too.

HI-PRO SPECIAL

¼ cup finely chopped onions
6 ounces hamburger meat
½ cup chopped spinach
2 eggs
   Pinch Lawry's seasoning salt
1 hard-boiled egg

Sauté onions in butter to medium done. Add hamburger and chopped spinach. Cook until done, stirring mixture. Add eggs last to all of mixture and scramble. Season with seasoning salt. Serve in a casserole and top with hard-boiled egg slices. 2 servings.

VENISON ROAST

1 5- to 6-pound venison roast

Sear roast in a hot oven (500 degrees) for 10 minutes. Use open baking pan. Reduce heat to 425 degrees and cook 30 minutes. Add Basting Sauce and cover loosely with foil so roast may be basted often while cooking. Cook allowing 20 minutes per pound. Serves 6 to 8.

Basting Sauce

Combine 1 cup consomme, 1 cup red wine, 3 tablespoons lemon juice and 4 tablespoons chopped onion. Add 1 clove minced garlic, pinch thyme, salt and pepper. Heat thoroughly.

West Covina, Calif.

Mount Baldy and the San Gabriel Mountains are the views from this Inn in the Los Angeles area. The Carousel, one of the world's largest theatres-in-the-round, is just next door. Top star entertainment in the world of musicals make it one of Southern California's greatest attractions. The Inn's Red Lion Dining room is popular with stars as well as audiences.

CABBAGE ROLLS

1 pound ground beef
1¼ teaspoons salt
⅛ teaspoon pepper
1 beaten egg
½ cup cooked rice
1 onion, chopped fine
1 medium-size cabbage
2 tablespoons butter
1-2 cups water or stock
½ teaspoon caraway seeds
2 tomatoes, peeled and cut

Mix together, lightly and thoroughly, the ground beef, salt, pepper and egg. Mix in the cooked rice and chopped onion. Steam the cabbage or place in boiling salted water, then drop in cold water. Carefully remove leaves and cut thick ribs so they will lie flat. Stack 2-3 cabbage leaves and place about ¼ cup of meat mixture on the center of leaves. Roll up leaves and tuck the ends in toward the center. Use wooden picks or skewers to fasten leaves securely or tie with string. Melt butter in heavy skillet and brown cabbage lightly on all sides. Add water and stock as needed. Add caraway seeds. Simmer for 45 minutes, adding tomatoes. If desired, thicken gravy with a flour and cold water paste. Season to taste. Serves 6.

Boulder, Colo.

This Inn is a popular summer and winter resort spot. There are football games in the fall (the Inn is opposite the University of Colorado), winter sports at Hidden Valley and yacht races in Grand Lake in August. The grandeur of the Colorado Rockies and the Continental Divide are yours to enjoy year-round. You'll be sorry if you don't save room for dessert after every meal.

PANCAKES

Sift 1½ cups flour, 3 teaspoons baking powder and ½ teaspoon salt. Add 2 beaten eggs and 1 pint milk. Then add ¼ cup melted butter. Pour batter in desired size pancakes, using medium hot griddle (preheated). When bubbles form turn pancakes and cook underside, until both sides are golden. Makes approx. 12-18 pancakes.

SOUR CREAM RAISIN PIE

1 cup sugar
1½ cups sour cream
3 egg yolks, beaten light
2½ tablespoons flour
1 teaspoon cinnamon
½ teaspoon salt
¼ teaspoon cloves
¾ cup raisins
Nut meats

Add sugar to sour cream and eggs. Sift dry ingredients together and add. Add raisins and nuts. Cook until thick. Pour into baked pie shell and top with Meringue. Bake in 400 degree oven for 8-10 minutes.

Meringue

Beat 3 eggs whites until frothy, adding ¼ teaspoon cream of tartar and pinch salt. Add 6 tablespoons sugar gradually. Whip until meringue is glossy. Heap on pie, spreading to edges.

Denver, Colo.
Colo. Blvd.

S. Colo. Blvd. at I-25

Denver's first rooftop revolving restaurant is atop this luxurious Holiday Inn. Only when the Penthouse food appears does one's eyes wander from the everchanging view of mountains and the Denver skyline. This tower of luxury in the "mile-high city" is designed for combining business with pleasure. Denver University and the U.S. Air Force Academy are nearby.

BEEF FONDUE

    2 pounds beef
      Olive oil
      Spiced soy sauce
    ¾ cup white wine
    ½ pound Swiss cheese, grated
    ½ pound mozzarella cheese, grated
      Kirsch

Dice meat in 1-inch squares. Marinate meat in olive oil and spiced soy sauce for 5 minutes. Rub casserole (heat-proof for top of stove or use an asbestos mat over low heat) with piece of garlic. Pour wine into casserole and heat until it bubbles. Stir constantly, add all of cheese and stir until smooth and creamy. Add dash of kirsch. Fill fondue pot with clear olive oil, spiced with soy sauce and simmer. Place marinated meat on serving plate garnished with lettuce. Place cheese sauce in individual dishes. Dinner guests dip meat in fondue pot and cook to suit their taste. Then they may dip it in cheese sauce if desired, or can dunk French bread. Serves 6.

Denver, Colo.-East

U.S. 40 & I-225 In Aurora

A world of fun and luxury awaits you at this Denver Inn. It's an Inn for vacationing away from downtown, yet it's near enough to spend carefree days sightseeing and evenings "on the town". The Inn is located opposite Fitzsimmons and Lowry Air Force Base. In an hour's drive you can picnic in the Rockies or fish in a clear mountain stream. The Inn's attractive restaurant awaits your return with fabulous entrees and desserts.

CREAM OF CHICKEN SOUP

    1 stewing chicken
    2 quarts water
    1 cup large diced onion
    2 carrots, quartered
    3 stalks celery, quartered
      Salt to taste
      Pepper to taste
    1 clove garlic, minced (optional)
    1 cup chopped mushrooms
    ¼ cup chopped onion
    ¼ cup plus 1 tablespoon flour
    ¼ cup chopped pimentos
    1 quart half and half

Wash chicken well and remove giblets. Place in pot with water and bring to boil. Add diced onion, carrots, celery, salt, pepper and garlic. Let return to boil, then turn heat down so that liquid is barely turning over. Continue cooking until chicken is tender. Remove from stock and strain stock. Skim fat and place 2 tablespoons in sauté pan. Set stock on low heat. Add chopped onion and chopped mushrooms to sauté pan and cook until onion is transparent. Add flour and cook until fat is absorbed and roux made. Add roux to stock. Boil 5 minutes and stir smooth. Add pimentos and chicken which has been cut into bite-size pieces. Simmer until heated and add half and half. Makes approximately 3 quarts.

Durango, Colo.

U.S. 160 & 550

Just step from your room to catch a fish. The Durango Holiday Inn is located on the banks of the Animas River. The Inn's chef will prepare your catch for dinner, if you can pass up the buffet of the day. It could be Italian, Mexican or Seafood. Durango is big game hunting country too. Don't miss a trip on the Narrow Gauge Train to the mining community of Silverton. Just 37 miles west are the greatest cliff dwellings in the world.

BAKED MEAT LOAF

    2 pounds ground beef
    3 eggs
    1 cup water
    1 tablespoon salt
    ½ tablespoon black pepper
    ½ cup parsley, minced
    1 large onion, chopped fine
    1 cup bread crumbs

Mix meat with eggs, water, seasonings and bread crumbs. Pack in a buttered loaf tin or form into a tight roll. Bake in a 350 degree oven for 1 to 1½ hours, or until brown and meat shrinks in pan. Make gravy from drippings in pan. Use 1 tablespoon flour smoothed in a small amount of water. Add to rest of drippings and stir until blended and thickened. May be served with tomato sauce, if preferred. Serves 6 to 8.

BAKED HALIBUT IN LEMON BUTTER

    8 halibut steaks, 8 ounces each
    1 pound butter or margarine
    4 lemons

Melt butter and squeeze lemons into butter. Place halibut in pan, pour juice and butter mixture over the halibut and bake in a 350 degree oven until done, about 1 hour. Serves 8.

Vail, Colo.

U.S. 6 & Vail Village Rd.

For alpine atmosphere, resort to the Vail Holiday Inn. Vail has more lift-served ski terrain than any other single ski mountain in North America . . . challenging high altitude golf . . . superb fly fishing . . . some of America's finest hunting. Get a taste of the international cuisine in the Gold Rush Dining Room, Swiss specialties in the Fondue Stube. Enjoy fireside music in the 1880's Den Bar.

CHEESE FONDUE

Rub fondue pot with fresh garlic clove. Put in 2 cups of dry white wine and bring almost to a boil. Add grated cheese as follows: ⅔ pound Emmental and ⅓ pound Gruyere. Stir continuously until cheese is entirely melted and mixed with wine. Take mixture of cornstarch and kirschwasser (approx. 1 to 2 teaspoons) and add slowly until fondue thickens. It is now ready to serve and should be maintained over a low flame.

Take French bread that has been exposed to air at room temperature for 8 to 10 hours and cut into 1 to 1½ inch squares. This bread is then secured on a long fondue fork and soaked in the Cheese Fondue, removed and popped into the mouth while still hot. Be careful though — if you drop your bread in the cheese, you must buy a round of drinks for everyone at the table!

COFFEE DOWNHILL

Take 1 ounce of light rum and add to it ¾ cup coffee. Garnish with a cinnamon stick and top off with whipped cream. An excellent after dinner drink or Apres Ski.

Bridgeport, Conn.

Interstate 95 & St. 25

The seafood is superb! Unusual recipes make any Neptune's feast fit for a gourmet. This downtown Holiday Inn also has live entertainment in its lounge. P. T. Barnum was once mayor of Bridgeport. The Barnum Museum contains mementoes of his "Greatest Show on Earth" and 28-inch-tall Tom Thumb. The Shakespeare Theatre is not far from the Inn.

FILLETS OF CUSK WITH CUCUMBER SAUCE

8 4-ounce fillets of cusk
10½ ounces canned mushroom soup
½ cup chopped, peeled cucumber
1 teaspoon chopped chives

Clean fillets, wash and pat dry with paper towels. Season and brush with butter on both sides. Prepare sauce. Warm soup, diluting with milk if too thick. Add cucumber and chives. Mix well and heat thoroughly. Place fillets on greased broiler and broil for 5 minutes on each side. Remove from broiler and place on serving platter. Top with cucumber sauce. Garnish with parsley and lemon wedges. Serves 4.

Darien, Conn.

Adj. Conn. Tpk. I-95

Be sure to try this Inn's famous Pompano dish. New England Seafood Stuffing makes shrimp an unforgettable delicacy. After dinner, enjoy live entertainment in the lounge. Yale Locks and Pitney-Bowes Postage Meters are just two of the 250 products of this city. Norwalk, where the derby hat was introduced, is only 3 miles away and still a hat manufacturing center.

NEW ENGLAND SEAFOOD STUFFING

(For Lobster or Shrimp)

1 small onion, chopped
1 green pepper, chopped
6 stalks celery, chopped
6 ounces cooking oil
1 pound grated bread crumbs
2 tablespoons paprika
Salt and pepper to taste
1 teaspoon garlic powder
1 tablespoon grated Parmesan cheese
½ cup sherry wine
1 teaspoon M.S.G.
½ cup cooked crab meat or canned shrimp pieces, or lobster
½ cup melted butter

Sauté onion, green pepper and celery in oil. To the bread crumbs, add remaining ingredients. Mix well. Add sautéed vegetab'es and drippings. Mix to medium moistness. Stuff cavity of split lobster, split jumbo lobster tails, or large butterfly shrimp. Bake in 400 degree oven, 12 to 15 minutes. Serve with butter. Serves 4 to 6.

Groton, Conn. (Mystic)

I-95, 404 Bridge St.

Stay in the heart of the Submarine Capital of the world. Visit the Mystic Seaport, the nationally famous restored fishing village and museum of American sailing ships and whaling industry. Tour the famous Thames River where atomic subs are launched and berthed. Gourmet dining and a nautical cocktail lounge await you here.

POMPANO EN PAPILLOTE

Clean 3 medium-sized pompanos. Cut into 6 fillets, removing heads and backbones. Simmer heads and backbones in 3 cups water until 2 cups of stock remain. Sauté fillets and 1 chopped shallot in 2 tablespoons butter. Add 2 cups white wine, cover and simmer slowly until fillets are tender (about 5 to 8 minutes). Sauté 1 cup sliced mushrooms, 1 cup diced cooked shrimp and ½ clove minced garlic in 2 tablespoons butter. Add 1½ cups chopped onions. Cook 10 minutes. Add pinch of thyme, 1 bay leaf and 1¾ cups fish stock and simmer 10 minutes. Blend 2 tablespoons flour in 2 tablespoons butter. Gradually add ¼ cup fish stock. Add to mushroom-shrimp mixture with wine stock drained from fillets. Simmer and stir until sauce thickens. Add 2 beaten egg yolks and ¼ cup white wine. Season with salt and pepper. Chill in refrigerator until firm.

Cut 6 parchment paper hearts 12 inches long and 8 inches wide. Oil paper well. Divide sauce into 6 portions, placing some on one side of each paper. Place a fillet on top of each portion. Fold over other half of paper heart and seal by folding over and pinching together all around. Lay sealed hearts on oiled baking pan. Bake at 450 degrees for 15 minutes. Cut paper open at table. Serves 6.

Meriden, Conn.

Wilbur Cross Pkwy., I-91

The food and silverware vie for attention at this Holiday Inn. The food is especially good and Meriden is known as the Silver City. Both sterling and plate emerge glistening from Meriden workshops. For fun on the slopes nearby, there's Powder Hill and Southington ski areas. Tours are popular through the unique former home of the late actor, William Gillette.

NEW ENGLAND CLAM PIE

2 quarts soft shell long neck clams
2 cups cubed raw potatoes
1 onion, finely chopped
  Salt and pepper to taste
1 teaspoon sugar
3 tablespoons butter
3 tablespoons flour
1 cup milk
  Pie pastry for a 1½ quart dish

Wash clams in several changes of water. Drain clams and place in a kettle. Add 2 cups cold water and bring slowly to a boil. When clams open, remove from the heat. Strain the clam broth through a double thickness of cheesecloth; reserve broth. Remove clams from shells and chop. Preheat oven to 400 degrees. Boil potato cubes and onion in salted water until tender. Drain, reserving 1 cup of potato water. Add salt, pepper, sugar, water, chopped clams, and clam broth. Bring to a boil. Blend butter and flour and slowly add to simmering stew. Bring milk to a boil and add to stew. Remove from heat. Butter a 1½ quart dish. Pour in clam mixture. Cover with rolled out pastry and prick with a fork. Bake 30 minutes at 375 degrees, or until pastry is golden. Serves 4 to 6.

Milford, Conn.

Boston Post Rd. at Conn. Tpk.

Milford Harbor is the abode of the clam, the oyster, and the summer vacationer. The Milford Holiday Inn has gourmet ways with clams and oysters to please summer vacationers. The Inn is only 5 minutes from the harbor and downtown Milford. Travelers enjoy the convenience of having a shopping center just opposite the Inn. Each summer the American Shakespeare Festival is held in nearby Stratford.

BEEF KABOBS

3 1-inch square pieces of tenderloin tips
3 small whole onions
3 1-inch square pieces of green pepper

Assemble on a 5-inch skewer: 1 piece of pepper, 1 piece of meat, 1 onion and repeat three times. Marinate kabobs in the following mixture for 5 hours.

Combine:

1 cup liquid beef consomme, undiluted
½ cup red table wine
½ cup soy sauce
1 mashed clove garlic
3 teaspoons fresh lime juice
2 teaspoons brown sugar

Oven bake kabobs at 375 degrees until browned, approximately 10 minutes, and finish under broiler. Serve 2 kabobs per person. Cooking kabobs in oven insures that pepper cooks properly without burning edges. The beef consomme has a nice browning effect and the lime juice adds a new tang to the marinade. Marinade for 6-8 kabobs.

New Haven, Conn.

(At Wilbur Cross Parkway)
Exit 59 off Wilbur Cross Pkwy.

A little story book cottage is your first impression as you approach this Holiday Inn with its alive-with-color exterior. Inside, superb cuisine and impeccable service make this Inn a favorite. Reservations must be made early for college weekends at nearby Yale University. Visitors are reluctant to leave — but when they do it is through West Rock Tunnel. West and East Rock Mountains reign in New Haven.

BRANDY SEAFOOD SAUCE

¾ cup mayonnaise
½ cup ketchup
¾ ounce brandy
2 dashes Tabasco

Blend mayonnaise and ketchup together with Tabasco sauce. When blended, add brandy for flavoring. This is an ideal sauce for crab meat cocktail. 1¼ cups.

CRAB MEAT SNACK

16 ounces Alaskan crab meat
¾ cup mayonnaise
½ cup ketchup
2 dashes Tabasco
32 Ritz crackers

Mix mayonnaise, ketchup and Tabasco together making a cocktail sauce. Portion crab meat on the Ritz crackers and top with approximately ¼ ounce sauce. Place on cooking sheet and then into 300 degree oven for 5 minutes. Serve as a cocktail snack. Simple but tangy, different and delicious. 8 party servings.

New Haven, Conn.
Downtown

(At Yale) 30 Whalley Ave.

This Holiday Inn is headquarters for many parents and friends visiting nearby Yale University. You'll enjoy touring the ivy clad buildings on the campus, but always be back at this Inn for gourmet fare. New Haven is the home of the Winchester Gun Museum. Exhibits trace the development of firearms from ancient China to modern times.

COCKTAIL CHEESE SPREAD

    1 pound Wisconsin Cheddar cheese
      spread
    ½ pound cream cheese
      Dash garlic powder
      Dash Tabasco
      Dash Worcestershire
    1 tablespoon horseradish
    1 ounce dry vermouth

Blend all ingredients together in a mixing bowl. Cream cheese makes mixture more spreadable. 3 cups.

STEAK SAUCE "RICHARD"

    ½ medium onion
    10 fresh mushrooms and stems, sliced
    1 fresh medium-sized tomato
      Salt and pepper to taste
      Dash garlic powder
    ½ ounce Burgundy wine

Chop onions fine and saute' slowly in margarine until clear. Add sliced mushrooms to onions and cook approximately 5 minutes. Chop tomato in small pieces and crush, then add to above mixture. Blend all ingredients until done, except wine. Just before serving add wine to mixture. 6 servings.

Waterbury, Conn.

At S. Elm just off I-84

You can order homemade Deep Dish Apple Pie, Rice Pudding and Bread Pudding for dessert in the Iron Gate Restaurant at this Inn. Be sure to try the delicious seafood au gratin dishes too. There's a live broadcast every Saturday night from the Inn's Nashville Room, dancing too. A miniature Bethlehem Village with a large lighted cross on Pine Hill may be seen from the Inn.

RICE PUDDING

    2 egg yolks
    ¼ cup butter
    ½ cup sugar
    1 cup cooked rice
    ½ teaspoon cornstarch
    ½ cup milk
    ½ cup raisins
    1 teaspoon vanilla
    ½ cup jelly

Beat egg yolks well. Cream butter and sugar and add egg yolks. Stir in the cooked rice. Add cornstarch to little bit of milk and blend with rest of milk and add vanilla. Add to rice mixture. Raisins are optional. Add last. Pour into a casserole greased with butter and bake at 350 degrees for 20 minutes. Let cool a few minutes. Beat jelly and spread over warm pudding. Spread meringue over warm rice pudding to seal edges of casserole. Bake at 325 degrees for 10 to 15 minutes. Serve warm. Serves 6.

Meringue

    2 egg whites
    4 tablespoons sugar
    ⅛ teaspoon baking powder

Beat egg whites stiff. Add sugar gradually, then baking powder.

Wilmington, Del.-North

U.S. 202 N.

You'll enjoy your stay in the Valley of the Brandywine. This popular Holiday Inn is only minutes away from an outstanding floral exhibit with fountains copied from Versailles. It's only 4 miles to Winterthur Museum, former home of Henry du Pont, with the finest collection of early American furniture in the world. You'll especially enjoy the regional dishes served at the Inn.

SAUERBRATEN

    4 pounds beef (rump, chuck or sirloin)
    1 cup vinegar
    3 cups water
    1 sliced onion
    3 tablespoons whole mixed spice
    ¼ cup salt
    1 sliced carrot
    ¼ cup white or brown sugar
    ½ cup flour
    2 ginger snaps
    ½ cup red wine

Mix together vinegar, water, onion, spice, salt and carrot. Soak meat in this brine for 3 or 4 days. Turn meat each day. Save brine for making good gravy. Grease heavy roasting pan. Roast meat at 300 degrees for about 2 hours, until meat is brown on both sides and almost done. Sprinkle sugar over meat and roast 5 to 10 minutes more, turning meat until sugar is dissolved and meat is brown. Take all brine in which meat was pickled and add flour and ginger snaps. Mix well and pour over meat. Roast meat for ½ hour more, or until gravy is creamy and thick. Remove meat and stir wine into gravy. Remove grease from gravy and strain. (If meat looks too dry during roasting, baste with pickling brine). Serves 8.

Wilmington, Del.-SW

I-95 at Del. 273 (Newark)

Canadian Blue Water Fillet of Flounder is only one reason visitors consider this Holiday Inn tops. The Horseless Carriage Restaurant with its candlelit decor is the scene of many a gourmet gathering. It's near the University of Delaware, Delaware State Park Race Track and only 9 miles from Wilmington. Sightseeing must: Cooch's Bridge, the scene of the only battle fought in Delaware during the Revolutionary War.

CANADIAN BLUE WATER FILLET OF FLOUNDER

    2 pounds fillet of flounder
    Melted butter
    Paprika
    Parsley flakes

Pour melted butter over flounder, sprinkle with paprika and broil for 4 minutes. Remove from broiler and pour 1 tablespoon of the sauce (below) over it. Re-broil for 2 minutes or until glazed. Sprinkle with parsley flakes and serve with remaining sauce. Serves 4.

Sauce

    ⅓ cup mayonnaise
    4 fillets of anchovy, chopped
    ¼ cup white wine
    1 teaspoon lemon juice

Combine all ingredients and use as directed above.

Washington, D.C. Downtown

1615 Rhode Island Ave. N.W.

Stay only 5 blocks from the White House. You can leave on tours right from the front door. Return for a dip in the Inn's pool, live entertainment direct from New York in the Rob Roy Lounge, outdoors on the Continental Terrace during the summer. It's no wonder so many Washingtonians have lunch at the Inn — international selections from every major country in the world are on the menu.

COSTELETTE DI VITELLO

    4 6-ounce veal chops
    1 beaten egg
      White bread crumbs
    8 slices proscuitto
    8 slices fontina or mozzarella
    4 tablespoons butter

Flatten chops until thin by placing between two pieces of wax paper and pounding. Dip in egg, then in bread crumbs. Place a slice of proscuitto and a slice of cheese on each chop. Spoon butter over each and season. Fold over and press edges together, or use additional flattened chop if chops are too small to fold. Sauté in butter until brown on each side. Place additional slices of cheese on top of each (if desired) and place in oven until cheese melts. 4 servings.

SCAMPI MARINARA

Boil 3 pounds shrimp for 5 minutes, peel and clean. Boil shells with water, adding ¾ small can tomato paste and 1 teaspoon salt. Reduce to ¾ of original amount and strain. Add ⅓ cup chopped pickles (small), ¼ cup chopped anchovies, 4 sprigs parsley (chopped), 1 clove garlic (minced), 4 pieces chopped zucchini and 2 tablespoons butter. Chop shrimp and add to sauce. Add rest of tomato paste and ⅓ cup dry white wine. Serve very hot with Italian bread. Serves 6.

Washington, D.C. Parkway NE

2700 New York Ave., N.E.

An adventure in eating around the world awaits you in the Old Angus Restaurant. The International Luncheons feature dishes from at least 2 different countries daily. Homemade breads are delicious extras. The heart of downtown Washington is only 2 miles from the Inn. Mt. Vernon is just a 20 minute drive, and the Lincoln Memorial is only 15 minutes away.

STUFFED CANTALOUPE

    2 cantaloupes, cut in halves and seeded
    1 bunch seedless white grapes
    2 cups Chicken Salad

Serve cantaloupe half with chicken salad in center. Serve grapes on side of plate and garnish with parsley.

Chicken Salad

    1 3-pound hen
    1 quart water
    1 tablespoon salt
    2 hard boiled eggs
    1 cup celery
      Mayonnaise

Put hen on to boil in deep kettle with water. Cover and simmer until tender, 2 to 3 hours. Turn occasionally. Season for last hour of cooking. Let cool in water. Remove meat from bones and cut fine. Add 2 tablespoons of fat from liquor chicken was cooked in. Add chopped eggs and celery. Fold mayonnaise in chicken lightly until it is moistened as desired. Makes 4 to 6 cups salad.

Alachua, Fla.

Interstate 75 & U.S. 441

Shrimp Remoulade is a delicious reason to stop at this Inn. There's excellent bass fishing at nearby Orange and Newman Lakes. Silver Springs, Six Gun Territory, the Florida State Museum, Medical Center and V.A. Hospital are all within minutes. An olympic size swimming pool and the Tiger's Den Lounge are popular places at the end of a day for travelers.

BREADED CALVES' BRAINS

2 pairs calves' brains
1 beaten egg
1 cup bread crumbs

Soak brains in cold water for ½ hour. Remove thick membrane covering them and be sure they are completely clear and white. Divide into 6 servings. Put in saucepan of boiling water. Add 1 teaspoon of salt and simmer for 15 minutes. Plunge into cold water. When cool, drain and season with salt and pepper. Dip into flour, then beaten egg. Roll in fine bread crumbs. Place in basket of deep fat fryer and cook at 375 degrees for 5 to 8 minutes. Serve with Ravigote or white sauce. Allow ¼ pound per person. (On menu Oct. through March)

MOUNTAIN OYSTERS

2 pounds lamb fries
2 eggs, slightly beaten
½ cup milk
1 cup breading

Wash lamb fries well. If large ones are used, slice ⅝-inch thick. Dip in batter of egg, milk and seasonings. Roll in breading. Drop in deep fat fryer at 325 degrees for 7 minutes.

For breading combine ⅓ cup corn flour, ⅓ cup wheat flour, 1 teaspoon baking powder, ⅓ cup soya flour and spices. Serves 4 to 6. (On menu Oct. through March)

Clearwater, Fla.

400 U.S. 19 South

If Red Snapper, Stuffed Florida Lobster and Shrimp Salad catch your eye, you'll be hooked on the delicious food at this Holiday Inn. The Sunday Buffet offers a minimum of 12 salads. All this (even sauna baths) is within minutes of sparkling white beaches, fresh water and deep sea fishing, regulation golf course and Industrial Park. The Philadelphia Phillies' training camp is just a mile away.

TOURNEDOS A LA BÉARNAISE

4 tournedos (cut from thinner end of chateaubriand 1¼ to 1½ inches thick, weighing approx. 4-oz. each)

Trim tournedos to round and tie. (After cooking remove string before serving). Sauté tournedos and arrange on round croutons which have been fried in butter. Cover top of each with 2 to 3 tablespoons Béarnaise Sauce. Serve with additional sauce. Serves 4.

Béarnaise Sauce

3 tablespoons water
3 tablespoons tarragon vinegar
½ chopped onion
4 egg yolks, slightly beaten
½ teaspoon salt
Dash of pepper
4 tablespoons butter, creamed

Combine water, vinegar and onion in a small saucepan. Heat to boiling, then remove onion. Gradually pour egg yolks on mixture. Add seasonings and cook over hot water, stirring constantly. When mixture thickens, add butter gradually and stir constantly.

Clearwater Beach, Fla.

521 Gulfview Blvd.

Right on the Gulf with a private beach, this attractive Inn has many extras . . . La Caravel Restaurant, Lounge, live entertainment and dancing. Star attractions among the entrées served in the dining room are seafoods. Ambrosia, though known as a holiday recipe, is a spring dessert here as fresh Florida fruits are popular any season. Juicy oranges and plump grapefruit start any guest's day off just right for Gulf fishing or sunning.

SOFT-SHELL CRABS

12 soft-shell crabs
2 tablespoons minced parsley
2 tablespoons minced chives
2 tablespoons minced celery leaves
2 tablespoons minced onion
1 small garlic clove, mashed
1 teaspoon salt
½ teaspoon pepper
½ teaspoon thyme
½ teaspoon tarragon
½ teaspoon nutmeg
1 quart milk
4 egg yolks, well beaten

Clean crabs and put them in a deep container. Combine vegetables with egg yolks and seasonings. Add to milk and pour over crabs. Place a biscuit board over container and let stand 30 minutes. Lift out crabs and roll in seasoned flour. Sauté in butter until golden on each side. Serve with tartare sauce. Allow 1 to 2 crabs for each serving.

FLORIDA AMBROSIA

3 cups Florida grapefruit sections, drained
   (about 2 grapefruit)
1½ cups Florida orange sections
1 cup purple grapes, halved
4 tablespoons sugar
½ cup flaked cocoanut

Alternate grapefruit sections, orange sections, grapes, sugar and cocoanut in a serving dish. Chill well. Serves 8.

Cocoa Beach, Fla.

At Cape Kennedy, U.S. AIA

Don't be surprised it you see an astronaut here. Cape Kennedy is only five miles away from this Inn on Cocoa Beach. The blaze of missile launchings can be seen for miles along the beach. You can still relax and enjoy excellent fishing, while history is being made nearby. An exhibit of the Air Force Titan, Thor, Snark and other headline makers may be seen at nearby Patrick Air Force Base.

SPECIAL FILET MIGNON

4 filet mignon
8 Dutch pearl onions
8 small whole potatoes
2 cups fresh green peas
1 cauliflower
½ cup Madeira Sauce

Sauté filet mignon in skillet to desired doneness. Then place in casserole and add Dutch pearl onions and other vegetables (cooked). Add Madeira Sauce, then place top over casserole. Place casserole on hot grill to steam vegetables for about 2 minutes. Serves 4.

Madeira Sauce

1 wine glass Madeira
1 cup Brown Sauce

Boil ingredients to ½ so alcohol can evaporate and sauce will have an excellent taste.

Brown Sauce

2 tablespoons butter
4 tablespoons flour
2 cups beef consomme

Blend flour in butter, add consomme gradually to thicken a little. Season. Makes 2 cups.

Crystal River, Fla.

1 mi. N. on U.S. 19 & 98

Fresh or salt water fishing? You can take your pick when you stay at this Holiday Inn on Crystal River . . . a mecca for scuba divers, water skiers and fishermen. Just minutes away is the Gulf of Mexico with its fighting big game fish. There are famous Indian mounds too. Some are located directly in back of the Inn. The menu always abounds with delicious seafood— your own catch, if you like.

BEEF A LA DEUTSCH

2½ pounds beef stew meat
½ cup olive oil
2 cups boiling water
1 large onion, sliced
½ stalk celery, chopped
2 green peppers, sliced
1 clove garlic, chopped fine

Cut beef in 1-inch strips. Sauté beef in olive oil over a quick fire. Add 2 cups boiling water. Simmer over low heat for 1½ hours or until fork tender. Add vegetables last ½ hour of cooking. Blend some of juice with 2 tablespoons flour. Stir in mixture and thicken until right consistency. Season to taste. Serves 6 to 8.

FRIED OYSTERS

1 pint oysters
2 eggs, slightly beaten
2 tablespoons milk
½ cup bread crumbs

Drain oysters and pat dry on paper towel. Make batter with eggs, milk, salt and pepper. Dip oysters in batter and then in fine dry bread crumbs or corn meal. Fry in deep fat fryer at 375 degrees for about 4 minutes. Serve with tartare sauce. Allow 6 to 8 oysters per serving.

Cypress Gardens, Fla.

U.S. Hwy. 27 at Dundee

The greatest shows on water take place only 5 miles from this Inn. Don't miss the water ski shows and aquatic tours at Cypress Gardens. The Bok Bird Sanctuary and Singing Tower are also nearby. Many enjoy touring citrus packing plants. This Holiday Inn is located in the most geographic center of the state. Unusual foods served in the restaurant delight every visitor.

GREEK SALAD

1 bunch romaine (washed and torn in bite-size pieces)
2 bunches leaf lettuce (washed and torn into bits)
2 to 3 tomatoes, quartered
3 to 4 sprigs water cress, minced
1 cucumber, sliced thin
3 little green onions, cut
2 to 3 little green salad peppers (pepperonicini)
6 black Greek olives
2 ounces feta cheese
4 to 6 anchovies
Oregano

Place ingredients in bowl in order listed. Sprinkle oregano over top lightly. Pour special dressing over all and mix lightly. Serves 6 to 8.

Greek Salad Dressing

½ pint olive oil
¼ pint vinegar

Whip together 5 minutes then add:
1½ teaspoons salt
¼ teaspoon garlic powder
1 tablespoon sugar
¾ teaspoon white pepper.

Place in jar and shake until well blended. Makes approx. 1 pint.

Daytona Beach, Fla. North

U.S. 1 N. Holly Hill

Deep sea and fresh water fishing, jungle cruises and speed races are within minutes of this Inn. It's a great place to vacation—Daytona's world famous beach just a 5 minute drive away. The Daytona International Speedway is also nearby. And you can mix business and pleasure at this Inn. It has sales showrooms. Be sure to try the Holiday Lamb sautéed in wine sauce.

ROAST PIG HOLIDAY INN

40-pound pig
    Salt and pepper
    Stuffing, if desired
3 to 4 ounces mustard
1 pound brown sugar
1 cup salad oil
3 tablespoons dill sauce
    Apple

Pig should be cleaned and dried, then several punctures made between ribs so seasoning will permeate. Place in large open roasting pan. Rub cavity with salt and pepper, then stuff with sage dressing. Make quart of mustard glaze by combining mustard, brown sugar, salad oil and dill sauce. Brush on lightly. Skewer mouth open so apple can be inserted later. Skewer ears and wrap in foil so they will stand erect. Wrap tail with wire so it will curl. Roast in moderate oven for 40 minutes a pound brushing with glaze as necessary. Puncture skin occasionally so fat will run out. Garnish with fruit when done and place apple in mouth to give festive appearance. Serves approximately 40. (10-pound pig serves 10 to 12).

Daytona Beach, Fla. Oceanside

905 S. Atlantic

Plunge into an unforgettable vacation directly on Daytona Beach. There are kitchenettes for easy oceanside living. It would take weeks to try every delectable dish on the Inn's menu, especially the seafood selections. There's much to see and do nearby, if guests can leave the sunning, fishing, live entertainment in the evenings, a game room and tennis at the Inn.

DILLY SHRIMP SALAD

¾ pound cooked shrimp
1 quart cabbage
½ cup green pepper
1 cup sour cream
1 tablespoon lemon juice
1 teaspoon Worcestershire sauce
¼ teaspoon salt
¼ teaspoon dill weed
    Dash of nutmeg
½ cup almonds

Peel and clean shrimp. Cut large ones in half. Shred cabbage, slice pepper, combine both with shrimp; chill. Combine sour cream, lemon juice, Worcestershire sauce and seasonings; chill. Add toasted, blanched slivered almonds and dressing to shrimp mixture. Toss lightly. Serve on salad greens. Serves 6.

CRAB SALAD BOWL

Thaw 1 pound crab meat and drain. Remove any remaining shell or cartilage. Break crab meat into large pieces. Combine 4 cups salad greens (torn), 2 tomatoes (cut in wedges), 1 cup corn chips, ½ cup pitted sliced ripe olives, 1 chopped onion, and crab meat. Toss lightly with Avocado Cream Dressing or favorite dressing. Sprinkle with ½ cup shredded Cheddar cheese and garnish with ripe olives. Serves 6.

Destin, Fla.

Hwy. 98 on Gulf

Destin is known as "the luckiest little fishing village in the world". King mackerel, Spanish mackerel, red snapper and pompano are easy catches. Of course picnickers, driftwood hunters, sea shell collectors, swimmers and sun worshippers find the beaches and exhilarating Gulf waters incomparable! Fishermen come from everywhere for the Destin Deep Sea Fishing Rodeo in October.

BAKED RED SNAPPER

Dress 2½ to 3 pound red snapper. Score diagonally. Place in baking pan with 1 cup water. Season. Bake at 350 degrees for 15 minutes.

Saute in 2 tablespoons butter: 2 chopped onions, 4 cloves mashed garlic, and 1 chopped green pepper.

Add 2½ cups tomatoes to onion mixture. Thicken with flour—butter paste and stir until smooth and thick. Simmer, adding ¼ teaspoon rosemary.

Pour above sauce over fish. Add lemon slices and bake 15-20 minutes at 350 degress. Serves 4-6.

MEXICAN CORN BREAD

1 cup corn meal
1 teaspoon baking soda
1 teaspoon salt
¾ cup buttermilk
2 eggs, well beaten
1 cup cream style corn
1 small can chopped green chilies
1 tablespoon melted butter
½ cup Cheddar cheese, grated

Sift corn meal, baking soda and salt together. Add milk, eggs, then corn, chilies and melted butter. Pour ½ of batter into greased 9" by 13" pan. Sprinkle cheese over it, then add rest of batter. Bake at 425 degrees for (approx.) 20 minutes. Serves 8.

Ft. Lauderdale, Fla.

Lauderdale-by-the-Sea, A-1-A Hwy.

The tropical way of life will set the mood for a fun holiday at this Holiday Inn directly on the ocean. Sun-Fun everyday — just a short drive away from golfing, races, fishing piers and cruises on land and sea! Your favorite drink in the Nautical Man-O-War Lounge or poolside sunken patio Bar. Have dinner for two in the elegant King Arthur Room.

CHICKEN A LA MADELINE

4 2-pound chickens
¾ cup olive oil
4 cloves garlic
1 teaspoon oregano
2 medium onions, chopped
2 pounds sliced mushrooms
1 cup sauterne or sherry
3 tablespoons chopped parsley
Accent to taste

Disjoint chickens and roll in seasoned flour (salt, pepper and Accent). Heat oil in skillet and brown chicken on all sides. Add chopped garlic and oregano. Cook 2-3 minutes. Remove chicken adding onions and mushrooms. Cook 5 minutes. Return chicken to pan. Add wine. Let simmer 20-30 minutes until chicken is done. Add parsley and Accent when serving. Serves 8.

BAKED RED SNAPPER

Clean fish and cut into serving-size pieces. Season with salt, pepper, olive oil, lemon juice and oregano. Sprinkle with crumbs. Place in buttered pan and cook under broiler 5-10 minutes. Remove and add 1 can tomato soup. Dilute soup with water or wine per two servings. Pour over fish and bake 20 minutes at 350 degrees. 2 servings to a pound of fish.

Ft. Lauderdale, Fla. U.S. 1

3355 North Federal Highway

With the surf only 3 minutes away, the pool at your doorstep and the Holiday Inn's own 45-foot cruiser at your disposal for cruises and fishing trips, how could you help but enjoy your stay here? For entertainment there are water games, aqua shows, fashion exhibits and breeze swept dining. Guests have access to four exclusive country clubs.

STEAK DIABLO

2 pounds beef tenderloin
½ cup salad oil
2 teaspoons soy sauce
¼ cup lemon juice
1 clove garlic
¼ teaspoon black pepper
1 teaspoon MSG
3 medium bell peppers, quartered
8 small onions
½ pound large mushroom caps
2 medium tomatoes, quartered

Cut beef in 1½-inch chunks. Marinate in salad oil, soy sauce, lemon juice, garlic, black pepper and MSG for 1 hour. Meanwhile blanch peppers, onions and mushroom caps. Place on skewers: 5 pieces of beef, 2 onions, 3 mushroom caps, 2 tomato quarters and 2 pepper quarters. Broil 7 to 8 minutes, turning skewers. Broil longer for well done meat. Serve with wild rice. Serves 4.

BRANDIED PEACHES WITH CHAMPAGNE

For that unusual dessert, place contents of 1 #2½ can of freestone peaches (3½ cupfuls) or 4 fresh peaches that have been peeled and seeds removed in a bowl with ½ cup brandy. Cover bowl tightly and chill for several hours before serving. Dish out peaches, pour one split of champagne over and serve. Serves 4.

Fort Myers, Fla.

2066 W. 1st

Seven miles of sandy beaches, excellent shelling, the Municipal Yacht Basin, and the home of Thomas A. Edison make Fort Myers a fun and interesting place to visit. Fresh orange juice (squeezed at your table) for breakfast, jam sessions and sing-ins in the Pago-Pago Lounge await you at the Holiday Inn on the Caloosahatchee River bank. Fishing is excellent, even from the Inn's own dock.

COLD BEEF STROGANOFF

1½ pounds cold roast beef
1 medium onion, sliced thin
1 pint sour cream
Curry Powder
Dry chives

Shred beef into thin strips and combine with onion and sour cream. Add salt and pepper to taste and dash M.S.G. Add curry powder and dry chives to taste. Mix all ingredients thoroughly. Place in covered dish. Marinate overnight. Serve as main course or as an appetizer.

WILD RICE

Wash 1 pound wild rice thoroughly in cold water. Drain, scald with hot water. Repeat. Add chicken stock (enough to cover 2 inches). Boil slowly for 30-35 minutes. Drain.

In a separate pan melt ½ pound butter and sauté: 1 medium-sized chopped onion, ½ stalk celery (chopped) and 1 cup mushroom stems and pieces. Add 2 tablespoons chopped pimento.

Add mixture to rice but avoid too much moisture as rice must be fluffy, before adding vegetables. Serves 8. This dish may be used with any kind of fowl or game.

Key West, Fla.

U.S. Highway 1

This Holiday Inn is located directly on the Gulf of Mexico with a private beach. Stone crab, shrimp, lobster, turtle steak, superb roast beef and tropical fruits entice throngs of visitors to the Inn's restaurant. The Barracuda Lounge is a favorite meeting place. Take the open-air Conch Tour Train to see the sights. Ernest Hemingway's home is nearby.

KEY LIME PIE

    4 eggs
    1 can Eagle Brand condensed milk
    ⅓ cup key lime juice

Beat egg yolks and the white of one until thick. Add condensed milk and beat again. Add lime juice and beat until thick. Beat the three remaining egg whites until dry and fold into above mixture. Pour into a baked pie shell and bake in a slow oven (325 degree) until set—about 15 minutes. Top with meringue and place in hot oven (400 degree) for 3 minutes to brown meringue slightly.

Meringue

Beat 2 egg whites with rotary beater until stiff, gradually adding 4 tablespoons sugar and salt until mixture holds a peak. Stir in ¼ teaspoon lime juice very lightly.

CONCH CHOWDER

Grind meat of 3 conchs. Cover with water and let boil for ½ hour. Dice 1 large onion, add 1 clove minced garlic and 1 diced sweet pepper. Add tomato sauce to moisten and combine with conch meat. Dice 2 cups potatoes and add to chowder mixture. Add 2-4 cups water, season and simmer until potatoes are done. Serves 6-8.

Lakeland, Fla.-North

910 E. Memorial, U.S. 92

Lakeland, Florida's Citrus Capital, abounds in recreational facilities. There are 11 lakes within the city limits. This Holiday Inn is on Parker Lake. The Prime Rib of Beef reigns in the dining room. There's live entertainment in the Swinging Saloon. See the champions in action during the daily water ski shows at Cypress Gardens, only a few miles away.

PICKLED SHRIMP

(Cocktail Party Fare)

    1 cup salad oil
    1 cup vinegar
      Juice of 3 lemons
    2 tablespoons sugar
    5 bay leaves
    1 teaspoon crushed peppercorns
    1 teaspoon dill seeds
    ½ teaspoon tarragon leaves
    1 teaspoon celery salt
    1 teaspoon dry mustard
      Cayenne pepper
    3 pounds cleaned and cooked shrimp
    6 medium-size onions, sliced

Combine all ingredients (except shrimp and onions) and simmer for 10 minutes. Add shrimp and simmer for 3 more minutes. Choose a large casserole with a lid. Make a layer of sliced onion, then a layer of shrimp until all are used. Pour the hot marinade over and be very sure that all shrimp and onions are covered. When cold, cover and place in refrigerator to "age". Chill at least 48 hours before serving. Slivers of pumpernickel are just right with this. Serves 18 to 24.

Lakeland, Fla. - South

3405 S. Florida Ave.

Chez Henri specialties are as well known as Wonder-full Lakeland. Unpack and enjoy 32 Florida attractions when you make this Inn your fun-quarters. Return each night and relax in comfort. From your first taste of Shrimp Rockefeller you'll know there will be no letdown as courses progress. Another evening, enjoy treats from the Holiday Inn Steaks Ranch. Try Viennese Wiener Schnitzel, a specialty of the Inn.

CHEESECAKE

    2 egg yolks, beaten
    1 teaspoon salt
    ½ cup sugar
    ½ cup milk
    2 tablespoons gelatin
    ½ cup cold water
    2 cups cottage cheese
    1 teaspoon vanilla
    1 lemon (juice and rind)
    2 egg whites
    1 cup cream, whipped

Make lining for cake pan with 1½ cups corn flakes, ½ cup butter and ½ cup sugar well blended. Save some for top. Chill crumb lined pan.
Stir egg yolks, salt, sugar and milk over boiling water. Add gelatin which has been softened in cold water. Cool until thick. Sieve cottage cheese, vanilla and lemon and add to mixture. Beat egg whites until stiff and fold in cream. Add to cheese and yolk mixture. Spoon into cheesecake pan. Sprinkle crumbs on top. Chill well. Serves 8 to 12.

LIME JELLO

Dissolve 1 package lime jello in 1 cup hot water. Cool slightly. Add 1 can applesauce and ½ cup sugar (scant). When thick and congealed some, add ½ pint whipped cream. Chill well before serving. Serves 4 to 6.

Leesburg, Fla.

U.S. 441 & 27

Just a "Fisherman's mile" from this Inn is one of the nation's largest fresh water fishing areas (Lake Griffin). The Inn arranges for guests to go bass fishing and guarantees a catch—enjoy your own for dinner in the Inn's Candlelight Restaurant. Citrus marmalade is a delicious breakfast treat. Be sure to see 2,000 square miles of central Florida from the Citrus Tower with its powerful telescope.

CITRUS MARMALADE

    1 grapefruit
    1 large orange
    1 lemon

Cut fruit into pieces (skins and all), removing seeds. Chop, using coarse blade in grinder. Cover with cold water and let stand 24 hours. Transfer fruit and liquid to large saucepan and cook about 20 minutes, or until peels are very tender. Let stand overnight. Measure fruit and liquid. For each cupful add ¾ cup sugar. Place in large saucepan and cook over low heat 10 to 20 minutes longer, or until 2 drops from syrup falling from a wooden spoon cling together and fall as 1 drop. Ladle into sterilized jelly glasses. 8 to 10 6-ounce glasses.

BEETS IN ORANGE JUICE

    1½ cups orange juice
    3 tablespoons sugar
    2 tablespoons flour
    1 tablespoon butter
    1 can sliced beets (1⅓ cups)

Put first four ingredients in top of double boiler over hot water. Cook until thick as custard. Drain juice from can of sliced beets and add beets to sauce. Let stand over hot water to heat beets thoroughly. Be sure to use sliced beets. Serves 4 to 5.

Marianna, Fla.

Hwy. 90 East

You can fish, swim, water ski and sun at the many nearby lakes and springs. The Gulf Coast is only an hour away. See exquisite nature-made lighted caverns festooned with fantastic formations in the nearby Florida Caverns State Park. Homemade breads and pastries make every meal special at this Inn. Be sure to try the Fried Oysters.

FRIED OYSTERS

1 quart select oysters
1 egg
2 tablespoons water
Buttered bread crumbs
Salt and pepper

Pick over oysters for bits of shell. Pour 1 cup water over them and drain. Dry with paper towel. Beat egg and add water. Dip oysters in egg mixture, then in seasoned crumbs. Repeat. Fry in deep fat at 375 to 385 degrees for 3 to 4 minutes. Serves 2 to 4.

ORANGE CHIFFON PIE

1 tablespoon gelatin
¼ cup water
4 egg yolks
½ cup sugar
1 tablespoon lemon juice
½ cup orange juice
1 teaspoon grated orange rind
4 egg whites
½ cup sugar

Soak gelatin in cold water. Beat egg yolks until light, add ½ cup sugar, citrus juices and rind. Beat until light, then cook stirring continuously until custard consistency. Add soaked gelatin and dissolve. Cool. When cool, add beaten egg whites to which remaining sugar has been added. Fill baked pie shell and chill. Serve with thin layer of whipped cream. Serves 6 to 8.

Miami, Fla.

2500 Brickell (U.S. 1)

All roads lead to this conveniently located Holiday Inn overlooking Biscayne Bay and the ocean. It's only a whisper away from downtown Miami. See denizens of the deep at the world famous Seaquarium. Go to sea for the big ones or go island hopping in a plane. Then come back to superb continental cuisine in the dining room and live entertainment in the lounge at this Inn.

LONDON BROIL

1 flank steak

Rub garlic over meat. Sprinkle with salad oil. Broil over charcoal grill or in oven 1½ inches from heat. Broil 5 minutes on each side. Spread with melted butter and season. Be sure to cut against grain in thin slices. Serve with Sauce below. Serves 4.

Sauce

Sauté ½ cup mushrooms in 2 tablespoons butter. Add 2 teaspoons cornstarch, then 1 cup beef bouillon or stock and thicken slightly. Add 2 tablespoons red wine and simmer. Pour over steak.

PORK CHOPS CREOLE

6 to 8 pork chops, 1-inch thick
2 tablespoons shortening
½ cup catsup
½ cup water
1 teaspoon Tabasco sauce
1 teaspoon Lee & Perrins sauce
2 tablespoons brown sugar
1 teaspoon salt
¼ teaspoon pepper

Wipe pork chops with damp cloth. Heat shortening in large skillets. Add pork chops and sauté until brown. Add all other ingredients. Cover and simmer for 1 to 1½ hours. Serves 6 to 8.

Miami Beach, Fla. 22nd St.

22nd St. & Collins Ave.

Miami Beach swings! Beautiful Japanese gardens, a private beach and luxurious accommodations assure a wonderful tropical resort vacation here. The Regency Lounge features top musical groups. For quick snacks in the sun, there's the Regency Patio overlooking the pool and beach. Tours for everything from nightclubs and Jai Alai to Network TV shows may be arranged at the Inn.

BEEF WELLINGTON

Trim and season a 3-pound beef filet. Braise in ¼ cup butter 5-8 minutes. Cool. Chop fine and sauté in butter: 1 onion, 4 shallots, 3 ounces chicken livers, 3 ounces pork and 1¼ pounds mushrooms. Add 3 ounces Chablis and 3 tablespoons minced parsley. Cover and refrigerate. Before using, add a 3-ounce can pâté de foie gras and 1 teaspoon Perigourdine Sauce.

Pastry

Blend 6 cups sifted flour and 2½ cups soft butter. Add ½ to 1 cup cold water and work into a ball. Refrigerate.

Perigourdine Sauce

Sauté 3 minced shallots in ¼ cup melted butter. Add a bay leaf or 2 cups Madeira. Simmer and add 3 cups consomme. Add 3 chopped truffles to ½ cup Madeira and pour into hot sauce.

Roll out pastry in a rectangular shape large enough for filet. Spread pâté de foie gras mixture over pastry, leaving a border. Place meat in center. Fold pastry over and seal seams with water. Place seam side down on a cookie sheet. Brush top and sides with egg mixed with a little cream. Prick with fork. Bake in a 400 degree oven for 25-30 minutes. Serve with Perigourdine Sauce. Serves 8.

Miami Beach, Fla. 87th St.

8701 Collins Ave.

You couldn't stay any closer to the ocean front! Enjoy an unobstructed view of the ocean, beach and inland waterway. Surfside, Bal Harbour, Sunny Isles are all conveniently close. Sightseeing, fishing, nightclub and overnight tours may be arranged at the Inn. Superb cuisine is served in the Terrace Room.

DEVILED CRAB

1 pound crab meat
½ cup diced onion
½ teaspoon salt
½ teaspoon pepper
Juice of ½ lemon
1 teaspoon mustard
1 teaspoon Worcestershire sauce
Dash Tabasco
½ cup bread crumbs
¼ cup crackers, crushed
¼ cup pimentos, chopped

Mix all ingredients with crab meat. Add enough Newburg Sauce to moisten well. Pack in crab shells and sprinkle tops with crushed crackers. Bake at 350 degrees until brown. Serves 6.

Newburg Sauce

3 tablespoons flour
Salt and pepper
2 tablespoons butter
1½ cups rich milk
2 egg yolks, slightly beaten
2 tablespoons white wine

Blend seasoned flour in melted butter, adding milk gradually. Cook until thickened a little. Add egg yolks and wine. Stir over low heat. Makes approximately 2 cups.

Miami Beach, Fla. 174th St.

17451 Collins Ave.

Surf, sand, sheltering palms, the largest beach on the Golden Strip and sensational food make this Holiday Inn popular with travelers from all over the world. And it has a fabulous feature . . . a unique crystal pool with large glass view ports through which lower floor spectators can watch swimmers or take wonderful pictures.

"GOLDEN STRIP" FAMOUS BUTTERFLY SHRIMP

2½ pounds shrimp (15-20 count)
2 eggs, beaten
1 cup flour
1 teaspoon paprika
¾ teaspoon salt
½ pint milk (or more)

Shell and clean shrimp. Split down back to butterfly, leaving tails on, if desired. Make batter with remaining ingredients. Dip shrimp in batter a few at a time. Cook in deep fryer of hot oil (375 degree) for 3 minutes. Serves 6 to 8.

COUNTRY FRIED CHICKEN

2 fryers (or favorite parts)
1 cup bread crumbs
2 whole eggs
Juice of 2 lemons
1½ cups flour (or more)
2 cups milk

Prepare chicken for cooking — wash and dry well. Cut up in serving size pieces. Season with salt and pepper. Lightly dust pieces in bread crumbs. Make batter of rest of ingredients listed. Dip chicken in batter. Cook quickly in deep fryer in 375 degree oil for about 15 minutes. (Cook large pieces first). Drain on absorbent paper. Serves 8.

Miami Beach, Fla. 180th St.

18001 Collins

There's swimming in the surf or pool . . . fun things to do in the recreation area . . . food and refreshments at the pool patio. Splendid seafood is the specialty everyday in the Inn's popular restaurant, overlooking the olympic-sized pool as well as the beach. It's easy to speed up a lazy pace here with sailfish or tarpon fishing.

CRAB MEAT NEWBURG

½ stick butter
1 tablespoon flour
2 cups heavy cream
2 eggs, separated
Dash paprika
¼ teaspoon salt
2 cups crab meat
¼ cup sherry

Blend butter and flour over low heat. Add cream gradually, egg whites and seasonings. Add crab meat and blend. Remove from heat and stir in egg yolks (beaten) and wine last. Serve on boiled rice. Serves 4 to 6.

BAKED CHICKEN AMANDINE

8 chicken halves
1 tablespoon chicken base
1 quart water
3 cups almonds
¼ pound butter

Bake chicken halves in pan 2 inches deep. Mix chicken base with water and pour over chicken before cooking. Bake 3 hours at 250 degrees. Cover with almonds which have been sautéed in butter. Brown under broiler 2 or 3 minutes before serving. Serves 8.

Miami Beach, Fla. 195th St.

19505 Collins Ave.

All the romance of the tropics is here. Most of the Inn's rooms have private balconies for sunning or enjoying the ocean view. There's a breeze cooled beach and a large salt filtered pool. Fish caught today are served tonight in the Inn's ocean view dining room. There's horse racing nearby during the winter months at Gulf Stream, Tropical and Hialeah Tracks.

STUFFED FLORIDA LOBSTER

4 lobsters
1½ cups Stuffing
Juice 2 limes
Melted butter
1 cup Drawn Butter

Have ready a large kettle hot salted water. Plunge lobster in head first. Cover and let come to boil again. Simmer 15-30 minutes. Cool, remove lobster. Place on back and split in half. Remove sac near head and intestinal vein. Clean under running water. Fill cavity of each lobster with stuffing to rounded top. Sprinkle with lime juice, salt and pepper. Place on buttered broiler, add butter and broil 5 inches from heat until heated through. Serve with pitcher of Drawn Butter. Allow 1 lobster for each person.

Stuffing

Mix lightly with fork 1½ cups bread crumbs, ½ teaspoon salt, pinch sage, 1 tablespoon Worcestershire sauce and 2 tablespoons melted butter.

Drawn Butter

Blend 2 tablespoons melted butter and 2 tablespoons flour. Add ½ teaspoon salt and dash pepper. Stir until smooth adding 1 cup fish stock or hot water slowly. Let come to boil. Add 1 teaspoon lemon juice and 2 tablespoons butter a little at a time.

Naples, Fla.

U.S. 41 at 10th Ave.

The chef's own recipe for pancake batter means no one can resist a hearty breakfast. This complete family resort is a great place to enjoy a vacation among tropical plants and palms. The ocean with 7 miles of public beach and a 1000 foot long fishing pier are near enough. Back at the Inn, delicious food in the Capri Room and music at the piano bar in the First Knight Lounge await you.

BROILED JUMBO SHRIMP

1 pound raw shrimp
1 cup Drawn Butter
½ teaspoon garlic salt
1 teaspoon lemon juice

Peel shrimp and wash. Place shrimp in a shallow pan of drawn butter. Sprinkle with garlic salt. Add lemon juice. Place in broiler or 500 degree oven for 2 to 3 minutes, turning once. Sprinkle with parsley and top with lemon slice dipped in paprika.

MIGNONNE OF BEEF

Slice tenderloin thin and saute' in butter. Season with a small amount of garlic. Place in a preheated casserole with wedges of toast under slices of meat. Pour over one half of meat a very rich Mushroom Sauce. Put mushroom button on top of each slice and parsley to decorate. Allow ⅓ pound beef per person.

Mushroom Sauce

Saute' ¼ pound mushrooms in 2 tablespoons butter. Remove mushrooms. Add 2 tablespoons flour to drippings and blend. Stir in slowly 1 cup water or stock. Cook until smooth and thickened a little. Season with Burgundy wine. Add mushrooms and pour over meat. Makes 1 cup.

Ocala, Fla.-South

U.S. 27, 441 & 301

Fly in for a holiday. Fresh orange juice is the only way to start everyday at the gateway to Florida's citrus industry. Superb cuisine in the Emerald Room and a relaxing atmosphere in the Fox and Hounds Lounge will make you want to stay longer than planned. Silver Springs, nature's underwater fairyland, is only 6 miles from the Inn. Visit the nearby Ocala Caverns too.

CHICKEN WITH ORANGE

2 frying chickens, cut up
¼ pound butter
2 large white onions
1 large can frozen orange juice
1 orange, peeled and sliced

Dredge chickens in seasoned flour and quickly brown in butter. Do not finish cooking. Take out of pan and keep warm. Slice onions thin and saute' in same pan until clear. Add orange juice concentrate and heat well. Add partially cooked chicken and orange slices. Place in 375 degree oven for 45 minutes to 1 hour. Turn several times to glaze. Garnish with orange slices and sauce in pan. Serves 8.

KIDNEY BEAN SALAD

1½ to 2 cups kidney beans, drained
½ chopped sweet pickle
⅓ cup chopped onion
4 tablespoons hard cooked eggs
4 tablespoons sweet pickle juice
½ cup mayonnaise

Combine beans, sweet pickle, onion and eggs and 3 tablespoons pickle juice. Toss lightly. Bend mayonnaise and 1 tablespoon pickle juice and toss lightly with first mixture to coat evenly. Set in crisp lettuce cups and garnish with sliced fresh onion rings. Serves 6.

Ocala, Fla.-West

Interstate 75 & St. Rt. 40

Ocala is the gateway to Florida's citrus industry. Visitors are welcome to see such notable horses as Kentucky Derby winners at the many thoroughbred horse farms in the area. There are gunfights galore in Six Gun Territory at Silver Springs, only 4 miles from the Inn. Step into the Inn's Iron Gate Restaurant for a feast in Florida. Enjoy live entertainment in the Lemon Tree Lounge.

BRAISED SHORT RIBS OF BEEF

Cut 5-6 pounds lean short ribs in 3-4 inch pieces. Dredge in seasoned flour, shaking off excess. Arrange in shallow roasting pan. Brown in preheated 500 degree oven 15-20 minutes. Check while cooking.

Place 2 tablespoons butter in flameproof casserole and cook vegetables slowly until tender:
1 cup coarsely chopped onion
1 cup coarsely chopped carrot
½ teaspoon garlic
⅛ teaspoon thyme
Stir while cooking.

Place browned ribs in 1 layer (if possible) over vegetables. Add 1 cup beef broth to roasting pan and stir all particles where meat was cooked. Pour in casserole. Bring to boil on top of stove. Add 2 bay leaves. Cover and place in 325 degree oven and cook 1 hour or until tender.

Place ribs on serving platter. Strain braising juices and vegetables in saucepan. Skim off fat. Season and pour over meat. Serves 6-8.

Orlando, Fla.-Midtown

929 W. Colonial Drive

Fresh citrus fruits and wonderful vegetables are served here within hours after they are picked. This Holiday Inn is located in the center of a fruit and truck farming region. 43 lakes are near the city. The restaurant is well known for its savory seafoods. The nearby Mead Botanical Garden is noted for its beautiful orchids.

CHESS PIE

½ cup melted butter
2 cups sugar
5 egg yolks, well beaten
1 tablespoon flour
1 tablespoon meal
1 cup milk
1 teaspoon vanilla

Cream butter and sugar. Add egg yolks, then flour and meal. Stir until well blended. Then add milk and vanilla. Place in unbaked pastry shell (9-inch). Bake at 425 degrees for 30 minutes or until filling is set. Cover with Meringue (leave rough) and place in 325 degree oven until delicately brown, about 10-12 minutes. Serves 8.

Meringue

Beat 5 egg whites until stiff, adding 3 tablespoons water while beating. Add ¾ cup sugar gradually and beat.

LAYERED SHORTBREAD

Cream ¼ cup butter and blend in 1 cup flour. Pat in 8½ x 6½ inch buttered pan. Bake in 300 degree oven until pastry is done. Mix and place on top:

1 cup coconut
1 cup broken nut meats
1½ cups dark brown sugar
2 well beaten eggs
½ teaspoon baking powder
½ teaspoon salt and 2 tablespoons flour

Bake at 325 degrees 25 minutes until filling is done. Leave in pan overnight. Remove and cover top with icing: ⅓ box of powdered sugar, butter (size of walnut), and a little sherry. Cut in squares. Makes 8-10.

Orlando, Fla.-South

U.S. 17, 92 & 441

Nostalgic memories of the Gibson Girl era are recalled in the Inn's colorful Pearce's Dining Room, with its gaslights and murals. Be sure to order Florida Lobster here. An individual loaf of bread will be brought to your table on a carving board. The nearby Ben White Raceway is the nation's largest winter training ground for harness racing.

CRAB MEAT EGG ROLL

1 pound crab meat
½ cup melted butter
½ medium onion, minced
2 cups milk
½ cup flour
    Salt and pepper
    Dash dry mustard
1 tablespoon lemon juice
2 tablespoons Worcestershire sauce
    French Pancakes

Saute onion in butter, adding milk and flour gradually. Season. Stir until sauce thickens. Mix crab meat with enough sauce to moisten well. Save remainder of sauce to serve over crab rolls. Unroll French pancakes and place 2 tablespoons crab meat mixture on each. Roll. Serves 8.

French Pancakes

Sift ¾ cup flour. Sift again with 1 teaspoon baking powder and ½ teaspoon salt. Combine 2 beaten eggs, ⅔ cup milk, and ⅓ cup water. Add to dry ingredients. Heat well greased 6-inch skillet. Add batter to barely cover bottom of pan. Cook over moderate heat until brown. Turn and brown under side. Grease pan again. Roll each pancake as cooked.

Palm Beach, Fla.

2770-2830 S. Ocean Blvd.

Scamper along the Inn's 350 feet of private beach, stop for cocktails or tasty tidbits at the pool snack bar. Order continental cuisine in the Orchid Room or outside on the terrace. A putting green and tennis courts are on the grounds. There's the "Paddlewheel Queen" for exciting lake and island cruises. The Henry Morrison Flagler Museum and Royal Poinciana Playhouse are near.

ORANGE BREAD SUR-LE-MER

¾ cup orange rind
1½ cups sugar
⅓ cup water
3 tablespoons butter
1⅓ cups orange juice
3 eggs, beaten
4 cups sifted flour
4 teaspoons baking powder
½ teaspoon soda
2 teaspoons salt

Remove thin orange rind and cut into thin slivers. Combine sugar and water, add rind. Stir constantly over heat until sugar dissolves. Cook slowly for 5 minutes. Add butter, stir until melted. Add orange juice and eggs. Sift dry ingredients into bowl. Add orange mixture and mix just enough to moisten ingredients. Bake in greased and lined loaf pan in 325 degree oven for 1 hour and 15 minutes. Turn on rack to cool. Makes 1 loaf.

BLEU CHEESE DRESSING

1 cup mayonnaise
6 ounces bleu cheese
½ cup sour cream
¾ cup milk
⅛ teaspoon salt
3 tablespoons vinegar

Beat ingredients together until smooth. Makes 2 cups.

Panama City, Fla. Downtown

U.S. 98 on St. Andrew Bay

Full-size growing palm trees and flower beds with exotic tropical plants are inside this Inn's dining room. The whole backside of the Inn is glass, so each room has a magnificent view of the Bay. Ground was actually pumped out of the water for the Inn's site. All the good foods of the Bay are served here, and famous old southern dishes too.

FRIED CUSTARD

(Serve with Fried Chicken)

12 eggs
¼ cup sugar
1 pint XX cream
   Pinch cinnamon
¼ cup rum
6 egg whites, whipped
½ cup nut meats, chopped fine
1 cup corn flakes, rolled

Beat whole eggs and add sugar, cream and cinnamon. Cook in double boiler. Add rum. Place in a flat pan and let set overnight. Cut in squares. Dip custard squares in egg whites, roll in nut and flake mixture and fry in deep fat. Serve hot. Serves 12.

CRANBERRY BREAD

Sift together 2 cups flour, 1½ teaspoons baking powder, ½ teaspoon soda and 1 teaspoon salt. Combine juice and rind of 1 orange with 2 tablespoons shortening and enough boiling water to make ¾ cup. Add 1 cup sugar to well beaten egg. Combine mixtures, dry ingredients last. Add 1 cup chopped nuts and 1 cup cranberries (each cut in half). Pour batter in well greased and floured loaf pan. Let stand 20 minutes before baking. Bake at 350 degrees for 70 minutes. 1 loaf.

Perry, Fla.

U.S. 19, Alt. 27 & 98 S.

Naturally this Holiday Inn specializes in seafood since it's right off
the Gulf Coast. Guests enjoy its
minutes-away-location from fishing
and water fun. Of course the Inn's
location is great for Florida sightseeing all day. It's only 38 miles
from the Jefferson County Kennel
Club with its popular dog racing.

MEAT LOAF WITH SAUCE

½ cup chopped onion
¼ cup chopped celery
¼ cup chopped green pepper
1 tablespoon butter
2 eggs, slightly beaten
⅔ cup milk
1 cup soft bread crumbs
2½ pounds lean ground beef
½ teaspoon black pepper
3 tablespoons catsup
1½ teaspoons salt

Sauté onion, celery and pepper in butter.
Mix eggs, milk and bread crumbs. Add to
sautéed mixture. Add beef and rest of ingredients. Mix lightly with fork. Place in
greased loaf pan or form into loaf and
place on buttered baking pan with sides.
2 strips of bacon may be placed on uncooked loaf if meat seems too lean. Bake
at 350 degrees for 1 hour. Serve with
Tomato Juice Sauce. Serves 6 to 8.

Tomato Juice Sauce

2 tablespoons cornstarch
1 pint tomato juice
1½ teaspoons salt
½ teaspoon pepper

Mix cornstarch with ¼ cup tomato juice.
Heat rest of tomato juice and add cornstarch mixture and seasonings. Stir until
sauce thickens. Makes 2 cups.

St. Petersburg, Fla. South

U.S. 19, 34th St. South

Coming by yacht? This Inn adjoins
the world's largest covered Marina.
Just dock your yacht in a covered
slip on the inland waterway. Arrive
by plane and the Inn provides free
transportation from the airport. By
car the Inn is easy to find just 1 mile
north of the Sunshine Skyway
Bridge. The Inn's Oyster Bar is
usually a first stop.

STUFFED SHRIMP

Place 6-8 cups water in a large kettle and
add seasonings:
¼ cup diced onion
1 clove mashed garlic
1 bay leaf
1 piece chopped celery and leaves
1½ tablespoons salt
Dash Cayenne
½ lemon (slices and juice)

Let come to a boil. Add 2 pounds (10 - 15
count) shrimp and simmer 12-15 minutes.
Cool in water. Drain and peel shrimp,
removing intestinal vein but leaving tails
on.

Pack Imperial Dressing around each shrimp
leaving tail showing. Dip in flour, then in
egg-milk mixture (2 beaten eggs and ½
cup milk). Dip in bread crumbs and fry
in hot oil in deep fryer until golden.
Place in buttered baking pan in a 350
degree oven for 5 minutes. Serves 12.

Imperial Crab Meat Dressing

Combine: 3-4 cups soft bread crumbs,
2 beaten eggs, ¼ cup soft butter, 1 tablespoon dry mustard, 1 tablespoon salt,
¾ teaspoon Accent, ½ teaspoon white pepper, 2 tablespoons Worcestershire sauce,
1 tablespoon chopped chives, ¼ teaspoon
celery seeds, ½ teaspoon hot sauce and
1-2 cups mayonnaise. Mix and fold in
1 pound shredded lump crab meat. Add
mayonnaise for right consistency to pack
around shrimp. Chill before using.

Sanford, Fla.

Seminole Blvd. & Palmetto St.

Every room has a waterfront view! There's a modern marina at your doorstep. Soak up the sun on the beautiful sand beach on St. Johns River. Everything is wrapped up for fun on Holiday Isle. Guests enjoy golfing privileges just 5 minutes away at the Mayfair Country Club. Sirloin is king in the Inn's restaurant.

GOPHER AND RICE

(FLORIDA TORTOISE)

1 gopher (Florida tortoise)
1 large onion, chopped
¼ cup chopped green pepper
    Pinch oregano
    Black pepper
    Salt
    Uncle Ben's Rice

Sauté onion in butter in heavy skillet. Add green pepper and seasonings. In another pot put turtle meat, peeled turtle legs and neck. Add water and cook until tender. Strain. Add liver (sliced) and unborn eggs to pepper and onion mixture. Measure stock and cover 1 inch above meat (diced). Add 1 cup rice for each two cups stock. Cook 20-25 minutes. Combine with first mixture.

To prepare gopher (a burrowing land tortoise found in Florida and other southern coastal states), cut head off tortoise, turn on back and saw four adjoining sections. Remove legs and meat with point of knife. Put necks and legs in boiling water to remove skin. Dice meat before using in recipe.

Sarasota-Bradenton Florida

N. Tamiami Trail, U.S. 41

A lot has happened since De Soto landed in Manatee County in 1541. Today Sarasota is the home of a circus. The Inn offers a beautiful view of Sarasota Bay, yacht club facilities and free boat accommodations in its own 50 slip marina. Naturally fish, fresh from the fisherman's line (your own line, if you like) are favorites in the Chart Room.

ASSORTED SEAFOOD NEWBURG

1 pound snapper fillet
1 pound grouper fillet
½ pound shrimp, cleaned
¼ pound butter
5 ounces sherry
1 tablespoon paprika
1½ cups Newburg Sauce

Cut seafood fillets in small pieces. Combine with shrimp. Sauté seafood in butter for about 15 minutes. Add sherry and paprika. Let simmer until tender. Combine with Newburg Sauce and season to taste. Serve in a casserole. Serves 6.

Newburg Sauce

2 tablespoons butter
2 tablespoons flour
1½ cups light cream or rich milk
2 egg yolks, beaten

Melt butter and stir in flour until blended. Add cream gradually. Stir a little sauce into egg yolks at a time and combine. Cook a little longer. Makes 1½ cups.

Silver Springs, Fla.

At entrance to Silver Springs

Guests are within easy walking distance of Florida's world famous Silver Springs, nature's underwater fairyland. Glass bottomed boats glide over the huge spring fed pool and offer colorful views of marine life. This Inn is a tropical paradise itself, where guests enjoy gourmet food and swimming beneath stately palms and Spanish moss.

FAMOUS PECAN PIE

¼ cup butter
1 cup white sugar
¼ scant teaspoon salt
2 eggs, beaten
1 cup white Karo syrup
1 cup chopped pecan meats

Cream butter and sugar. Add salt, eggs, syrup and nuts. Mix well. Bake in unbaked pastry shell for 1 hour at 300 degrees. Serves 6.

Pastry

1⅓ cups flour
   (sifted before measuring)
½ teaspoon salt
½ cup shortening
3 tablespoons ice water or milk

Spoon sifted flour into measuring cup. Do not pack. Combine with salt. Cut in shortening. Sprinkle with water until all is used. Use fork to blend and make into a ball. Roll out on floured board about 1½ inches larger than pie plate. Ease dough into plate. Fold excess under rim of plate. Crimp and flute edges with fingers. 1 shell.

Tallahassee, Fla.
Apalachee

U.S. 27 S.

Spanish decor in the Holiday Inn's Cafe de Sol, El Cid Dining Room and Flamenco Room is very fitting—DeSoto spent the winter of 1539-40 in this capital city area. Stately old homes and elaborate plantations with huge live oaks make the city popular with visitors. Southern fried chicken, pecan pie, and hot biscuits make this Inn popular.

DEVILED CRABS

1 pound crab meat
2 boiled eggs
1 cup bread crumbs
   Worcestershire sauce
   Tabasco sauce
½ teaspoon salt
2 tablespoons Durkee's dressing
2 tablespoons mayonnaise

Mix crab meat and mashed boiled eggs. Then add ½ cup bread crumbs, Worcestershire sauce, Tabasco sauce, salt, dressing, and mayonnaise. Put this mixture into shells. Cover crabs with ½ cup crumbs and melted butter. Bake 15 minutes in a moderate oven. Serves 4.

CHOPS BAKED WITH CHERRIES

4 thick loin pork chops
1 cup raw rice
1 #2 can sour red cherries
1 tablespoon sugar
   Grated peel ½ lemon
   Dash cinnamon

Season and brown chops on both sides. Place in bottom of casserole the uncooked rice. Pour cherries and juice over rice. Sprinkle sugar, lemon peel and cinnamon over this and arrange chops on top. Cover and bake for 1¼ hours at 350 degrees. Serves 4.

Tallahassee, Fla. Downtown

U.S. 90 West

Live it up right downtown at this beautiful high-rise Holiday Inn. It's only 3 blocks from Florida State University. The Capitol and Governor's Mansion are only a few blocks away. After a busy day in the capital city, take a dip in the Inn's luxurious swimming pool. Dine on gourmet fare in the dining room. Enjoy live entertainment in the lounge.

SEAFOOD GUMBO

½ cup celery, diced
¾ cup onion, diced
½ cup green pepper, diced
¼ cup margarine
　Salt and pepper to taste
1½ teaspoons oregano
¾ teaspoon thyme
1½ teaspoons M.S.G.
　1 teaspoon gumbo file
3¼ cups canned tomatoes
1¼ cups okra
　3 quarts court bouillon
　　(liquid used for poaching fish)
¼ cup cornstarch
½ cup crab meat
　5 to 6 cups cooked rice

Sauté celery, onion and green pepper in margarine. Add salt, pepper, oregano, thyme and M.S.G. Fold in gumbo file and add tomatoes, okra and court bouillon. Simmer for 15 minutes and thicken to desired consistency with cornstarch (blended with a little bouillon). Then add crab meat Serve over cooked rice. Serves 10 to 12.

Tampa, Fla.-Apollo Bch.

U.S. 41 S. of Tampa

You don't have to cross the street to reach Tampa Bay. This Inn is on it. Some rooms are only 30 feet from the water. You can battle the famous fighting tarpon right off the beach during season. Dinner by sunset in the Gold Room is unforgettable. You'll find out why people drive for miles to savor the Stuffed Lobster and Prime Rib. There's entertainment in the Apollo Lounge.

ORANGE TREAT

1 pound butter
1 box brown sugar
4 eggs
2 cups sifted flour
　Juice of 1 orange
　Rind of 1 orange, grated
1 teaspoon vanilla
3 cups uncooked oatmeal

Cream butter, add sugar gradually until fluffy. Beat in eggs, one at a time. Add flour and orange juice alternately. Add grated rind and vanilla. Fold in uncooked oatmeal and place in oblong greased pan. Bake at 325 degrees for 25 minutes.

Cool and top with Orange Butter Cream Frosting: Cream 1 stick butter, adding 1 box powdered sugar. Beat until light. Add 1 teaspoon vanilla and stir in 3 tablespoons orange juice or more until right consistency to spread. 24 portions.

CRANBERRY ORANGE SALAD

Stir 1½ cups boiling hot water into 1 package strawberry Jello. Chop 1 can cranberry jelly (16 ounce size) and add to Jello while hot. Quarter orange, remove seeds, and put through grinder. Add to Jello mixture. Place in mold and chill. Unmold on lettuce and serve with mayonnaise. Serves 8.

Titusville, Fla.

U.S. 1 S.

Bring your telescope or binoculars. You can look across the Indian River and watch the excitement at Cape Kennedy. International cuisine is the order of everyday in the Captain's Table Restaurant. Enjoy live entertainment in the Apollo Lounge. This is a great place to relax, yet so close to where the race for space goes on.

BOHEMIAN STYLE CHICKEN

2 tablespoons butter
2 tablespoons flour
1½ cups chicken broth
   Salt and pepper
1 clove garlic, minced
2 cups shredded chicken
½ cup green pepper (strips)
1 tomato, sliced
½ cup mushrooms (stems-pieces)
½ teaspoon oregano
½ teaspoon paprika

Make a roux of butter and flour. Add broth gradually and thicken. Season. Add chicken, peppers, tomato and mushrooms. Simmer 30 minutes. Sprinkle with oregano and paprika. Serves 4.

HAM AND MACARONI AU GRATIN

Blend 2 tablespoons butter and 2 tablespoons flour. Add 2 cups milk gradually and stir until smooth and thick. Add 2 cups cooked macaroni and 1 cup cooked cubed ham. Season to taste. Add ½ cup grated cheese and simmer a few minutes. Place in buttered casserole and sprinkle with ½ cup grated cheese. Bake in 400 degree oven until brown and bubbly. Serves 6.

Wildwood, Fla.

I-75 at St. 44 Interchange

Picture orange groves encircling crystal lakes set in rounded hills and you'll know what to expect in Wildwood. There's no hustle and bustle around this Holiday Inn. Take your time enjoying the delicious food. Southern Fried Chicken is a must on the menu. There's a buffet too. Expect excellent fishing in nearby lakes. The Inn will prepare and serve your own catch.

FRIED CHICKEN LIVERS

1 pound chicken livers
   Flour
¼ cup butter
   Salt and pepper

Wash chicken livers thoroughly. Cut in half and soak in cold water for a few minutes. Wipe on paper towel. Dip in flour and sauté in butter about 8 to 10 minutes. Serves 4, or more if used as cocktail fare.

POMPANO

1 pound pompano (fillets)
   French dressing
   Salt and pepper

Place fillets on oiled broiler pan. Brush with French dressing. Season. Place under broiler and broil 12 to 14 minutes, depending on thickness of fillets. It is not necessary to turn during broiling. Garnish with lemon wedges and parsley. Serves 2 to 3.

Winter Haven, Fla.

U.S. Highway 17 S.

This Inn's 3-miles-away location from Cypress Gardens makes it a favorite with vacationers. At Cypress Gardens visitors may cruise in electric boats. There are several water ski shows daily. You have a lot to look forward to back at this Inn too. The food served in Vic's Open Hearth Restaurant is fabulous.

PAELLA VALENCIANA

1½ pounds jumbo shrimp (washed well)
3 chickens, cut up
1½ pounds lean pork, cubed
2 cups Uncle Ben's Rice
1½ pounds lobster meat
1 can whole clams (in shells)

Combine 3 cups water with 12-ounce bottle of beer and 1 cup dry sauterne wine in a large saucepan. Add shrimp, 2 carrots, 2 small onions, 3 parsley sprigs, 2 bay leaves, 2 teaspoons salt and 5 peppercorns. Bring to a boil and simmer 45 minutes. Let shrimp cool in stock. Later strain stock and save to use. When stock is cool, peel and clean the shrimp. Meanwhile in a Dutch oven, heat ½ cup olive oil and brown cut up chicken and pork on all sides. Remove chicken and pork and add 2½ cups chopped onions, 4 garlic cloves, 1 cup green peppers, ¼ cup chopped parsley and cook until onions are tender but not browned. Then stir in 1 teaspoon saffron, 1 teaspoon paprika, 1 teaspoon oregano, 1 teaspoon pepper and 2 teaspoons salt. Arrange chicken and pork in heat proof earthenware casserole. Preheat oven to 350 degrees. Put 5 cups stock in casserole with chicken and pork. Bring to a boil. Then add rice, stirring continuously. Bring back to boil, add lobster, shrimp and clams. Bake covered about 1 hour. Rice should be moist. Serves 12 or more.

Albany, Ga.

U.S. 19 & 82

Enjoy quail hunting on nearby plantations. The Holiday Inn chef will prepare yours for dinner. You'll enjoy a stay at this Inn in the heart of Albany, in the heart of Georgia. Radium Springs, the largest natural spring in the state, is only four miles away. Over 700,000 pecan trees are located at nearby Papershell Pecan Groves.

CRANBERRY PINEAPPLE SALAD

3 tablespoons gelatin
1 quart cranberry juice
1 small can crushed pineapple
1 can whole cranberry sauce

Dissolve gelatin in ¼ cup cranberry juice. Heat remainder of juice and dissolve gelatin. Cool. Add pineapple and cranberry sauce. Pour in mold. Chill. Serves 10-12.

FLANK STEAK ALBANY

2 1-pound flank steaks, about 1 inch thick
½ cup Worcestershire sauce
1 tablespoon liquid smoke
1 teaspoon salt
1 teaspoon pepper

Trim edges and score crosswise. Marinate overnight in Worcestershire sauce, liquid smoke and seasonings for best results. Charbroil to desired doneness. Serves 6.

QUAIL SOUTHERN

4 quail
¾ cup flour
1 tablespoon salt
1 tablespoon paprika
¼ teaspoon pepper

Parboil quail until tender. Drain. Combine flour and seasonings in paper bag and place one bird in bag at a time and shake until bird is covered. Fry in heavy iron skillet with melted shortening or cooking oil to cover. Turn once. Cook until golden brown. Serves 4.

Athens, Ga.

U.S. 129, 78, 29 and 441

This Holiday Inn is built on soil where warring Creek and Cherokee nations once fought. The Inn is adjacent to the campus of the University of Georgia. You can expect delicious food in the southern tradition in the Inn's elegant restaurant overlooking the patio and heated pool. Holiday Inn guests are invited to use the facilities of the Athens Country Club.

SWISS STEAK

Dredge 6 cube steaks in seasoned flour. Place steaks in heavy skillet with 2 tablespoons cooking oil and brown on both sides. Chop coarse: ½ onion, ¼ bunch celery and 1 green pepper and add to steaks. Sauté until tender. Pour ½ cup hot tomato juice and 1 pint beef stock or bouillon over steaks. Cover. Place in 325 degree oven until tender (about 1½ to 2 hours). Place steaks on serving platter. Blend flour-water paste in juices if gravy needs thickening. Serves 6.

POTATO PANCAKES

    3 potatoes
    ½ onion
    3 tablespoons parsley
    1 beaten egg
    2 tablespoons flour
    1 teaspoon salt
    ⅛ teaspoon pepper
      Dash Accent
    ¼ teaspoon baking powder

Wash and peel potatoes. Grate or place in a fine grinder with onion and parsley. Add egg. Sift flour, salt, pepper, Accent and baking powder. Add to mixture using a little cream if needed to make right texture for dropping on hot griddle. Makes cakes size of top of cup. Turn once with pancake turner to brown both sides. 4 to 5 portions.

Atlanta, Ga.-Downtown

Interstate 75 & 85

Enjoy dinner in the round. French cuisine is the specialty in the Inn's round dining room with a gazebo. Since the Inn is right in the heart of downtown Atlanta, many a business decision is made over the delicious buffet breakfasts and buffet luncheons. Atlanta's new Civic Center is only 3 blocks away. Springtime is a beautiful time to visit, when the peach trees along the streets are in full bloom.

FRISCIA'S LASAGNE

Put enough water in a pan to barely cover 6 pieces of lasagne. Bring to a boil, adding 1 tablespoon salt along with lasagne. Cook until tender (about 15 min.). Drain lasagne carefully. Allow to cool in rice colander. Rinse in warm water.

Sauce

Brown 2 medium onions (chopped fine) and 1 garlic bud (chopped fine) in ½ cup cooking oil until light brown in color. Add 1 pound ground beef and brown. Add 2 cups beef stock (bouillon), 1 cup tomato paste, 1 pint whole tomatoes and juice, and 1 pint tomato purée. Season with 1 tablespoon salt, dash pepper, 1½ teaspoons oregano, ½ teaspoon M.S.G. and simmer over low heat 1 hour, or until flavors blend. Remove from heat.

Cut lasagne into 2 pieces crosswise and line baking pan with 3 pieces (whole cut in half). Cover with half of meat sauce and 1 cup cottage cheese. Repeat, adding rest of meat sauce and another cup of cottage cheese. Sprinkle 1 cup grated Cheddar cheese over top and 1 cup grated Parmesan cheese on very top. Place in a 375 degree oven for 40 minutes, or until brown. Serve hot. 10 servings.

Atlanta, Ga.-NW

I-75 N., U.S. 41 N.

Whether on your way to Kennesaw Mountain Battlefield or here to visit Georgia Tech, you'll be glad you stopped at this Holiday Inn. Let them serve you southern style in the Pavillion Dining Room. The Bikini Lounge is a favorite place with local residents as well as visitors. The Georgia Tech campus is only 2 miles from the Inn.

SHRIMP GUMBO

    4 ribs celery with leaves, chopped
    2 onions, chopped coarse
    1 green pepper, chopped
    2 tablespoons margarine
    2 tablespoons flour
    2 cups tomatoes, canned
    8 cups fish stock (or water)
    1 teaspoon pickling spice
    1 bay leaf
    2 pounds raw shrimp
      (shelled, deveined and cut)
    3 cups okra, chopped
    2 tablespoons oil
    ½ teaspoon gumbo filé
    ½ teaspoon white pepper
    1 to 2 teaspoons salt

Sauté celery, onions and pepper in margarine in a heavy pot until all are tender. Add flour and cook until flour is brown. Squeeze tomatoes into small pieces and cook slowly for 15 minutes in a separate saucepan. Add fish stock, pickling spice, bay leaf and shrimp to sauté kettle. Last, add tomatoes. Cook 1½ to 2 hours at simmer stage after boil is reached. Sauté okra in oil. Dissolve gumbo filé in a little water. Add remaining ingredients to sauté pot. Bring to a boil. Then remove from heat. Do not refrigerate while hot. Serve hot in bowls with rice. Serves 8.

Atlanta, Ga.-South

I-75, U.S. 19, 85 & 41

White dogwood and wooded foothills of the Blue Ridge Mountains attract visitors to this region. The food served in the Magnolia Dining Room lures people to the pleasant surroundings of this Holiday Inn. It's the Inn to stay away from the hustle and bustle, but close enough (10 miles) to the business district for convenience.

DEVILED CRAB

    1 pound crab meat
    2 tablespoons lemon juice
    4 tablespoons chopped onion
    2 tablespoons chopped green pepper
    2 tablespoons chopped celery
    4 tablespoons butter
    2 tablespoons flour
    1 cup top milk
    ¼ cup crushed crackers
    1 teaspoon dry mustard
    1 teaspoon salt
    1 teaspoon Lea and Perrins
    ½ teaspoon Tabasco
    1 tablespoon chopped pimento
    ½ cup soft buttered bread crumbs

Pick over crab meat for shells. Sprinkle with lemon juice. Let stand while preparing rest of ingredients. Sauté onion, pepper and celery in 2 tablespoons butter until onion is golden. Make cream sauce, blending 2 tablespoons butter with flour. Add milk gradually and cook until thickened. Add crackers. Mix crab meat and sautéed mixture. Combine with cream sauce and add seasonings. Add pimento. Place in shells or ramekins. Sprinkle with bread crumbs and bake in 350 degree oven for 10 to 12 minutes. Serves 8.

Augusta, Ga.

A beautiful antique canopy bed is in the bridal suite. There's superb food for your eating pleasure. Live entertainment creates an atmosphere of gaiety in the lounge. Augusta is the "Golfing Capital of the Nation". It hosts the Masters Golf Tournament. The Manse, the boyhood home of Woodrow Wilson, is an interesting place to visit.

POTATO SALAD

    6 to 8 potatoes, boiled and diced
    ¼ cup green pepper, chopped fine
    ⅓ cup celery, chopped fine
    1 pimento, chopped fine
    2 hard boiled eggs, chopped coarse
    1½ teaspoons grated onion
    1 teaspoon salt
    ¼ teaspoon white pepper
    1 tablespoon mustard
    1½ teaspoons Durkees Dressing
    ¾ cup mayonnaise (or more)

Combine potatoes with chopped vegetables and eggs, adding grated onion and seasonings. Toss all ingredients until well blended. Add dressing and mayonnaise. Toss until it is well mixed with other ingredients. Line bowl with lettuce leaves, then toss salad in bowl lightly. Garnish with parsley and a bit of sieved hard cooked egg. Serves 6 to 8.

Mayonnaise

Beat 2 egg yolks and add few drops vinegar. Add salad oil, drop by drop, into egg mixture, beating constantly, until ¼ cup is used. Gradually increase amount of oil, beating all the time until 1 pint (in all) is used. As mixture thickens, add ¼ cup vinegar and 1 tablespoon lemon juice, a little at a time. Add 1 teaspoon salt and dash pepper. Makes 2 cups.

Bremen-Carrollton, Ga.

Men have no excuse for not being well dressed around here. Bremen is the Men's Clothing Capital of the South. To make purchasing even easier for visitors, this Holiday Inn has a men's outlet store on the premises. (Beware of the restaurant's Fried Chicken if you don't want to buy larger sizes). There's a popular private club in the Inn too.

GEORGIA FRIED CHICKEN

    2 2½-pound fryers
    2 teaspoons salt
    1 teaspoon pepper
    1 cup flour
    2 cups shortening (more if needed)

Disjoint chicken and cut into thighs, breasts, wings, and drumsticks. Save back and neck for broth later. Wash chicken thoroughly and dry with paper towel. Place flour and seasonings in paper sack. Drop in a few pieces of chicken at a time and cover each piece thoroughly. Use heavy iron skillet and melt shortening about 1 to 1½ inches deep. Heat grease and put in pieces of chicken. Brown quickly on one side, then on other. Lower heat and cook until done; depending on pieces of chicken. Thick pieces require more time so should be placed in pan at same time. When chicken is fried, pour off all but 2 tablespoons shortening. Add 3 tablespoons flour and blend. Add 2 cups rich milk gradually and season to taste. Cook until gravy is smooth and thick. 6-8 servings.

Callaway Gardens, Ga.

U.S. 27 S. at Pine Mountain

A beautiful land of lakes, beaches, birds and flowers in a green woodland awaits you at Callaway Gardens. The 2500 acre preserve has 11 lakes for fishing and boating and an excellent golf course. The mountain air will give you the appetite to appreciate the food served here. It's as bountiful and picture-pretty as the surrounding scenery.

PINE MOUNTAIN CORN BREAD

    2 cups Pine Mountain corn meal
    2 teaspoons baking powder
    1 teaspoon salt
    1⅔ cups milk
    1 egg
    ¼ cup melted shortening

Mix dry ingredients. Add milk and beaten egg. Then add melted shortening and pour into sizzling hot greased pan, muffin or corn stick pans and bake in a hot (450 degree) oven for 18 to 20 minutes. Serves 6 to 8.

BANANA BREAD

    1 stick real butter
    1 cup sugar
    2 eggs, beaten
    1 cup flour
    ½ teaspoon salt
    3 soft ripe bananas, mashed
    1 cup chopped pecans
    1 tablespoon vanilla
    1 teaspoon soda dissolved in 1 table-
        spoon hot water

Soften butter to room temperature overnight. Cream butter, add sugar and beaten eggs. Sift flour and salt into mixture. Add bananas, pecans and vanilla. Add soda solution last. Pour in greased, floured loaf pan. Bake in 325 degree oven for 1 hour. Makes 1 loaf.

Columbus, Ga.

U.S. 27, 280 S.

Although you may relax by a pool in a "Riviera" setting at this Inn, it's located in a charming old city in America. The Chattahoochee River still turns the wheels of the city's factories. The excellent food at the Inn grows in popularity each week. Servicemen at nearby Fort Benning will vouch for that.

SWEET AND PUNGENT PORK

    1½ pounds cubed pork
    2 eggs, beaten
    1 cup flour
    1 teaspoon salt
        Peanut oil
    3 green peppers, cut in strips
    2 cups canned pineapple chunks
    ¾ cup brown sugar
    1 cup vinegar
    3 tablespoons molasses
        Freshly ground black pepper
    3 tomatoes, peeled and diced
    1 tablespoon cornstarch

Combine eggs, flour, salt and ¼ cup water. Add pork cubes and stir until coated. Fry pork in 2 inches of hot oil (375 degrees) for 3 minutes or until golden brown. Drain pork and keep in a warm place. Combine green peppers, pineapple (drained), brown sugar, vinegar, molasses, black pepper and 1½ cups water. Bring to a boil, stirring constantly. Add tomatoes and simmer for 5 minutes, stirring occasionally. Combine cornstarch with ¼ cup cold water and stir in green pepper mixture. Cook until thickened, stirring constantly. Add pork and simmer for 15 minutes. Serves 6.

Dalton, Ga.

Interstate 75 and Walnut Ave.

The "Tufted Textile Center of the World" is a great place to come on business and bring the whole family. Dalton's Holiday Inn is within five minutes of downtown and the Inn provides free transportation to and from if requested. The Baked Virginia Ham with Tropical Fruit Sauce is a "must try" on the Inn's menu. The best deer hunting in North Georgia is at nearby John's Mountain.

CLAM CHOWDER

2½ cups chopped clams (#2 can)
2½ cups clam juice (#2 can)
3 cups water
1 cup potatoes, cubed
2 onions, diced
½ cup carrots, diced
¾ cup celery, diced
    Salt, white pepper and Accent
1 pint cream
¾ cup instant mashed potatoes

Add cubed potatoes, onions carrots, and celery to water and cook until tender. Add clams and clam juice. Season with salt, white pepper and Accent. Bring to a boil. Use instant potatoes to thicken. Bring milk to a boil. Add to chowder just prior to serving. Serves 10 to 12.

TROPICAL FRUIT SAUCE

¾ cup claret
1 cup grape jelly
⅛ teaspoon cinnamon
⅛ teaspoon nutmeg
    Salt
    Pepper
1 orange

Simmer wine, jelly and seasoning for 15 minutes. Peel orange, removing white membrane. Cut and peel in strips and add to sauce, then add sliced orange (seeded). This is excellent for ham or duck. Makes 1½ cups.

Gainesville, Ga.

On U.S. 23

Southern hospitality means extras unlimited at this Holiday Inn. Visit the poultry center at the foothills of the Blue Ridge Mountains. Pan for gold in the old Cherokee Nation. Or go to Lake Lanier by small cruiser with box lunches aboard. There's even more here — fresh homemade bread (individual loaves to cut at your table).

HOMEMADE BREAD

1 package dry granular yeast
1 cup lukewarm water
2 tablespoons sugar
2 teaspoons salt
½ cup shortening (scant)
3 to 4 cups flour (approximately)
1 beaten egg white

Dissolve yeast in warm water. Add sugar, salt and shortening to remaining water. Then add 1 cup flour. Add yeast-water mixture and stir well. Thoroughly fold in egg white, then add flour to make dough. Turn on floured board and knead until satiny. Place in greased bowl and lightly grease top. Cover and let stand until double in bulk (in warm place). Knead down. Shape into 2 small loaves and place in well greased loaf pans. Permit loaves to rise until double in bulk. Start cooking in slow oven for about 10 minutes, then set oven at 350 degrees and bake 25 minutes. Remove from oven and brush with melted butter if desired. Makes 2 small loaves.

Jesup, Ga.

U.S. 301 South

If you're on your way to the Georgia coast this Holiday Inn is the place to stop—for a day, a week, even longer. Excellent food is one reason you'll want to stay. You're near enough to visit the historic Midway Church, built by Puritans in 1754. The Fort Frederica National Monument on St. Simon's Island has the preserved ruins of the fort built in 1739.

GEORGIA POT ROAST

    5 pounds beef (cut in chunks)
    ¼ cup flour
    ¾ quart tomato purée
    ½ pint beef stock
    ⅓ cup celery tops
    2 cups whole small potatoes, cooked
    1 cup carrots, cooked
    2 cups tiny whole onions, cooked

Roll beef in seasoned flour and brown in shortening. Pour in tomato purée, stock and celery tops. Bake in covered pan 2 to 3 hours at 350 degrees. Add vegetables and cook another 15 minutes uncovered. Thicken gravy if desired (blend 2 tablespoons flour in ¼ cup water and add to juices). Serves 8.

FRENCH PORK TENDERLOIN

    2 pounds pork loin (end cuts)
    4 tablespoons flour
    1 cup tomato purée
    ½ cup bread crumbs

Slice pork in ½-inch thick slices. (Remove bones). Pound with mallet to flatten. Dredge in seasoned flour. Next dip into tomato purée (soy sauce, ginger or allspice may be added to purée if desired). Then roll in bread crumbs. Fry in deep fat at 350 degrees until brown—about 5 minutes. Serves 6.

McDonough, Ga.

I-75 & State 155

You'll know you're in the middle of Georgia when you look from your window and see the beautiful southern countryside. This Holiday Inn offers southern hospitality and southern dishes . . . Chicken and Dumplings, Strawberry Shortcake, Talmadge Ham (from Henry County). There's much to see and do with the International Raceway, Hampton Downs, Lake Spivy and Stone Mountain nearby.

SKILLET CHICKEN SUPREME

    1 12-oz. package wide noodles
    6 whole chicken breasts, split
    4 slices boiled ham, cut
    ¼ cup butter or margarine
    ¼ cup Fresca or water
    1 pint dairy sour cream
    2 tablespoons flour
    1 teaspoon salt
    ¼ cup snipped parsley
    1 2-oz. jar sliced pimento
    1 3-oz. can whole mushrooms

Cook noodles and drain. Tuck piece of ham into slit of each chicken breast, where breast bone was removed. Secure with toothpicks. Preheat skillet with cover over low heat on stove. Melt butter. Arrange chicken, skin side down. Pour Fresca or water over chicken and cook covered for 30 minutes, or until chicken is tender. Meanwhile, combine sour cream, flour and salt. Then add parsley and pimento and mix gently. Remove chicken from skillet. Place noodles in skillet and mix gently with pan drippings. Stir in half of sour cream mixture. Arrange chicken, skin sides up, on top of noodles. Top chicken with remaining sour cream mixture. Place 1 mushroom on top of each chicken breast. 12 servings.

Macon, Ga.-Central

Ga. Hwy. 87

The Village Tavern awaits the pleasure of your company. Relive the days when dining was a gracious experience in the Country Squire Restaurant. This Holiday Inn is only 5 minutes from downtown Macon and on scenic Riverside Drive. The Ocmulgee National Monument is only 2 miles from the Inn. Macon is only 6 miles from the geographical center of the state.

CHICKEN MONTE CARLO

2 fryers (split in half)
2 tablespoons butter
1 cup Madeira Wine Sauce

Prepare chickens for baking. Season. Sauté in a heavy pan over medium heat in butter turning once to brown each side. Place in a large casserole or heavy baking pan with cover. Pour Madeira Wine Sauce over chickens and bake covered at 350 degrees for 1½ to 2 hours, or until tender. Baste with sauce occasionally. Serves 4.

Madeira Wine Sauce

2 tablespoons butter
⅓ cup minced onion
¼ cup minced celery
2 tablespoons flour
1 cup canned tomatoes
1 cup bouillon
½ cup Madeira

Sauté onion and celery in butter, adding flour and seasonings. Blend well, add tomatoes, bouillon and wine. Cook until well mixed and thickened. Makes approximately 2 cups.

Rome, Ga.

707 Turner McCall Blvd.

Be a guest in an old historical city of seven hills and three rivers. This luxurious Holiday Inn is located on the banks of the Oostanaula River and downtown. The Inn's Taproom invites you to relax and enjoy delicious seafood specialties and sandwiches. Be sure to see the Romulus and Remus Statue which was given to the city by Rome, Italy.

BEEF BORDELAISE

3 cups cooked roast beef
2½-ounce can mushrooms
   (stems and pieces)
2 tablespoons butter
2 tablespoons flour
   Freshly ground pepper
   Salt
1½ to 2 cups Bordelaise Sauce

Sauté beef and mushrooms in butter. Add seasoned flour and blend. Add Sauce to right consistency and simmer 30 to 40 minutes, adding more sauce as needed. Serves 6.

Bordelaise Sauce

2 tablespoons butter
2 tablespoons shallots, minced
¾ cup dry red wine
1 to 1½ cups brown sauce
1 tablespoon minced parsley
   Salt
   Cayenne

Sauté shallots in butter, add wine and reduce one half while simmering. Add brown sauce, parsley and seasonings. Makes 1½ to 2 cups.

Statesboro, Ga.

U.S. 301 & 25

Travelers enroute north or south find this Holiday Inn convenient and relaxing for an overnight stop. The food is fabulous in the Gourmet Steak Room. Bubbly casseroles are just as delicious as the steaks. Interesting places nearby include Magnolia Spring State Park and Yam Grandy State Park. Statesboro is not far from Savannah and the beach.

TURKEY TETRAZZINI

    2 cups cooked turkey, diced
    ¼ pound spaghetti
    ½ cup mushrooms, sliced
    4 tablespoons butter
    4 tablespoons flour
    1½ to 2 cups milk
    1 pimento, diced
      Seasonings
    ½ cup Parmesan cheese

Cook spaghetti until tender. Drain. Sauté mushrooms in half of butter. Blend flour in rest of butter and add milk gradually. Cook until it thickens. Add mushrooms and butter, then pimento and turkey. Season. Combine with spaghetti and place in greased shallow baking dish. Sprinkle with cheese. Bake in 350 degree oven until well heated and browned, about 15 to 20 minutes. Serves 4.

GEORGIA PECAN PIE

Combine 2 cups dark Karo syrup, 1 cup sugar, 4 tablespoons butter and ½ teaspoon salt. Bring to boil. Beat 6 eggs, add 1 teaspoon vanilla and 2 cups pecan halves. Add to hot mixture and pour into 2 unbaked pastry shells. Bake 10 minutes at 450 degrees then turn oven to 300 degrees and bake 20 minutes. Let cool and serve. 2 pies.

Thomasville, Ga.

U.S. 19 S., Downtown

You can anticipate the unexpected at this Holiday Inn. There's music everywhere—even from the bottom of the pool. Quail come up to the Inn's putting green to challenge sportsmen. You may order quail on the menu any day of the year. The Inn will arrange hunting trips and prepare your own game. Each year Thomasville hosts one of the largest Rose Festivals in the nation.

QUAIL BAKED IN WINE

    ½ cup butter
    2 small onions, minced
    2 whole cloves
    1 teaspoon peppercorns
    2 cloves garlic, cut fine
    ½ bay leaf
    6 quail, cleaned and trussed
    2 cups white wine
    ½ teaspoon salt
    ⅛ teaspoon pepper
      Few grains cayenne
    1 teaspoon minced chives
    2 cups cream

Melt butter, add onions, cloves, peppercorns, garlic and bay leaf. Cook for several minutes. Add quail and brown on all sides. Add wine, salt, pepper, cayenne and chives and simmer until tender, about 30 minutes. Remove quail to hot serving dish. Strain sauce, add cream and heat to boiling point. Pour over quail. Allow 1 quail for each serving.

Valdosta, Ga.

I-75 at Ga. 94 Interchange

No wonder this Inn is known as the "swinginest" place in southern Georgia. Commercial travelers are greeted with a free drink when they register. The Executive Club offers sauna baths, weight lifting equipment, pool tables and ping pong on the house (Inn). There are two swimming pools. Gourmet food is served on the terrace at night, overlooking the Inn's 20 acres of beautifully landscaped grounds.

ROAST LEG OF SPRING LAMB

5- to 6-pound leg of lamb
Slivers of garlic
1½ cups Lake Country red
dinner wine
3 to 4 tablespoons flour
2 to 3 cups water

Wipe leg of lamb and dry well. Cut deep slits along leg of lamb about 1 inch apart. Stuff gashes with slivers of garlic. Roast lamb in shallow pan at 325 degrees allowing 35 minutes per pound. After first hour remove garlic and baste with ¼ cup wine. Baste every 20 minutes until wine is used (use ¼ cup each time) and lamb is desired doneness. Remove lamb from pan. Pour off fat. Add flour to pan and blend with pan drippings, adding 2 to 3 cups water gradually. Cook and stir until gravy is smooth. Season to taste. (Fresh dill may be used instead of garlic if preferred). Serves 10 to 16.

Honolulu, Hawaii Airport

3401 Nimitz Highway

When palm trees, surf and sun beckon, be off to this Holiday Inn. Make reservations on the isle. Then soak it up—the sun never sets on fun and relaxation. The sea is at your doorstep. Hawaiian dishes as well as All-American favorites await you in the Ani-Ani dining room. Let them entertain you Hawaiian style in the Kalama Lounge.

HALEKULANI SALAD

Take 1 fresh Hawaiian Pineapple and cut horizontally. Core the fruit meat and rinse the shell in water. Fill the shell with the freshly cut pieces of pineapple, mango, papaya and orange. Garnish with slices of apple and bananas. Center with cottage cheese or fruit sherbet and sprinkle with shredded coconut. Serves 1-3.

MAHI-MAHI MACADAMIA

Cut fresh fillet of Mahi Mahi (dolphin) in 4 8-ounce portions. Sprinkle with butter and lemon and broil until golden brown. Garnish with macadamia nut pieces and serve with steamed island rice and tartar sauce. Serves 4.

TERIYAKI STEAK

6 8-ounce cube steaks
Marinate for 6 to 8 hours.

Marinade: ½ soy sauce and ½ water. Dice finely: garlic, ginger, onions, sugar and bay leaves and add to marinade.

Broil steaks to desired doneness and serve with Hawaiian steamed rice. Serves 6.

Waikiki Beach, Hawaii

Kalakaua Ave., on island of Oahu

Swim in waters once the playground of Hawaii's Kings and Queens. Ride outrigger canoes and try to master the surf. This luxurious 23-story Holiday Inn overlooks two of Hawaii's world famous landmarks . . . Waikiki Beach and Diamond Head. The first floor dining room features Baked Avocado Kilauea, Chicken Kamehameha and Barbecued Teriyaki Steak.

MAI TAI

1½ ounces 86 proof light rum
1½ ounces 86 proof gold rum
 1 ounce Trader Vic's Orgeat Syrup
 ½ ounce lemon juice
 ½ ounce lime juice
 ½ ounce orange curacao

Fill giant old-fashioned glass with crushed ice. Add a cherry, slice of fresh pineapple, pour in all ingredients and stir. Float ½ ounce of rum (151 proof) on the top. Garnish with mint. Only one to a customer!

POLYNESIAN BAKED CHICKEN

 2 frying chickens, cut up
 1 cup orange juice
 2 tablespoons lemon juice
 ½ cup brown sugar
 1 fresh pineapple, cubed
 1 fresh papaya, cubed

Shake chicken parts in paper bag with 1 cup of flour and 1½ teaspoons seasoning salt. Melt ½ pound butter. Rub 2 tablespoons into a large baking dish. Place chicken in dish and brush with remainder of butter. Bake 50 minutes at 350 degrees. Combine juices, sugar, 1 tablespoon soy sauce and 1 tablespoon cornstarch in a saucepan. Bring to a boil, stirring constantly. Cook until clear and thickened. Add fruit and pour over chicken. Bake 10 minutes. Serves 4-6.

Boise, Idaho-Airport

Vista Ave. off U.S. 30

This Holiday Inn is a favorite. There's live entertainment in the lounge and superb food in the dining room. Take time to visit the many interesting places in Idaho's capital. The State Historical Museum, Boise Art Museum, and Julia Davis Park are worth your while. The Gothic First Methodist Church has 24-karat gold windows.

SWEDISH MEAT BALLS

 3 cups stale bread, diced fine
 1 cup cold milk
 ¾ cup onion, diced fine
 3 tablespoons margarine
 ½ pound ground lean pork
 1 pound ground beef, chuck
 1 teaspoon salt
 ¼ teaspoon ground nutmeg
 ½ teaspoon white pepper
2½ tablespoons parsley, chopped fine
 3 eggs, slightly beaten
1½ pints chicken stock, hot

Soak bread in milk. Saute onion in margarine. Mix meat, onion and bread. Add salt, nutmeg, pepper, parsley and eggs. Mix well and form into balls. Place in rows in buttered baking pan. Add chicken stock and cook for 25 minutes in 400 degree oven. Remove balls. Strain stock for sauce. Serve with Cream Sauce. Serves 8.

Cream Sauce

Blend ¼ pound margarine and ½ cup flour. Add 1 quart stock (adding water if not 1 quart). Cook until smooth and thick. Add ¾ cup half and half. Stir well and strain over meat balls. Season, adding 1 tablespoon chopped parsley last.

Bloomington-Normal, Illinois

Intersection U.S. 66 & Ill. 9

Illinois State and Illinois Wesleyan University make Bloomington's Franklin Avenue the only street in the world with a university at each end. The Illinois Republican Party was born here. From hors d'oeuvres to pastries, each meal is a gourmet adventure. The dining room is literally "packed" when the menu includes Hungarian Goulash or Veal Fricassee.

BEEF SALAD

    1 pound roast beef (ground)
    ½ cup salad dressing
    ⅛ cup grated onion
    ¼ cup sweet pickle relish
    1 tablespoon Worcestershire sauce
    ¼ cup diced celery
      Salt, pepper, onion & garlic salt

Blend ingredients in mixing bowl, adding more salad dressing if needed. Chill. Serve on hot toasted buns or as a stuffing in tomatoes. Serves 8 to 10.

BRAISED SIRLOIN TIPS

    1½ pounds steak tips, 1½ inch strips
    ¾ cup onions
    ¼ cup celery
    ½ cup carrots
    ½ green pepper
    1 cup tomato puree
    ¾ pint beef stock
    ⅓ cup mushrooms

Sprinkle salt, pepper and flour over steak tips. Brown in ¼ cup butter over medium heat for 12-18 minutes. Chop onions, celery, carrots and green pepper. Add to meat and braise 15 minutes. Add tomato purée and beef stock. Simmer 1 hour. (Cover skillet). Slice mushrooms and sauté in 2 tablespoons butter. Add to meat mixture and serve. Serves 6.

Carbondale, Ill.

E. Main St. on Rt. 13 E.

The excellent casseroles will delight you, along with the Braised Beef— a house specialty in the Embers Restaurant. There's live entertainment in the lounge. The nearby Crab Orchard Lake Recreation Center offers fishing, camping and fine hunting (goose, quail and duck). The Inn is also near golf courses. Carbondale is a University town too.

LARGE MOUTH BASS

Clean fish well. Leave whole or cut in fillets. Allow ¾ pound fish per serving.

Broiled

Place fish skin side up on heavily oiled rack on broiler pan. Place beneath unit 5 to 8 minutes, depending on thickness of fish. Use wide spatula and turn fish. Season with melted butter blended with lemon juice or French Dressing. Replace on broiling unit and cook 10 to 12 minutes, depending on thickness of fish. Serve on hot platter.

Baked

Rub garlic in cavity of good size fish that is clean and ready to bake. Blend ingredients for stuffing and place in fish cavity:

    4 tablespoons soft butter
    ½ cup hot milk
    2 cups soft bread crumbs
    1 teaspoon paprika
    ½ cup minced celery
    2 tablespoons minced onion
    1 tablespoon minced parsley and add
      juice of 1 lemon last.

Sew cavity loosely allowing for expansion. Place on well oiled foil in baking pan. Sprinkle with salt and lemon juice. Bake in 375 degree oven allowing 15 minutes per pound. About 15 minutes before done, add more lemon juice. (Enough stuffing for 4-pound fish). Serves 4 to 5.

Champaign-Urbana, Ill.

I-74 & Neil St. Exit

This Inn is only 5 minutes from the University of Illinois and 15 minutes from Chanute Air Force Base. It's a favorite place with students, airmen and tourists. Everyone finds the east dining room with Chinese decor and imported Chinese screens a charming place with unforgettable food. The "Airman of the Month" is a special feature at the Inn.

BROILED CHICKEN WITH WINE SAUCE

2 broilers, split in half
¼ cup butter, melted
2 cups Wine Sauce

Clean broilers and pat dry with paper towels. Sprinkle with seasonings. Place skin side down on well oiled foil in baking pan or broiler rack. Place under preheated broiler. Allow 12-15 minutes for each side to cook. Baste with melted butter and turn once allowing longer time for cooking when skin side is up. Baste with butter after turning. Serve Wine Sauce over chicken and use extra sauce in sauce boat. Allow ½ broiler for each person.

Wine Sauce

2 cups top milk
2 tablespoons butter
2 tablespoons flour
½ cup dry white wine or sherry

Heat milk to boiling point. Blend butter and flour in a little cold milk. Gradually add to hot milk and stir well, until it thickens. Add pinch salt and wine. Makes 2½ cups.

Chicago, Ill. Des Plaines

Touhy Ave. & U.S. 45

Des Plaines is 25 miles from downtown Chicago, yet only 3 miles from O'Hare International Airport. The daily luncheons are delicious and different (Round of Beef French Market, Baby Back Ribs, Chicken Hong Kong). There's live entertainment in the Pirates Cove lounge. Tours are available to all points of interest in Chicago.

TRIO SALAD

(Chicken-Tuna-Potato)

Chicken Salad

Toss 2 cups diced cooked chicken, ½ cup finely chopped celery, ⅓ cup chopped pimento and 2 diced hard boiled eggs with 1 cup mayonnaise. Add 1 teaspoon salt. Serve on crisp lettuce garnished with pickles, olives and radish roses. Serves 6.

Tuna Fish Salad

Flake 2 cups well drained tuna fish. Add ½ cup finely chopped celery, ¼ cup pickle relish, ½ teaspoon salt and paprika. Toss with ½ cup mayonnaise. Serve in nests of lettuce and garnish with celery curls and green pepper rings. Serves 6.

Potato Salad

Season 8 diced cooked potatoes, add 3 eggs (hard boiled and chopped). Toss with ¼ cup minced green pepper, ¼ cup minced onion and salad dressing to moisten. Season to taste. Serve on lettuce leaves with 1 teaspoon minced parsley on top. Sieve hard cooked egg over all. Serves 6.

Chicago, III.-Elmhurst

U.S. 20, Jct. I-90 & I-294

Elmhurst, "the City of Trees", is only 18 interstate miles from downtown Chicago. People travel for many more miles to enjoy the Inn's Sunday Morning Brunch. A hot loaf of French bread welcomes guests when they are seated for dinner in the El Conquistador Dining Room. There's live entertainment each weekend in the El Conquistador Lounge.

SILVER DOLLAR PANCAKES

1½ cups milk
3 tablespoons melted butter
2 eggs
¾ teaspoon salt
2 tablespoons sugar
2½ teaspoons baking powder
1½ cups flour, sifted

Place milk, melted butter and beaten eggs in bowl and mix. Add dry ingredients sifted together all at once. Add more milk to make batter like cream if necessary. Heat griddle moderately hot. Pour pancakes size of silver dollars. Turn when pancakes are full of bubbles. Brown underside. Serve with choice of syrups. Makes approximately 24 pancakes.

CREAMED BEEF

2 ¼-pound packages chipped beef
6 tablespoons butter
4 tablespoons flour
3 cups rich milk

Pull beef apart in pieces and sauté in butter. Add flour to small amount of milk and blend. Add to beef, then add rest of milk gradually. Stir until sauce is creamy and smooth. Pour over toast at serving time. Serves 6 to 8.

Chicago, III. Kennedy Expwy.

1 S. Halsted St.

Be sure to order Breast of Chicken Parmesan in the garden-like setting of this Inn's Green Lantern Restaurant. There's live entertainment and dancing in the Lounge. All of Chicago is at your doorstep (free parking at the Inn). Lake Michigan is only 10 blocks away. Tours are available through the Merchandise Mart.

LOBSTER CASSEROLE

1 pound lobster meat
¼ cup butter
Pinch paprika
1 teaspoon flour
1 ounce sherry
3 cups hot milk
Melted butter
Bread crumbs

Sauté lobster meat in butter, add paprika and flour and cook 1 minute. Add sherry and milk, bring to a boil and simmer for a few minutes. Season with salt, pepper and M.S.G. Grease casserole with melted butter and sprinkle with bread crumbs. Add lobster, then Bread Crumb Topping. Bake at 400 degrees until Bread Crumb Topping is brown. Serves 4.

Bread Crumb Topping

½ cup bread crumbs
Salt and pepper
M.S.G. (pinch)
½ teaspoon paprika
2 tablespoons sherry
1 teaspoon lemon juice
Dash Worcestershire sauce

Mix all ingredients and cover top of casserole. Sprinkle melted butter over all.

Chicago, Ill.
Lake Shore Dr.

644 N. Lake Shore Dr.

Come up in the world. Come up to The Pinnacle . . . the revolving restaurant on the 33rd floor of this Inn for a breath-taking view of the Chicago skyline and Lake Michigan. The International entrees are well worth the climb too. This luxurious Holiday Inn is only 5 minutes from the bustling Loop, just 3 blocks from the famed shops of Michigan Avenue.

VEAL ROULADE ROMANOFF

    16 thin escalopes of veal
     1 cup chopped onion
     1 pound chopped mushrooms
     3 ounces butter
     ½ pound chicken livers or pâté maison
         (goose liver pâté)
     8 ounces butter
       Salt and pepper

Sauté onion and mushrooms in 3 ounces butter until almost dry. Let cool. Add chicken livers and sauté in 8 ounces of butter. Stir well and season. Use 1-2 ounces of stuffing, depending on size of roulade desired. After stuffing, roll veal in flour and brown in butter in skillet. Place in 350 degree oven for 8-10 minutes. Flame with Madeira wine (1 cup) and add Espagnole Sauce to desired reduction. 8 servings.

Espagnole Sauce

Blend 2 tablespoons flour and 2 tablespoons butter. Add 1 cup brown stock and thicken. Season with salt and pepper. Cook 1 tablespoon of each (chopped ham, celery, carrot) in butter. Then add ⅓ cup stewed tomatoes and cook 5 minutes. Add to sauce and strain, if desired. 1 cup.

Chicago, Ill.
Lawrence Ave.

U.S. 14 & 41 N.

This Holiday Inn is right on Lake Michigan. There's a beautiful view any season since the Inn overlooks Lincoln Park too. Chicago's famous "Loop" is only 10 minutes away. You can expect an authentic Scottish theme (complete with Scotch plaid carpet) in the Highlander Restaurant and Highland Fling Lounge.

SHRIMP REMOULADE

     1 pound chilled shrimp
        (cooked, peeled and deveined)
    1½ cups Remoulade Sauce
        Salad greens
     2 tomatoes, quartered
     2 hard boiled eggs, sliced

Place shrimp on crisp salad greens and top with whole shrimp, tomato wedges, egg slices and Remoulade Sauce. Serves 6 to 8.

Remoulade Sauce

     1 cup mayonnaise
     ½ tablespoon Dijon mustard
     1 teaspoon lemon juice
     2 tablespoons chopped capers
     2 tablespoons chopped gherkins
     1 teaspoon chopped tarragon
     2 teaspoons chopped parsley

Season mayonnaise with mustard. Combine with other ingredients. Let stand at least 4 hours or more before using. Makes approximately 1½ cups.

Chicago, Ill.
Mt. Prospect, Ill.

200 E. Rand Road

"Like climbing, the essence of fine dining is elusive. Join us in a hearty tasty meal . . . forget the time . . . Live a Little!" That's your invitation to the Matterhorn Restaurant—and it's something to yodel about. The menu itself is a treat. You're invited to order your steaks by the ounce. Try Fondue for Two—Swiss or Fondue Bourguignonne. The Inn is near the Arlington Race Track.

SWISS FONDUE

    12 ounces Rhine wine
     8 ounces mild Cheddar cheese, grated
    24 ounces Gruyere (Swiss) cheese, grated
     4 tablespoons kirschwasser
     2 tablespoons clear gel
       Salt to taste
    ⅛ teaspoon white pepper
    ⅛ teaspoon nutmeg (optional)

Cut a fresh garlic clove in half and rub inside of fondue pot with it. Pour wine in pot. Heat until tiny bubbles begin to form on the bottom and sides of pot. Add cheeses and stir until completely melted. Mix clear gel with kirschwasser and blend into cheese mixture, until it reaches a very smooth and glossy appearance. Add seasonings. Serve with cubes of French bread and fondue forks. Serves 2 to 6.

VEAL PICCATA

Heat 2 tablespoons oil in a skillet until very hot. Toss 16 ounces veal round or strips (cut ¼x¾x1½) in 1 ounce flour, until well coated. Shake off excess. Place meat and ¼ cup diced onions immediately in hot oil and brown well. Drain off excess oil and add ½ cup Marsala wine. Evaporate wine, add seasonings to taste and ½ cup 40% cream. Continue cooking until sauce is smooth and glossy, about 2 minutes. Serve with buttered noodles. Serves 2 to 3.

Chicago, Ill.-NW
Rolling Meadows

I-90 & Rt. 53

Rolling Meadows is rightly named. The Arlington Race Tack is only 5 minutes away. There's live entertainment in the Fox's Den Lounge. The Black Fox Dining Room with its country French decor is popular with local residents and visitors alike. Just try to resist the homemade bread, hot blueberry muffins and garlic bread.

PEPPER STEAK EN CASSEROLE

    2 pounds prime beef tenderloin
    ¾ pound fresh mushrooms
    2 large green peppers
    2 large Bermuda onions
    1-2 cups brown gravy
    1 teaspoon Accent
    1 teaspoon beef base
    1 teaspoon Worcestershire
    1 cup tomato juice
    ½ cup Burgundy

Sprinkle steaks (sliced 2″ x 3″ x 2″) with salt and pepper, then dredge in flour. Sauté in 3 tablespoons hot oil in heavy skillet over medium heat. At the same time in separate skillet sauté mushrooms (sliced), peppers (quartered) and onions (quartered) in 2 tablespoons bacon drippings or hot oil. When tender add rest of ingredients, adding Burgundy last. Let simmer 5 minutes. Serve over bed of saffron rice with tomato garnish. Serves 4-6.

BLACK FOX FRENCH TOAST

Cut 6 slices homemade bread ½ inch thick. Trim crusts. Dip in: 2 beaten eggs, 2 tablespoons powdered sugar, pinch salt, and ¼ cup cream. Grill on buttered griddle until golden on each side. Sprinkle with powdered sugar. Serve with syrup. 3 servings.

Chicago, III.-Skokie

W. Touhy Ave., Skokie, III.

International cuisine is the order of everyday in the Black Bowler Dining Room. Take time to take a gourmet tour from Polynesia to Italy, through Germany and New England. Homemade bread and fresh Strawberry Tarts are baked daily. The Inn is 18 miles from downtown Chicago and only 7 miles from O'Hare International Airport.

POLYNESIAN CHICKEN

Split 6 broiler chickens in half and season with salt and pepper. Combine the following ingredients and baste chicken while baking at 375 degrees for an hour:

1½ cups pineapple juice
3 tablespoons soy sauce
2 tablespoons Kraft oil
1 tablespoon sugar
½ teaspoon garlic powder
½ teaspoon ginger

Combine the following ingredients, bring to a boil, and then simmer for 45 minutes:

¾ cup undrained crushed pineapple
2½ cups water
¼ cup cornstarch
2 teaspoons chicken soup base
¼ cup slivered almonds
¼ cup shredded coconut
1 tablespoon sugar

Serve ¼ cup sauce over each piece of chicken. 12 servings.

LUAU CHICKEN SALAD

Combine 2 cups diced cooked chicken, 1 cup drained pineapple chunks, 1 cup diced celery, ¼ cup chopped toasted almonds, ¼ cup flaked coconut, 1 cup Kraft mayonnaise and toss lightly, mixing well. Chill. Fill pineapple boats and serve with assorted finger sandwiches. Serves 6.

Chicago, III. - South Lansing, III.

U.S. 6, I-80 & I-94 at Torrence

Many places are high on the list of things to see in Chicago. This Holiday Inn is a must with people who have tried barbecue in the Tivoli Restaurant. A special barbecue sauce is blended to perfection and basted over baby back ribs. Enjoy a bowl of homemade navy bean soup on a cold windy day. No matter the season, the fare is always excellent. Downtown Chicago is only a half hour away.

BARBECUED BABY BACK RIBS

Place 10 pounds fresh baby back ribs in a large pot and cover with boiling water. When water returns to a boil, reduce heat and simmer 30 minutes. Remove ribs from pot and place on cookie sheet. Oil ribs lightly and brown both sides in oven or under broiler. Place ribs flat in roast pans (inside rib down) and cover with Barbecue Sauce. Bake in 350 degree oven 1 to 1½ hours, or until tender. Turn once and baste with sauce. 12 servings.

Barbecue Sauce

¾ cup minced onion
1 tablespoon minced garlic
1½ quarts hot brown stock
¼ cup sugar
½ tablespoon dry mustard
1 teaspoon black pepper
½ cup cider vinegar
1 quart tomato sauce or purée
Juice from 1½ lemons
½ cup Worcestershire sauce
½ tablespoon barbecue spice

Sauté onion and garlic in ½ cup oil in a sauce pot. Add 6 tablespoons flour to make a roux. Add hot stock, stirring until smooth. Dissolve sugar, mustard and pepper in vinegar. Add tomato sauce, vinegar mixture and lemon juice to brown sauce. Add Worcestershire sauce and barbecue spice. Simmer 30 minutes. Add salt to taste.

Chicago, III.-West

On U.S. 12 & 45

There's an Italian Festival each Thursday night featuring authentic Italian dishes and pastries. Eggs Benedict and Baked Chicken a la Craddock are favorites on the menu everyday. O'Hare International Airport is only 7 minutes away. Try to be in Chicago during the Old Town Art Fair, the nation's largest outdoor art gallery, in June.

CRAB MEAT A LA KING

½ pound crab meat
¼ cup diced green peppers
¼ cup diced onions
3 tablespoons butter
3 tablespoons flour
2 cups milk
2 beaten egg yolks
2 tablespoons chopped pimentos
2½ tablespoons sherry
4 tablespoons buttered bread crumbs

Sauté peppers and onions in butter. Add flour which has been blended with ¼ cup milk, then add rest of milk gradually and stir. Add egg yolks and bring to a slow boil. Stir until thick. Season, add pimento, crab meat and sherry. Serve in shells with buttered bread crumbs on top. Place under broiler for crumbs to brown. Serves 6.

DEEP DISH CORN BREAD

Add 1 cup boiling water to 1 cup corn meal. Cool. Add 2 tablespoons sugar, 3 tablespoons melted shortening, 2 egg yolks and 1 cup milk. Beat.

Sift 1 cup flour, 1 teaspoon salt and 2 teaspoons baking powder. Add to mixture. Beat 2 egg whites and fold into mixture. Pour into buttered pan and bake 30-45 minutes at 400 degrees. Serve immediately. Serves 6-8.

Chicago Heights, III.

2 blks. N. U.S. 30, St. Rd. 1

Chicago is only 46 minutes away but no one ever goes for a meal. The Inn's house special, Grecian Cheese Cake, is a gourmet treat. It's worth staying over for the sausage, biscuits and fried apples served at the Sunday Morning Brunches. 12 kinds of fish leave nothing to be desired at the Fish-orama each Friday night. Chicago Heights is a city of factories.

VEAL PARMIGIANA

1 onion, chopped fine
½ pound butter
¼ cup sauterne
1 tablespoon garlic powder
1 tablespoon leaf oregano
2 cups diced tomatoes
1 cup tomato purée
3-4 pounds veal cutlets
   (8 ounce pieces)
½ cup milk
   Bread crumbs
   Cooking oil

Sauté onion in butter until lightly brown. Add sauterne. Boil 5 minutes. Add garlic powder, oregano and other seasonings. Simmer 5 minutes. Add tomatoes and purée. Simmer ½ hour. Lightly bread veal in coating of milk and bread crumbs. Fry until golden in cooking oil. Cover bottom of pan with sauce. Arrange veal cutlets on top of sauce. Grate mozzarella cheese on hand grater. Sprinkle over veal. Bake in 350 degree oven about 20 minutes or until cheese is golden. Serve with extra sauce on side. Serves 6-8.

Danville, Ill.

400 N. Vermilion St.

You'll be glad this Holiday Inn has sauna baths and an inviting swimming pool after a day of sightseeing in and out of Danville. An art gallery, museum and the Red Mask Theatre are within walking distance. Salt mines are only 15 miles away. This is one of the largest coal mining areas in the U.S. French pastries and the Sunday buffet breakfasts make guests linger at this Danville Inn.

CHICKEN WITH PEPPER

    4 cups cooked chicken, bite-size
    2 cups sliced mushrooms
    5 tablespoons butter
    2 cups chicken broth
      Salt and pepper
    ½ teaspoon oregano
    ½ teaspoon curry powder
    1 onion, sliced in rings
    3 small green peppers, cut in strips
    4 tablespoons toasted almonds, slivered

Sauté mushrooms in 2 tablespoons butter until soft. Add chicken, broth, salt and pepper, oregano and curry. Blend remaining butter with 2 teaspoons flour. Slowly stir into the chicken mixture and stir over a low fire for 10 minutes. Add onion rings and pepper strips, leaving last for only 3 minutes to retain firm body. Add toasted almonds on top. Can be served on toast squares or on a rice bed, as desired. Serves 6 to 8.

De Kalb, Ill.

1212 W. Lincoln Hwy.

Delicious food is served in the Winged Ear Dining Room, The Husky Coffee Shop, and Keyboard Banquet Rooms. Radio fans enjoy the recipes for the wonderful cuisine over "The Mixing Bowl", a local recipe program the Inn sponsors. Since the Inn is just across the road from the University, football crowds find it a perfect place to gather. An excellent putting green is available for guests.

FRUIT PLATE

    6 Bartlett pear halves
    1 cup Royale Ann cherries
    4 tangerines (sections)
    2 ounces brandy
    1 cup cottage cheese
    1 pint cranberry sherbert

Carefully mix together equal quantities of pear halves, cherries and tangerine sections. Reserve juice and add to brandy. Pour over fruit. Let chill overnight. Serve over crisp lettuce on a serving plate with cottage cheese and (or) sherbert in center. Serves 4 to 6.

BUFFET JELLO SALAD

    1 can pineapple tidbits
    1 glass jar spiced peaches
    2 boxes pineapple-orange Jello
    2 cups ginger ale

Drain pineapple and peaches. Save juice. Add enough water to make two cups of liquid. Heat juice to boiling, dissolve Jello in it. Then add ginger ale. Cool until slightly thickened. Then add peaches (sliced) and pineapple tidbits. Pour into a decorative mold to set. Chill. Serve on lettuce. 8 to 10 servings.

East St. Louis, Ill.

657 E. Broadway

This Inn, just across the river from downtown St. Louis, is a popular location for visitors in either state. It's justly proud of its fine German dishes — you'll revel in the perfectly prepared creations. Even a plain American favorite is served flamboyantly here. The salads and choice of dressings delight luncheon guests while fritter-type sandwiches are a compliment to the chef!

SWISS STEAK CREOLE

    2½ pounds top round
    2 cups tomatoes
    1 medium onion, diced
    1 green pepper, diced

Select top round 1½ inches thick and cut into 6 portions. Score meat with knife on each side and season. Dredge each piece in flour and pound it with edge of plate or meat tenderizer. Sauté in a heavy skillet, which has been greased with suet or shortening. Brown on both sides. Pour ½ cup brown gravy (beef broth or water) over meat. Add remaining ingredients. Cover and cook until fork tender (2 hours or more). Add a little water from time to time to keep meat from sticking. (It may be cooked in a 325 degree oven if preferred). Serves 6.

MONTE CRISTO SANDWICH FRITTER

Prepare 2 sliced chicken and Swiss cheese sandwiches. Trim crusts from each. Dip in egg wash (2 egg yolks beaten with 1 to 2 tablespoons water added gradually). Using a heavy frying pan with a small amount of butter, brown sandwiches on each side. Place in moderate oven until cheese melts. 2 sandwiches.

Edwardsville, Ill.

Jct. I-270 and Ill. 157

This Holiday Inn is in the rolling countryside on a bluff overlooking St. Louis, only 15 miles away. It is adjacent to the Southern Illinois University campus. The Inn provides free courtesy car service to St. Louis, the Municipal Airport, nearby Illinois private fields and to industrial plants in the surrounding Illinois area. You can sip into something cool seven days a week in the cocktail lounge.

HOMEMADE BREAD

    2 yeast cakes
    2½ cups milk
    2½ cups water
    ¼ cup sugar
    ⅓ cup shortening (melted)
    12 cups flour, or more
    1½ tablespoons salt

Dissolve yeast cakes in ½ cup milk. Scald rest of milk and cool until lukewarm. Add water and dissolved yeast, sugar, melted shortening and 4 cups of the flour. Beat vigorously 1 to 2 minutes. Cover and allow to rise ½ hour. This aids in producing a fine textured bread. After 30 minutes, add salt and remaining flour and knead 5 minutes or until elastic to touch. Cover and let rise double in bulk. Shape into loaves. Let rise double in bulk. Brush with milk and bake in a preheated 375 to 400 degree oven for 50 minutes to 1 hour. Makes 4 loaves.

Freeport, Ill.

U.S. Hwy. 20 East

In 1858 Abraham Lincoln and Stephen A. Douglas held their famous Freeport is a manufacturing center coln the Debater" stands as a memorial in Freeport's Taylor Park. Freeport is a manufacturing center and trade hub, less than 2 hours from Chicago. You can enjoy live entertainment in the Red Fox Tavern. Excellent food is the standard fare in the Torch Lite Restaurant.

OLD-FASHIONED DINNER

6-pound corned beef brisket
3 white turnips
1 cabbage
6 potatoes
6 beets
6 onions
4 carrots

Cover meat with cold water, heat rapidly to boiling, then remove foam, reduce heat and simmer until tender, 3 to 4 hours. Prepare vegetables, cutting turnips into quarters and cabbage into eighths. Cook beets in boiling water until tender. About 45 minutes before serving, skim fat from liquid. Add vegetables except beets and cook until vegetables are tender. Drain and add beets. Serves 10.

CORN FRITTERS

2 eggs
⅔ cup milk
1 teaspoon salt
1 cup cooked corn
1 teaspoon melted butter
1 cup flour
1 teaspoon baking powder

Beat eggs slightly, add milk, salt, corn and melted butter. Add flour sifted with baking powder. Beat until smooth. Drop by spoonfuls into deep hot fat and fry 3 to 5 minutes. Serves 6 to 8.

Jacksonville, Ill.

U.S. 36, 54 & Ill. 104

Abraham Lincoln addressed many audiences on the lawn of Jacksonville's Central Park. There are markers to show where General Grant camped with his troops . . . where Daniel Webster made a public address in 1837. They all would have enjoyed this Holiday Inn's delicious food. Do take a tour through the only ferris wheel factory in the world.

CHOP SUEY

1½ pounds pork steak
1½ pounds round steak
2 tablespoons butter
1 tablespoon brown gravy mix
¼ cup soy sauce
1 cup chopped onion
2 cups celery, sliced thick
1 can chicken broth
1 can mushrooms (1 cup)

Cube meat and brown in butter in a heavy skillet. Add gravy mix, soy sauce, onion, celery and chicken broth. Cook slowly until meat is tender. Add mushrooms and seasonings. Serve on cooked rice or noodles. Serves 6 to 8.

SUMMER CANDY

2 pounds powdered sugar
1 stick margarine or butter
1 can coconut flakes
4 cups pecans, chopped fine
1 can Eagle Brand milk
1 teaspoon vanilla
2 packages Hershey chocolate chips

Cream sugar and butter. Add coconut, pecans, milk and vanilla. Mix well and roll in small balls. Leave in refrigerator overnight. Melt the chocolate chips over warm water. Dip balls in chocolate. Place on waxed paper to cool. Makes 40.

Joliet, Ill.

U.S. 66, 52 & Interstate 55

In Joliet on business? This Holiday Inn is only minutes away from major industry, research, business and educational facilities. You can come home to the Scotch Pub for relaxation and outstanding food in the Red Lion Dining Room at your home away from home. Golf and indoor ice skating are only half a mile away.

PUFFED MUSHROOMS

1 pound medium-size fresh mushrooms
1 egg
1 cup milk
1 cup bread crumbs

Wash mushrooms and let air dry. Beat egg and milk mixture. Place mushrooms (stems and all) in milk mixture, then in bread crumbs and seasonings. Let stand 10 minutes. Fry in deep fat at 350 degrees for 3 to 4 minutes. Serves 2 to 4.

HAWAIIAN RIBS

2 slabs spareribs, cut across
  Glazing Sauce
1 can pineapple chunks, drained
2 green peppers, cut in squares

Rub spareribs (3-4 pounds) with salt and garlic. Brown under broiler on both sides. Cut into 2 rib pieces and roast in oven for ½ hour at 350 degrees. Drain excess grease from pan and pour Glazing Sauce over ribs. Roast 20 minutes more. Move ribs to side of pan. Toss in pineapple chunks and green peppers (½-inch squares). Cook 5 minutes more. Serve over rice. Serves 4.

Glazing Sauce

Combine pineapple juice from can, 3 tablespoons brown sugar, 2 tablespoons molasses, 2 teaspoons instant bouillon, 2 cloves minced garlic, ¼ cup vinegar, ½ teaspoon powdered ginger, 2 tablespoons soy sauce, 1 teaspoon M.S.G., 1 teaspoon anise seeds and boil 10 minutes. Thicken with cornstarch paste (3 tablespoons cornstarch plus ¼ cup water).

Kankakee, Ill.

Jct. U.S. 54 & I-57

Dining is a relaxing treat in this Inn's veranda . . . a screened-in sidewalk cafe by the pool. Chuck wagon dinners and poolside fashion shows are fun for all. There are fashion shows inside during the winter months. This is the largest gladiolus producing area in America. There's a Momence Gladiolus Festival in August featuring parades with floats made entirely of gladioli.

SHISH KEBAB

2 pounds loin or leg of lamb, cut in
  1½ inch cubes
2 tomatoes, cut in fourths
2 onions, cut in 8 chunks
1 green pepper, cut in 1 inch pieces
8 large mushroom caps (optional)
  Marinade

Put lamb cubes, tomato sections, onion chunks and green pepper pieces in a glass or earthenware bowl. (Do not marinate mushroom caps). Pour Marinade over mixture and marinate 4-6 hours or overnight. Drain. Put on long skewers alternately, adding mushrooms caps. Brush with oil and broil about 15-20 minutes, so that all sides are browned. Serve on bed of rice or pilaff. 4 to 6 servings.

Marinade

1 cup claret wine
½ cup oil
¼ teaspoon pepper
1 teaspoon salt
1 teaspoon marjoram
¼ teaspoon oregano
1½ teaspoons rosemary
¼ teaspoon sweet basil
¼ teaspoon ginger
1 clove garlic

Combine and blend all ingredients.

121

La Salle-Peru, Ill.

Interstate 80 & U.S. 51

Nickel beer is back—during the Special Sandwich Buffet each day at noon. The Hearth Buffet takes over at dusk. Dinner includes a decanter of wine, compliments of the Inn. There's no doubt about it, this Holiday Inn is a fun place to stay. Shuffleboard and swimming are at your doorstep. The Indian PowWow at Starved Rock State Park is a sight to see every September

DEVILED BEEF RIBS

Trim and separate the individual cooked beef ribs from the bones left over after carving a beef roast. They should all have meat but little fat left on after they are trimmed. Marinate overnight in a good, tart Italian oil and vinegar dressing. Place in a row in a baking pan, meat side up. Brush well with butter, and then coat with coarsely ground bread crumbs which have been seasoned with dry mustard, salt, pepper and paprika (to individual taste). Drizzle with additional butter and bake at 400 degrees for 30 minutes.

CRANBERRY ICE

1 quart cranberries
2 cups sugar
¼ cup lemon juice
1 teaspoon lemon rind

Cook cranberries in ½ cup water until the skins are broken. Rub through a sieve until a smooth pulp. Stir in sugar, lemon juice, lemon rind and 2 more cups of cold water. Pour into a freezing tray and freeze until firm. Stir about 3 times while freezing. Serves 6 to 8.

Macomb, Ill.

N. Lafayette on U.S. 67

This Holiday Inn is the place to stay near major industries and only 5 minutes from Western Illinois University. Macomb is the home of Haeger Potteries, Inc. Guided tours are conducted daily through the largest art pottery in the world. Homemade Breakfast Cinnamon Rolls make guests look forward to getting up in the mornings.

CINNAMON ROLLS

1¼ cups lukewarm water
1 package dry yeast
⅓ cup sugar
½ cup soft shortening
1 teaspoon salt
1 egg, beaten
4 cups flour

Place water and yeast in bowl. Add sugar, shortening, salt and beaten egg. Add flour (sift before measuring). Beat well and let rise until double in bulk.

Punch down and roll dough ¼ inch thick (on floured board) in oblong shape. Sprinkle with 1 cup sugar and 1 teaspoon cinnamon mixed (more cinnamon if desired). Add ½ cup raisins or currants and pour ½ cup melted butter over all. Roll like jelly roll, making long roll. Cut each piece 1-1½ inches thick. Place in buttered pan. Sprinkle additional cinnamon and sugar over top, adding more melted butter. Let rise double in warm place. Bake in 400 degree oven for 15 minutes or until brown. Makes 2 dozen.

Dough may be used for plain rolls or may be kept in refrigerator several days for later use.

Moline, Ill.

Hwys. 150, 6, 92 & I-280

The Inn's location in "the Plow City" is only 10 minutes from famous Black Hawk Park and a view of the Mississippi and Rock Rivers. John Deere located his plow factory in Moline just 4 years after the city was laid out in 1843. The old Rock Island Arsenal on an island in the Mississippi is still in operation (daily tours). The Quint Cities airport is only 1 minute away.

CHEESE BLINTZES

    2 eggs
    ½ cup water
    ½ cup milk
    ½ cup flour
      Pinch Salt

Combine either in blender or with egg beater to mix thoroughly. Pour into slightly greased, heated frying pan (about 6 inches). Fry very thin pancakes on one side until top bubbly. Place each on tea towel, browned side up. When all are done, add filling.

Filling

    ¾ pound dry cottage cheese
    1 whole egg
    1 teaspoon cinnamon
      Salt and sugar to taste

Blend ingredients together. Place tablespoon of filling in center of each pancake. Fold outer edge of circle toward center, fry in butter with folded sides down first, until golden brown on both sides. Serve with sour cream and jelly. These may be frozen successfully. Makes about 18 to 20.

North Chicago, Ill. Waukegan

2315 Green Bay Road

Downtown Chicago is only 30 minutes away. Boating, swimming and other water sports await you at the Great Lakes. This Inn offers free transportation to and from the fun. The Inn's Open Hearth Dining Room features a beautiful log burning fireplace as well as delicious food. The Sip-'N-Sail Lounge is a popular meeting place right off the lobby.

HAM BALLS IN PEACH HALVES

Mix 1 cup crushed corn flakes with 1 tablespoon brown sugar, ¼ teaspoon cloves, and ½ cup evaporated milk. Add beaten egg, then 1 pound ground ham, ½ pound ground pork (lean). Mix well. Shape in balls to fit in peach halves (9 fresh or canned). Place ham balls in greased baking pan and bake at 350 degrees for 30 minutes. Place peaches cut side up with butter in each in pan the last 15 minutes of baking time. When serving, place 1 ham ball in each peach. Makes 4 servings.

ORANGE BLOSSOM CAKE

    1⅓ cups sugar
    2 eggs, beaten
    1½ cups flour
    ½ teaspoon salt
    1½ teaspoons baking powder
    ½ cup water
    1 teaspoon vanilla

Gradually add sugar to eggs. Sift flour with salt and baking powder. Add water alternately with flour to egg mixture. Add vanilla. Pour into greased cupcake tins. Bake at 350 degrees for 12-15 minutes, until done. Remove from tins.

Orange Dip

Sift ¼ pound confectioners sugar, add juice and rind of 2 oranges and 2 lemons. Cream well. Dip hot cupcakes and place on waxed paper. Allow to dry. Makes 12 or more.

123

Olney, Ill.

Jct. U.S. 50 & Ill. 130

Traveling families and businessmen going to nearby industrial areas find this Holiday Inn's location excellent. Children beg to stay longer because of the Inn's wading pool, bouncing animals and horse swings on the playground. Everyone enjoys the daily smorgasbord featuring 42 delectable dishes. The Antique Show each fall draws antique lovers from miles around.

LEMON FILLED CAKE

    ½ cup butter
    1½ cups sugar
    3 eggs
    2½ cups flour
    3 teaspoons baking powder
    ½ teaspoon salt
    1 cup sweet milk
    1½ teaspoons vanilla

Cream butter and add sugar gradually. Beat until fluffy. Add eggs, one at a time, and beat after each addition. Sift dry ingredients and add to first mixture alternately with milk and vanilla. Divide into 2 equal parts. Pour into greased layer cake pans. Bake at 375 degrees for 25-30 minutes.

Cool and split each layer. Fill with the following:

    2 eggs, slightly beaten
    1 cup sugar
    ¼ cup flour
    2 cups sweet milk
    1 teaspoon lemon flavoring

Add eggs to sugar and flour, then add milk. Cook ingredients until thickened. Add flavoring. Frost with your favorite icing.

Peoria, Ill.

Interstate 74 & Ill. 116 W.

The Caterpillar Tractor Co., the world's largest manufacturer of earth moving equipment, is right next door. Hiram Walker & Sons, Inc. is only minutes away. Tours may be arranged through both. Live entertainment is featured nightly in the Inn's Red Fox Tavern. Prime Ribs, Barbecued Ribs and Southern Style Hash always draw a crowd to the Colonial Dining Room.

MONTE CRISTO SANDWICH

    2 slices fresh white bread
    2 ounces sliced boneless ham
    2 ounces sliced turkey breast
    2 tomato slices
    ⅓ cup extra thick cheese sauce

Cut one slice of bread diagonally. Place bread slices on a platter to form a diamond shape. Place ham and turkey slices on bread and top with tomato slices. Ribbon hot cheese sauce across sandwich, sprinkle lightly with paprika and place in broiler for 1 to 2 minutes. Garnish with parsley sprig. Serves 1.

"REUBEN" SANDWICH

    2½ ounces corned beef, sliced thin
    1 slice Swiss cheese
    1 tablespoon sauerkraut
    2 slices rye bread

Prepare corned beef brisket: Wash well. Cover with cold water. Bring to a boil slowly. Cover and simmer until tender, about 3 to 3½ hours for 4-pound piece. Cool in water it was cooked in. Slice with sharp knife long way of meat. Place slices of corned beef with Swiss cheese and sauerkraut on rye bread. Grill until bubbly. Serve with horseradish and pickle sticks. A 4-pound piece serves 8.

Quincy, Ill.

U.S. 24 & St. 57-104

You're in luck when you stop at this Inn with its clover leaf shaped pool, in the heart of downtown Quincy. There's fun for all on Quincippi Island. Back at the Inn, live entertainment awaits you in the Sidewheeler Lounge, patterned after an old packet steamer. The River Room offers gourmet food plus a view of the Mississippi River.

BIBB LETTUCE SALAD

2 heads bibb lettuce
¼ cup chopped green onions
2 slices bacon, cooked crisp
⅓ cup Italian dressing, garlic flavored
2 Triscuits (crackers)
3 hard-boiled eggs (sliced or chopped)

Wash lettuce thoroughly by separating leaves. Dry between towels or in a salad basket. Tear lettuce and place in chilled salad bowl. Add rest of ingredients, eggs last. Toss salad in dressing until all leaves are coated. Serves 4 to 6.

Italian Dressing

6 tablespoons olive oil
1 clove garlic, mashed
2 tablespoons wine vinegar
Juice of ½ lemon
1 teaspoon salt
1 teaspoon pepper
¼ teaspoon basil

Place oil in deep bowl, add garlic. Remove bits of garlic after stirring well. Add rest of ingredients and blend. Keep in refrigerator until time to use. ⅓ cup.

Rockford, Ill.

U.S. 51 South

Stay at this Holiday Inn and enjoy the "Forest City" with its 80 parks and 37 public golf courses! There's year round swimming, a putting green and well equipped playground at the Inn. Dine in the superb Crown Room, enjoy a snack in the Coffee Shop, or relax in the Orbit Room and Flight Deck Lounge. Rockford is one of the leading machine tool centers in the world.

THICK BAKED PORK CHOP

4 ¾-inch thick loin pork chops
Seasoned flour
½ cup catsup
4 tablespoons brown sugar
Pinch dry mustard

Flour chops and place in shallow pan. Combine mixture of catsup, brown sugar and dry mustard. Blend and place 1 tablespoon of this mixture on heart of chop. Pour water into pan, cover and bake in oven for 1 hour at 350 degrees. Remove cover for last 15 minutes to brown. Place on plate and garnish each with a spiced whole crab apple and sprig of parsley. Serves 4.

BAKED SQUASH

Cut 4 acorn squash in halves. Scrape out seeds and string portions. Place in shallow pan. Sprinkle with salt and butter insides of each using 4 tablespoons softened butter. Mix 1 cup sugar with ⅓ cup brown sugar and sprinkle on squash. Add water to cover bottom of pan. Sprinkle with cinnamon and nutmeg. Cover pan and bake in 350 degree oven for 1 hour. Allow ½ squash for each serving.

Springfield, Ill.-East

U.S. 66 Bypass

You'll know you're in the Land of Lincoln. There's the Lincoln Dining Room, Railsplitter Lounge and a rustic rail fence surrounding the Inn's Coffee Shop. Only 20 miles away is the reconstructed village of New Salem, where Lincoln lived. It's fun to come back to an olympic size indoor swimming pool, hot homemade bread and gourmet cuisine.

COQ AU VIN

    1 2½-pound chicken
    ¼ pound salt pork
    1 clove garlic, lightly crushed
    8 pearl onions, raw and peeled
    ½ pound mushroom caps, small
    8 ounces red wine
    ½ cup water or chicken stock
       Bouquet garni: 1 sprig parsley,
       ½ sprig thyme, ¼ bay leaf

Disjoint chicken. Place diced salt pork in heavy stewpan and cook over moderately high heat until partially rendered. Add garlic clove, brown light, and then remove. Dredge chicken pieces in flour seasoned with salt and pepper. Add chicken pieces to stewpan and brown well on both sides. Remove from pan and reserve. Add onions and washed drained mushrooms to pan in which chicken was sautéed and cook until lightly colored. Add wine and water. When particles have been smoothed in liquid and it starts to boil, return chicken to pan, add bouquet garni, and cover. Simmer gently for ½ hour, or until tender. Or cover and bake in 350 degree oven until tender. Remove bouquet garni and season.

The sauce should be thin and served sparingly as it is very rich. Serves 4.

Springfield, Ill.-South

625 E. St. Joseph St.

Visit the only home Lincoln ever owned and the 1st Presbyterian Church with its Lincoln pew. Businessmen find the Inn a favorite place to stay while visiting nearby industries in Illinois' capital and important coal fields in Ohio. Everyone enjoys the delicious food and dinner music in the dining room. The Knight Room Lounge is popular.

ROQUEFORT DRESSING

    1 pint mayonnaise
    1 cup sour cream
    ½ teaspoon white pepper
    1 teaspoon garlic powder
    1 tablespoon onion salt
    ½ pound Roquefort

Whip mayonnaise, cream, pepper, garlic powder and onion salt. Shred cheese and stir in lightly. Makes 4 cups.

SAVORY DRESSING

(For Pork Roast or Fowl)

    8 to 10 cups stale bread
       Broth to moisten
    ½ teaspoon thyme
    1 teaspoon poultry seasoning
    ½ cup minced onion
    1 cup celery, cut fine
    2 eggs
    ½ cup melted butter

Moisten bread slightly in broth. Then add thyme, poultry seasoning, onion and celery. Add beaten eggs and butter last. Use as a stuffing or cook in a buttered baking dish at 350 degrees for 25 to 30 minutes.

Anderson, Ind.

I-69 & 109 Bypass

There's a lot of traffic inside this Inn — along the buffet table. No wonder. The daily luncheon buffets are outstanding and night owls enjoy the late night buffet snacks three nights a week. Monday night is Italian Night in the Royal Family Court dining room. The Inn is only 5 minutes from Anderson's General Motor plant.

SPAGHETTI

2 onions, diced
1 green pepper, diced
1 clove garlic, mashed
½ stick butter
1 pound round steak, ground
   Salt
   Pepper
3 cans tomato paste
9-ounce package spaghetti
   Parmesan cheese

Sauté onions, green pepper and garlic in butter in a heavy iron skillet. Add round steak, season and brown. Combine tomato paste with first mixture, adding water or tomato juice if too thick. Simmer for 1½ to 2 hours with lid on skillet over very low heat. Stir frequently to prevent sticking. Cook spaghetti in deep kettle of boiling salted water for 7 to 10 minutes. Drain in colander. Serve sauce over spaghetti with Parmesan cheese, if desired. Serves 4 to 6.

Bloomington, Ind.

St. 37 North

Indiana University is only minutes away from this Holiday Inn. Also of interest in this area is the artists colony and the handcraft industries located nearby. Sports enthusiasts enjoy the "Little 500" Bicycle Race. Everyone enjoys the year round comfort and convenience at this Inn. Everything is great—from food to fun.

ROULADE OF BEEF

2 pounds bottom round of beef
   Mustard
1 garlic clove, minced
1 medium onion, chopped fine
1 tablespoon butter
1 teaspoon salt
½ teaspoon white pepper
½ teaspoon caraway seeds
4 slices dill pickle, thinly sliced
4 strips bacon
4 tablespoons cooking oil
¾ cup consomme
¼ cup tomato purée
1 bay leaf
1 peppercorn
½ cup Burgundy wine

Use 8-ounce strips of bottom round tenderized. Rub with prepared mustard and sprinkle with finely diced garlic and onion sautéed in butter. Season with salt, white pepper and caraway seeds. Lay a thin slice of dill pickle on each strip and roll. Wrap with strip of bacon and secure with toothpicks. Fry in skillet with cooking oil and then transfer to pan and add consomme to which a little tomato purée has been added. Add bay leaf and peppercorn. Simmer until tender. While simmering, add a little Burgundy wine. Remove beef, strain sauce and thicken a little. Serve sauce over meat. Serves 4.

Crawfordsville, Ind.

U.S. 231 & Interstate 74

Take a hike through the woodland wonders of the Shades State Park. Drive through a covered bridge. Visit General Lew Wallace's study, where he wrote Ben Hur in 1880. Return to the Holiday Inn for home-made pies, biscuits, blueberry muffins and gourmet buffets everyday at noon. Children are delighted with the Inn's wading pool, swings and sandbox.

CHEESE CASSEROLE

Cover a 7-inch baking dish with 1 table-spoon of French dressing. Place the following in this dish, in the sequence listed:

1 slice toast
1 slice Swiss cheese
2 slices turkey
2 slices tomato
½ green pepper, diced
1 slice toast
1 tablespoon French dressing
2 slices ham
1 slice American cheese
2 strips fried bacon
1 slice mild Cheddar cheese

Top with American Cheese Sauce and place in 350 degree oven for 5 minutes. Then put under broiler for 2 minutes, until cheese melts and runs down the sides. Serves 1.

American Cheese Sauce

Blend 2 tablespoons butter and 2 table-spoons flour. Stir 1½ cups milk in slowly. Add 1 cup grated cheese, ½ teaspoon salt, ½ teaspoon dry mustard and dash of both cayenne and paprika. Stir sauce until cheese is melted and sauce is thickened. For 4-6 servings.

Evansville, Ind.-North

2508 U.S. 41 North

Santa Claus, Indiana with its color-ful park, Toyland, Circus and Deer Farm is a neighbor. During the yuletide season the Inn keeps gifts at the desk for the young and young in heart. It's not unusual to see Santa having breakfast here. The Inn's holiday buffet includes such special treats as Noel Chicken Loaf and Christmas Tree Salad.

HOLIDAY FRUITCAKE

1 cup butter
2 cups sugar
6 egg yolks, beaten
1 teaspoon soda
1 teaspoon cinnamon
1 teaspoon allspice
2½ cups flour
1 cup buttermilk
1 pound raisins
1 pound currants
5 ounces lemon, crystallized
5 ounces citron, crystallized
5 ounces orange, crystallized
1 cup nuts (pecans or walnuts)
6 egg whites, beaten stiff
½ cup brandy or port wine

Cream butter and sugar. Add egg yolks. Mix soda and spices with about half the flour and add alternately with the butter-milk. Mix the rest of the flour with raisins, currants, fruits and nuts and add. Last, add the beaten egg whites, folding them in. Place in a well greased deep tube cake pan and bake in a 250-275 degree oven about 2 to 2½ hours, until top is gently browned. When cool, put in earthen crock with a cloth well dampened with brandy or port wine. Makes 1 large cake.

Fort Wayne, Ind.-East

On U.S. 30 E. & 24 E.

No wonder this Inn is so popular. Luncheon specials include Chicken and Dumplings, Beef Stew, Corned Beef and Cabbage. There's a Fish Fry each Friday night and Spaghetti is the Saturday night special. The playground's merry-go-round makes a hit with children. Johnny Appleseed is buried only 3 miles from Fort Wayne.

NEW ENGLAND CLAM CHOWDER

½ cup diced celery
1 cup diced potatoes
½ cup diced onion
2½ cups frozen clams (chopped)
  or 1 quart shucked chowder clams
3 cups fish stock

Place all ingredients in fish stock and simmer slowly. Prepare 1 quart light cream sauce and add slowly to fish stock. Add thyme and season to taste. Add shredded carrots or diced peppers for eye appeal. Serves 8.

ESCALLOPED HAM AND EGGPLANT

1 eggplant
1 medium onion, diced
¼ cup shortening
2½ cups diced ham (cooked)
1½ cups applesauce
  Pinch sage (optional)
1 cup bread crumbs
2 tablespoons butter

Blanch eggplant in salt water, remove and dice eggplant. Sauté onion in shortening. Combine eggplant, ham and applesauce with lightly browned onion. Pour into greased baking pan, top with bread crumbs, dot with butter and bake at 350 degrees for 35 minutes. Serves 6.

Fort Wayne, Ind. Northwest

Calif. Rd. on I-69

Mixed Grill is undoubtedly the most popular dish on the menu in the Harvest Grill Dining Room. Antique furnishings in the lobby and dining room, organ music in the Comrade in Arms Lounge and a swimming pool especially for children make this a family Inn too. General Anthony Wayne's historic fort is a site to see nearby.

HAM CROQUETTES WITH ORANGE SAUCE

1½ pounds ham (when ham is cut)
¼ cup green peppers, minced
¼ cup onions, minced
¼ cup cracker crumbs
2 eggs

Chop ham through coarse grinder. Combine ham, green peppers, onions, cracker crumbs and eggs. Form croquettes and roll in flour. Deep fry until golden brown. Serve with Orange Sauce. Serves 4 to 6.

Orange Sauce

6 tablespoons tart jelly
3 tablespoons sugar
  Grated rind 2 oranges
2 tablespoons orange juice
2 tablespoons lemon juice
  Salt
  Cayenne
2 tablespoons sherry or port wine

Mix jelly, sugar and orange rind. Beat. Add orange juice, lemon juice, dash salt and cayenne. Stir until mixed. Add sherry or wine if desired.

Gary, Ind.-East

U.S. 12 & 20

As you approach Gary on the Indiana Toll you will glimpse the fiery steel mills. Only 15 miles east of Gary is Indiana Dunes State Park . . . a 3 mile beach of white sand on Lake Michigan and 20,000 acres of shifting dunes and densely forested terrain. Gourmet food and a popular lounge await you at this Inn 1½ blocks from the heart of downtown.

WEST INDIAN PORK CHOPS

    4 double pork chops
      (6 oz. each)
    ¼ pound Swiss cheese,
      sliced thin
    ¼ pound baked ham,
      sliced thin
      Flour
    1 egg
    3 tablespoons milk
    ⅔ cup bread crumbs
    3 tablespoons Parmesan cheese
      Salt
      Shortening

Cut a deep pocket in each chop and stuff with a slice of cheese and ham. Then seal each chop. Dredge meat with flour. Beat egg with milk and dip each chop in mixture. Mix bread crumbs, cheese and salt. Roll pork chops in mixture. Fry uncovered in hot shortening for about 20 minutes, reducing heat after browning on each side. Cook until meat is done. Serve with broiled tomato half filled with mushrooms if desired. Serves 4.

Hammond, Ind.

Calumet Ave., U.S. 41

Hammond is on the southeast edge of Chicago—close enough to enjoy the city's year round attractions Calumet Harbor and Calumet Park Beach are even closer. There's excellent fishing at nearby Wolf Lake and Powder Horn Lake. Be sure to try the Pepper Steak at this Holiday Inn. Of course it's just one of many delicious features on the menu. The Inn's lounge is a most popular place in the evenings.

BAKED LASAGNE

    1 pound large lasagne noodles
    2 tablespoons olive oil
    1 pound ground beef
    1 tablespoon cooking oil
    2 teaspoons marjoram
    2 teaspoons oregano
    1 tablespoon salt
    1 teaspoon sugar
      Chopped parsley
    1 cup tomato paste
    1 cup cottage cheese or ricotta
    1 pound mozzarella cheese

Oil noodles with olive oil before placing in boiling water. Cook, then drain. Cook beef in cooking oil, add spices, salt, sugar, parsley and tomato paste. Line bottom of casserole with noodles. Add layer ground beef, cottage or ricotta cheese. Place six slices mozzarella cheese next. Add noodles and repeat. Cover and bake in 350 degree oven 35 minutes. Serves 10-12.

Indianapolis, Ind. Airport

2501 S. High School Rd.

Enjoy foods from Germany, Switzerland, France or Iran while watching planes land and depart for distant places. Dining in the Chanteclair gourmet room atop this Holiday Inn is unexcelled. The Chef de Cuisine has won awards here and in Europe. Many of his award winning dishes are prepared at your table side. Indianapolis' most complete wine cellar awaits your selection.

ALASKA KING CRAB COCKTAIL

1 pint mayonnaise
1 cup whipped cream
1 cup chili sauce
1 tablespoon chopped mango chutney
1 teaspoon Worcestershire sauce
½ teaspoon M.S.G.
1 can Alaska king crab

Combine above ingredients and spoon over individual servings of chilled crab meat. Lobster meat or diced white turkey may be substituted for king crab. Serves 4.

SHRIMP HUBERT

1 tablespoon sherry
Juice of half a lemon
½ teaspoon Worcestershire sauce
2 drops Tabasco sauce
Salt and pepper to taste
Dash garlic

For each serving, prepare above marinade for 8 large peeled and deveined shrimp; marinate for 30 minutes. Wrap each shrimp in one half slice bacon; place on skewer. Broil at low heat about 15 minutes. Turn a couple of times until done. Avoid burning bacon. Serve with curried rice.

Indianapolis, Ind.-Dwtn.

U.S. 40, 36, 52, 421

So many lines of nationwide traffic intersect Indianapolis that this city is often called the crossroads of America. This Holiday Inn is right downtown — just across the street from the State Office Building. There's a Hoosier twang to the food served — it's so good that it's talked about around the Inn's piano bar after dinner.

HUNGARIAN STYLE STUFFED BELL PEPPERS

4 pepper cases
2 tablespoons butter, melted
2 tablespoons onion, minced
½ pound cooked ground beef
1 cup cooked rice
1 garlic clove, crushed
1 teaspoon salt
½ teaspoon pepper
2 tablespoons buttered bread crumbs

Cut tops off peppers (stem ends) and remove seeds and membrane. Drop in pan of hot water and cook 5 to 8 minutes. Remove and drain well. Combine butter, onion, beef, rice and seasonings. Stuff peppers. Sprinkle bread crumbs on top, if desired. Bake in pan with hot water covering the bottom in a 350 degree oven for 15 to 18 minutes. Serve with Tomato Sauce. Serves 4.

Tomato Sauce

Melt 2 tablespoons butter and blend with 2 tablespoons flour. Cook 2 cups canned tomatoes, 1 tablespoon minced onion, 1 tablespoon minced celery and 1 chopped carrot until tender. Strain and add to flour roux. Cook until thickened. Makes approximately 1 to 1½ cups.

Indianapolis, Ind. Speedway

W. 16th St., U.S. 136 N.W.

This Holiday Inn is a meeting place for sports fans — it's just opposite the famous Motor Speedway, scene of the Annual Memorial Day 500 Mile Auto Race. Extraordinarily good food and a convenient location make this Inn a popular place with people who come from all parts of the world. Indianapolis is one of the largest cities in the U.S. not on a navigable river.

SAUERBRATEN-POTATO BALLS

Season a 3-pound beef shoulder. Heat but do not boil:

- 2 bay leaves
- 1 sliced onion
- ½ cup sugar
- 1 garlic clove
- 1 cup Burgundy
- 1 teaspoon peppercorns
- 2 cups vinegar

Place meat in crock. Cover with marinade. Leave in refrigerator 1 week, turning once a day. Place meat and marinade in kettle with cover. Add water if needed. Simmer 2-3 hours until tender. Thicken stock by adding 4 tablespoons Graham cracker crumbs mixed in a little water. Add 1 cup sour cream. Serve with potato balls. Serves 8 or more.

Potato Balls

Sift ⅔ cup flour and 3 teaspoons baking powder. Add:

- 2 cups mashed potatoes
- 1 teaspoon melted butter
- ¼ cup milk
- Salt to taste

(Test for right consistency to drop from spoon).

Drop by spoonfuls into 2 quarts boiling salted water. Do not boil after adding potato balls. Remove cooked balls. Roll in bread crumbs. Serve hot. For 6-8 persons.

Jasper, Ind.

U.S. 231 & Ind. 45 South

"Real" German food makes this Jasper Holiday Inn a very popular Inn. It's served amidst rough sawn planking and wood ceiling beams, decorated with authentic beer steins. At nearby St. Meinrad is the Archabbey of St. Benedictine Order. Over a century old, it has its own stone quarry, printing plant, bakery, meat packing and dairy farm.

KARTOFFELSALAT

(Potato Salad)

- 8 or 9 potatoes
- 1 teaspoon finely chopped parsley
- ½ teaspoon finely chopped onion
- ½ teaspoon finely chopped chives
- 2 tablespoons salad oil
- 1 tablespoon wine vinegar
- ¼ cup hot stock

Boil potatoes in their skins, peel and slice thin. Place in layers in a salad bowl, sprinkle each layer with parsley, onion, chives, salt and pepper. Mix the oil and vinegar, add hot stock and pour over salad. Mix lightly, garnish with cucumber slices and serve hot and fresh. Serves 6 to 8.

APPLE SNITZEL

Pare 8 tart apples and slice in horizontal slices ½ inch thick. Core each slice. Make a batter of 1 slightly beaten egg and 1 cup beer. Dip apple slices and roll in 1 cup flour. Fry in ¾ cup heated shortening until golden brown. Roll in mixture of 1 cup sugar and 2 teaspoons cinnamon. Serve hot. Serves 8.

Kokomo, Ind.

Hwy. 31 S. Bypass

Many composers have written songs about Indiana and a popular one is about this little city on Wildcat Creek. In 1894 Elwood Haynes built the first clutch driven auto here. Children especially enjoy seeing "Old Ben," a huge stuffed Hereford steer who weighed 4720 lbs. in life and stood 6 feet 4 inches high, in Highland Park. Everyone enjoys the hospitality at this Inn.

TALK OF THE TOWN STEAK

    3 pounds top round, ground coarse
    ½ tablespoon seasoning salt
    ¾ teaspoon liquid smoke
    8 slices bacon

Sprinkle seasoning salt over meat, then sprinkle liquid smoke over meat. Form into patties 1-inch thick. Wrap each with bacon and secure with toothpicks. Broil to doneness desired. Sprinkle with garlic butter and serve. Serves 8.

MEAT PIE TOPPING

    1½ cups corn meal
    1½ cups flour
     4 teaspoons baking powder
     1 teaspoon salt
     2 tablespoons sugar
     3 eggs, separated
    1¾ cups milk
     6 tablespoons shortening, melted

Sift dry ingredients. Beat egg yolks, add milk and shortening. Combine with dry ingredients. Beat egg whites and fold into mixture. Spoon over meat pies. Bake at 400 degrees until filling is hot and corn bread topping is done and crisp. Makes enough for 1 large casserole or 8 small ones.

Marion, Ind.

Hwys. 9 & 37 at Quarry Rd.

Whole loaves of French bread are brought to the tables in the famous Scotch and Sirloin Room. Marion is located on the west bank of the Mississinewa River. It is the home of one of the largest manufacturers of Christmas decorations in the U.S. Marion's Easter Pageant has a cast of over 2,000.

FRENCH BREAD

    1 ounce dry yeast
    2 teaspoons salt
    2 teaspoons sugar
    2 cups lukewarm water
    4 cups sifted flour, or more

Dissolve yeast, salt, and sugar in lukewarm water. Mix in flour gradually until mixture will absorb no more flour. Knead dough on floured board until light and elastic (3 or 4 minutes). Let rise for 1 hour in greased bowl covered with a damp cloth. Place in a warm spot. Butter a baking sheet and sprinkle with corn meal. Shake off excess meal. Without working dough too much, divide into 4-ounce portions. Let rise for 45 minutes. Mark a row of diagonal slits across top of loaves with sharp razor. Brush lightly with butter and bake in a preheated oven (450 degrees) for 5 minutes. Reduce heat to 375 degrees and bake another 35 minutes. To get a crust on bread that is as tender as it is crisp, put large shallow pan of hot water on lowest rack of oven during baking. Makes 4 loaves.

Muncie, Ind.

Jct. U.S. 35 & St. 3 & 67

Established in 1833, Muncie was named for the Muncie Indians, who once lived in the area. Today it is an industrial center where automobile equipment, airplane engines and glass fruit jars are among some of the things produced. The Ball Brothers, who became wealthy by manufacturing glass canning jars, gave the state the campus of Ball State University. The campus is near the Inn.

TOASTED SALMON ROLL

Cut rolls in half lengthwise. Put serving of salad on bottom half and spread. Sprinkle cheese lightly over salad. Butter top half of roll. Broil roll until cheese is melted and top half toasted.

Roll Dough

Dissolve 1 package dry yeast in 1 cup lukewarm water. Add ⅓ cup sugar, ¼ cup shortening, 1 teaspoon salt and 1 beaten egg. Add 4 cups flour (sift before measuring). Let dough rise double in bulk in warm place. Punch down. Roll out on floured board. Make each roll about 6 inches long and 4 inches wide. Place in greased pan on the slant. Let dough double in bulk in a warm place. Bake at 375-400 degrees for 8 to 10 minutes. 6-8 rolls.

Salmon Salad

Drain oil off a #1 can red sockeye salmon. Flake. Add 1 teaspoon lemon juice, 1 cup diced celery, 3 chopped hard-boiled eggs, ¾ cup mayonnaise, ½ teaspoon salt, and ⅛ teaspoon pepper. Mix. Makes approximately 2 cups.

South Bend, Ind.

U.S. 31 at Exit 8

An arched bridge over a beautiful creek takes you to this Inn's swimming pool. The playground teems with fun things to do . . . merry-go-round, slide, animals on springs, to name a few. With Notre Dame University less than 2 miles away, the Inn delights football fans with European cuisine before and after games.

EUROPEAN PANCAKE

    2 cups flour
    1 teaspoon sugar
      Pinch salt
    6 whole eggs
    1 extra egg yolk
    1 cup milk
    2 tablespoons melted butter

Sift flour, sugar and salt. In depression of flour, break eggs and extra yolk. Blend with wooden spoon until smooth. Gradually add, while stirring, milk and melted butter. Blend well—should be as heavy oil. Drop about 8 tablespoons on a heated griddle, allowing to spread to size of 9-inch dinner plate. When lightly brown on one side, and top slightly set, turn and allow to cook 1 minute.

Spoon (previously prepared) 3 tablespoons cottage cheese with walnut chunks across the center of pancake, fold both edges toward center and finish cooking. Place on serving plate, sprinkle with powdered sugar and top with red currant sauce, orange sauce or desired flavor. Prepare sauce by adding 1 tablespoon water to 3 tablespoons any desired flavor jelly or preserves, and heating. Makes 10 to 12 pancakes.

Terre Haute, Ind.

U.S. 41 & 150 S. & I-70

"On the Banks of the Wabash" was inspired and written here. This industrial center is proud of its Early Wheels Museum, which exhibits antique and classic automobiles. Visitors also enjoy the Swope Art Gallery. Everyone enjoys the city's Holiday Inn. There are a menu of reasons the dining room is so popular.

LOBSTER AND SHRIMP SALAD

1 cup shrimp, cut in pieces
½ cup lobster, cut in pieces
1 cup celery, diced
    Mayonnaise to moisten
2 tablespoons lemon juice

Combine shrimp, lobster, celery and mayonnaise. Season to taste. For each serving line plate with lettuce. Put ½ cup Chinese noodles in center of lettuce and a serving of salad on top of noodles. Garnish with tomato wedges, quartered hard-boiled eggs and stuffed celery. Place mayonnaise and capers on top of each salad. Serves 4.

SCRAMBLED EGGS SANTE FE

Place 5 to 6 pieces diced (¾") cold boiled potato, 1 tablespoon diced onion and 1 teaspoon raw diced green pepper in a pan and fry until light brown. Break 2 eggs over above mixture and scramble lightly. Season with salt. Serve on 2 slices of breaded grilled green tomato. Note: If green tomatoes are not available, add cubed ripe tomatoes when eggs are added. One portion.

Valparaiso, Ind.

U.S. 30 West

Entertainment six nights a week at the piano bar makes this Inn popular with local guests and travelers. The Chuckwagon Dinner is a house specialty—prime ribs of beef, fried chicken and baked ham are the meat choices. The Inn even has its own bowling lanes. The famous Indiana Dunes are only minutes away.

MOSTACCIOLI WITH MEAT SAUCE

1 pound mostaccioli
6 tablespoons cooking oil
2 cups finely chopped onion
2 pounds ground beef
4 cups tomato sauce (4 8-oz. cans)
3 cups hot water
½ teaspoon crumbled basil or
    ¼ teaspoon oregano
½ cup bread crumbs
2 cups shredded American cheese
2 teaspoons salt
¼ teaspoon pepper

Cook mostaccioli in 2 quarts boiling salted water until almost tender—about 12 minutes, stirring occasionally. Then drain and rinse with warm water. While mostaccioli is cooking, heat oil in a heavy skillet. Add onion and cook and stir until transparent. Then add meat and cook. Then add tomato sauce, water and basil and bring to a boil. Remove from heat and add crumbs, cheese, salt and pepper. Add cooked mostaccioli and pour into a baking dish. Sprinkle top with grated Parmesan cheese and bake in a 350 degree oven for about 30 minutes, or until contents are bubbling and top is lightly browned. Serves 8.

Vincennes, Ind.

U.S. 41 N. & 50 Cloverleaf

Take time to see historic Vincennes with 250 years of history. During the Revolutionary War, Vincennes was the center of the storied exploits of George Rogers Clark. There are 42 historic places to visit —tours originate from the Inn during the summer. Everyone who comes to this Inn should try the Cheesecake. It vies in popularity with the uniquely prepared selection of vegetables on the menu.

SAUERKRAUT RELISH

⅓ cup vinegar
1 cup sugar
2 cups drained sauerkraut
1 cup chopped celery
¼ cup chopped green pepper
¼ cup chopped red pepper
¼ cup chopped onion

Cook vinegar and sugar together long enough to dissolve sugar. Cool. Pour over other ingredients. Allow to set overnight. Delicious appetizer. (Refrigerate). Serves 4 to 6.

DELMONICO APPLES

(An old French recipe)

Applesauce (fresh or canned)
⅓ as many sliced canned peaches as applesauce

Mash these two ingredients well. Crumble almond macaroons through fruit and add brown sugar to taste. Pour in casserole (not too deep). Dot with butter, slivered almonds and macaroon crumbs. Bake very slowly in a 300 degree oven for 2 hours. When served as a dessert, as this Holiday Inn does, add whipped cream topping. This was originally served as an accompaniment with turkey or chicken at Christmas or holiday season.

Wabash, Ind.

Wabash St., St. Rd. 15 S.

In pioneer days when a traveler rode by a log cabin in the Indiana backwoods, an occupant would peer out and call "Who's there?". To the passerby, unaccustomed to the Indiana twang, it sounded like "Hoosier?". Hence Indianians came to be called Hoosiers, friendly people who always welcome visitors. Wabash and this Holiday Inn are no exceptions.

WESTERN STEAK PLATTER

(Steak - Potatoes - Eggs)

Steak

Have 6 breakfast steaks cut ½ to 1 inch thick. Use heavy iron skillet adding enough grease to lightly cover bottom and keep steaks from sticking. Brown steaks on each side, then cook over low heat to desired doneness. Pour melted butter over steaks and sprinkle with parsley, salt and pepper. Serves 6.

Potatoes

Cook 6 potatoes in small amount of boiling water. Peel and mash with potato masher. Add ½ cup hot top milk, a little at a time, beating continuously. Season with salt and pepper and 2 tablespoons butter. Then beat some more. Serves 6.

Eggs

Heat ¾ cup top milk and 4 tablespoons butter. Beat 6 eggs lightly. Add 1 teaspoon salt and ⅛ teaspoon pepper. Combine with milk mixture and stir over medium heat until set, but not hard. Serves 6.

Ames, Iowa

On U.S. 69 & 30 off I-35

"Land where the tall corn grows" is true of this rich farming country. And you can be sure that this Holiday Inn's restaurant uses the golden kernels to stir up delicious dishes. Farm fresh vegetables and excellent beef add to the popularity of the 24-hour restaurant. The Inn is near Iowa State University.

BEEF STEW

3 pounds boneless beef, cubed
⅓ cup cooking oil
2 cups beef stock or bouillon
1 tablespoon paprika
1 tablespoon salt
¼ teaspoon pepper
2 cups potatoes, peeled & diced
1½ cups diced carrots
1½ cups tomato paste
1 cup onion, diced
½ cup chopped celery
2 tablespoons cornstarch

Sauté beef in oil in a heavy skillet. Brown on all sides. Add stock and cook slowly until meat is tender (1-1½ hours). Add seasonings, then vegetables and cook until they are done. Carefully add thickening for gravy (blend cornstarch in a small amount of water and add gradually to stock). Serves 8.

BLACKBERRY WHIPPED JELLO

Dissolve 2 packages of Royal Blackberry Jello in 1 pint boiling water. Put in mixing bowl and add 1 pint packed finely crushed ice and whip on high speed for 20 minutes. Pour into molds and refrigerate 3 to 4 hours or until set. Remove from molds and serve in parfait glasses with whipped cream. Serves 8.

Burlington, Iowa

Jct. U.S. 61 and 34

There's something for everyone to enjoy in and around Burlington. Sportsmen enjoy the excellent deer and duck hunting. Fishermen are not disappointed. You'll have to make 6 turns in 1 block if you drive through Snake Alley, the crookedest block in the world. A beautiful sunken lobby with a huge fireplace awaits you at this Inn. Be sure to try the homemade Strawberry Pie.

BARBECUED RIBS

4 pounds spareribs
1 cup Barbecue Sauce

Place ribs on broiler rack over hot coals on charcoal grill. Baste with sauce and barbecue very slowly. Turn and brush with sauce often. Cook at least 30 to 45 minutes. The oven may also be used. If so, place ribs on rack in shallow pan. Bake at 350 degrees for 1 hour. Turn and baste frequently. Serves 4.

Barbecue Sauce

1 cup tomato sauce
½ clove garlic, minced
1 teaspoon prepared mustard
¼ teaspoon salt
Dash black pepper
Dash paprika
2 tablespoons lemon juice
1 teaspoon Worcestershire sauce
2 tablespoons vinegar
2 tablespoons onion, minced
¼ to ½ teaspoon Tabasco
1 cup water

Mix all ingredients. Cover and bring to a boil. Lower heat and simmer 25 minutes. Makes 1 cup.

Cedar Rapids, Iowa

U.S. 30 & 218

City fathers put the city and county buildings and the Memorial Coliseum on an island in the river to create an unusual civic center. Oatmeal mills established in 1870 were the start of the thriving cereal-processing industry in the city today. The Cedar Rapids Holiday Inn is established as "the" place to eat. Its 24-hour restaurant is popular night and day.

BAKED LAMB WITH RICE

(Pisto Arni Pilaf)

Brown 2- to 3-pound lamb roast in ¼ cup butter. Place in a baking pan, sprinkle with **seasonings and dot with ¼ cup butter. Add** 2 cups tomatoes, cover and bake at 350 degrees for about an hour or more, until meat is nearly done.

Bring 1 can consomme and 3 cups water to a boil and add to meat. Stir in 2 cups rice and season to taste. Cover and bake about 30 minutes longer, or until rice is tender. Serves 6.

BUTTER TEA COOKIES

(Kourabie Thes)

Soften 1 pound sweet butter at room temperature. Put in electric mixer and beat well. Add ½ cup confectioners sugar and beat until fluffy. Add 2 egg yolks and beat thoroughly. Sift 6 cups cake flour and 1 teaspoon baking powder and add to butter mixture. Add 1 cup chopped browned almonds. Sprinkle dough lightly with 1 ounce whiskey and knead thoroughly. Roll out dough and cut into diamond shapes or roll into balls and center with a whole clove. Bake on cookie sheet at 350 degrees for about 20 minutes. Sprinkle liberally with confectioners sugar. Makes about 4 to 5 dozen.

Clinton, Iowa

Hwys. 30 & 67

Agriculture, industry and business meet in Clinton. Everyone tries to meet at this Holiday Inn at noon for its famed Luncheon Buffets. Two different bands are featured in the Lions Den Lounge every week. Nearby the Rhododendron Showboat-Museum is just across a gang plank for your enjoyment. Clinton is on the mighty Mississippi. Help celebrate Riverboat Days the first week in July.

BEEF ROULADE

    1 beef loin approx. 8 inches long
       Mustard (French's preferably)
    ½ cup raw onions, diced
    ½ cup bacon, diced
    ¼ cup pickles, diced
    2 tablespoons flour
    2 tablespoons butter
    3 tablespoons olive oil
    2 tablespoons warm water
    2 tablespoons tomato paste
    1 tablespoon beef base

Slice loin very thin (allow 2 pieces per person). Spread mustard on it, then salt and pepper. Sprinkle onions, bacon and pickles. Roll meat up tight and fasten with two toothpicks. Turn rolls in flour and fry in skillet with butter and olive oil. Brown on all sides. Transfer rolls to deep pan. Add water to skillet and stir well. Pour over roulades. Add salt, pepper, tomato paste and beef base. Add water to cover and simmer until tender (30-40 minutes). Add flour with little water and blend until smooth. Stir into gravy and simmer 4 minutes. Add ½ cup Burgundy. Serve with buttered noodles and Iowa corn. Serves 6.

Des Moines, Iowa-South

2101 Fleur Drive

Every room has a lakeside view. This Holiday Inn is located right on Gray's Lake offering ice skating in the winter and water sports in the summer. Festive daily buffets include 14 colorful salads. There are two outdoor pools, and one indoor for year round swimming. Des Moines is the home of Drake University. "West Point for Women", Fort Des Moines, where WAC officers are trained is nearby.

MUSH BISCUITS

4 cups corn meal
1 cup cold water
3 cups boiling water
1 scant cup shortening
½ cup sugar
1 teaspoon salt
¼ cup warm water
1 teaspoon sugar
1 package dry yeast
6 cups or more sifted flour

Mix corn meal with cold water to dampen. Add to salted boiling water and cook over medium heat about 10 minutes. Stir occasionally. Add shortening, ½ cup sugar and salt. Let cool to lukewarm. Add warm water and 1 teaspoon sugar to dry yeast. Let stand 20 minutes and add to corn meal mixture when it is lukewarm. Measure sifted flour and add 2 cups at a time to mixture. Stir well until of consistency to knead. Place on floured board and knead well. Place in greased bowl with cloth on top and put in a warm spot. Let rise until double in bulk. Punch dough down and roll on floured board. Cut with biscuit cutter. Place on greased cookie sheet and let rise until light. Bake at 375 degrees for 20 to 25 minutes, until brown on top. Makes about 4 dozen.

Dubuque, Iowa

Dodge St., U.S. 20 W.

Delicious food and a beautiful view attract visitors to this Inn. You can expect homemade bread and superb buffets daily. A Trappist Monastery is nearby where the monks have tilled their fields since 1840. They still bake their famous bread nearly every visitor carries away after a tour of the grounds. The Inn will arrange excursions on a Mississippi river boat.

HOLIDAY INN BREAD

1 yeast cake
¼ cup water
2 cups scalded milk
1 tablespoon shortening
2 tablespoons sugar
6 cups sifted flour (approx.)
2 teaspoons salt

Soften yeast in ¼ cup water. Add shortening and sugar to scalded milk. Cool. Stir in 2½ cups flour, then softened yeast. Add salt. Add flour until dough is stiff enough to handle. Turn on floured board. Knead until smooth, adding more flour if necessary. Place in greased bowl and let rise double in bulk. Knock down and make into loaves and place in 2 greased bread pans, or form in loaves on a flat pan. Let rise again. Bake at 450 degrees for 10 minutes, then 350 degrees for 30 minutes, or until bread shrinks from sides of pan. Remove from pans and place on rack to cool. Makes 2 loaves. Brush with melted butter.

Iowa City, Iowa

Interstate 80 & U.S. 218

Sightseers enjoy staying adjacent to Herbert Hoover's Birthplace and Museum. The Inn is also near the University of Iowa. Iowa's famous Amana Colonies (comprising 25,000 acres) are only about 11 miles from the Inn. The Colonies are well-known for their superb workmanship in woolen articles and furniture products. Find out why this Inn is well-known for its Cheesecake.

HOT GERMAN POTATO SALAD

6 potatoes
¼ pound bacon, preferably side bacon
¼ cup bacon fat
¼ cup green onion, chopped fine
¼ cup chopped celery
⅓ cup vinegar
⅓ cup water or bouillon
2 teaspoons sugar
½ teaspoon salt
⅛ teaspoon paprika
⅛ teaspoon pepper, freshly ground
1 tablespoon chopped parsley

Cook potatoes in jackets in covered saucepan with water until they are done but not mushy. Peel and slice them while hot. Keep warm. Cook bacon (chopped fine) until crisp. Remove and add to potatoes. Sauté onions and celery in bacon grease (¼ cup only). Add vinegar, water, sugar and seasonings. Bring to a boil and pour over potato mixture. Toss lightly and serve with chopped parsley or chives. Serve hot. Serves 6.

IOWA CORN

Choose fresh corn, moist and juicy. Remove husks and threads. Place in a deep kettle of ½ milk and ½ water. (Have liquid about 2 inches deep and boiling hot). Add 1 tablespoon sugar and bring to a boil again. Cook 5 to 10 minutes, depending on age of corn. Drain and serve with butter, salt and pepper.

Mason City, Iowa

U.S. Hwy. 18 W.

"Seventy-six Trombones" resound each June during the North Iowa Band Festival. The "Music Man" was born in Mason City. Visit the Meredith Wilson footbridge and the house where he was born. North Iowa Aviation Days are held in July. Visitors and local residents enjoy the daily noon buffets at this Inn. Homemade rolls and pastries make every meal special.

CHOCOLATE PIE

¼ pound butter
9 ounces powdered sugar
¼ pound shortening
3 eggs
¼ teaspoon cinnamon
1 teaspoon vanilla
⅓ cup English walnut meats
1½ ounces melted chocolate
1 cup whipping cream

Thoroughly cream butter and powdered sugar. Add shortening and cream again. Then add eggs, cinnamon, vanilla, nut meats and melted chocolate and thoroughly beat and stir well. Cool. Place in a baked pie shell and chill for 1 hour. Before serving top with whipped cream.

Pastry

Sift 2 cups flour and 1 teaspoon salt together into a quart bowl. Work ⅔ cup soft shortening into flour mixture with fork or pastry blender. When mixture resembles coarse meal, add ¼ cup cool water. Stir with fork until dough follows fork around bowl. Roll out on lightly floured pastry cloth or board.

(Divide pastry into 2 parts to use in pie above). Line pie pan and pinch edge to flute. Prick bottom and sides and bake at 450 to 475 degrees for 10 to 12 minutes. 1 large pastry shell or top and bottom of regular size pie.

Newton, Iowa

Interstate 80 & State 14

F. L. Maytag built the first motor-driven washing machine here in 1911. The Maytag historical display is of special interest to visitors when touring the plant. Visit Pella, Iowa's Dutch village, only 30 miles away. Tulip time at Pella in May is a gala occasion. Children enjoy seeing the boyhood home of Wyatt Earp in Pella. Everyone looks forward to returning to this Inn and its excellent evening buffets.

CHICKEN CASSEROLE

(Chicken Brunch)

1 4- to 5-pound hen
1 cup cream of chicken soup
½ cup chicken broth
1⅓ cups celery, diced fine
¾ cup slivered almonds
4 hard-boiled eggs
　Few grains white pepper
　Accent
　Seasoning salt
1 cup mayonnaise

Boil hen — it is less dry than if roasted. Use deep kettle and add water to partially cover. Bring water to boil. Cover and simmer 2-3 hours, adding salt last half of cooking time. Cool cooked hen. Take meat from bones and dice. Mix with soup, broth, celery, almonds, sliced eggs and seasonings. Fold in mayonnaise. Add ½ cup crushed potato chips and place in buttered casserole adding more crushed potato chips on top. Bake 1 hour at 325 degrees. Serves 8-10.

Okoboji, Iowa

Highway 71 North

This is a golfer's dream Inn. It's located right on a beautiful 18-hole championship golf course. A view of Lake Okoboji, indoor and outdoor swimming pools, sauna baths and a snowmobile are added attractions. It's the Inn's own special sauce that makes the Barbecue Ribs and Chicken so extra special. French doughnuts are served every Sunday morning.

ROYAL CHOCOLATE CREAM PIE

1 quart vanilla ice cream
2 tablespoons ice cold milk
1 4-ounce package chocolate instant pudding
1 Graham cracker pie crust
½ pint whipping cream
½ ounce creme de menthe

Place ice cream in mixer with milk and turn on medium speed until mixed. Add pudding and blend. Pour into pie shell. Whip cream and add creme de menthe, if desired. Put on top of pie. Decorate with shaved chocolate. 1 pie.

Graham Cracker Crust

1¼ cups Graham cracker crumbs
3 tablespoons sugar
⅓ cup butter

Combine crumbs and sugar. Stir in melted butter and blend well. Pack firmly into a 9-inch pie pan, covering sides and bottom. Chill before filling for 1 hour.

Ottumwa, Iowa

U.S. 34 & 63

Archeologists and linquists frequent Ottumwa to try their hand at reading ancient cuneiform writing. The clay Babylonian tablets are found in Ottumwa's library. This Holiday Inn is a great place to stay. It's only 2 blocks from downtown. Italian dishes are featured each Thursday night. Homemade bread is a daily feature. Try to be here for the Antique Airplane Fly-In on Labor Day.

LASAGNE

    1 pound lasagne noodles
    1 pound mozzarella cheese
    2 pounds ricotta cheese
    ¼ pound Romano cheese, grated

Cook noodles as directed on package. Pour Sauce in bottom of large baking pan or casserole. Place layer of noodles (3 strips) then layer of mozzarella cheese, then ricotta cheese. Repeat with more sauce, noodles (crosswise), then cheese. Use noodles last and spread sauce on top. Sprinkle Romano cheese on last. Bake at 350 degrees for 20 to 30 minutes. Serves 8.

Sauce

Heat 2 tablespoons olive oil in skillet and sauté 1 cup finely diced onions and 2 minced garlic cloves. Add ½ pound lean beef and ½ pound lean pork (which have been ground together) and sauté. Place 2 small cans tomato paste, 2 cups water and 3½ cups tomatoes in a large kettle. Add meat mixture and cook for 25 minutes, adding 1 teaspoon salt, ½ teaspoon pepper and 1 diced green pepper. Simmer for 1½ to 2 hours, until thick.

Sioux City, Iowa

I-29 at Isabella St. Exit

There are two big swimming pools (indoor and outdoor) so everyday is a good day for a dip. A bounteous buffet is served every meal (even breakfast), plus menu service. The Inn has a picturesque location near the Missouri River. Sioux City is perched on the bluffs at the confluence of the Missouri and Big Sioux Rivers.

ROULADE

(German Rolled Meat)

    2 pounds round steak, sliced thin and
        cut in serving pieces
    ¼ onion, diced
    2 strips bacon, diced
        Pickle relish
        Salt and pepper
        Flour
    2 tablespoons hot fat

On each serving piece of meat place some onion, bacon and relish. Then roll, enclosing the contents. Secure with toothpicks. Season to taste and roll in flour. Brown meat in hot fat on all sides. Add boiling water to half cover the meat and add seasoning to water to taste (dashes of allspice, ground cloves, nutmeg, paprika, sage and bay leaf). Cover and simmer for 2 hours or until tender. Add water if necessary. Thicken gravy with flour, if desired. Serve with cooked noodles. 4 to 6 servings.

RASPBERRY PARFAIT PIE

Dissolve 1 package raspberry Jello in 1 cup hot water. Add 1 pint vanilla ice cream, spooning into hot Jello until melted. Add 1 package frozen raspberries (which have been thawed) and stir to mix. Pour in a baked 9-inch Graham cracker pie shell (cooled) and refrigerate until set. Garnish with ½ pint whipped cream and raspberries. Serves 6.

Waterloo-Cedar Falls Iowa

U.S. 218 & Waterloo Road

It's not where to eat in Cedar Falls, but where to eat at this Holiday Inn. Ye Coffee House has delicious food served promptly. The Round Table offers excellent cuisine for leisurely dining. Sales groups find The King's Tavern a perfect spot to meet and eat. Visitors are invited to tour the John Deere Tractor Works and the Rath Meat Packing Company.

MILLION DOLLAR CAKE

    2 tablespoons quick Nestles cocoa
    2 ounces red food coloring
    ½ cup butter
    1½ cups sugar
    5 eggs well beaten
    2½ cups cake flour
    1 cup buttermilk
    1 teaspoon vanilla
    1 teaspoon salt
    1 teaspoon soda
    1 tablespoon vinegar

Make paste of cocoa and food coloring. Cream butter and sugar thoroughly in mixer. Add well beaten eggs and beat until fluffy. Add cocoa mixture, then flour (sifted 3 times after measuring) alternately with buttermilk. Add vanilla and salt. Then add soda which has been dissolved in vinegar (blend in by hand). Bake in a greased loaf or layer cake pans. Bake 45 minutes at 350 degrees for loaf; 20 to 25 minutes at 375 degrees in 2 layer cake pans. Frost when cool. Makes 1 loaf or 2 layers.

Frosting

Sift 1 box powdered sugar with 3 tablespoons cocoa. Cream 1 stick butter, add sugar-cocoa mixture. Then add 3 tablespoons (or more) strong coffee, 1 beaten egg yolk and 1 teaspoon vanilla. Beat well in mixer.

Lawrence, Kansas

Jct. U.S. 59 & Kansas 10

Parents and friends visiting Kansas University find this Holiday Inn a great place to stay — it's adjacent to the campus. The Inn's elaborate daily buffets are as bountiful as delicious. Lawrence, set on the western edge of the trans-Mississippi hardwood forests, is known for its abundance of beautiful trees and homes. Lawrence also has one of the few ski slopes in this part of the country.

SOUTHERN SAUCE

(A Bar-B-Q Sauce for Ribs, Chicken, Pork Chops, Lamb Chops or any Wild Game)

    ½ medium-sized onion, chopped fine
    1 garlic clove, mashed
    ½ teaspoon rosemary
      Water
    2 14-ounce bottles Heinz Chili Sauce
    1 teaspoon dry mustard
    2 tablespoons white sugar
    2 tablespoons brown sugar
    2 tablespoons wine vinegar
    ¼ cup honey
    ¼ cup liquid smoke
    3 dashes Worcestershire sauce

Simmer onion, garlic and rosemary leaves in water (enough to cover onion) until onion is tender. Place in mixing bowl, add rest of ingredients and blend slowly for 5 minutes.

Precook meat until nearly tender in skillet, browning both sides. Place in a baking pan in layers, covering each layer with Southern Sauce. Cover and bake at 375 degrees for 30-40 minutes. Makes 2 pints of sauce.

Mission, Kansas

Jct. U.S. 50 & 69

This Inn is only 15 freeway miles from downtown Kansas City, Missouri. Make it your headquarters for sightseeing and entertainment. Start the day with hot homemade biscuits for breakfast. The Old Shawnee Indian Mission is only 2 miles away. Professional casts star at the outdoor Starlight Theatre during the summer months in Swope Park. You can enjoy live entertainment in the Inn's private Red Slipper Club.

CHUCK WAGON CHILI

```
1 pound red kidney beans
¼ cup suet
1 pound ground beef
1 onion, cut fine
1 clove garlic, mashed
  Salt
  Pepper
4 cups tomatoes
2 tablespoons chili powder
```

Wash beans, cover with cold water and soak several hours or overnight. Heat suet in large skillet and cook beef in it, stirring continuously until all of beef is browned. Add onion and garlic and brown with meat. Then add salt and pepper. Cook beans covered in water in which they were soaked until tender (about 2½ hours). Add tomatoes during last hour, as water cooks low. Extra tomato juice may be added if too low. Blend chili powder with a bit of cold tomato juice and add to beans. Add beef and onion last, stirring continuously until thoroughly mixed and right consistency for chili. Makes 5 to 6 cups.

Topeka, Kans.—Dwtn.

914 Madison

A Presidential chef in the kitchen is reason enough to plan a visit to this Inn. You'll feel like visiting royalty in this high-rise when you receive the same tableside service given to Presidents. Homemade soups, country style sausage and charcoal broiled steaks are choice. Homemade carrot cake reminds you there's a choice of desserts to sample. The Inn's Country Kettle Dining Room is a gathering place for legislators from the nearby State Capitol.

LEG OF LAMB

```
8-pound leg of lamb
2 oranges
12 dried prunes
```

Trim some fat from leg of lamb. Rub leg with cut orange halves. Season with salt and pepper. Place in roasting pan and add prunes. Do not add water. Bake at 275 to 300 degrees for 35 minutes per pound. 10 to 12 servings.

CARROT CAKE

```
3 cups sifted flour
2 teaspoons soda
2 teaspoons cinnamon
½ teaspoon salt
2 cups sugar
2 teaspoons vanilla
1½ cups cooking oil
2 cups finely grated raw carrots
1 cup crushed pineapple
1½ cups chopped nuts
3 eggs
```

Mix flour, soda, cinnamon and salt. Mix sugar, vanilla and oil. Add ½ of dry ingredients to sugar, vanilla and oil. Mix well. Add carrots, pineapple and nuts. Mix well. Add remaining dry ingredients and eggs (one at a time) and blend. Pour ingredients into well greased and floured 10-inch tube pan. Bake at 350 degrees for 70 minutes. 18 servings.

Topeka, Kans.-North

Jct. U.S. 24 & 75

Fine old shade trees give visitors a friendly welcome in this busy capital city. Sportsmen enjoy a taste of the wildlife at this Inn. Bring your own pheasant, duck, quail, and the Inn will prepare it with fabulous wild game recipes. The 24-hour restaurant is popular with everyone. The famed Menninger Foundation is only 3 miles from the Inn.

LASAGNE, HOLIDAY INN STYLE

    1 pound ground beef
    1 pound ground pork
    ¼ cup olive oil
    ½ cup onion, chopped fine
    1 clove garlic, chopped fine
    2 teaspoons parsley, chopped
    3 cups tomato paste
    1 quart water
    2 pounds lasagne, cooked & drained
    2 pounds mozzarella cheese, sliced
    1½ pounds ricotta

Sauté beef and pork in olive oil with onion, garlic and parsley. Add tomato paste, water, salt and pepper and simmer for 1½ hours. Place lasagne in casseroles, alternate layers of sauce, mozzarella and ricotta. Sprinkle top with grated Romano cheese. Bake in a 375 degree oven for 20 minutes, or until cheese is melted. Serves 12.

CHAMPAGNE PUNCH

Combine 1 quart sauterne wine, 1 cup curacao, 1 #2 can cherries (pitted), 1 quart champagne and 2 quarts soda water. Pour into bottles, close and chill quickly. Serve in chilled champagne glasses. 25 servings.

Topeka, Kans.-South

U.S. 75 at Kansas Tpk.

The Atchison, Topeka and Santa Fe Railroad calls Topeka home. And this Holiday Inn is a popular traveler's home away from home. Everyone finds the Inn relaxing, the food superb and an air of friendliness when they stop for a meal or visit. Nearby Ft. Riley, established in 1852 as a camp center, was one of the largest cavalry schools in the world. The Inn is only 2 miles from downtown.

BEEF STROGANOFF WITH BUTTERED NOODLES

    2 pounds cooked beef
    2 tablespoons butter
    2 tablespoons onions, minced
    1 cup mushrooms
    1½ teaspoons salt
    2 teaspoons paprika
      Dash pepper
      Dash nutmeg
    1 teaspoon M.S.G.
    1 tablespoon tomato paste
    1 cup sour cream
    2-6 tablespoons red wine
    3 cups cooked buttered noodles or wild rice

Cut beef into 1x2½ inch strips. Use heavy skillet and sauté beef in butter, adding onions and mushrooms. Add seasonings. Stir in tomato paste and sour cream. Add wine last (use amount desired). Heat thoroughly. Serve on nest of buttered noodles or wild rice. Serves 6.

Wichita, Kans.-East

Wichita was called the "Magnetic City" in 1888. It is known as the air capital of the world. This Holiday Inn is conveniently near the Boeing, Beech and Cessna factories. It's also close to McConnell Air Force Base. The dining room looks like an English pub and offers the same hearty traditional welcome (and food).

SPLIT PEA SOUP

1 pound split peas
3 quarts beef or chicken stock
½ cup carrots, grated
1 cup celery, chopped
½ cup onion, chopped
1 bay leaf
1 teaspoon sugar
½ teaspoon pepper
Salt to taste

Soak peas overnight in water to cover. Drain and add liquid to stock to make 3 quarts. Add peas and simmer 3½ hours in a covered vessel. Add rest of ingredients and simmer another ½ hour. Strain soup through a sieve. Makes 2 to 2½ quarts.

OLD-FASHIONED BEEF STEW

Sauté 2 pounds boneless chuck in 2 tablespoons cooking oil until browned. Add 4 cups hot stock and simmer 2 to 3 hours. Add 1 cup cubed carrots, 2 cubed onions, 1 cup cubed or chopped celery and 1 bay leaf. Cook over low heat, adding 1 pound tiny whole potatoes, 1 cup tomatoes, 2 teaspoons salt and ½ teaspoon pepper. Cook 30 to 40 minutes over low heat, until potatoes are done. Serves 6.

Wichita, Kans. - Plaza

This beautiful 27-story Inn is the tallest building in Kansas. Located in the downtown area Garvey Center, it is opposite the Convention Center. Diners have a spectacular view from all sides in the 24th floor dining room, one of the Inn's three restaurants. There's also the Penthouse Club high in the air with live entertainment, the Coffee Shop and Ship's Tavern on the street level. For fun there's a swimming pool, shuffleboard court and putting green on the 6th floor.

BREAST OF CHICKEN PETITE MARMITE

Skin 3 chicken breasts, halve them, and remove the bones, including the wing tips — leave the main wing bones. Put the 6 prepared breasts between two sheets of waxed paper and pound them thin with the flat side of a cleaver. Put 2 tablespoons mashed banana on each fillet and fold the meat over the filling to form 6 cutlets of even shape. Dip the cutlets in flour, then in 3 beaten eggs. Roll them about in fresh fine bread crumbs. In a skillet, add ½ pound of butter. Sauté the chickens on one side until golden brown. Then turn the cutlets over and put in a baking dish with the butter from the skillet. Bake the chicken in a hot oven (400 degrees) for 10 minutes, or until tender. Serves 4 to 6.

VINEGAR PIE

Lightly beat together 4 eggs and ½ cup sugar. Add 2 teaspoons vinegar, ½ teaspoon salt and ¼ teaspoon nutmeg. Gradually add 3 cups hot milk. Pour mixture into pastry lined pie plate. Bake in 450 degree oven for 5 minutes, reduce heat to 350 degrees and cook 20 to 25 minutes.

Bowling Green, Ky. Midtown

U.S. 31 W. Bypass

You'll find good food and fun at this Holiday Inn. It's within easy access to the many attractions in and around the area. Visit historic Mammoth Cave with its limestone caverns and underground rivers and lakes. Take in Diamond Caverns and Horse Cave. Come back to this Inn for a refreshing dip in the pool, a dinner you'll remember, and live entertainment in the lounge.

CHEF'S SALAD DRESSING

1 pint corn oil
1 clove fresh garlic, mashed
1 egg
1½ teaspoons dry mustard
1½ teaspoons fresh lemon juice
1½ teaspoons A-1 sauce
1½ teaspoons Lea & Perrins sauce
1 teaspoon tomato catsup
1 teaspoon Tabasco sauce

Marinate oil and garlic overnight in c covered jar. Mix other ingredients and add oil slowly. Makes 2 cups.

CODFISH BALLS

1 cup salt codfish,
    soaked and shredded
2 cups potatoes, diced
1 egg, beaten
2 teaspoons butter, softened

Cook codfish and potatoes in boiling water until potatoes are soft. Drain and mash. Add egg, salt (if needed), pepper and butter. Beat with fork until smooth and fluffy. Form into cakes. Dip into flour. Then fry in deep fat, heated to 375 degrees, for 1 minute. Drain on absorbent paper. Serves 6.

Elizabethtown, Ky. North

Jct. U.S. 62 & Interstate 65

Elizabethtown residents say they are "In the Heart of Kentucky" and "Close to Everywhere". Within an hour's drive are 25 local and state historical points of interest . . . Abraham Lincoln's birthplace, My Old Kentucky Home, Fort Knox. Sightseeing visitors always try to be back at this Inn for its noon buffets. Kentucky Country Ham and homemade rolls are making the Inn famous.

BAKED KENTUCKY COUNTRY HAM

10- to 12-pound ham
Currant jelly
Sherry (optional)

Wash and brush country ham well. Place skin side up in large kettle. Cover with cold water and place lid on top. Let come to boil and simmer for 15 minutes for each pound of ham. Let cool in water. Place ham in shallow pan and remove skin. Rub all over with currant jelly to which a little sherry has been added. Bake uncovered in 275 degrees oven for 1 hour. Each pound of ham with bone serves 2.

FRENCH PUDDING

½ cup butter
1½ cups powdered sugar
2 eggs, beaten
½ pound vanilla wafers, crushed
½ pint heavy cream, whipped
    or dessert topping mix
1 cup crushed pineapple
1 cup chopped nuts

Cream butter and sugar. Add eggs. Press half the wafer crumbs in bottom of 8"x11" x2" greased pan. Spread sugar mixture over crumb layer. Add layer of whipped cream and cover wtih layer of pineapple. Top with remaining crumbs and sprinkle with nuts. Refrigerate for 24 hours. 12 servings.

Elizabethtown, Ky.
South

Jct. U.S. 31 W., St. 61, I-65

Stay in the middle of things. This Inn is at the Hub of Kentucky, only a short drive from major tourist attractions. Visit Fort Knox. Tour the Abraham Lincoln National Historical Park and see the log cabin where Lincoln was born. Homemade breads and pastries highlight every meal in the French Quarter and in the Candlelight Dining Rooms.

SCALLOPED EGGS GOLDENROD

    3 tablespoons butter
    3 tablespoons flour
    2 cups milk
    ½ teaspoon salt
    1 dash Tabasco
    1 tablespoon Worcestershire sauce
    8 eggs, hard-cooked
      Buttered bread crumbs

Make a cream sauce by melting butter and blending flour. Gradually add milk and stir until sauce is smooth and has thickened. Add seasonings.
Run eggs through a ricer or chop fine. Add to cream sauce. Pour into buttered casserole. Cover top with buttered bread crumbs and bake at 375 degrees until bubbly. Serves 6.

SOUTHERN TURKEY HASH

Heat 2 cups turkey stock, add 1 cup finely chopped celery, 1 finely chopped onion, ½ lemon (juice and rind), and seasonings. Cook until onion and celery are tender. Add ½ loaf bread toasted and minus crust to part of stock. Add 2 cups cooked turkey (cut in good size pieces) to remaining stock. Combine and add 2 tablespoons butter. Serves 4 to 6.

Frankfort, Ky.

U.S. Highway 60

Kentucky's capital is nestled along the banks of the Kentucky River. Its many fine homes include Liberty Hill, designed by Thomas Jefferson. The State Capitol Building houses the Historical Society Museum. Daniel Boone and his wife Rebecca are buried in Frankfort. Just west of downtown, this Holiday Inn welcomes guests with old-fashioned hospitality and delicious food.

STUFFED SHOULDER OF LAMB

    5 ounces salt pork, diced
    4 tablespoons onion, finely chopped
    2 tablespoons celery, finely chopped
    1 tablespoon parsley, finely chopped
    ½ cup apples, finely chopped
    3 tablespoons sugar
    2 tablespoons salt
    ½ teaspoon white pepper
    1¼ cups bread crumbs
      Egg yolks, beaten
      5-pound lamb shoulder, boned & rolled

Pan fry salt pork until crisp. Remove pieces from skillet. Cook onion, celery and parsley in pork drippings until tender. Remove and put apples in skillet, sprinkle with sugar and cook until tender. Mix all with salt, pepper, bread crumbs and egg yolks to moisten, cool. Wipe meat with damp cloth and sprinkle with salt and pepper. Put stuffing into cavity, sew edges together. Place in open roast pan. Roast in a moderately hot (375 degree) oven for 2½ to 3 hours. Will serve 10 6-ounce portions.

Lexington, Ky.-East

Jct. 25 Bypass & U.S. 60

Most of Kentucky's famed thorough-bred horse farms admit visitors. This Kentucky Bluegrass region is well known for its natural beauty and romantic history too. Be sure to visit Ashland, the home of Henry Clay. This Holiday Inn, only 5 minutes from downtown, is a perfect host in the Bluegrass. Enjoy excellent food in the gracious dining room, entertainment nightly in the patio lounge and pool side service.

HOT BROWN

Bluegrass Country Special

1 quart milk
1 stick butter
½ cup flour
　Salt to taste
　Pepper to taste
6 slices toast
1 cup grated cheese
12 slices bacon, cooked
6 slices cooked chicken
　(or enough for 6 sandwiches)
6 slices tomato

Let milk come to a boil. Blend flour in butter over low heat in a saucepan. Add milk gradually and stir until it thickens and is smooth. Season. Use individual buttered casseroles. Place a slice of toast in bottom of each casserole. Sprinkle grated cheese on toast. Then add chicken, 2 slices of bacon and a slice of tomato for each serving. Cover with sauce. Sprinkle more cheese on top. Run under broiler until hot and bubbly. Serves 6.

Louisville, Ky.-Central

Newburg Rd. at Watterson Expwy.

Downtown Louisville is only 6 minutes from the Inn. Make your reservations early for the Kentucky Derby at nearby Churchill Downs. Enjoy trotting at Louisville Downs. Then step into the Port O Spain, the Inn's dining room. Unforgettable dinners are yours for Doubloons and Pieces of 8. There's live entertainment nightly in the Buccaneer Lounge.

FROG LEGS

4 pounds frog legs
2 tablespoons lemon juice
4 tablespoons butter
2 tablespoons chopped parsley

Frog legs must be really fresh! Before using, the feet must be cut off with scissors and legs washed thoroughly. Sprinkle with salt, pepper and lemon juice. Chill for a few minutes in a covered dish. Sauté legs in hot butter in a skillet, but do not let them get too brown. Turn to cook on both sides. Toss parsley over them and serve. Serves 6-8.

LAMB CHOPS

6 center cut loin chops
2 tablespoons butter
　Seasonings
½ cup chopped mint leaves
　Mint jelly

Use chops 2½-inches thick and trim. Lightly brush both sides of loin chops with butter, salt and pepper. Broil on hot grill, quickly browning on both sides, then lower heat and cook until doneness desired. When done, toss mint leaves on top of chops and serve with mint jelly. Serves 6.

Louisville, Ky.
Downtown
927 S. 2nd Street

This Inn is right downtown in Derby City — only minutes away from the Fairgrounds and Churchill Downs. Take a cab from the airport (the Inn picks up the tab). The Back Door Restaurant serves meals you'll remember as fondly as your horse that won. Take time to visit the museum at Churchill Downs (it's open when the horses are not running) and the Tobacco Warehouses.

KENTUCKY HODGE PODGE

    3 tablespoons butter
    2 tablespoons flour
    2 cups strong chicken stock
      Salt and black pepper
    1 teaspoon hot mustard
    ⅛ teaspoon cloves
    2 cups cream
    ¼ teaspoon grated nutmeg
    ½ teaspoon sugar
    ¼ teaspoon cayenne or Tabasco
    4 chopped hard-cooked eggs
    3 cups cooked, diced chicken or turkey
    ½ cup sherry or Madeira

Melt butter, add flour and stir to make a paste. Slowly add stock and cream. Make a thick sauce. Place over hot water and add seasonings and eggs. Fold in chicken or turkey. Add wine and let cook until meat is thoroughly heated and sauce at the boiling point—do not let boil. Serves 8.

MINT JULEP

    4 sprigs mint
    1 lump sugar
    1 tablespoon water
    2 ounces bourbon

Crush mint leaves, sugar and water in a tall glass or mint julep cup. Fill with crushed ice. Add bourbon. Do not stir. Garnish with fresh mint sprig. Serves 1.

Louisville, Ky.
Riverbluff
U.S. 42, I-264 & I-71

Silks of Derby winners are on display in this Holiday Inn's famous Tack Room Restaurant. The Saddle Room overlooks the pool and patio, while the Stirrup Room features a spacious ground level entrance for large exhibits. The Inn is only minutes away from Churchill Downs. Buffet and party preparations add something extra to gala occasions here. The food is delicious everyday.

CHICKEN LIVER CARUSO

Tenderly sauté 1 pound chicken livers in 2 tablespoons butter until done. Cook a 9-ounce package of spaghetti (as directed on package) unti done. Wash with cold water to remove starch. Place in buttered casserole with chicken livers on top. Cover with Caruso Sauce and sprinkle Parmesan cheese over all. Place under broiler until brown. Serves 4.

Caruso Sauce

    1 onion, diced
    1 green pepper, cut in thin strips
    1 clove crushed garlic
    2 tablespoons butter
    ½ cup mushrooms
    1 cup canned tomatoes
      Salt and pepper
    ½ teaspoon Lea & Perrins sauce
      Parmesan cheese
    1 ounce sherry
      Pinch sugar

Sauté onion, pepper and garlic in butter until done, but not brown. Add mushrooms and tomatoes and cook. Season. Makes approximately 2 cups.

Louisville, Ky.-South

I-65 & Fern Valley Rd.

Select your own steak for open charbroiling. Enjoy patio dining overlooking the pool. This Holiday Inn is near the airport and downtown Louisville, within minutes of Churchill Downs. Ford, General Electric and other commercial plants are nearby. But you'd never know it — the woods and greenery block all views of traffic and commercial surroundings. There's live entertainment nightly.

SWEETBREADS A LA KING

    1 pound sweetbreads
1½ cups water
    1 teaspoon salt
    1 tablespoon vinegar
    3 tablespoons butter
½ cup mushrooms
    4 tablespoons fat
    4 tablespoons flour
2½ cups milk
    1 teaspoon salt
¼ teaspoon pepper
    3 eggs

Soak sweetbreads in cold water for 1 hour. Drain. Add 1½ cups water, 1 teaspoon salt, vinegar and simmer for ½ hour. Drain. Remove membrane and cut in pieces. Sauté mushrooms in butter for 5 minutes (use separate pan). Simmer flour in fat for 10 minutes without browning. Heat milk, add to roux, whip smooth, and add other ingredients. Season. Hard boil eggs and cut coarse. Add to creamed sweetbreads. Can be served in puff shell or with hot biscuits. Serves 5 to 7 persons.

Louisville, Ky.-SE

U.S. 60, 150 & 31 E.

The Kentucky Derby, the Great Steamboat Race plus nearby Mammoth Cave are all good reasons to visit Louisville. Free bus service to Churchill Downs on the "Big Day" is just one of many delightful extras at this Holiday Inn. On Sundays there's a country style dinner wtih a choice of chicken, country ham or pan-fried steak. Nearby Bardtown is where Stephen Foster wrote "My Old Kentucky Home".

SEAFOOD DELIGHT

½ pound lobster meat
¼ pound scallops
½ pound shrimp (green)
½ pound haddock

Cook fish in a 350 degree oven about 12 to 15 minutes. Dice fish coarse and place equal portions in small casseroles. Top with Cheddar Cheese Sauce. Serves 6 to 8.

Cheddar Cheese Sauce

2 tablespoons butter
2 tablespoons flour (level)
1 pint milk
1 cup Cheddar cheese, grated

Blend flour into melted butter, add milk and stir until thick. Add Cheddar cheese, salt and pepper to taste. Stir until blended. Makes 2½ cups.

PORK CHOP A LA OIGNON

Brown center cut pork chops in skillet. Top each with a slice of onion, salt, pepper and Accent. Cover bottom of pan with tomato juice, arrange chops in pan and cover with tomato soup. Brown in oven about 15 minutes.

Madisonville, Ky.

U.S. 41 North

Western Kentucky's coal fields and oil wells are responsible for many visitors to this area. Visitors may tour the mines of the West Kentucky Coal Company on weekdays. This is also the home of the largest steam shovel in the world. The gigantic Kentucky Dam forms the 184 mile Kentucky Lake. This Inn is located near enough to everything — close enough to return for every delicious Kentucky meal.

CHICKEN LIVERS SAUTE'

2 pounds chicken livers
1 cup cream
1 teaspoon salt
Dash pepper
Flour
Shortening
2 ounces Madeira wine

Pour cream over chicken livers and place in refrigerator for 24 hours. Drain, season livers and dredge in flour. Pan-fry in shortening until golden brown. Sprinkle with wine and serve. Serves 8 to 10.

CHESS PIE

3 eggs
2 cups sugar
2 tablespoons flour
1 teaspoon salt
1 cup milk
1 teaspoon vanilla
¼ pound butter or margarine

Cream eggs, sugar, flour and salt together. Add milk, vanilla, butter and cook in double boiler until butter melts. Pour in an unbaked pie shell and put in a preheated 400 degree oven, then turn to 275 degrees and bake about 30 minutes. Serves 6.

Mayfield, Ky.

St. 121 & Mayfield Bypass

Kentucky Lake, Barkley Lake and Land Between the Lakes are within minutes of this Inn. Guests at the Inn enjoy golf privileges at the Mayfield country clubs. It's no wonder everyone starts back for the Inn at the first sign of hunger. The Honey Cured Kentucky Ham with Red Eye Gravy and Hot Biscuits is a delicious way to start or end a day.

GERMAN CHOCOLATE PIE

1 package (4-oz.) Baker's German Sweet Chocolate
¼ cup butter
1⅔ cups evaporated milk
1½ cups sugar
3 tablespoons cornstarch
⅛ teaspoon salt
2 eggs
1 teaspoon vanilla
2 8-inch Graham cracker pie shells
1⅓ cups Baker's Angel Flake Coconut
½ cup chopped pecans

Melt chocolate with butter over low heat, stirring until well blended. Remove from heat. Gradually blend in milk. Mix sugar, cornstarch, and salt thoroughly. Beat in eggs and vanilla. Combine with chocolate mixture. Pour into pie shells. Combine coconut and nuts. Sprinkle over filling. Bake at 375 degrees for 45 minutes. Filling will be soft, but will set while cooling. Cool at least 4 hours before cutting. Pastry shells may be used if desired. 2 pies.

Owensboro, Ky.

Highway 60 West

The fascinating chant of tobacco auctioneers, historic places to visit, and this beautiful Inn on the Ohio River make Owensboro a great vacation spot. Businessmen enjoy the Inn's location in the center of Kentucky oil fields. Everyone enjoys the food . . . Kentucky favorites and international fare. The popular cocktail lounge features live entertainment.

ONION PIE

(Zwiebel Kuchen)

Combine 1½ cups flour, ¾ teaspoon salt and 1½ teaspoons caraway seeds. Add ½ cup shortening and cut into flour until mixture resembles coarse corn meal. Stir 2-3 tablespoons water in lightly with fork, and stir until mixture adheres and follows fork around bowl. Turn onto floured board and roll ⅛ inch thick. Fit into 10-inch pie pan. Bake in 425 degree oven for 10 minutes, or until light brown.

Pie Filling

3 cups peeled onions
3 tablespoons melted butter
½ cup milk
1½ cups sour cream
1 teaspoon salt
2 eggs, well beaten
3 tablespoons flour

Slice onions thin. Sauté in butter until golden. Spoon into pastry shell. Add milk, 1 cup sour cream and salt to eggs. Blend flour with remaining sour cream. Combine with egg mixture. Pour over onions. Bake in 325 degree oven for 30 minutes, or until firm in center. Garnish with crisp bacon. 8 servings.

Paducah, Ky.

U.S. 45 E., 60, 62 & 68

Blueberry Pancakes with genuine Kentucky Country Smoked Ham! That's the way most guests start the day at this Holiday Inn. Many start the day early — fine fishing and boating facilities are only minutes away at Kentucky Dam Lake, one of the largest man made lakes in the world. For your shopping convenience, the Inn is located in the heart of Cardinal Point Shopping Center.

PADUCAH HOLIDAY INN SALAD

2 small packages gelatin
1 medium can crushed pineapple
1 cup sugar
Juice of 1 lemon
⅔ cup blanched almonds, chopped
⅔ cup American cream cheese
⅔ pint cream, whipped stiff

Soften gelatin in 1 cup cold water and dissolve over hot water. Pour juice off pineapple, heat pineapple juice, sugar and lemon juice. When hot, add gelatin and stir until entirely dissolved and hot—do not boil. When mixture is cold, place in refrigerator. When it begins to set, add almonds, grated cheese, pineapple and whipped cream. Fold gently and pour into shallow pan. Leave in refrigerator overnight. Serves 10-12.

Dressing

½ cup whipped cream
½ cup finely chopped celery
½ cup Miracle Whip

Mix and leave overnight in refrigerator Makes 1 cup. Serve over any fruit salad.

Alexandria, La.

U.S. 71, 165 & 167 Bypass N.

Indians and trappers once came by flatboat to trade at Alexander Fulton's store. Now visitors come to enjoy this Holiday Inn. The Inn specializes in seafood and is famous for its Chicken Pie. There are many hot wells nearby. Their hot mineral waters have been credited with near miracle cures. Alexandria was once called "Les Rapides" because it is at the rapids of the Red River.

CHICKEN POT PIE

Boil about 15 minutes in water to cover:
  1 cup celery, diced fine
  1 cup onions, diced fine
  1 cup potatoes, diced medium
Strain and throw away water.

Blend ¼ pound melted margarine and ½ cup flour. Add: 2 quarts hot water, 3 tablespoons chicken base, ¼ teaspoon white pepper. Stir and bring to boil.

Add: 1 pint diced carrots and 1 pint green peas to strained vegetables above. Combine with hot stock above.

In each individual casserole place: 1 large piece dark turkey meat or chicken meat. Cover with vegetable sauce. Add 1 large piece white turkey or chicken meat. Add more sauce if needed to fill casserole. Cover pie with pastry. Prick center with fork to allow steam to escape while cooking. Usually when sauce bubbles through, pie is ready to serve. Cook at 450 degrees about 12 minutes. Makes 12 small pies.

Baton Rouge, La.-North

Rt. 61 & 190 Bypass

Along the highways leading to Baton Rouge strawberry venders are a familiar sight. Strawberry Pancakes are the specialty at this beautiful Inn with its open dining room and tropical plants. The Inn's football buffet is the way to enjoy a showcase of delicious dishes while enroute to the Sugar Bowl or a Louisiana State University game.

STRAWBERRY PANCAKES

  1 egg, well beaten
  1¼ cups milk
  2 tablespoons soft shortening
  1¼ cups flour
  1 teaspoon sugar
  1½ teaspoons baking powder
  ½ teaspoon salt
  2 cups Strawberry Filling
  1 cup cream, whipped
Beat all ingredients with a rotary beater until smooth. Add extra milk if batter is so thick pancake will not roll. Brown each side on a hot griddle. Place 1 tablespoon Strawberry Filling on each pancake and roll. Serve 2 pancakes for each portion and top with whipped cream and a large whole strawberry. Makes 6 to 8 pancakes.

Strawberry Filling

Crush 1 pint washed and hulled strawberries and add 1 cup powdered sugar. Makes approximately 2 cups.

Baton Rouge, La.-South

U.S. 61 & Interstate 12

Whether in Louisiana's capital city for business or pleasure, you'll enjoy your stay at this ultramodern Holiday Inn. Elaborate buffet dining and an exciting a la carte menu are featured in the King Edward Dining Room. There's a lot of talk about LSU football games in the Captain Cove Lounge. A Gift Shop in the lobby completes a convenient picture.

CRAWFISH ETOUFFEE

4 pounds cleaned, peeled crawfish
½ cup salad oil
1½ cups chopped onions
1½ cups chopped bell peppers
¾ cup chopped celery
1 cup flour
1 gallon water
¼ bottle Lea & Perrins sauce
Tabasco sauce to taste
1½ teaspoons M.S.G.
1 teaspoon garlic powder
1 teaspoon red pepper (cayenne)

Using 2-gallon pot, cover bottom with oil. Add onions, peppers, celery, salt and pepper. Cook until onions are clear. Add flour to make roux. Then add water, Lea & Perrins sauce, Tabasco sauce, M.S.G., garlic powder and red pepper. In separate pot, place cleaned and peeled crawfish and cover with crawfish fat and water. Bring to a boil and remove from fire. Add to vegetables and bring to boil, then remove from fire and allow to cool. Heat when serving. Makes approximately 24 to 28 cups.

Lafayette, La.

U.S. Highway 90 East

This Inn on the Old Spanish Trail is near Longfellow's "Evangeline Oak". The Live Oak Society has its headquarters in Lafayette. Only live oaks at least 100 years old may be members — they pay annual dues of 25 acorns. As one would expect, this Holiday Inn specializes in Creole foods. The Inn is adjacent to the airport.

FAMOUS CREOLE SAUCE

1 cup olive oil
½ cup salad oil
4 onions, diced
2 green peppers, diced
3 cups celery, diced
1 garlic pod, mashed
2 #2½ cans whole tomatoes
2 small cans tomato paste
2 bay leaves
½ teaspoon sage

Place oil in black iron pot. Fry onion, pepper, celery and garlic until all are tender. Add whole tomatoes (which have been mashed) and tomato paste. Add 1 quart water, bay leaves and sage. Cook not less than 2 hours. Add ½ teaspoon sugar. Season with salt, black and cayenne pepper. Makes approximately 6 cups.

Shrimp Creole

Peel 3 or 4 pounds of 31-35 count shrimp. After sauce is finished, place shrimp in the sauce and cook 14 minutes. Add ¼ cup chopped shallots and ¼ cup chopped parsley. Serve in casserole with steamed rice. Serves 10 to 12.

Lake Charles, La.

Bypass 90 E. off I-10

Located in a vast petro-chemical empire, visitors who come from all over the world enjoy Bayou Country hospitality at this Holiday Inn. And more. The Garden Room Smorgasbord features 52 epicurean delights. This is duck hunting country and the Inn will serve yours with Cajun Rice Dressing. Try to be here in mid-July for "Contraband Days".

CAJUN DIRTY RICE

6 chicken livers
2 chicken gizzards
1 large onion, diced
2 ribs celery, cut up
2 cloves garlic, split
½ green pepper
4 tablespoons butter
1 cup chicken broth
1 teaspoon salt
Dash cayenne
½ teaspoon Worcestershire sauce
2 tablespoons flour
2 cups cooked rice
Chopped parsley

Grind livers and gizzards with onion, celery, garlic and pepper. Mix and saute in 2 tablespoons butter until cooked. Add a little chicken broth and cook slowly. Season. Blend flour in rest of butter and let brown, add a little broth and add to mixture, thickening a little. Add rice. Simmer for 10 to 15 minutes, adding more broth if too dry. Serve with chopped parsley to add color. Serves 6.

Monroe, La.

U.S. 80 & 165

When in Louisiana travelers expect to find superb seafood in the great French tradition. They are not disappointed in the Davis Dining Room of this Inn. Nectarine Pie is another reason to stop here. The Davis Pancake Room is always crowded with guests enjoying 17 varieties of unsurpassed pancakes. The Monroe Natural Gas Field is one of the world's largest.

CURRY OF SHRIMP

2½ pounds medium shrimp
¼ pound margarine
1 tablespoon curry powder
1½ teaspoons garlic powder
½ teaspoon salt
1½ teaspoons cornstarch
1 cup beer
2 cups water

Peel and devein fresh boiled shrimp. Sauté in margarine, add curry powder, garlic powder, salt and blend in cornstarch. Cook 5 minutes. Add beer and water and simmer 15 minutes. Serve over rice or use as hors d'oeuvres. Allow 1 pound shrimp in shell for 4 portions.

HONEY PECAN PIE

4 large eggs
¾ cup sugar
2½ tablespoons flour
2 cups honey
1½ teaspoons vanilla
¼ teaspoon salt
1⅛ cups chopped pecans

Beat eggs until light. Mix sugar and flour. Add to eggs and beat well. Add honey, vanilla, salt and pecans. Pour into an uncooked pie shell. Bake in a 425 degree oven for 10 minutes, reduce heat to 325 degrees and bake 45 minutes. Makes 1 large pie or 1 regular pie and 1 small pie.

New Orleans, La.-East

Chef Menteur Hwy., U.S. 90 E.

Gourmets traveling to or from the Gulf of Mexico always enjoy this Inn's wonderful food. Lake Ponchartrain's cool breezes make patio eating delightful. Downtown New Orleans is just a few minutes away. Louisiana waterways are a sportsman's paradise. Cruise on an inland lake or go to sea off the coast.

HOT SEAFOOD CANAPÉ

1 bunch shallots, chopped fine
1 stick butter
Pinch thyme
2 bay leaves
Dash cayenne
½ pound crab meat, cooked
2 chopped pimentos
Dash Tabasco
2 heaping tablespoons flour
¼ cup milk
½ ounce brandy
½ ounce sauterne wine
Toast rounds
½ cup American cheese, grated

Sauté shallots in ½ stick of butter. Add thyme, bay leaves, dash of cayenne and sauté for 3 minutes. Remove bay leaves and add shredded crab meat, pimentos and dash Tabasco. Blend flour and rest of butter. Add milk and cook until it thickens a little. Combine mixtures, adding wine and brandy. Spread on toast rounds. Top with grated cheese. Broil quickly so cheese will melt. Makes approximately 1 cup.

New Orleans, La. French Quarter

124 Royal Street

Don't wait too long . . . the gumbo is getting cold! Every guest who has visited this Inn agrees you must hurry and enjoy the delicious regional specialties. You'll find Bratwurst, Shrimp Remoulade, Beef Teriyaki and Red Beans with Rice are excellent. For a bird's eye view of the New Orleans French Quarter, go into the Bird Cage for a drink or bite into one of its famous sandwiches. This is an "up in the air" outdoor dining terrace.

CRAB GUMBO

1 dozen hard shell crabs
6 large tomatoes, skinned & quartered
1 onion, chopped
2 pints finely sliced okra
1 bay leaf, chopped fine
½ red pepper pod, seeded

Scald crabs and clean them, removing the "dead man's fingers" . . . spongy substances and sand bags on under part. Cut off claws, crack, and crack body in quarters. Season with salt and pepper. Heat 2 tablespoons cooking oil in a heavy skillet. Throw in crabs (bodies and claws). Cover closely and after 5 to 10 minutes, add tomatoes. Add onion and sprigs of parsley and thyme, stirring occasionally to prevent scorching. After 5 minutes, add okra. When well browned, add bay leaf. Pour in 2½ quarts boiling water, add pepper pod, place on low heat and let simmer for about 1 hour. Season with cayenne and salt. Pour into a tureen and serve with boiled rice. Serves 6 to 8.

YELLOW BIRD

Combine in mixer glass: 1 ounce white rum, ¾ ounce triple sec, ¾ ounce Galliano, ½ ounce fresh lime juice and 6 ounces pineapple juice. Shake well and pour over crushed ice. Garnish with pineapple spear and maraschino cherry. 1 serving.

New Orleans, La.-West

Airline Hwy., U.S. 61 West

This Holiday Inn is only a few minutes from the International Airport (free transportation), yet conveniently close (12 minutes) to the romance of the "Queen City of the South". Guests enjoy the Inn's private balconies and sunlit patio. It has extra services too—it arranges sightseeing tours, theatre and sports reservations and it has a gift shop.

SHRIMP CREOLE

    4 tablespoons bacon drippings
    2 medium-sized onions, minced
    1 green pepper, minced
 1½ cups celery, minced
    1 clove garlic, minced
    1 quart tomatoes
    3 tablespoons tomato paste
    3 cups cooked shrimp

Sauté onions, pepper, celery and garlic in bacon drippings until they are transparent. Add tomatoes and tomato paste. Let mixture simmer to a thick consistency (30 to 45 minutes). Add a dash Tabasco. Add freshly cooked shrimp about 15 minutes before serving. Serve with fluffy cooked rice. Serves 6 to 7.

SHRIMP PROVENCALE

    21 jumbo shrimp
     3 cloves garlic, minced
     2 tablespoons parsley, minced
     1 cup butter

Peel and clean shrimp. Butterfly: split down back and leave tails on shrimp. Sauté shrimp, garlic and parsley in butter until cooked (5-8 minutes). Season. Serves 3.

Ruston, La.

Interstate 20

This beautiful Inn with all ground floor rooms is a welcome sight for travelers on Interstate 20. The red carpeted dining room rolls out homemade rolls and pastries. During the summer the tantalizing aroma of peach cobbler lets you know "it's peach country". Wintertime guests are greeted with a roaring fire in both the lobby and dining room.

SOUR CREAM RAISIN PIE

    ½ cup seedless raisins
    ½ cup nut meats
    1 cup sugar
 2½ tablespoons flour
    1 teaspoon ground cloves
 1½ cups sour cream
    3 egg yolks, beaten

Chop raisins and nuts. Mix together. Sift dry ingredients and add to raisins and nuts. Pour sour cream over mixture and blend. Place in double boiler and bring to boil over hot water. Add egg yolks gradually and stir constantly until mixture is thick. Let cool. Pour into baked pastry shell. Top with meringue. Bake in 325 degree oven 10-15 minutes. Serves 6-8.

Meringue

Beat 3 egg whites until stiff. Add 6 tablespoons sugar gradually and beat until glossy.

Pastry

Mix 2½ tablespoons shortening, ½ teaspoon salt and 1½ cups flour. Blend until crumbly.

Add ¼ cup ice water. Roll lightly on floured board ⅛ inch thick. Place in pie pan. Crimp edges. Prick bottom. Bake at 475 degrees for 10-12 minutes.

Shreveport-Bossier City, La.

150 Hamilton Lane (I-20)

Shreveport and Bossier City are both only 1 mile from this Inn. Transportation to and from the airport (8 miles) is compliments of the Inn. The Inn is also near the Convention Center. There's a well-worn path around the dining room at this popular Inn. The Smorgasbords are exceptional — exceptionally outstanding.

GREEN BEAN LA LOUISIANNE

6½ cups cut green beans
1 pint chicken stock
1 cup sliced onions
¼ cup margarine
¼ cup flour
    Yellow food coloring
¼ cup slivered almonds
¼ cup pimento

Drain beans well, rinse and soak in salted chicken stock overnight. Sauté onion in melted margarine. Thicken ½ cup chicken stock with flour. Add rest of stock, blend then cook until it has light gravy consistency. Add yellow food coloring to give extra rich appearance. Add sautéed onions, almonds and pimento. Heat well and serve on platter or place in buttered casserole and cook covered at 350 degrees until heated through. Serves 10-12.

Shreveport, La.-North

Market St. on U.S. 71 N.

Shreveport is named for Captain Henry Miller Shreve, who rammed his steamboat through 200 miles of Red River driftwood to open up navigation to the town. Today Shreveport is one of the leading oil and gas centers in the nation. Old southern plantation hospitality greets guests here. You'll welcome the food and atmosphere of the bygone era.

OVEN SMOKED HAM

1 14-16-pound ham
1 pint cider vinegar
2 cups Wrights liquid smoke
6 medium onions
3 cups brown sugar
6 bay leaves
½ cup bread crumbs
4 teaspoons dry mustard

Place ham skin side down in pan with false bottom so that water can circulate. Cover with cold water, vinegar and one cup liquid smoke. Add onions, 2 cups brown sugar and bay leaves. Simmer 20 minutes to the pound. When done, allow to cool in mixture, then remove skin. Put in whole cloves after removing ham from water. Mix together remaining brown sugar, crumbs and mustard and moisten with liquid smoke. Add 1 cup liquid smoke and bake in a hot oven (400 degrees) until glazed. (1 pound with bone serves 2—boneless 3 to 4).

SOUTHERN FRIED APPLES

Slice 8 apples. Add ½ cup water and cook in covered frying pan until almost tender. Remove cover and cook until nearly dry. Add 6 tablespoons butter, 1 cup brown sugar and ½ cup raisins and fry until tender. Serves 6 to 8.

Shreveport, La.-West

Bounteous buffets everyday at noon appeal to hungry travelers in a hurry. Everyone is delighted with the Inn's savory southern dishes. The Red Horse Tavern is a popular gathering place at night. The Inn is only 5 minutes from downtown, 1 mile from the airport and near the State Fairgrounds. Every sightseer should visit the Louisiana State Museum.

STUFFED SPRING CHICKEN

Wash 2 2-pound whole fryers and dry. Stuff each with Dressing and sew cavity loosely. Rub with softened butter, season and place in shallow roasting pan. Cook at 450 degrees until brown, reduce heat to 350 degrees and cook until tender. (Approx. 1½ hours). Remove from pan and keep warm.

Cook necks and giblets in 1 cup water for stock. Baste chicken with stock while baking.

To pan drippings add and blend for gravy:
2 tablespoons flour
1 cup milk
Stock as needed
Seasonings

Cut each fowl in half. Pour sauce over and serve. Serves 4.

Dressing

Moisten 3 cups bread crumbs with ½ cup milk. Squeeze dry. Sauté ½ cup minced onion, and ½ cup minced celery in ⅓ cup butter. Add ¼ teaspoon thyme, 1 teaspoon salt and ¼ teaspoon pepper. Add dry bread and minced parsley. Stir in 1 beaten egg. Add hot broth for right consistency to handle. Makes 2 cups.

Auburn-Lewiston, Maine

Lewiston, Maine's second largest city, grew beside the waterfalls in the Androscoggin River. The area has important textile and electronic industries. This Holiday Inn is conveniently close to Lewiston and Auburn so both cities' residents can enjoy its excellent seafood entrees. Casco Bay and the Atlantic are only a short drive away.

STUFFED OYSTERS AU GRATIN

2 dozen large oysters
6 egg yolks, hard-boiled
6 pieces cooked bacon, minced
Salt to taste
1 tablespoon chopped parsley
½ cup crumbs
1 cup Velouté Sauce

Split oysters in the thick part and stuff with a mixture of egg yolks, bacon, salt and chopped parsley. Dip in freshly grated bread crumbs. Place four in scallop shell and pour over a Velouté Sauce flavored with anchovy butter. Sprinkle with crumbs and brown in 400 degree oven for 5 minutes. Serve hot. Serves 6.

Velouté Sauce

Melt 2 tablespoons butter, add 3 tablespoons flour and dash salt and pepper. Blend over low heat and add 1 cup chicken broth. Bring to boil and thicken. Add 2 tablespoons butter creamed with 1 teaspoon anchovy paste, dash lemon juice and cayenne. Add ⅓ cup cream last.

Augusta, Maine

Western Ave. and I-95

Feast on fabulous Maine seafoods. Fresh catches from the sea are delivered daily to this Inn — and other produce of Maine. Do order Maine shrimp, clams on the half shell, baked stuffed Maine lobster and Maine corn. Maine apples are in the Waldorf salad and apple cider. If you stay a week you can play a different golf course everyday. Get the jump on winter at nearby Sugarloaf and Squaw Mountains.

LOBSTER NEWBURG

2 cups fresh Maine lobster meat
4 tablespoons butter
3 tablespoons flour
½ teaspoon salt
⅛ teaspoon nutmeg
    Dash cayenne pepper
¼ teaspoon Accent
1½ cups light cream
2 to 3 tablespoons sherry

Cut lobster in bite size pieces. Cook in butter in a heavy skillet over low to medium heat, slowly to draw the color slightly. Combine flour and seasonings and sprinkle over lobster. Add cream or tall can undiluted evaporated milk, stirring constantly. Cook until thickened. Add sherry slowly while stirring. Serve on toast, in patty shells, or with curried rice. Serves 4 to 5.

CRAB MEAT STUFFING FOR LOBSTER

Slowly fry 2 slices diced bacon until golden brown. Add ¼ cup chopped onion and ¾ cup chopped celery and cook over low heat until tender. Add 1 cup soft bread crumbs, salt and pepper. Combine 1 cup Maine crab meat with melted butter and 2 beaten eggs. Add to first mixture, stirring to blend. Use this as a stuffing for 4 to 6 baked stuffed lobsters.

Baltimore, Md. Downtown

Howard & Lombard

Enjoy an ever changing view of the city's skyline and gourmet cuisine in the La Ronde Restaurant atop Baltimore's 13-story downtown Holiday Inn. Then there's the "English Pub" for men only. "The Night Club" features live entertainment. All this, and you can stay right across the street from the Civic Center too.

SUPREME DE VOLAILLE

2 8-ounce boneless chicken breasts
10 butter patties
8 ounces lump crab meat
4 ounces Smithfield ham, julienne
1 cup cooked wild rice
¼ cup heavy cream

Skin and flatten chicken breasts. Place butter in an oval copper chafing dish and heat until bubbly, but not brown. Place chicken breasts in center of pan and surround them on one side with crab meat, the other side with ham. Sauté slowly until done, about 5 minutes, being careful not to break crab lumps in the process. Add a pinch of salt and pepper, then dry sherry to taste. Simmer slowly until juices are absorbed. Remove pan from fire and pour brandy from bottle into pan. Place pan back on fire and tilt just so flame touches pan and ignites the brandy. Again, turn chicken and other ingredients to absorb brandy. Place wild rice on center of platter and place chicken breasts on top of rice, then crab meat and ham. Add cream to remaining sauce in pan and stir well, until cream is boiling. Pour sauce over top of chicken and serve. 2 servings.

Baltimore, Md.-East

Pulaski Hwy., U.S. 40 E.

This Inn is just west of the Harbor Tunnel. It's conveniently located for everyone. Businessmen enjoy being close to the harbor, mills, refineries and warehouses. John Hopkins Hospital is within minutes. Sightseeing visitors like to make the Inn their headquarters. The delicious food and excellent service are why people keep coming back to this Inn too.

NEW ENGLAND STYLE BAKED BEANS

1½ pounds California pea beans
¼ pound fat salt pork
1 medium-size onion
1 teaspoon dry mustard
1 teaspoon baking soda
1 tablespoon salt
⅓ cup dark molasses
1 tablespoon sugar
   (if sweet bean is desired)

Soak beans in cold water overnight. Bring just to a boil in same soaking water. Place salt pork in one piece in bottom of two-quart clay bean pot. Next place onion in pot. Drain beans, reserving soak water, and fil pot only ⅔ full, as beans will swell. Add other ingredients and fill pot with reserve water. Cover and bake in a slow 275 degree oven for about 8 hours. Watch constantly, as water must cover beans at all times. Remove cover the last hour for additional browning. 6-8 servings.

Baltimore, Md. Glen Burnie

State 2. 6600 Ritchie Hwy.

It's not unusual to see a sea of uniforms in this Inn's popular restaurant. The U.S. Naval Academy is only 15 miles away. The Inn offers guests free transportation to the Academy and to the State Capitol. The sight to see nearby is the U.S.S. Constellation, the oldest ship in the world still afloat. It was built in 1797 and served in every conflict up to and including World War II.

SAUERBRATEN

3 pounds beef shoulder
   Garlic, if desired
1 teaspoon salt
   Pepper
2 cups vinegar
2 cups water
½ cup sliced onion
2 bay leaves
1 teaspoon peppercorns
¼ cup sugar
1 cup sweet or sour cream

Rub meat with a cut surface of garlic, salt and pepper and place in bowl. Heat vinegar, water, onion, bay leaves, peppercorns, and sugar together, but do not boil. Pour hot mixture over meat, cover bowl, and let stand in cool place 4 to 8 days, turning meat each day. Drain, saving vinegar mixture. Brown meat in cooking oil, add ½ strained vinegar, cover pan and simmer until tender (2 to 3 hours), adding vinegar as required to keep liquid about ½ inch deep in pan. Strain liquid and thicken with 2 tablespoons flour for each cup of liquid. Cook until thickened and add cream. Serves 6.

Baltimore, Md.-North

Loch Raven Exit 29 off I-695

The Inn's Highlander Restaurant (kilts and all) on Loch Raven Boulevard gives guests a bit of Old Scotland with its haggis, shortbread, broths and woodcock. Succulent oysters and soft-shelled crabs from Chesapeake Bay vie in popularity. Downtown Baltimore is only 20 minutes away. Visitors enjoy the nearby Sherwood Gardens with some 150 year old boxwood.

MARYLAND STUFFED CUCUMBER BOAT

    2 cucumbers, medium-sized
    1 cup crab meat
    ¼ cup diced celery
      Salt
      Pepper
    ½ cup mayonnaise
    4 pimento strips

Split cucumbers lengthwise. Remove seeded center and score outside with a fork. Stuff center of cucumbers with Maryland backfin crab meat, seasoned with diced celery, salt and pepper, and held together with mayonnaise. Place on a bed of lettuce. Garnish with carrot curls placed through large sandwich picks and stuck in the centers of the cucumbers in the form of a sail. Place a pimento strip on either side of sails. Serve with lemon wedges and olives. Serves 2-4.

Baltimore, Md.-NW

U.S. 140 at Interstate 695

Make your reservations early at this Inn for the weekend of the "Preakness" . . . the world's richest purse for 3-year-olds at the nearby Pimlico Race Track. Racing has been conducted at Pimlico every spring and fall since 1870. This Holiday Inn is especially popular for its German dishes. Its location is excellent too, only 8 miles from downtown Baltimore.

CHEESE BLINTZES

Place six eggs in a bowl and beat until frothy. Add: 1½ teaspoons salt, 1½ cups milk, 1½ cups sifted flour. Stir until smooth.

Grease 6½-inch skillet and heat. Pour 2-3 tablespoons batter in pan and tilt to distribute over bottom. Cook until pancake is firm. Place on buttered plate brown side up. Repeat cooking pancakes, greasing skillet each time. As they cook place 1 tablespoon filling on edge of each and fold over, tucking sides and ends firmly. Approx. 36 pancakes.

To make filling beat:

    7 ounces cottage cheese
    9 ounces pot cheese
    9 ounces cream cheese
    1 teaspoon soft butter
    2 eggs
    1 tablespoon sugar
    ½ teaspoon salt

To serve, heat a little butter in large skillet. Fry blintzes golden brown on both sides. Serve at once with sour cream or applesauce. Fry only number required. Blintzes will stay fresh in refrigerator several days. Blintzes freeze well.

Baltimore, Md.-Pimlico

5422-5430 Park Heights Ave.

Stay next door to the famous Pim-lico Race Track. The Preakness Dining Room and Winners Circle Lounge at this Inn reflect the racing theme — waitresses dressed in jockey silks and boots serve you. The Inn's menu is planned around the historic Woodlawn Vase . . . the oldest racing trophy. Inside, splendors of another kind are described. Try all the superbly prepared Chesapeake Bay specialties. Select your own lobster from the live lobster tank.

SEAFOOD PIMLICO

½ pound lump crab meat
½ pound lobster claw meat
½ pound raw shrimp, shelled
4-6 tablespoons butter
2 tablespoons chopped parsley
2 tablespoons chopped shallots
2 tablespoons mushrooms, cut up
Salt and pepper
6 ounces Marsala wine

Blend seafood over low heat in melted butter in a skillet. Add remaining ingredients and simmer until wine evaporates, leaving only aroma in seafood.

Sauce: Beat 2 to 3 egg yolks, add 1½ cups cream and 2 ounces sauterne. Blend into smooth, almost fluffy mixture. Gently add hot seafood morsels. Serve over fluffy rice. 6 to 8 servings.

SHRIMP A LA CHEF

Marinate peeled and deveined shrimp in a mixture of oregano and sherry for about 10 minutes. Dip shrimp in an egg wash* and bread in cracker meal. Then dip the shrimp in beer and again in cracker meal with finely chopped parsley. Cook shrimp in hot, deep fat for a few minutes. Serve with cocktail sauce and lemon wedges. Allow 1 pound shrimp in the shell or ½ pound shelled shrimp for 3 or 4 small servings.

*Egg plus 1 tablespoon water. Beat lightly.

Baltimore, Md.-West

U.S. 40 W.

Delectable seafood from the Bay area becomes gourmet cuisine in the Inn's restaurant. Nearby, visitors enjoy the Enoch Pratt Free Library, founded in 1892. This is just opposite the first Roman Catholic Church in the U.S. Edgar Allen Poe's home is open to the public and his grave is in the Westminister Churchyard.

BAKED STUFFED LOBSTER TAIL

1 8-oz. lobster tail
2 tablespoons butter
4 ounces crab meat

Split boiled lobster tail down center. Remove meat and chop it. Melt butter, add lobster and crab meat. Season. Refill lobster and bake in a moderate oven for 20 to 25 minutes. Garnish with lemon wedge and parsley. 1 serving.

POT ROAST OF BEEF

1 6-pound top round roast
4 tablespoons shortening
1½ teaspoons paprika
3 teaspoons salt
1 cup diced onion
½ cup diced carrots
½ cup diced celery
1 clove garlic
1 teaspoon mixed pickling
¾ cup tomato paste

Wipe meat with damp cloth. Make paste of shortening, paprika and salt. Spread paste over meat, then sear on all sides in heavy pot. Add vegetables and seasonings. Add 1 pint water and bring to boil, then simmer until done, about 3-4 hours. Use flour-water paste to thicken juices, adding more water if needed. Heat thoroughly. Add tomato paste while thickening. Strain. Serves 12.

Bowie, Md.

U.S. 301, 50 at Md. 3

Maryland's most colorful race track is adjacent to this Holiday Inn. It's only 15 minutes from Washington, D.C. and just 12 minutes away from Annapolis. Marlboro and its tobacco auctions are nearby. The most delicious Pennsylvania Dutch food is right here. You can order such treats as Ham smoked over sassafras and hickory, fabulous Pennsylvania Dutch Chicken.

CORN FRITTERS

(Welschkan Fritters)

    2 cups corn, cooked
    1 egg
    1 teaspoon sugar
    ½ teaspoon salt
    1½ teaspoons pepper
    3 tablespoons shortening
    ¼ cup flour
    ½ teaspoon baking powder

Mix the corn, egg, sugar, salt and pepper in a mixing bowl. Melt 1 tablespoon shortening and add. Sift flour and baking powder together and add to above. Melt rest of shortening in frying pan. When hot, drop batter by the tablespoon into hot shortening. Fry on both sides, then drain on absorbent paper. Chopped ham may be added to batter for main course, or fritters may be served as a vegetable with chops. Serves 4 to 6.

College Park, Md.

9137 Baltimore Blvd.

"Where Flavor Goes Eiffel Tower High" is really true in The Gourmet restaurant of this Holiday Inn. A new world of culinary delights served indoors and outdoors pleases every guest. A sightseeing representative is on the premises to help arrange tours for the Washington, Maryland and Virginia area. The Inn is adjacent to the University of Maryland.

COQ AU VIN BOURGUIGNON

Quarter a 2-pound young capon. Season and roll in flour. Brown in butter using heavy skillet. Add 2 chopped shallots and cook until brown. Add 8 ounces Burgundy and let cook 5 minutes. Add 1 cup chicken broth. Sauté ½ pound fresh mushrooms in butter and add. Let all cook 15 minutes over low heat, until juices thicken. Serves 2-4.

BAVARIAN CREAM

    1 pint milk, boiling hot
    ⅔ cup sugar
    10 egg yolks, beaten well
    5 drops vanilla
    1 tablespoon gelatin
    2 tablespoons water
    1 pint whipped cream

Boil milk. Mix sugar with egg yolks and vanilla. Beat until mixture is fluffy, adding boiling milk slowly, stirring constantly. Cook in double boiler until mixture thickens. Add gelatin dissolved in water. Stir until gelatin dissolves. Let cool thoroughly. Fold whipped cream in custard with upward movement. Serves 10-12.

Frederick, Md.

U.S. 40 W. & 15 & 70 S. Bypass

This college town is full of historic memorabilia. Defiant Barbara Fritchie flew the U.S. Flag as "Stonewall" Jackson's army tramped past her house. Her pluck earned Confederate cheers. Maryland Fried Chicken is a delicious reason why visitors always seem to be back at this Inn for dinner.

MARYLAND CHICKEN WITH CORN DODGERS

2 frying chickens, disjointed
1 cup cream

Dredge chickens with seasoned flour and place in heavy skillet with hot cooking oil. Fry until golden. Remove chicken from pan, pour off excess oil, leaving gravy essence in pan. Add cream and flour paste. Add rest of cream when blended. Simmer several minutes and stir while thickening. Season and pour over chicken. Serves 6-8.

Corn Dodgers

Combine 1 cup water ground corn meal, 1 teaspoon salt, 1½ teaspoons sugar, and 1 tablespoon butter or bacon drippings (or more). Boil 1 cup water and pour over dry ingredients. Beat until blended. Pack in greased loaf pan. Chill.

Slice corn meal mush into 1-inch slices, then cut in diamond shape. Dip in beaten egg, then in flour. Brown on both sides in hot cooking oil. Garnish the edge of chicken platter with corn dodgers, adding parsley. Makes about 16-18.

Hagerstown, Md.

U.S. 40, 900 Dual Hwy.

In the "heart of history", this Inn offers unsurpassed food in an exciting location. It's near the Antietam Battlefield, Fort Frederick, Harper's Ferry and Barbara Fritchie's home. There's a view of the Blue Ridge Mts. from both the restaurant and the banquet room. Hagerstown has the largest pipe organ factory in the world.

SWISS STEAK

2 pounds round steak
⅓ cup flour
1 teaspoon salt
   Dash pepper
½ cup butter
1 onion, sliced
1 carrot, sliced
½ cup celery, chopped
½ cup beef suet
2 cups water or
1 #2 can tomato juice
¼ cup mushrooms

Mix flour with salt and pepper and pound into steak. Melt butter and sauté onion, carrot and celery until tender. Cut suet in small pieces and brown in skillet, then put in steak and brown on both sides. Pour in water or tomato juice. Add sautéed vegetables and mushrooms. Cover and bake in a slow oven (350 degrees) for 1½ hours, or until tender. Serves 6.

Salisbury, Md.

Delmar Blvd. N., Rt. 13

Sauna baths, live entertainment in the lounge, and fabulous food in the Eastern Shore dining room await you at this Holiday Inn. A sea of white is always the scene around the Inn in February—Salisbury hosts the National Indoor Tennis Tournament. There's excellent hunting and fishing in the area.

CHICKEN CACCIATORA

    2 chickens (young fryers)
    ¼ cup olive oil or salad oil
    1 teaspoon salt
    ½ teaspoon pepper
    1 tablespoon flour
    2 medium-size onions, chopped fine
    2 cloves garlic, mashed
    1 teaspoon rosemary
    ¼ cup parsley leaves, chopped
    3 tomatoes, cut in pieces
      (or 1½ cups canned tomatoes)

Wash chicken, cut in serving pieces. Sprinkle with salt, pepper and a little flour. Heat oil in heavy skillet, add chicken and brown on all sides. Add onions and slowly cook until onions are tender. Add garlic, rosemary and parsley leaves. Cook and stir well for about 5 minutes. Then add tomatoes, cover and cook 30 minutes slowly until chicken is done. Add tomato juice if more liquid is needed. Serves 6.

Boston-Cambridge, Mass.

1651 Mass., Cambridge, Mass.

Take a dip in the Holiday Inn's year round heated swimming pool. Relax in an invigorating sauna bath. Enjoy your stay in the scientific and educational center of Massachusetts. Just be sure you're always near the Inn for dinner. The homemade bread and individual chess pies are not to be missed. Harvard University is only 3 blocks from the Inn.

INDIVIDUAL CHESS PIES

    ½ pound butter
    2 cups granulated sugar
    6 eggs, beaten
    2 cups seedless raisins
    2 cups chopped walnuts
    1 teaspoon vanilla extract

Cream butter and sugar into a thick, rich consistency. Add eggs and beat until fluffy. Fold raisins and nuts lightly into mixture, then add vanilla. Line 8 individual aluminum molds with pastry. Fill shells and bake in a 425 degree oven for 10 minutes, then 350 degrees until done.

Rich Pastry

    2 cups unsifted flour
    1 teaspoon salt
    ⅔ cup shortening
    ¼ cup cool water

Sift flour and salt into bowl. Add shortening. Blend until it is like coarse meal. Add water and stir with fork until dough forms a ball. Roll out lightly on floured board. Enough for 8 small pies.

Boston, Mass. Framingham

30 Worcester Tpk. Rt. 9

You'll think your'e stepping back into the days of King Arthur when you step into this Inn's Round Table Room. You'll know you're in New England when you try the fabulous seafood served. Boston is only 30 minutes away and the Inn is convenient to many colleges. There's a buffalo farm at nearby Marlborough.

NEW ENGLAND CODFISH BALLS

½ pound dried codfish
2½ cups potatoes, diced
1 egg, well beaten
½ tablespoon butter

Soak codfish in cold water overnight. Drain and pull fish to shred it. Boil potatoes and fish in saucepan of water until potatoes are tender but not mushy. Drain and shake until they are dry. Add egg. Mash thoroughly, add pepper, butter and salt if needed. Use fork and beat until mixture is fluffy and light. Drop by spoonfuls in hot deep fat and cook 1 minute, until golden. Do not cook too many at a time. Drain on paper towel. Serve with Tartare Sauce. Serves 6.

Tartare Sauce

Combine 1 tablespoon chopped parsley, 1 tablespoon minced onion, 1 tablespoon capers, 1 tablespoon chopped olives, 1 tablespoon chopped cucumber pickle, and add to 1 cup mayonnaise. Makes 1¼ cups.

Boston, Mass.-Newton

Rt. 128 S. & Mass. Pike

Here's high-rise luxury overlooking beautiful New England golf courses, only 10 minutes from downtown Boston. There's a piano bar at the Inn. Sightseeing in Boston is endless, but a sauna bath at the Inn is the way to end a day. The Inn is noted for regional type food with a slight trace of European influence.

BEEF BITS IN ALE, NEWTON BARN

2½ pounds beef (bottom round)
½ cup olive oil
2 large onions, chopped
2 teaspoons prepared mustard
½ cup tomato paste
1 cup flour
1½ cups Ballantine ale
3 cups beef broth
1 cup celery, cut
1 cup carrots, cut
1 cup silver skin onions

Cut beef in 1½ inch cubes. Place in heavy skillet with hot oil and cook until brown. Add chopped onion and simmer 3 minutes. Add mustard and tomato paste. Stir until meat is covered. Add flour and mix well. Add ale and simmer for 10 minutes, until alcohol evaporates. Add beef stock, dash oregano, thyme, rosemary and 2 bay leaves. Cook 1 hour, then add vegetables. Cook 1 more hour. Season to taste with salt and pepper. Serve with mashed potatoes or noodles. Serves 8.

Lenox-Pittsfield, Mass.

U.S. 7 & 20. Pittsfield Rd.

This Inn is at the entrance to Berkshires. Snow skiing, ice skating, boating, tennis and picnic areas are all within a few miles of the Inn. The Summer Berkshire Festival ranks among the greatest. In Lenox the Boston Symphony and famous soloists fill the green lawns of Tanglewood with music. The menu at this Inn is filled with delicious delicacies.

CELERY STEAK

Cut 1 pound boneless sirloin or round steak into 2 x ½ x ¼ inch strips. Rub with salt, pepper and flour. Brown in hot cooking oil using heavy skillet. Remove from pan and keep warm.

Sauté 1 green pepper (in strips), 1 cup onion rings, 1½ cups sliced celery in same pan until tender. Add meat and season with chopped ginger, tumeric, lemon juice, adding 1 cup hot beef broth. Simmer covered until tender. Serves 3-4.

APPLE RUM FLOAT

2 cups applesauce
1 cup light brown sugar
1 cup broken pecans
1 cup seedless raisins
⅔ cup dark rum
2 teaspoons cinnamon
1 teaspoon nutmeg
⅛ teaspoon allspice
4 egg whites
½ cup granulated sugar

Preheat oven to 325 degrees. Combine applesauce, brown sugar, pecans, raisins, rum and spices in a saucepan. Bring to a boil. Spoon into a 6-cup casserole. Beat egg whites until stiff and gradually beat in the granulated sugar. Pile lightly on top of pudding in casserole. Bake 15-20 minutes until meringue is brown. Serve at once. Serves 6.

Leominster, Mass.

Mass. Rt. 2 & 12

People from all over the world meet at this Holiday Inn. It's "the" place to stay in Leominster. And Leominster has a lot of visitors. It's known as the "Plastics Capital of the World". Delicious food and a convenient location are two more reasons this Inn is so popular. There are many famous Revolutionary sites nearby.

BAKED STUFFED JUMBO SHRIMP

24 raw shrimp
6 ounces crab meat
¾ cup butter
1½ teaspoons paprika
½ teaspoon salt
¼ teaspoon white pepper
Dash cayenne
2 cups fresh bread crumbs
6 ounces dry sherry

Peel, devein and leave tails on shrimp. Cut pockets through center of backs. Chop crab meat fine, and mix with remaining ingredients. Stuff shrimp with crab meat mixture and place in shallow pan, backs up. Bake at 450 degrees for about 5 minutes. Serves 6-8.

CLAMS CASINO

36 cherry stone clams
6 slices raw bacon, minced
¼ cup diced green pepper
½ cup diced pimento
1 teaspoon minced shallots

Arrange clams in shells on a bed of rock salt. Sprinkle with bacon, green pepper, pimento and shallots. Bake in a hot 400 degree oven for 10 to 12 minutes, or until bacon is golden brown. Serves 6.

Seekonk, Mass. (Providence, R.I. - East)

U.S. 6 off I-195

This Inn's menu is where the real interest lies, though it's near interesting sights and on the direct route to Cape Cod. The best introduction to the delicious specialties is Seafood Delight for Two . . . a sampling of five native foods from the sea. Baked Boston Scrod and Stuffed Lobster are cooked expertly and lavishly sauced. Traditional Baked Indian Pudding à la Mode is a 3-star dessert.

SEAFOOD DELIGHT FOR TWO

Boiled Lobster

Whole 2½-pound lobster

Prepare fish stock with water, sliced onion, shallots, carrots, salt, pepper, herbs and white wine. Strain. Throw lobster into boiling stock and boil 8-10 minutes. Simmer 15-20 minutes, depending on size. Serve halved lengthwise, claws broken, with melted butter.

French Fried Shrimp

1 pound cleaned and deveined shrimp

Beat 2 eggs, add ½ cup flour, ¾ teaspoon salt and dash freshly ground pepper. Stir in 1 teaspoon butter and 1 teaspoon rum or Worcestershire sauce. Dip shrimp in batter. Fry until golden in deep fat. Drain on absorbent paper.

Clams Fried In Beer Batter

1 to 2 cups shucked clams

Place 1 cup flour, 1 teaspoon salt and 1 tablespoon paprika in a bowl. Gradually add 1 bottle beer, beating until batter is smooth. Dip clams lightly in flour, then in beer batter. Drop into hot oil and cook quickly. Drain on absorbent paper.

Scallops and Crab Legs complete platter.

Worcester, Mass.

Dwtn. at Southbridge & Myrtle Sts.

The pastry chef at this Holiday Inn is known for his delicious cherry pies. Guests going to and from the industrial metropolis of Worcester and nearby college students are all aware of this favorite pastry. Skiers who come in from wintry winds find hearty dishes to enjoy. There's no season for the popular à la carte dinner menu. Even lunch becomes the finest hour for travelers in a hurry. You'll always take time for a piece of cherry pie and coffee.

CHERRY PIE WORCESTER

1 to 1½ cups sugar
2½ tablespoons flour
¼ teaspoon salt
1 quart tart red cherries or 1 can red pie cherries

Mix sugar, flour and salt together. Wash cherries and pit them. Line pie pan with pastry and add cherry mixture (flour, sugar, salt and cherries). Cover with top crust. Bake at 450 degrees for 10 minutes, then reduce temperature to 350 degrees and bake 25 minutes longer.

Pastry

Sift 3 cups flour with ¾ teaspoon salt and blend in ⅔ cup shortening with pastry blender or two knives. Add 4 to 5 tablespoons water, a little at a time, until dough will hold together. Divide into 2 parts. Roll out on floured board to fit 9-inch pie pan.

TINY CHERRY TARTS

Soften 1 cup butter and 2 3-ounce package cream cheese. Beat until creamy. Add cups sifted flour, blending after each cup. Work until dough is smooth. Chill well in covered container or wrap well before chilling. Shape into 1-inch balls and place on baking sheet. Make a well in each ball with thumb. Bake at 425 degrees for 12 15 minutes, or until golden. Cool. Drain cherry preserves and use to fill wells. Make 3 dozen.

Adrian, Mich.

U.S. 223

This Inn is easy to find — just a half hour off the Ohio Turnpike. Sports fans know it's the place to stay — close to the Irish Hills Sports Park and the Michigan International Speedway. The Inn is next door to Adrian College, just minutes from Siena Heights College. It only takes one meal to find out why this is the town's favorite dining spot.

RED SNAPPER AMANDINE

    4 6-8-ounce red snapper fillets
    ½ cup margarine
    ½ teaspoon onion juice
    ¼ cup blanched almonds
    1 tablespoon lemon juice

Wash and dry fish, dust lightly with salt and flour. Heat half the margarine and onion juice in a heavy skillet, cook fish until light brown. Remove fish and place on a hot serving dish. Pour off excess grease in pan, add remaining margarine, finely slivered almonds and brown slowly. Add lemon juice. When mixture foams, pour over fish. 4 servings.

CHOCOLATE PARTY COOKIES

    1 bar German sweet chocolate
    1 beaten egg
    1 cup powdered sugar
    1 teaspoon butter
    1 teaspoon vanilla
    1 package colored miniature marsh-
      mallows

Melt chocolate and add egg, sugar, butter and vanilla. Add marshmallows and let set for a few minutes. Press into 2 rolls with greased fingers, sprinkle with chopped nuts and coconut. Wrap in waxed paper and chill in refrigerator. Slice when ready to serve. 2 dozen or more.

Albion, Mich.

Interstate 94 & 28 Mile Rd.

Albion is between two cities (Battle Creek and Jackson) so you can enjoy the advantages of country and city living. The Inn's restaurant is an Inmans. Try the Beef Tenderloin en Brochette flamed at your table, homemade cheese and bread and you'll know why Inmans is synonymous with extraordinary dining. Old barn wood decorates the bar where you can enjoy organ and piano music.

BROILED SHRIMP STUFFED WITH CRAB MEAT

    1 pound jumbo shrimp
    ¾ cup dried bread
    ¼ cup diced onion
    ¼ cup essence mushrooms
    ¼ cup sauterne
    1 cup fresh crab meat
    1 clove minced garlic

Peel, devein and split uncooked shrimp. Put bread, onion and mushrooms through a fine sieve. Add sauterne and season with salt and pepper. Mix into fine paste. Cook crab meat and shred. Add to mixture and blend in garlic last. Stuff shrimp. Top each with butter and broil 4-5 minutes to a golden brown. Serves 4-6.

CHICKEN LIVERS BORDELAISE

Sauté ¼ cup minced onions and ¼ cup fresh sliced mushrooms in butter until golden brown. Dust 1 cup chicken livers in seasoned flour and add to mushroom-onion mixture. Sauté about 10 minutes until livers are thoroughly cooked. Add 1½ ounces Burgundy. Cook until wine is reduced. Serve in casserole with pilaf. Serves 2.

Ann Arbor, Mich.-West

I-94, Exit 172

The University of Michigan campus and Medical Center are near this Holiday Inn. Of particular interest at this outstanding educational institution is the Baird Carrillon (the bells ranging from 12 pounds to 12 tons peal out in regular recitals). Football season always draws a crowd to this Inn. Superb dining awaits you year round—truly gourmet fare.

TUNA STROGANOFF WITH RICE

    1 lemon (juice of)
   12 ounces white meat tuna
      (drained bite-size)
   ¼ pound butter
    1 cup onions, minced fine
    1 tablespoon flour
   ⅔ cup tomato paste
  1 ⅔ cups water
   ¼ teaspoon garlic seasoning
    1 teaspoon salt
  1½ teaspoons Worcestershire sauce
   ⅓ cup sugar
   ¾ teaspoon paprika
  1½ cups dairy sour cream

Sprinkle lemon juice over drained tuna. Sauté onions in butter over low heat for 5 minutes. Blend in flour. Add tomato paste, water, garlic seasoning, salt, Worcestershire sauce, sugar and paprika. Blend and bring to a boil. Add sour cream, then fold in tuna. Serve in casserole with rice. Serves 6.

Battle Creek, Mich.

Interstate 94 at Capital

You don't have to order cereal for breakfast, but more breakfast food is made in Battle Creek than in any other city in the world! Take a tour through the nearby Kellogg plant and Kellogg Bird Sanctuary. The Sirloin Steak and African Lobster Tail combination entree is the answer for the undecided at dinner. Everyone decides to order homemade pie.

ERNIE MOORE'S BOARDWALK

    2 pieces rye bread
      Tossed salad
    2 slices turkey breast
    2 slices ham
    3 slices tomato
    2 slices Swiss cheese
    2 slices raw bacon
   ½ tomato
      Parmesan cheese

Place rye bread in the center of a steak platter. Completely cover the rye bread with an ample portion of tossed salad. Place turkey breast over lettuce. Place slices of ham over turkey, then slices of tomato over ham, Swiss cheese over tomato, then raw bacon. Place ½ tomato on the raw bacon. Sprinkle with Parmesan cheese. Place on a metal tray and put in the broiler until bacon has been cooked to a golden brown and the Swiss cheese has melted. Serve Thousand Island dressing on the side. For variation, after removing from the broiler, shrimp or lobster may be added. 1 serving.

Benton Harbor, Mich.

I-94 Exit 28 & U.S. 31

You'll be glad you "picked" this Holiday Inn in Benton Harbor . . . home of the world's largest open air cash-to-grower fruit market. Lake Michigan is within minutes. Children enjoy the nearby House of David Amusement Park. You can look forward to a putting green, shuffleboard and sauna baths at this Inn. The Chuck Wagon buffet on Sundays always draws a hungry crowd.

FRESH STRAWBERRY PIE

1 cup sugar
¼ cup cornstarch
¼ teaspoon salt
1 cup water or less
6 cups strawberries, hulled

Mix sugar, cornstarch and salt in saucepan. Slowly stir in water (using less if berries are juicy). Add 2 cups halved strawberries. Cook over low heat stirring constantly and mashing berries until mixture thickens and boils 3 minutes. Remove from heat and cool slightly. Layer remaining 4 cups berries (cut side down) in even design circles in baked pastry shell. Spoon cooled strawberry glaze over berries. Chill 1 hour. Serve plain or top with ice cream or whipped cream. Makes 1 9-inch pie.

Pastry

1½ cups sifted flour
3 tablespoons water
½ cup shortening
½ teaspoon salt

Make a paste with ¼ cup of the flour and water. Cut shortening into the dry flour and salt until pieces are size of small peas. Add flour paste and mix until dough comes together and can be made into a ball. Roll out and bake in a pie pan for 10 to 12 minutes at 450 degrees.

Dearborn, Mich.

U.S. 12 & 24. Michigan Ave.

Tours to the nearby Ford Motor Plant may be arranged at this Holiday Inn. Be sure to visit the Henry Ford Museum too, an exceptionally fine museum of Americana. Greenfield Village adjoins the museum. It can be viewed from a horse drawn carriage, on foot, or from the Paddle-wheeler "Suwanee". This Inn awaits your return with excellent Prime Rib (to name only one tempting entree on the menu) and live entertainment in the Lounge.

STEAK EN BROCHETTE

2 pounds beef tenderloin
12 mushrooms
12 small onions
3 green peppers, cut
(strips 1 inch wide)
3-4 tomatoes, quartered
4-6 skewers
2 tablespoons butter

Cut beef in cubes. Sauté mushrooms in butter if fresh mushrooms are used. Place beef, mushrooms, onions, pepper, and tomatoes on skewers and repeat until skewers are serving size desired. Brush meat and vegetables with melted butter and season. Charbroil or place on broiler rack in oven. Cook until meat is doneness desired and vegetables are tender. Serves 4-6.

Detroit, Mich.-Airport

Indus. Expwy., Romulus, Mich.

Industrialists coming and going to the automobile capital of the world find this Holiday Inn most convenient. It's adjacent to the Detroit Metropolitan Airport. The "Five Nation's Favorites" on the menu delight guests. Sightseeing tips: The Henry Ford Museum and Ford Rotunda are open daily during the summer months.

IMPERIAL CHOW MEIN

6 large black mushrooms
1 pound beef tenderloin
1/3 teaspoon sugar
1 teaspoon salt
1 teaspoon M.S.G.
1/3 cup soya sauce
1/3 cup cooking oil
3 slices fresh ginger root
3 stalks scallions, chopped
2 stalks celery, sliced
1 green pepper, sliced
1 pound fresh bean sprouts
2 tablespoons cornstarch

Wash mushrooms and cover with water. Soak 2-3 minutes. Boil 1 hour and cool. Save water. Slice mushrooms. Season meat with sugar, salt, M.S.G. and soya sauce. Place 3 tablespoons cooking oil in skillet and add seasoned meat (cut in 1/8 inch slices). Do not overcook meat. Remove to warm dish. Add rest of cooking oil and cook finely chopped ginger lightly. Add scallions, celery and pepper, then mushrooms. Add bean sprouts. Cook uncovered for 3 minutes. Season to taste. Add beef and mix well. Dissolve cornstarch in 1/2 cup cold water and add to thicken. Pour over Hong Kong noodles. Serves 6.

Detroit, Mich. Downtown

1331 Trumbull

Saturday night is Italian Night at this Holiday Inn. Even avid sports fans find it hard to leave the spaghetti for games at Tiger Stadium, only 4 blocks away. Convenience is the best way to describe this Inn, with the heart of downtown Detroit only ¾ mile away, and the bridge and tunnel to Canada within 5 minutes.

DEVILED EGGS A LA RUSSE

Serve deviled egg halves on a bed of lettuce with slices of tomato. Cover the eggs with Russian or Thousand Island dressing.

Russian Dressing

2 tablespoons celery, chopped
2 tablespoons green pepper, chopped
2 tablespoons sweet pickles, diced
1 tablespoon pimento
2 tablespoons chili sauce
1 tablespoon tomato catsup
1 cup mayonnaise

Mix ingredients (except mayonnaise). Then blend in mayonnaise with 1 teaspoon confectioner's sugar. Makes 1½ cups.

ORANGE FLAMBÉ

Cut an orange in half and section out as you would a grapefruit. Cut a small piece from the bottom of the orange so it will sit flat on the plate. Top with a scoop of orange sherbet and place on top of this a lump of sugar which has been soaked in pure lemon extract. When served, the lump of sugar is lighted with a match. Serves 1.

Detroit, Mich.
Northland

West Eight Mile Road

This is a gourmet's haven—from the homemade soup to the strawberry tarts. The Friday Fish Fry Buffet is served from a rowboat. Alligators and turtles are made of hand molded homemade bread. There's a daily Soup and Sandwich buffet in the Library Lounge (it's a lounge that looks like a library that isn't very quiet in the evenings because of the live entertainment).

CORNED BEEF

5-pound piece beef brisket
6 peppercorns
½ clove garlic

Select piece of brisket with streak of fat running through it for best flavor. Wash well under running water. Place in deep kettle and cover with cold water. Add peppercorns and garlic clove. Bring to boiling point, remove the foam that forms on top, then cover and simmer until meat is tender. Some boiling water may need to be added to keep meat covered. Allow 3 hours or longer. Cook in stock. When serving, slice thin as desired and add a little stock if more moisture is needed. The stock is excellent to use in cooking cabbage. Serves 8 to 10.

FRESH HORSERADISH SAUCE

½ cup cream
4 tablespoons horseradish, grated
1½ tablespoons vinegar
½ teaspoon salt
Dash cayenne

Beat cream until stiff. Mix horseradish, vinegar, salt and cayenne. Add to cream and blend. Makes approximately ½ cup.

Detroit, Mich.
Southfield

I-696 John Lodge Expwy.

Windsor, Canada is just across the Detroit River. But you'll find it hard to leave this Inn with its beautiful Spanish decor. Slip into a swivel rocking chair and relax over something cool in the Red Wing Hockey Lounge. Find out why guests keep coming back to enjoy the fine food. This is a fisherman's dream world—there are over 400 lakes in this county.

ROAST PRIME RIB

5- to 6-pound standing rib roast
Seasonings

Wipe meat, season and place on rack in open pan with fat side up. Cook in 325 degree oven at 22 to 24 minutes a pound, depending on doneness desired. If meat thermometer is used, Rare: 140 degrees, Medium: 160 degrees, Well Done: 170 degrees. Do not let thermometer touch bone. Serve with Yorkshire Pudding. Serves 8 to 10.

Yorkshire Pudding

1 cup flour
½ teaspoon salt
2 eggs
2 tablespoons beef drippings
1 cup milk

Sift flour and salt. Blend well beaten eggs, 1 tablespoon drippings and milk. Add to flour and beat several minutes in mixer or with rotary beater. Use cake pan or muffin tins, well greased. Add other tablespoon of drippings in bottom of pan or tins. Pour in batter. Bake at 450 degrees for 20 minutes. Serves 8 to 10.

Detroit, Mich.-Warren

32035 Van Dyke. St. 53

A lot of people leave here knowing a lot more about cars — the General Motors training school is very near this Holiday Inn. Of course you can see the famous auto assembly lines in action in Detroit, just a few minutes away. Make this Holiday Inn your headquarters while you sightsee. The Family Style Chicken Dinners served are delicious.

SKILLET BROWNED CHICKEN

    2 chickens (fryers)
      Cooking oil or shortening
 1½ to 2 cups hot milk or water

Wash chickens, cut in serving pieces. Dredge with flour and add seasonings. Place in heavy skillet with hot cooking oil to nearly cover. Brown quickly on each side and let cook until done at lower heat. Do not overcrowd pieces in skillet. When all pieces are done, keep chicken warm and pour off grease except 1 to 2 tablespoons. Add 2 tablespoons flour, and scrape all bits of chicken from bottom of pan and stir well. Add hot milk or water and make gravy. Serves family of 6.

SNOW-WHIPPED POTATOES

 6 to 8 potatoes
    2 tablespoons butter
 ½ cup rich milk or cream

Peel potatoes and cut in quarters. Place in saucepan with enough boiling water to cover. Heat milk and butter. Use potato masher or put through a ricer when potatoes are done. Add hot milk and butter gradually. Beat well. Leave just moist enough so potatoes will look snow-whipped in peaks. Season and serve. Serves family of 6.

Flint, Mich.

St. 121 at U.S. 23 & I-75

This Inn is a favorite with busy people who come to the "Vehicle City", and for those who work in this industrial city too. There's a good reason for the Inn's popularity — outstanding food. The Inn is located across the street from several General Motors Plants (Flint is the largest General Motors plant city in the world).

YANKEE POT ROAST

    2 pounds round steak
      (1½ to 2 inches thick)
    3 tablespoons bacon drippings
    4 potatoes, pared, quartered
    6 carrots, scraped
    6 onions, cleaned

Flour steak generously. Place in hot iron kettle with bacon drippings. Brown on both sides quickly. Cover and place in 300 degree oven for 3½-4 hours. About 1 hour before done add potatoes, carrots and onions. If gravy 'around meat not thickness desired add 1 tablespoon flour with little water when meat and vegetables are done. Serves 4-6.

BROILED CHICKEN

Cut 1 chicken in half. Season with salt and pepper. Dust with flour and dot with butter. Arrange chicken on broiler pan, cut side up.

Broil, allowing 15-18 minutes for each side (skin side requires more time). Baste with ¼ cup cream last half of broiling time. Serves 2.

Grand Haven-Spring Lake Michigan

940 Savidge Street

Beautifully located on the water, this Inn has a marina which can accommodate 40 boats. Begin your discovery of this fishing paradise by taking a cruise boat or charter for Coho and Chinook salmon fishing. Start each day with French Toast - it's almost a breach of tradition not to sample it! Enjoy exquisite meals in the Dragon Restaurant with its Nordic atmosphere.

FRENCH TOAST

    4 eggs
    1½ cups milk
    ½ teaspoon salt (scant)
    16 slices dry white bread

Beat eggs until creamy, add milk and beat approximately 3 minutes. Add salt and mix well. Soak bread in mixture for about 30 seconds — don't shake off excess. Cook on lightly buttered grill or fry pan over medium heat until crispy on both sides. Cut diagonally and overlap on plate. Dust lightly with powdered sugar. Serves 8.

BROILED SALMON STEAKS

    2 pounds salmon, 1-inch steaks
    ¼ cup oil
    2 tablespoons lemon juice
    1 teaspoon grated lemon rind
    ½ teaspoon salt
      Pinch dry marjoram
      Pinch pepper

Rinse salmon. Dry thoroughly. Combine remaining ingredients for marinade. Pour marinade over steaks and let stand for 15 minutes. Turn once. Place on greased broiler rack about 2 to 3 inches from heat. Allow 10 to 15 minutes for broiling, until fish flakes easily when touched with a fork. Turn once while cooking and brush with marinade. Serve with melted butter and lemon slices. Serves 4 to 6.

Grand Rapids, Mich. South

250 28th St. S.W.

Test your gourmet taste in this Inn's luxurious Americana dining room. Try the Coffee Shop for informal dining. Only 5 minutes from downtown, the Inn is at the Gateway to Michigan's Water Wonderland. Hundreds of lakes, streams, parks and beaches are within easy driving distance. Visit the world's only Furniture Museum in Grand Rapids.

BAKED MACARONI IN CHEESE SAUCE WITH MUSHROOMS

    2 cups elbow macaroni
    1½ quarts water, boiling
    1 small can mushrooms
    2 tablespoons butter
    1 tablespoon onion, minced
    ⅔ cup flour
    3 cups milk
    1 teaspoon salt
      Pinch paprika
      Pinch dry mustard
    ½ teaspoon Worcestershire sauce
    6 ounces Cheddar cheese, cubed

Add macaroni to salted water and cook until tender, about 18 minutes. Drain broth from mushrooms. Melt butter in saucepan, add onion and fry until golden. Then add mushrooms and fry 5 minutes. Add flour, stir until smooth, simmer slowly for 5 minutes. Add milk, bring to a boil while stirring very smooth, then add salt, paprika, dry mustard, Worcestershire and cheese. Reduce heat and stir until all is blended thoroughly. Drain macaroni for 5 minutes. Add to sauce mix and place in casserole. Sprinkle with bread crumbs, butter and paprika. Brown in a 400 degree oven for 25 minutes. Serves 6.

Jackson, Mich.

Jct. I-94 & U.S. 127

Nightly specials in the dining room make every meal a special event. Jackson is situated on both banks of the Grand River. The city's major attraction is Sparks Foundation County Park with its world famous Illuminated Cascades. Every evening the rainbow-hued waters rise high and tumble down a giant stairway.

STUFFED SPANISH PEPPERS

6 large green peppers
3 tablespoons butter
1 small chopped onion
1 tablespoon chopped parsley
6 tablespoons chopped ham
3 hard-boiled eggs, chopped
1 cup hot cream
6 chopped mushrooms
1 tablespoon lemon juice
½ cup bread crumbs, buttered

Cut off tops of peppers and scoop out insides. Parboil for 10 minutes. Put butter in frying pan and add onion, parsley, ham and eggs. Fry 9 minutes, stirring often. Add hot cream and mushrooms. Let come to a boil. Stir in lemon juice and stuff peppers. Cover with bread crumbs and bake in a 400 degree oven until crumbs are brown. Serves 6.

GERMAN POTATO SALAD

Sprinkle ¼ cup minced onion and ¼ cup minced parsley over 6 sliced cooked potatoes in frying pan. Season, adding dash Worcestershire sauce. Dice 4 strips crisp cooked bacon, add ¼-½ cup white vinegar and ¼-½ cup chicken broth. Heat. Mix carefully with potatoes, taking care not to break slices. Serve warm. Serves 4-6.

Kalamazoo, Mich.
Crosstown

220 E. Crosstown Pkwy.

One side of the menu in the Viennese Lantern Dining Room has "American Favorites", the other side has "Foreign Favorites" . . . Paniertes Wiener Schnitzel, Zwiebel Rostbraten, Szekely Gulasch. You can choose your own appetizers from the Gourmet Table. The Inn is located mid-town in Kalamazoo halfway to anywhere in the Mall City.

CHICKEN FRICASSEE

1 heavy stewing hen
1 small box frozen peas
1 small box frozen pearl onions
1 small box frozen little carrots

Wash chicken well, cut up as for frying. Place chicken in a large pot, add water to half cover the chicken, and bring to a boil. Add 1 large carrot, 2 stalks celery, 1 medium onion (all diced) and boil until tender. Remove chicken from stock and cool. Skim excess fat from stock and make a roux of the 2 tablespoons fat and 3 tablespoons flour.

Cook all of the frozen vegetables until nearly done and strain. Make the sauce by adding roux to stock, stir until fairly thick. Beat 3 egg yolks with some of the hot sauce until smooth, then add to sauce. Remove chicken from bones and cut into bite-size pieces. Squeeze juice of ½ lemon into finished sauce, add vegetables and chicken, reheat and serve. May be served with buttered noodles or tea biscuits. Serves 6 to 8.

Lansing, Mich.-East

3121 E. Grand River Rd.

Coming to Lansing on business? This Holiday Inn is only minutes away from major firms in Michigan's "Capital City". A luxurious pool and a popular cocktail lounge are for your relaxation at the Inn. Spaghetti is the specialty each Monday night. Everyone enjoys the Friday Fish Frys too. Michigan State University, the oldest land grant school in the country, is only 3 minutes from the Inn.

CREAMED HAM AND TURKEY AU GRATIN

4 tablespoons butter
1 green pepper, shred fine
1 cup mushrooms
2 tablespoons flour
1 cup turkey broth
1 cup top milk
1 pimento, sliced thin strips
1 cup cooked turkey, diced large
1 cup cooked ham, diced large
2 eggs, hard-boiled
   Salt and pepper
2 tablespoons sherry (optional)
½ cup buttered bread crumbs
½ cup grated cheese

Melt butter in heavy skillet. Sauté green pepper and mushrooms. Remove, add flour and blend. Add broth, cook until thickened, then add milk and cook. Add pimento, turkey and ham, then sliced eggs, seasonings and sherry last. Heat 1 minute. Place in casserole or individual casseroles. Combine cheese and crumbs. Sprinkle on top. Run under broiler until crumb-cheese mixture is brown. Serves 6 to 8.

Lansing, Mich.-South

S. Penn. & Cedar. Exit I-96

Among the beautiful elm and chestnut trees stands Michigan's impressive granite Capitol, open daily to the public. This Holiday Inn is conveniently located for sightseeing. Guests enjoy Spanish decor in the Inn's La Fiesta Room. Spaghetti, Perch and Fried Chicken vie for popularity—all are delicious. There's live entertainment in the lounge.

PERCH

2 pounds perch
1 cup corn meal or flour
1 teaspoon salt
1 cup cooking oil (or more)

Wash fish well, wipe dry with paper towel. Place corn meal and salt in a paper sack. Add fish, one at a time, and shake to cover well. Then place in heavy skillet of hot oil 1 inch deep. Keep fish apart, cooking a few at a time. Turn carefully with spatula as fish brown. Test for doneness with fork to see if it flakes. Cook 8 to 10 minutes, depending on thickness of fish. Serve wtih Tartare Sauce. Serves 4 to 5.

Tartare Sauce

1 cup mayonnaise
2 tablespoons chopped onion
2 tablespoons chopped capers
2 tablespoons chopped parsley
1 tablespoon chopped pickles
1 tablespoon chopped olives

Mix and serve with fish. Makes 1½ cups.

Marquette, Mich.

Wash. St. & U.S. 41 Bypass

Leave on a snowmobile safari or in a horse drawn sleigh right from the Inn. Try a martini garnished with spiced mushrooms in the Viking Ship Lounge. Take a free sauna bath then leap into a snow bank in the Viking tradition. Lake Superior is right at your doorstep here. Be sure to order a "Pasty" . . . the old original Cornish miner meat pie.

CRAB HARWELL

1 can (very small) crab meat
3 to 4 tablespoons mayonnaise
Lemon juice to taste
6 large mushroom caps

Blend crab meat, mayonnaise and lemon juice. Wash mushroom caps. Broil open side up for 5 minutes, 3 or 4 inches from flame. Remove and stuff with crab meat mixture. Dot with Cheddar cheese and broil 3 to 4 minutes more. Serve immediately.

PASTY

Blend ¼ cup lard into 3 cups flour. Add 1 cup finely ground suet. Mix well. Add 1-2 teaspoons cold water to make dough a little more moist than ordinary pastry. Divide dough into 4 pieces. Roll each size of dinner plate.

Mix 1 pound diced beef and ½ pound diced pork. On ½ of each piece of dough place a layer of finely chopped potatoes (½ inch thick). Season and add thin layer sliced turnips, very thin layer chopped onion, a sprinkle of parsley. Cover with ¼ of meat mixture. Season again. Top each with piece of butter size of walnut. Fold uncovered portion of dough over filled portion. Crimp edges. Pasty should be shape of half moon. Make 1 inch slit in top of dough. Place on greased cookie sheet. Bake at 400 degrees for 1 hour. Makes 4 servings.

Midland, Mich.

U.S. 10 & Eastman Rds.

Midland is the home of Dow Chemical Co. and Dow Corning (tour available). It's no wonder this Inn can take reservations in several languages — guests are from all over the world. A diamond shaped pool, sauna baths and the Valhalla Lounge are for relaxation in this ultramodern Inn. There are buffet breakfasts and luncheons for those in a hurry.

CREAM OF PUMPKIN SOUP

3 cups chicken stock
¼ cup minced onion
3 cups pumpkin
1½ cups crushed pineapple
Light cream

Bring chicken stock to a boil. Add onion to butter and sauté in frying pan. Combine with stock, adding pumpkin and pineapple. Simmer about 20 minutes, until soup starts to thicken. Add cream until desired consistency. Place 1 teaspoonful whipped cream on each bowl when serving. Serves 4-6.

BAKED CHICKEN HOLIDAY

1 2-pound chicken, quartered
Butter
1½ cups sliced mushrooms
½ cup sliced onion
¼ cup water

Roll chicken in flour. Fry in a heavy skillet with butter until golden brown, turning frequently. Place in Dutch oven, cover with mushrooms and onions. Add water and cover tightly. Bake in a 350 degree oven for about 1½ hours. Serves 2-4.

Mount Pleasant, Mich.

Jct. M 20 & U.S. 27

Tee off on this Inn's own 18-hole golf course. Try your luck in the lakes right on the Inn's property. You'll never run out of things to do here. Enjoy relaxed, gourmet dining in the Fireside Room, live entertainment in the lounge. The Inn is only 1 hour from major ski areas — only 20 minutes from day and night skiing at Mott Mountain.

LAKE MICHIGAN WHITEFISH

Place a 2-pound whitefish on an oiled rack above 1½ to 2 inches of Court Bouillon. Use a fish steamer or piece of cheesecloth to protect fish from breaking. Simmer 15 to 20 minutes with cover. Test doneness of fish. If it does not look translucent when pricked with a fork, it is nearly done. Remove fish and keep warm until ready to serve. Serve with Whitefish Sauce. 4 servings.

Court Bouillon

    3 quarts water
    1 tablespoon butter
    2 teaspoons salt
      Juice of 1 lemon
    2 peppercorns
    1 bay leaf
    ¼ cup diced onion

Combine ingredients and bring to a boil. Then simmer for 20 minutes. Use for steaming fish.

Whitefish Sauce

Strain leftover court bouillon. Use 2 cups, adding 1 cup rich milk and ¼ cup milk which have been blended with 2 tablespoons flour. Stir over low heat in a saucepan until sauce is thickened. Two finely diced hard-boiled eggs may be added, if desired. Also seasonings.

Saginaw, Mich.

On Rt. M-81 W.

You're in the "bean pot" of the nation, where beans are the king of the crops. This Holiday Inn has a gourmet way with beans, but its fresh perch, homemade bread, rolls and biscuits have gained fame throughout Saginaw Valley. Skiing at Apple Mountain is only 2 miles away. The Bavarian Festival in nearby Frankenmuth is fun for all in the fall.

PAN-FRIED LAKE PERCH

    1½ pounds perch, fillets

Dip fillets in egg and milk mixture. Dredge in flour and cracker crumbs which have been mixed. Fry in 365 degree cooking oil until golden brown. Time will vary according to thickness of fillets. Serve with lemon wedges and tartare sauce. Serves 4.

GREEN BEAN CASSEROLE

    2 pounds sliced green beans
    1 cup water chestnuts, sliced
    1 can bean sprouts, drained
    ½ pound fresh mushrooms, sliced
    1 medium-sized onion, chopped
    2 cups medium cream sauce
      Grated cheese
      Salt
    1 can French fried onions

In a 2-quart casserole, place half of beans (cooked), half of water chestnuts, half of bean sprouts, half of mushrooms and half of onions. Cover with half of cream sauce. Sprinkle lightly with salt and cheese. Repeat each layer. Bake at 375 degrees for 30 minutes or until bubbling hot. Top with onion rings the last 10 minutes. Serves 6.

Traverse City, Mich.

Downtown on the Bay

Sail in during the summer! Use a snowmobile in the winter. End any day with a splash in the Inn's heated pool. Every room overlooks Grand Traverse Bay. Front door fishing is year'round — there's ice fishing too. Any season is the time for a dazzling array of trout dishes. Another very special specialty of the Inn (guests often ask for the recipe) is Chicken Creole Sauce. Just five minutes away is Holiday's Family Ski Resort — night skiing and a special children's program.

TROUT WITH ALMONDS

```
6  pounds lake trout fillets
2  cups flour
1  tablespoon salt
1  teaspoon white pepper
1  tablespoon M.S.G.
¼  teaspoon garlic powder
1  cup butter
1½ pounds almonds
1  cup Rhine or Riesling wine
```

Clean and wipe, but do not wash the trout after cutting into portion sizes. Dredge in seasoned flour. Mix flour, salt, white pepper, M.S.G. and garlic powder.

Using a large heavy frying pan, heat ½ cup of the butter to bubbling point. Brown trout for 4 minutes on each side. Put trout in a warm oven to keep hot.

Skin and slice almonds. Using a small fry pan, heat remaining butter until deep golden brown. Then saute the almonds until golden, tossing them about so that they will all color equally. Add wine to the almonds and heat. Pour over cooked trout and serve. Serves 8 to 10 people.

Duluth, Minn.

250 S. 1st Ave. E.

A loaf of homemade bread is brought to your table as soon as you are seated in this Inn's restaurant. You can enjoy a beautiful view of Lake Superior, the Aerial Bridge and delicious food served buffet style all at the same time. For fun, take a tour around Lake Superior, take in a pop concert in the Leif Erickson Park. Downtown Duluth is within walking distance.

SPAGHETTI LOAF

Boil 2 cups broken spaghetti with 1 clove garlic in salted water until tender. Remove garlic, drain spaghetti and rinse.

Melt ½ pound sharp American cheese in 1⅔ cups milk, over boiling water. Add 2 beaten eggs. Add ¾ teaspoon salt, ¼ cup minced parsley, 1 tablespoon grated onion and spaghetti. Mix thoroughly. Pour into buttered loaf pan. Bake in 350 degree oven for 1 hour. Serves 6.

TUNA EN CASSEROLE

```
1  medium onion
4  tablespoons cooking oil
4  tablespoons flour
2  cups tomato juice
1  teaspoon sugar
¾  teaspoon salt
   Few grains cayenne
   Juice of 1 lemon
1  cup flaked tuna
2  cups mashed potatoes
```

Chop onion, add to cooking oil and cook until tender. Blend in flour and add tomato juice, sugar, paprika, salt, cayenne and lemon juice. Cook, stirring constantly, until thickened. Add tuna and pour into casserole. Cover with seasoned potatoes. Bake in a moderate 350 degree oven for about 20 minutes, or until potatoes are browned. Serves 4.

Minneapolis, Minn.
Central

1313 Nicollet Ave., Downtown

Here's an island of comfort right in downtown Minneapolis. After a busy day, enjoy a dip in the round indoor pool, take a sauna bath, sip something cool in the Brandywine Lounge. Dine lavishly on superb continental food in the rooftop Starlite Room. The Inn really comes to life later in "Pierre's". The University of Minneapolis is only 20 minutes away.

LASAGNA, MARINARA SAUCE

- 8 ounces lasagna noodles
- 1 pound ricotta cheese
- 8 ounces mozzarella cheese
- ½ cup Parmesan cheese

Cook noodles in boiled salted water for 25 minutes, or until tender, stirring frequently. Drain and arrange in a shallow 2½-quart baking dish. Make 3 layers each of cooked noodles, ricotta, mozzarella (sliced thin), Marinara Sauce and Parmesan cheese. Bake in a preheated slow 325 degree oven for about 45 minutes. Makes 6 servings.

Marinara Sauce

- 1 medium onion, minced
- 2 garlic cloves, minced
- 2 tablespoons olive oil
- 1 pound ground beef
- 3½ cups Italian style tomatoes
- 1 can (Counes) tomato paste
- 2 cups water
- 1 tablespoon salt
- ⅛ teaspoon cayenne
- 1 teaspoon sugar
  Pinch ground basil
- 1 bay leaf

Brown onion and garlic lightly in oil in saucepan. Add meat and cook until browned. Stir with a fork. Add remaining ingredients and simmer uncovered for 1½ hours. Remove bay leaf.

Moorhead, Minn.
Jct. I-94 & U.S. 75

Try a delicious meal in the Bon Vivant Room in this charming Holiday Inn. There's excellent hunting within a mile of the Inn and the chef will prepare your game (pheasant, duck, etc.). Minnesota's fabulous lake country is less than an hour way. Fort Abercrombie, frontier fort of the Red River, is 30 miles from the Inn.

BAKED CHICKEN WITH WILD RICE DRESSING

4- to 5-pound roasting chicken

Wash chicken thoroughly. Cook giblets in separate saucepan with 1 cup water until tender. Rub fowl with salt. Stuff with Wild Rice Dressing and sew cavity. Tie legs and wings close to body. Rub with soft butter. Bake in shallow pan with ½ cup water for 2-3 hours at 350 degrees (about 35 minutes per pound). Make gravy using flour-water paste to thicken juices, adding water or milk. Serves 6-8.

Wild Rice Dressing

- 1 tablespoon green pepper, chopped
- 2 tablespoons onion, chopped fine
- 2 tablespoons celery, chopped
- 2 tablespoons butter
- 1 cup hot broth (or more)
- 1 teaspoon salt
- ¼ teaspoon pepper
- 2 cups cooked wild rice
- 2 cups bread crumbs, toasted

Sauté pepper, onion and celery in butter. Add to broth. Add seasonings to cooked rice and lightly toss in bread crumbs. Stir in broth gradually. Use to stuff any fowl. May be baked in casserole at 350 degrees for 20 minutes. Serves 8.

St. Paul, Minn.

Exit I-94 at Marion St.

There's never a dull moment at the St. Paul Holiday Inn. Visitors make this luxurious 10 story high-rise their headquarters when enjoying the famous St. Paul Winter Carnival, the Minnesota Twins and the Viking football games. The Inn even hosts the Carnival Skating Rink in its back parking lot during the Carnival. Be sure to order the exquisite "'Bird of Paradise for Two". Downtown and the Capitol Building are just blocks from the Inn.

BIRD OF PARADISE FOR 2

    2 chicken breasts
    1 whole fresh pineapple
    2 carrots, 8 inches
    1 cup steamed wild rice
    ½ cup nuts
    2 cups Pineapple Sauce

Place chicken breasts in a shallow pan skin side up. Cover with foil. Bake 25 to 30 minutes at 325 degrees. Remove foil. Place 2 inches from heat and broil 12-15 minutes until brown. Cut whole fresh pineapple in equal halves lengthwise. Hollow out center of pineapple and reserve pieces to be used later. Slice carrots lengthwise ⅛ inch thick into 10 strips. Notch strips to obtain tail feather and wing effect. Empty ½ cup rice into each piece pineapple and place 1 breast of chicken on each half. Arrange carrot strips, pineapple pieces and nut meats. Pour sauce over chicken. Serves 2.

Pineapple Sauce

Blend 4 teaspoons cornstarch and ¼ cup sugar in ½ cup of pineapple juice. Add 1½ cups of juice and cook until it thickens.

Winona, Minn.

U.S. 61, 14 and State 43

Few have achieved the reputation of the restaurant at this Inn — it is filled with local guests year' round. Linahan's Restaurant has charm, outstanding food and a gifted chef, who is dedicated. The meat is excellent — cooked to the exact degree of doneness requested. The entire menu merits praise — complete with homemade pies and a wine to complement each course. Located on the Great River in the picturesque Hiawatha Valley opposite Sugar Loaf Mountain — this is a spot to remember when traveling.

PRIME RIB ROAST

6 to 8-pound prime rib roast

Remove meat from refrigerator at least ½ hour before cooking. Place in shallow roasting pan (no cover) and cook in 325 degree oven without basting. (Allow 18 to 30 minutes per pound, depending on doneness desired). Never cook more than three hours ever, for even a very large roast. Let roast rest ½ hour in warm place before carving. Serve roast prime rib of beef, au jus (heat juices left in pan, add a little water if needed). Allow ½ to 1 pound per person.

POTATOES AU GRATIN

    5 pounds baked potatoes, cooled
    1½ quarts, half and half
    ½ pound Parmesan cheese, grated
       White pepper and salt

Peel and chop potatoes. Combine with half and half and season to taste. Cook over low heat 15 minutes (do not boil). Pour into baking pan, cover completely with grated cheese, sprinkle with paprika and drizzle melted butter over top. Place under broiler until browned. For a buffet party of 20 to 25 persons.

Biloxi, Miss.

92 W. Beach. U.S. 90

Delicious gourmet dishes at this Holiday Inn make each day complete on the famous Mississippi Gulf Coast. Biloxi is the coast's oldest town. Ship Island, Biloxi Light House and Beauvoir, the home of Jefferson Davis, are historic sites to see. Young and old enjoy watching the Shrimp Fleet and visiting the Biloxi and Gulfport Harbors.

GULF FLOUNDER STUFFED WITH CRAB MEAT DRESSING

4 1-pound flounder

Clean and bone flounder. Stuff with dressing. Sew sides with coarse needle and thread. Top with crumbled bleu cheese. Bake at 400-450 degrees for 15-30 minutes or until fish is done. Baste with butter while cooking. Place 3 to 4 cooked shrimp on top of each flounder to heat last 3-4 minutes of cooking time. Serves 4.

Crab Meat Dressing

½ medium onion, minced
½ cup celery, minced
2 tablespoons butter
1 cup cream
1 cup rich chicken stock, hot
½ pound crab meat, shredded
½ teaspoon salt
　　Dash black pepper
½ to 1 cup cracker meal

Sauté celery and onion in butter. Heat cream and add to boiling hot stock and combine with crab meat and seasonings. Cook until crab meat is tender over medium heat. Slowly stir in cracker meal and sautéed onion and celery. Cook until thick. Cool slightly. 2 cups.

Clarksdale, Miss.

State St., U.S. 61 N.

In 1954 Holiday Inns of America decided to build the first Holiday Inn outside of Memphis, Tennessee in Clarksdale. Its Restaurant serves some of the best food in the rich Delta Country. It's not unusual to see a wild turkey or deer on a car parked at the Inn. To catch a fish is as easy as dropping a line into Moon Lake.

VEGETABLE SOUP

2 tablespoons margarine
½ cup onions, chopped coarse
½ cup celery, chopped coarse
2 quarts hot water
1 cup cut green beans
1 cup kernel corn
1 cup green lima beans
1 cup diced carrots
1 cup green peas
1¾ cups tomatoes, squeezed
¼ cup dry soup mix
¼ cup cut macaroni
1½ tablespoons beef base
1½ tablespoons chicken base
3 tablespoons tomato paste
　　Dash white pepper
¼ teaspoon salt

Sauté onions and celery in margarine until tender, about 10 minutes. Place in kettle of water. Add green beans, corn, lima beans, diced carrots, green peas and tomatoes. Bring to a boil. Add dry soup mix and cut macaroni. Dissolve beef base and chicken base in hot water, then add to first mixture. Add tomato paste, white pepper and salt. When soup comes to a boil, reduce heat to simmering point and simmer 10 to 12 minutes. 3 quarts.

Columbus, Miss.

Hwy. 45 N. at 5th Ave. N.

On Sunday local people always come to this Holiday Inn for dinner — it's a way of life in the "Friendly City", as Columbus is called. Commercial guests consider the Inn their second home. Guests always find the soup excellent, and the ham, grits and biscuits delicious. A Pilgrimage to ante-bellum homes in the spring begins at the Holiday Inn.

BONELESS CHICKEN STUFFED AND ROLLED WITH RICE

1 2-pound chicken (or breasts)
1 cup cooked rice
½ cup chicken giblets, cooked
½ teaspoon salt
½ teaspoon black pepper
1 teaspoon ground cumin
½ cup chopped green pepper and celery

Combine rice, giblets (ground), seasonings, green pepper and celery. Place on boned chicken. Roll so filling is completely enclosed. Use covered casserole for baking. Bake at 300 degrees for 1½ hours. Cover may be removed for last ½ hour to brown chicken more, if desired. Serve with Mushroom Sauce Supreme. Serves 2 to 4.

Mushroom Sauce Supreme

2 tablespoons butter
3 tablespoons flour
¼ teaspoon salt and pepper
1 cup chicken broth
¼ cup sliced mushroom caps
⅓ cup heavy cream
1 egg yolk, slightly beaten

Melt butter in a small heavy saucepan. Add flour, seasonings and blend. Cook one minute, add broth gradually and cook for 15 minutes over low heat. Add mushrooms and cream. Just before serving, add egg yolk and heat. Makes 1½ cups.

Greenville, Miss.

U.S. 82 E., W. of Hwy. 61

The anticipated fried chicken, grits and corn bread are all on the menu, but it's the festive display of salads at the noon buffets that are most impressive. The "Cotton Pickin" Big Steak Specials are always favorites with local guests and travelers. The Greenville Harbor is called the "Million Dollar Mile".

SPOON BREAD

1 cup corn meal
3 cups milk, scalded
1 teaspoon butter
1 teaspoon sugar
1 teaspoon salt
3 beaten egg yolks
3 beaten egg whites

Scald milk and add meal. Cook and stir in double boiler for a few minutes. Then add butter, sugar, salt and egg yolks. Fold in stiffly beaten egg whites. Pour in buttered pan and bake at 350 degrees for 1 hour. Serves 6.

SWEET POTATO BISCUITS

1 cup mashed sweet potatoes
⅔ cup milk
4 tablespoons melted butter
1¼ cups flour
2 tablespoons sugar
3½ teaspoons baking powder
½ teaspoon salt

Mix mashed potatoes, milk and melted butter. Add remaining ingredients, sifted all together, to make a soft dough. Turn out on a floured board and toss lightly until outside looks smooth. Roll out ½-inch thick and cut with floured biscuit cutter. Place on a greased pan and bake at 450 degrees for 15 minutes. Makes 12 biscuits.

Greenwood, Miss.

Hwys. 82 & 49 E. Bypass

You can expect superb southern food here. The Friday night buffet features Catfish and Hush Puppies. Twenty fishing lakes within 10 miles of the Inn entice visitors to bring their fishing gear. Sightseeing is also fun in this area. Visit the home of Greenwood Leflore, the Indian who founded the city. All visitors enjoy being here during the cotton market.

TURKEY AND HAM AU GRATIN

    6 thin slices baked ham
    6 thin slices turkey
   24 stalks asparagus (cooked)
 1½ cups Rich Cream Sauce
  ½ cup Cheddar cheese (grated)

Place ham and turkey in casserole over asparagus stalks. Cover with cream sauce. Sprinkle cheese on top. Bake at 350 degrees until brown. Serves 6. May also be used in individual casseroles.

Rich Cream Sauce

 2½ tablespoons butter
 2½ tablespoons flour
    1 cup turkey stock or milk
   ½ cup cream

Melt butter, add flour and stir until blended. Stir in turkey stock or milk. Then add cream. Cook until sauce is smooth and thick. Stir while cooking. Makes 1½ cups.

Hattiesburg, Miss. North

U.S. 49 and Interstate 59

This hilltop Holiday Inn is a favorite with parents and friends visiting the nearby University of Southern Mississippi. No wonder. The food is fabulous. The Inn goes Italian each Monday night—guests enjoy a complete Italian dinner, including a glass of wine. People look forward to the Sunday Breakfast Buffets all week. You'll enjoy the live entertainment in the Sevilla Lounge during your stay here.

HATTIESBURG HAM

Place 1½ pounds sliced cooked ham on a flat baking sheet. Sprinkle with 2 tablespoons chopped onion and dot with 1 tablespoon butter. Place in a 400 degree oven and bake for 15 minutes. Remove from oven, cover ham slices with 2 sliced hard-boiled eggs. Pour 1 cup catsup over eggs and sprinkle ½ tablespoon anise seeds over catsup. Top with 2 tablespoons grated cheese. Place in 375 degree oven for 20 minutes, or until cheese is lightly browned. Serves 4 to 6.

SNOB HILL CHERRIES

    2 cups Graham cracker crumbs
   ½ cup margarine
   ½ cup cream cheese
   ½ cup sugar
 1½ cups whipped cream
    2 tablespoons sugar
    1 teaspoon vanilla
    4 cups cherry pie fililng

Mix cracker crumbs and margarine but reserve a few crumbs for top later. Mix cream cheese and ½ cup sugar. Whip 2 tablespoons sugar, vanilla and whipped cream until thoroughly mixed. Pat cracker crumb mixture into ungreased pan. Pour cherry pie filling into pan and add layer of creamed cheese mixture and whipped cream mixture. Sprinkle lightly with cracker crumbs. Chill thoroughly. Serves 12.

Hattiesburg, Miss. South

Broadway Dr., U.S. 11 & 49

Many a bride remembers this Inn where she tossed her bouquet on her wedding day! Receptions, banquets, dinners and dances are all popular at this Inn in the Hub City (3 large railroad lines cross here). Colleges take credit for a lot of Hattiesburg visitors. Both the University of Southern Mississippi and Wm. Carey College are near the Inn.

SHRIMP IMPERIAL

1¼ pounds shrimp, cooked
1¼ pounds scallops, cooked
1 pint Cream Sauce
2½ tablespoons sherry wine
Paprika

Cut each shrimp into 3 individual pieces. Cut each scallop into 4 pieces. Combine cream sauce and sherry. Add scallops and shrimp to sauce. Put in a casserole and sprinkle with paprika. Bake 5 to 7 minutes in a 400 degree oven. Serves 10.

Cream Sauce

3 tablespoons butter
4 tablespoons flour
⅛ teaspoon pepper
⅛ teaspoon salt
2 cups scalded milk

Melt butter, add flour, salt and pepper. Mix to a smooth paste. Add scalded milk, stir, and cook over low heat until thick. Use immediately or cool. Makes 2 cups.

Jackson, Miss.-North

I-55 N., U.S. 51 N.

The food served in the Colony Dining Room is excellent. Visitors and local residents enjoy the Inn's popular Red Fox Tavern. Things to see in Jackson include the Mississippi State Capitol and the Governor's Mansion (it served as headquarters for Sherman and Grant during the Civil War). The Old Capitol now houses the State Historical Museum.

SPECIAL SALAD

Leaf lettuce
Salad greens, torn
4 hard-boiled eggs, cut in wedges
4 tomatoes, cut in wedges
1 ounce American cheese
12 strips crisp bacon
4 slices turkey breast
8 queen olives
12 raw onion rings
Parsley
8 flat anchovies
Paprika

Line 4 salad bowls with crisp lettuce leaves so that lettuce protrudes above edges of bowls. Fill with salad greens. Bring to a peak in center of bowl. Place egg and tomato wedges at opposite sides of bowls. Slice cheese into strips ¼-inch wide and place on top of salad at random. Crumble and sprinkle bacon on top of salad. Slice turkey into ¼-inch strips and place on top. Garnish salad with olives, onion rings, parsley and anchovies. Dust lightly with paprika. Serve with the salad dressing of your choice. Serves 4.

Jackson, Miss.-SW

2649 U.S. 80 West

Look down on Mississippi's capital from this Holiday Inn, high atop a hill in Jackson. There's scheduled limousine service to downtown (10 miles). Take the road to yesterday and enjoy all the reminders of Jackson's historic past. Steaks cooked over an open grill are favorites in the Heritage Dining Room. The Red Fox Tavern features live entertainment.

SEAFOOD DE JONGHE

¼ pound butter, softened
1 clove garlic, mashed to pulp
⅓ bunch parsley, minced
1 cup fine bread crumbs
¼ cup dry white wine
¼ pound crab meat, cooked
½ pound shrimp, cooked and peeled
1 cup buttered croutons

Cream butter, add garlic paste, parsley and bread crumbs. Blend well. Form into loaf and chill. Place crab meat and shrimp in shallow baking dish which has been buttered and sprinkled with croutons. Cut chilled butter mixture and place over all. Sprinkle with paprika. Cook in 400 degree oven for about 15 minutes. Serves 4.

PAN ROASTED OYSTERS

Melt ½ cup butter in sauté pan. Add ½ cup chopped chives and ¼ cup chopped parsley. Then add 32 oysters and cook until oysters curl around edges. Remove oysters and add 1 tablespoon flour to pan and blend. Then add ½ cup white wine and cook for 5 minutes, or until thickened. Pour sauce over oysters. Serves 4.

Laurel, Miss.

U.S. 11 & Interstate 59 N.

Laurel is known as the "City Beautiful" because of its stately homes and lovely lawns. This Holiday Inn is designed to make you feel like a personal guest in one of the south's most gracious homes. Take time to linger over the fine food cooked the southern way. The Lauren Rogers Memorial Library has a valuable collection of European and Japanese art.

CRAB MEAT CARIBBEAN

½ pound bacon
1 cup chopped green onions
1 cup chopped green peppers
1 chopped garlic clove
4 ripe tomatoes, peeled and chopped
½ pound Virginia ham, small pieces
1 teaspoon dried basil
1½ pounds lump crab meat, cooked
¼ cup rum
½ cup sour cream

Cut bacon in small pieces. Fry until cooked through but not crisp. Remove bacon pieces and add onions, peppers and garlic. Then add tomatoes, ham and basil. Simmer 15 minutes. Add crab meat and rum. Cook until crab meat is heated through. Add sour cream and heat. Serve crab meat over Pilaf in a casserole. Serves 6.

Pilaf

Sauté ¾ cup celery and ¾ cup onions (both cut small) in ¼ pound butter until tender. Add 1 teaspoon paprika, dash egg color, 2 cups chicken stock and 1 cup rice. Bring to a rolling boil. Stir often. Cover and put in oven at 400 degrees for 20 minutes, until rice has absorbed all of liquid. Makes 3-4 cups.

McComb, Miss.

Delaware Ave. at I-55

Each spring a lighted Azalea Trail is followed by hundreds of visitors through the residential area of McComb. Everyone in town lights his yard for 3 days. And an Azalea Ball is held each year. There's a well-worn path around the buffet tables at this Holiday Inn. Unusual casseroles and homemade cobblers, puddings and pies demand seconds.

CHICKEN LAS VEGAS

4 chicken breasts, bone removed
2 tablespoons flour
2 tablespoons margarine
1½ cups sweet milk
1 cup grated cheese
½ teaspoon salt
⅛ teaspoon paprika
2 tablespoons butter

Blend flour and margarine. Add milk gradually and cook until thickened for a cream sauce. Add grated cheese. Season. Roll boned chicken with toothpicks and broil in butter until well done. Serve with cream sauce. Serves 4.

STUFFED CABBAGE ROLL

1 cup onions, chopped
1 cup celery, chopped
1 cup bell pepper, chopped
4 tablespoons butter
2 pounds ground beef
2 cups cooked rice
15-20 steamed cabbage leaves

Saute' onions, celery and bell pepper in butter. Add ground beef and cook slowly until done. Add cooked rice and roll in steamed cabbage leaves. Place casserole on top of stove, add 1 cup catsup or tomato sauce, and heat thoroughly. Serves 8 to 10.

Meridian, Miss.-NE

U.S. 45 N.

There's "atmosphere" dining in the Fountain Room at this Holiday Inn. Designed like an outdoor patio with trellises and fountains, this Room is perfect for enjoying delicious food. Men in uniform are frequent guests for dinner. The U.S. Naval jet training base for Navy and Marine Corps fliers is nearby. It's open to visitors who make advance reservations.

WESTERN SPECIAL

4 slices turkey
4 slices ham
8 toast points
1 cup Cheddar Cheese Sauce
8 slices crisp bacon

Place ham and turkey on toast. Cover with cheese sauce. Then place bacon strips on top. Serve with crisp green salad on the side.

Cheddar Cheese Sauce

Blend 2 tablespoons butter and 2 tablespoons flour. Add 1 cup milk gradually and stir over moderate heat until it thickens. Add ½ cup sharp Cheddar cheese (grated) and stir until sauce is smooth.

SOUTHERN PECAN PIE

1 cup (scant) sugar
2 tablespoons flour
3 eggs, slightly beaten
⅔ cup Karo syrup
½ cup chopped pecans
2 teaspoons vanilla

Blend sugar, flour and eggs. Then blend in remaining ingredients. Pour into a very short pastry shell. Bake at 450 degrees for 10 minutes, then at 350 degrees for 30-35 minutes. Serves 6 to 8.

Meridian, Miss.-South

U.S. 45 S. at Tom Bailey Dr.

The food is outstanding. Find out for yourself at the Holiday Buffet luncheons each weekday at noon. The special buffets make any dinner a special occasion. Though General Sherman once sacked the city and said "Meridian no longer exists", an aviation training center and textile industry give proof of its importance today.

COCKTAIL-SIZE MEAT BALLS

Combine 1½ pounds ground meat (ground very small), 1 well beaten egg, 1 teaspoon salt, and 1 tablespoon catsup. Soak 1 slice crumbled bread in ¼ cup water. Then add to first mixture and mix lightly with a fork. Form into meat balls and brown on all sides in cooking oil.

Sauce

    3 tablespoons olive oil
    1 small onion, diced fine
    1 crushed garlic clove
    ¼ teaspoon salt
    ¼ teaspoon oregano
    1 teaspoon flour
    1 beef bouillon cube
    1 cup water
    1 teaspoon dry mustard
      Dash of bitters
    2 jiggers rye whiskey
    1 jigger sweet vermouth

Cook onion and garlic in olive oil until just tender. Add salt, oregano, flour, beef bouillon cube, water, mustard, bitters, whiskey and vermouth. Cook slowly and make a smooth, thick sauce. Add meat balls to sauce and refrigerate for 24 hours. Heat slowly in chafing dish and serve hot as hors d'oeuvres. Makes approximately 2½-3 dozen small meat balls.

Pascagoula, Miss.

U.S. Hwy. 90 E. at 14th St.

Be sure to visit the Old Spanish Fort built in 1718 on Krebs Lake. This is the land of fish, fun and friendliness, but important industries too. Pascagoula is well-known for ship building and has a historic seafood industry. So you can expect excellent seafood at this Inn. Do try the Horn Island Seafood Platter and a broiled Gulf flounder for sure.

MISSISSIPPI GULF COAST GUMBO

    ½ cup flour
    3 tablespoons olive oil
    1 small minced onion
    1 pound raw, peeled shrimp
    6 cups hot water
      Salt
      Pepper
    1 small green pepper, minced
    1 bunch green onions, minced
    3 sprigs parsley, minced
      Pinch file' (powdered sassafras)

Roux is the base for all French gumbo and many other dishes. To make roux, brown flour in olive oil. Then add onion and brown lightly. Add shrimp and simmer until shrimp are done (about 20 minutes). Then add hot water, salt, pepper, green pepper, green onions, and parsley. Cook another 5 minutes and remove from heat. Add a pinch of file'. Serve in soup bowls and put 1 large spoonful of cooked rice in the center of each. The real French gumbo does not use fresh okra, however, if desired, chop 2 cups okra and 1 large fresh tomato and stew down in 2 tablespoons olive oil until brown and all moisture from okra has disappeared. Then add to main kettle. (No file' is used with okra). 6 servings.

Sardis, Miss.

Interstate 55 at Miss. 315

Vacationers on their way to New Orleans and the Mississippi Gulf Coast are glad to find this Holiday Inn on their direct route. It's a favorite with fishermen and hunters too. The Inn will clean and fry your fish to suit your taste, dress quail and prepare with wine. The world's largest Dirt Dam is only 8 miles away. For fishing, water skiing and camping, there's the Sardis Lake Reservoir nearby.

HASH BROWN POTATOES

Medium-size potatoes
Onion salt
Paprika
Melted butter

Select medium-sized potatoes, making sure they are all more or less the same size. Put them in a large container and boil until done, but not mushy. (They are really better if you take them off just before you think they are done). Run cool water over them immediately and allow the water to run until potatoes are cold. Peel potatoes and run them through a medium shredder —do not shred too fine. Add onion salt to taste, and store in the refrigerator. When ready to cook them, scoop a cupful into individual cooking rings, sprinkle paprika on bottom of grill, add potatoes, pour a small amount of melted butter on top, and sprinkle again with paprika on top. Allow them to cook until golden brown on the bottom, turn and cook the top.

Vicksburg, Miss.

On 80 E. at U.S. 61 & I-20

Step on a rich red and black carpet. Slip into a red captain's chair. Gaze through the window at the Battle of Vicksburg Park. And enjoy superb southern food in this Inn's unique Heritage House dining room. Be sure to order ham, grits and hot biscuits for breakfast. A showboat melodrama is presented on the world's largest riverboat in the spring and summer.

STUFFED SHRIMP

Peel and devein 16 raw shrimp. Split and stuff 8 with mixture below.

Blend ingredients:

1-pound can Geisha Girl crab meat
½ cup diced boiled shrimp
1 cup cracker crumbs
⅓ cup grated Romano cheese
1 teaspoon black pepper
2-3 dashes Tabasco
3 raw eggs
2 tablespoons parsley flakes
⅔ cup minced onions

Flatten stuffing on shrimp after filling. Place a shrimp on top of each. Dip in egg-milk wash (1 beaten egg + ¼ cup milk). Roll in flour. Cook in deep fat 6-8 minutes. Serves 4.

MISSISSIPPI HUSH PUPPIES

Mix 2 cups self-rising white corn meal and 1 tablespoon sugar. Add 1 small chopped onion, 1 well beaten egg and ¾ cup milk. Drop mixture from tablespoon into hot grease or fat. Serves 6.

MISSISSIPPI RIVER CATFISH

Allow ¾ to 1 pound catfish for each person. Flour well washed catfish. Beat 2 eggs. Add 1 pint milk and beat. Dip catfish in mixture. Roll in corn meal. Fry in hot fat until brown and done.

Cape Girardeau, Mo.

Jct. I-55 & William St.

Enter Cape Girardeau beautifully, along the picturesque highway from Jackson — a rose garden extends for 10 miles. This Holiday Inn is located in the Cape countryside, yet is only minutes from the business area. People say it's the special basting sauce that makes the Inn's charcoaled steak so superb. There's a putting green as well as a shuffleboard on the grounds.

MISSOURI PECAN CREAM PIE

1 cup sugar
2 tablespoons flour
2 egg yolks, beaten
1½ cups milk
1 tablespoon butter
½ cup ground pecans
1 teaspoon vanilla
1 baked 9-inch pastry shell
Meringue

Mix sugar and flour; add egg yolks and milk. Add butter and pecans. Mix well and cook until thickened, stirring constantly. Add vanilla. Pour into pie shell. Top with meringue and bake at 350 degrees until meringue is golden brown. 6 servings.

Meringue

Beat 2 egg whites until frothy, add ¼ teaspoon salt and beat. Add ¼ cup sugar gradually and beat until meringue holds stiff peaks. Spread over pie to cover all filling.

Columbia, Mo.-East

I-70 & Providence Road

Columbia is known as College Town, U.S.A. This Holiday Inn is home to the many parents and friends visiting the University of Missouri (3 miles from the Inn), Stephens College (2 miles), and Christian College (2 miles). There's a well-worn path around the Inn's laden round buffet table everyday at noon. Mexican foods and Country Ham are always favorites in the Camelot Room.

BOONE COUNTY COUNTRY HAM

4 ham steaks
1 cup water or coffee

Heat a heavy iron skillet until it sizzles. Grease lightly with a piece of ham fat. Put in ham steaks but do not let them overlap. Sear on both sides. If ham steaks are thick, add water to cover, place lid on skillet and simmer a few minutes. Otherwise lift ham out and then pour in 1 cup water and stir to get all ham drippings for gravy. Serve with gravy poured over ham. May use coffee for red eye gravy. Serves 4.

MEXICAN SCRAMBLED EGGS

4 eggs
2 tablespoons butter
1 teaspoon onion, minced
1 tomato, chopped
½ teaspoon chili sauce
½ teaspoon salt

Beat eggs with whisk. Melt butter in frying pan and sauté onion and tomato. Add seasoning to beaten eggs and pour into frying pan. Cook over low heat stirring constantly. Serves 4.

Columbia, Mo.-West

I-70 at Conley Lane Exit

The University of Missouri, Stephens College and Christian College are all within 10 minutes of this Inn. During football season there's a "quick buffet" for the many sports fans in town. Every Friday night is International Night. It could be a German, Mexican, Southern (barbecue) or a St. Patrick's Day Buffet. This is a favorite stopping place for tourists too. Columbia is at the edge of the Ozarks.

CHICKEN OKRA GUMBO SOUP

    1 quart chicken stock
    ½ cup chicken, chopped
    1½ cups canned tomatoes, sieved
    2 ounces rice, washed
    2 teaspoons salt
    1 onion, chopped fine
    ½ cup celery, chopped fine
    1 cup cooked or frozen okra
    ½ green pepper, chopped fine
    ¼ teaspoon pepper

Bring stock to a boil and add above ingredients. Simmer for 30 minutes. Then add ½ cup cooked peas (frozen or fresh). Serves 6 to 8.

POUND CAKE

    2 cups soft butter
    2 cups sugar
    10 eggs
    4 cups cake flour
    ½ teaspoon salt
    ½ teaspoon mace
    ½ teaspoon lemon juice

Cream butter and sugar until smooth. Add eggs one at a time, beating well after each addition. Beat one extra minute after all are added. Add flour which has been sifted with mace and salt. Mix carefully. Add lemon juice if desired. Place in buttered bundt or tube pan. Bake at 300 to 325 degrees for 1¼ to 1½ hours.

Hannibal, Mo.

4141 Market St., Dwtn.

Don't be surprised if you see youngsters painting fences in this town— you're in Tom Sawyer and Huckleberry Finn country! Mark Twain's home and the famous cave every child should see are nearby. The chef at this Inn raises his own vegetables so he knows they're always fresh. He even has a strawberry patch. The vegetable soup is excellent. Homemade bread, biscuits and desserts are hard to resist.

SANDBAR SQUASH

    16 zucchini squash
    1 cup tomato juice
    6 tomatoes, diced
    1 onion
    ½ green pepper, seeded

Scrub squash and cross cut into approximately 1-inch cubes. Place in ½ inch boiling salted water. Cook 5 minutes, drain and set aside. Place tomato juice and tomatoes in large pan. Add julienne onion and diced green pepper. Place squash in pan, season with pepper and Accent. Boil until vegetables are tender and juice has been reduced. 8 servings.

MARK TWAIN BISCUITS

    2 cups flour
    1 yeast cake
    1½ teaspoons baking powder
    1 teaspoon salt
    ½ teaspoon soda
    1 to 2 teaspoons sugar
    ¼ cup shortening
    ¾ cup buttermilk

Measure flour after sifting. Dissolve yeast in ¼ cup warm water. Sift all dry ingredients. Mix shortening in dry ingredients with pastry blender. Add yeast and stir well. Add buttermilk. Place in greased bowl, cover and refrigerate for several hours or overnight (will keep 1 to 3 days). When ready to use, roll out biscuits on floured board, cut and place in a greased pan. Let rise 30 minutes. Bake at 450 degrees 10 to 12 minutes. 12 to 16 biscuits.

Independence, Mo.

13900 E. U.S. 40

Wagon trains heading west touched off at Independence. During Gold Rush days stagecoaches on their way to California stopped here. Today visitors find this Holiday Inn the perfect place to stop — and stay for a holiday. Its shaded acreage invites relaxation and traditional food is graciously served. The Truman Library with Museum is nearby. Downtown Kansas City is only 12 miles away.

CHEESECAKE

    4 eggs
    1 cup sugar
    2 teaspoons vanilla
    1½ pounds Philadelphia cream cheese

Beat eggs until light. Add sugar and vanilla and beat well. Add cream cheese and blend. Fill a Graham cracker crust ⅔ full and bake 40 minutes at 350 degrees. Do not overcook! Let cool 10 minutes. Cover with a mixture of: 2 cups sour cream, 1 teaspoon vanilla, 4 tablespoons sugar. Bake 10 minutes at 400 degrees. Serves 8-9.

PRUNE CAKE

    1 cup vegetable oil
    1½ cups sugar
    3 eggs
    2 cups flour
    1 teaspoon cinnamon
    1 teaspoon nutmeg
    1 teaspoon allspice
    1 teaspoon soda
    1 cup buttermilk
    1 teaspoon vanilla
    1 cup prunes, cooked

Blend oil and sugar. Add eggs and blend well. Sift dry ingredients together and add alternately with buttermilk. Add vanilla and prunes (seeded and chopped). Pour into a well greased pan. Bake at 300 degrees for 45 minutes to 1 hour. Let cool in pan. 1 cake (13x9x2).

Jefferson City, Mo.-SW

1937 Christy Lane

The Walnut Room in this Holiday Inn offers an unforgettable view as well as memorable food. It overlooks a beautiful wooded valley, yet the Inn is only a short distance from the heart of the Capital City. Jefferson City is at the Gateway to the Lake of the Ozarks. Missouri's recreation center is only an hour's drive away.

APPLE DUMPLINGS

    2 bottles 7-Up (7 oz. ea.)
    1½ cups sugar
    ¼ teaspoon cinnamon
    ¼ teaspoon nutmeg
    ¼ cup margarine or butter
    6 medium apples
    2 cups flour
    1 teaspoon salt
    2 teaspoons baking powder
    ¾ cup shortening
    ½ cup milk

Combine 7-Up, sugar, cinnamon and nutmeg in a saucepan. Cook over medium heat, stirring constantly, until sugar is dissolved. Add margarine and stir until melted. Set aside. Pare and core apples, but leave whole. Sift flour, salt and baking powder and cut in shortening. Add milk all at once and stir until moistened. Roll out and cut into six 7-inch squares and place apple in center of each square. Combine 6 tablespoons sugar, 1 teaspoon cinnamon and sprinkle about 1 teaspoon of this mixture in the center of each apple. Dot with 3 tablespoons butter. Fold corners of pastry to center and pinch edges together. Arrange in a 9x13x2 inch baking dish. Pour syrup into pan. Bake at 425 degrees for 35 minutes. Serve warm with sauce. Makes 6 dumplings.

Joplin, Mo.

On U.S. 71, Range Line Rd.

The "Dugout", the Inn's lounge, is a popular place with its white baseball top tables, gourmet sandwiches and live entertainment. Fondue Bourguignonne and Chateaubriand delight gourmets in the dining room. You can expect homemade biscuits and sweet rolls for breakfast — the Inn has its own baker. Joplin is known as the city that lead and zinc built.

HOT AND BROWN SANDWICH

Split 6 English muffins, butter and place them in a baking pan. Cover with sliced chicken breast, sliced ham and tangy Cheese Sauce. Place 12 slices of bacon over cheese sauce and put under broiler for 5 minutes. Serves 6.

Cheese Sauce

¼ cup butter
6 tablespoons flour
¼ teaspoon dry mustard
3 cups milk
1 cup diced sharp Cheddar cheese

Melt butter and add flour and mustard. When smooth, add milk gradually and cook until thickened and smooth. Add cheese, salt and pepper. Heat until cheese is melted.

FRENCH SILK PIE

¼ pound butter
¾ cup sugar
1 ounce Hershey's Chocolate, melted
2 eggs
1 baked pie shell
1 cup whipped cream

Cream butter and sugar. Add chocolate. Then add eggs, one at a time, on medium speed of mixer. Place in a baked pie shell and top with whipped cream. Chill. Makes one 8-inch pie. Serves 6.

Kansas City, Mo. Airport

1st St. at Broadway, U.S. 71

Fly in and stay only 500 feet from the airport, 8 blocks from downtown Kansas City. Once you have your feet on the ground in this luxurious Inn, start your stay in the dining room. There's nothing like a Kansas City Steak in this Kansas City Holiday Inn. There are impressive views of the city from the 80th floor of the City Hall, and from the platform of the Lincoln Memorial.

CHICKEN EN CANTALOUPE

2 chicken breasts
2 tablespoons butter
1 cantaloupe
1 pint rich cream
2 tablespoons sherry
6 asparagus spears, cooked
4 fresh mushrooms, sautéed

Fry chicken slowly in butter. Cover each with ½ ripe cantaloupe and bake 15 minutes at 350 degrees. Remove cantaloupe and chicken and add cream and seasonings to pan drippings. Boil in a stew pan, stirring constantly, until thickened. Add sherry. Place chicken breast in each cantaloupe half on serving plates. Strain sauce over them and serve with asparagus and mushrooms. Serves 2.

WILD GOOSE

Clean 1 wild goose and cut into serving pieces. Place in heavy skillet. Add ¼ cup dry white wine, 1 tablespoon meat sauce and water to cover. Cover and cook until tender (1½-2 hours). Brown 1 minced onion in 2 tablespoons butter, add 2 tablespoons flour and stir well. Slowly add 1 cup broth and 1 cup tomato juice. Add ½ green pepper (minced) and 6 sliced ripe olives. Cook until thickened. Add ¼ cup sherry. Serve sauce over cooked goose with wild rice. Serves 8-10.

Kansas City, Mo.-South

Blue Ridge Blvd. & U.S. 71 S

Ideally located at Truman Corners Shopping Center, this Holiday Inn offers the ultimate in convenience. You can enjoy the city yet come back to this relaxing Inn away from it all. You'll want to come back for dinner anyway, once you get a taste of what's served in the dining room. Kansas City sightseeing musts: Liberty Memorial, Kansas City Museum, Ft. Osage, Nelson Gallery of Art and Swope Park.

CHEESE SOUP

½ cup carrots
¼ cup onions
½ cup margarine or butter
1 tablespoon salt
½ teaspoon pepper
½ teaspoon paprika
⅓ cup flour
1 pint milk
1 pint Cheese Whiz
1 quart chicken stock
1 teaspoon Lea & Perrins
1 teaspoon Lawry's
1 teaspoon Accent

Chop carrots and onions extra fine and saute in 2 tablespoons butter. Add salt, pepper and paprika. Make a roux with the remaining butter and flour. Bring milk to a boil and thicken with the roux. Add Cheese Whiz, chicken stock and seasonings to the first two mixtures which have been combined. Makes approximately 2 quarts.

Kansas City, Mo.-SE

E. U.S. 50 at 63rd St.

This is the place to stay in Kansas City if you'd like to be just a stone's throw from the renowned Swope Park with its zoo and Starlight Theatre. The Inn is located on the scenic "Old Santa Fe Trail" overlooking the downtown Kansas City skyline. Country Club Plaza is just 10 minutes away. You can expect the finest in food, service and hospitality too.

ZUCCHINI CASSEROLE

½ pound bacon (cut and fried)
1 cup minced onion
2 pounds zucchini, sliced ¼" thick
6 slices tomatoes
2 cups cracker crumbs
1 pound grated Cheddar cheese

Saute onion in 4 teaspoons bacon grease. Arrange in casserole alternate layers of zucchini, tomatoes, bacon, cracker crumbs, onion and cheese. Season. Repeat above 3 times — with Cheddar cheese on top. Bake 1 hour at 325 degrees. Serves 8 to 10.

CORN PUDDING

Sliced bread
1 #2 can cream style corn
2 tablespoons minced onion
1 pound sharp cheese, grated
6 well beaten eggs
1 teaspoon paprika
1 teaspoon dry mustard
1 teaspoon salt
5 cups milk
¼ cup melted butter

Arrange layer of sliced bread on bottom of buttered baking dish. Mix corn and onion, then place layer over bread. Top this layer with cheese. Repeat procedure twice. Combine remaining ingredients and pour over the top. Bake 1 hour and 15 minutes at 325 degrees. Serves 6 to 8.

Lexington, Mo.

NW Corner St. 13 and U.S. 24

Lexington is steeped in Civil War history. See the cannonball lodged in the courthouse. The Inn arranges tours through the Lexington Civil War Battlefield, the Anderson House (now a museum) and the many historic homes. Visitors enjoy the Wentworth Military Academy parades every Sunday. This Inn's Civil War decor features "both sides". (Missouri was a "fence-sitting" state).

SWISS STEAK

This 3-century-old recipe is called Schmor Braten. Rub ½ cup seasoned flour into 3-pound round steak about 2½ inches thick. In a heavy skillet heat 2 tablespoons drippings and brown meat on all sides. Place meat in heavy kettle and add: 2 cups boiling water, 1 large thinly sliced onion and bouquet garni (bay leaf, sprig thyme, celery leaves, blade garlic, 2 cloves, tied). Cover and simmer 1 hour.

Stir in 1 cup tomato purée, 1 teaspoon mustard, 1½ tablespoons catsup. Cover and simmer 1 hour, or until meat is tender. Thicken gravy, if needed, and add additional stock, if desired. Serves 8.

HUSH PUPPIES

2 cups fine corn meal, sifted
2 teaspoons baking powder
1 teaspoon salt
1½ cups milk
½ cup water
1 extra large onion, chopped fine

Sift corn meal, baking powder and salt together. Combine milk and water and stir in alternately with the onion. (1 teaspoon celery seed and ½ teaspoon garlic salt may be added for flavor). Add more sifted corn meal if necessary to make a soft but workable dough. Dip hands in flour and mold pieces of dough into pones (oblong cakes about 5" long, 3" wide and ¾" thick). Fry in deep hot fat or oil until well browned on all sides. Serve hot. Makes about 30 hush puppies.

Poplar Bluff, Mo.

U.S. 60 & 67 North

An oversized fireplace and beautiful paintings give the proper background for the fabulous buffets served in the Red Coals Restaurant. Large graceful trees enhance the view at the Open Flame "Gas Lite" patio parties. The Inn is a popular dining place for the whole area. Lake Wappapello, a fisherman's paradise and land of plenty for the hunter, is only a few miles away.

SELECT SHRIMP BROIL

2 pounds 10-15 count shrimp
1 cup butter
1 tablespoon lemon juice
1 tablespoon chopped parsley

Split shrimp in shell. Separate shell from shrimp, leaving intact. Wash thoroughly. Dip complete shrimp in lemon butter sauce (cream butter adding lemon juice and parsley for sauce). Place on sheet pan and sprinkle with paprika. Broil 8 minutes. Serve with Wine Sauce, salad or slaw, and potatoes. Allow 6 shrimp per person.

Wine Sauce

2 cups milk
4 egg yolks
4 tablespoons sherry

Scald milk. Add egg yolks, well beaten. Be sure to take milk from heat before mixing. Add red pepper and salt to taste. Add sherry, mixing well. Keep at 90 degree temperature. Serve with Shrimp Broil. Makes approximately 2 cups.

St. Joseph, Mo.

On Interstate 29 & U.S. 71

You'll be welcomed in the Roundhouse Dining Room with a glass of wine and a relish tray. Take time to "read all about it" in the Roundhouse Gazette . . . news for sightseeing in St. Joseph and the menu. The barbecued ribs and homemade tarts are "must trys". There's live entertainment and a baby grand piano on stage in the Gaslight Depot Lounge. The Pony Express and the world's first mail car started here.

GOLDEN SPIKE BROCHETTE

    4 6-ounce round steaks
    1 cup red wine
    1 onion, pieces
    2 green peppers, cut in eighths
    3 tomatoes, cut in wedges

Marinate steaks in wine for 18 to 24 hours. Cut each steak into quarters, Assemble meat and vegetables on skewers (onion, meat, green pepper, tomato wedge, onion, etc.) a single brochette should have 4 onion pieces, 4 chunks of meat, 4 pieces of green pepper and 4 tomato wedges. Broil for 11 minutes for medium done. Top with Mushroom Sauce. Serves 4.

Mushroom Sauce

    2 tablespoons butter
    ½ slice onion
    2 tablespoons flour
    1 cup stock
    ½ cup sliced mushrooms

Saute onion in butter until brown. Remove onion. Stir in flour and brown it, adding stock slowly. Stir and cook until sauce is smooth and boiling. Add sliced mushrooms which have been sautéed in butter. Season with salt, pepper and dash of Worcestershire sauce, if desired. 1½ cups.

St. Louis, Mo. Downtown

2211 Market, U.S. Hwy. 40

All of downtown St. Louis is at the doorstep of this Holiday Inn (the river front, Busch Memorial Stadium, Kiel Auditorium). You'll step back into the early St. Louis river boat days when you step into the River Room. Gourmet dinner menus make the River Room outstanding. Free hors d'oeuvres are served during cocktail hour in the River Room Lounge.

SWEETBREADS
WITH LEMON BUTTER SAUCE

    1 pair sweetbreads
      Salt
    2 tablespoons lemon juice
      Flour
    4 tablespoons butter

Wash sweetbreads in running water and drain well. Place in kettle of hot water in which salt and lemon juice have been added and brought to a boil. Lower heat when sweetbreads are added and simmer 15 to 20 minutes. Drain and put in cold water for a few minutes. Remove skin and membrane. Save stock. Dry sweetbreads and break into large pieces. Roll in seasoned flour and saute in butter until golden brown. Serve with Lemon Butter Sauce. Serves 2.

Lemon Butter Sauce

    1 cup stock
    4 tablespoons butter
    ½ lemon (juice)
    1 wine glass white wine

Reduce the stock in which sweetbreads were parboiled to one half. Add butter and mix well. Season, add lemon juice and wine. Boil up and pour over the sweetbreads.

St. Louis, Mo. Midtown

Lindell Blvd. at Taylor

This Holiday Inn turns cartwheels (wine and pastry cartwheels) to please you in the luxurious de Ville Room Restaurant. There's an outstanding menu too. The Cocktail Plaza in the middle of a reflecting pool is a delightful place for relaxation. Gaslight Square, the Municipal Opera and the St. Louis Zoo are very near.

CHOCOLATE ECLAIRS

½ cup butter or margarine
1 cup boiling water
1 cup bread flour
4 eggs

Add butter to water and cook until butter melts. Add all of flour at once. Stir vigorously until ball forms in center of pan. Cool a little. Add eggs, one at a time, beating after each addition. Mixture should be stiff. Put in pastry tube for eclair shape or use eclair pans. Use cookie sheet. Bake 40 to 50 minutes at 400 degrees. When cool split and fill with custard and add Chocolate Frosting to tops. Makes 8 to 10.

Eclair Filling

Scald 2 cups milk. Mix ⅔ cup sugar, ½ cup flour, ½ teaspoon salt and 2 beaten eggs. Add to milk and cook, stirring continuously, until mixture becomes quite thick. Cool and add 2 tablespoons rum or vanilla.

Chocolate Frosting

Melt 1 square unsweetened chocolate with 2 tablespoons butter and 3 tablespoons light cream over low heat. Stir in 1½ cups powdered sugar and beat until smooth and creamy.

St. Louis, Mo.-North

On U.S. 140 at I-70, Bridgeton

Country French decor in the La Grange Restaurant is the perfect setting for the superb food served. The Hostess Sirloin Steak is always in most popular demand. Live entertainment makes the Le Riveau lounge fun for travelers and local guests. The Holiday Inn is within 15 miles of all the attractions and entertainment in St. Louis. See the Cardinals play in Busch Stadium. Visit the City Art Museum.

BEEF A LA HOLIDAY

24 cubes beef tenderloin
1 tablespoon cooking oil
2 tablespoons onions, chopped
4 tablespoons mushrooms, chopped
½ cup boiling water
6 cups noodles, cooked
4 tablespoons garlic butter
1 tablespoon parsley, chopped

Brown tenderloin cubes in oil (just enough oil to keep from sticking) in heavy skillet. Sauté onions and mushrooms in frying pan with butter. Add to beef cubes. Rinse frying pan with boiling water and add to beef mixture. Cook and stir 5 minutes. Sauté cooked noodles in garlic butter in saucepan. Add chopped parsley. Place beef tenderloins over cooked noodles and serve. Serves 6-8.

SAUTÉED TROUT WITH WATER CRESS BUTTER

6 trout
4 tablespoons butter or margarine
¼ cup chopped water cress
½ teaspoon Tabasco sauce
¼ teaspoon salt

Melt butter. Add water cress, Tabasco, salt and heat through. Serve over sautéed trout. Garnish with lemon wedges. Serves 6.

St. Louis, Mo.-NE

I-270 Hazelwood, Mo.

Businessmen visiting McDonnell Aircraft and Emerson Electric find this Holiday Inn a most convenient place to stay. The Inn provides free transportation to and from the airport only 5 miles away. There's everything from Old-Fashioned Beef Stew to gourmet Tenderloin Tips with Mushroom Sauce on the menu. Live entertainment makes the Lounge a popular place after dinner.

OLD-FASHIONED BEEF STEW

    2 pounds boneless beef
    2 tablespoons cooking oil
    6 carrots, cubed
    4 potatoes, cubed
    1 onion, diced
    1 cup celery, diced
 1½ teaspoons salt
    ½ teaspoon pepper
    ⅛ teaspoon thyme
 1½ cups water

Dip meat in flour and brown in oil on all sides. Add vegetables, seasonings and water. Place in casserole and bake 1½ hours at 350 degrees. If gravy is not thick enough, add flour to a bit of water and blend. Add to gravy in casserole and cook a little longer to thicken. Serves 8.

TENDERLOIN TIPS

Sauté ½ cup chopped onions and 1 cup mushrooms in ¼ cup cooking oil. Remove and brown 2 pounds tenderloin tips, which have been lightly dusted with flour. Cook 8 to 10 minutes. Add salt and pepper to taste, ¼ teaspoon garlic powder if desired. Make a roux of ¼ cup water and 2 tablespoons flour and add to pan with 1 cup water gradually and thicken. Serve with buttered noodles. Serves 6.

St. Louis, Mo.-South

Jct. 66, 61, 50 & Bypass 50

German specialties that have been favorites with St. Louis families for over forty years are served everyday. Be sure to order the Sauerbraten. The Inn has not one, but two luxurious swimming pools. Sightseeing in St. Louis should include Forest Park (1400 acres with Zoo and Open Air Theatre) and Shaw's Garden (more than 12,000 plants).

PEPPER POT STEAK

    2 pounds round steak, ½" slices
    4 tablespoons cooking oil
    2 large onions, cut in ½" cubes
    2 blades celery, cut in ½" cubes
    3 tablespoons flour
    1 cup beef stock (or bouillon)
    ½ cup soya sauce
    2 ripe tomatoes, cut in wedges
    2 large green peppers, ½" cubes

Season cut up steak with salt and pepper. Sauté steak in hot oil until brown. Add onions and celery. Then add flour and brown. Add beef stock and soya sauce and cook for 3 to 4 minutes. Add tomatoes and peppers and cook until tender, about 10 to 20 minutes. Makes 6 servings. Serve with Fried Rice.

Fried Rice

    1 cup rice
    ⅓ cup chopped onion
    2 tablespoons butter
    ½ teaspoon salt
 2½ cups consomme

Sauté rice and onion in butter until brown. Add consomme (canned may be used). Add salt, cover and cook until dry over very low heat (about 20-25 minutes). Serve with Pepper Pot Steak. Serves 4-5.

St. Louis, Mo. - West

I-270 at St. Charles Rock Rd.

Enjoy a "Captain K" sandwich. It's picture pretty, served on a wooden board, a hard egg roll filled with choice meats, cheeses and extra treats. Sea and stream entrées are in perfect harmony with the charming Golden Galleon Restaurant at this Inn. Do visit the Sea Dog Lounge. Then enjoy the Inn's many German Specialties . . . Wiener Schnitzel à la Holstein, Sauerbraten and Der Sizzler.

SEAFOOD NEWBURG

2 dozen oysters
2 dozen scallops (each cut in three pieces)
2 teaspoons chopped shallots
½ cup butter
12 mushroom caps (cut in halves)
3 cups Cream Sauce
3 dozen cooked shrimp (each cut in half)
1 tablespoon paprika
3 cups cream
3 egg yolks (beaten)
8 tablespoons sherry

Blanch oysters and scallops, then strain through a colander. Place juice in a pot and allow to reduce 5 minutes. Saute shallots in a little butter, then add rest of butter and mushrooms; simmer slowly until done. Add Cream Sauce and juice, then shrimp and rest of seafood. Add paprika and blend, then cream and slowly cook for 5 minutes. Add egg yolks which have been beaten with wine. Serves 12.

Cream Sauce

6 tablespoons butter
6 tablespoons flour
1½ teaspoons salt
3 cups milk

Place butter in saucepan and add flour as butter melts. Blend, add salt and milk. Stir over low heat until it thickens. 3 cups.

Springfield, Mo.

U.S. 66 & 65

A busy four lane highway is near this Inn, but 16 acres of rolling green lawn offer complete rest and quiet, 5 minutes from downtown. Gourmet cuisine and a children's menu make it popular with families. Yon can sip into something refreshing in the Red Slipper Lounge. Springfield is the Ozarks' market basket. Hill country crafts and household arts are displayed during the Ozark Empire Fair.

SAVORY SWEETBREADS

2 pounds calf sweetbreads
1 lemon, juice and all
1½ teaspoons pickling spices
1½ teaspoons salt
4 tablespoons butter
1 cup canned mushrooms, sliced
4 ounces dry sherry

Place sweetbreads, lemon and juice, pickling spices (tied in bag) and salt in a big pot with cold water to cover. Use a lid to fit inside pot to keep sweetbreads under water while cooking. Bring to a boil. Skim once in a while. Let sweetbreads simmer 20 minutes. Drain and save stock. To handle easily, place in cold water 8-10 minutes. Drain and remove skin and membrane. Sauté sweetbreads in butter in a skillet until slightly brown. Add mushrooms. Deglaze skillet with sherry, getting all particles from sides and bottom of pan. Add Cream Sauce and season to taste. Serve in casserole with toast points. Serves 8.

Cream Sauce

Blend 4 tablespoons butter and 4 tablespoons cornstarch. Add 1 cup stock (left from sweetbreads) gradually. Stir until it thickens, adding 1 cup top milk. Season. Makes 2 cups.

Table Rock Lake, Mo.

Kimberling Bridge on Hwy. 13

From each room and private patio there's a breath-taking picture of Table Rock Lake's blue-green mirror. This Inn has a lot to offer in the heart of Shepherd of the Hills Country. A private boat dock, marine facilities, riding stables, bowling lanes and starlight cruises on the lake all await your pleasure. There's a private dinner and dancing club on Pier 13. Breakfast is ready for the early risers.

CAMPING OUT SPECIAL

3 strips bacon
2 pieces bread
1 slice cheese
1 tablespoon peanut butter
2-3 slices tomato

Fry bacon until slightly crisp. Toast bread. Place bacon on toast with 1 slice cheese on top. Spread peanut butter on one side of second piece of toast. Warm cheese until soft. Place tomato on cheese with peanut butter on top. 1 portion.

FRANKFURTER CURL

Cut slices running parallel on edge of frank about ½ inch apart. Drop frank in hot oil and cook until lightly brown on both sides, and until it becomes a circle. Place on a regular hamburger bun. Fill the center of the circle with pickle relish. Pour favorite barbecue sauce over relish and frank. Add shredded lettuce and top of bun and serve. Allow 1 or 2 for each serving.

Great Falls, Mont.

On Bypass 87-89

Everyone knows about the fabulous fishing in Montana. Word is quickly spreading about this Holiday Inn's delicious picnic lunches to take along on fishing trips. The daily buffets are excellent too. Home-made bread is baked twice a day. No visitor should miss seeing the nearby Giant Springs — they flow 388 million gallons a day. Visit the C. M. Russell Art Gallery too.

CARROT SALAD

6 medium carrots, scraped and grated
3 tart apples, peeled, grated
¾ cup white raisins
½ cup crushed pineapple
⅓ teaspoon salt
Mayonnaise

Combine carrots and apples. Add raisins and pineapple (if desired). Mix with salt and mayonnaise and chill. Serve on lettuce leaves. Serves 4 to 5.

GREEN PEA SALAD

2 cups green peas
¼ cup onion, chopped
4 hard-boiled eggs, chopped
¼ cup sweet pickles, chopped
¼ cup sharp cheese, diced
½ cup celery, chopped
½ cup mayonnaise
Salt to taste

Combine all ingredients and toss lightly. Serve on lettuce leaves. Serves 8.

Grand Island, Neb.
Midtown

2503 South Locust

Choose your own steak to be charcoaled over the open grill in the Kopper Kettle Restaurant. For the best Fried Chicken, order it here. After dinner enjoy live entertainment in the lounge. The Inn is close to Riverside and Stuhr Museum. Grand Island is located in the rich Platte Valley. The town is an island 20 miles long in the middle of the Platte River.

ROCK CORNISH GAME HENS

    4 Rock Cornish hens
    4 tablespoons butter
    1 teaspoon salt
    ½ cup cream
    ½ cup butter
    1 can beef bouillon
    1 tablespoon Worcestershire sauce
    1 lemon (juice)
    1 large onion, chopped

Prepare hens for cooking. Rub inside with part of butter and salt. Dip each in cream, then roll in flour. Brown over medium heat in a heavy skillet with rest of butter. Place in a Dutch oven or casserole. Add beef bouillon and remaining ingredients. Bake 45 minutes to 1 hour in a slow 275-300 degree oven. Serve with Mock Wild Rice. Serves 4.

Mock Wild Rice

Heat skillet, cover with olive oil and add ½ can French's parsley flakes, 2 dashes garlic salt, 1 chopped onion, and 1 cup long grain rice (uncooked). Sauté until rice is brown. Pour into casserole and add 1 cup water and 1 can undiluted beef consomme. Season. Bake at 275-300 degrees for 1 hour. Add more liquid, if needed Serves 4 to 6.

Lincoln, Neb.
5250 Cornhusker Hwy.

Delicious food specialties with gourmet sauces and dressings make this a favorite stopping place for diners who want unusual dishes. The Inn is 4 miles from downtown Lincoln, the second largest city in Nebraska. The "Cornhuskers" battle for gridiron glory at the University of Nebraska. Lincoln is the home of the Ralph Mueller Planetarium.

SAUTÉ OF BEEF STROGANOFF

    1 pound beef tenderloin tips
        (strips ½" thick, 2" long)
    1 large onion, finely chopped
    1 green pepper, diced
    ½ pound mushrooms, cooked
    ½ pint tomato juice
        Dash lemon juice
        Dash Worcestershire sauce
    1 cup sour cream
    ½ cup Burgundy

Season meat generously with salt, pepper and Accent seasoning. Sauté sliced beef tenderloin in butter. Then add finely chopped onion, green pepper and mushrooms. Dust with a little flour, then add tomato juice, dash of lemon juice and Worcestershire sauce. Simmer slowly (do not boil) for about 1 hour. Then add sour cream and Burgundy. Serve from a chafing dish on a bed of steamed rice with toasted rye bread. Serves 3 to 4.

FLAMING SHISH KABOB

Alternate juicy beef tenderloin cubes, whole large mushrooms, little whole onions and cherry tomatoes on a flaming dagger Charbroil to desired doneness. Allow 1 dagger for each person.

North Platte, Neb.

U.S. 83 & Interstate 80

For pheasant hunting at its best, come to North Platte. This Holiday Inn is headquarters for hunters and knows how to keep them happy — with delicious food. The menu offers everything from exotic dishes to All-American fare. Homemade rolls and pies are baked daily—they're always gone at the end of the day! The fun place in the evenings is around the Inn's piano bar.

ROAST WITH SAUCE ROBERT

4- to 5-pound beef roast
    (inside round)
½ cup barbecue sauce
1 cup brown gravy
2 tablespoons Heinz 57 sauce
1 tablespoon A-1 sauce

Roast meat in preheated oven at 350 degrees uncovered until done to your taste (30 to 40 minutes a pound). Drain fat from roaster but retain meat juices. Add barbecue sauce, brown gravy and sauces. Simmer over low heat for 5 minutes. Strain (or not) and serve separately with meat. Serves 10 to 12.

BANANA NUT BREAD

1 cup sugar
½ cup butter or margarine
2 beaten eggs
2 cups sifted flour
1 teaspoon soda
3 tablespoons sour milk
3 mashed bananas
1 cup chopped nuts

Cream sugar and butter. Add eggs and beat well. Sift flour and soda together and add alternately with sour milk. Add mashed bananas and nuts. Mix well. Pour into a greased loaf pan. Bake in a 350 degree oven for 1 hour. Cool before slicing.

Las Vegas, Nev.

3740 Las Vegas Blvd. S.

Everyone has to stop once and awhile in Las Vegas. This Holiday Inn is right on "The Strip", so stop for a swim in either of its two pools. Stop and relax in the Red Fox Tavern. Stop for a snack or dinner in the Red Coals Restaurant. City Tours and Night Club Tours may be arranged at the Inn, also day-long tours to Hoover Dam, Lake Mead and the Grand Canyon.

CHICKEN POLYNESIAN

2 2-pound chickens (fryers)
2 tablespoons melted butter
2 tablespoons soy sauce

Split chicken into 4 halves and season. Mix butter and soy sauce and brush chicken with it. Sprinkle with paprika and broil until delicately brown and chicken is done. Place in shallow baking dish, skin side up, cover with foil and bake for 30 minutes at 325 degrees. Remove foil and broil about 10 to 15 minutes.

Polynesian Sauce

1 can chunk pineapple
1 green pepper
¼ cup chopped pimentos
¼ cup pineapple juice
½ cup mandarin orange sections
½ cup brown sugar
2 tablespoons cider vinegar
½ teaspoon powdered ginger
    Pinch garlic powder
2 tablespoons cornstarch
1 cup shredded coconut, toasted

Mix all ingredients except coconut and simmer for 15 minutes. Cover top of broiled chickens with sauce and sprinkle toasted coconut on top of each. Serve with rice or potatoes. Serves 4.

Manchester, N.H.

21 Front St. on Everett Tpk.

Guests at this Inn can track a deer or hook a trout in the morning and make a business call in downtown Boston the same afternoon. 2 ski areas and 11 ice skating facilities are within the city limits. A most frequented Manchester attraction is the Currier Gallery of Art. The Inn's Old English dining room features traditional New England fare. Homemade bread too.

NEW ENGLAND BOILED DINNER

```
4 pounds corned beef
1 cup water
2 onions, sliced
1 head green cabbage
6 potatoes
6 medium turnips
6 carrots
  (cook 6 beets separately)
  Tomato flowers
  Parsley
```

Wash corned beef thoroughly. Cover with boiling water and soak 1 hour. Prepare vegetables, paring and quartering cabbage and potatoes. Pare turnips, cut up if large. Scrape carrots and cut up if large. Place meat on rack in large kettle, cover with cold water, cover and let come to a boil. Simmer slowly for 2 hours. Arrange vegetables around corned beef, onions, turnips, potatoes, carrots, then cabbage on top. Season. Steam vegetables with meat until done (about 30 to 40 minutes). Place meat in center of platter and arrange vegetables around it. Place cooked beets on platter too. Garnish. Serves 8.

Portsmouth, N.H.

I-95 & Woodbury Ave.

Come aboard the Helm Restaurant for the best seafood ever! The nautical decor will make you think you are dining at sea. Exquisite Mediterranean dishes are also on the menu. The same waters that launched ships for John Paul Jones are launching vessels for today's Navy in Portsmouth. There are many historic homes to visit with costumed guides.

STUFFED GRAPE LEAVES

```
1 pound fresh grape leaves or
  1 12-ounce jar
¾ pound lamb, ground
1 cup uncooked rice
½ teaspoon ground cinnamon
½ cup water
  Lamb bones
2 garlic cloves, sliced
2 cups lamb broth or chicken bouillon
```

Wash and blanch fresh grape leaves, or rinse bottled ones. Combine meat, rice, cinnamon, salt and pepper to taste with water. Place 1 teaspoon of the mixture in the center of each leaf and roll up, beginning with bottom (where stem has been removed), then folding in sides, and ending with top point. Roll tight enough so that leaves hold together, but allow for swelling of rice. Place bones on bottom of casserole, cover with garlic. Arrange rolls on top, close together, in as many layers as necessary. Press down firmly, add broth and cook (uncovered) for 1 hour. Makes 10 or more servings.

Mint Sauce

Add 2 tablespoons fresh lemon juice, 1 minced garlic clove, and a few minced mint leaves to liquid in pot for last few minutes grape leaves are cooked. Serve sauce hot or cold with squeeze of lemon.

Atlantic City, N.J.

Jct. Expwy. & Boardwalk

Stay at an unsurpassed location in Atlantic City — on the Boardwalk, overlooking the ocean, adjacent to the Convention Hall. The Casa Del Sol Restaurant and Cocktail Lounge are "tops of the walk" with superb cuisine served 23 floors above the ocean. You can walk from the Boardwalk right into the Caribbean Restaurant and Lounge.

FRESH LOBSTER COOKED IN BURGUNDY WINE

```
12 ounces cooked lobster, cut
 2 tablespoons butter or oil
 2 shallots, minced
½ cup Burgundy wine
 2 teaspoons Italian tomato paste
 1 chicken bouillon cube
 1 cup hot water
 1 cup brown sauce
 8 pearl onions
 8 button mushrooms
   Maggi seasoning, few drops
 2 small tomatoes, peeled and cut
½ clove garlic
 1 pinch rosemary
 1 spray parsley, chopped fine
 1 bay leaf
 1 pinch black pepper
```

Saute lobster in butter or oil while covered. Add shallots, salt and pepper and cook for a few minutes. Add wine and let simmer until wine is absorbed. Add tomato paste, bouillon cube and hot water and brown sauce. Simmer until thickened. Add remaining ingredients and continue to simmer about 3 minutes. Remove garlic and serve in casserole with baked orange, flavored rice and kumquats. Serves 2.

(Old French Market style recipe).

Gloucester City, N.J.

U.S. 130 S., Walt Whitman Bridge

A beautiful dining room sets the stage for gourmet dinners. Casual outdoor living and relaxation on terraced gardens are part of the scene too. Located at the Walt Whitman Bridge, the Inn is convenient to all major industries on both sides of the Delaware River. Historic Philadelphia, the International Airport and the Garden State Race Track are all nearby.

BEEF TENDERLOIN KEBAB

```
2-3 pounds beef tenderloin
¾ cup wine
 2 tablespoons olive oil
 4 Bermuda onions
 4 green peppers
 6 solid tomatoes
```

Cut beef into squares, add wine, olive oil and season to taste. Cut onions lengthwise in medium-size pieces. Mix together and let stand overnight in refrigerator. Arrange beef, onion pieces, green peppers (cut in pieces) on skewers. Put tomatoes on separate skewer. Broil over charcoal, turning often until desired doneness. Serves 6.

SOUR-SWEET POT ROAST

Flour and season a 4- to 5-pound top round of beef with 3 tablespoons flour, 1 teaspoon salt and ¼ teaspoon pepper. Brown in 2 tablespoons hot cooking oil over medium heat. (Use heavy skillet).

Slice 2 medium-sized onions over meat and add:

```
 1 bay leaf
 4 whole cloves
¼ cup red wine vinegar
¼ cup water
```

Cover and cook slowly. Baste often. Cook until tender (2-3 hours). Add more water if needed while cooking. Serves 10.

Jersey City, N.J.

At entrance to Holland Tunnel

Diamond Jim and Lillian Russell are only memories, but the Trolley Room in this Inn brings the Gay Nineties to life. There's an authentic Trolley Car, and a conductor serves "Velvet Swings" and "Gibsons". Rooms are sound proofed so guests will not be disturbed by the passing parade of 25,000 cars on their way to Manhattan. This Inn is only 5 minutes from New York City, just a few minutes away from the Port of New York.

FETTUCINI

1 pound egg noodles
3 ounces butter
½ pint sour cream
½ pint heavy cream
1 tablespoon chives, chopped fine
3 ounces grated Parmesan cheese

Boil the noodles, cool and drain. Melt slowly the butter in aluminum saucepan, add the drained noodles, sour cream and heavy cream. Simmer and bring to a boil. Let boil, stirring for 3 minutes. Add chives. pepper and stir and add Parmesan cheese. Since Parmesan cheese is often salty, be careful in adding salt. It is essential that fettucini be served immediately. Serves 4.

MOUSSE GLACÉE

3 whole eggs
4 egg yolks
1 pound powdered sugar
¾ cup filberts, toasted
1 pint heavy cream

Place eggs and sugar in mixer and whip well for 15 minutes. Add and blend in finely chopped filberts. Whip the heavy cream separately until stiff. Fold gently into egg and sugar mixture. Place in a mold and freeze until stiff. When hard, remove from mold, cut and serve. Serves 8.

Kenilworth, N.J.

Exit 138 Garden St. Pkwy.

Rare, medium or well done? Steaks and roasts are exactly as you like them at this Holiday Inn. The Inn has gained fame for its superb prime ribs and beef sirloin. The spacious dining room overlooks the beautiful Garden State Parkway. Newark Airport is only 3 miles away. Ask about the Chartered Tour Service. The Inn is near Nomahagen Park and Echo Lake. A shooting range is also nearby.

COQ AU VIN

Chicken in Wine Sauce

2 onions, diced
6 slices bacon, diced
3 tablespoons butter
1 3-pound roasting chicken
   (cut in serving pieces)
¼ cup cognac or brandy
1 tablespoon flour
½ bottle red wine
   Bouquet garni
   (bay leaves, thyme, parsley)
1 clove garlic, chopped
1 can button mushrooms

Place onions and bacon in top of stove casserole or frying pan with cover and lightly brown in butter. Remove onion and bacon and brown chicken in remaining grease to a golden brown on all sides. Pour cognac over the chicken and set aflame. Sprinkle with flour and stir. Then add wine. When liquid begins to simmer, return the bacon and onion. Add the bouquet garni and garlic. Cover casserole and simmer gently for about 45 minutes, or until chicken is tender. Shortly before serving remove bouquet garni and add mushrooms. Serve hot. Serves 4 to 6.

Moorestown, N.J.

Exit 4 N. J. Tpk.

Here's country club living at a most convenient location. This Inn is only minutes from Philadelphia and its many historic sights. And it's near the Garden State Race Track. Antique hunters find this area a storehouse of forgotten treasures. Once you get a taste of the seafood, you too will always try to be nearby when hunger strikes.

OYSTER DELIGHT

    6 tablespoons butter
    1 teaspoon paprika
    1 teaspoon salt
    ½ teaspoon celery salt
    1 teaspoon coarsely ground pepper
    4 dozen oysters with their liquid
    2 teaspoons Worcestershire sauce
    1½ cups cream

Melt butter in skillet over very low heat. Add paprika, salt, celery salt and ground pepper. Add oysters with their liquid and cook until edges begin to curl. Add Worcestershire sauce and cream. Serve in Toast Cups and garnish with lemon wedges. Serves 6.

Toast Cups

    12 slices fresh bread

Place fresh bread in muffin tins, forming shape of a four corner roll. Place in oven (425 degrees) until brown. Allow to cool and serve oysters.

SHRIMP SALAD

Combine 2 pounds cooked cleaned shrimp, 3 cups pineapple tidbits, 3 cups diced celery, ⅔ cup mayonnaise and salt and pepper to taste. Serve on lettuce leaves or in scooped out tomatoes. Serves 4 to 6.

Phillipsburg, N.J.

U.S. 22 E. of Phillipsburg

You'll be aware of modern luxury the minute you enter this Holiday Inn. And you'll be surrounded with fun things to do. There are skiing, slalom courses and cross-country trails. A Summer Theatre is nearby. Plan a day's sightseeing tour and visit Ingersoll-Rand, J. T. Baker Chemical Co., Bell and Howell, and Koh-I-Noor Pencil Co. And the highlight of every visit — incomparable cuisine at this Inn.

EGGPLANT PARMIGIANA

    2 eggplants
    2 eggs, lightly beaten
    ¼ cup water
    1 cup bread crumbs
    ¼ cup butter, melted
    4 tablespoons olive oil
    2 cups Tomato Sauce
    1 cup mozzarella cheese
    ¼ cup Parmesan cheese

Wash eggplants, dry—but do not peel. Slice in ½-inch thick slices. Add water to beaten eggs. Dip eggplant slices in bread crumbs, egg, then in crumbs again. Sauté slices in butter and olive oil, using a heavy frying pan. Brown on both sides. Place in a buttered casserole using a layer of eggplant slices, layer of Tomato Sauce, layer of cheese. Repeat. Top with Parmesan cheese. Cook in a 325 degree oven for 20-25 minutes. Serves 6.

Tomato Sauce

Sauté ¼ cup chopped onion and ¼ cup chopped green pepper in 2 tablespoons butter. Add 2½ cups canned tomatoes. Stir until well blended. Season and add a pinch of sugar. Makes 2 cups.

Albuquerque, N.M.-East

12901 Central Ave.

Ski buffs enjoy being so near Sandia Crest with its 7,500 foot chair lift. The numerous Indian Reservations in the area offer endless hours of sightseeing. The Inn will arrange for you to board America's longest Tramway (12 miles). The University of Mexico is only 6 miles away. Find out the delicious difference between Spanish and Mexican food in the Coronado Dining Room.

PINTO BEANS

1 pound pinto beans
½ pound salt pork, finely diced
1 clove garlic, mashed
1 tablespoon chili powder

Wash and pick over beans. Add cold water to cover and soak overnight. Drain, place in a heavy kettle, add cold water to cover and bring to a good boil. Add salt pork. Cook 40 minutes. Add hot water if needed. Add chili powder and salt. Simmer until beans are tender (about 2 to 3 hours). Serves 4 to 6.

MUFFINS

2 cups flour
4 teaspoons baking powder
1 tablespoon sugar
⅓ cup shortening
1 egg, beaten
1 cup milk

Sift dry ingredients and cut in shortening with blender or knives. Add egg and milk. Stir into dry ingredients. Bake in hot greased muffin pans for 20 minutes at 375 degrees. Fold in a cup of fresh berries or diced fruit for a good variation. (Sprinkle a little flour over any juicy berry to prevent discoloration of batter). Makes 12 muffins.

Carlsbad, N.M.

U.S. 62 & 180 S.

Carlsbad Caverns National Park is just minutes away. Tour information is available at the Inn. The complete walking tour takes about 4 hours and includes luncheon in the lofty underground dining room. After a day of sightseeing, drop in the Inn's "Silver Stallion" Saloon. Authentic Spanish food as well as American favorites (steak and lobster) and homemade bread await you in the Coronado Dining Room.

MEXICAN PINK BEANS

2 pounds beans
1 ham bone
1 large Bermuda onion (leave whole after removing outer leaves)
1 clove garlic
  Chili powder to taste
1 small can hot tomato sauce

Wash beans thoroughly and soak overnight. Drain and place in heavy kettle with water to cover with ham bone, onion, garlic, and chili powder. Cook for an hour over low heat. Add hot water, if needed, salt and more chili powder, if desired. Add tomato sauce last. Simmer slowly until beans are done but do not overcook. They should hold their shape and water should cook low. Pieces of ham can be cut off and added to beans when serving. Serves 18-20.

HOMEMADE BREAD

Scald 2 cups milk and cool until lukewarm. Add 1 yeast cake, ¼ cup sugar and ¼ cup melted shortening. Then add 2 cups water and 6 cups flour. Beat 3 minutes. Cover and let rise 1½ hours. Knock down, add 6 or more cups of flour with 1½ tablespoons salt sifted in. Knead on floured board until dough is elastic to touch. Cover and let rise until double in bulk. Shape into loaves and let rise again until double. Bake at 400 degrees for 1 hour. Makes 4 loaves.

Hobbs, N.M.

200 S. Linam St.

This Holiday Inn welcomes you to the land that was already old when the Spanish Conquistadores came. You'll discover a great place to stay when you stop at this Inn. It's right in the heart of downtown Hobbs. The Strata Restaurant is famous for its varied menu. You can order everything from Hot Tamales with Homemade Chili Sauce to Southern Fried Chicken and Yankee Pot Roast.

SPANISH OMELETTE

    2 teaspoons butter
    4 eggs
    3 tablespoons milk
    ¾ teaspoon salt
    ½ teaspoon baking powder

Measure butter and place in frying pan or omelette pan. Heat pan several minutes. Separate eggs, beat yolks, add milk, salt, baking powder and mix well. Beat egg whites and then fold into mixture. Pour mixture in frying pan, cover and cook 5 minutes. Remove cover and cook 6 more minutes. Cut through center and fold over. Pour Spanish Sauce over it and garnish with parsley. Serves 2 to 3.

Spanish Sauce

    3 tablespoons butter
    5 tablespoons flour
    1½ cups stock or water
    ½ cup tomato juice
    1 tablespoon green pepper, minced
    2 tablespoons tomatoes, crushed
      Salt and pepper

Melt butter, add flour and brown a little. Add stock, tomato juice, green pepper and tomatoes. Thicken a little, stirring continuously. Season to taste. Makes 1½ cups.

Las Cruces, N.M.

U.S. 70, 80 & 85, W.

There's always a wide variety of guests at this Inn. The Inn is in the heart of the fertile Mesilia Valley of the Rio Grande (where the old Spanish road, El Camino Real, once ran.) The area is famous for paper shell pecans, grown and shipped from the largest pecan orchard in the world. Meals at the Inn's Gaslight Restaurant are as colorful as New Mexico's glorious color from dawn to dusk. The pool-side parties are great.

CHEESECAKE

    3 packages Philadelphia cream cheese
      (small size)
    3 whole eggs, lightly beaten
    1 cup sugar
    1 teaspoon vanilla
    1 Graham cracker crust

Cream Philadelphia cream cheese, eggs and sugar. Add vanilla and pour into Graham cracker crust. Bake at 375 degrees for 15 minutes. Pour Topping over hot cheesecake and bake at 500 degrees for 5 minutes.

Graham Cracker Crust

Combine 1¼ cups Graham cracker crumbs and 3 tablespoons sugar. Stir in ⅓ cup melted butter and blend. Pack mixture firmly in bottom of 9-inch spring form pan and up about 1 inch on sides. (Butter pan sides so mixture will adhere).

Topping

Combine 2 cups sour cream, ⅔ cup sugar and 2 teaspoons vanilla.

Santa Fe, N.M.

Cerrillos Rd., U.S. 85 S.

Ancient narrow streets of adobe homes with patio gardens hold the history of the Indians, Spanish and Old West. The surrounding area is famed for hunting, fishing, skiing, horseback riding and hiking. The Santa Fe Ski Basin is just 16 miles north. Guests at this Inn look forward to the buffet dinners . . . showcases of delicious foods (from mild to real hot). There's a piano bar in the lounge.

SPAGHETTI SAUCE WITH CHICKEN GIBLETS, LIVER AND PORK LOIN END

2 large onions
2 tablespoons salad oil
½ cup chicken giblets
1 cup pork trimmings
1 cup chicken livers
2 large bell peppers
2½ cups canned tomatoes
1 28-ounce can tomato juice
1 can (2½ oz.) mushrooms
    Garlic powder
    Sweet basil
    Salt and pepper
½ pound spaghetti (cooked)

Chop onions and brown in salad oil. Run the giblets and pork trimmings through a meat grinder with coarse holes. Cut liver and bell peppers into small pieces. Add to the browned onions and simmer until tender. Add tomatoes, tomato juice and mushrooms. Add garlic powder, sweet basil, salt and pepper to taste. Cook until thick. Serve over spaghetti. Serve with a sprinkling of Romano or Parmesan cheese, garlic bread and butter and a good tossed green salad with vinegar and olive oil. Serves 4 to 5.

Albany, N.Y.-No. 1

Albany-Schenectady Rd.

Be prepared for succulent prime ribs of beef and unusual specialties at this Inn. It's no wonder statesmen, tourists and executives make this Inn their first choice. Sightseers enjoy the Port of Albany, Saratoga Spa (the famous Saratoga Race Track and historic Battlefield of the Revolutionary War), and the State Capitol Building.

LOBSTER CUTLETS

½ pound lobster meat, chopped
½ pound shrimp, chopped
½ teaspoon tarragon leaves
½ tablespoon paprika
½ tablespoon salt
1 medium onion, chopped fine
¼ pound mushrooms, chopped fine
½ clove garlic, minced
1 ounce sherry
2 eggs, well beaten

Sauté lobster, shrimp, tarragon leaves, paprika, salt, onion, mushrooms and garlic in butter until all water evaporates. Add sherry, then Cream Sauce. Let simmer 10 minutes. Remove from heat and add eggs. Let cool completely. Make into 3-ounce cutlets. Bread and sauté in butter. Makes 12 or more cutlets. Serve with Newburg Sauce.

Cream Sauce

Melt ¼ pound butter, add ¼ pound flour and blend. Add 1 pint hot milk gradually and cook until it thickens.

Newburg Sauce

Melt 2 tablespoons butter and blend in 2 tablespoons flour. Then add 2 cups half and half. Cook over very low heat. Add part of sauce to 2 well beaten egg yolks. Then combine with rest of sauce. Add salt, pepper and a dash of nutmeg. Then add 3 tablespoons sherry last. Makes approximately 2 cups.

Binghamton, N.Y. - East

U.S. 11 and N.Y. 17, East

Watch the chef carve a Steamship Roast with showmanship and lightning speed. Some of the most delicious specialties of this Inn are served at noon. Notables in the evening include Filet of Beef with a brandy flavored stuffing. Over 35 different salads are prepared here, so expect a wide variety on the Smorgasbord.

STUFFED FILET OF BEEF

3 to 4-pound filet of beef (at least 3 inches in diameter)

Cut slit in beef to within ¼ inch of ends and deep but be careful not to cut through. Spread stuffing in cavity but not too full. Tie loosely with string in 1-inch spaces or use skewers. Place in roasting pan and bake in preheated 400 degree oven approximately 1 to 1½ hours. Remove strings or skewers and place filet on hot platter. Be sure to put slit side down. Fat may be skimmed from pan where filet was cooked. Add a little water and stir particles in pan to get additional sauce to pour over filet when serving. Serve with Béarnaise Sauce in extra sauce boat. Serves 8.

Stuffing for Filet of Beef

Crumble ½ to 1 cup imported Roquefort cheese. Sauté 2 tablespoons fresh chives (chopped fine) in 1 tablespoon butter. Add to cheese and blend. Combine with 1 tablespoon chopped almonds, pinch garlic powder, ½ teaspoon salt, ⅛ teaspoon pepper, pinch Accent and pinch oregano. Moisten with enough brandy for right consistency to spread in slit of beef.

Béarnaise Sauce

Combine ½ tablespoon tarragon, 2 minced shallots, dash pepper, ¼ cup wine vinegar and white wine. Boil until only 2 tablespoons left. Beat 3 egg yolks until thick. Strain into vinegar mixture and beat. Add 1 tablespoon melted butter (cold) and thicken over low heat. Beat in ½ cup melted butter (cold) gradually. Season.

Binghamton, N.Y. - West

N.Y. 17 on Vestal Pkwy.

For guests who really appreciate Italian cookery . . . fettucini, scallopini and spaghetti . . . this Holiday Inn is the answer. Excellent American dishes are served here too. The restaurant is bright and cheerful and the service is good. Try any dish, you'll find them as delicious as described. Many a bride has a more memorable day because of her wedding reception at this Inn.

BAKED SPANISH PORK

1 full loin of pork, butt ends removed

Using a shallow roasting pan, place roast fat side up. Roast meat in 350 degree preheated oven and cook until meat is done, allowing 35 minutes per pound. Just before meat is done, take pork out of oven and place on heat proof platter on which part of rice mixture (below) has been spread. Spread rest of rice on top of meat. Return to oven for last part of cooking.

After removing pork from oven, pour juices in jar. Fat will rise to the top. Place 2 tablespoons of the fat in same pan on stove and stir to loosen particles where meat was cooked. Add ¼ cup flour and brown. Add 1 to 1½ cups liquid (including pan juices which were poured in jar). Stir until thickened. Allow ½ to 1 lb. per person.

Rice for Pork

4 cups Uncle Ben's Rice
1 large onion, diced
¼ cup bacon fat
½ stalk celery, diced
1 bell pepper, diced
1-2 quarts hand crushed tomatoes
1 teaspoon Tabasco
1 teaspoon sweet basil
2-3 teaspoons salt
½ teaspoon pepper

Cook rice. Brown onion in bacon fat. Add to rice. Boil rest of ingredients until thickened. Add to rice and stir over low heat.

Buffalo, N.Y.-Amherst

Tonawanda, N. Y.

This Holiday Inn is only 15 minutes from scenic Niagara Falls. (The Inn arranges limousine tours to the Falls for guests). During the summer months there are festivals almost weekly at the Falls, also weekend fireworks displays on the Canadian side. You can expect unusual regional foods (Stuffed Cabbage Rolls, Roulade of Beef) as well as homemade breads, pastries and desserts at this Western New York Inn.

GOAMKI

(Stuffed Cabbage Rolls)

1 large head cabbage
1 large onion
½ pound butter
2 pounds ground beef
2 cups cooked rice
2 tablespoons salt
1 tablespoon pepper
2 tablespoons Accent
2 eggs

Boil whole head of cabbage for 15 minutes, or until cabbage leaves begin to break away from core. Remove from water and peel off cabbage leaves carefully and allow to cool. Sauté onion in butter until limp but not brown. Cool and combine with ground beef, rice, salt, pepper, Accent and eggs. Mix thoroughly. Spread out cabbage leaves and place approximately ½ cup filling in each leaf (depending on size of leaf). Wrap carefully and place in casserole pan. Cover the cabbage rolls with 1 #2 can of drained sauerkraut (2½ cups) and cover this with 1 #2 can tomatoes (2½ cups), juice and all. Cover and bake at 350 degrees for 2½ to 3 hours. Allow to remain under refrigeration at least 24 hours before using to allow flavors to blend. When serving place 1 tablespoon sour cream over each cabbage roll. Serves 8 to 10.

Buffalo, N.Y. International Airport

Cheektowago, N. Y.

This Inn's location is great for businessmen. It's right at the airport, right in the middle of a busy industrial area. Everyone starts lunch or dinner with the fabulous homemade soups served at this Inn. A fresh loaf of hot rye bread is served with every dinner. Jack's Place (the Inn's Lounge) is the place to enjoy live entertainment and dancing.

FRENCH ONION SOUP

½ pound onions, thinly sliced
4 tablespoons butter
2 teaspoons flour
1 teaspoon salt
½ teaspoon pepper
½ teaspoon sugar
1 quart beef broth
1 bouillon cube
½ cup white wine (optional)
6 slices toast, preferably
   French bread (day old)
   Grated Parmesan cheese

Sauté onions in butter until tender and yellow. Blend in flour and seasonings. Add broth, bouillon cube and wine. Simmer slowly for 30 minutes. Toast bread on both sides. Place one in each individual casserole and cover with soup or use big tureen. Sprinkle with cheese. If oven proof casseroles are used, place under broiler to melt cheese. Serves 6 to 8.

Cortland, N.Y.

River St., Exit 11 on I-81

This Inn is in the heart of New York's ski country. It's surrounded by excellent ski resorts. And after a day on the slopes there's nothing like a bowl of hot chili at this Inn. It's delicious. But you don't have to ski to have a good time. Sightsee. Both Howes Caverns and the Baseball Hall of Fame are near the Inn. Cornell University is just a half hour away.

CHILI CON CARNE

1 to 2 cloves garlic, minced
½ to 1 cup onions, sliced
1 cup green pepper, diced
2 tablespoons salad oil
1 pound ground beef
1 to 2 large cans tomato sauce
    Chili powder to taste
    Salt to taste
2 #2 cans red kidney beans

Saute' garlic, onion and green pepper in hot oil for 5 minutes or until soft. Stir occasionally. Add ground beef, cook slowly until lightly brown and stir often, breaking meat apart. Mix in tomato sauce and seasonings. Cook tightly covered over low heat for 20 minutes. Add kidney beans (undrained), stir well and simmer uncovered for 20 to 25 minutes. 6 to 8 servings.

STRAWBERRY PIE

Blend 1 heaping cup of flour, ½ cup butter and 3½ tablespoons powdered sugar. Press in a pie pan with fingers. Bake at 350 degrees until slightly brown, about 20 minutes.

Place 1 pint hulled strawberies in baked crust. Add 1 cup sugar and 3 tablespoons cornstarch to another pint of hulled strawberries and boil until clear and thick. Pour over berries in crust. Cool, cover with whipped cream and serve. 1 pie.

Liberty, N.Y.

Exit 100, Rt. 17 Quickway

It's a Ski Chalet. It's a Summer Spa. This luxurious Holiday Inn in the Catskills is the place to get with it, away from it all. You're within minutes of major ski areas — Grossinger's slopes are only 500 feet away. The Inn has a private preserve for deer, bear and woodchuck hunting. Enjoy special access to private streams for great fishing. The Holiday Inn Restaurant makes gourmets' dreams come true. There's a complete Chinese menu too.

CAESAR SALAD

2 bunches romaine
1 clove garlic
1 slice bread
1-2 ounces olive oil
1 soft-boiled egg (1 minute)
    Salt
    Pepper
1 tablespoon lemon juice
2 teaspoons Worcestershire sauce
1 tablespoon Parmesan cheese

Wash romaine well. Dry and wrap in paper towel. Place in refrigerator. Rub wooden salad bowl with fresh garlic. Make croutons by cubing bread and toasting in 1 teaspoon olive oil. Tear romaine in small pieces, add soft-boiled egg and toss. Sprinkle with salt and pepper. Add lemon juice, olive oil, and Worcestershire sauce. Sprinkle cheese and croutons over all. Mix lightly. Serves 4.

Newburgh, N.Y.

I-84. Exit 17

The restaurant at this Holiday Inn is special. The food is so unusual (and unusually good) you'll want to come back again and again. It's located 2 miles from the heart of downtown, between Stewart Air Force Base and West Point. And it's close enough to the heart of Metropolitan New York for easy commuting. There are sauna baths at the Inn when you return.

BREAST OF CAPON WITH MUSHROOMS BONNE FEMME

```
4 capon breasts
   (from 3½ to 4 pound roasters)
   Seasonings
   Flour
4 tablespoons butter
1 tablespoon shallots, minced
1 tablespoon onion, chopped fine
8 medium-sized sliced mushrooms
1 bay leaf
1 cup white wine
   Butter and flour
1 teaspoon chopped parsley
```

Bone the breasts of roasters, taking care not to cut the nerve that holds the fillet. Cut the wing at the joint. Season and dip in flour. Saute in a heavy skillet using 4 tablespoons butter. Remove from pan and place in warm bowl. Add shallots, onion, mushrooms and bay leaf to skillet and brown over low heat. Add wine and stir all particles left in pan when chicken was cooked. Replace chicken and cover pan. Simmer until chicken is done (about 20 to 30 minutes). Dot with butter and flour and baste chicken. Sprinkle with chopped parsley. Serves 4.

New York, N.Y. Coliseum

440 W. 57th St.

There's rooftop swimming, free underground parking and everything in between at this Holiday Inn, in the heart of Manhattan. The Inn is only 2 blocks from the Coliseum, within a 10 minute walk of Lincoln Center, Central Park, and the Broadway theatre district. There's a 6-foot loaf of French bread for guests to slice for sandwiches at noon.

CORNISH HEN MIKI MOKA

```
6 game hens (1½ pounds each)
1 cup uncooked wild rice
1 large onion, chopped
1 stick butter
¾ cup diced lapchong
   (Chinese sausage)
¾ cup water chestnuts, chopped
½ cup light rum
1½ cups broth (made from necks, gizzards
   and hearts of game hens)
```

Wash wild rice and cook uncovered in 3 cups water over low heat for ½ hour. Drain. Saute onion in ⅛ of butter. Add to wild rice. Cook game hen livers in rest of butter. Remove, chop and add to wild rice. Combine wild rice with diced lapchong and water chestnuts. Season with salt, pepper and M.S.G. Stir in ¼ of the rum. Stuff and truss birds. Rub generously with butter. Roast in a hot (400 degree) oven for 40 minutes, basting frequently with ¼ cup rum and ¼ cup water. Remove hens and place on a warm platter. Add broth to pan drippings, thicken with a cornstarch paste (1 tablespoon cornstarch mixed with ¼ cup water). Season to taste with salt, pepper and M.S.G. Serve gravy separately with game hens. Serves 6.

Olean, N.Y.

2711 W. State St. Hwy. 17 W.

Located in the foothills of the Allegheny Mountains, this Inn has reason to boast about its beautiful scenery. (Olean hosts the Miss New York State Pageant too). Excellent skiing is nearby at Grosstal and Holiday Valley ski areas. This Holiday Inn has gained fame for its delicious and varied buffets. There's music nightly around the piano bar in the lounge.

CARROT BREAD

    3 cups sifted flour
    2 teaspoons baking powder
    2 teaspoons soda
    ¼ teaspoon salt
    2 teaspoons cinnamon
    2 cups sugar
    1 cup salad oil
    3 beaten eggs
    3 cups grated carrots
    1 cup chopped nuts (optional)

Sift together flour, baking powder, soda, salt and cinnamon. Set aside. Mix together sugar, salad oil and eggs. Add to this the dry ingredients and blend well. Add the grated carrots and chopped nuts. Mix until well blended. Pour into greased pans and bake in a preheated 350 degree oven for about 1 hour. 3 small loaves.

KING ARTHUR DRESSING

    ½ cup sugar
    1 tablespoon salt
    1 tablespoon dry mustard
    ½ onion, minced
    ½ clove garlic, minced
    1 cup Wesson Oil
    ¼ cup white vinegar

Sift dry ingredients together, add onions and garlic. Pour oil slowly and add a little vinegar at the same time. Spice with ½ tablespoon celery seed, dash Tabasco and ½ teaspoon Worcestershire sauce. Mix. 1¼ cups.

Plainview, L.I., N.Y.

On Sunnyside Blvd.

All of the excitement of Manhattan is only 35 minutes away. A 10 minute drive south will take you to Jones Beach and Fire Island. Long Island Sound is just 10 minutes north. Indoor and outdoor swimming pools and sauna baths are right here. The Inn is famous for its smorgasbord luncheons. Gourmet sandwiches are served in the lounge.

WILD RICE STUFFING

    3 cups cooked wild rice
    ½ cup butter
    1 cup chopped onion
    1 cup diced celery with leaves
    ½ teaspoon Tabasco sauce
    ½ teaspoon poultry seasoning
    5 cups bread crumbs
    2 tablespoons chopped parsley
    ¼ cup chicken bouillon

Melt butter, add onion, celery, Tabasco, poultry seasoning and 1½ teaspoons salt. Cook until onion is tender, not brown. Combine with bread crumbs and parsley, add bouillon and rice. Toss lightly with fork until well mixed. Yield is enough for 1 12-pound turkey, using ¾ cup stuffing per pound dressed weight. Place stuffing in foil; seal edges tightly. Bake in moderate 350 to 375 degree oven for 35 minutes or in slow oven at 325 degrees for 45 minutes. Place in turkey and sew securely.

PUMPKIN PIE

Mix ½ cup sugar with 1 teaspoon salt, ¼ teaspoon cloves, ¼ teaspoon nutmeg, and ¼ teaspoon ginger. Add to 2 cups cooked pumpkin. Beat 3 eggs and add to mixture. Then add 2 tablespoons melted butter and 1 cup milk. Turn into a pastry lined pan and bake at 425 degrees for 30 to 45 minutes. Serve with cheese or whipped cream. Serves 6 to 8.

Rochester, N.Y.-NW

1525 Ridge Road West

Having fun here is a snap — this is "Kodak City". This popular Inn is known as "The Big One on the Ridge". It's renowned for its delicious food. Just order Eggs Benedict for a start. Then be sure to try a Kummelwelk Sandwich for lunch. For dinner in Les Chandles dining room may we suggest a whole lobster with Chef's dressing and a glass of champagne.

EGGS BENEDICT

3 English muffins
6 slices ham, broiled
6 poached eggs
1 cup Hollandaise Sauce

Split muffins and toast. Cut ham same size as muffins and place on each muffin half. Slip a poached egg on each and cover with Hollandaise Sauce. Serves 3.

Poached Eggs

Place water or milk to cover in shallow pan or frying pan. Bring almost to boiling point and add salt. Break 6 eggs in a dish, one at a time, and carefully slip into the water. Cover and steam until white has jellied. Remove from water with perforated spoon.

Hollandaise Sauce

½ cup butter
Juice of ½ lemon
3 egg yolks, beaten
½ cup boiling water

Melt butter over low heat and add lemon juice and pinch of salt. Slowly add egg yolks, beating continuously. Add boiling water and cook, beating until thick. Makes 1 cup.

Rochester, N.Y.-South

4950 W. Henrietta Rd.

There are pictures to take home from the "Kodak City", but no picture can describe the excellent food served at this Holiday Inn. Once a week is "Italian Night" at the Inn. Red checkered tablecloths are the setting for a choice of Italy's regional specialties. Visitors enjoy tours through the Eastman Kodak camera works and the 50-room George Eastman home, a photography museum.

VEAL PARMESAN

3 eggs
1 cup milk
2 tablespoons Parmesan Cheese
4 to 6 veal cutlets
½ pound mozzarella cheese

Whip eggs with milk, Parmesan cheese, salt and pepper into a batter. Dip veal cutlets into batter and then into bread crumbs. Repeat. Fry cutlets in a quarter-inch of melted shortening until golden brown. Remove and drain. Then place cutlets on a shallow pan with a layer of Spaghetti Sauce. Add a layer of sauce over the cutlets, then cover each cutlet with a thin slice of mozzarella cheese. Place in a 350 degree oven until cheese has melted. Remove and serve. Serves 4 to 6.

Spaghetti Sauce

Fry pork chop in ¼ cup cottonseed oil. Brown well. Add 4 cups tomato purée, 3 cloves garlic, ½ teaspoon black pepper, 1 teaspoon basil, ½ teaspoon oregano, ½ teaspoon salt and 2 tablespoons Parmesan cheese. Cook at bubbling point 20 minutes.

Add 3-4 cups tomato purée and 1-2 cups water. Bring to boil, stir well and simmer 3 hours adding 1 tablespoon sugar. Sauce should cook down until thick. Approx. 2½ pints.

Stony Brook, L.I., N.Y.

Nesconet-Port Jefferson Hwy.

Chances are everyone in the area goes to this Holiday Inn between 2 and 10 on Sundays. The Sunday Buffets in the Camelot Room are marvelous. Long Island Duck is always a feature. Shore dinners, duck, steaks and ribs of beef are popular features everyday. There's something for everyone nearby . . . beaches, deep sea fishing, horseback riding, snow skiing, museums and golf.

DUCKLING BIGARDE

In mixing bowl combine: ⅓ cup orange marmalade, 1 tablespoon soy sauce, 1 teaspoon salt.

Roast 3½-4-pound L. I. Duckling (quartered) in 450 degree oven for 15 minutes. Reduce heat to 400 degrees and cook 30 minutes (until tender). Baste with half of orange sauce while cooking.

Brown 1 tablespoon flour in 1 tablespoon butter over low heat. Stir in ¾ cup Chablis, 1 tablespoon wine vinegar, and ¼ cup consomme. Bring to boil. Stir constantly and simmer 10 minutes. Add remaining orange sauce. Cover and cook 10 minutes more. Add ¼ teaspoon pepper.

Peel and cut 1 orange into wedges. Cook in boiling water 3 minutes. Drain.

Remove duckling to serving platter. Garnish with orange wedges. Pour excess fat off juices in pan. Add more stock to pan if needed for sauce, to serve hot in sauceboat with duck. Serves 4.

CAMELOT POTATO SALAD

Combine 7 cups sliced boiled potatoes, ⅓ cup chopped chives, 1 teaspoon salt, dash pepper, 2 tablespoons grated onion and ½ cup salad dressing. Stir well and chill. Combine 2 ounces Rhine wine, ½ cup chopped celery, ½ cup sour cream, and ½ cup mayonnaise. Chill. Combine mixtures and serve. Serves 8.

Syracuse, N.Y. Downtown

Exit 18 off I-81

Syracuse grew up in a giant-sized salt marsh at the south end of Lake Onondaga. Today it is one of the top manufacturing cities of the East. Excellent service, gourmet food and a most convenient location make this beautiful Inn a towering success in the heart of downtown. Syracuse University is only 4 blocks away. The War Memorial Convention Center is 6 blocks.

VEAL CUTLET MOZZARELLA

- ½ cup onion, chopped fine
- 2 ounces olive oil
- 2 cloves garlic, chopped fine
- 1 #2½ can tomatoes, whole
- 9 ounces tomato paste
- 6 veal cutlets
- ½ cup margarine
- 6 slices mozzarella cheese
- ⅓ cup Parmesan cheese

Sauté chopped onion in olive oil until clear and tender. Add garlic, canned tomatoes and tomato paste. Sprinkle with pinches of sugar, oregano, thyme, white pepper and marjoram. Add 1 teaspoon salt. Blend thoroughly and simmer about 30 minutes. Keep warm.

Add 1½ teaspoons salt to 2 eggs and beat until well blended. Dip veal cutlets in beaten eggs, then in dry bread crumbs. Sauté immediately in margarine until nicely browned on both sides. Remove from sauté pan, add slice of mozzarella cheese on top of each and place cheese side up in the sauce. Sprinkle Parmesan cheese over top of sauce. Bake covered in a 350 degree oven for about 45 minutes, until veal is tender. Lift veal cutlets out of sauce with a wide spatula. Place on cooked spaghetti. Pour sauce over all. Serves 6.

White Plains Elmsford, N.Y.

Tarrytown Rd. Rt. 119

Unforgettable dinners in the Winchester Dining Room always begin with homemade soup and usually end with Ice Cream Pie or Cheesecake. The menu teems with a variety of American and Continental cuisine for in between. Hot homemade rolls complete the delicious picture. But there are other reasons so many people stay at this Inn. New York City is only a 30 minute drive.

HOMEMADE VEGETABLE SOUP

    1 soup bone (beef shank)
    1 cup celery, diced
    1 cup carrots, shredded
    1 cup potatoes, diced
 1½ cups tomatoes
    4 green onions, diced
    2 tablespoons parsley, chopped
    1 turnip, peeled and diced
    ½ head cabbage, shredded

Place soup bone in heavy kettle, add cold water to cover, then salt. Bring water to a good boil and reduce heat. Simmer 2 hours. Add vegetables and simmer 1 hour, adding seasonings when vegetables are added, more later, if needed. Cut pieces of meat in small pieces for each bowl. Serves 8 to 10.

ICE CREAM PIE

Fill baked pie shell with favorite flavor of ice cream. Use very hard ice cream and take care not to break crust. Pile meringue over all, making sure it touches crust all around. Put under broiler for a few minutes until it browns. Serve at once, or place in freezer. Serves 6 to 8.

Meringue

Cook 6 tablespoons sugar and ½ cup water until you can spin a thread. Pour slowly over 3 egg whites (beaten with a pinch of salt and ¼ teaspoon cream of tartar). Beat until thick — about 5 to 8 minutes.

Yonkers, N.Y.

Exit 6 N. Y. St. Thruway

It's hard to check out of this Inn, once you check into what's in store for guests here. There are two plush swimming pools (outdoor and indoor). The Inn's Health Club is completely equipped with sauna baths, sun lamps and massage facilities. Gourmet cuisine and a fascinating view of the valley below await you in the "Restaurant in the Sky". All this is only 30 minutes from Broadway.

SALTIMBOCCA ALLA ROMANA

 2½ pounds veal, sliced thin
    8 slices prosciutto
    3 to 4 tablespoons butter
    2 tablespoons shallots
    2 wine glasses Marsala

Pound cutlets thin and sprinkle lightly with flour. Cover each slice with a thin slice of prosciutto (ham). Hold together with toothpicks. Sauté in butter until light brown on both sides. Add shallots and sauce as meat cooks. Add wine and water. Simmer until thickened. Season to taste. Serves 8.

BONED CHICKEN WITH WINE SAUCE

    1 chicken
    2 tablespoons butter
    1 teaspoon shallots, minced
    8 ounces white wine
    ½ cup soup stock

Bone chicken, breast and legs separately. Season and sauté in butter until done. Remove chicken and add shallots, wine and soup stock. Boil until thickened. Pour over chicken. Serve with pilaf and a whole mushroom on each piece of chicken. (If fresh mushrooms are used, sauté in butter until done). Season. Serves 4.

Asheville, N.C.-East

U.S. 70, 74 E., Tunnel Rd.

There's a real merry-go-round on the playground for the soda pop set. A heated pool, ping pong and shuffleboard await grown-ups. The Great Smoky Mountain Park is near and the Flat Rock Vagabond Players give nightly performances during the summer months. Guests at the Inn have golfing privileges at the Asheville Country Club. And you can expect unsurpassed food at the Inn too.

SUPERB WAFFLES

    3 eggs
    1½ teaspoons sugar
    ½ cup cooking oil
    1 cup buttermilk
    2 cups flour
    ½ teaspoon baking powder
    ½ teaspoon baking soda
    ½ teaspoon salt

Separate eggs. Beat whites until quite stiff with sugar. Combine yolks, oil, buttermilk and dry ingredients and beat well. Add stiffly beaten egg whites, gently folding into the batter. Do not beat. Cook in hot waffle iron. Makes 5-6 waffles.

HONEY FRENCH DRESSING

    1 cup sugar
    ½ tablespoon dry mustard
    ½ tablespoon paprika
    ⅜ teaspoon salt
    ½ cup honey
    ½ cup vinegar
    1½ tablespoons lemon juice
    ¾ tablespoon celery seed
    ½ tablespoon grated onion
    1½ cups Wesson oil

Mix sugar, mustard, paprika, salt, honey, vinegar, lemon juice, celery seed and onion. Then gradually add Wesson oil. Makes approximately 1 pint.

Charlotte, N.C. North

N. Tryon, Exit 85, Sugar Creek Rd.

Charlotte was once a gold mining center. Today it is a textile capital. Businessmen and visitors enjoy free transportation to and from the airport (10 miles) almost as much as the delicious food served at this Holiday Inn. The Mint Museum of Art is nearby. It is a restoration of the building occupied in 1835 by an original branch of the U.S. Mint. The birthplace of James K. Polk is only a few minutes away.

SWEET POTATOES IMPERIAL

    4 sweet potatoes
    1 cup corn syrup
    2 ounces Cointreau
    1 teaspoon cinnamon
    4 pats butter
    ⅓ stick butter
    1 red apple
    8 maraschino cherries

Boil sweet potatoes in their jackets. When done, remove from heat and peel. Cut in half lengthwise and place each half beside the other in a shallow baking dish. Make a mixture of corn syrup, Cointreau and cinnamon. Pour over the sweet potatoes and dot each one with butter. Place in the oven and bake for approximately ½ hour, basting frequently wtih the syrup. When potatoes are candied, remove from the heat. In a skillet, melt ⅓ stick of butter. Take small red apple and remove the core. Do not peel. Slice it evenly in ½ inch slices and saute' in the butter until golden in color. Place a slice of apple on top of each potato and a maraschino cherry in center of the apple. Serve hot. Serves 8.

Charlotte, N.C.
West (Airport)

6045 Wilkinson Blvd.

This Holiday Inn opens the door to a world of contemporary living in a city with a rich and colorful history. The Inn's quiet southern charm is near the airport and only a short distance from downtown. Guests return again and again for the Inn's delicious pastries. There's live entertainment in the lounge. The Children's Nature Museum is nearby.

SOUR CREAM APPLE PIE

Prepare pastry to line a 12x8x2 inch baking dish to within ¼ inch from top, having straight top edge. Wash, core and pare 1½ pounds crisp apples. Then cut into wedges ½ inch thick. Arrange the apples on pastry. In small bowl, mix ½ cup granulated sugar, ½ teaspoon cinnamon and 3 tablespoons flour. Sprinkle over apples, then spoon on 1 cup commercial sour cream. Bake 1 hour in a 400 degree oven until apples are done. Cool slightly, then cut into squares to serve. Makes 8 to 10 servings.

CHOCOLATE PECAN PIE

3 slightly beaten eggs
1 cup light corn syrup
½ cup granulated sugar
1 teaspoon vanilla
⅛ teaspoon salt
1 cup chopped pecans
½ cup semi-sweet chocolate

Combine eggs, syrup, sugar, vanilla and salt in a mixing bowl. Blend well. Stir in the pecans and chocolate morsels. Pour into an unbaked pie shell. Bake at 375 degrees for 40 to 45 minutes. Serves 6.

Durham, N.C.
Downtown

605 W. Chapel Hill St.

The Charcoal Hearth Restaurant at this downtown Inn welcomes you in the American tradition with an "open fire". The Festa Room where fine Italian foods are served is known as the "Mecca of Gourmets". Duke University and Hospital are only 1 mile from the Inn. Research Triangle Park is nearby. Durham is the home of American tobacco and there are daily guided tours through tobacco companies.

VEAL CUTLETS, HUNTERS STYLE

2 tablespoons melted butter
¼ cup olive oil
2 pounds veal cutlets
1 cup celery, chopped
1 cup carrots, chopped
½ cup onions, chopped
1 tablespoon parsley, minced
Salt and pepper to taste
½ pint dry sherry
1 tablespoon tomato paste

Combine melted butter and olive oil in a hot skillet. Place veal cutlets in skillet and brown on both sides. Add celery, carrots, onions, parsley, salt and pepper. Cover and simmer 10-15 minutes. Mix sherry and tomato paste and stir in mixture above. Cover and simmer gently until veal cutlets are tender. Remove skillet from heat. Thin gravy with a little stock if desired. Simmer an additional 5 minutes. Serves 6.

Fayetteville, N.C.

U.S. 301 & I-95

Watch your own steak sizzle to delectable perfection right before your eyes in the Copper Hearth Restaurant. Relax with something cool in the Stein Room. The daily life of Fayetteville citizens revolves around The Market House. It's in the center of town and occupies the site of the capitol of North Carolina from 1789-1793. There is a marker in Fayetteville showing where Babe Ruth hit his first home run in professional baseball.

FRESH PORK HAM (BOILED)

Wipe an 8- to 12-pound fresh pork ham with a damp cloth. Sprinkle with salt freely. Place in a kettle of simmering water so that ham is just covered. Do not allow water to bubble. Allow 25 to 30 minutes per pound for medium-sized ham. Allow ½ to 1 pound per person for serving.

HOLIDAY YELLOW SQUASH

6 to 8 yellow crook neck squash
1 teaspoon salt
1 onion, chopped

Slice small, tender yellow crook neck squash. Sprinkle with salt and simmer slowly in a covered skillet, in the squash's own juice which heat will extract. Just before squash is done and ready to take up, sprinkle onion over squash. Simmer slowly for a few more minutes. Serves 6 to 8.

Gastonia, N.C.

Exit U.S. 29 & 74 off I-85

This downtown Inn welcomes you to the Heart of the Piedmont. Gastonia is one of the largest textile spinning centers in the world. (Visitors enjoy the many garment outlets at local mills). Holiday Inn guests especially enjoy the Cattleman's Steaks and Prime Ribs of Beef in the English Pub style dining room. Homemade demi-loaves of bread and hot muffins are delicious extras.

SAUTÉED DANISH HAM AND KING CRAB MEAT

2 3-ounce pieces Danish ham
6 tablespoons crab meat (from legs)
2 tablespoons butter
Salt and pepper
Dash Worcestershire sauce

Dice ham, mix with crab meat and sauté in butter. Season. Place in individual casseroles and cover with bread crumbs. Brown in a 350 degree oven for 5 minutes. 2 servings.

TROUT AMANDINE

1 rainbow trout
Lemon Butter Sauce
¼ cup slivered almonds

Dip trout in butter. Place in ovenproof dish and bake in 450 degree oven for 15 minutes. Baste with Lemon Butter Sauce. When trout is done, cover with slivered almonds and Lemon Butter Sauce. Serves 1.

Lemon Butter Sauce

4 tablespoons melted butter
1 tablespoon lemon juice
Few drops Tabasco
¼ teaspoon salt

Combine butter and seasonings over low heat. Makes ⅓ cup.

Greensboro, N.C.
North
U.S. 29 & 16th St.

Memorable experiences in good eating await you at this Holiday Inn. And it's in the heart of downtown too. The city is named for General Nathaniel Green of the Continental Army. Today Greensboro is famous for its furniture markets. The Greensboro Historical Museum contains period rooms, an early store, the Dolly Madison collection, and the drugstore in which the noted author, O'Henry, worked as a boy.

POTATO A LA NORTH

½ whole onion, medium-size
½ green pepper, medium-size
½ pound bacon, chopped fine
2 cups instant mashed potatoes
   Seasonings to taste
   Parmesan cheese

Chop onion fine. Remove seeds and membrane from pepper and chop fine. Fry bacon until crisp and dice fine. Combine above ingredients. Prepare potatoes according to directions on package. If fresh potatoes are used, peel 5 to 6 medium-size potatoes and boil in water until tender. Drain and mash with potato masher and add ¼ to ½ cup hot milk. Beat until fluffy. Add other mixture and season. Mix well. When serving, sprinkle Parmesan cheese on top. Serves 6 to 8.

Greensboro, N.C.
South
I-85 at U.S. 220 & I-40

Furniture markets in the area bring businessmen from all over the country. This Holiday Inn is a convenient place to stay and the food is excellent. The Inn takes pride in serving anything from an informal snack to a gourmet dinner. Located just 2 miles from downtown, the Inn is a fun place for sightseers. The Guilford Courthouse National Military Park preserves the site of a Revolutionary War battle. Guided tours are available through a cigarette factory.

SHRIMP DE JONGHE

1½ pounds shrimp
2 cups boiling water
1 teaspoon salt
2 slices onion
   Bay leaf
   Clove
1 teaspoon vinegar
½ cup butter
½ cup salted crackers, crushed
¼ cup parsley, chopped fine
¼ cup dry sherry
   Dash Worcestershire sauce
   Paprika

Wash shrimp. Peel and take out black line. Place in boiling water with salt, onion, bay leaf, clove and vinegar. Cover and simmer 8 to 10 minutes. Drain. Cream butter, add crackers, parsley, wine and paprika. Place shrimp in buttered baking dish and dot with butter and cracker mixture. Bake in a 400 degree oven for 20 to 25 minutes. Serves 5 to 6.

Hickory, N.C.

This Holiday Inn offers mountain tours to guests as a special service. The Chamber of Commerce arranges tours through textile and furniture plants. Hickory is also a Hosiery Center. Lake Hickory and Linville Falls and Caverns are nearby. Fine foods are prepared to your taste in the Inn's Open Hearth Restaurant.

POTATO-LIVER LOAF

    1½ pounds liver
    2 tablespoons fat
    ¼ cup finely chopped onion
    ¼ cup finely cut celery
    ¼ pound pork sausage
    1 teaspoon salt
    1 cup mashed potatoes
    1 beaten egg

Brown the liver lightly in fat. Chop liver, onion and celery by hand or put through a food chopper, depending on the texture desired. Brown the onion and celery in fat and add to the liver. Add rest of ingredients, using enough milk or tomatoes to moisten the mixture well. Pack firmly into a loaf pan and shape. Bake in a moderate 350 degree oven for 1½ to 2 hours. Serve with Spanish Sauce. Serves 6.

Spanish Sauce

Brown 2 tablespoons chopped onion in 2 tablespoons butter or bacon drippings. Blend in 1 tablespoon flour. Add 2 cups cooked tomatoes, ½ cup finely cut celery, ½ cup chopped green pepper, salt and pepper. Cook about 20 minutes over low heat or until sauce is rather thick. Makes about 2 cups.

High Point, N.C. - No. 1

Choice steaks and delectable seafood make evening dining especially enjoyable at this beautiful Inn. High Point is a large furniture and hosiery manufacturing center. This Inn is only 5 minutes from the Furniture Expo. The High Point Municipal Park offers dancing, swimming, rides, a large playground, picnic area, fishing and excursions on a fabulous old boat.

FILLET OF FLOUNDER

    10 fillets of flounder, flattened
    10 noodle cakes, fried in butter
    ½ cup cooked shrimp, diced
    ½ cup dry sherry

Season each fillet. Spread about 1 tablespoon Fish Farce over each fillet and fold in two. Place in a well buttered pan and cook over a low flame for 15 to 20 minutes. Remove fillets and place each on a noodle cake on a heated platter. Reduce juices in pan by boiling for a few minutes. Add the diced shrimp. Stir in Mornay Sauce and wine. Add a pinch of salt and cayenne pepper. Pour this sauce over fillets and glaze in a 500 degree oven or under broiler. Serves 10.

Fish Farce

Sauté ¾ cup mushroom pieces in 2 tablespoons butter. Blend in ¼ cup flour and add ½ cup cream gradually. Stir in buttered bread crumbs until stuffing is right consistency. Add a little onion juice and seasonings. 1 cup.

Mornay Sauce

Melt ¼ cup butter. Blend in ¼ cup flour. Add 2 cups half and half gradually and stir until smooth and thickened. Stir in ¾ cup grated Cheddar (or Swiss) cheese and season. 2 cups.

Morganton, N.C.

Interstate 40 & Hwy. 18

Arrive on Friday and you're in luck. "Harvest of the Sea" buffets each Friday night feature such delicacies as Crab Legs au Gratin and Shrimp Newburg. The Family Buffets on Sundays last all day long. Morganton is located at the foot of the Blue Ridge Mountains—this Inn arranges mountain tours for guests. There's excellent trout fishing in the many nearby streams.

SHE-CRAB SOUP

1 pint milk + 1 pint cream
2 stalks celery, grated
2 teaspoons onion, grated
½ stick butter
⅛ teaspoon mace
⅛ teaspoon white pepper
2 cups white crab meat
4 tablespoons sherry
½ cup crab roe

Bring milk and cream to a boil. Sauté celery and onion in butter and blend. Combine mixtures and thicken. Add seasonings and crab meat. Add sherry and crab roe last. Stir well. Serve hot. Serves 6 to 8.

HOMEMADE BREAD

2 cups milk
1 yeast cake
¼ cup sugar
¼ cup shortening
2 cups water
12 cups flour

Scald milk. Cool until lukewarm. Add yeast, sugar and melted shortening. Add water and ½ of the flour. Beat 2 to 3 minutes. Cover and let rise 1½ hours. Add 1½ tablespoons salt and remaining flour. Knead until elastic to touch. Cover and let rise until double in bulk. Shape into loaves and let rise again until double in bulk. Bake at 400 degrees for 1 hour. Makes 4 loaves.

New Bern, N.C.

Jct. U.S. 70 and 17

The broad Neuse River flows behind this Inn. It's yours for fishing, moonlight cruises or just for the beautiful view. Walk 6 blocks into yesterday, into the restored first capitol of North Carolina, Tyron Palace. The Inn's popular Charcoal Hearth Restaurant invites you to make your choice at the steak display and watch it sizzle to perfection over an open fire. Seafoods from the coastal waters are served fresh daily.

BACKFIN CRAB MEAT AU GRATIN, EN CASSEROLE

4 tablespoons butter
4 tablespoons flour
1½ cups milk
2 egg yolks
1 teaspoon salt
Lemon Juice
Dash Worcestershire sauce
Onion juice
1 pound crab meat
½ cup cream
1 ounce sherry
½ cup buttered bread crumbs
¼ cup grated American cheese
Paprika

Melt butter, add flour and blend. Slowly add milk and stir until thickened. Beat egg yolks, add salt, a few drops of lemon juice, dash of Worcestershire and a little onion juice. Combine with first mixture. Cook over low heat, adding crab meat and cream. Stir all. Add sherry last. Place in a buttered casserole and sprinkle with bread crumbs, cheese and paprika. Bake at 350 degrees until cheese melts and bread crumbs are toasted. Serves 4.

Raleigh, N. C. - Dwtn.

320 Hillsboro Street

Your horoscope forecasts an evening of pleasure when you dine at "The Twelve Signs" rooftop restaurant in this Holiday Inn. Soaring nineteen stories high, the new circular Inn is the capital city's highest building. While dining, guests enjoy a panoramic view of Raleigh. The restaurant's zodiac theme is quite fitting as guests are "under the stars" while enjoying Chicken Capricorn, Gemini Beef and Steak Diane.

CHICKEN CAPRICORN

1 chicken
2 tablespoons shortening or oil
1 clove garlic, crushed
¼ pound sliced mushrooms
1 tablespoon lemon juice
2 tablespoons butter
⅓ cup brandy
2 cups red wine
1 bay leaf
8 to 12 pearl onions

Cut chicken into 8 parts. Heat shortening or oil, add garlic and mushrooms. Sauté 3 minutes. Add chicken, lemon juice, salt, pepper and butter. Cover and cook over high heat for 5 minutes. Reduce heat, add brandy and simmer until reduced. Add wine, bay leaf and onions. Cover and cook until tender. Remove chicken. Bring sauce to a boil for 5 minutes then pour over chicken. Allow ½ chicken for each serving.

STEAK DIANE

Cut 4 to 6 pieces of beef about ¼ inch thick from the tenderloin. Melt 2 tablespoons butter, add 1 tablespoon chopped shallots (or green onions), 1 clove garlic (juice of) and ¼ cup sliced mushrooms. Season. Cook steaks 2 minutes on each side in sauce, then remove and keep warm. To sauce add ½ teaspoon dry mustard, ½ teaspoon lemon juice and ½ cup finely chopped green onions. Heat 1 minute. Add 3 tablespoons sherry and ¼ cup cognac. Flame and serve sauce over steaks. Serves 1 to 2 persons.

Rocky Mount, N.C. Downtown

425 N. Church St.

The famous June German, a full dress dance, has been held annually in Rocky Mount for over 60 years. Over 5000 people attend, but by bid only. A new tradition is breakfast at this Inn after the June German. Hot biscuits, fried chicken and other southern specialties tempt travelers everyday. Jim Thorpe made his professional baseball debut with the Rocky Mount Railroaders.

POULTRY STUFFING

2 cups soft bread crumbs
½ teaspoon chopped parsley
2 tablespoons chicken fat
Salt and pepper
Sage
3 tablespoons finely diced celery
1 teaspoon chopped onion
2 teaspoons poultry seasoning

Combine ingredients, adding sufficient water or broth to make stuffing pack readily. If desired, a well beaten egg may be added. The giblets may be chopped and added to the stuffing.

SOUTHERN BROWNIES

1 cup plus 2 tablespoons butter
6 squares unsweetened chocolate, melted
2 cups sugar
5 beaten eggs
2 teaspoons vanilla
1¾ cups sifted cake flour
1 teaspoon salt
1½ cups walnuts or pecans, chopped

Melt butter and chocolate. Add sugar, eggs and vanilla and beat thoroughly. Sift flour and salt together. Add and beat until smooth. Fold in nuts. Pour into a greased 15x10x1 inch pan and spread evenly. Bake 20 to 25 minutes in a moderate 350 degree oven. Cool slightly. Cut into 2-inch squares. Yields 3 dozen.

Rocky Mount, N.C. North

U.S. 301 & 301 Bypass N.

At nearby Tarboro, an ancient cotton press once operated by mule power is preserved for posterity. You're in tobacco country and it's fun to attend a tobacco auction. Take a tour through a cigarette factory. Excellent fishing is not far away in the Pamlico Sound. Excellent food and a relaxing atmosphere are good reasons to make this Holiday Inn your headquarters.

PINEAPPLE CREAM CAKE

2¼ cups self-rising cake flour
1¼ cups sugar
1 cup milk
½ cup shortening
2 eggs
1 teaspoon almond extract

Grease and flour bottom of two 8-inch round cake pans. In mixing bowl, combine flour, and sugar. Add milk and shortening. Blend well. Beat 1½ minutes at low spead. Add eggs and almond extract, continue beating 1½ minutes. Pour batter into pans. Bake at 350 degrees for 30 to 35 minutes, until cake springs back when lightly touched. Cool 5 minutes, remove from pans, cool completely. Split layers in half crosswise, making 4 thin layers. Fill and frost with Pineapple Cream Filling and Topping.

Cream Filling and Topping

Combine 2½ cups crushed pineapple and 1 package coconut cream pudding or pie filling mix. Cook and stir constantly until thick. Chill.

Prepare 1 package dessert topping mix, using ½ cup cold milk and ½ teaspoon almond extract. Stir in ¼ cup maraschino cherries. Combine half of topping with pineapple mixture. Spread between layers and on top of cake. Frost sides of cake with plain topping mix. Chill.

Salisbury, N.C.

U.S. 29 Bypass at I-85

The buffets at this Holiday Inn are exceptional — exceptionally elaborate and delicious. Local residents know where to go on Sunday if they want to see everyone—to the Sunday Buffet at this Inn. Of course visitors enjoy excellent food throughout their stay. The Inn's Tiki Lounge is a fun place to relax. Sightseeing visitors enjoy being near "Towel City" (textile manufacturers).

CREOLE PORK AND SPAGHETTI

2 cups minced onion
2 pounds pork shoulder, ground
1 quart cooked spaghetti
1½ cups cooked tomatoes
2 cups grated cheese
1 teaspoon salt
1 cup dry bread crumbs
¼ cup butter

Brown onion and meat in hot skillet with butter. Mix with spaghetti, tomatoes, cheese and salt. Place in greased baking dish. Sprinkle crumbs on top, dot with butter and bake in 350 degree oven for 30 minutes. Serves 8 to 10.

DUTCH STEWED POTATOES

3 onions, sliced
3 tablespoons melted butter
1½ teaspoons salt
Dash or 2 of pepper
1½ teaspoons minced parsley
6 cups diced uncooked potatoes
1 quart boiling water
2 tablespoons flour

Sauté onion in butter for 5 minutes. Add salt, pepper, parsley and potatoes. Cover with boiling water and cook until tender. Thicken with flour, which has been mixed with a little cold water. Serves 8 to 10.

Southern Pines, N.C.

U.S. 1 South

Fox hounds and red coated hunters are usual sights around here. This is the sandhill region where fox hunting is a favorite sport. It's not surprising that this Inn's Red Fox Tavern is a favorite place to meet after the hunt. Golf, tennis, polo and riding are popular as well. The Inn arranges golfing privileges for guests. Dinner is served with a continental flair at the Inn.

SOFT-SHELL CRAB AMANDINE

12 soft-shell crabs
½ cup butter
¾ cup almonds, blanched
1 teaspoon paprika
1 teaspoon salt

Wash crabs thoroughly and dry well on absorbent paper. Dredge in seasoned flour. Sauté in butter, using a heavy skillet. Cook 2 to 3 minutes on each side until crabs are crisp on edges and browned a little. Remove to a hot serving platter and add paprika and salt. Add shredded almonds to juices in pan. Sauté and stir until golden color. Pour almonds and pan juices over crabs. Serve garnished with flowered lemons and chicory. 4 to 6 servings.

SOUR CREAM CHEESECAKE

Beat 2 eggs, add ½ cup sugar, ¾ cup cottage cheese, 6 ounces cream cheese and ½ teaspoon vanilla. Beat well. Pour the batter into a spring form pan lined with Graham cracker shell and bake in a moderate 350 degree oven for 20 minutes. Cool for 5 minutes. Combine 1½ cups thick sour cream and 2 tablespoons sugar and flavor with vanilla. Pour over cake and bake in a hot 475 degree oven for 5 minutes. Cool. Serves 8.

Wilmington, N.C.

U.S. 17 & 74, 4215 Market

Bring your camera, binoculars too. You can see the Atlantic Ocean, the U.S.S. North Carolina Battleship Memorial berthed on the Wilmington waterfront, and beautiful Azalea Gardens from this Holiday Inn. The Inn arranges an exciting 6-hour tour for guests during the summer months. It includes a spectacle from the Battleship's amphitheatre at night. The seafood is superb at the Inn.

LOBSTER THERMIDOR

2 1½-pound boiled lobsters
   or 3 cups lobster meat
1 cup milk
¼ cup butter
2 tablespoons flour
3 egg yolks, beaten
½ cup cream
½ cup soft bread crumbs
½ teaspoon lemon juice
3 tablespoons sherry
1 teaspoon salt
½ teaspoon cayenne
⅓ cup Parmesan cheese

Boil lobster and remove meat. Scald milk. Melt butter in skillet and cook lobster meat 5 minutes. Add flour, then milk and stir until well blended. Combine egg yolks with cream and bread crumbs. Add to lobster mixture and cook until thickened. Add lemon juice, sherry and seasonings. Fill lobster shells and place in baking pan. If no shells, use shallow casserole. Sprinkle Parmesan cheese on top and cook under broiler until bubbly and hot. Serves 4-6.

Wilson, N.C.

U.S. 301 South

Tobacco auctioneers' chants are heard throughout this part of North Carolina from August until October. Visitors are welcome to the sales held in over 26 communities. Many furniture factories are also in the area. For a taste of true North Carolina hospitality, this Holiday Inn is the place to visit. Try its gourmet ways with fish for sure.

MEAT BALLS IN TOMATO SAUCE

    1 pound finely ground beef
    1 tablespoon onion
    1 cup dry white bread crumbs
    1 beaten egg
    1 teaspoon salt
    1 teaspoon white pepper
    ½ teaspoon oregano
    ½ teaspoon garlic powder
    ¼ teaspoon sage

Mix meat with onion, bread crumbs, egg and seasonings. Shape into small balls and arrange on a sheet pan. Bake for 15 to 20 minutes at 350 degrees. Drain off grease. Place in a baking pan, cover with Tomato Sauce and bake for 10 to 20 minutes. Serve with hot spaghetti. Serves 4 to 5.

Tomato Sauce

    1 or 2 onions, diced fine
    1 large can tomatoes (2½ cups)
    1 can tomato paste
      Salt to taste
    1 teaspoon paprika
    1 tablespoon sugar
    ½ teaspoon white pepper
    1 clove garlic
      Oregano to taste
      Water, as needed

Combine and cook for 1 hour. Then blend and stir in 3 tablespoons flour and ¾ cup water.

Bismarck, N.D.

U.S. 10 at Memorial Bridge

Year round swimming is something in North Dakota. Located on the bank of the Missouri River, the Inn offers everything from a heated indoor pool to saunas, sun lamps and a putting green. The continental cuisine is outstanding in the Red Lion Dining Room. (Be sure to order the French Toast for breakfast). Sights to see include the western part of the beautiful Badlands and where General Custer took his last stand.

SOUR CREAM MEAT LOAF

    3 pounds ground beef
    2 cups soft bread crumbs
    ¾ to 1 cup milk
    1 whole onion, minced
    1 teaspoon salt
    1 teaspoon pepper
    3 eggs, slightly beaten
    1 carton sour cream

Soften bread crumbs in milk. Add to meat and sasonings. Stir in eggs. Place in greased loaf pans. Bake in 350 degree oven for 1 hour, or until loaf shrinks from sides of pan and is brown. Take out of oven 15 minutes before it is done and spread sour cream over top of each loaf. Bake 15 minutes more. Makes 2 loaves. Each serves 6.

GREEN GODDESS DRESSING

    ¼ cup parsley, minced
    ¼ cup onion, minced
    3 to 4 onion tops, minced
    2 tablespoons cider vinegar
    ¼ cup lemon juice
    1 teaspoon garlic salt
    ½ teaspoon pepper
    2 cups mayonnaise
    8 ounces sour cream
    1 dash green food coloring

Mix all ingredients together and let stand in refrigerator for a short time before using. Makes approximately 3 cups.

Akron, Ohio - West

Exit 11 S. of Ohio Tpk.

You can expect award winning food and an atmosphere of gracious living at this Akron Inn. The many businessmen and tourists visiting this important city need a place like this Inn to relax. Akron is the largest rubber manufacturing center in the world, and has the largest cereal mill. Tours of tire and rubber factories may be arranged.

POMPANO EN PAPILLOTE

1-pound pompano
¼ pound crawfish
¼ pound shrimp
   Salt
2 onions
¼ pound butter
2 tablespoons flour
½ pint boiled sweet milk
2 egg yolks, beaten
¼ teaspoon nutmeg
2 ounces sherry

Boil crawfish and shrimp in shells 10 minutes with 1 tablespoon salt. Then strain and shell. Clean and wash thoroughly. Chop crawfish, shrimp and onions very fine. Fry in 4 tablespoons butter, adding flour, milk, egg yolks, nutmeg, sherry and 1½ teaspoons salt. Keep stirring with a wooden spoon until done, then allow to cool.

Now halve pompano and skin, removing bones completely. Slice each half into quarters. On each piece of paper place 3 generous spoonfuls of paste, then place a slice of pompano. Spread more paste, then another slice of pompano. Spread paste over top. Pour melted butter over this and fold paper to form a bag with crimped edges. Place in well buttered pan and cook for 18 minutes in a hot oven. Serve while hot on paper. Serves 4.

Bowling Green, Ohio

1550 E. Wooster St. on I-75

This Inn's Red Fox Dining Room is well known for its steaks—but other specialties are just as ordered. Be sure to try Lobster and Capon Oriental or Braised Beef Tips and Vino Mushrooms. There's a seafood buffet on Fridays. The Inn is only ¾ mile from the airport and transportation is on the Inn. Bowling Green State University is also nearby. The University's Ice Arena is open to the public. There's also a golf course on the campus.

LOBSTER AND CAPON ORIENTAL

2-3 tablespoons butter
½ onion, chopped fine
½ green pepper, chopped fine
½ red bell pepper, chopped fine
½ pound cooked lobster meat, cubed
¼ pound cooked chicken, cubed
½ cup sherry
2 tablespoons Parmesan cheese

Sauté onion and peppers in butter. Add lobster and chicken. Then add sherry. Make Medium White Sauce and add as needed to meat and fish mixture. Cook slowly for about 15 minutes, then place in a casserole dish. Top with Parmesan cheese. Brown under broiler. Approximately 4-5 servings.

Medium White Sauce

Blend ¼ cup butter and ¼ cup flour. Add 1 pint hot milk gradually. Add 2 beaten egg yolks and stir until all is thickened. Season. Makes 2 cups.

Cambridge, Ohio

I-70 at Ohio Rt. 209

Commercial travelers look forward to the relaxing atmosphere and outstanding food at this Holiday Inn, near an industrial area. It's located 2 miles from downtown Cambridge, not far from Astronaut John Glenn's boyhood home. There's live entertainment in the Inn's lounge. Cambridge is near a popular vacation and resort region on Seneca Lake.

PORK-PINEAPPLE BROCHETTE

```
3  pounds lean pork shoulder
1  teaspoon Worcestershire sauce
2  cloves fresh garlic
1  teaspoon oregano leaves
36  pineapple tidbits (canned)
```

Trim the fat from the pork shoulder completely. Cut in 1-ounce cubes, roll in flour and sauté in a skillet with a little shortening. Add Worcestershire sauce, garlic (finely chopped), oregano leaves, salt and pepper. Leave in skillet until all sides of the meat are nicely brown and tender. **Do not overcook.** Allow 4 cubes of meat, 3 pineapple tidbits on each skewer. Glaze with Sweet-Sour Sauce when serving. Serves 10.

Sweet-Sour Sauce

Blanch 1 cup each: julienne celery, julienne onion, and julienne green pepper until tender but crisp. Then drain. Place 2 cups canned pineapple juice, ½ cup cider vinegar, ½ cup sugar, 1 teaspoon ground ginger and ½ cup soya sauce in a saucepan. Blend and bring to a boil. Add 1 tablespoon potato starch, blend in and simmer 3 or 4 minutes and remove from heat. Add the blanched celery, onion, green pepper and 1 cup water chestnuts (sliced ⅛ inch thick). Blend. Keep hot for serving. Makes approximately 1½ quarts.

Canton, Ohio

St. Rt. U.S. 30

Professional Football Hall of Fame games are popular in this industrial city. No wonder. Professional football was first organized in Canton. Jim Thorpe, Duke Osborne and Guy Chamberlain are among the greats belonging to the first professional team organized here. This Holiday Inn is in the heart of downtown and only minutes from the football Hall of Fame. Adventures in good eating await you in the Inn's dining room.

CANADIAN CHEESE SOUP

```
1½  tablespoons flour
1½  tablespoons melted butter
½  teaspoon dry mustard
1½  tablespoons Worcestershire sauce
1  tablespoon salt
1½  quarts milk
1½  cups Cheddar cheese
1½  tablespoons cooking sherry
```

Blend flour and melted butter. Add dry mustard, Worcestershire sauce and salt. Blend well. Add milk, stirring constantly until it thickens. Bring to scalding point, but Do Not Boil. Add cheese thinly sliced or grated. Mix well and add the sherry. Makes 2 quarts. A salad of grapefruit sections, slices or orange and avocado on lettuce with French Dressing is a good accompaniment.

Chillicothe, Ohio

U.S. Hwy 23, N. Bridge St.

Dine in the luxurious Great Ohio Seal Room. Superb food in an elegant setting has made this Holiday Inn a delightful dining spot. The decor is historical and appropriate. (The first State Constitution was written and the first Capital established in Chillicothe). Guests at the Inn enjoy the President's Lounge or refreshments on the patio. Do take a "Skyline Drive" through nearby Paint Valley.

SAUSAGE MEAL-IN-A-DISH

1 pound pork sausage
4 medium-size pared potatoes, thinly sliced
2 medium-size onions, thinly sliced
2½ cups cream style corn
1 teaspoon salt
⅛ teaspoon pepper
½ teaspoon paprika
1 can tomato soup
1 cup chopped green pepper

Shape sausage into 10 or 12 small patties. Brown in heavy skillet over medium heat. Place potatoes, onions and corn in alternate layers in a greased 2-quart casserole, sprinkling each layer with salt, pepper and paprika. Lay browned patties around rim of casserole. Pour undiluted soup over top. Sprinkle with chopped green pepper. Cover and bake in a moderate 350 degree oven for 1 hour, or until potatoes are tender. Makes 6 to 8 servings.

Cincinnati, Ohio Downtown

I-75 dwtn. at 8th & Linn

In the early days sidewheel steamers brought cargoes to this busy river port. Today the Queen City, enthroned on 7 hills above the Ohio River, is still a great commercial center. The Little Foxes Rooftop Night Club features live entertainment atop this high-rise downtown Inn. Meals fit for a King (at Peasant's prices) are served in the Inn's main floor King's Room.

STUFFED RAINBOW TROUT, SINGAPORE STYLE

4 boneless brook trout
4 tablespoons butter
4 ounces salad oil
4 glazed pineapple rings
4 spiced crab apples

Season trout with salt and pepper, inside and outside. Dredge in flour and shake off excess. Heat oil and butter in a frying pan and cook trout slowly on top of stove until golden brown on one side. Turn over and finish cooking in moderate oven for about 8 minutes. When cooked, place on platter and discard excess oil. Put pilaff on top of trout, glazed pineapple rings on top of rice, and cover with Curry Sauce. Top with spiced crab apples. Serve with banana fritters. Serves 4.

Curry Sauce

Sauté 2½ tablespoons finely diced onion in ¼ cup margarine until clear. Add ¼ cup diced apple and 1 tablespoon curry powder. Blend ¼ cup flour into mixture. Add 1-2 tablespoons fresh coconut (shredded) and 2 cups chicken stock. Cook 5 minutes, stirring constantly. Add ¼ cup cream and salt to taste. Strain. Serve hot. 2 cups approximately.

Cincinnati, Ohio
North
I-75 N. at Sharon Rd. Exit

After a day of business (or sight-seeing) in Cincinnati, it's fun to come home to this Holiday Inn. Tee off on the Inn's own 18-hole par 3 golf course. Sip into something refreshing and enjoy live entertainment in the Red Slipper Lounge. Visitors agree this Inn is a great place to stay overnight or for a long visit. Gourmets consider themselves lucky whenever they stop here.

BEEF TENDERLOIN STROGANOFF

2 pounds beef tenderloin tips
1½ tablespoons salad oil
⅓ cup finely diced onion
1 medium clove garlic
¾ cup cooked mushrooms, sliced
2 tablespoons paprika
1 tablespoon salt
2 heaping tablespoons flour
3 ounces vodka
1 pint brown gravy
1 pint sour cream

Trim rough membrane and fat off tenderloin tips. Cut trimmed pieces of tenderloin into strips approximately ½ inch wide by 2 inches long by ¼ inch thick. Sauté strips in hot salad oil until they are golden brown. Add onion, garlic and mushrooms and simmer about 2 minutes. Add paprika, salt and flour and blend well. Add vodka and brown gravy and blend. Bring to a boil. Then add sour cream and simmer over low heat for about 2 minutes, until meat is tender. Serve with pilaff or noodles. Serves 6.

Cincinnati, Ohio
Northeast
I-71, Mason, Ohio

This popular Holiday Inn is within the Greater Cincinnati area. There are sights to see in every direction, a shopping center close by. More than 10,000 mounds left by prehistoric Ohio Indians are just a sightseeing trip away. The largest is the Serpent Mound, a simulated snake measuring more than 1,330 feet. There's live entertainment in the Inn's Lounge.

CHEDDAR CHEESE SOUFFLÉ

3 tablespoons margarine
3 tablespoons flour
½ teaspoon salt
1 cup milk, heated
1 cup Cheddar cheese, grated
3 egg yolks, well beaten
3 egg whites

Make a roux of margarine and flour. Remove from heat and cool. Add salt to hot milk, bring to a boil, then add grated cheese. Stir until melted. Remove from heat, add egg yolks. Mix well. Let cool. Beat egg whites until stiff. Turn mixer on low and slowly pour cooled cheese mixture into egg whites. Mix only enough to blend whites into cheese mixture. Pour into buttered casserole and bake in pan containing hot water below. Bake at 350 degrees for 30 to 40 minutes. Serves 8. Serve with Tomato Sauce.

Tomato Sauce

Sauté 2 diced carrots, 1 diced onion, 2 pieces diced celery, 1 garlic clove (cut in half) and 2 tablespoons parsley stems in 2 tablespoons bacon grease. Add 2 cups tomato purée, simmer 10 minutes. Add 4 cups chicken stock, 2 teaspoons salt, ¼ teaspoon white pepper, ¼ teaspoon thyme, ½ bay leaf and ¼ teaspoon oregano. Bring to boil. Thicken with flour-butter roux, add ham bone and simmer 2 hours. Strain. 1 quart.

Columbus, Ohio
North

I-71 & State Rt. 161

Downtown Columbus is only 15 expressway minutes away. The Inn arranges special tours for guests to visit the Ohio State Capitol Buildings. Columbus is also the home of the world's largest rose garden, the Park of Roses. The Inn's homemade soups are a delicious way to start dinner in the President's Dining Room. Be sure to try the Broiled Mountain Trout on the menu.

SNAPPER SOUP

5-pound snapper turtle
3 tablespoons beef extract
3 quarts stock
2 carrots, chopped
2 stalks celery, chopped
3 onions, chopped
½ teaspoon marjoram
Salt and pepper to taste
2 cups tomato purée
Dash of Tabasco
1 bay leaf
2 cloves garlic, minced
2 lemons (24 thin slices)

In large kettle, cook the snapper in 3 quarts of water. Cook in its shell for 1½ hours. When meat is tender, remove snapper from pot and let it cool. Pick snapper meat from shell, keep warm, and set aside. Put shell back in snapper stock with beef extract, beef stock, carrots, celery, onions, marjoram, salt, pepper, tomato purée, Tabasco, bay leaf and garlic. Let simmer for 30 minutes and strain. Mix ½ cup melted butter and 1½ cups flour and beat into soup until smooth. Cut snapper meat into small pieces and add to soup. Chop 3 hard-cooked eggs and add to soup. Stir in 1 cup sherry and lemons. Let soup simmer for one half hour. Serve hot. Serves 12.

Columbus, Ohio
West

4601 W. Broad St., U.S. 40 W.

If you approach a row of poplars you'll know you're on the right road to this popular Holiday Inn. When you see a courtyard and fountain you're here. All-American food at its best awaits you in the dining room at this Inn only 5 miles from downtown. When in Columbus, be sure to visit the Capitol. A 10-acre park surrounds the Capitol in the middle of the city.

NAVY BEAN SOUP

Wash 1 pound of navy beans. Place in 3 quarts cold beef stock and bring to a boil. Add ham hock or bacon grease and ⅓ large minced onion. Boil beans until tender and add ⅓ cup diced cooked ham. Season to taste. Cook slowly for 2 hours, stirring occasionally. Remove ham hock from pot and dice any extra ham on it and add to soup. Makes 3 quarts.

COCOANUT CREAM PIE

2 cups milk
⅓ cup cornstarch
1 cup sugar
3 egg yolks, lightly beaten
½ teaspoon salt
1 teaspoon vanilla
½ pint cream, whipped
2 tablespoons fresh cocoanut, grated

Scald milk. Mix cornstarch, sugar and egg yolks. Add milk gradually and stir until it thickens. Cool a little. Add salt and vanilla and cool. Place in baked pastry shell and cover with sweetened whipped cream (add 2 tablespoons sugar to cream after whipping). Sprinkle cocoanut on top. Chill thoroughly. Serves 6.

Dayton, Ohio
North

U.S. 25 N. (I-75)

Dayton is the home of aviation — it was home to the brothers who invented the first successful airplane. The Air Force Museum is at Wright-Patterson Air Force Base, and the Wright Brothers Memorial is nearby. Dayton is also the home of James Ritty, inventor of the cash register. For those in a hurry the Yucatan Sandwich is a special treat at this popular Inn. A gourmet sauce makes the prime rib of beef unusually delectable.

YUCATAN SANDWICH

4 slices bread
4 slices turkey (white meat)
2 tomatoes, sliced
4 slices bacon, cooked
1 cup grated American cheese

Toast bread and place on an ovenproof platter. Add slices of turkey and 2 slices of tomato on each. Pour Supreme Sauce (below) over and add a slice of bacon on each side. Sprinkle grated cheese generously on top. Add a dash of paprika. Place under broiler until bubbly.

Supreme Sauce

2 tablespons butter
3 tablespoons flour
   Seasonings
1⅓ cups half and half
1 egg yolk, lightly beaten

Melt butter and add flour mixed with seasonings. Stir until well blended. Add milk gradually, stirring constantly. Bring to a boil and boil for 2 minutes. Add egg yolk just before serving. Makes about 1 cup.

Hamilton-Fairfield
Ohio

Dixie Hwy., Fairfield, Ohio

Baked Alaska (for 2) and the Hunter's Grove Nut Ball are specialties of the Inn. A roaring fire is a pleasant extra in the dining area during the winter months. A buffet luncheon goes on all day Sunday so early and late risers may enjoy the exciting variety of foods. Sports fans enjoy staying so near the Cincinnati Baseball Club.

HUNTERS GROVE
VEAL PARMESAN

6 veal cutlets
2 tablespoons oil
6 tomato slices
6 Provolone cheese slices

Lightly flour veal cutlets and dip in seasoned Egg Batter. Sauté in oil. Top with sliced tomato, Provolone cheese. Use dish lined with Tomato Sauce. Sprinkle grated Parmesan cheese on top. Serves 6.

Egg Batter

3 eggs, well beaten
   Pinch parsley flakes
   Dash lemon juice
1 tablespoon grated Parmesan cheese
   Dash thyme

Blend all ingredients together.

Tomato Sauce

2 tablespoons butter
2 tablespoons flour
1 cup tomato juice

Melt butter, add flour and blend. Add tomato juice slowly. Stir over low heat until thick. Season. Makes 1 cup.

Lima, Ohio

Interstate 75 & 81 West

No wonder this Inn's Ole Masters Dining Room is so popular. Monday night is Italian night with complimentary wine. There's a Fish Buffet each Friday night featuring Fried Perch and Baked Haddock. Lima is known as the pipeline center of the nation. It's the location of many industrial concerns. Wapakoneta, the home of Neil Armstrong (the first man to set foot on the moon), is only 15 miles from Lima.

IMPERIAL CHOW MEIN

3 whole chicken breasts, (cooked)
    or equivalent chicken meat
½ cup butter
3 cups mixed Chinese vegetables
1½ cups Brown Sauce
2 cups celery, julienne strips
½ cup mushrooms
    Salt and Pepper
1 teaspoon sugar
    M.S.G.
2 tablespoons soy sauce

Cut chicken in fine thin strips. Use heavy skillet and sauté chicken in ¼ cup of the butter. Add Chinese vegetables and Brown Sauce. Cook celery and mushrooms in remainder of butter. Combine mixtures and add seasonings. Cover and cook slowly, adding soy sauce. Serve on large platter with fried noodles surrounding it. Serves 6-8.

Brown Sauce

Brown 2 tablespoons flour in 2 tablespoons cooking oil. Gradually add 1 cup chicken stock and season. Cook until sauce thickens.

Mansfield, Ohio

U.S. Rt. 30 at Laver Rd.

Travelers enroute to Lake Erie's shores enjoy a stop at this Inn. They always remember the restaurant's delicious apples and berries served in a variety of enticing dishes. Nearby farms raise and ship Christmas trees all over the country. The Inn is easily accessible to excellent fishing as well as boating. Two ski areas are nearby.

BAKED SWISS STEAK WITH VEGETABLE GRAVY

¾ cup chopped celery
1 cup chopped carrots
¾ cup chopped onion
¼ cup butter or cooking oil
6 4-ounce cube steaks

Boil vegetables in small amount of water until tender. Flour steaks well and brown in hot oil or butter, using a heavy frying pan. Place steaks in a baking pan when done. Thicken gravy with 2 tablespoons flour mixed to a smooth paste with an equal amount of cold water and add to frying pan. Add 1 cup boiling water and stir all particles in pan. Then add cooked vegetables. Pour over steaks and bake for 1 hour at 325 degrees in a covered casserole. Serves 6.

CANDIED FRUIT SAUCE

1 cup dried apricot halves
1 pint water
1 1-pound can applesauce
1 cup Heinz Candied
    Krink-L-Chips, minced

Simmer apricots in water until tender. Purée. Combine with applesauce and pickles. Chill. Serve over hot or cold roast pork. Makes 1 quart.

Marion, Ohio

1065 Delaware Avenue

Warren G. Harding, 29th President of the U. S., once published the "Marion Star". Many of the original furnishings may be seen in the house, which was his home when he made the famous front porch campaign. The site of the Wyandot Mission is an interesting place to visit. Superb food at this Holiday Inn is a good reason to make it your vacation or business headquarters. It only takes one complete meal to know you should always save room for dessert.

SPICY APPLE CAKE

½ cup shortening
2 cups sugar
2 eggs
2 teaspoons vanilla
2 cups flour
2 teaspoons soda
2 teaspoons nutmeg
2 teaspoons cinnamon
1 teaspoon salt
¼ cup hot water
5 cups canned sliced apples,
   chopped fine and drained
1 cup chopped walnuts or raisins

Cream shortening and sugar together. Add slightly beaten eggs and vanilla. Sift together dry ingredients and stir half into sugar mixture. Beat in half of hot water. Add remaining dry ingredients and the rest of the hot water. Mix well. Fold in apples and nuts or raisins. Pour into 2 greased 9-inch pans. Bake in moderate oven (350 degrees) for 50 minutes. Serve with whipped cream topping or ice cream. Makes 16 to 18 servings.

Middletown, Ohio

I-75 at Ohio Rt. 122

Stop for a meal here and you'll probably decide to spend a night or two. It's hard to leave the hospitality and delicious food at this Holiday Inn. Of course regular visitors know to stop at this delightful Inn on the way to Dayton or going north from Cincinnati. Visitors and local residents enjoy the live entertainment in the Red Slipper Lounge. Sightseers enjoy visiting the nearby Miamisburg Mound.

HERRING AND BEET SALAD

½ cup mayonnaise
¼ onion
1 apple
1 cup dill pickles
1 cup herring fillets (plain)
1½ cups cooked potatoes
   (do not overcook)
1 cup beets
   Pepper
   Salt
1 head Boston lettuce

Put mayonnaise in stainless steel mixing bowl. Dice onion in ¼" pieces. Peel, core and dice apple and mix with mayonnaise and onion. Dice whole dill pickles in ¼" pieces and drain. Dice herring, potatoes and slice beets in ¼" pieces and drain. Mix all ingredients together with a fork very gently. Do not over mix. Add salt and pepper to taste. Garnish platter with lettuce; place salad on platter, then garnish top with mayonnaise. Care must be taken to drain all ingredients well as salad should not be too moist. Serves 6 to 8.

Napoleon, Ohio

St. 108, North Scott St.

You can order a Josephine Steak in the Emperor Room at Napoleon's Holiday Inn. That is, if you can forego the exciting buffets. Guests are invited to spend an Evening in Old Italy. Dark beer and Alpine hats make the Holiday Bierstube a festive German occasion. There's a romantic Hawaiian Luau too, and more. All this and the Inn's own tennis courts await you in Napoleon. Lake Erie is not far away.

JOSEPHINE'S MUFFINS

2 cups flour
¾ teaspoon salt
4 teaspoons baking powder
1 egg
¼ cup sugar
1 cup milk
⅓ cup melted shortening

Sift dry ingredients. Beat egg thoroughly, add sugar, milk and shortening. Combine the two mixtures and stir, but do not over mix. Pour into greased muffin pans and bake in a 400 degree oven for 25 minutes or until brown. Makes 12 muffins. For a nice variation, add ¾ cup chopped apple, ¼ teaspoon cinnamon or ¼ teaspoon nutmeg.

RICE MEAT BALLS

1 pound ground beef
½ cup uncooked rice
1 small onion, diced very fine
2 tablespoons green pepper, diced
1 tablespoon butter
2½ cups (#2 can) tomatoes

Combine meat, rice and season. Sauté onion and pepper in butter. Add to first mixture and form into small balls. Add tomatoes and ½ teaspoon celery salt to sauté pan and stir well, mashing tomatoes to a pulp. Place meat balls in casserole, add tomatoes and cover. Add more water if needed. Bake at 350 degrees for 1 hour. Makes 8 to 12 meat balls, depending on size desired.

Newark, Ohio

Heath Village, St. Rt. 79

This Holiday Inn is just a few blocks away from Mound Builders State Park with its famous Eagle Effigy Mound. Also, Octagon State Park with its unusual Octagon Mound. Archeologists are fascinated with their findings, and with the food at this Inn. You can expect wonderful pumpkin pie. Hawaiian, French and German Smorgasbords are delicious and different.

PETITS POIS AUX CELERI

3 tablespoons melted butter
3 tablespoons onion, chopped fine
3 tablespoons ham, chopped fine
2 cups celery soup, condensed
½ teaspoon parsley flakes
⅔ cup milk
½ teaspoon salt
Dash white pepper
4½ cups young green peas, cooked

Pan-fry onion and ham in butter until onion is transparent. Combine soup, parsley, milk and seasonings. Add to onion and ham mixture. Then add peas and heat thoroughly. 8 to 10 servings.

PEPPER STEAK

4 sirloin steaks (individual size)
3 tablespoons freshly ground pepper
Salt
3 tablespoons butter
¼ cup cognac
½ cup brown sauce

Salt and pepper steaks thoroughly. Sauté in butter to doneness desired. Place steaks where they can be kept warm. Add cognac to skillet juices (remove excess butter first) and ignite. When flame is gone, add brown sauce. Pour over steaks. 4 servings.

Springfield, Ohio

W. North St., U.S. 40

Cheesecake is a delicious reason why you should stop at this Holiday Inn. Of course there are many other tempting dishes to delight gourmets too. This Inn is only ¼ mile from the heart of downtown. Sightseers enjoy visiting the Pennsylvania House where stagecoaches stopped in the last century. The Ohio and Zane Caverns with their spectacular formations are both nearby.

CREAM CHEESECAKE

3 pounds cream cheese
4 large eggs
1 cup sugar
1 ounce arrowroot
2 teaspoons vanilla
½ lemon (rind grated)
½ lemon (juice) or more
Graham cracker crumbs

Place cream cheese in a mixing bowl and add eggs, sugar, arrowroot, vanilla, lemon juice and rind. Mix until smooth. Lightly grease a 10-inch (round) or 9-inch (square) spring pan and sprinkle Graham cracker crumbs on sides and bottom. Leave about ⅛ inch of Graham cracker crumbs in bottom. Put cheesecake batter into pan and bake in a 375 degree oven for 35 minutes. Remove from oven and let cool for 15 minutes.

Topping

1 pint sour cream
⅓ cup sugar
½ ounce arrowroot
2 teaspoons vanilla

Mix sour cream, sugar, arrowroot and vanilla. Spread on cheesecake and bake in a 375 degree oven for 6 minutes. Remove from oven and cool completely before removing from pan. Makes 1 cheesecake.

Toledo, Ohio
No. 1 (Lemoyne)

No. 5 Interchange of Ohio Tpk.

The Interstate and airport are at this Inn's front door. A private helicopter landing field is adjacent. Indoor and outdoor swimming pools plus sauna baths are on the premises. Sportsmen enjoy excellent hunting nearby while tourists revel in the many historic sites. All enjoy returning to the Inn for delicious food. Toledo is a major port on Lake Erie. It is called the city of glass because of its glass industries.

HAM LOAF

1½ pounds ham
¾ pound pork shoulder
2 eggs, well beaten
1 cup milk
2 cups bread cubes
1 small onion, diced
1 can tomato soup

Have meat ground together. Add eggs, milk, bread cubes and onion to meat. Mix well and put in a greased loaf pan. Pour tomato soup over loaf and bake for 2 hours in a moderate oven. This is good hot or cold. For a dressing over the loaf, mix 1 cup Eagle Brand Dressing with 2 tablespoons horseradish which has been drained. Serves 8.

Eagle Brand Dressing

Beat 2 eggs well, then add ¾ cup vinegar and 2 tablespoons mustard and beat again. Then add 1 can Eagle Brand milk and ½ cup melted butter. Store in a cool place. This dressing is also good in potato salad or deviled eggs. May be mixed with ½ cup commercial salad dressing.

Van Wert, Ohio

The Inn's Isaac Van Wart Dining Room, named for the Revolutionary War hero, features authentic German cuisine. (A mistake made in 1834 changed the spelling to Van Wert). Johnny Appleseed is believed to have passed this way, hence the Inn's Johnny Appleseed Coffee House. The popular Mad Anthony Lounge honors General "Mad" Anthony Wayne. Van Wert's Borden Co. plant supplies the world with all of its Liederkranz.

ROULADE

(Stuffed Beef Roll)

Use 3 slices top round of beef cut ⅜ inch thick. Place flat on table and sprinkle with Burgundy and let set 5 minutes. Rub with yellow prepared mustard (½ teaspoon on each slice). Sprinkle lightly with 1 teaspoon salt, ½ teaspoon garlic powder, ½ teaspoon white pepper. Let set while making dressing.

Tear 10 slices of bread in large pieces adding 1 large minced onion. Combine 1 beaten egg with 2 cups hot water. Add enough to bread mixture to make moist. Place in buttered loaf pan and bake at 375 degrees for 30 minutes. Cool.

Divide dressing into 3 portions. Place on each slice of meat, making furrow in center. Add strip of Kosher dill pickle to each furrow. Roll meat like a jelly roll and wrap each with 2 slices of bacon. Place in shallow roaster. Cover and cook at 350 degrees for 45 minutes. Uncover and cook 30 more minutes. Remove from oven. Thicken drippings with roux (1 tablespoon flour + 1 tablespoon cornstarch and 1 cup cold water). Simmer 5 minutes. Place roulades on serving tray and pour gravy over all. Add sprinkle of minced parsley. Serve remainder of sauce in gravy boat. 2 pounds beef serves 6.

Warren-Niles, Ohio

In 1860 Stephen Foster and his family lived in Warren. It's the home of Halsey W. Taylor, inventor of the drinking fountain. This Holiday Inn, between Warren and Niles, is the home of the popular "Pub" Lounge and Restaurant. There's dancing at night and superb food always. Guests are greeted at dinner with hot miniature loaves of homemade bread.

BLANQUETTE DE VEAU

1½ pounds veal, breast or shoulder
2 small carrots
1 onion stuck with 1 clove
1 bouquet garni
¾ cup butter
3 tablespoons flour
½ cup mushrooms
1 cup onions (8-10 small ones)
1 cup white stock
3 egg yolks
½ teaspoon lemon juice
½ teaspoon nutmeg, grated

Cut meat in 1½- to 2-ounce pieces and put in cold salted water to cover (use 1½ tablespoons salt to 2 pints water). Bring gently to a boil, stirring and skimming carefully. Add carrots, onion and bouquet garni. Cover and simmer for 1½ hours. Melt ⅓ cup of the butter, add the flour and cook for a few seconds. Gradually add 1 cup veal stock and stir until boiling. Then simmer for 15 minutes, skimming frequently. Place veal in serving dish. Add garnish of mushrooms and small onions cooked in white stock. Keep hot. Thicken the sauce with rest of butter, egg yolks, lemon juice and nutmeg. Strain and pour over veal. Serve with pilaf, noodles or spaghetti. 4 servings.

Clinton, Okla.

Hwy. 66, 40 West

The menu goes on and on at this Holiday Inn. But you never have to worry about making the right choice. Every dish is delicious. The Inn is only 2 miles from the heart of downtown Clinton and transportation to and from the airport (4 miles) is compliments of the Inn. The Foss Dam and Reservoir is nearby and offers a recreation area, fishing, swimming and water sports.

CRAB IMPERIAL

1 cup mayonnaise
¼ finely chopped green pepper
¼ cup finely chopped onion
½ teaspoon dry mustard
2 tablespoons lemon juice
½ teaspoon salt
Dash pepper
2 cups cooked crab meat
2 hard-cooked eggs, chopped
4 medium-size avocados
1 cup soft bread crumbs
2 tablespoons melted butter

Combine mayonnaise or salad dressing, green pepper, onion, mustard, lemon juice, salt and pepper. Add crab meat and eggs. Cut each avocado in half, remove seed. Cut a thin slice off bottom of each so avocado will stand. Brush cut surfaces with 1 tablespoon lemon juice. Mound crab meat mixture on avocado halves. Combine bread crumbs and melted butter or margarine and sprinkle over crab meat. Bake in a moderate 350 degree oven for 10 to 15 minutes, or until crumbs are lightly browned. Serve at once. Serves 8.

Muskogee, Okla.

U.S. 69

Muskogee is in the heart of the Cherokee nation. This Holiday Inn is near five civilized tribes' headquarters. Be sure to visit Sequoyah's Home. The cabin, built by Sequoyah around 1830, houses relics relating to the tribal statesman and inventor of the Cherokee alphabet. Live entertainment in the Inn's lounge and excellent food in the dining room make this Inn a popular stopping and staying place. There are many lakes in the area for fishing and water sports.

GAZPACHO

3 cups chopped fresh tomatoes
1 cup chopped green pepper
½ cup chopped onion
½ cup chopped cucumber
1 clove garlic, crushed
4 cups chicken broth
¼ cup lemon juice
¼ cup olive oil
2 teaspoons salt
1 teaspoon paprika
Few grains cayenne pepper

Combine ingredients and serve well chilled. (Use blender or food chopper if desired.) Serve in ice cold cups with Croutons. Makes approximately 2 quarts or little more.

Croutons

Dice 2 pieces of bread and saute' in butter until brown. Place in sack and toss with 1 teaspoon salt and 1 teaspoon grated Parmesan cheese.

Oklahoma City, Okla.
Downtown

Main St. at Dewey St.

This high-rise Holiday Inn in the heart of downtown combines top flight luxury and comfort with all the hospitality and fun of the Sooner State. You can tour the gourmet world in La Fiesta Restaurant—it's International Night every night. Hot blueberry muffins are a specialty of the Inn everyday. Do drop in the Inn's popular La Cantina Club too. The Inn's downtown location puts shopping at your doorstep. The Civic Center is only 2 blocks away.

SHRIMP CACCIATORA

1 pound raw shrimp,
    shelled & cleaned
1 medium onion, minced
½ medium green pepper, minced
2 cloves garlic, minced
¼ cup olive oil
1 can (19 ounces) tomatoes
1 can (10¾ ounces) spaghetti
    sauce with mushrooms
½ cup dry red wine
2 teaspoons pepper
¼ teaspoon allspice
1 bay leaf
¼ teaspoon ground thyme
    Dash cayenne
    Hot cooked spaghetti
        (9-ounce package)

Put shrimp in salted cold water and bring to a boil. Drain. Cook onion, green pepper and garlic in oil for 5 minutes. Add remaining ingredients, except shrimp and spaghetti. Simmer uncovered for about 20 minutes. Add shrimp and heat. Serve on spaghetti. Serves 6.

Oklahoma City, Okla.
West

Interstate 40 at Meridian

650 square miles of Oklahoma are inside the city limits of Oklahoma City. There's fun for all ages inside and around this Inn. Delicious daily buffets, sauna baths and plenty of playground equipment await guests. There's live entertainment in the Pirates Cove Lounge. The Inn is in the center of an industrial area, next to the State Fairgrounds.

BEEF STROGANOFF

2 pounds round steak
½ cup butter or shortening
1 cup minced onions
1 pound mushrooms, sliced
¾ cup water
½ cup red wine
1 cup sour cream

Pound flour and 1 teaspoon salt into steak. Cut into 2 ¼-inch strips. Brown in half the butter. Place in a 3-quart pan. Brown onions and mushrooms in remaining butter. Mix water, wine and 1 teaspoon salt, and add to meat. Cover and simmer 30 minutes. Add mushrooms and onions and simmer until meat is tender. When ready to serve, add sour cream. Heat and serve over hot buttered noodles. Serves 6.

MEAT LOAF SUPREME

Soak 1 cup bread crumbs in ½ cup evaporated milk. Mix 1½ pounds ground beef, 1 chopped onion, 1 teaspoon salt, ¼ teaspoon garlic powder and ¼ teaspoon pepper. Add 2 beaten eggs and ½ of an 8-ounce can tomato sauce. Combine mixtures. Form into a loaf and place in a shallow pan. Pour rest of tomato sauce over loaf and bake in a 350 degree oven for 1 hour and 15 minutes. Baste while cooking. Serves 4 to 6.

Tulsa, Okla.
Downtown

17 W. 7th at Boulder

Enjoy luxurious accommodations, underground parking and an indoor pool in the heart of downtown Tulsa. Dine on gourmet fare in the La Cantina Supper Club with its outdoor patio. You'll be delighted with the "Cheese and Bread Board" served before dinner. The Inn is only 2 blocks from the Civic Center. The Philbrook Art Center, Tulsa Garden Center and Mohawk Zoo are all nearby.

COLD CHERRY SOUP

    1 quart fresh pie cherries
    4 ounces triple sec
    ⅓ cup cornstarch
    ½ teaspoon cinnamon
    ¼ teaspoon cloves
    ½ teaspoon tarragon
    ½ cup sour cream

Pit cherries and simmer in 1½ quarts cold water until cooked. If canned cherries are used, add water to juice to make 1 quart. Drain cherries and place juice in a saucepan. Soak cherries in triple sec. Make a paste with cornstarch and a little water. Add to juice and add sugar to taste. Cook until thickened some. Chill well. Combine cherries, seasonings and juice. Add sour cream last. Serves 6.

LIVER KREFELD

Cut 1 pound liver with scissors in match like strips. Heat 2 tablespoons salad oil in a skillet. Add 4 thinly sliced onions and cook until golden. Add ½ cup sliced mushrooms and liver. Cook about 3 minutes, until liver is just browned. Add 2 thinly sliced tomatoes and cook a little longer. Season with salt and pepper. Serve over rice. Serves 4.

Tulsa, Okla.
West

U. S. 66 Alt. 75, I-44

There's lots of room to roam over the beautiful grounds of this Holiday Inn. The continental cuisine is superb in the Gaslite Supper Club with Gay 90's decor and live entertainment. Homemade rolls and pastries from the Inn's own ovens are too tempting not to take seconds. Tulsa, often called the Oil Capital of the World, was an Indian Village (Tulsey Town) in 1880.

WINE SPAGHETTI DINNER

    1 tablespoon olive oil
    1 large onion, chopped
    1½ pounds ground beef
    ½ pound fresh mushrooms
    ¼ cup butter
    1½ cups tomatoes
    1½ cups tomato paste
    ½ green pepper, diced
    4 cloves garlic
    ½ tablespoon Worcestershire sauce
    ½ tablespoon Angostura bitters
    ½ tablespoon sugar
      Salt and pepper to taste
    ½ teaspoon celery salt
    2 bay leaves
      Dash cayenne
      Dash oregano
    ½ cup dry red wine

Place olive oil in a heavy skillet and stir in chopped onion and meat. When nearly done, add mushrooms which have been sautéed in butter. Add tomatoes, tomato paste, pepper, garlic and seasonings. Add wine. Cook over very low heat for 3-4 hours. Add more liquid if necessary. Stir occasionally to keep from sticking. Serve over cooked spaghetti. Sprinkle Parmesan cheese on top. Sauce serves 8 to 10.

Eugene, Ore.

I-105 at Coburg Road

When in Eugene, you're in the heart of the orchard country. This Holiday Inn dips in the fruit basket and nut bowl to make delectable desserts, as well as jams and jellies. You'll enjoy the taste of native grown peaches, plums, apples and cherries. Hendricks Bridge, Fern Ridge Reservoir, Dexter Dam and Lookout Point Reservoir are just a few nearby interesting places to visit. The University of Oregon is in this bustling lumber city.

PEACH PUDDING

4 cups sliced peaches
½ cup water
1 cup sugar

Combine peaches, water and sugar and bring to a boil. Spice with cinnamon.

Batter

1 cup sugar
1 cup flour
1 teaspoon baking powder
¼ teaspoon salt
2 tablespoons shortening
½ cup milk
1 teaspoon vanilla

Mix all ingredients thoroughly and pour into a greased baking dish. Pour hot fruit over batter and bake at 350 degrees for 40 minutes. The batter rises to the top during baking. Serves 6 to 8.

BRANDIED PEAR SLICES

Core and slice 3 fresh Anjou, Bosc or Comice pears. Melt 3 tablespoons butter in a chafing dish and sauté pear slices until tender. Sprinkle with ¼ cup sugar and add ¼ cup halved walnuts. Stir gently to glaze. Add 2 tablespoons apricot brandy to 1 cup heavy cream (whipped). Serve over hot pears in compotes. Garnish with walnut halves. Serves 6.

Portland, Ore.

Interstate 5 & U.S. 99

Ice skating and skiing on Mt. Hood and year round golf await you. And more. Wonderful salmon fishing trips are arranged by the Innkeeper for guests at this Holiday Inn. The Inn is also next to the Coliseum and near Lloyd Center. Superb cuisine in the Inn's dining room makes every meal unforgettable. Portland, the City of Roses, is the western gateway to the Columbia River Highway and Mt. Hood.

STRAWBERRY ROULADE

Beat 5 egg yolks, adding ⅔ cup sugar. Beat 5 egg whites and add ⅔ cup sugar gradually. Combine mixtures. Add 1½ cups flour (sift into mixture and fold). Add 3 teaspoons melted butter and 1 teaspoon lemon flavoring. Place batter on greased paper in a shallow baking pan. Bake at 400 degrees for 15 to 20 minutes. Remove from oven and turn on a cloth sprinkled with powdered sugar. Cool and cover with a thin layer of red jelly (about 1 glass) that has been beaten with a fork. Spread Filling on cake and roll. Decorate with whipped cream and whole strawberries if desired. Serves 8.

Filling

Wash 1 pint strawberries (save 6 to decorate). Remove hulls, crush and mash lightly with a fork. Add ¼ cup granulated sugar. Soak 1 tablespoon gelatin in 2 tablespoons water. Dissolve over hot water. Add to berries and chill thoroughly. Whip 2 cups cream and add 4 tablespoons sugar. When berries have partially set, fold the cream into mixture.

Salem, Ore.

U.S. 99 at Mission

Salem is the Cherry Center of the state. And this Holiday Inn serves them in preserves, pies, salads, flambé or just freshly picked for guests to enjoy. The Inn is right downtown in the Capital City. It's not hard to find something from Oregon to take home. Linen yarn, twine, fishnets and shoemaker's thread are all made here.

ELEGANT CHERRY ROLLS

    1 cup scalded milk
    ⅛ to ¼ cup butter
    ⅛ to ¼ cup sugar

Mix 1 yeast cake with ¼ cup water. Scald milk, adding butter, sugar and 1 teaspoon salt. Cool to lukewarm. Gradually add flour to make a thick batter. Add yeast mixture and 1 beaten egg. Beat, stirring in about 3½ cups flour in all.

Knead dough on floured board. Swirl in greased bowl to grease top. Cover and let dough rise double in bulk in a warm place.

Roll dough into a 12x8 inch triangle, dot with 1 teaspoon soft butter and fold dough. Repeat twice. Roll ¼ inch thick. Cut into 2-inch rounds. Place on greased cookie sheets and let rise in a warm place for 30 minutes. Then press indentations in center of each roll and fill with Cherry Filling. Bake at 350 degrees 15-18 minutes. Make icing by combining 1 cup sifted confectioner's sugar and 2 tablespoons cream. Drizzle over baked rolls. Makes 24 rolls.

Cherry Filling

Cut fresh or canned red cherries from seeds to make 4 cups. Cook in a little water until soft. Add 1 cup sugar, 3 tablespoons cornstarch, ¼ teaspoon salt and cook until thick, stirring constantly. Add ¼ teaspoon almond flavoring. Cool.

Allentown, Pa.

Rt. 22 at Jct. of Rt. 309

The quaint charm of the Pennsylvania Dutch countryside, traditional food and a luxurious swimming pool make this Inn popular. It's only 5 minutes from an 18-hole golf course and near the Trexler Game Preserve with the largest herd of buffaloes in the country. During the American Revolution the Liberty Bell was hidden in Allentown. Today the Liberty Bell Shrine has a copy of the bell.

RED VELVET CAKE

    ¼ pound butter
    1½ cups sugar
    2 eggs
    2 teaspoons cocoa (level)
    2 ounces red food coloring
    1 teaspoon vanilla
    1 teaspoon salt
    1 cup buttermilk
    2 cups cake flour, sifted
    1½ teaspoons baking soda
    1 tablespoon vinegar

Cream butter, sugar and eggs. Make a paste of cocoa and food coloring. Add to creamed mixture, Mix salt with vanilla, add to buttermilk alternately with flour. Mix soda with vinegar and add last, folding in. Bake in 2 layers in greased layer cake pans for 30 minutes at 350 degrees. Spread icing between layers, on top and sides. Makes 1 2-layer cake.

Icing

Blend 5 tablespoons flour with a small amount of milk, adding 1 cup of milk gradually. Cook until it thickens. Let cool. Cream 1 cup butter, 1 cup granulated sugar and 1 teaspoon vanilla. Then add flour and milk mixture and beat until fluffy and spread on cake.

Altoona, Pa.

2915 Pleasant Valley Blvd.

Altoona is the home of the famous Horseshoe Curve, one of the greatest engineering feats of the world. Blue Knob, the state's largest and most popular ski resort, is only 20 minutes from the Inn. You only have to step into the Inn's Tack Room to enjoy exotic Polynesian dinners, Roast Prime Rib of Beef carved right at your table and Flaming Sword dinners.

POLYNESIAN DINNER

2 medium pineapples
4 raw African lobster dainties
2 cooked breasts of chicken
¼ cup butter
½ cup sliced mushrooms
½ cup chopped onion
1 tablespoon all purpose flour
¼ cup light cream
¼ cup white or light wine
1 5-oz. package sliced almonds

Cut pineapples in halves, leaving on spines. Scoop out the meat to make boats of about ¾ inch thickness. Remove shell from lobsters, clean and devein. Cut lobster and chicken in ½-inch cubes. Sauté onions and mushrooms in butter over medium heat for 5 minutes. Add lobster, chicken, salt and pepper. Braise until lobster is done. Stir in flour, add wine and cream, and cook, stirring until mixture thickens. Fill pineapple boats with mixture, top them with almonds, and bake in a preheated 400 degree oven until mixture bubbles. (Be sure to cover spines of pineapples with foil before placing them in the oven). Serve with steamed rice. Garnish with sugared pineapple. Serves 4.

Bedford, Pa.

Bedford Exit 11, I-70 & I-76

This Inn has a Pennsylvania Dutch cook so delightful dishes are in store for you. An L-shaped heated swimming pool, a nine-hole putting green and sauna baths are fun for all. The Inn is near Blue Knob ski slopes and Bedford Springs Resort. The many antique shops, covered bridges, caves and coke ovens make sightseeing endless. Ask about the walking tours too.

APPLE BUTTER

12 large apples
1½ quarts water
5 cups sugar (or more)
6 cups apple cider
2 teaspoons cinnamon
1 teaspoon allspice
2 teaspoons cloves (ground)

Wash, quarter and cook apples in water until soft. Run through coarse sieve, discarding skins and seeds. Add half as much sugar as pulp. Heat cider to boiling point and add sugar-apple mixture, stirring often to prevent scorching. Add spices as butter thickens. Cook until thickened. Butter will become thicker after it gets cold and should be thick enough to spread. Makes about 4 pints.

SMIERKASE

2 quarts milk
2 quarts warm water
Cream
Seasonings

Place milk in a warm (but not hot) place and allow to sour until whey separates from the curd. Drain curd in cheesecloth bag. Pour warm water over it and drain, hanging it over a bowl to catch the drippings. Repeat warm water procedure and let drain again. Let drip until curd feels firm in bag. Place on ice and remove from bag after thoroughly chilled. Add cream and seasonings to taste (and chopped chives or chervil if desired). Beat until it is creamy and smooth. Makes about 1 pint of cottage cheese.

Bethlehem, Pa.

Route 22

You can stay for a week and never see the same menu in this Inn's fabulous El Cetro dining room. Whether you order from the open charcoal hearth or try an international dish, be sure to save room for the finale. The Deleitoso Final is a special dessert menu. Bethlehem is on the threshold of the Poconos and the Pennsylvania Dutch Country. Christmas in Bethlehem is unforgettable. Visitors also enjoy touring the Moravian Settlement.

CEREZA LLAMEANTE

1 can big black bing cherries
5 ounces red currant jelly
2 tablespoons lemon juice
1 pint vanilla ice cream
⅓ cup Spanish brandy

Beat jelly, add lemon juice and a small amount of cherry juice. Place in chafing dish over direct heat. Add drained, pitted cherries. When heated, pour brandy over sauce and ignite. Shake pan and stir with ladle after flame dies. Spoon over hard balls of ice cream which have been placed in serving dishes. Serves 6.

LEMON MERINGUE PIE

Mix 2 tablespoons cornstarch with 1 cup sugar. Place in double boiler with 3 egg yolks, juice and rind of 1 lemon and 1½ cups hot water. Stir until well blended. Cook until mixture will barely run off spoon.

Add 1½ tablespoons butter and stir. Cool slightly. Pour into a baked pie shell. After filling has set, spread Meringue over top of pie and bake at 325 degrees for 10 to 12 minutes. Serves 6.

Meringue

Beat 3 egg whites until stiff. Add 6 tablespoons sugar gradually, then ⅛ teaspoon baking powder. Pile in peaks on pie.

Erie, Pa.
Downtown

18 W. 18th St.

Since every good Pennsylvania Dutch farm has a pantry room filled with homemade foods, this Holiday Inn's restaurant is named the Dutch Pantry. Dutch recipes are taste treats for the whole family. And the Inn is only 10 minutes from the heart of thriving Erie. It's close to Presque Isle State Park with its beaches, boating, picnicking and sports facilities.

SHOO-FLY PIE

(Schuuflei Boi)

¾ cup flour
½ teaspoon cinnamon
⅛ teaspoon nutmeg
⅛ teaspoon ground cloves
½ cup sugar
½ teaspoon salt
2 tablespoons shortening
½ tablespoon soda
¾ cup water
½ cup Gold Label molasses
1 well beaten egg

Combine flour, cinnamon, nutmeg, cloves, sugar and salt with shortening. Work together with hands to make crumbs. Dissolve soda in water. Add molasses to the soda and water. Then add egg. Line a 9-inch pie tin with pastry. Pour ½ the liquid into pie tin and put ¼ of the crumbs on top. Stir. Pour remaining liquid in and top with remaining crumbs. Do not stir. Bake at 400 degrees until crust starts to brown (10 minutes). Finish baking at 325 degrees until firm. Serves 6.

Gettysburg, Pa.

U. S. 140 & 15

Stay in the heart of historic Gettysburg. Tours through the historic battlefields may be arranged at the Inn. You can see where the most desperate fighting by the 170,000 men of the North and South took place in July, 1863. After visiting the bullet shattered Jennie Wade House during the day, you can slip into a captain's chair in the Inn's Jennie Wade Dining Room. Be sure to save room for the homemade Cheesecake.

CHEESECAKE

4 8-ounce packages cream cheese
⅔ cup sugar
4 eggs
½ cup real lemon juice

Mix softened cream cheese with sugar. Add eggs one at a time, beating well after each addition. Then add lemon juice and beat for 30 minutes in all. Bake at 350 degrees for 35 minutes using spring mold that has been greased with butter, filled with Graham Cracker Crust on bottom, and dusted with Graham cracker crumbs on sides.

Topping

2 cups sour cream
2 tablespoons sugar
1 teaspoon vanilla

Combine and mix together thoroughly and put on top of cooked cheesecake. Bake at 450 degrees for 10 minutes.

Graham Cracker Crust

1 cup Graham cracker crumbs
1 tablespoon sugar
2 tablespoons butter, melted

Mix butter and sugar with crumbs and press in bottom of greased cheesecake pan.

Hazleton, Pa.

Rt. 309

Make this Holiday Inn your headquarters for sightseeing trips to the nearby victorian mansion home of pioneer railroad builder, Asa Packer, and Flagstaff Park. Parents enjoy staying so near Wilkes College and Kings College. Delicious food and live entertainment in the Lounge will make you glad you chose to stay at this Inn.

CRAB CAKES

2 slices bread with crust removed
1 pound crab meat
1 teaspoon seafood seasoning
1 teaspoon salt
1 tablespoon mayonnaise
1 tablespoon Worcestershire sauce
1 tablespoon chopped parsley
1 tablespoon baking powder
1 beaten egg

Break slices of bread into small pieces and moisten with milk. Mix with remaining ingredients and shape into 4-ounce cakes. Fry quickly in butter until brown. Makes 6 to 8 cakes.

POTATO CAKES

4 potatoes
1 tablespoon grated onion
1 large egg
⅓ cup all purpose flour
¾ teaspoon salt

Peel potatoes and grate very fine, for approximately 3 cups. Squeeze and drain. Add onion, egg, flour and salt to potatoes. Beat until well blended. Place ½ inch fat into skillet and drop batter by heaping tablespoons into fat. Fry until crisp and brown on both sides. Remove cakes and place on paper towel to absorb grease. Serve hot with sour cream or warm applesauce. Serves 4.

Irwin, Pa.

U.S. 30 at Irwin Exit 7 of Pa. Tpk.

Irwin's Holiday Inn is famous for its table side service. Enjoy roast prime rib of beef carved right before your eyes, sauce served from a flaming chafing dish and salad tossed while you watch. Sightseers enjoy touring western Pennsylvania's bituminous coal area and industrial region. There are ski slopes to enjoy during the winter months.

BOXTY

    1 cup raw potato, pared
    2 teaspoons lemon juice
    1 cup sifted flour
    1 cup mashed potatoes
    1 teaspoon salt
    2 teaspoons baking powder
    1 slightly beaten egg
    1 cup buttermilk
    ¼ cup melted butter

In a small bowl, toss grated potato with lemon juice to coat well. Put into cheesecloth and press to squeeze out as much liquid as possible. In a large bowl, combine flour and mashed potatoes, beating well with a spoon. Add raw potato to flour mixture along with salt and baking powder. Add egg and buttermilk, beating to mix well. Slowly heat a heavy skillet. To test temperature, drop a little cold water into skillet—water should roll off in drops. Lightly grease skillet with some butter. Drop batter, 1 tablespoon for each pancake, into skillet. Cook 3 minutes on a side, or until nicely browned. 7 portions.

Johnstown, Pa.

1540 Scalp Ave. Rt. 56 E.

Built on steps going down a hill, this Holiday Inn is in the center of the Laurel Highlands. The Laurel Mountain ski resort is only 30 minutes away. The University of Pittsburgh is only 1 mile away in Johnstown. The Inn's Camelot dining room delights guests with international food every night. There's top entertainment in the lounge too.

PIGS IN BLANKET

    1 quart oysters, drained
      Seasonings
      Bacon strips
      Lemon juice

Pat oysters dry and season. Wrap a ½ strip of bacon around each and attach with toothpicks. Arrange on rack in pan. Broil until bacon is crisp. Turn once. Sprinkle a few drops of lemon juice over them before serving. Serve hot. Allow 6 to 8 oysters for each serving. As cocktail party fare, will serve more.

HOT ROLLS

    1 quart sweet milk
    1 cup sugar
    1 cup shortening
    1 yeast cake
    1 teaspoon soda
    1 teaspoon salt
    1 teaspoon baking powder

Heat milk, sugar and shortening to boiling point but do not boil. Let cool until milk is lukewarm. Add yeast cake and enough flour to make a batter. Let rise 2 hours. Add some flour with baking powder, salt and soda sifted in it and make a dough. Place in refrigerator. Make out rolls 2 hours before baking. Place in greased pan and bake 15 to 20 minutes at 375 degrees. Makes 2 to 3 dozen, depending on size of rolls.

Lancaster, Pa. - North

U.S. 222 at St. Rt. 501

You can expect fasnachts, schmier-kase, lotwarrick, shoo-fly pie, even an "Apple Schnitzing" party at this Inn in the heart of Pennsylvania Dutch and Amish Country. The Inn will arrange tours (in an antique surrey bus, if you like) to see Amish craftsmen, Farmer's Markets and Hex signs. People still cling to traditions dating back to the 1600's in the nation's oldest inland city.

LOBSTER THERMIDOR

    2 live lobsters (1¼ lbs. each)
    4 tablespoons cooking oil
    1 medium onion, chopped fine
    ½ cup dry white wine
    2 tablespoons flour
    1 teaspoon salt
    ½ teaspoon cayenne pepper
    ¾ cup milk
    ¼ cup cream
    1 pinch dry mustard
    1 pinch paprika
    1 cup grated Parmesan cheese

Wash lobsters in cold water. Split in half, starting in the center of the head. Place split side down in the oil, which has been heated in a pan. Cover and cook slowly for 12 minutes. Remove slowly and carefully.

Take lobster meat from the shell and cut up roughly.

Melt 2 tablespoons butter in a pan. Add the onion and cook until soft, without browning. Add the wine and cook slowly until the wine has evaporated.

In another pan, heat 1 tablespoon butter. Stir in the flour, salt and pepper. Stir until smooth and add the milk. Stir over the heat until the mixture comes to a boil. Add this and the cream, mustard, paprika and 2 tablespoons cheese to the onion mixture. Reduce it to a thick, creamy consistency by adding a little of the lobster stock. Mix lobster meat into this and fill the shells. Sprinkle well with grated cheese and put butter on top. Serves 2.

Ligonier, Pa.

Loyalhanna St., U.S. Rt. 30

Storybook Forest, historical Ft. Ligonier, Forbes Road Gun Museum, Idlewild Park and 8 ski areas are all nearby. History lingers in the Inn with its old musical instruments, guns and letters with odd postmarks on display. An old carriage in the Camelot Dining Room creates the right atmosphere for the excellent traditional food served.

STUFFED SHRIMP

    1 pound green jumbo shrimp
    ½ cup chopped onion
    1 teaspoon prepared mustard
    ¼ cup whipped cream
    ¼ cup mayonnaise
    1 cup imperial or king crab meat
      Salt and pepper

Peel and devein shrimp. Wash and clean, leaving tails on, and cut pockets through center backs. Sauté onion in butter. Add to mustard, whipped cream, mayonnaise and crab meat. Season. Stuff shrimp with mixture and bake at 375 degrees for 12 to 15 minutes. After baked, place a spoonful of mixture on top of each shrimp and bake 2 minutes longer. Season more, if desired. Serves 4 to 6.

COLE SLAW DRESSING

    1 pint mayonnaise
    ½ cup white vinegar
    ½ cup salad oil
    ¼ teaspoon salt
    ¼ teaspoon white pepper
    ⅛ teaspoon garlic powder
    1 teaspoon celery seed
    ¼ cup sugar

Combine all ingredients and mix well. Pour over shredded cabbage and toss thoroughly. Makes 3 cups.

New Hope, Pa.

Route 202

Original Finnish saunas, tennis, and gourmet cuisine in the Riverboat Room await you at this Inn. Guests enjoy live entertainment in the intimate, torch lit Frenchman's Cove cocktail lounge. Snow skiing is only 3 miles away and excellent hunting and fishing are nearby. But there's even more in store for visitors in this area . . . the Phillips Mill art exhibits, the Bucks County Playhouse and rides on mule-drawn barges on the Old Delaware Canal.

SHRIMP CREOLE

1 green pepper, minced
1 onion, minced
1 clove garlic, crushed
2 tablespoons butter
1 tablespoon flour
1 can (2½ cups) tomatoes
2 carrots, diced fine
2 stalks celery, diced fine
2 teaspoons parsley, chopped
1 bay leaf
¼ teaspoon thyme
1 teaspoon salt
Dash cayenne
1 pound shrimp, raw and shelled

Use heavy iron kettle with close fitting top for best results. Sauté pepper, onion and garlic in butter. Blend in flour. Add remaining ingredients and seasonings. Add shrimp last. Cover and cook slowly for 1 hour, adding more tomato juice if sauce seems too thick. Stir occasionally to keep from sticking. Serve over rice or with rice as a side dish. Serves 4 to 6.

New Kensington- Tarentum, Pa.

Exit #5 Pa. Tpk. Rt. 28 N.

Watch your steak, lobster or chicken as it is broiled slowly on the Old Hickory Hearth. Or order dinner at pool side. Enjoy live entertainment until 1 a.m. in the Lounge. Be a guest at this Inn, nestled on a wooded 8-acre site overlooking the Allegheny River. Penn State and New Kensington College are within minutes.

BEEF A LA WINSTON

4 pieces sirloin (4 ounces each)
½ cup Horseradish Sauce
½ cup potato chips, chopped fine
4 tablespoons butter
2 cups Pilaf

Marinate beef for 5 hours in Horseradish Sauce. Dip in breading of finely chopped potato chips. Sauté in butter until golden brown on each side. Serve with Pilaf and garnish with cherry tomatoes. Serves 4.

Horseradish Sauce

1 cup French dressing
2 teaspoons horseradish

Combine ingredients and mix.

Pilaf

2 tablespoons butter
½ cup uncooked rice
1 cup beef bouillon

Cook rice and butter in frying pan until rice is brown. Add boiling hot bouillon and cook slowly until all liquid is absorbed and rice is soft. Season with salt and pepper.

New Stanton, Pa.

U.S. Rt. 119 at I-70 S.

Serve yourself at the Inn's Beef and Beer Bar. Some of the popular sandwiches are named for industries in this area. If you prefer, there are 13 sandwiches named for the original states. In the dining room, the Old English style menu features Savories, Sallats, Broilen Fish, Beefe Stake, and Pound Cayke with Rum Sause. Nearby Keystone Park and Laurel Mountain provide exciting year-round recreation.

ROAST BEEF

Select sirloin of beef for a roast. Leave fat on. Rub meat with salt, pepper and a little flour. Arrange on a rack with pan beneath and place in a preheated 325 degree oven. Cook 18 to 35 minutes per pound. Never cook over 3 hours, even a very large roast. Allow ½ to 1 pound for each serving. Serve with Yorkshire Pudding.

YORKSHIRE PUDDING

1 cup sifted flour
½ teaspoon salt
1½ cups milk
2 beaten eggs

Preheat oven to 450 degrees 20 minutes before putting pudding in oven—place a 9x13" baking dish in oven to heat.
Mix flour and salt. Stir in milk combined with eggs. Add a little of roast drippings. Beat until smooth. Pour batter into hot baking dish. Put back in oven and bake 25 minutes. Serves 6 to 8.

DEEP FRIED CRAB CAKES

Melt 3 tablespoons butter, blend in 5 tablespoons flour, add 1½ cups milk and cook, stirring constantly until thick. Add salt, pepper, 1 beaten egg, dash celery salt and 1 teaspoon grated onion. Cook until thick, adding 2 cups cooked crab meat when done. Form into cakes, dip into flour then spread with mayonnaise on both sides and roll in dry bread crumbs. Brown in hot butter in heavy skillet. Serves 4 to 6.

Philadelphia, Pa. City Line

Rt. 1 & Schuylkill Expwy.

Guests have an ever changing view as they dine in the revolving Empire Room. It usually takes a complete revolution to decide what to order. The menu offers everything from a Pennsylvania Dutch Dinner to Fillet Sole Sauté Banania. Test drive the Inn's own golf course. The Inn is located on the edge of the city.

SCAMPI FRADIAVOLO

Peel 5 pounds jumbo shrimp, leaving fantail. Split open, remove vein, season and brush with olive oil. Coat with fine bread crumbs. Broil 3 inches from heat 4-5 minutes on each side. Serve with Fradiavolo Sauce. 6-8 servings.

Scampi Sauce Fradiavolo

¼ cup olive oil
2 tablespoons shallots, minced
2 tablespoons leeks, minced
½ cup onion, minced
½ cup celery stalks, chopped
1 clove garlic, mashed
½ cup red wine vinegar
½ cup tarragon vinegar
1½ cups tomato purée
2½ cups rich brown gravy
4 tablespoons bay leaves
¾ teaspoon thyme
¾ teaspoon oregano
1 teaspoon whole black pepper
3 tablespoons French mustard
1 teaspoon lemon juice
Salt to taste

Put oil in flameproof casserole and sauté shallots, leeks, onion, celery and garlic. Add 2 vinegars and reduce ⅓. Then add tomato purée, brown gravy, bay leaves, thyme, oregano, and pepper. Cook slowly for 2 hours over low heat. Stir occasionally. Remove from heat. Add remaining ingredients. Cool, then refrigerate until ready to use. Makes 3½ pints.

Philadelphia, Pa. Penn Center

18th & Market, Downtown

This is a most unusual Inn — right in the heart of Philadelphia with everything for meetings. A 600 seat theatre is located on the subterranean level. There's a French sidewalk cafe. Magnificent buffets of international flavor always draw a crowd to the dining room. There are wines of the world to taste with excellent cheeses — even an International Coffee Bar.

ESCARGOTS BOURGUIGNONNE

Place snails (prepared for cooking) in clean shells. Close openings with Snail Butter. Leave in refrigerator for butter to harden. When serving, place on baking sheet covered with salt and place snails opening upwards. Bake in 375 degree oven for 5 to 6 minutes, until butter boils. Serve at once. Allow 8 per serving.

Snail Butter

Slightly cream 1 cup butter and combine with 1 clove finely grated garlic, 2 tablespoons minced parsley, 2 tablespoons minced shallots, salt and pepper.

QUICHE LORRAINE

10 slices cooked bacon
1½ cups diced Swiss cheese
4 eggs
1 tablespoon flour
2 cups light cream

Line a pie pan with pastry and refrigerate for 1 hour. Crumble bacon into bits and sprinkle ½ on pastry. Sprinkle ½ of cheese on bacon. Put eggs, flour, cream, ½ teaspoon salt and ¼ teaspoon pepper in blender and mix well. Pour into pastry shell, adding rest of bacon and cheese. Bake approximately 40 minutes at 350 degrees, or until top is brown and mixture set. Test for doneness — when knife comes out clean, it's done. Serves 4 to 6.

Pittsburg, Pa. Airport

Parkway West at Rts. 22 & 30

When you land at the Greater Pittsburgh Airport you'll only be 5 minutes from this Holiday Inn. Downtown Pittsburgh is just 10 minutes away. American and continental cuisine is right here at the Inn. There are endless tourist attractions in Pittsburgh. Visit the University of Pittsburgh campus with its 42 story "Cathedral of Learning".

CHICKEN KIEV

6 whole chicken breasts, boned
1 teaspoon salt
¼ teaspoon pepper
2 tablespoons chopped parsley
¼ teaspoon garlic powder
½ cup almonds, chopped fine
¾ cup butter
1 tablespoon flour
1 egg, beaten
1 cup milk

Lightly season chicken breasts with salt and pepper, then with chopped parsley, garlic powder and part of almonds. Cover each breast with 2 tablespoons butter. Roll breasts and tie. Roll in flour and dip in batter made of 1 tablespoon flour, 1 beaten egg and 1 cup milk. Mix well. Add rest of almonds. Deep fry in hot oil (350 degrees) for 12 to 15 minutes. Serve on bed of saffron rice and garnish with spiced peaches. Serves 6.

Reading, Pa.

U.S. 222 N. 5th St. Hwy.

Expect traditional Pennsylvania Dutch food and you won't be disappointed at this Holiday Inn in the heart of the Pennsylvania Dutch Country. Today one of Reading's 600 products is pretzels. The region's spring waters are given credit for their famous taste. Daniel Boone was born on a farm only a few miles from town.

BAKED FILLET OF FLOUNDER MARINARA

6 flounder fillets
¼ cup onion, sliced
2 tablespoons butter
4 or 5 cups whole tomatoes
¾ teaspoon salt
¼ teaspoon white pepper
½ teaspoon oregano
½ teaspoon chopped parsley
½ bay leaf

Sauté onion to a light golden color in butter. Add crushed tomatoes. Combine with other ingredients and simmer for 30 minutes. Bake flounder fillets at 400 degrees on an oiled or buttered platter for 12 to 30 minutes. Pour marinara sauce over flounder fillets and serve. Serves 6.

PENNSYLVANIA DUTCH STEW

Fry 2½ pounds of smoked sausage in braising pan until golden. Add flour to make a roux. Slowly add 1 quart warm milk making a gravy as it thickens.

Add vegetables: ¾ pound diced potatoes, ½ pound sliced carrots, ½ pound cooked peas. Season with salt and white pepper. Simmer 5-15 minutes, depending on size of vegetables. Serves 8-10.

Scranton, Pa.-East (Dunmore)

I-81 E., Tique St. Exit

Whether in Scranton for business or vacation, this Holiday Inn serves you right. There is a "must order" in the Lord Dunmore dining room. It's Rice Pudding. If you don't like rice or pudding, this delicious treat will change your mind. The Inn is near Marywood College and the University of Scranton. Many ski slopes are nearby.

BROILED LAKE TROUT

Place fish skin side up on heavily oiled rack on broiler pan. Rub with olive oil and salt. Broil fish 3 inches from heat for 5 to 8 minutes, depending on thickness of fish. Turn it with a wide spatula. Season other side. Cook 10 to 15 minutes, until done. Serve with lemon butter sauce: combine 4 tablespoons melted butter with 1 tablespoon lemon juice and 2 teaspoons chopped parsley. (Enough sauce for 2 to 4 trout). Allow 1 trout per person.

RICE PUDDING

3 eggs
½ cup brown sugar
½ teaspoon salt
1 teaspoon vanilla
3 cups milk
1 cup cooked rice
⅓ cup raisins
Nutmeg

Beat eggs slightly, add sugar, salt and flavoring. Scald milk and add to first mixture. Add rice and raisins last. Place in a buttered casserole. Sprinkle nutmeg on top. Place in pan of hot water and bake at 325 degrees for 1¼ hours. Stir once after first 30 to 40 minutes of baking. Serve warm. 6 servings.

Sharon, Pa.

Rt. 18 at Interstate 80

Antique chandeliers, rough hewn ceiling beams and a water wheel set in mortared soft coal are special treats in the Hermitage Dining Room. Homemade bread is an especially delicious extra. Scalloped Oysters, Irish Stew and Glazed Ham Loaves are only a few of the daily noon buffet features. A championship golf course is just a highway away (across). Visitors enjoy the many scenic and quaint Amish farms in the area.

GLAZED HAM LOAF

```
1    pound cured ham, ground
     (all fat removed)
1½   pounds fresh pork ham, ground
     (all fat removed)
1    cup toasted bread crumbs
¾    teaspoon prepared mustard
1    teaspoon salt
1    cup milk
2    eggs, well beaten
2    teaspoons green pepper,
     chopped fine
```

Mix all ingredients well and shape into a loaf. Place in well greased baking dish and bake 1 hour at 300 degrees. Makes 1 large loaf. Serves 8.

Sauce for basting and glazing:

```
½    cup brown sugar
½    cup water
¼ to ½ cup vinegar
1    tablespoon dry mustard
```

Bring all ingredients to a boil. Baste loaf and pour over loaf when serving.

State College, Pa.

U.S. 322 S., S. Atherton St.

Ski enthusiasts enjoy being only 5 minutes from the Skimont slopes. The Inn has a Ski Smorgasbord every Saturday evening. Everyone wears informal clothes and feasts before a roaring fire. Fifteen countries are represented in beverages served in the bar. Lighted tennis courts, 2 swimming pools and live entertainment will add to your fun. The Inn is also near Penn. State University and only 1 mile from town.

DEEP SEA SCALLOPS

```
1    pint scallops
     Flour
     Seasonings
2    tablespoons butter
¼ to ½ cup sherry
     Drawn Butter
     Lemon garnish
```

Clean scallops by dipping in cold water quickly. Remove bits of shell and pat dry on absorbent paper. Lightly flour and season scallops. Sauté in butter in a heavy skillet for 5 minutes, or until light brown. Place scallops in a casserole. Add sherry to juices and butter in skillet. Stir well and pour over scallops. Heat thoroughly. Top with Drawn Butter when serving. Add lemon garnish. Serves 3 to 4.

Drawn Butter

Blend 2 tablespoons butter and 2 tablespoons flour, adding salt and pepper. Slowly stir in 1 cup hot water. Add 1 teaspoon lemon juice and, bit by bit, add 1 tablespoon butter. Makes 1 cup.

Wilkes-Barre, Pa.

Exit 36 NE Ext. Penn. Tpk.

This Holiday Inn has a great location for everyone. Downtown Wilkes-Barre and the Pocono Downs Raceway are only 1 mile away. It's just opposite the Veterans Hospital. Guests enjoy free transportation to and from the airport 5 miles away. Many are attracted when the Wilkes-Barre Historical and Geological Society presents the dramatic history of the valley and the story of coal. The Inn's delicious food attracts people everyday.

POLLO ACOSTO
(Chicken Acosto)

2 boneless chicken breasts
3 slices bacon
4 ounces smoked ham, sliced thin
¼ cup pimento strips
3 thin slices dill pickle

Pound chicken breasts flat. Place bacon slices so they parallel each other, lengths touching. Place 1 chicken breast on top of bacon, layer ham, strips pimento and pickle slices. Top with another chicken breast. Roll jelly roll fashion and fasten bacon securely with toothpicks. Roll into flour, dip in beaten eggs, then in bread crumbs. Refrigerate to handle easily. Fry in deep fat at 325 degrees for 8 minutes. Cool slightly. Slice the roll into thirds, discarding ends. Pour Filbert Sauce over roll and garnish. Serves 2-3.

Filbert Wine Sauce

Melt 4 tablespoons butter. Add 4 tablespoons sliced filberts and 4 tablespoons sliced mushrooms. Sauté 5 minutes. Finely chop 2 cooked chicken livers and add to sauce. Add ⅓ cup dry sherry and ½ cup Burgundy last. Simmer 15 minutes.

Williamsport, Pa.

Rt. 220 N. & E. 3rd.

Be sure to try Pennsylvania Dutch Style Chicken Waffles. Homemade bread and garlic bread are also special features at this Holiday Inn in Williamsport, the birthplace of Little League Baseball. Your team members will want to visit the Little League Museum. For hunters, the Allegheny Mountains abound in deer, grouse and turkey. Streams teem with bass and trout. Golf, bowling, ice skating and boating are all nearby.

PENNSYLVANIA DUTCH CHICKEN POT PIE

1 4- to 5-lb. stewing chicken
4-5 carrots, thickly sliced
4-5 large potatoes, thickly sliced
3 large onions, ½ inch slices
2 tablespoons flour
Salt and pepper
Pastry

Boil hen (which has been salted) until thoroughly tender. Use covered vessel with 1 quart water. Bring to a boil, then let it simmer until leg bone is loose (about 35 minutes per pound, depending on size and age of hen). Cool. Strip meat from bones and cut in medium-size pieces. Reserve liquid. Save giblets or cook separately and cut to use in gravy, if desired. Cook carrots, potatoes and onions. Use a deep casserole. Make a layer of vegetables, layer of chicken, and repeat until all have been used.

Make a sauce with flour and 2 tablespoons chicken fat from stock. Add 2 cups broth and stir until thickened. Add seasonings to taste. Pour over chicken and vegetables. Cover with pastry and bake in a 350 degree oven for 20 to 30 minutes, until pastry is brown. Serves 8 to 10.

York, Pa. - Rt. 30

Rt. 30 E., 2600 E. Market St.

York is a city of colonial houses, markets and museums. Visitors also enjoy Hershey and Gettysburg Battlefield tours and the many Dutch Amish attractions. This York Holiday Inn blends modern luxury with old-fashioned Pennsylvania Dutch hospitality. You can expect traditional food of the area in the dining room. It's as interesting as the area.

YORKSHIRE CHICKEN

1 2½- to 3-pound young chicken
¼ cup flour
2 teaspoons salt
1½ teaspoons ground sage
¼ teaspoon pepper
¼ cup cooking oil
1 cup sifted enriched flour
1 teaspoon baking powder
1 teaspoon salt
3 eggs, well beaten
1½ cups milk
¼ cup butter or margarine
¼ cup chopped parsley

Prepare chicken for cooking. Cut in pieces. Combine ¼ cup flour, 2 teaspoons salt, sage and pepper. Coat chicken. Brown in half of cooking oil. Place in a 2-quart casserole. Sift 1 cup flour, baking powder and 1 teaspoon salt. Combine eggs, milk, melted butter and parsley. Add to flour mixture. Stir until smooth. Pour over chicken and bake at 350 degrees for about 1 hour. Serves 4.

Providence, R.I. (So. Attleboro, Mass.)

Jct. I-95 & U.S. 1A

You'll be glad you decided to stop and stay at this Inn—the first Holiday Inn built in New England. It's an old hand at serving excellent food. The lounge features live entertainment. The area tempts everyone to explore. See the church with a bell cast by Paul Revere. Take a look at a widow's walk.

BAKED FRENCH MEAT PIE

1 pound hamburger meat
½ pound ground pork
½ medium onion, chopped
½ teaspoon Accent
½ teaspoon ground cloves
2 medium potatoes

Melt chicken or beef cube in ½ cup warm water. Add to hamburger, pork, onion and seasonings. Simmer until well done. Drain off fat. Dice potatoes and add to meat mixture and mix well. Line a 10-inch pie pan with pastry, fill, cover and brush with egg wash. Bake at 375 degrees until brown. Serves 6 to 8.

HICKORY PECAN PIE

3 large eggs
1 cup light brown sugar
¼ cup melted butter
1 cup white karo
¼ teaspoon salt
1 teaspoon rum extract
2 ounces pecans

Mix all ingredients well. Pour into unbaked pie shell and sprinkle pecans over the top. Bake at 400 degrees for 10 minutes, then reduce to 350 degrees and bake until set. Serves 6 to 7.

Providence, R.I. Downtown

I-95 at Atwells Ave., Exit 21

The white marble State House on a nearby hill contains such treasures as the parchment charter granted by King Charles II in 1663. Newport tours may be arranged at the Inn. Located on Narragansett Bay, the Inn is near the ocean and white sandy beaches. It also has an indoor pool, superb food and dancing nightly in the Captain's Quarters.

BROILED SCROD

Arrange 4 scrod fillets (young filleted cod) on a well buttered pan. Sprinkle generously with fresh lemon juice. Pour a little melted butter over each fillet, season with salt and light dusting of paprika. Broil about 4 inches from broiling unit for 6 minutes or until scrod flakes easily with a fork. Remove to a heated platter (using a wooden spatula). To make lemon butter, melt about 2 or 3 tablespoons butter per person and add fresh lemon juice to taste. Serve hot over the scrod and sprinkle with chopped parsley. Serves 4.

GEN'S COUNTRY BREAD

Sift 1¼ cups sifted all purpose flour and 1 teaspoon salt together and mix with ½ pound mixed candied fruit (chopped) and 1¼ cups almonds or pecans (chopped fine).

Beat 3 eggs thoroughly, then add ½ cup sugar, a little at a time, and continue beating until mixture is smooth and fairly thick. Stir in 1 teaspoon vanilla, 1¼ teaspoons pure orange extract and flour combination. Pour into a well greased and floured loaf pan. Bake in a preheated 325 degree oven for 50 to 60 minutes. Remove from pan immediately and cool on cake rack. Allow 2 hours before cutting. Cut in thin slices. This makes a good breakfast bread. Makes 1 loaf.

Allendale, S.C.

U.S. Hwy. 301 North

This Inn is located in a state with rare beauty and charm. It's near the Savannah River where the snowy heron and white egret nest and feed. But time does not stand still. It's not unusual to see scientists dining at the Inn. Like a wayside Inn of old, the Inn offers hospitality and features recipes handed down by word of mouth. Allendale hosts the Masters Tournament.

NUT CAKE

¾ pound butter
2 cups sugar
6 eggs
4 cups flour
1 teaspoon baking powder
½ teaspoon salt
1 teaspoon nutmeg
1 wine glass of whiskey
1 quart nuts
1 pound white raisins

Cream butter and sugar. Add eggs, one at a time, beating thoroughly after each addition. Sift together dry ingredients and add to mixture. Add whiskey, nuts and raisins. Bake in a well greased and floured tube or loaf cake pan at 350 degrees for 1½ hours. 1 cake.

Charleston, S.C. Airport

I-26 & West Aviation Ave.

Historic Charleston, the charming old city by the sea, is filled with things to see and do. Visit Fort Sumter, the National Monument on a tiny man made island in Charleston Harbor reached only by boat. The Gullah accents of the farmers are as colorful as their flowers, fruits and vegetables at the City Market. There's delicious food cooked southern style.

OLD-FASHIONED CHICKEN AND DUMPLINGS

1 3- or 4-pound hen
1 quart water
1 tablespoon salt
1 cup flour
2 teaspoons baking powder
1 teaspoon salt
½ cup milk

Cook giblets in 1 cup salted water until tender, and save for gravy. Wash hen and place in covered kettle with water and 1 tablespoon salt. Bring to boil, then simmer until tender and leg bone moves easily, about 2 hours depending on size of hen. Let cool in broth. Remove chicken from bones and cut in large size pieces. Keep warm in a little broth. Sift flour and baking powder and 1 teaspoon salt. Stir in milk. Have broth at boiling point and drop dumpling batter in broth. Cook, uncovered 10 minutes, add chicken, cover and cook 10 minutes more. Remove to serving platter. Thicken broth left with 1 tablespoon flour mixed with ¼ cup milk. Stir until right consistency for gravy. Add chopped, cooked giblets, using extra broth they were cooked in, if needed. Serves 4.

Charleston, S.C. Downtown

Meeting St. at Calhoun St.

Stay in the center of things in quaint Old Charleston. This Holiday Inn is only 1 block from the Civic Center, yet excellent fishing is only 1 mile away. The fresh seafood served in the Inn's La Porte de Fer Restaurant will soon be as famous as the city's historical homes. The Citadel is only 2 miles from the Inn.

PINEAPPLE CHEESE SALAD

1 envelope Knox plain gelatin
1 tablespoon sugar
¼ teaspoon salt
2 tablespoons lemon juice
1 cup crushed pineapple
⅔ cup cream cheese (or grated)
½ cup cream

Put ¼ cup cold water in a bowl and sprinkle gelatin on top. Add sugar, salt, ½ cup hot water and stir until dissolved. Add lemon juice and pineapple. Place in refrigerator, and when it begins to stiffen, stir in cheese and cream (or evaporated milk). Place in refrigerator until firm. Serve on lettuce. Serves 6.

HUSH PUPPIES

1 cup yellow corn meal
¼ cup flour
¼ teaspoon baking powder
¼ teaspoon paprika
1 teaspoon salt
1 teaspoon sugar
¼ cup chopped onion

Pour 1 cup plus 2 tablespoons boiling water into mixed dry ingredients. Add onion. Stir to mix thoroughly. Drop by tablespoonfuls into 350 degree cooking oil. Serves 6.

Charleston, S.C.
South

U.S. Ocean Hwy. 17 S.

Charleston is famous for its beautiful gardens near this Inn. The Magnolia Gardens are known the world over. Lagoons of black onyx water and centuries old cypress trees are found in Cypress Gardens. The massive Middleton oak is unforgettable in the Middleton Gardens. Guests enjoy relaxing strolls through this Holiday Inn's own lush gardens almost as much as the marvelous food in the Camelot Room. There's a barbecue pit for cookout fun.

SHE-CRAB SOUP

1 pound white crab meat
¼ pound crab roe, chopped

Melt ½ pound butter in a skillet. Sauté 4 chopped scallions or onions and cook until tender. Add crab meat, then crab roe. Let cook until heated through. Add 2½ tablespoons flour to ¼ cup milk and blend. Then add about 2 quarts milk or cream which has been heated. Add crab meat mixture to hot milk or cream. Stir until it thickens a little. Serve hot. Serves 8 to 10.

SHRIMP PILAU

1 cup green pepper, chopped
2 cups long grain rice, uncooked
1¼ quarts water
¼ cup chopped onion
2 tablespoons chicken base
½ teaspoon pepper
1 teaspoon Worcestershire sauce
1½ pounds shrimp, cooked
¾ cup mushrooms, sliced

Lightly sauté green pepper in ½ cup margarine over low heat. Add rice and cook until rice is slightly browned. Add water, onions, chicken base, pepper, and Worcestershire sauce. Cover and cook until rice is light and fluffy, about 30 minutes. Add shrimp and mushrooms, simmer until thoroughly heated. Serves 10 to 12.

Columbia, S.C.
Southwest

Cayce, S.C. U.S. 21, 76 & 321

Start the day here with hot home-made biscuits. Country ham with red eye gravy is delicious any time in the Gold Stallion Restaurant. This Inn is a favorite with parents and friends visiting the University of S.C. only 3 miles away. The Stable Taproom is a popular gathering place. Visitors enjoy Woodrow Wilson's boyhood home (now a museum).

POT ROAST

1 package frozen carrots
1 package frozen June peas
¼ cup mushrooms
1 onion
2 cups rice, cooked
8 slices roast beef, cooked
2 cups gravy

Cook vegetables as directed on packages. Sauté mushrooms and onion in butter. Add to rice in a casserole. Place layer of drained vegetables, then meat and add hot gravy. Serves 6.

OLD-FASHIONED BEEF STEW

1½ pounds beef round
3 baking potatoes
1 pound carrots
1 pound green peas
Beef broth

Cut meat in 1½-inch cubes. Sprinkle with salt and pepper and roll in flour. Melt some of fat from meat (can use 2 tablespoons cooking oil) in a heavy pan. Brown meat well on all sides. Cover with boiling water. Reduce heat and cook slowly. After 1½ hours, add vegetables, diced or sliced. Add beef broth (bouillon cube and water) to make more liquid. Season and cook until vegetables are done. Serve in a casserole. Serves 6.

Florence, S. C. - I-95

Ya'll come! Biscuits are baked right in the middle of the room by a hooped-skirted hostess when the daily noon buffet is served. The Emporium Restaurant features country "vittles" — everything from collard greens and country sausage to lace corn bread and blueberry cobbler. Before dinner you can sip something cool with a seafood appetizer in the seaworthy atmosphere of the Crow's Nest Lounge. You can bed down in a king-size, if requested. Five golf courses are nearby for tee time.

VEGETABLE SOUP

½ pound fat back (salt pork)
6 cups canned tomatoes, peeled
3 cups baby lima beans
3 cups yellow corn
3 cups cut okra
    Salt and pepper

Cut fat back into strips and add to 1 quart water in a pot. Mash tomatoes and add to mixture. Boil over high heat for 30 minutes. Add lima beans and corn. Let boil again for 30 minutes. Add okra and 1 quart water. Boil 10 to 15 minutes. Reduce heat and let simmer for approximately 15 minutes. Add salt and pepper to taste. 12 to 15 bowls. (Good warmed over).

CRACKLING CORN BREAD

2 cups self-rising corn meal
1 cup cracklings (fried pork rinds)
2 eggs, beaten
2 teaspoons sugar
⅔ cup milk
1 cup water

Combine corn meal, cracklings, eggs, sugar, milk and water. Mix until stiff. Grease a frying pan or grill to avoid sticking. Drop batter, one tablespoon at a time, on pan or grill. Fry 2 to 3 minutes on each side. Approximately 8 servings.

Georgetown, S. C.

Moss covered highways, old plantations, the Rice Museum with its Town Clock, and Live Oak Walk at Brook Gardens are sights to see in this historic city. But no trip in the Low Country is complete without tasting She-Crab Soup at this Inn with its plantation cook. Old Smoky Pilaff, a steamed rice dish with sausage in a seasoned broth, never fails to delight guests. There are touches everyone appreciates — piping hot old southern spoon bread for lunch!

SHE-CRAB SOUP

2 pounds shrimp
1 quart milk
2 tablespoons butter
½ pint heavy cream
1 cup crab roe
½ pound white crab meat
2 tablespoons Worcestershire sauce
    Sherry

Wash and boil shrimp. Drain off liquid and add milk to shrimp liquid. Bring to boil and thicken slightly. Add butter, cream, crab roe, crab meat and Worcestershire sauce. Add teaspoon of sherry to each cup before serving. 15 to 20 servings.

OLD SOUTHERN SPOON BREAD

1 cup corn meal
⅓ cup flour
3 cups boiling water
2 tablespoons sugar
½ pound butter
5 eggs, beaten slightly
½ teaspoon salt

Blend above ingredients. To this add 2 cups cold milk, then 3 teaspoons baking powder, which have been blended in a little milk. Bake in a well greased casserole at 375 degrees for 45 minutes to 1 hour. Makes 10 servings.

Greenville, S.C.
Pleasantburg

U.S. 291 & 276

The Reedy River runs through the heart of Greenville. This Holiday Inn is located on the edge of the picturesque city, 2 miles from the business district. Southern dishes are a specialty of the Inn. But unusual treats such as Red Snapper with Coconut are on the menu as well. Greenville hosts the Annual Southern Textile Exposition in October. Nearby Table Rock State Park is a botanist's paradise.

SKY-HI LEMON PIE

    4 tablespoons cornstarch
    4 tablespoons flour
    ½ teaspoon salt
 1½ cups sugar
 1½ cups boiling water
    2 tablespoons butter
    5 egg yolks, slightly beaten
    ⅓ cup lemon juice
    1 9-inch baked pie shell
    5 egg whites

Combine cornstarch, flour, salt and sugar. Add a little hot water to blend, then rest of water gradually. Cook over hot water for 20 minutes, remove and add butter and egg yolks. Continue to cook over hot water until thick. Cool and add lemon juice and grated peel. Pour into pie shell. Beat egg whites to soft peak stage, then beat in ½ cup sugar gradually. Add 1 teaspoon lemon juice. Pile on pie roughly and high. (For Sky-Hi, add 2 more egg whites and 2 tablespoons sugar). Bake about 5 minutes at 425 degrees. Watch closely. Whipped cream may be used in place of meringue. Serves 6.

Orangeburg, S.C.

430 John C. Calhoun Dr.

Enjoy a lazy susan laden with delicious treats, while you decide what to order in the Golden Gate Dining Room. This Holiday Inn is only minutes away from the heart of downtown. Edisto Gardens, a city park on the banks of the North Edisto River, is a beautiful place to visit. Camellias and azaleas burst into bloom beneath the moss draped live oaks in late March and early April. Excellent deer and quail hunting is only 2 miles away.

CHOCOLATE CREAM ROLL

    6 eggs, separated
    ¾ cup sugar
    ½ cup cocoa, scant
    ¼ cup flour
    ½ teaspoon salt
    1 teaspoon baking powder

Beat egg yolks until thick, add ¼ cup sugar and then beat until lemon colored. Measure cocoa, flour, salt and baking powder and sift on wax paper. Add to beaten yolks. Beat egg whites stiff, adding ½ cup sugar gradually. Fold egg whites into egg yolk mixture. Flavor with 1 teaspoon vanilla.

Line well greased jelly roll pan with greased wax paper and spread batter evenly in pan covering corners. Bake in 375 degree oven 12 minutes. Turn out on fresh tea towel covered with sifted powdered sugar. Roll cake with tea towel. Cool on rack. When cold unroll cake, spread with Filling and reroll without towel. Decorate with whipped cream. Serves 8.

Filling

Whip 1 pint cream. Reserve part for decorating in pastry tube. Add ¼ cup sifted powdered sugar to remainder and a little sherry or vanilla.

Spartanburg, S.C.

Junction I-85 & I-26

Bubbly peach cobblers, peach preserves, even fresh peaches and cream for breakfast are served here. In the spring the fruit trees are a beautiful sight to see in this Peach Capital. During the summer months the town's packing sheds are full of peaches, and visitors are welcome. Spartanburg is also a very important textile center. Wofford College and Converse College are both located here.

FRESH PEACH COBBLER

    3 to 4 cups fresh peaches
      Sugar to taste
    2 teaspoons lemon juice
      Pinch salt
1½ tablespoons flour
    ¾ cup water
    ¼ pound butter, melted

Peel and slice peaches. Sprinkle with sugar, lemon juice and salt. Let stand while preparing pastry. Blend flour into a little of water, then add rest of water and stir until smooth. Add to peaches. Place peaches in a buttered baking pan. Pour melted butter over all. Roll pastry medium thin, cut in strips and place on cobbler. Place in a 350 degree oven for 45 minutes. If top is not brown, bake 10 to 12 minutes more at 425 degrees. Sprinkle with extra sugar. Serves 6-8.

Pastry

Sift 2¼ cups flour with 1 teaspoon salt. make a paste of ⅓ cup flour and ¼ cup ice water. Cut ¾ cup shortening in rest of flour. Stir in flour paste. Roll out on floured board. Pastry may be used in bottom of baking pan and then folded over peaches, if desired.

Sumter, S.C.

U.S. 76, 378, 521

Do try the Carolina Low Country She-Crab Soup here. It's a traditional dish of the area and a specialty of the Inn in "The Gamecock City". Sumter is named to honor Gen. Thomas Sumter, the "Gamecock" of the American Revolution. The Palmetto Pigeon Plant the largest in the world, attracts thousands of visitors yearly.

CAROLINA LOW COUNTRY SHE-CRAB SOUP

    1 medium onion, chopped
    1 pound white crab meat
    2 quarts plus 1 pint milk
    1 stick butter
    ¼ pound crab roe, chopped
    ½ cup sherry

Sauté onion over low heat in half of butter, until soft but not brown. Add crab meat and heat. Heat milk in top of double boiler, but do not boil. Add crab meat mixture and rest of butter to hot milk. Season to taste with Worcestershire sauce and sprinkle with salt. Stir 1 teaspoon corn starch into ½ cup cold milk. Pour into soup to thicken. Add crab roe and sherry. Stir together thoroughly. Sprinkle a little paprika on each serving. Serve piping hot. Serves 10 to 12.

BAKED STUFFED SQUAB

    6 squab
1½ cups chopped onion
    3 cups corn bread, crumbled

Clean squabs. Cut giblets and boil with onion in 1 cup water for 15 minutes. Moisten corn bread with 2 tablespoons vinegar and giblet water. Add giblets and onion. Season and stuff squabs. Tuck ends behind each. Brush with butter and a sprinkle of flour. Bake in covered roaster at 425 degrees for 45 minutes. Turn to brown evenly. Serves 6.

Aberdeen, S.D.

U.S. 12, 2727 6th Ave. S.E.

No wonder people in Aberdeen have the Holiday Inn "habit" — the daily buffets and salad bars are gourmet feasts. The Friday Night Fish Buffets feature Fillets of Ocean Perch. Hunting and Aberdeen go hand in hand — it's in the heart of the pheasant hunting belt. Hunters from coast to coast make this Holiday Inn their headquarters, while they pursue the ring-necked pheasant each fall.

RING-NECKED PHEASANT

2 pheasants
1 tablespoon salt (for soaking)
Melted butter (cooled)

Cut each skinned pheasant into four pieces (2 legs with thighs and 2 breasts). Soak in cold water to which salt has been added for about 2 hours before preparing. Wash well. Take a small pan of flour and add seasonings. Coat each piece well with mixture. Dip each in melted butter, place on a baking sheet and oven broil until tender at 450 degrees. Remove from oven and drain from grease. Serve with Cream Sauce. Serves 2 to 4.

Cream Sauce

Combine 1 quart beef stock gravy or stock, 1 can mushroom soup, 1 onion (thinly sliced), 1 small can mushrooms and ½ cup sherry. Place broiled pheasant pieces in roasting pan and pour Cream Sauce over them. Leave uncovered in 250 degree oven for 30 to 40 minutes.

BEER BATTER FOR FISH

2 beaten eggs
1 bottle beer
1 teaspoon salt
1 tablespoon paprika
Flour for a medium thick batter

Combine all above ingredients to make a batter. Dip fish in batter, drain in a colander. Fry fish in deep fat until brown.

Mitchell, S.D.

I-90 W. Interchange Access Rd.

Stuffed Veal Birds, Julienne Fillet of Perch and Chicken and Dumplings are part of the bountiful buffets in the Windjammer Dining Room. Live entertainment in the Shipwreck Lounge and sauna baths await you here. Tours to the Corn Palace leave from the Inn. The entire exterior and portions of the interior are covered with corn. Top talent from Hollywood and Broadway are featured during the annual festival held at the Corn Palace.

PHEASANT CARLYLE

1 ring-necked pheasant
   (picked, cleaned and singed)
½ gallon water
1 medium onion, diced
3 to 4 stalks celery (and leaves)
4 to 5 carrots
   Seasonings
1 cup cider vinegar
2 bay leaves

Make stock of water, vegetables and seasonings. Cook until vegetables are tender. Add cider and bay leaves. Marinate pheasant in liquid 4 hours or overnight. Remove and stuff bird with Dressing. After stuffing bird, roast 15 to 20 minutes per pound at 350 degrees. Baste with leftover marinade. Allow 1 pound of bird per person. Use drippings in pan for gravy, add a flour-water roux, blend, then add water or stock. Sherry may be added if desired.

Dressing

Grind 3 cups cooked kernel corn with vegetables in stock. Add 3 cups soft bread crumbs moistened with 1 beaten egg and ½ cup soft butter. Add a dash of nutmeg, sage, black pepper and salt. This is enough dressing for more than 1 pheasant.

Rapid City, S.D.

I-90 at LaCrosse St. Exit

You can see the scenic Black Hills from this Inn. You're in "Cowboy and Indian country" — where Wild Bill Hickok, Calamity Jane and Sitting Bull once lived. Since everyone is in a hurry to see the sights, breakfast, lunch and dinner are served buffet style during the summer months. The museum at the S.D. School of Mines displays a flexible rock which tourists are invited to bend.

BEAN SOUP

Bring 4 cups water to a boil, add 2 teaspoons salt, 1 tablespoon minced salt pork, 1 tablespoon minced ham and ¼ pound dried navy beans. Cook slowly for 2 hours. Add 2 tablespoons chopped celery, 2 tablespoons chopped carrots, 2 tablespoons chopped onion, ½ teaspoon seasoning salt, ½ teaspoon paprika and ½ teaspoon pepper. Simmer for 30 minutes. Use blender or sieve if desired. Thin with boiling water or milk if too thick. Season to taste. Makes 5 to 6 cupfuls.

MACARONI SALAD

- 1 cup macaroni
- 1 tablespoon green pepper, chopped
- 1 tablespoon green onion, chopped
- 1 tablespoon pickle or relish
- 2 tablespoons pimento, chopped
- 1 cup celery, diced
- ½ cup American cheese, grated
  Salt and pepper
- 2 hard-boiled eggs, chopped

Break macaroni in pieces 2 inches long. Cook as directed on package. Drain well. Toss other ingredients into macaroni and use enough mayonnaise for right consistency. Serve on lettuce. Serves 5 to 6.

Sioux Falls, S.D.

Hwy. 38 At W. Ave.

You'll never miss a flight when you stay at this Inn — the airport is next door. The Inn is also located on the direct route to the famous Black Hills. This Inn is tops in preparing wild game (pheasant, duck, venison, etc.) for its hunter guests. Children enjoy seeing where Jesse James jumped a canyon nearby to escape the law.

CHINESE PEPPER BEEF

- 1 quart beef stock
- ¼ cup soy sauce
- 1 to 1½ pounds cooked beef
- 1 cup cold water
- 2 tablespoons cornstarch
- 2 large green peppers
- 1 large onion

Bring beef stock to a boil, add soy sauce. Cut beef into small strips and add to stock. Bring to a boil. Add cornstarch to cold water, add to stock and beef. When it has thickened, remove from heat. Cut peppers and onions into strips and add to thickened stock and beef. Serves 4.

VENISON

Marinate venison steaks in:

- 1 cup red wine
- 2 tablespoons oil
  Sliced onion
- 2 bay leaves
- ½ teaspoon salt

Heat all ingredients and blend well. Cool before using.

Brush steaks with butter and sprinkle with seasonings. Brown in hot skillet. Reduce heat and cook until tender. Before done, add ½ cup hot water. Cover skillet and allow meat to steam. Thicken juices for gravy.

Bristol, Tenn.
South

Turkey with corn bread dressing and giblet gravy, Tennessee country ham with red eye gravy, and homemade bread await you at this Holiday Inn. The famous Barter Theatre, where many a star is born, is at neighboring Abingdon. Bristol Caverns, Steele Creek Park, and Davy Crockett's birthplace are all nearby. Bristol is also the home of Sullins College, King College and Virginia Intermont College.

TENNESSEE COUNTRY HAM

    8-ounce country ham steak
    ¼ cup coffee
    ¼ cup water

Place ham (only **country cured** ham) in a large iron skillet and slowly brown on both sides. Mix coffee and water. Pour over steak while it is frying. Let simmer for 1 minute. Remove steak when done to sizzling hot platter and pour "red eye" gravy over it. Garnish with crab apple. 1 serving.

CORN BREAD DRESSING

    ½ cup celery, chopped
    ½ cup onion, chopped
    1 tablespoon butter
    3 cups corn bread, crumbled
    1 cup white bread, dry bits
    2 whole eggs, beaten
    1 tablespoon poultry seasoning
    2 cups turkey or chicken broth

Sauté celery and onion in butter until tender but not brown. Add corn bread, bread, eggs, and seasoning. Hot broth is added to the dry ingredients until right consistency is reached—not too dry or too moist. Place in baking dish. Leave rough on top. Bake in 400 degree oven for 30 minutes. Dressing for 8 to 12.

Chattanooga, Tenn.
East

Take the Enchanted Trail through tunnels, along bluffs, and over a spectacular suspension bridge in Rock City Gardens on nearby Lookout Mountain. Civil War soldiers fought the "Battle above the Clouds" atop Lookout Mountain. It's fun to take the Incline Railway to see the battlefields. You'll need time to try more than a few of the excellent entrées on this Inn's menu.

FRENCH FRIED ONIONS

    4 to 5 onions
    Salt
    Pepper
    ½ cup milk
    ½ cup flour or bread crumbs
    1 quart hot cooking oil

Peel and cut onions in ¼ inch slices and separate into circles. Season, dip in milk, then into flour or bread crumbs. Fry in 390 degree hot cooking oil until golden brown. Shake onto a sheet of paper to absorb extra fat. Serves 4.

FRENCH FRIED POTATOES

Wash and pare potatoes (sweet or Irish). Cut into lengths and leave ¼ inch thick. Dry with paper towels. Cook in warm cooking oil (325 degrees) until tender but not brown. Remove from heat, spread on paper and cool. Preheat oil to 390 degrees, add potatoes, cook until golden brown. Shake off oil. Sprinkle with salt if Irish potatoes, sprinkle with sugar if sweet potatoes. Serve hot.

Chattanooga, Tenn. South

2100 S. Market St. at I-24

Historic Lookout Mountain may be seen from all sides of this Inn. Take the Incline Railway to the top. You can take along a Holiday Inn picnic lunch or return to the Inn for lunch at pool side. Wonderful southern cooked dinners (Tennessee Country Ham, Fried Chicken) are served in the Red Coals Restaurant. There are the Choo Choo Coffee Shop and Caboose Lounge to start and end your days.

REMOULADE SAUCE

½ cup mayonnaise
½ cup creole mustard
2 hard-boiled egg yolks
⅔ cup olive oil
½ cup finely chopped celery
½ cup finely chopped onion
2 tablespoons minced parsley
1 tablespoon capers
2 tablespoons chopped dill pickle
1 clove garlic, minced very fine
Juice of 1 large lemon
Few drops pepper sauce
1 tablespoon paprika
Red pepper to taste

Combine mayonnaise, mustard, powdered egg yolks and oil. Add remaining ingredients and blend thoroughly. Serve with shrimp or any cold fish. Note: If a sharper type of mustard is used, the amount may be decreased as desired. Also, a small amount of horseradish may be added. Yields 2 cups.

Chattanooga, Tenn. Southeast

U.S. 41 & Interstate 75

This Holiday Inn is on the direct route to Florida but overnight guests usually decide to stay longer. It takes a while to try the many tempting entrées on the menu. Lookout Mountain is only a few miles away. Take a trip to the top on the Incline Railway. View seven states from Lover's Leap in Rock City. See Lookout Mountain Caves and Ruby Falls (the 145-foot falls are reached by unusual underground elevator).

SWEDISH MEAT BALLS

1 pound cooked beef, ground
1 pound hamburger meat
4 eggs
   Oregano
   Cumin
   Salt and pepper
1 cup celery
1 medium onion
1 green pepper
1 cup mushrooms
½ cup cooking oil

Combine meat. Beat eggs and add. Blend seasonings in mixture and add rest of ingredients, except cooking oil. Form into small balls. Brown in cooking oil in heavy skillet. Place on serving platter when done. Add 2 tablespoons flour to pan drippings (pouring off excess grease before adding). Brown flour. Add 1 cup of milk for cream gravy and stir until thick. Serves 6-8.

Small meat balls are excellent as appetizers for cocktail parties.

Clarksville, Tenn.

U.S. Highway 41-A

Partake of superb food served in delightful surroundings. Take a dip in the beautiful inner court swimming pool. This Holiday Inn is only a half mile from downtown and near Ft. Campbell. Dunbar Cave Park is just east of town. There's much to do and see in the nearby Kentucky Lake country. As you approach Clarksville the tobacco fields will let you know this is a tobacco growing center.

EGGS BENEDICT

For each serving, split and toast an English muffin. Top with a thin slice of broiled ham. Place a poached egg on the ham. Pour Classic Hollandaise Sauce over all. Serve immediately!

Classic Hollandaise Sauce

½ cup butter
¼ teaspoon salt
   Dash cayenne
1 tablespoon lemon juice
2 egg yolks

Beat butter in top of double boiler (not over heat or hot water) until creamy. Add salt and cayenne. Add lemon juice, a few drops at a time. Beat constantly. Add egg yolks, one at a time, beating until sauce is light and fluffy. Place over hot, not boiling, water for a few minutes and stir constantly until glossy. (Water shouldn't touch top pan—and don't let sauce stay over hot water too long). Serve warm. Makes about ¾ cup.

Columbia, Tenn.

U.S. Highway 31 North

Have a real southern breakfast in your room — you'll enjoy being pampered here. Parents visiting the nearby Columbia Military Institute find this Inn unexcelled for comfort and dining. Visitors enjoy touring the James K. Polk home with 1800's furniture and relics. Rattlesnake Falls and the Lewis National Monument are also interesting.

CHICKEN BREASTS BAKED IN WINE

4 whole chicken breasts, split
1 can cream of chicken soup
1 can cream of mushroom soup
1½ cups sherry wine
2 cloves garlic, pressed

Mix soups together, add sherry and garlic. Place chicken breasts in a casserole and and cover with soup mixture. Then sprinkle minced parsley and slivered almonds on top. Cover and cook in oven 1½ hours at 350 degrees. Serve with rice and extra sauce in a gravy boat. Serves 4.

SALMON LOAF DELUXE

1-pound can flaked salmon
½ cup buttered bread crumbs
½ teaspoon salt
2 tablespoons melted butter
   Dash black pepper
2 eggs, slightly beaten
½ cup milk
   Pinch sage
2 tablespoons chopped onion
1 teaspoon lemon juice
1 tablespoon minced parsley

Drain salmon and mix with other ingredients. Pack in a greased baking dish and bake 40 minutes at 350 degrees. Serve with sliced hard-boiled eggs on top. Heat 1 can mushroom soup and pour over loaf. Serves 6.

Gatlinburg, Tenn.

Airport Road

This Inn is nestled in the mountains just one mile from the entrance of the magnificent Great Smoky Mountains National Park. Recreational facilities are unlimited. Thrill to the sight of a native black bear. Fish in crystal clear trout streams. Ski in the winter. Enjoy exploring, hiking, camping, swimming, mountain museums. The Inn's special Pancake Breakfast is the way to start each fun day.

TENNESSEE PUDDING

    1 teaspoon soda
    ½ cup buttermilk
    2 cups white sugar
    2 sticks margarine (or butter)
    4 eggs, beaten
    3½ cups flour
    1 cup chopped nuts
    1 cup chopped dates
    1 cup shredded coconut

Dissolve soda in buttermilk. Cream margarine and sugar and add to buttermilk mixture. Add eggs. Sift flour into mixture. Then add nuts, dates and coconut. Bake in a greased tube pan at 300-350 degrees for 1½ hours. Pour hot Sauce over hot cake and leave until it cools before removing from pan. 1 cake.

Sauce

    1½ cups orange juice
    ½ cup sugar

Heat orange juice and sugar over low heat until sugar dissolves. Stir while heating.

Greeneville, Tenn.

U.S. 11 East Bypass

Visit the birthplace of Davy Crockett, now a state park off U.S. 11 East. Tour the home and Tailor Shop of Andrew Johnson, the 17th President of the U.S., in Greeneville. Attend one of Greeneville's large Tobacco Markets. Be sure to find out why Tennessee Country Ham is the "most ordered" in the Inn's Davy Crockett Dining Room.

FISH FRY

    8 fish, washed and cleaned
    1 cup corn meal
    1 quart cooking oil

Sprinkle salt and pepper on fish and in cavities. Roll in corn meal. Place in heavy skillet with hot oil over medium heat. Brown one side then turn with wide spatula to avoid tearing or breaking whole fish. Brown other side. Remove from stove and place on paper towel to drain. Serve hot and crisp. For 4 to 6 persons, depending on size of fish.

COLE SLAW

Chop 1 head cabbage fine and cover. Chill in refrigerator. Just before serving, mix with Sour Cream Dressing to moisten well. Add 1 grated raw carrot, ½ teaspoon celery seeds, 1 tablespoon minced onion and ¼ green pepper (cut fine). Serves 8.

Sour Cream Dressing

Mix 2 tablespoons sugar, 1 teaspoon salt, 2 tablespoons vinegar, 1 teaspoon mustard and 2 tablespoons lemon juice. Whip 1 cup sour cream. Then add ingredients previously mixed. Mix with cabbage for slaw. Makes 1 cup.

Jackson, Tenn. I-40

I-40 & U.S. 45 Bypass

This is the home town of railroad engineer Casey Jones. Visit the railroad museum and see the whistle he was blowing when his beloved "Old 382" was derailed. Jackson is a college town too. Union University and Lambuth College are both near this Inn. It's also near Owens Corning Fiberglass Plant. You can expect southern hospitality the minute you enter the lobby of this popular Inn.

CASEY JONES SOUTHERN FRIED CHICKEN

    1 frying-size chicken
      Salt
      White or black pepper
    ½ cup milk
    1½ cups sifted flour
      Paprika

Cut chicken into serving pieces. Rub with salt and pepper. Dip in milk. Season flour and put in a paper sack. Put a few pieces of chicken in sack at a time and shake until all are coated. Fry in deep 400 degree fat until golden brown. Serve with Cream Gravy. Serves 4.

Cream Gravy

Pour all grease off, leaving drippings of where chicken was fried. Add 1 tablespoon flour and stir until all drippings are blended with flour, adding a little grease if needed. Add 1 cup milk (scalded) gradually and stir until gravy is thickened. Season. Strain if desired.

Jackson, Tenn. North

U.S. 45 N.

Tennessee Country Ham and Waffles are tops at this Inn for breakfast, lunch or dinner. There are 12 acres of playground for family fun. The famous in song and story Casey Jones lived here. His home is now a museum of railroad memorabilia. The Inn is near both Lambuth College and Union University.

CHILE CON QUESO DIP

    3 tablespoons butter
    1 large onion
    1 cup canned tomatoes
    1 can Ro-Tel
    1 teaspoon cumin seed
    3 pods garlic
    1 tablespoon Tabasco sauce
    1½ pounds Old English cheese

Dice and fry onion in butter until soft. Add remaining ingredients (except cheese) with the cumin seed and garlic either mashed or ground. Cook slowly for 30 minutes. Add grated cheese and heat thoroughly until cheese dissolves and dip is smooth. Makes approximately 4 cups.

SEAFOOD COCKTAIL SAUCE

    1 pint chili sauce
    ½ pint tomato catsup
    ¼ bottle Heinz 57 sauce
    ½ tablespoon Worcestershire sauce
    1½ tablespoons horseradish
    2 tablespoons prepared mustard
    ½ cup finely chopped celery
      Juice of 1 lemon
      Tabasco sauce to taste

Combine all ingredients and place in refrigerator to chill before serving. Makes 1½ pints.

Kingsport, Tenn.

U.S. 23 at U.S. 11 Cloverleaf

Typical old south bell boys assist you in getting settled in your room. Try out the putting green or take a dip in the L-shaped heated pool. Then relax in one of the two dining rooms at this Inn. You can select your own steak from the steak cart. There are many regional specialties too. The whole family will enjoy nearby Warrior's Path State Park.

BEEF STROGANOFF

- 2½ pounds bottom round steak, ½" thick
- 2 tablespoons butter or margarine
- 1 cup chopped onion
- ½ clove garlic, minced
- 1½ teaspoons paprika
  Dash black pepper
- 2 cans mushroom soup
- ½ cup water
- 1 cup sour cream
- 5 cups cooked noodles

Slice round steak into thin strips, about 1 inch long. Sauté in butter. Stir in onion, garlic, paprika and pepper. Stir soup until smooth and slowly blend in water to make a smooth sauce. Add to meat. Cover meat and simmer for 1 hour, or until meat is tender. Stir occasionally. Mix a little hot sauce into sour cream and stir into meat mixture. Do not boil. Serve with hot noodles. Serves 10.

Knoxville, Tenn. Downtown

Chapman Hwy. at Blount Ave.

No wonder this Inn is popular. It's only 2 blocks from downtown. There's helicopter service from the airport. The University of Tennessee is within walking distance. It's just across the street from the Baptist Hospital. The Inn is famous for its "Beef Buffet" served at noon in the Twin Lantern Restaurant.

SPOON BREAD

Combine 1½ cups sifted corn meal, ½ teaspoon salt, 1½ tablespoons sugar and a dash of nutmeg. Stir in 1½ cups scalded milk. Add 2 beaten egg yolks and stir in ¼ cup melted butter. Beat 2 egg whites until stiff but not dry. Fold into corn meal mixture. Bake in a greased casserole at 350 degrees for about 45 minutes, or until done. Serves 6 to 8.

SHRIMP DE JONGHE

Run the following through a food mill:
- ½ pound butter
- ½ bunch parsley
- 5 cloves garlic
- 5 scallions
- 5 slices white bread, trimmed
- ½ teaspoon salt
- ½ teaspoon pepper
  Dash Tabasco
  Dash Worcestershire sauce

Stir in ¼ cup sherry wine. Roll in wax paper and place in refrigerator. Later place 1½ pounds of shrimp that have been boiled, peeled and deveined in a casserole. Add a dash of sherry. Cut previously prepared butter roll and lay over shrimp. Sprinkle with paprika. Bake at 350 degrees until golden brown. Serves 4 to 6.

Knoxville, Tenn.
Northeast

Asheville Hwy., U.S. 70

Unsurpassed scenic beauty is just outside your window at this Holiday Inn. It's near the Great Smoky Mountain area. For unforgettable cuisine in a relaxing dining atmosphere, the Red Coals Restaurant is the answer. The Cup and Saucer Coffee House serves delicious southern breakfasts. The tree shaded campus of the University of Tennessee is near the Inn.

SOUTHERN FRIED CHICKEN

2 disjointed fryers
2 cups flour
1 teaspoon curry powder
1 teaspoon nutmeg
2 teaspoons paprika
1 teaspoon oregano or thyme
  Salt and pepper to taste
3 eggs, beaten
2 cups milk
1 cup shortening or cooking oil
½ to 1 cup water

Mix dry ingredients thoroughly. Beat eggs into the milk. Heat shortening or cooking oil in a heavy skillet. Dip chicken in milk mixture and then in the flour mixture—be sure to coat thoroughly. Cook in melted shortening over medium heat until brown on all sides. Pour off excess shortening. Lower heat, add water and simmer until tender — about 20 minutes. Serve on platter garnished with spiced peach halves filled with cranberry sauce. Serve country gravy in sauce boat with biscuits and honey. Serves 4 to 6.

Manchester, Tenn.
U.S. 41 & Interstate 24

Casual outdoor living, relaxing hours on the patio and the finest of foods will make you glad you stopped at this Inn. It's halfway between Chattanooga and Nashville. Watch for beautiful horses as you drive along. Manchester is in the heart of Tennessee Walking Horse Country. Golf, fishing and hunting are all conveniently close to the Inn.

GARLIC GRITS

1 cup grits, cooked
1 roll garlic cheese
1 stick margarine
2 whole eggs
½ cup milk

Melt garlic cheese and margarine. Add to eggs which have been beaten and added to milk. Add mixture to cooked grits. Crumble corn flakes on top before baking. Bake in a 300 degree oven for 30 to 40 minutes. Serves 6.

OLD-FASHIONED POUND CAKE

Whip 3 cups sugar and 1 pound butter until light and creamy. Add 10 eggs, 2 at a time, and mix well each time. Add 1 teaspoon vanilla and 1 teaspoon pure lemon extract at one time and mix well. Sift 4 cups sifted flour (plain), ¼ teaspoon baking powder and ¼ teaspoon baking soda together and add to mixture all at one time. Mix on low speed for one minute. Scrape down sides of mixing bowl and mix on medium speed for two minutes. Add 6 ounces fresh or frozen orange juice last and mix on low speed for at least one minute. Pour mixture into well greased and floured tube pan (10-inch). Bake at 350 degrees for one hour, or until done. 1 cake.

Memphis, Tenn.
East

Off I-240 & I-40, 4941 Summer

Stay where it all started. Southern hospitality awaits you at the first Holiday Inn in the world. Chicken and Dumplings and Southern Fried Skillet Chicken are the specialties in the Scotsman Restaurant. The Trophy Tavern specializes in relaxing guests after a busy day. Golf and bowling facilities are close at hand.

CHICKEN AND DUMPLINGS

    1½ cups all purpose flour
    ½ teaspoon salt
    ¼ cup shortening
    ¼ to ½ cup water
    2 quarts chicken broth
    2 pounds cooked chicken
      Salt and pepper
      Pinch sage

Sift flour with salt. Cut in shortening with fork or pastry blender. Add water to make right consistency. Roll out thinly on a floured board. Cut into strips about 2 inches long and 1 inch wide. Add to 2 quarts of chicken broth. Cook covered until dumplings are done. Add 4 cups chicken (pieces, not diced) and season with salt and pepper. Add sage, cover and simmer. If broth is too thin, blend in 1 tablespoon flour with ¼ cup water and add while cooking at last. Serves 8.

Memphis, Tenn.
I-55

I-55 & 1441 Brooks Road

If you don't order Swedish Meat Balls here you'll miss a treat. There are delicious daily buffets at noon. Everyone gathers around the piano bar at night in the Black Eagle Lounge. Memphis is on the mighty Mississippi River and abounds with things to do and see. Graceland, home of Elvis Presley, is only a mile from the Inn.

STOBA

(Stewed Meat and Potatoes)

    2 pounds veal or lamb, diced
    1 tomato, chopped
    2 tablespoons ketchup
    2 potatoes, cubed

Cut meat in serving size pieces. Sauté in heavy skillet with 2 tablespoons oil and 2 tablespoons butter. Add 1 minced onion, 1 minced garlic clove, 1-2 diced hot peppers, 2 cloves, 2 tablespoons vinegar, salt and nutmeg. Add ¾ cup hot water and simmer covered until meat is nearly done. Add tomato and ketchup. Place potatoes on top of meat and simmer with cover until potatoes are soft. Add more water as needed to keep stew gravy right consistency. Serves 6.

AREPA DI BACOBA

(Banana Pancakes)

Make batter of ¾ cup flour, 3 eggs (beaten) and 1 pint milk. Add 3 mashed bananas. Grease griddle with butter before frying pancakes and each time thereafter. Fry round pancakes on preheated griddle (medium heat). Sprinkle with 1 tablespoon cinnamon mixed with 1 tablespoon sugar when ready to serve. Makes 10 to 12 pancakes.

Memphis, Tenn. - Jr.

Lamar at Semmes (U.S. 78)

You're never too late to order something good to eat here. The Holiday Grill is open 24 hours a day. The Inn is near the airport and travelers enjoy being able to order a steak, sandwich or breakfast at any hour. Motorists like its location only ¼ mile from Interstate 240. The Inn is close to the Coliseum and Memorial Stadium.

HOLIDAY JR. CHEESEBURGER

1½ pounds lean beef (ground)
1 teaspoon salt
1 teaspoon seasoning salt
¼ teaspoon black pepper
6 slices Cheddar cheese
6 hamburger buns

Mix meat and seasonings. Form into flattened cakes ¾ inch thick. Place on hot grill for 5 minutes, turn and cook for 5 minutes on other side, unless rare meat is desired. Spread split buns with soft butter. Toast. Place hamburger meat on bottom bun, add slice of cheese and run under broiler for a few minutes, until cheese melts. Place top on bun. Serves 6.

Variation: use slice of thin Roquefort cheese for Roquefort-burger.

Memphis, Tenn. Medical Center

969 Madison Ave.

There's always a doctor in the Inn. No wonder. This Holiday Inn is so close to the Baptist Memorial Hospital and the University of Tennessee Medical Center. Downtown Memphis is only 2 miles away. Everyone finds the DeSoto's View Restaurant a great place to eat. DeSoto's View Lounge on the 19th floor is the popular place to relax and sip into something refreshing.

LAMB MEAT BALLS

1 pound lean lamb
3 large onions
1½ cups rice (cooked)
½ cup Cheddar cheese, grated
1 teaspoon dill, chopped
1 teaspoon parsley, chopped
4 eggs, beaten until frothy

Grind lamb and onions. Combine with rice, cheese, dill, parsley, pepper and salt. Knead mixture thoroughly and form into balls or egg shapes. Roll meat balls in flour, then dip in eggs. Fry meat balls in heavy skillet to which ¼ cup shortening has been added. Fry over medium heat until they are golden on all sides. Serves 4 to 6.

ROBERT E. LEE SANDWICH

On a large slice of rye bread place a leaf of lettuce, top with sliced white turkey, 4 slices hard-cooked egg, and sprinkle with chopped stuffed olives, and place 2 slices of broiled bacon on either side. Pour over a souffle cup of 1000 Island Dressing and garnish with a spiced crab apple and ripe olives. One portion.

Memphis, Tenn.
Midtown

1262 Union

Tennessee Country Ham is just one reason this Inn's Bull 'n Bear Restaurant is so popular. People in Memphis also know where to go on Sundays for the best Chicken Dinners. The Inn's location is another reason for its popularity. It's opposite the Methodist Hospital and only 1½ miles from the Coliseum. There's a fine zoo at nearby Overton Park.

BAKING POWDER BISCUITS

    2 cups all purpose flour
    3 teaspoons baking powder
    ½ teaspoon salt
    ⅓ cup shortening
    ⅞ cup milk
       (1 cup less 2 teaspoons)

Measure all ingredients accurately. Sift flour, measure, re-sift 3 times with dry ingredients, the last time into mixing bowl. (Three siftings prevent yellow specks of crust caused by incomplete blending of baking powder). Cut shortening into dry ingredients with a pastry blender or 2 knives until particles are size of rice. Pour milk in all at once. Stir quickly and vigorously. Turn dough out immediately onto a lightly floured pastry board or table. Knead quickly 6 to 8 times. Roll out ½ to ¾ inch thick. Cut with biscuit cutter, then place on a greased shallow baking pan. Bake in a 425 degree oven for 12 to 15 minutes, or until golden brown. Makes 18 to 24 biscuits.

Memphis, Tenn.
Poplar I-240

U.S. 72, 5679 Poplar Ave.

Local businessmen in the area and regular visiting executives know where to go at noon — to the Businessmen's Buffet. There's always a delicious variety of meats, but no one can ever pass by the Roast Beef. There's live entertainment in the lounge every night. Nearby Germantown hosts a nationally known Horse Show annually.

ARROZ CON POLLO

    3 pounds chicken (joint cuts)
    1 cup olive oil
    1¼ cups onion, finely diced
    2 cloves garlic, minced
    ½ cup celery, finely diced
    ½ cup bell pepper, finely diced
    2 quarts chicken broth
       Salt to taste
       Pepper to taste
    1 teaspoon oregano
    2 pounds uncooked rice
    1 small can pimentos
    2 tablespoons parsley, minced
    ½ cup sliced almonds
    1 cup cooking sherry

Brown chicken in oil. Remove from pan and sauté onion, garlic, celery and pepper until tender in same oil. Add broth, salt, pepper, oregano and chicken and cook for 10 minutes covered. Add rice, pimentos, parsley, almonds and sherry. Cook for 30 minutes or until rice is tender or liquid is gone. Serves 8.

Memphis, Tenn.
Riverbluff

At foot of Memphis-Arkansas Bridge

The distinctive Roman Dining Room on the top floor of this Inn is a most delightful place to dine in Dixie. Don't miss the Chariot Buffet served at high noon! Statues, fountains and a revolving globe bring ancient Rome to the modern world. And you overlook the Mississippi River and Memphis skyline while you dine. The Cotton Carnival is the nation's party to attend in Memphis each spring.

CHEROKEE CHOWDER

¼ cup white salt pork, cubed
1 small hen or fryer
1 bay leaf
¾ pound boneless lean pork, julienne strips
1 onion, cut in wedges
1 large green pepper, ½" slices
½ red pepper, ½" slices
1 cup minced raw carrots
3 medium potatoes, pared and diced
2 cups whole kernel corn

Sauté salt pork cubes in a heavy pot, but do not brown. Cut hen in half so it will lie flat. Place in pot with pork and cover with water. Drop bay leaf in and bring to a boil. Then cook over low heat until chicken falls off bones. Remove chicken from stock. Put pork strips into pot with stock. Bring to boil, then simmer until pork is tender. Remove pork and add vegetables. Cook until they are done and potatoes thicken stock. Return shredded chicken and pork to pot, adding more water if needed. Serves 12 or more.

Memphis, Tenn.
Rivermont

W. Ga. Ave. & Riverside Dr.

Each room's balcony atop this luxurious Inn affords a view of the Mississippi River or the Memphis skyline. Holiday Hall, Mid-America's most modern convention facility, is adjacent to the Inn. Capt. Isaac Rawlings' Table (an 1819 cafe) delights guests with old southern favorites. Gourmet cuisine and a dance band are enjoyed in the Rivermont Club.

STEAK DIANE

1 12-ounce sirloin steak
8 butter pats
1 onion, finely chopped
3 ounces fresh mushrooms, chopped
English mustard
Lea and Perrins sauce
Tabasco
Garlic salt
Cognac
⅓ cup brown gravy
Finely chopped parsley

Trim fat from meat and pound with mallet. Season. Heat 8 butter pats in chafing dish until golden. Cook steak quickly on each side (no longer than 60 seconds on each side). Remove steak and place between 2 plates to keep warm. Add onion and mushrooms to chafing dish and stir as they cook. Add mustard, Lea and Perrins sauce and dash of Tabasco. Add garlic salt.

Replace steak in pan and cook 90 seconds on each side. Stir sauce well. Flambée with cognac. To insure proper flaming effect place most of sauce on side of pan closest to you. Place opposite side of pan directly above flame. Add cognac and when it ignites tilt pan slowly toward you. Flaming cognac will burst into high flame. As soon as flame dies add brown gravy to sauce and stir well. Cover steak with sauce when serving. Add parsley. Serves 1.

Memphis, Tenn.
South

S. Bellevue, U.S. 51 S.

This Inn is near enough to the city for convenience (5 miles), yet far enough away to avoid congested traffic. It's a good place to stay when you desire an early start south or west. The Inn is on the direct route to the bridge over the Mississippi River. And it's close to the airport and the industrial area too. For dining try the southern delicacies in the Holiday Restaurant.

APPLE PIE

    6 medium-size apples
    ⅔ cup sugar
    1 tablespoon cornstarch
    ¼ teaspoon cloves
    ¼ teaspoon cinnamon
    ⅛ teaspoon nutmeg

Peel and core apples. Cut in thin slices. Sift dry ingredients over apples and stir gently so they are all coated. Place in an unbaked pie crust. Add 2 tablespoons melted butter and 1 tablespoon lemon juice. Cover pie with upper crust. Add extra sugar and cinnamon on top. Bake in a 450 degree oven for 10 minutes. Reduce heat to 350 degrees and bake 40 to 50 minutes, until pie is done. Serves 6.

ASPARAGUS AU GRATIN

Place 2 pounds drained asparagus, fresh cooked or canned, in a buttered baking pan. Make a cream sauce by blending 2 tablespoons butter and 2 tablespoons flour and adding 1 cup milk gradually. Season with ¼ teaspoon salt and dash of pepper. Cook over medium heat until it thickens. Pour over asparagus. Top with ½ cup buttered bread crumbs and ½ cup grated Cheddar cheese. Bake at 375 degrees until crumbs are brown. Serves 6.

Memphis, Tenn.
Southeast

3728 Lamar in Holiday City

This could be the busiest Holiday Inn of all. It's next door to the headquarters for the Holiday Inn International system. "Holiday City" is a complex of 75 acres in Memphis, Tenn., U.S.A. The Holiday Inn University is nearby. Naturally this Inn hosts guests from all over the world, hence the Journeyman Restaurant. Banquet facilities are appropriately called Founders' Hall.

HOLIDAY BLINTZES

Stuff thin Pancakes with Cottage Cheese Filling (place a spoonful of filling on each and roll up, tucking ends in). Fry in butter. Then place in a casserole and pour Hot Fruit Sauce over each. Makes 24.

Pancakes

    3 eggs
    1 cup flour
    1½ cups milk

Beat eggs well, adding a pinch of salt, 2 tablespoons sugar and all of flour. Add milk slowly with ½ teaspoon vanilla. Melt 2 tablespoons butter in a small frying pan (preferably crepe pan) and add to pancake mixture, blending well. Pour in batter to cover bottom of pan and cook quickly on one side. Then place on a thick towel, brown side up. Wipe pan each time with a greased cloth after cooking.

Cottage Cheese Filling

Beat 1 egg, adding 1 pound cottage cheese, 2 tablespoons sugar, ½ teaspoon cinnamon and a little vanilla or grated lemon rind. Beat well. Makes 2 cups.

Hot Fruit Sauce

Combine 1 cup sugar and 1 tablespoon cornstarch. Add a pinch of salt, ½ cup hot water and blend. Stir in 1 cup fruit juice and 1 cup drained fruit cocktail. Add 2 tablespoons lemon juice. Makes 3 cups.

Morristown, Tenn.

Hwy. 11 E., West of 25 E.

Tennessee Sugar Cured Ham with Red Eye Gravy and Hot Biscuits is a delicious way to start (or end) a day here. The Inn is located in the heart of an industrial district, yet only 2 miles from downtown. The airport is also only 2 miles away. Sightseers enjoy visiting the birthplace of Davy Crockett only 1 mile from town. Fishing is excellent in both Cherokee and Douglas Lakes. Morristown has the first overhead sidewalks in the U.S.

DAVY CROCKETT'S BEAR STEW

Wash a 2- to 3-pound piece of bear meat in cold water. Cut off fat. Soak in 2 quarts water to which ½ cup vinegar has been added. Soak 30 minutes. Drain and wipe dry. Fry meat in big heavy iron skillet until brown on all sides. Add 1 chopped onion, 1 chopped green pepper, 2 stalks celery (cut pieces), and 1 clove minced garlic. Then add seasonings. Cook until onion is soft. Then add 2 cups tomatoes, ¾ cup tomato paste and a dash of Tabasco. Simmer covered for 2 to 3 hours or until meat is tender. Serves 6.

BUTTERMILK BISCUITS

2 cups sifted flour
1 teaspoon baking powder
½ teaspoon soda
1 teaspoon salt
4 tablespoons shortening
¾ cup buttermilk

Heat oven to 425 degrees. Sift flour, baking powder, soda and salt. Cut shortening into flour. Stir milk into mixture with a fork until flour leaves sides of bowl. Turn out on a floured board and pat ½ inch thick. Cut with floured biscuit cutter and place on lightly greased baking sheet. Bake 12 to 15 minutes. Makes 14 to 16.

Nashville, Tenn.
Capitol Hill

On Hwys. 431, 41A & 31 West

This Inn is right downtown and across from the state capitol too. Nashville has made its state capitol and surroundings a mecca for tourists. The Inn is also near the Grand Ole Opry. Tender steaks, fresh seafood and wonderful breakfasts have made the Inn's Parthenon Restaurant most popular. There is an exact replica of the Greek Parthenon housing an art gallery in Nashville's Central Park.

PIMENTS VERTS FARCIS

(Stuffed Green Peppers)

2 large green peppers
1 small onion, chopped
1 tablespoon butter
⅓ cup long grain rice
1 cup hot broth
1 tablespoon tomato, chopped
1 cup leftover chicken, ground
1 tablespoon chopped parsley
2 tablespoons grated Swiss cheese

Split the green peppers in two down the sides, remove all seeds and parboil. In saute' pan, lightly brown the onion in butter. Add the rice and let simmer 5 minutes while stirring with a wooden spoon. Pour in the hot broth, season with salt and pepper, cover the pan and let simmer in the oven for 20 minutes. When the rice is cooked and nearly dry, add the tomato, chicken, parsley and correct the seasoning. Add more broth for moisture. Blend well and fill each half of peppers. Sprinkle a little grated Swiss cheese over them, place in a baking pan and add a little water. Bake at 350 degrees for about 20 minutes. 2 servings.

Nashville, Tenn. Southeast

U.S. 41 & 70 S.

Arrive by plane and the Holiday Inn Coach will meet you. You'll be off to enjoy Tennessee Holiday Inn hospitality and fine food in La Fonda Restaurant. A world of country music awaits you in Nashville. Each week top performers play to a packed house at the famous Grand Ole Opry. Be sure to visit the Country Music Hall of Fame and Museum. Sightseeing should include The Hermitage (home of Andrew Jackson).

ORANGE AMBROSIA

2 cups hot water
1 package gelatin, lemon flavor
¼ cup sugar
    Pinch salt
1 tablespoon lemon juice
½ cup orange juice
2 tablespoons grated orange rind
1 cup evaporated milk, whipped
2 oranges, segments

Refrigerate evaporated milk a few hours prior to use so it may be easily whipped. Dissolve gelatin in hot water. Add sugar, salt, lemon juice, orange juice and rind. Cool to consistency of molasses. Whip well. Fold in whipped evaporated milk and orange segments. Chill. Serves 6.

HONEYCOMB PUDDING

Mix 1 cup flour, 2 teaspoons baking powder and ½ cup sugar. Add 3 tablespoons molasses, ¼ cup butter and ¼ cup heated milk. Then add 1 teaspoon cinnamon, ¼ teaspoon allspice, ¼ teaspoon salt and 2 slightly beaten eggs. When ready to bake add 1 teaspoon soda which has been dissolved in a small amount of water. (Do not add baking soda until ready to bake). Pour in greased pan and bake at 350 degrees for 30 minutes. Can be served plain or with sauce or whipped cream. Serves 6.

Nashville, Tenn. West End Ave.

1800 W. End Ave., U.S. 70

Free covered parking facilities with direct-to-rooms elevator service makes weather no worry here. Be sure to order pancakes for breakfast — they're a specialty of the Inn. Downtown Nashville is only 10 blocks away and Vanderbilt University is just 4 blocks. Visit the Hermitage, home of Andrew Jackson.

BREADED SHRIMP

2 pounds shrimp (18 to lb.)
2 eggs
½ cup flour
¾ teaspoon salt
¼ teaspoon freshly ground pepper
1 teaspoon butter or olive oil
1 tablespoon brandy

Thaw raw shrimp by submerging in cold water. Remove shell down to last joint; just before tail. Using a sharp paring knife, cut shrimp down center of back (almost completely through shrimp). Remove dark vein by scraping with blade of knife. Spread or flatten shrimp in form of butterfly.

Beat eggs until light. Beat in flour, salt, and pepper until smooth. Stir in butter and brandy or Worcestershire sauce. Dip a few shrimp at a time in the batter. Fry in deep fat heated to 375 degrees until golden brown (about 3 minutes). Drain shrimp on paper towels. Serve with fried onions, lemon wedges or mayonnaise seasoned with catsup or horseradish. Serves 6 to 8.

Oak Ridge, Tenn.

St. Hwy. 62 W. & 95

Don't be surprised if you share a family-size Sunday dinner with a famous scientist at this Inn — even a genius enjoys homemade biscuits and corn bread. You're in "Atomic City". Tours leave from the Inn for the Oak Ridge National Lab plants and for a visit to the nearby Atomic Museum. This Holiday Inn is also near the Great Smoky Mountain area. The L-Bow Room is a favorite gathering place and offers live entertainment.

JALAPENO CORN BREAD

    3 cups corn meal
    3 eggs
2½ cups grated Cheddar cheese
    1 large onion, grated
    4 jalapeno peppers,
        crushed with fork
    1 #2 can whole kernel corn,
        drained

Mix above ingredients in large bowl. Add 3 cups of milk and ½ cup of hot oil. Place in deep skillet and bake for 45 minutes at 350 degrees. Serves 12. Recipe may be cut in half if desired.

6 CUP SALAD

    1 cup fruit cocktail
    1 cup marshmallows
    1 cup crushed pecans
    1 cup sour cream
    1 cup cottage cheese
    1 cup coconut, shredded

Drain half the juice from the fruit cocktail and mix all the ingredients together. Serve on salad greens with a favorite dressing. Serves 6 to 8.

Abilene, Tex.

U.S. 80 West

Expect a Texas-size welcome and Texas-size steaks broiled right before your eyes in the Red Coals Restaurant. The Inn is next to the Dyess Air Force Base. Many historical places of interest are not far away — Old Abilene Town (about 10 miles), Buffalo Gap, Butterfield Trail and the Western Overland Stage Route. Abilene is also the home of Abilene Christian College and Hardin-Simmons University.

SPEZZATO DI POLLO
ALLA CACCIATORA

(Chicken in Red Wine)

    5-pound pullet, disjointed
    ¼ cup olive oil
    ¾ cup chopped onions
    1 green pepper
    1 clove garlic, minced
1½ teaspoons salt
    ½ teaspoon black pepper
    ¼ teaspoon oregano
    1 cup peeled, chopped tomatoes
    ¾ cup dry red wine
    ¼ pound sliced mushrooms

Wash and dry the chicken. Heat the oil in a Dutch oven or deep skillet. Brown the chicken in it. Add the onions, green pepper, garlic, salt, pepper and oregano. Cook 10 minutes. Add tomatoes and wine and cover. Cook over low heat for 30 minutes, or until chicken is almost tender. Add mushrooms, re-cover and cook 15 more minutes. Add more seasonings if needed. Serve with buttered noodles. Serves 4.

Alvin, Tex.

Intersection St. Hwy. 6 & 35

Houston is only 15 miles away. The Astrodome is just a 20 minute drive. No wonder so many people choose this Inn for business and vacation headquarters. It's also near beaches and fishing, Galveston and Freeport. And it's only 12 miles from NASA headquarters. There's free courtesy car service to the Houston International Airport (17 miles away). Seafood Gumbo is a "must order" during your stay. The Coffee Shop is open round-the-clock.

OKRA AND TOMATOES

½ cup chopped onion
¼ cup chopped green pepper
2 garlic buds, chopped fine
1 pound sliced okra
¼ cup Wesson oil (or more)
1½ teaspoons flour
½ teaspoon black pepper
Salt to taste
3 ounces tomato purée
1½ cups tomatoes, canned

Simmer onion, green pepper, garlic buds and sliced okra in Wesson oil for 10 minutes. Then add flour, black pepper, salt, tomato purée and tomatoes. Simmer for about 20 minutes. Serves 6.

BLUEBERRY MUFFINS

1 cup shortening
1¾ cups sugar
½ cup egg whites
1½ cups all purpose flour
1½ teaspoons baking powder
½ cup milk
1 individual box corn flakes
1¼ cups well drained blueberries

Cream shortening and sugar at room temperature. Add egg whites and mix well. Add half of flour (sift first) and mix. Add remaining flour (sifted with baking powder) and milk. Then add corn flakes (or Post Toasties) and mix well. Fold in blueberries. Bake in greased muffin tins at 400 degrees for 15 minutes. Makes approximately 24.

Amarillo, Tex.
East

U.S. 60 & 66 on I-40 Bus. Rt.

This Inn's Villa Restaurant is known for its fabulous food. There's a special menu featuring Mexican food. Meet your friends in the relaxing Old English atmosphere of The Red Fox Tavern. Enjoy year round swimming in an enclosed heated pool. Amarillo has grown from a cattle town to a railroad shipping center for cattle, wheat and leather products in the Texas Panhandle.

TROUT PUFFS

Mix 1½ pounds cooked trout (chopped fine), 1 tablespoon melted butter, ½ cup bread crumbs, 1 teaspoon salt, ½ teaspoon pepper and 1 teaspoon lemon juice. Blend in 3 beaten eggs. Pour into greased custard cups and place in pan of hot water. Bake at 350 degrees for 30 minutes. Remove from cups and serve piping hot. Serves 4.

VILLA FROZEN DELIGHT

1 package lemon Jello
1 package lime Jello
1½ cups hot water
1 can #303 crushed pineapple
1½ cups mandarin oranges
½ package miniature marshmallows
1 package Dream Whip
Parmesan cheese

Pour hot water into both packages of Jello and dissolve. Add crushed pineapple and mandarin oranges (juice and all). Mix well. Spread a layer of marshmallows over top. Cover with Dream Whip or whipped cream. Sprinkle with Parmesan cheese and place in freezer until solid. This is excellent for a buffet. Serves 8 to 10.

Amarillo, Tex.
Midtown

U.S. 60, 66E, 87 & 287 N.

You'll get a Texas-size welcome at this Holiday Inn only 2 minutes from downtown Amarillo. Favorite foods are served in the Red Coals Restaurant. When in Amarillo be sure to visit the Palo Duro Canyon State Park. Scenic drives, bridle paths and trails are found throughout the park. The Panhandle Plains Historical Museum contains relics from the early days of West Texas ranching.

CORN BREAD

½ cup flour
3 teaspoons baking powder
¼ teaspoon soda
1 teaspoon salt
1 tablespoon sugar
1 cup corn meal
1 beaten egg
1½ cups sour milk or buttermilk
4 tablespoons melted shortening

Sift together the flour, baking powder, soda, salt and sugar. Then add the corn meal, beaten egg and milk to make a stiff batter. Add the melted shortening and beat until well mixed. Pour into a greased shallow pan. Bake in a hot oven (425 degrees) for about 25 minutes. Break into squares and serve with butter. Makes 9 squares.

Amarillo, Tex.
West

Amarillo Blvd., U.S. 66

Cattlemen feel right at home here. A display of famous cattle brands is part of the striking decor between the Inn's lobby and mezzanine. You'll see John Chisholm's "Bug on a Rail", Stephen Austin's Spanish brand and the brand of the XIT Ranch (at one time the world's largest ranch with 3,000,000 fenced acres). Continental cuisine and western favorites are served in the Continental Club.

SWISS VEAL EN CASSEROLE

1½ pounds bottom round veal.

Cut milk fed veal into strips ¼ inch thick. (Set veal in freezer until firm enough to slice). Season well, adding paprika. Dip in 2-3 well beaten eggs. Place veal in heavy skillet (not crowded) and sauté in butter for 3 minutes. Turn and cover with very thin slice of imported Swiss cheese. When melted and veal is cooked, place in buttered casserole over Swiss Tomato Sauce. Serve with buttered noodles. Serves 4.

Swiss Tomato Sauce

1 small bunch celery,
chopped with tops
1½ large Bermuda onions,
chopped fine
2 bell peppers, diced
2 cans whole peeled tomatoes
½ cup sherry
⅔ cup sugar
2 teaspoons rosemary, ground
1 teaspoon thyme

Combine celery, onions, bell peppers, and salt and pepper to taste. Sauté in small amount of butter until tender. Add tomatoes (broken up) and 1½ cups water. Combine with rest of seasonings and simmer 1 hour or longer, adding more water if needed. Cook until sauce thickens.

Arlington, Tex.

FM Hwy. 157, 903 N. Collins

Stay midway between Dallas and Fort Worth—just around the corner from the nationally famous Six Flags over Texas, Turnpike Sports Stadium and the industrial district. Dallas and Fort Worth are both less than 20 minutes away from this Holiday Inn. The Holiday Room is a haven for the hungry in a hurry. Relax and feast on gourmet cuisine in the beautiful Mediterranean Room overlooking the pool. Two championship golf courses are just a chip shot away.

SHRIMP COCKTAIL SUPREME

Allow 1 pound of fresh shrimp for 4 servings. Wash well and peel off shells. Devein using knife or toothpick. Put shrimp in seasoned boiling water and simmer for 5 to 12 minutes. (Season water with salt, parsley, onion, bay leaf and clove). Cool shrimp in water. Drain and chill. Serve with Cocktail Sauce.

Cocktail Sauce

½ cup tomato catsup
3 tablespoons cider vinegar
8 drops Tabasco
   Salt and pepper to taste
2 teaspoons chopped chives
¼ cup finely chopped celery

Mix all ingredients and let stand for several hours before using. Makes ¾ cup.

DIP A LA MARY

1 pound cream cheese
1 cup Sour Cream
1 bottle Pick-A-Pepper Sauce

Mix softened cream cheese and sour cream. Then mix in Pick-A-Pepper Sauce. Serve in bowl with chips or toasted tostados with cocktails.

Austin, Tex.
South

20 N. Interregional & Interstate 35

Surround yourself with luxury in the round — this beautiful Inn is octagonal shaped. It towers 13 stories beside Town Lake. Dining on the top floor affords beautiful views as well as gourmet cuisine. The Inn is also near the University of Texas campus and the Texas State Capitol. The capitol is a domed structure second only in size to the U.S. Capitol in Washington. Visitors enjoy seeing Austin from the 370-foot observation tower on the University campus.

CHICKEN A LA MURRY

1 2¼-pound fryer, halved
1 stick melted margarine
1½ cups fresh bread crumbs
3 tablespoons Parmesan cheese
1 lemon
1 tablespoon parsley, minced

Clean chicken in cold water and pat dry. Season with salt and pepper. Dip in melted margarine. Cover with bread crumbs mixed with Parmesan cheese, as much as will cling to chicken. Place in shallow pan in preheated 325 degree oven, skin side down. When it starts to brown and bubble, turn until bottom is golden brown. Squeeze lemon juice on chicken and let bubble until golden brown. Serve with minced parsley. Be sure oven is preheated. Time in oven is about 45 minutes. Serves 2 to 4.

Baytown, Tex.

Hwy. 146 at Republic St.

Game fish are waiting to be battled off Galveston Bay and the Texas Gulf Coast. You can expect wonderful seafood at the Inn's restaurant, fun in the Club Holiday Bar. The Inn is only ½ mile from downtown, 10 minutes from the Humphrey Airport, and 30 minutes from the Houston Airport. It's near the San Jacinto Battleground.

CHEESECAKE

    2½ pounds cream cheese
    1¾ cups sugar
     3 tablespoons flour
    1½ teaspoons grated orange rind
    1½ teaspoons grated lemon rind
     ¼ teaspoon vanilla extract
     2 egg yolks
     5 eggs
     ¼ cup heavy cream

Combine cream cheese, sugar, flour, grated orange and lemon rind and vanilla. Add egg yolks and eggs, one at a time, stirring lightly after each addition. Stir in cream. Pour into Cookie Dough Pastry. Bake in a very hot oven (500 degrees) for 12 to 15 minutes. Reduce temperature to 200 degrees and continue baking 1 hour. Cool. Makes 12 generous servings.

Cookie Dough Pastry

Combine 1 cup sifted flour, ¼ cup sugar, 1 teaspoon grated lemon rind and ¼ teaspoon vanilla. Make a well in center and add 1 egg yolk and ½ cup butter. Blend. Chill thoroughly. Roll out ⅛ inch thick and place over oiled bottom of a 9-inch spring cake pan form. Bake in a 400 degree oven for 20 minutes. Cool, butter sides, add cake form and place over base. Roll remaining dough ⅛ inch thick and cut to fit sides.

Beaumont, Tex.

I-10 at U.S. 69, 287 & 96

The Port of Beaumont provides world wide shipping of petroleum, natural gas, sulphur, salt, water, timber and sand. The Laffite Club in the Inn brings back the days of Pirate Jean Laffite with a towering mast, weathered sails and a captain's bar. Enjoy the finest seafood cuisine by candlelight in Le Chateaubriand Room. Nearby, the Spindletop Monument and Outdoor Oilfield Museum are located where "oil became an industry in 1901"— the Lucas Gusher ran wild for 8 days.

SHRIMP CREOLE

     6 tablespoons Wesson oil
     3 tablespoons flour
     1 white onion, finely grated
     1 green pepper, chopped
     1 clove garlic, minced
     2 pounds raw shrimp,
        shelled and deveined
     1 can tomato paste
     ½ teaspoon Accent
        Salt and pepper
        Worcestershire sauce

Make a roux of oil and flour. Add onion, pepper and garlic. Stir well until blended for about 5 minutes over low heat. Now add raw deveined shrimp. Mix with the sauce and continue cooking over low heat until shrimp are coated on all sides with the mixture. Add tomato paste and sufficient water to make a good sauce. Simmer for 30 minutes, stirring occasionally. Add Accent, salt, pepper and Worcestershire to suit your taste. Serve with rice. Serves 8.

Big Spring, Tex.

U.S. 80 at I-20

This Holiday Inn's location was once a camp site for early expeditions on the Santa Fe Trail. Air Force men from the nearby base and cattlemen from neighboring ranches like the welcome they receive here. And you will too. The food is superb. Big Spring hosts an Annual Rattlesnake Hunt in April with trophies and prizes.

LOBSTER SALAD WITH AVOCADO DRESSING

12 ounces Philadelphia cream cheese
1 can tomato soup
2 tablespoons gelatin
1 cup water
¾ cup finely chopped celery
¾ cup finely chopped green pepper
2 tablespoons grated onion
3 tablespoons lemon juice
1 large can lobster
1½ cups mayonnaise
2 tablespoons Durkees dressing

Mash cheese in soup and heat. Soak gelatin in water and add to soup mixture. Add celery, pepper, onion, lemon juice, lobster, mayonnaise and Durkees dressing. Season highly with salt, Tabasco sauce and Worcestershire sauce. Mold and chill until firm. Serve on lettuce with Avocado Dressing. Serves 8.

Avocado Dressing

Mash 1 large avocado lightly with fork. Add 3 tablespoons whipped cream, 1 tablespoon lemon juice and 1 teaspoon prepared mustard. Beat thoroughly, adding salt and a dash of Tabasco. Makes approximately 1 cup.

Brownsville, Tex.

3135 N. Expressway

Romantic old Mexico is at your doorstep. This Inn is on the shortest route to Mexico City for 70% of the people in the states. A hostess offers information and help on "things to see" and "what to do" in Mexico. The best of Mexican cuisine is served right here at the Inn. Guests enjoy golf privileges at the Brownsville Country Club.

GUACAMOLE DIP OR SALAD

6 black rough avocados (or the equivalent of small green or black)
1 3-ounce package Philadelphia cream cheese, softened
1 bunch or 8-10 green onions
6-8 drops Tabasco (if desired)

Peel and mash avocados with old-fashioned potato masher. Mix cheese and avocados and blend well. Sprinkle at least ½ teaspoon salt and add juice of ½ lime. Add chopped onions and onion tops and mix well. Taste. Add 1 teaspoon more salt, plus more lime juice, if needed. Add Tabasco and serve with king-size Fritos. This may be refrigerated (covered with foil) for hours before serving. If dip does turn black on top, just stir real well and black disappears. This may be served on lettuce leaves or stuffed in tomatoes. Makes 2 to 3 cups.

FRIJOLES

Wash 1 pound pinto beans, cover with water and soak overnight. Drain. Combine beans with ¼ cup bacon fat, ¼ teaspoon pepper, 1½ teaspoons sugar, ½ cup tomato catsup, 1 chopped onion, 1 teaspoon salt, ¼ teaspoon ground cumin seed and 1 teaspoon chili powder. Add cilantro to taste. Add water to cover and bring contents to a boil. Reduce heat and simmer for 4 to 5 hours. Serves 8 to 10.

Brownwood, Tex.

U.S. 67, 84 & 377 E.

Big Bend Trail takes you right to this Holiday Inn. It's located right downtown, almost in the center of the big state of Texas. It's hard to decide what to order in the dining room—the menu teems with exciting dishes. Guests also enjoy the Inn's Red Fox private club. The Inn is near Lake Brownwood.

CHICKEN NEW ORLEANS

1 2-pound fryer, serving portions
1 stick butter
½ cup green onion tops, chopped
1 cup diced celery
1 garlic button, minced
2 cups steamed rice

Season chicken pieces with salt, pepper, and dash cayenne. Dust well with flour. Place in skillet with half of butter and brown on both sides. Place in baking dish. Sauté onion tops, celery and garlic in same skillet. Add ½ cup of water. Stir well. Pour over chicken. Place in 350 degree oven and bake until tender, 35-40 minutes. Serve with rice. Add chopped parsley when serving. Serves 3-4.

BLUEBERRY CREAM CHEESE PIE

½ pound Philadelphia cream cheese
½ pound powdered sugar
1 pint whipping cream
Graham cracker crust
1 cup sweetened and cooked blueberries

Have Philadelphia cream cheese at room temperature and whip in mixer. Then add powdered sugar and whip. Add whipping cream and whip to a stiff consistency. Pour in a Graham cracker crust. Top with sweetened and cooked blueberries, which have been thickened as for a pie. Refrigerate. Makes 1 large pie.

Corpus Christi, Tex. Airport

Exit I-37 at Corn Prod. Rd.

Here's where to stay near the airport but within the city limits. Tours may be arranged at the Inn to visit Corpus Christi's many places of interest. Be sure to visit Port Aransas, home of the world's largest shrimp fleet. Go treasure hunting on nearby Padre Island. The Mexican border is only 3 hours away so you can expect authentic Mexican food here. Shrimp are caught and served the same day.

PARGO RELLENO

(Stuffed Red Snapper)

1 4-pound red snapper
3 tablespoons finely chopped onion
6 tablespoons butter
4 cups small bread cubes
1 cup minced cucumber
2 teaspoons chopped capers
Powdered cloves
1 teaspoon sage
¼ cup toasted almonds
4 tablespoons white wine

Rub snapper inside and out with garlic salt and freshly ground pepper. For the stuffing, sauté onion in butter until soft but not brown. Add bread cubes (without crusts, dried overnight). Add a little freshly ground black pepper, salt, minced cucumber, capers, sage, a light dusting of powdered cloves, sage, and toasted almonds.

Mix thoroughly in a bowl. Moisten with white wine. Stuff the fish rather lightly and sew. Score both sides at one portion intervals and bury a trimmed slice of bacon. Make a paste of butter, freshly ground almonds and white wine and spread ⅛ inch thick all over the fish. Bake in a moderate oven and baste with butter and white wine. Serves 4 to 5.

Corpus Christi, Tex.
Emerald Beach

1102 South Shoreline Blvd.

You can check into a suite with your own private swimming pool here. Or you might prefer a cabana facing the bay. There's an olympic-size swimming pool and beautiful private beach for all guests. Dining is elegant in the unique Club Seville. The center of downtown is only 8 blocks away. Water skiing and deep sea fishing are at your doorstep. The surf is always up nearby.

LOBSTER FIGARO

    1 pound lobster meat, diced
    2 lobster shells, halved lengthwise
    1 cup cooked vegetables
    ½ cup mayonnaise
      Dash Tabasco
      Dash Worcestershire sauce
    1 tablespoon lemon juice
    1 pimento, sliced
    4 strips anchovy fillets
    4 stuffed olives
    2 hard-boiled eggs, chopped

Mix the cooked vegetables with the mayonnaise and spread on the bottoms of the lobster shells. Mix half of the Figaro Sauce with the lobster meat and add Tabasco sauce, Worcestershire sauce and lemon juice. Spread the lobster mixture over the layer of vegetables in the shells. Spread remainder of the Figaro Sauce over tops of the lobster shells and smooth with a knife or palette. Garnish the tops with pimento, anchovy fillets and olives (sliced). Arrange chopped eggs and chopped parsley around edges. Serves 4.

Figaro Sauce

Mix well together: 1 cup mayonnaise, 2 tablespoons tomato paste, ½ teaspoon anchovy paste, 1 clove garlic (ground fine with salt), 1 teaspoon lemon juice, dash of Tabasco, dash Worcestershire sauce, ½ teaspoon chopped parsley and ¼ teaspoon chopped tarragon.

Corpus Christi, Tex.
Shoreline

1401 North Shoreline Drive

Balcony rooms overlook Corpus Christi Bay and the ship channel with continuous ocean going traffic. The Inn's Hyperbolic Paraboloid roof line simulates gull's wings in flight. There's excellent fishing from the sea wall in front of the Inn. Bring in your own catch for dinner, or try the Inn's delicious seafood specialties. Popular annual attractions include the Tarpon Festival, Buccaneer Days and Jazz Festival.

STUFFED MUSHROOMS WITH CRAB MEAT A L'AURORE

    ½ cup butter
    ½ chopped onion
    1 pound lump crab meat
    ¼ cup grated Parmesan cheese
    1½ pints Heavy Cream Sauce
    20 large mushroom caps
    ½ lemon, juice
      Salt and pepper
    ½ cup heavy tomato purée
    1 chopped hard-boiled egg
    1 tablespoon chopped parsley

Melt ¼ cup butter slowly, adding chopped onion. Simmer a few minutes. Place crab meat in pan together with onion and let simmer slowly for 10 minutes. Add ½ of cheese and ½ of Cream Sauce. Mix slowly. Place mushrooms in casserole with rest of butter. Sprinkle with lemon juice and seasonings. Bake 10 minutes. Remove from oven and place a filling of crab meat mixture in each mushroom cap. Combine remaining Cream Sauce and tomato purée. Pour over mushrooms. Sprinkle mushrooms with chopped egg, cheese and parsley. Bake slowly 10 minutes. Serves 5-6.

Heavy Cream Sauce

Blend 6 tablespoons melted butter and 6 tablespoons flour in a heavy skillet. Add 3 cups milk gradually. Season. Stir until thickened. 1½ pints.

Dallas, Tex.
Central

4070 N. Central Expressway

The center of downtown Big "D" is only 3 minutes from this luxurious Holiday Inn. It's also near the SMU campus, Cotton Bowl, State Fair Park and the Dallas Memorial Auditorium. What's in the Inn for you? Gourmet dining in the elegant surroundings of the Embassy Room. There are banquet and convention facilities for up to 1,000 persons. All this and the Inn also houses the art gallery of Dmitri Vail.

CHEESECAKE

1 pound cream cheese
4 eggs, separated
1 cup sour cream
1 teaspoon vanilla
1 cup sugar
2 tablespoons flour
¼ teaspoon salt
1 Graham cracker crust

Soften cream cheese. Beat egg yolks until thick and lemon colored. Add sour cream, vanilla and ¾ cup of sugar. Add flour and salt. Blend until smooth, then add cream cheese and blend thoroughly. Beat egg whites stiff, adding ¼ cup of sugar gradually. Fold into other mixture. Bake at 325 degrees for 1 hour in buttered cheesecake pan, which has been lined with Graham cracker crust on bottom and sides. After cake has cooled add Strawberry Topping if desired. Place in refrigerator until ready to serve. 1 cake.

Strawberry Topping

1 pint strawberries
½ cup sugar
1 tablespoon cornstarch
¼ cup water

Wash and hull berries. Cut in halves. Boil with sugar, cornstarch and water. Stir continuously until sauce is quite thick. Cool before adding to cake.

Dallas, Tex.
East

I-20, Mesquite, Tex.

Casual attire is the order of the Inn — even in the elegant dining room featuring authentic Spanish food. The Inn's location provides easy access to the many points of interest nearby. Fair Park and the Cotton Bowl are only 5 minutes away. Downtown Dallas is just a 10 minute drive. Fun for the whole family is a short half hour's drive to Six Flags Over Texas.

TEXAS STEAK

Have steak cut 2 inches thick. Use sirloin, porterhouse, t-bone, club, tenderloin or rib. Take steaks out of refrigerator at least ½ hour before cooking. They should be at room temperature.

Cook over open grill or broil under cooking unit of stove (at least 2 to 3 inches below). Sear steak on each side. Then cook 15 minutes for rare steak, 20 to 22 minutes for medium and 35 for well done, depending on thickness of steak and heat. Turn once while cooking. If meat seems to be browning too fast, move rack away from heat at least one more inch. When done, place on heated platter, spread with soft butter and season. Serve immediately. Good aged beef requires no marinade. Serve with Béarnaise Sauce, if desired.

Béarnaise Sauce

In a small saucepan, heat ½ cup butter to bubbling stage. Place 4 egg yolks, 2 tablespoons lemon juice, ¼ teaspoon salt, pinch of cayenne, 1 teaspoon chopped tarragon, and 1 teaspoon chopped parsley in blender. Blend at high speed. Add hot butter in a slow steady stream through opening in top of blender or remove cover if no opening. Makes nearly 1 cup.

Dallas, Tex.
Love Field

Lemmon Ave. Opp. Love Field

Guests have a commanding view from this Inn's Pilot's Table Restaurant and Skyriders Club — jets are continuously arriving and departing. Incidentally, the Inn is not under flight pattern. Dallas is an important aviation center and the site of a Naval Air Training Station and Air Base. People fly in here from all over the world and are never disappointed with the Inn's continental cuisine.

SHRIMP DE JONGHE

½ cup butter
½ teaspoon salt
¼ teaspoon pepper
¾ cup fine dry bread crumbs
2 cloves garlic, crushed or minced
1 tablespoon finely chopped parsley
1½ teaspoons finely chopped chives
1 teaspoon minced onion
¼ teaspoon Worcestershire sauce

Cream butter, salt and pepper until butter is softened and fluffy. Add ½ cup bread crumbs and blend well. Stir in garlic, parsley, chives, onion and Worcestershire sauce. Wrap mixture in wax paper, roll into a cylinder about the size of half dollar and put into refrigerator until ready to use. Use reserve crumbs for topping. Makes 1 cylinder (approximately 1 cup).

Spread 1½-2 pounds fresh raw shrimp (cleaned, cooked and peeled) in a shallow baking dish or in individual dishes. Dot with butter mixture and bake at 375 degrees for 20 to 25 minutes, or until golden. Serves 4 to 6.

Dallas, Tex.
Market Center

N. Industrial Blvd. & I-35

Going to market? This is the Inn to stay only 2 blocks from the Apparel Mart, Trade Mart and Furniture Mart. It's located right at the edge of the industrial area too. But you don't have to go to market to enjoy the superb Mexican dishes served in the western dining room. Find out why Enchiladas and Carne Asada are the most ordered.

ENCHILADAS

12 to 18 tortillas
½ cup salad oil
1½ cups grated Cheddar cheese
1 onion, chopped
2½ cups chili con carne
½ teaspoon chili powder

Dip tortillas in hot salad oil until softened. Drain well. Mix cheese with the onion. Spread each tortilla with Chili Con Carne and roll up. Place open side down in buttered casserole. Pour rest of chili on rolled tortillas. Sprinkle with cheese and onion mixture. Season with chili powder. Bake in 350 degree oven until bubbly, about 10 minutes. Allow at least 2 for each person.

Chili Con Carne

1 pound ground beef
¼ cup salad oil
1 tablespoon onion, chopped
1 clove garlic, chopped
4 red chile pods
1 teaspoon cumin seed, ground
2 teaspoons salt
½ tablespoon chili powder
1 tablespoon corn meal
1 tablespoon flour

Brown beef in oil, adding onion and garlic. Cook until all is brown. Soften chile pods in warm water to remove seeds and add. Stir seasonings in mixture, then blend in corn meal and flour. Add 1 cup water and simmer until quite thick. Makes 4 cups.

Dallas, Tex. Northwest

I-35 E. & U.S. 77

If you want to stay in the heart of the Greater Northwest Dallas industrial area, this is the Inn. Enjoy free transportation to and from the airport 8 miles away. Let them entertain you in the Captain's Corner, the Inn's popular private club. Texas-size steaks are featured in the Captain's Table Dining Room. There are daily luncheon buffets.

FRENCH FRIED SHRIMP

1½ pounds shelled shrimp
½ cup fine cracker crumbs
½ teaspoon garlic salt
1 teaspoon salt
¼ cup flour
2 eggs plus 2 tablespoons water
Cooking oil

Remove dark vein from jumbo shrimp. Combine crumbs, salts and flour. Dip shrimp in beaten eggs and water mixture, then in crumbs. Place in deep fat frying basket and cook 5 to 8 minutes, depending on size of shrimp. Deep fat should be heated 365 degrees for frying shrimp. Drain on absorbent paper. Serve with Shrimp Sauce. Serves 4 to 5.

Shrimp Sauce

½ cup catsup or chili sauce
3 tablespoons lemon juice
1 tablespoon horseradish
2 drops Tabasco
Few grains garlic salt
¼ teaspoon salt
2 teaspoons Worcestershire sauce

Mix all ingredients and place in individual servers.

Dallas, Tex. West

183 at Loop 12, Irving, Tex.

A two-hole Pitch and Putt Golf Course is on the grounds. There are outdoor patio dinners from charcoal broilers. The Terrace Dining Room inside offers a fascinating array of dishes, including Polynesian and Mexican. The only thing halfway about this Inn is its location. It's between Dallas and Fort Worth. And it's between Six Flags Over Texas and the Texas State Fair Grounds.

PORK CHOPS, HAWAIIAN

4 5-ounce pork chops
1 tablespoon cooking oil
1 tablespoon chopped onion
1 tablespoon sliced almonds
½ cup pineapple juice
½ cup pineapple chunks
1 tablespoon sugar

Dust pork chops with seasoned flour. Cook in hot oil until brown on both sides. Add chopped onion and almonds and continue to cook for 2 minutes. Add remaining ingredients. Cover and cook over low heat until pork chops are tender. Serves 4.

CHICKEN AND RICE MEXICALI

1 2-pound fryer
3 tablespoons cooking oil
2 tablespoons chopped onion
1 teaspoon paprika
¼ cup white rice
1 small bell pepper, julienne
1 cup peeled tomatoes
1 pinch powdered garlic
1 cup chicken stock

Heat oil in French skillet. Cook chicken until brown on both sides. Add chopped onion, paprika and rice and continue cooking for 3 minutes. Add remaining ingredients and salt and pepper to taste. Cover and continue to cook at low heat until rice is done. Makes 2 generous servings.

Del Rio, Tex.

U.S. 90 and 227

Expect South of the Border flavor in the food served here. Enjoy western specialties . . . ranch beans and smoky bar-b-que dishes, plus all the Mexican favorites that "chiles" complement. The most pampered way to explore this enchanting country is to stay at this Inn. Just across the Rio Grande you'll find Cuidad Acuna and Mexican National Parks. On the Texas side, take time to enjoy recreation at Amistad Dam and Reservoir.

PORTUGUESE TORTILLAS

    6 cups Chili con Carne
   16 corn tortillas
    8 slices onion
    8 slices tomato
    2 cups longhorn cheese

Make Chili con Carne and keep hot. Cut tortillas in quarter-inch strips. Deep fry in hot oil until crisp. Chop onion and tomatoes. Grate cheese. Add to hot chili con carne to form a creamy sauce. Place strips of tortillas on dinner plates. Pour hot sauce over the tortilla strips and serve hot. Serves 4.

Chili con Carne

    2 pounds ground beef
    ½ cup chopped onion
    2 tablespoons cooking oil
    6 chiles (or 2 to 3 tablespoons chili
      powder)
    1 clove garlic, crushed
    1 teaspoon oregano
    ¼ teaspoon ground cumin seed
      Salt

Have beef ground coarse. Brown meat and cook onion in hot oil. Soak chiles in warm water to cover until soft (15 to 20 minutes). Drain and remove seeds. Grind chiles, garlic and oregano to make a paste. Add ½ cup water and ½ cup water in which chiles were soaked. Combine with beef mixture. Add cumin seed and salt to taste. Cover and simmer for about 1 hour.

Denison, Tex.

U.S. 75 and U.S. 69

Dwight D. Eisenhower was born in a two story frame house only a mile from this Inn. His home has been restored and is now in the Eisenhower Birthplace State Park. The Dallas-Fort Worth metro area is only an hour's drive away. Try to resist the hot homemade cinnamon rolls served here. Everything is delicious . . . steaks, Mexican food and especially the homemade lemon pie.

PEKING ROAST

(Old Chinese Recipe)

    3-pound beef brisket
      (or inexpensive cut of roast)
      Onion buds
      Garlic cloves
      Vinegar
      Strong black coffee
      Salt
      Pepper

Tie brisket into compact shape. Cut slits completely through roast and stuff with onion and garlic buds. Place in glass bowl, cover with vinegar and leave covered in refrigerator for 24 to 48 hours. Drain vinegar and brown roast on top of stove in greased heavy skillet until browned all over (very brown). Then place in roaster and cover with strong black coffee. Cover roaster and cook 6 to 8 hours at 250 degrees. Do not use salt and pepper until last hour of cooking. To make excellent dark gravy, thicken with 2 tablespoons flour blended in ¼ cup water. Serves 4 to 6.

Denton, Tex.

I-35, U.S. 77, Dallas Hwy.

It's not surprising that the "Plantation Service" here charms visitors. Whether in Denton for pleasure or business, you'll find traditional hospitality at this Holiday Inn. Huge steaks are just one popular entrée on the menu. North Texas State University and Texas Woman's University are both nearby. The Inn is only 35 minutes from Dallas. Transportation is available from Love Field, 33 miles away.

COO COO PIES

(Chicken or Turkey Turnovers)

2 cups cooked turkey or chicken
2 tablespoons flour
2 tablespoons butter
1 pint hot milk
  Salt
  Pepper
½ cup mushrooms, stems & pieces
  (sauté in butter if fresh)

Blend flour and butter. Add to hot milk gradually and stir until thickened. Season. Mix enough of sauce with chicken or turkey and mushrooms so it will be moist for turnovers. Let cool. Roll Pastry in large sheet ¼ inch thick. Cut into 6-inch squares. Place ⅓ cup (or more) turkey or chicken mixture on each. Turn each square and seal, pricking edges to form turnover. Bake in a 425 degree oven for 20 to 30 minutes, until pastry is brown and cooked. Serve with cream sauce left to which mushrooms have been added. Serves 6.

Pastry

Sift 2 cups flour and 1 teaspoon salt. Add ¾ cup shortening and cut in with fork. Add 6-8 tablespoons water until ingredients hold together. Knead lightly. Form into ball. Chill and roll.

El Paso, Tex.
Airport Interstate

I-10 at Airways Blvd.

Welcome to a wonderful world of contrasts . . . the easy living of Mexico and the fast excitement of El Paso. The Inn's architecture blends into the landscape on three levels. You can expect lanterns and carved chests from Mexico, picturesque bridges, waterfalls and striking decor throughout the Inn. Flaming foods in the Club Holiday are memorable. The Inn is adjacent to the airport. It's near Juarez, Mexico and Carlsbad Caverns.

CARNE ASADA

Charcoal broil a 9-ounce filet mignon for each serving. Paint often with Bourbon-Butter Sauce. When cooked to desired doneness, place ½-inch thick slices of canned green chiles on steak and garnish with sautéed mushrooms. Serve with Frijoles Refritos (fried beans) and guacamole.

Bourbon-Butter Sauce

Combine ¼ pound butter and 1½ ounces bourbon. Cream the butter to consistency of mayonnaise.

DELMONICO ENTRECOTE

For each portion charcoal broil a 12-ounce center cut rib eye steak to suit taste. Just before steak is removed from broiler, cover with a thick layer of Roquefort Sauce. Let the crumbs of Roquefort melt slightly as it is served.

Roquefort Sauce

Crumble ½ pound Roquefort into 1 pint olive oil. Add 1 large clove quartered garlic. Let marinate overnight. Shake well before using each time. Makes approximately 3 cups sauce.

Ft. Worth, Tex.
Midtown

U.S. 80, 180 & I-20

Texas Christian University is only 2 minutes from this popular-with-parents-and-students Holiday Inn. The Inn is only 5 minutes from downtown Fort Worth. You can expect Texas-size welcomes (and steaks) in the Inn's Copper Hearth Restaurant. The Texas West is said to have begun in Fort Worth, one of the greatest of all the old cow towns.

BEEF BRISKET

6-pound beef brisket
1 tablespoon salt
1 ounce Accent
2 teaspoons black pepper
1 tablespoon chili powder
1½ teaspoons bay leaves (ground)
1 tablespoon garlic powder
1 tablespoon cornstarch
3 tablespoons beef base

Mix ingredients and rub into beef brisket the day before cooking meat. Do not baste or turn meat while cooking. Cook at 250 degrees for 2-3 hours. After cooking place in refrigerator. After grease comes to top skim all of it off. Add water to make "Au Jus" and serve heated with reheated beef. 6-8 servings.

BARBEQUE RIB SAUCE

2 teaspoons sage
1½ tablespoons sugar
1½ teaspoons salt
1½ teaspoons black pepper
2 tablespoons lemon juice
2 tablespoons paprika
1 tablespoon cornstarch
1 ounce Accent
1 tablespoon chicken base

Mix ingredients and rub into ribs or chicken the day before cooking. Cover and place in refrigerator. When cooking do not baste or turn. Cook at 250 degrees until done (1-2½ hours). 1 cup seasoning.

Ft. Worth, Tex.
West

U.S. 80-180 W. at Tex. 183

It's cowboy country and western foods (especially steaks) rank first in popularity at this Holiday Inn. But the Venetian Club is something else. The old world elegance and charm of canal laced Venice has come to Texas. Guests enjoy continental dining, dancing and entertainment. Shoppers enjoy being within a block of Neiman-Marcus (Ft. Worth Branch).

LASAGNE A LA VENETIAN

1 pound ground beef
1 pound ground pork
¼ cup finely chopped onion
1 clove garlic
2 tablespoons salad or olive oil
2 tablespoons grated Parmesan cheese
3 tablespoons chopped parsley
½ teaspoon oregano
1 teaspoon sweet basil
1 teaspoon salt
2 teaspoons ground pepper
2 14-ounce cans whole tomatoes
2 6-ounce cans tomato sauce

Sauté onion and garlic in oil until golden. Remove garlic. Add ground meat, breaking apart with fork. Cook until browned, then pour off excess grease. Add 2 tablespoons Parmesan cheese and parsley. Mix well, then add oregano, basil, salt and pepper. Stir in tomatoes and tomato sauce. Simmer for 1 hour, covered. Preheat oven to 375 degrees. Lightly grease a large casserole. Prepare 1 large package lasagne noodles according to directions on package. Layer ingredients in baking dish in the following order: lasagne noodles, 6 ounces mozzarella cheese, 6 ounces Provolone cheese, meat sauce, 1½ cups cottage cheese, 1½ cups Parmesan cheese. Bake 45 minutes. Serves 24 for a buffet.

Galveston, Tex.

600 Strand. Adj. to Yacht Basin

Galveston's Holiday Inn is located in the family resort area of Galveston Island. There's a large swimming pool, picnic area and a view of over 100 sailing crafts at their marina from the Inn. 32 miles of sandy beach, outstanding fishing and Country Club golf privileges are nearby. Exceptional seafood is the order of everyday in the Captain's Table Dining Room. The University of Texas Medical Branch is opposite the Inn.

SEASHELL GALVESTON

1 pound ground beef
1 pound fresh or frozen shrimp
1 medium onion, chopped
1 green pepper, diced
   Butter
1 small can diced mushrooms
½ teaspoon salt
½ teaspoon pepper
½ teaspoon rosemary
½ teaspoon oregano
2 ounces sauterne wine
2 tomatoes
½ head lettuce

Sauté beef, onion, and green pepper in butter over a medium high heat until brown. Remove from pan and repeat process with shrimp and mushrooms. Mix beef, onion and green pepper with shrimp and mushrooms. Add all spices. Add wine and let simmer for 5 minutes. Shred lettuce and tomatoes and add to mixture. Toss lightly until warm. May be served in an abalone shell with hot French rolls and a Rosé wine. Serves 4.

Greenville, Tex.

Interstate 30 and U.S. 69

What a shame travelers going through Greenville on the Old Chisholm Trail of yesteryear couldn't stop at this luxurious Holiday Inn. A warm welcome and every modern comfort keeps the Inn in step with the aerospace industry in the city. The homemade cream pies are unforgettable. Lake Tawakoni is only 15 minutes away and offers fishing, boating, duck hunting and water birds.

ASPARAGUS MOUSSE

2 cups green asparagus (canned)
1 cup hot liquid
   (asparagus liquid plus water)
1 tablespoon gelatin (dissolved in ¼ cup cold water)

Heat liquid and pour over dissolved gelatin. When partially set, fold in ½ cup mayonnaise, ½ cup whipped cream, 1 teaspoon salt and 2 tablespoons lemon juice. Add asparagus (cut in pieces) and pour in mold. Serve with mayonnaise whipped with a little lemon juice. Serves 12.

TEXAS GRITS

1½ cups grits
1½ sticks butter
1 pound grated Cheddar cheese
3 teaspoons savory salt
2 teaspoons salt
   Paprika
   Dash Tabasco sauce
3 beaten eggs

Bring 6 cups of water to a boil, add grits slowly and cook until done. Add remaining ingredients, except eggs. Stir until cheese and butter melt. Beat eggs and add. Turn into greased baking dish. Bake at 250 degrees for 1½ hours. Serves 8-10.

Houston, Tex.
Astroworld

Interstate 610 & Kirby Drive

A world of fun awaits you at this Inn near the Astrodome (the 8th Wonder of the World). Tours of the Astrodome, as well as tours of Houston, NASA, Galveston, and deep sea fishing parties may be arranged at the Inn. Delicious food and live entertainment in the Rhubarb Club of this luxurious Inn make it the "sportiest place to stay."

IMPERIAL CRAB

1¼ pounds crab meat flakes
5 ounces haddock fillet, cooked
⅔ cup (scant) white bread cubes
3 large eggs
½ teaspoon dry mustard
1½ teaspoons Worcestershire sauce
¾ cup mayonnaise
2 teaspoons salt
¼ cup green peppers, diced
¼ cup canned pimentoes, diced
1½ teaspoon granulated sugar
½ teaspoon Spanish paprika
⅛ teaspoon cayenne pepper

Flake crab meat and remove any cartilage. Flake cooled haddock to size of crab meat. Mix lightly but thoroughly. Add diced bread and toss lightly. Mix all other ingredients separately. Add to crab mixture. Mix lightly, but well. Pack a scant ⅔ cup into each shell or ramekin. Cover lightly with mayonnaise. Sprinkle top with paprika and brown under broiler until mixture is thoroughly heated or bake at 400 degrees until golden brown, approximately 20 minutes. Sprinkle top with chopped parsley when serving. Serves 8.

Houston, Tex.
North

U.S. 75, 90 & I-45

A relish tray and individual loaf of bread welcome you into the private Club Casbah for dinner. Authentic Spanish food is gourmet fare in the Empire Room Restaurant. Fishermen guests enjoy having the chef prepare their own red snapper, flounder or trout for dinner. Everyone enjoys a slide into the pool at the end of a day.

ARROZ CON POLLO
A LA VERACRUZANA

(Chicken and Rice)

2 fresh fryers (no more than two pounds)
2 cups cooking oil
3 cups rice (Uncle Ben's)
4 cloves garlic
1¼ cups chopped onions
3 cups fresh tomatoes, chopped
1 tablespoon salt
1 tablespoon white pepper
1 cup tomato juice
½ cup capers
¾ cup stuffed olives
5 tablespoons hot sauce
½ tablespoon cumin seeds

Cut chicken into small pieces and boil until tender. Drain chicken and save broth. Heat cooking oil in a large frying pan. Add rice and fry to a golden brown. Add garlic (whole cloves) and chopped onions. Fry for 5 minutes. Add chopped tomatoes, salt and pepper and chicken pieces. Pour remaining chicken broth and tomato juice into rice mixture. Add capers, stuffed olives, hot sauce and cumin seeds. Cook over low heat (do not stir) until rice is fluffy and tender. Serves 6 to 8.

Houston, Tex.
West

I-10W & U.S. 90W, Katy Frwy.

Guests always enjoy excellent service as they savour delicious cuisine amid lush tropical plants and trees in the Capri Dining Room. Chestnut Shrimp are the highlight on every buffet table. The Inn is 9 miles from the heart of downtown and only 20 minutes from the Astrodome. Everyone enjoys a trip to the Port of Houston.

CHESTNUT SHRIMP

    10 to 12 large raw shrimp
     1 beaten egg
     1 tablespoon water
    ¼ cup flour
    ½ cup crushed saltine crackers
    ¼ teaspoon garlic powder
     2 teaspoons parsley flakes
    ¼ cup sliced almonds
    ¼ teaspoon Accent
       Salt and pepper to taste

Peel and devein shrimp. Wash thoroughly. Dip in egg batter (egg beaten with water), then in flour and in batter again. Combine remaining ingredients for breading mixture. Dip shrimp in mixture. Fry in shortening to cover until golden brown (2 to 3 minutes). Serve with broiled tomatoes and rice. Serves 2 to 3.

TART ORANGE SALAD

Dissolve 1 6-ounce package orange Jello in 1 cup boiling water. Sprinkle ¼ cup sugar over 2 cups diced oranges and let set for 10 minutes. Drain 1 cup crushed pineapple, but save juice. Add enough water to pineapple juice to make 1 cup and add to Jello. When Jello begins to set, add fruit and chill. Serve on crisp salad greens. Serves 6 to 8.

Houston, Tex.
West Loop

3131 W. Loop, S. (I-610 S.)

Don't pass by the luncheon buffets in the Pin Oak Restaurant here. The line-up offers Steamship Round of Beef, Charcoal Broiled Flank Steak, Fried Oysters, Prime Rib and more. The Pin Oak Club hosts two dance bands nightly, one for cocktail hour, another for later on. Daily tours are arranged at the Inn to the nearby Astrodome, San Jacinto Battleground, including a tour of the Battleship Texas.

RED SNAPPER PONTCHARTRAIN
(New Orleans Style)

    1½ pounds red snapper fillets
    12 shrimp (15-20 count)
     2 cups Alaskan king crab meat

Flour red snapper fillets and fry in a buttered skillet until golden brown. Sauté shrimp and crab meat in ½ pound margarine.

Combine 2 cups Pontchartrain Sauce with crab meat and shrimp. Place ½ cup of this mixture on each browned red snapper fillet. Pour ½ cup sauce on each stuffed fillet and place in a 350 degree oven for 15 minutes. Serves 4 to 6.

Pontchartrain Sauce

    ½ cup flour
     4 cups beef bouillon
     3 cups water
     2 tablespoons paprika
       Dash salt
     1 teaspoon Accent
       White cherry wine to taste

Mix flour with a little water for thickening. Add flour-water mixture to bouillon and water. Add seasonings and stir until right consistency. Add wine. Makes 4 cups.

Laredo, Tex.

U.S. 81 N. & Interstate 35

This is a romantic city of bull fights and fiestas on the Rio Grande River. The Inn is only 5 minutes from the International Bridge to Mexico. In the Inn's lobby, personnel from a Mexican insurance agency advise and help those going to Mexico. Mexican specialties delight everyone in the dining room.

CHOCOLATE CREAM PIE

2 cups sweet milk
1 cup sugar
2 ounces unsweetened chocolate
¼ teaspoon salt
2 tablespoons cornstarch
2 tablespoons pastry flour
½ cup warm milk
1 beaten egg
2 beaten egg yolks
1 teaspoon vanilla
2 tablespoons butter
2 egg whites
4 tablespoons sugar

Place sweet milk, sugar, chocolate and salt on stove and bring to a boil. Dissolve the cornstarch and pastry flour in the warm milk. Add the warm milk slowly, forming a paste so it will have no lumps. Add eggs and egg yolks to flour-cornstarch mixture. Mix until smooth. When chocolate mixture comes to a boil, thicken with cornstarch mixture slowly, beating with a wire whip, and continue cooking until thick. Remove from heat and add vanilla. Break butter into small pieces and let melt on top. Beat egg whites. Add 4 tablespoons sugar and whip until medium stiff. Fold into chocolate mixture. Mix until smooth and place in a baked pie shell. When cool, place in refrigerator and chill. Top with whipped cream and serve. Serves 6 to 8.

Longview, Tex. - I-20

Interstate 20 at Estes Pkwy.

Stay only 3 minutes from downtown. R. G. LaTourneau College is within 6 blocks, and Kilgore College 12 miles. There's excellent fishing at nearby Cherokee Lake, Lake of the Pines and Caddo Lake. Find out why Italian Spaghetti and Meat Balls is the most popular dish on the menu in the Captain's Table Dining Room.

FRUIT AND GINGER ALE SALAD

4 3-ounce boxes lemon Jello
1½ cups boiling water
½ cup cold water
½ cup orange juice
1 cup ginger ale
3 cups fruit salad (#2½ can)

Dissolve Jello in boiling water. Add cold water, orange juice and ginger ale. Let congeal slightly. Add fruit salad and chill until set. Serve on lettuce leaf with fruit salad dressing. Serves 12.

VEAL CASSEROLE WITH RICE

2½ pounds boneless veal
½ cup fat
½ cup chopped onion
1¾ cups tomato purée
½ pint sour cream
1 teaspoon paprika
2 tablespoons all purpose flour
1 tablespoon salt
¼ teaspoon ground black pepper
3 cups stock

Cut veal in 1-inch pieces and brown in fat. Add onion and tomato purée. Combine sour cream, paprika, flour, salt and pepper. Beat together and add to first mixture. Then add stock and simmer for 1½ hours. Serve in casserole with steamed rice. Serves 8 to 10.

Lubbock, Tex.
Parkway

U.S. 82 E. & 62

The highlight of the Alamo Dining Room is a beautiful mural of Texas history covering one entire wall. But the aroma and sizzle of steaks quickly turns guests' minds from battles and victories to steaks and pastries. It's fun to adjourn to the Roman Club after dinner. The world's only Prairie Dog Community is located in nearby MacKenzie State Park.

EGGS HOLIDAY

Sauté 2 tablespoons sliced mushroom buttons and 2 tablespoons shallots in 2 tablespoons butter until slightly browned. Add 6 slightly beaten eggs to which 3 tablespoons of fresh cream have been added. Cook until the desired doneness of eggs is reached, stirring with a fork during cooking. Serves 3 to 4.

PEPPER STEAK EN CASSEROLE

    4 5- to 6-ounce filet mignon
    8 tablespoons mushrooms
    8 tablespoons onion
    8 tablespoons green pepper
    3 peppercorns
    ¼ to ½ cup butter
       Deep fried baby new potatoes

Slice mushrooms, onion and green pepper in uniform pieces. Crush peppercorns. Sauté this mixture in a small amount of the butter until tender. Cut each fillet into 2 thin slices. Quickly brown to seal in juices. Place in individual casseroles and top with sautéed vegetables. Bake in a 350 degree oven for a few minutes to blend flavors. Top with potatoes and serve en casseroles. Serves 4.

Lubbock, Tex.
South

Slaton Hwy., Hwys. 84 & 87 S.

Where but in Texas would a Holiday Inn have a 20-foot hitching post for its guests? It's not unusual to see 10 or more horse guests contentedly munching grass, while their owners enjoy a meal in the Inn's Red Carpet Restaurant. Of course there's a parking lot for those who arrive by car. But this Inn wants to please everyone. The Inn is only 10 minutes from downtown, just 4 miles from Texas Tech.

JALAPENO HORS D'OEUVRES

Use Jalapeno packed in oil and wash thoroughly, using rubber gloves to protect hands. Split lengthwise and remove seeds. Mix together equal parts of light meat tuna and grated Cheddar cheese, using only enough mayonnaise to hold the mixture together. Stuff pepper halves with the tuna mixture and serve cold.

RANCH STYLE BEANS

    2 pounds dried kidney beans
    1 large onion, chopped
    ¼ cup salt
    1 tablespoon chili powder
    1 teaspoon garlic powder
    1 cup sugar
    ½ pound butter

Boil kidney beans 3 hours in enough water to cover. Drain and save liquid. To the liquid add onion, salt, chili powder, garlic powder, sugar and butter. Boil for 1 hour and strain. Add the strained liquid back to the beans and boil for 1 more hour. Serves 10 to 12.

Marshall, Tex.

Jct. of I-20 & U.S. 59

The Sun Up Coffee Shop lives up to its name—serving hearty breakfasts to fishermen at dawn. Fish are always waiting at nearby Lake O'Pines, Caddo Lake, Lake Murval and many smaller lakes. The Gallant Knight features open hearth cooking. Guests are greeted in the dining room with a relish tray, whipped butter (made with honey) and homemade bread served on individual cutting boards. Visitors enjoy the Jefferson Pilgrimage.

GALLANT KNIGHT CHICKEN

    6 6-oz. boneless chicken breasts
    2 tablespoons sweet basil
    ¼ pound butter
    1 small can mushrooms, pieces & stems
    1 cup white wine (sauterne)
    8 slices mozzarello or white American cheese (2-oz. slices)
    Salt and pepper to taste

Place chicken in shallow pan. (Do not flour chicken.) Sprinkle sweet basil over chicken. Dot chicken with butter. Place in a preheated 375 degree oven until brown. Remove from oven and add mushrooms and wine. Put back into reduced 325 degree oven for 15 minutes. Remove from oven, then place sliced cheese on top of each piece of chicken. Put back into oven until cheese is melted. Serve immediately. Serves 6 to 8.

TONY'S VEAL BIRDS

Pound 6 4-ounce veal cutlets with a mallet. Place on each cutlet: 1-2 small anchovies and 2 strips mozzarella cheese (cut in ¼ inch strips). Roll cutlets into fingers. Use toothpicks to hold together.

Sauté veal birds in butter, adding 2 teaspoons sweet basil. Remove veal from pan after browning. Add 1 cup Burgundy to pan. Cook for 10 minutes. Serve sauce on the side. Serves 6.

McAllen, Tex.

2000 S. 10th, On St. 336

Bull fights are just a border away in Reynosa (7 miles). But you'll find it hard to leave this luxurious Holiday Inn. McAllen has a bountiful citrus crop so anticipate fresh fruits for breakfast. The dining room is popular for its authentic Mexican and American foods. There's dancing and nightly entertainment in the El Toreo Club. Excellent hunting and year round fresh water fishing are nearby.

FRIJOLES

Cook 2 cups pinto beans in 5 cups water until tender. Pour off remaining water. Mash beans and add ½ teaspoon salt and ¼ teaspoon black pepper.

SPANISH RICE

Fry 2 cups Uncle Ben's Rice until brown. Add 3 cups water and cook until rice is done. Then add ¼ cup tomatoes, 1 whole green pepper (chopped fine), ½ teaspoon cumin seeds, ¼ teaspoon garlic and salt to taste.

CHILI SAUCE

Cook 1 pound hamburger until tender. Add 5 cups water and simmer for 10 minutes. Then add ½ cup chili powder, 1 teaspoon cumin seeds, 1 whole garlic pod (chopped fine), ½ teaspoon salt, ¼ teaspoon black pepper and 2 teaspoons cornstarch. Cook over low heat until thick.

TACOS

Fold tortillas and fry until crisp. Sauté ½ pound hamburger until done. Add 1 whole chopped green pepper. Cook until tender and remove from heat. Mix in 2 whole tomatoes (chopped fine) and ½ head lettuce (chopped fine). Put in tacos.

Mt. Pleasant, Tex.

I-30, U.S. 67 & U.S. 271

Bring your rod and reel. This Inn has its own fishing lake. You can enjoy your own catch for your dinner if you like. The Inn offers Country Club golf privileges too. There's a commanding view of Holiday Lake and Texas longhorns grazing on the other side from the dining room. The Vintage Dining Room features delicious East Texas dishes. Mt. Pleasant hosts 3 annual horse shows.

FISHERMAN'S CATCH

6 fish
  Buttermilk
⅓ cup flour
⅔ cup corn meal
  Salt and pepper

Wash fish well and dip into buttermilk. Then coat in flour and corn meal which have been mixed with seasonings. Fry in a heavy skillet or kettle of hot fat 2 to 3 inches deep. Fry until brown on both sides.

CORN BREAD

1 cup boiling water
2 cups corn meal
2 eggs, beaten
1 cup buttermilk
½ teaspoon soda
1 teaspoon salt
2 tablespoons butter

Pour boiling water over corn meal and stir until it is like thick mush. Mix eggs and buttermilk to which soda has already been added. Stir well, adding salt and butter. Pour into a large hot pyrex pie pan or skillet, which has been greased with 1 tablespoon cooking oil or bacon drippings. Bake in 350 degree oven for 45 minutes. Cut in wedges. Makes 1 large pie pan of corn bread.

Odessa, Tex.

5901 E. U.S. 80

This luxurious Holiday Inn is 4 miles from downtown, between Odessa and Midland. Pioneers on westward bound wagon trains and Indians once passed near these panoramic vistas. You may enjoy the same nights of starry splendor. The Odessa Meteor Crater is nearby. The 500-foot wide crater was created when a million ton meteor struck the earth. Flaming foods are a specialty of the Inn.

HOLIDAY INN DEVILED CRAB

6 crab shells
1 tablespoon butter, melted
2 tablespoons flour
⅔ cup milk
2 egg yolks, beaten
1 cup crab meat, chopped
1 cup mushrooms, chopped
2 tablespoons sherry wine
1 teaspoon parsley, chopped
  Salt
  Pepper
4 tablespoons melted butter
5 tablespoons bread crumbs

Blend butter and flour and add milk to make a cream sauce. Cook over medium heat until thickened, adding egg yolks gradually. Let boil a couple of minutes, stirring constantly. Cool and chill 2 hours. Mix crab meat, mushrooms, sherry, parsley and season. Stir this mixture into sauce. Fill crab shells. Mix 4 tablespoons melted butter and bread crumbs and sprinkle over top. Bake in a 400 degree oven for 10 to 12 minutes. Serves 6.

Paris, Tex.

N. Loop 286, Hwy. 271

Visitors smell clover as they approach this Inn in the honey bee country of the Red River Valley. Daily trips are made to the Farmers' Market in nearby Blossom for fresh vegetables served at the Inn. Texas steaks and rib roasts are old favorites here. A marker nearby shows the tree Davy Crockett slept under on his way to the Alamo.

BREAST OF TURKEY MORNAY

On a very thin slice of baked ham, place 3 medium asparagus spears and top with a slice of turkey breast. Pour Sauce Mornay over all and sprinkle with 2 generous tablespoons of Parmesan cheese and sprinkle lightly with paprika to add a touch of color. Just before serving, put under broiler until bubbly and golden brown. Garnish with spiced apricots and a sprig of parsley. Serves 1.

Sauce Mornay

Mix 3 slightly beaten eggs with a little cream and combine with Béchamel Sauce. Cook and stir constantly until it just reaches the boiling point. Add 2 tablespoons butter and 2 ounces sherry wine. To achieve the golden brown, reserve a small portion of the Mornay sauce and fold in 2 tablespoons whipped cream and spread it over the top before putting under the broiler. Makes 1½ cups.

Béchamel Sauce

Melt 2 tablespoons butter and stir in 2 tablespoons flour. Add ½ cup milk and ½ cup meat stock or vegetable stock. Cook until smooth. Season with salt and pepper. An egg yolk may be added (slightly beaten) but do not boil after addition. Makes 1 cup.

San Angelo, Tex.

Concho Dr. at Concho River

The only thing this Inn overlooks is the Concho River. The spacious dining room has a view of the river and city park. Everything is at your doorstep and delicious southern dishes are inside. The Inn is ½ a mile from Ft. Concho. The Ft. Concho Museum displays equipment used by soldiers stationed here during pioneer days. San Angelo's Experimental Educational System is world renowned.

HAM AND MACARONI CASSEROLE AU GRATIN

    ½ pound (1½ cups) macaroni
    2 tablespoons butter
    ¼ cup diced onion
    ¼ cup diced celery
    ¼ pound diced cooked ham
    2 tablespoons chopped red peppers
      Salt and pepper
    1½ pints Supreme Cheese Sauce
      Cracker crumbs

Cook macaroni and wash. Sauté onion and celery in butter until soft, but not browned. Mix macaroni, onion, celery, ham, red peppers, salt and pepper to taste. Add. Stir in Supreme Cheese Sauce. Put in baking dish, top with cracker crumbs and bake in a 350 degree oven for 35 minutes. Serves 6 to 8.

Supreme Cheese Sauce

Heat 1 pint milk, 1 cup chicken stock (or chicken base) and salt and pepper to taste. Bring to a boil. Thicken with a roux (2 tablespoons butter and 2 tablespoons flour) to a heavy consistency. Stir in ¼ teaspoon paprika, ⅛ teaspoon nutmeg and 1 cup Cheese Whiz. Do not boil. Makes 1½ pints.

San Antonio, Tex. - NE

PanAm Hwy. I-35, U.S. 81

Fresh bread and pastries are baked right here at this Inn. And you'll be delighted with the culinary masterpieces served in the dining room. The Inn's unique Cork Lounge is the spot for relaxing. There are sights and sites to see nearby . . . Fort Sam Houston and Brackenridge Park. And this is the place to remember the Alamo. Downtown San Antonio and the airport are both only 15 minutes from the Inn. Transportation to and from the airport is compliments of the Inn.

CHICKEN LIVERS ROLANDÉ

    1 pound diced livers
    ¾ pound butter
    2 tablespoons white wine
      Cream Sauce
    3 cups boiled rice (white)
    ½ cup grated cheese

Sauté livers in butter with white wine. Add Cream Sauce. Cover bottom of a casserole with boiled white rice. Place chicken livers over rice. Sprinkle with grated cheese. Place in hot oven for 15 minutes. Serves 6.

Cream Sauce

Melt 3 tablespoons butter, add 2 tablespoons flour and blend well. Add 2½ cups boiling milk and stir until thick. Season with salt and pepper to taste. Makes 2 cups.

Sherman, Tex.

U.S. Highway 75 North

Flaming Steak Kabobs or sizzling Steaks are treats in this Inn's Brandin' Room. The Chestnut Room offers an international menu. Hot-from-the-oven sweet rolls are passed continuously. Nearby Lake Texoma is an outstanding recreational area. About 1876 the Butterfield Mail Line through Sherman made it a very important city.

BEEF STROGANOFF

    4 pounds filet of beef (¼" strips)
    ½ cup butter
    ½ cup minced onion
    ½ teaspoon garlic powder
    ¼ to ½ cup flour
      Beef stock or bouillon
    2 tablespoons butter
    2 tablespoons flour
    1 pound mushrooms
    1 pint sour cream

Place butter in sauté pan, add beef, onion and garlic powder. Dredge with flour. Sauté beef until brown. Cover with half water and half beef stock. Cook until tender. Blend butter and flour for roux and add to small amount of stock, then to mixture. Cook over moderate heat until it thickens. Season. Remove from heat and add mushrooms and sour cream. Serve over noodles or with wild rice. Serves 12.

THOUSAND ISLAND DRESSING

    1 quart mayonnaise
    ½ cup sweet relish
    ¾ cup catsup

Mix all ingredients and chill before serving. For a Louie' Dressing, add ½ cup strained honey. Makes 1 quart.

Sweetwater, Tex.

I-20 and Georgia Ave.

It's hard to lasso a room during the Annual Rattlesnake Roundup in March. It's the largest of its kind in the world. Sweetwater hosts the world's largest Junior Indoor Rodeo and Texas' largest All-Girl Rodeo. Mexican food is the specialty of the Inn. Be sure to order the Acapulco Platter, the most popular dish on the menu. Spanish decor and a figure eight swimming pool are two more extras at this popular Inn.

CHILE CON QUESO DIP

½ cup onion, chopped
2 tablespoons butter
2 teaspoons green chile pepper, minced
1 cup tomatoes
   (canned whole tomatoes)
1 clove garlic, mashed
1 teaspoon salt
1 cup water
1 pound American cheese, grated
1 pound Cheddar cheese, grated

Sauté onion in butter. Add chile peppers, tomatoes and garlic, then seasonings. Add water and simmer for 10 to 15 minutes. Blend flour with a little water and add with cheese. Keep warm in a chafing dish. Makes about 4 cups.

AVOCADO DIP

1 large avocado
½ cup sour cream
½ teaspoon salt
1½ teaspoons lemon juice
   Dash hot pepper sauce

Cut avocado in half. Remove skin and seed. Place avocado in blender and then add remaining ingredients. Makes 1 cup.

Temple, Tex.

I-35 at Adams

A demitasse of soup, hush puppies and Oysters "Ernie" (compliments of the Inn) keep you deliciously occupied while you await steaks from the open grill in the dining room. Piping hot mini-loaves of homemade bread keep coming to your table. You can enjoy all of this on the Bird Creek Battle site. (The battle between Capt. John Bird and Indians was fought on the premises of the Inn).

OYSTER HORS D'OEUVRES

Select 24 oysters. Sprinkle with salt and pepper and dredge in flour. Brown oysters on both sides in butter, using a heavy skillet. Pour hot Sauce over oysters and serve immediately.

Sauce

3 tablespoons melted butter
⅓ cup fresh lemon juice
1 cup A-1 sauce
½ cup Lea and Perrins
2 jiggers sherry or Madeira

Mix all ingredients well. Heat until mixture reaches bubbling point.

ANGEL KISSES

Beat 1 cup egg whites (room temperature) with ½ teaspoon cream of tartar until they form moist peaks when mixer is raised. Beat in ¾ cup sifted granulated sugar, about 1 tablespoon at a time. Add ½ teaspoon vanilla and beat until glossy and stiff. (Not grainy.) Drop mixture by spoonfuls (12 in all) onto cookie sheet (covered with brown paper). Bake at 250 degrees for 50 minutes. Cool 10 minutes with oven door open. Remove and store in tightly covered container. Use with fruit or ice cream filling. Serves 12.

Texarkana, Tex. North

The Texas-Arkansas State Line runs through the center of the U.S. Post Office Building here. Take pictures of your family and friends standing in two states at the same time. Arkansas is only 1,000 yards from this Holiday Inn. The Inn's guests enjoy golfing privileges at the nearby Texarkana Country Club. Shrimp en Cheddar, Roast Beef au jus and Red Snapper are the most popular entrées in the appropriately named dining rooms (Arkansas Room and Texas Room).

CHICKEN LIVERS IN WINE

Sauté ½ pound whole raw mushrooms and 2 sweet peppers (chopped) in 3 tablespoons melted butter for 3 minutes. In another pan, sauté 2 pounds chicken livers in 6 tablespoons butter for 2 minutes. Combine the mushrooms and liver mixtures, ½ cup red wine, 1 bay leaf and salt and pepper to taste, and simmer for 10 minutes. Serve on hot buttered toast points. Serves 8.

STUFFED PORK CHOPS

Have the butcher cut 6 loin pork chops about 1½ inches thick and slit them to make pockets for stuffing. Sauté 1 large onion, finely chopped, in 3 tablespoons butter until it is soft but not brown. Stir in ¾ cup soft bread crumbs, 2 tablespoons chopped parsley, a pinch of nutmeg, and salt and pepper to taste. Remove the mixture from the heat and bind it with 1 egg, lightly beaten.

Fill the chops with stuffing and close the pocket with wood or metal skewers. Put the stuffed chops in a shallow baking dish and bake in a moderate 350 degree oven for about 1 hour, or until they are well cooked and browned. Serves 6.

Texas City, Tex.

This Inn is only minutes away from the city's major industries, yet overlooks Galveston Bay and Texas City Dykes. As an extra service the Inn informs guests of fishing prospects and weather bureau information. (There's excellent fishing at the Inn's door). The Anchor Room Restaurant is famous for its fresh seafood dishes. Guest privileges are extended for the Inn's Caravan Club.

FRESH SEAFOOD NEWBURG

¼ pound margarine
⅛ teaspoon paprika
¼ cup flour
1½ pints hot milk
½ cup sliced mushrooms
½ pound codfish
¼ pound shrimp (raw)
¼ pound lobster
½ pound scallops
¼ pound crab meat (dark)
½ tablespoon chopped chives
¼ teaspoon garlic powder
2 egg yolks, slightly beaten
1 tablespoon sherry

Melt margarine and add paprika. Blend in flour. Add hot milk and stir until smooth. Add mushrooms, if desired. Boil codfish, shrimp, lobster and scallops in water to cover until tender (5 to 12 minutes). Drain and add crab meat. Mix chives and garlic powder in cream sauce. Just before serving add egg yolks and sherry. Pour over seafood mixture and stir lightly. Serves 6 to 8.

Tyler, Tex.

Hwy. 69 North and Loop 323

A shaded patio for outdoor dining is popular beside this Inn's giant-size 3-way swimming pool (diving—swimming — small fry wading). Whether breakfast, lunch or dinner, the menu for every meal at the Inn's restaurant is full of good things to eat, new dishes to try. Tyler's Municipal Rose Garden has 23,700 rose bushes of over 350 varieties. There's a Rose Festival in October.

CHICKEN WITH GREEN RICE

Wash 6 chicken breasts and dry. Remove skins. Place in greased pan and season with margarine, salt, pepper and paprika. Broil at 350 degrees for about 45 minutes. The chicken should be tender and golden brown. Just before serving, pour some Mushroom Sauce over each piece and place back in oven for 5 minutes. Serve with Green Rice Squares. Serves 6.

Mushroom Sauce

Blend 2 tablespoons flour with drippings in pan. Add ½ cup mushrooms (pieces and stems or buttons) and sauté longer. Add 1 cup light cream and thicken a little. Season more if needed. Makes 1 cup.

Green Rice Squares

  3 cups rice, cooked
  1 green pepper, ground fine
  6 sprigs parsley tops, cut fine
  1 tablespoon onion juice
  ½ cup half and half
  2 beaten eggs
  ¼ pound American cheese, grated
    Salt and pepper

Combine rice with other ingredients, except cheese. Place in well greased square cooking pan. Sprinkle with cheese and bake at 350 degrees for 30 minutes. Cut in squares. Serves 6.

Victoria, Tex.

2705 E. Houston, Hwy. 59

There are supposedly more millionaires per thousand in this area than in any other part of the U.S. But there are other reasons you'll enjoy your visit here. Fresh Gulf trout are caught and served the same day at this popular Holiday Inn. Buffets feature food from every country. There's live entertainment in the Hunt Club. Daily tours leave for the Mission Church of La Bahia, which was important in the Texas Revolution.

PEPPERED ROUND

  3-pound beef roast
  1 teaspoon freshly ground pepper
    Dash peppercorn
    Dash M.S.G.
    Dash pepper sauce

Marinate roast in vinegar and water for 8 hours. Take out of marinade and prepare for roasting. Add seasonings. Use shallow roasting pan with rack preferably, so roast will not stick. Put roast fat side up in a preheated 325 degree oven and cook 30 to 40 minutes per pound, depending on doneness desired. Serves 4-6.

FRESH TROUT

Clean and wash trout. Leave whole or cut into fillets, if large. Dip in seasoned flour. Sauté in melted butter in a heavy skillet until nicely browned. Add more butter if needed and turn fish carefully with broad spatula. Serve with lemon wedges and chopped parsley. Allow 1 whole trout per person, or 1 or 2 fillets, depending on size.

Waco, Tex.
Southwest

4909 W. Waco Dr., U.S. 84 W.

Waco is in the heart of Texas and this Holiday Inn is in the midst of everything. It's only minutes away from the most major industries in the downtown section. Baylor Stadium is just ½ a mile. Lake Waco is only a short 5 minutes away. You can expect Texas-size portions in the Iron Gate Restaurant. The Red Fox Tavern is the place the Baylor games are replayed.

FRENCH FRIED ONION RINGS

    6 jumbo onions
    1 egg, beaten
  1½ cups milk
    3 ounces beer
      Flour

Skin onions and cut crosswise into slices approximately ⅓ inch thick. Separate the slices.

Combine egg, milk and beer. Dip onion slices into mixture and place them in flour to coat thoroughly.

Cook for 3 minutes or until brown in deep fryer at 350 degree heat. Fry only a few at a time. Place on paper towels to drain well. (The advantage of beer in dip is that the yeast from the beer will fluff onion rings to generous size with true crispness). Sprinkle with salt if desired. Serves 6-8.

CHARBROILED HAM STEAK

Charbroil to perfection a center cut of ham approximately 8-9 ounces. A few minutes before removing ham from broiler, place 2 canned pineapple rings (in natural juice) on broiler. Streak broiler lines on both sides of pineapple rings. Place on ham steak. Serves 1-2.

Wichita Falls, Tex.
U.S. 287 & 82 & St. 79 E.

A world of good food and excellent service awaits you at this Holiday Inn only 10 minutes from downtown Wichita Falls. Some say the steaks are the best ever. Others rave over the specialties cooked with wine. The Sheppard Air Force Base is nearby. There's fun for the whole family at Lake Kemp.

BROILED CHICKEN

Boil 2 fryers (cut in half) in the following for about 12 to 15 minutes:

    2 bay leaves, crushed
    1 tablespoon poultry seasoning
    1 cup vinegar
    1 tablespoon salt
    2 large white onions, quartered
    1 cup water (or more)

Remove from water. Dry. Broil to a golden brown, or until done (about 8 to 10 minutes). Baste while broiling with a sauce made from this mixture:

    1 cup salad oil
    1 cup sauterne wine
    1 tablespoon honey
    1 tablespoon catsup
    1 teaspoon tarragon

Serve with drippings from pan. Serves 4.

LE COQ AU VIN

Season 2 breasts of chicken and roll in flour. Heat butter in saucepan and add chicken. Add ½ cup mushrooms (stems and pieces), 4 small white onions, and ¼ cup diced salt pork to pan. Cover and allow to cook slowly for 15 minutes. Drain all the fat from saucepan. Then add 1 cup red wine, 1½ cups brown gravy and a bouquet garni and cook for 15 minutes. Season to taste and serve. Serves 4 to 6.

Burlington, Vt.

Jct. U.S. 2 & I-89, Exit 14 E.

Arrive by ferry for fun across beautiful Lake Champlain. You'll be in the land of red clover, maple sugar, Morgan Horse Farms, country auctions and covered bridges. 8 major ski areas are within a few miles. An adventure in gourmet dining awaits you at this Holiday Inn. Start the day with Vermont maple syrup covered pancakes. Scallops reign as hors d'oeuvres, in casseroles, or broiled. Vermont turkey and Maine lobster vie with baked Grecian chicken for popularity.

BROILED SCALLOPS SPANOS

    1 quart scallops
    ½ cup bread crumbs
    2 tablespoons grated cheese
    ⅔ cup drawn butter
      Amontillado sherry

Slice fresh scallops to ¼-inch thickness. Season with salt, pepper, garlic powder and Accent. Combine bread crumbs and cheese and cover scallops lightly. Pour drawn butter over all. Place in steel sizzling platter and sprinkle with sherry. Then place under broiler for 8 to 10 minutes, or until brown. Serves 6.

RIZOGALO

(Greek Rice Pudding)

Cook ⅓ cup rice in ⅓ cup boiling water until water is absorbed. Add 1 quart hot milk, dash salt and cook slowly until rice is tender. Add ¾ cup sugar and heat until sugar is dissolved. Remove pan from heat.

Beat 2 eggs and stir them into a little of mixture. Add ¼ cup butter and stir until butter melts. Pour into rice mixture.

Stir over heat until creamy. Add 1 teaspoon vanilla and pour into dessert dishes. Add sprinkle of cinnamon. Serves 6.

Alexandria, Va. Richmond Hwy.

Richmond Hwy. U.S. 1-S.

Guided tours of both Washington and Alexandria leave from the Inn daily. Mt. Vernon, George Washington's beautiful home overlooking the Potomac River, is only 10 minutes from the Inn. Old Town Alexandria, the nation's first seaport, is within 5 minutes. Gracious charm and delicious food await you in Billy Budds family room restaurant. After a day of sightseeing, take a dip in the Inn's heated pool, aim for the putting green, or just relax and make yourself at home.

MOUNT VERNON MEAT LOAF

    ½ cup cream
    2 cups soft bread crumbs
    ½ cup water
    2 eggs, well beaten
    2 teaspoons salt
    ¼ teaspoon pepper
    ½ cup chili sauce
    2 tablespoons horseradish
    ½ cup finely chopped onion
    ¼ cup finely chopped parsley
    1 pound ground beef
    ½ pound ground pork
    ½ pound ground veal

Combine cream, bread crumbs and water; let stand 5 minutes. Add remaining ingredients. Mix thoroughly. To shape, pack mixture lightly into medium-sized (1½ quart) mixing bowl. Turn out onto lightly greased baking pan. Gently score design into top with wooden spoon, if desired. Bake at 350 degrees for 1¼ hours. Remove to warm serving platter, pour ¼ cup chili sauce over, decorate with pimento strips. Serves 8.

Alexandria, Va.
Telegraph Rd.

Capitol Beltway (I-495)

Historic Colonial Alexandria is only ½ mile from this Holiday Inn. George Washington kept a townhouse here. Bygone days are reflected in Gadsby's Tavern, Carlyle House and the Apothecary Shop. This is the land of frosted mint juleps, ham and beaten biscuits mixed with old-fashioned hospitality at this Inn.

SCOTCH BEEF ROLL

2½ pounds round steak ¾" thick
2 small onions, chopped fine
2 carrots, diced
2 stalks celery, chopped fine
3 potatoes, diced
  Salt and pepper to taste
1 cup water
1 #2 can tomatoes (2½ cups)

Pound flour into steak, spread mixed vegetables onto prepared meat. Season. Roll and tie. Place in roasting pan. Add water and pour tomatoes over roll. Bake 3 hours at 350 degrees. Slice and serve with sautéed mushrooms. Serves 8.

BAKED CRAB MEAT SALAD EN CASSEROLE

1½ pounds lump crab meat
1 small onion, chopped fine
1 cup celery, chopped fine
½ teaspoon salt
¼ teaspon pepper
2 tablespoons Worcestershire sauce
1 cup mayonnaise
3 tablespoons chopped pimento
2 tablespoons melted butter
1½ cups dry bread crumbs

Mix all ingredients together. Place in buttered casserole and cover with buttered bread crumbs. Bake at 350 degrees for 30 minutes. Serves 8.

Arlington, Va.

2485 S. Glebe Rd. & I-95

Tours leave this Inn four times a day for Washington, D.C. — only 5 minutes away. The airport, Arlington Cemetery, the Pentagon, Mt. Vernon, George Washington University and American University are all within minutes. But this Inn has more than just a great location. Superb Grecian food is featured in the Charcoal Hearth Restaurant. Tip for hunters: For years guests have brought their buffalo meat to be prepared here.

PASTITSIO

2 pounds ground beef
2 onions, chopped fine
¾ cup tomato paste
½ teaspoon cinnamon
½ teaspoon allspice
½ teaspoon mint leaves, chopped
½ teaspoon parsley, chopped
1½ pounds macaroni, cooked
1 cup hard cheese, grated coarse

Sauté meat and onions in ¼ cup butter over medium heat in a heavy skillet. Add tomato paste, which has been blended with 1 cup water, cinnamon, allspice. Add salt and pepper. Cook 15 minutes, until thickened. Cool. Add 2 beaten eggs. Beat 2 more eggs and add to macaroni. Add mint and parsley. Place half of macaroni mixture in buttered casserole. Sprinkle with cheese and add a layer of meat sauce. Repeat. Pour ½ cup butter over top, then add Sauce (below). Sprinkle rest of cheese and additional cinnamon if desired. Bake at 400 degrees for 30 minutes. Serves 8.

Sauce

Heat 1 cup milk and 2 tablespoons butter for a few minutes. Gradually blend 2 tablespoons flour with 1 cup milk and stir. Add 2 well beaten eggs. Combine mixtures. Cook slowly until thick. Season.

Bristol, Va.
West

With many colleges and the Barter Theatre nearby, this Holiday Inn has guests from nearly every state during the year. Visitors also enjoy the TVA lakes, Davy Crockett's birthplace, Bristol Caverns and the Rocky Mount Historical Museum. Lush Chinese decor welcomes guests to the dining room in this downtown Inn. Everyone enjoys the fortune cookies. Specialties of the Inn are predominantly Cantonese.

CANTONESE CHICKEN

    2 pounds chicken breasts, split
    ½ teaspoon thyme
    ¼ teaspoon leaf sage
    ⅓ cup flour
      Cooking oil or peanut oil
    1 #2 can tiny new potatoes, drained
    1½ cups water
    1 small onion, sliced thin
    1 package frozen cut string beans
    ½ cup water chestnuts, sliced
    1 small piece ginger root or
    1 teaspoon dried ginger root

Mix thyme and sage with flour. Dredge chicken breasts in seasoned flour. Heat cooking oil or peanut oil in a heavy skillet and sauté chicken breasts for 25 minutes over moderate heat. Place chicken in shallow buttered casserole. Brown new potatoes in skillet and then add to casserole. Add rest of flour to skillet and stir particles left in skillet. Add water gradually and stir until smooth. Add onion, green beans and water chestnuts to casserole. Sprinkle with ginger. Pour gravy over all and bake in a 375 degree oven for 20 minutes. Serves 4.

Charlottesville, Va.
U.S. 29 N. & 250 Bypass

In the picturesque foothills of the Blue Ridge Mountains, this Inn is only minutes away from the airport and downtown, just 3 blocks from the University of Virginia. Monticello, designed and built by Thomas Jefferson, and Ashlawn, the plantation home of James Monroe, are within a few miles. Sightseeing tours may be arranged at the Inn. Southern charm coupled with sauna baths will welcome you here. Do try the delicious homemade pies.

OLD VIRGINIA SPOON BREAD

    2 cups milk
    1 cup white ground corn meal
    1 teaspoon salt
    1 teaspoon sugar
    2 tablespoons shortening
    3 eggs, separated
    2 teaspoons baking powder

Scald milk. Sift in the corn meal, slowly to avoid lumps, and cook until thickened. Add salt, sugar, shortening and beat egg yolks. When thoroughly blended, add baking powder and fold in the stiffly beaten egg whites. Turn into a well greased baking dish and bake in a 400 degree oven for 25 to 30 minutes. Serve with a spoon from dish in which it was cooked. Should be served at once as it falls like a souffle. Serves 6.

SMITHFIELD HAM LOAF

    2 pounds raw ham, ground
    1 pound raw pork, ground
    1 cup milk
    1 cup soft bread crumbs
    1 egg for every pound of meat
      Pepper
      Dry mustard

Mix well and after loaf is in baking dish, pour ¾ can tomato soup over top. Bake slowly for 2 hours with pan in a another pan which contains water to about ½ inch depth. Serves approximately 12.

Danville, Va.

U.S. 29-A Bypass & U.S. 58

A wooden bridge spanning a pool in the lobby is the only way to go— into the Holiday Room with its open charcoal hearth. Enjoy a crock of cheese and crackers while you decide between a bowl of Old-Fashioned Brunswick Stew and a slice of Virginia Ham. Expect the best Italian dishes in the Casa Italian Room and you won't be disappointed. Inquire at the Inn's desk about attending tobacco auctions.

LOBSTER NEWBURG

    ¼ cup flour
    ¼ cup butter
    1 cup milk or cream
    3 egg yolks, slightly beaten
    2 tablespoons sherry
    2 cups cooked lobster meat

Make a roux with flour and butter. Add hot milk or cream. When it begins to thicken, add egg yolks, sherry, salt and cayenne. Add lobster meat and serve over toast points or puff paste cutouts. Serves 4 to 6.

CHOCOLATE PECAN PIE

    2 ounces Bakers chocolate
    2 ounces (½ stick) butter
    ¾ cup sugar
    1 cup Karo syrup
    3 eggs
      Pinch salt
    1 teaspoon vanilla
    ¼ pound pecans, chopped coarse

Melt chocolate and butter over hot water. Combine sugar and syrup in a saucepan, bring to a boil and stir. Boil 2 minutes. Remove from heat, add chocolate mixture to hot syrup and blend. Combine eggs and salt. Beat well. Add chocolate mixture slowly, stirring constantly. Add vanilla and nuts. Stir well. Pour into an unbaked pie shell and bake at 375 degrees for 35 to 45 minutes, or until crusty and there is a puffed appearance on top.

Emporia, Va.

Intersection I-95 & U.S. 58

Hot breads, sweet rolls, real country ham and grits start your day here. Apple pie, pecan pie and pickled beets are specialties of the Inn. Emporia is right on the way to historic sites. You can expect to see tobacco, soy bean, cotton and peanut crops along your way. Emporia was once 2 villages. It still has two shopping sections as in the past.

INDIAN PUDDING

    3 cups milk
    3 tablespoons corn meal
    ⅓ cup dark molasses
    ½ cup sugar
    1 beaten egg
    1 tablespoon butter
    ¼ teaspoon salt
    ½ teaspoon ginger
    ½ teaspoon cinnamon
    ½ cup milk
      Whipped cream or ice cream

Scald 3 cups milk. Combine corn meal, molasses and stir into hot milk. Cook until thickened. Remove from heat. Add sugar, egg, butter, salt, ginger and cinnamon and mix thoroughly. Pour into a buttered baking dish and bake in a slow 300 degree oven for 30 minutes. Pour in ½ cup milk. Continue baking for 2 hours more. Serve hot. Top with whipped cream or ice cream. Serves 8.

Fredericksburg, Va.

U.S. 1 & Interstate 95

Hold hands with history while you enjoy ultra modern comfort in the heart of historic Fredericksburg. The city changed hands seven times during the Civil War Battle of Fredericksburg. George Washington's famous cherry tree incident happened here. Return to today at this Inn. Choose your own steak to be broiled on the open hearth in the Colonial Dining Room.

JAMBALAYA WITH SHRIMP

    2 pounds shrimp
    4 tablespoons butter
    2 tablespoons flour
    3 chopped onions
    1 clove garlic, chopped
    ¼ cup cooked ham
    2 cups canned tomatoes
      Salt
      Pepper
    1 teaspoon oregano
    2 cups rice
    3 cups broth or fish stock

Melt butter in a heavy skillet with a tight lid. Blend the flour in the hot fat and add the peeled and chopped onion and garlic. Cut the ham into strips and add to the onion mixture. Cook slowly until the onion is soft. Add the canned tomatoes and cook for about 10 minutes, until blended and thickened. Season to taste with salt, pepper and oregano. Add the washed rice. Use fish stock or meat broth. Cover kettle and lower heat to simmer. Let rice and seasoning cook slowly. Shell shrimp and wash well. Add to rice 9 minutes before rice is done. Serves 8.

Hampton-Newport News, Va.

I-64, Hampton, Va.

After a launching at the Newport News Shipyard, everyone goes to this Inn. The Port of Hampton Roads is connected with foreign ports by regular steamship service—this Holiday Inn offers a fascinating array of foods from other countries. Visitors enjoy the Mariners Museum in Newport News. It has one of the world's greatest collections of marine articles. Williamsburg, Va. is only 20 minutes from this Holiday Inn.

LOBSTER THERMIDOR

    2 1¼-pound lobsters
    2 chopped shallots
    1 small glass white wine
    ½ pint double cream

Cook lobster in fish stock. Cut them in half and break off the claws. Remove all the meat from the claws and the bodies and reserve the bodies without spoiling the shells. Cut the meat into small dice. Brown the shallots lightly in butter, and add the white wine. Reduce this to a quarter, then add the double cream and 1 cup Béchamel Sauce. Season with salt, cayenne pepper and chopped chervil and reduce well, until it coats the spoon. Add the meat to the sauce and continue cooking for a minute or two. Remove from the heat and finish off with a little mustard powder. Fill the shells with this mixture, sprinkle with grated Gruyere cheese and glaze under broiler. Serves 4.

Béchamel Sauce

Melt 1 tablespoon butter in a heavy pan. Stir in 2 tablespoons flour and blend. Add 1 cup hot milk and stir until it thickens. Add salt and pepper and a dash of fresh nutmeg. Last, add ¼ cup cream if desired. Heat to boiling. Makes 1 cup.

Lynchburg, Va.
North

U.S. Hwy. 29

This Inn is a favorite stopping place in central Virginia with its view of the Blue Ridge Mountains. It's located only 8 miles south of Sweet Briar College. Historic Appomattox, the Natural Bridge and Peaks of Otter are all nearby. Broiled live Maine Lobster stuffed with delicious crab meat dressing has made this Inn famous. There are exotic Polynesian dishes too.

JUMBO SHRIMP STUFFED WITH CRAB IMPERIAL

1 pound shrimp, 15 count
3 tablespoons onion, chopped fine
3 tablespoons green pepper, chopped fine
3 tablespoons celery, chopped fine
2 tablespoons butter
1 cup backfin crab meat
¼ teaspoon pepper
1 teaspoon salt
1 teaspoon MSG
½ cup (approx.) heavy Cream Sauce

Clean and devein shrimp. Sauté vegetables in butter. Fold in crab meat, pepper, salt, MSG and Cream Sauce. Be careful not to break crab lumps. Stuff each shrimp with 2 tablespoons of mixture. Sprinkle with paprika and broil until shrimp are done (about 6 to 8 minutes) and stuffing is hot and brown. Allow 5 shrimp per person. Makes 2 to 3 servings.

Cream Sauce

3 tablespoons butter
3 tablespoons flour
1 cup hot milk

Blend butter and flour. Add hot milk and stir over low heat until thick. Season. Makes approximately ½ to 1 cup.

Lynchburg, Va.
South

Rt. 29, Expressway

Nearby colleges take credit for many guests at this Inn. Randolph Macon is only 4 miles away, Lynchburg College (4 miles), Sweet Briar (16 miles), and Community College (3 miles). Businessmen enjoy its location in the center of industrial Lynchburg. The Inn is headquarters for the Lynchburg Sightseeing Tour. All this and delicious food is served in the Medallion Room.

BREADED VEAL

1½ pounds veal steak (⅜″ thick)
1 egg plus 2 tablespoons water
½ cup bread crumbs
¾ teaspoon salt

Cut veal into serving size pieces. Dip in egg beaten with water, then in crumbs mixed with salt. Place one layer thick in fryer or heavy skillet of cooking oil. Fry at 365 degrees or over medium heat on stove 4 to 6 minutes, until well browned. Drain on absorbent paper while cooking other pieces. Serve with Brown Sauce. Serves 4.

Brown Sauce

Melt 3 tablespoons butter with 5 tablespoons flour and stir until flour browns. Add 1½ cups water gradually and stir until thickened. Add seasonings. Sautéed mushrooms may also be added. If cream sauce is desired, use milk instead of water.

Martinsville, Va.

U.S. 220 North

Businessmen and tourists find warm hospitality, personalized service and delicious food here. The Inn is located near the industrial area with furniture manufacturing plants and textile mills. Racing fans enjoy the stock car races held annually at the Martinsville Speedway. Fairstone State Park is nearby—unusual stones shaped like a cross are found atop Bull Mountain.

SOUTHERN SUPPER

Corn Bread

1½ cups corn meal
1⅓ teaspoons salt
1 teaspoon sugar
1½ cups boiling water
⅛ cup butter
5 eggs, beaten
2 cups milk
1 teaspoon baking powder

Mix corn meal, salt and sugar. Scald with boiling water. Add melted butter. Add eggs to milk. Combine mixtures. Add baking powder. Pour into greased baking pan. Cook 30-40 minutes at 350 degrees. Serves 6-8.

Fried Apples

Green cooking apples
2 cups sugar
¼ pound butter

Peel and slice 4 cups green cooking apples. Add 2 cups sugar. Cook in an iron skillet slowly in ¼ pound butter until light brown. Stir occasionally. Serves 6.

Country Sausage

1½ pounds freshly ground pork sausage

Mold sausage into patties. Sauté them in a heavy skillet until done. Turn once while cooking and do not cook too fast. Serves 6.

Norfolk, Va.
Virginia Beach

Hwy. 13, Virginia Beach, Va.

Virginia Beach is only 15 minutes away. Daily tours are available through the Norfolk Naval Station and Naval Air Station, the world's largest naval military installation. The Inn's courtesy car takes guests to the tour buses, also to the airport adjoining Norfolk's Gardens-By-The-Sea. Don't miss the Inn's special "all you can eat" dinner each Saturday evening. It features the "Holiday Inn Hunk-O-Steak".

BAKED SEAFOOD SALAD

1 cup cleaned, cooked shrimp
1 cup cooked crab meat
½ to ¾ cup chopped green pepper
¼ cup minced green onion
1 cup thinly sliced celery
1 cup mayonnaise
1 teaspoon Worcestershire sauce
½ teaspoon salt
¼ teaspoon pepper
½ cup soft bread crumbs
1 tablespoon melted butter

Heat oven to 350 degrees. Cut shrimp in halves lengthwise. Flake crab meat. Combine, then add green pepper, onion, celery, mayonnaise, Worcestershire sauce, salt and pepper. Spread in a 10x6x2 inch baking dish. Toss bread crumbs with melted butter and sprinkle over salad. Bake 30 minutes, or until browned. Serve with parsley sprigs and lemon quarters. Note: This salad may be assembled and refrigerated until approximately 45 minutes before serving, then baked 30 to 40 minutes. Makes 4 generous servings.

Petersburg, Va.
South

This Inn is located in one of America's most historic spots. Petersburg played a part in the Revolutionary War, the War of 1812 and the War Between the States. The Petersburg Battlefield is the largest in the U.S. (170 square miles). Blandford Church and Centre Hill Mansion are popular tourist attractions. Petersburg is also within easy access to the seashore and the mountains. Traditional Virginia food is served at the Inn.

CHOCOLATE RUM CHIFFON PIE

Melt 2 ounces unsweetened chocolate over boiling water with 1 tablespoon strong black coffee. Stir until chocolate is melted and smooth. Then stir in ⅔ cup sugar, pinch of salt and ½ cup hot milk and cook for 3 minutes, stirring constantly. Stir in 1 envelope gelatin softened in ¼ cup cold water.

Then stir mixture over cracked ice until it is cool and thickened. Beat in 2 tablespoons rum and fold in 1½ cups cream (whipped). Pile into a baked pie shell and cover with a topping of whipped cream and sprinkle with chocolate chips. Serves 6 to 8.

ORANGE CHARLOTTE

Soften 1½ tablespoons gelatin in ⅓ cup cold water and dissolve in ⅓ cup boiling water. Strain and add 1 cup sugar, 3 tablespoons lemon juice and 1 cup orange juice. Chill in pan of ice water. When set, whip until frothy. Then add 3 stiffly beaten egg whites and fold in 2 cups cream (whipped). Turn mixture into a mold lined with fresh orange sections. Chill. When ready to serve, unmold and decorate with mint leaves. Serves 8.

Roanoke, Va.
Downtown

Watch your own breakfast being prepared in this Inn's exhibition cooking area. Dine on the patio and enjoy a beautiful view of the Shenandoah Valley while you indulge in Virginia food at its best. Visit the log cabin home of Booker T. Washington, writer, educator and founder of the Tuskegee Institute.

LOBSTER THERMIDOR

2 live lobsters, 1¼ lbs. ea.

(To kill lobsters, cut spinal cords by inserting pointed knife where tail and body meet). Wash lobster in cold water. Split each in half, starting at center of head. Place split side down in 4 tablespoons cooking oil which has been heated in a pan. Cover and cook slowly for 12 minutes.

Remove from pan and take lobster meat from shells. Cut up roughly and place shells on hot serving dish to keep warm.

Melt 2 tablespoons butter in a pan and add: 1 finely chopped onion and ½ cup dry white wine. Cook until wine has evaporated. In another pan, heat 1 tablespoon butter and stir in: 2 tablespoons flour, 1 teaspoon salt and ½ teaspoon cayenne. Stir until smooth and add ¾ cup milk. When mixture comes to a boil add: ¼ cup cream, pinch dry mustard, pinch paprika and 2 tablespoons Parmesan cheese. Combine with onion mixture. Add lobster stock if too thick.

Fold lobster meat in sauce and fill shells. Sprinkle with Parmesan cheese (grated) and add melted butter to top of each shell. Brown quickly under broiler. Serves 2.

Roanoke, Va. North

U.S. Hwy. 11 & 220 North

Roanoke is nestled in a bowl like region between the Blue Ridge and Allegheny Mountains. Only the beautiful scenery at this Inn (5 miles out from downtown) vies with the excellent food served. It's the place to stay for parents and friends visiting Hollins College, only 1 mile away. See the world's largest man-made star atop Mill Mountain. The nearby Wildheim Game Farm houses a living exhibit of rare and exotic birds, and small animals.

CHICKEN LIVER PÂTÉ

Place 1 pound chicken livers in a saucepan and cover with water. Cover pan and simmer 15-20 minutes, or until tender. Drain and wash.

Grind chicken livers and 1 hard-boiled egg. Place in mixing bowl and add: 2 tablespoons minced onion, 1½ teaspoons dry mustard, 1 teaspoon salt, ½ teaspoon nutmeg, ⅛ teaspoon cayenne pepper. Mix well. Add ½ cup softened butter and blend. Pack in bowl or crock. Serve with crackers. Makes approximately 1 pound.

BAKED APPLES

Wash, core and peel 4 apples. Place ends down in pan for steaming. Add 2 cups sugar to 1 cup boiling water, adding peelings, cores and 1½ teaspoons strawberry flavoring. Stir until sugar is dissolved, strain and pour over apples.

Place in 400 degree oven and bake covered for 30-45 minutes, until apples begin to soften. Turn apples with fork, and press down to close hole. Sprinkle with ¼ cup granulated sugar. Bake at 450 degrees another 30-40 minutes. Baste frequently. Remove as soon as apples can be pierced with fork. **Do not overbake.** Place in dessert dishes. Strain juice from pan over apples. Serves 4.

Salem, Va.

Exit 40, I-81 at Rt. 619

You can't miss Salem. It's on your way to and from so many major cities. You'll be glad you stopped after you've had a taste of the relaxing atmosphere and delicious food. Beautiful scenery surrounds Salem any season of the year. Visitors are especially entranced with the flaming fall colors. Dixie Caverns are nearby, and Roanoke College is only 3 miles away. You're in luck if you're in the area during a Song Festival.

MEAT LOAF SWIRL

    2 pounds ground beef
    ¼ cup chopped onion
    ½ cup milk
    1 slightly beaten egg
    2 teaspoons salt
      Dash pepper
 1½ cups soft bread crumbs
 1½ cups shredded raw potato
    2 tablespoons snipped parsley
    1 slightly beaten egg
    1 teaspoon sage
    ½ teaspoon salt
    ½ pound ground pork
    ¼ cup chopped onion

Combine first 6 ingredients and mix well. On foil, pat beef mixture into a 10-inch square. Combine remaining ingredients and mix well. Spread over meat. Roll up, using foil as help. Place seam side down in a shallow pan. Bake at 350 degrees for 1 hour and 15 minutes. Makes 8 to 10 servings.

Staunton, Va.
Downtown

N. Central Ave. & Lewis St.

Take time to stroll back into history, up and down the hills in Staunton. Old-fashioned hospitality and traditional food of Virginia await you at this Holiday Inn. Mary Baldwin College and Stauton Military Academy are within minutes of the Inn. Be sure to visit the birthplace of Woodrow Wilson.

FRIED CHICKEN

```
2 young frying chickens
¾ cup flour
1 teaspoon salt
¼ teaspoon pepper
3 tablespoons fat
1 cup water
```

Clean and cut chickens into halves or quarters. Wash carefully and dry, shake in bag with flour, salt and pepper. Brown chicken quickly in fat. Reduce heat, add water and simmer slowly until tender, about 30 minutes. Remove lid and let chicken fry slowly. Serve with cream gravy. Garnish with corn oysters or small corn fritters and broiled bacon. Serves 4 to 6.

YORKSHIRE PUDDING

```
1 cup beef drippings
3 eggs
1½ cups milk
2¼ cups flour
1½ teaspoons salt
¼ teaspoon white pepper
1 teaspoon nutmeg
```

Put drippings in a roast pan. Add beaten eggs, milk and flour. Add salt, white pepper and nutmeg. Pour in preheated pan (9x9 or equivalent and about ½ inch deep) and bake at 450 degrees for about 30 minutes, or until inserted knife comes out dry. Serve with Prime Rib or Roast Beef.

Waynesboro, Va.
Jct. U.S. 250 & I-64

Bring your camera. The views from this Inn atop Afton Mountain are magnificent. You look down on the beautiful Shenandoah Valley, the rolling Piedmont area, and the fabulous Blue Ridge Mountains. The Inn has its own ice skating rink and sauna baths. Gourmets especially enjoy the Flaming Sword of Beef with Wine Sauce in the Inn's popular Angus Barn Restaurant. Monticello, Ashlawn and the area's many caverns await sightseers.

FLAMING SWORD OF BEEF

```
2 pounds prime filet chunks
1 cup Red Wine Sauce
2 tablespoons cooking oil
12 large mushroom caps
12 small onions
1 cup large stuffed olives
2 green peppers, chunks
  Seasonings
¼ cup warmed cognac
6 tomatoes
  Buttered bread crumbs
```

Marinate beef in Red Wine Sauce for 1 hour. Heat oil in large skillet and sauté mushrooms 1 minute on each side. Remove and drain. Add onions to same skillet and sauté half done. Thread six skewers with marinated beef chunks and alternate with olives, mushrooms, onions, and green peppers according to color and size. Brush with marinade and season. Charcoal broil 8-10 minutes, depending on doneness of meat desired. Remove skewers from heat and sprinkle with cognac and flame. Serve on flaming skewers, placing one half a broiled tomato (with buttered crumbs on top) on each serving plate. Serves 6.

Red Wine Sauce

Combine: 1 cup dry red wine, ¼ cup vinegar, 1 cup olive oil, 1½ teaspoons salt, 1 teaspoon pepper, pinch thyme, pinch marjoram. Let stand several hours before using. Keeps several days.

Williamsburg, Va.
East

Capitol Landing Rd.

Ride in 18th century carriages. Watch craft workers in colonial dress at work in the restored shops. Children especially enjoy the daily militia drills and the musket and cannon shoots at the old Magazine. Back at this Inn you'll have the opportunity to order old favorites . . . Brunswick Stew, Sally Lunn Bread, Corn Pudding and Brandied Sweet Potatoes.

BRANDIED SWEET POTATOES

6 sweet potatoes
⅓ cup butter
⅓ cup brandy

Select medium-sized sweet potatoes. Bake until soft at 400 degrees for 1 to 1½ hours. Cut off the tops and remove pulp with a spoon. Whip the potatoes, butter and brandy together until light and fluffy. Season with salt and pepper. Fill potato shells and dust with buttered bread crumbs and nutmeg. Reheat until brown. Serves 6.

OLD WILLIAMSBURG GINGER-MOLASSES CAKE

1 cup sugar
1 cup butter
3 eggs
1 cup sour milk
2 cups molasses
3½ cups flour
2 teaspoons soda
½ teaspoon salt
1 tablespoon ginger

Mix sugar and butter thoroughly. Beat eggs into mixture. Add sour milk and molasses alternately with flour sifted with soda, salt and ginger. Bake in a greased pan in a slow oven for about 40 minutes. Makes 1 cake.

Williamsburg, Va.
West

Richmond Rd. at Wythe Ave.

Walk on the same old cobblestones that echoed the footsteps of Thomas Jefferson, Patrick Henry and George Washington. Then return to this Inn for jet age conveniences. Enjoy typical Old Williamsburg recipes and gracious dining. The Inn is only about 1,000 feet from the College of William and Mary.

SAVORY OYSTER SOUP

1 quart oysters
1 quart milk
2 tablespoons flour
2 eggs, beaten

Place oysters in saucepan with 3 tablespoons butter. Season with salt and pepper. Cover pan and cook slowly until oysters' gills begin to curl. Heat milk. Blend flour and 2 tablespoons butter and add to hot milk. Stir until thickened. Slowly add this to oysters and season. Then add eggs. Serves 4.

TOMATO-MUTTON CHOPS

4 mutton chops
4 tomatoes
Cracker meal

Place peeled and chopped tomatoes in buttered casserole. Season with salt and pepper, adding a trace of sugar. Bake in a 350 degree oven until heated thoroughly and done. Broil mutton chops until both sides are brown, allowing 12 to 15 minutes for 1-inch chops (rare is best). Serve on hot platter. Spoon cover chops with tomatoes and add a sprinkle of cracker meal. Serves 4.

Winchester, Va. - East

I-81 and U.S. 50 E.

Everybody loves apples! Just wait until you've tried them for breakfast, lunch, dinner and snack treats at this Holiday Inn — you'll find out how really wonderful apples can be. While you're in the area, visit the beautiful Shenandoah Valley and enjoy the scenic Skyline Drive. Come in the spring for apple blossom season or in the fall for harvest time. Hospitality and good food are year'round at this Inn.

WINCHESTER APPLE PIE

    5 to 7 tart apples
    2 tablespoons flour
    ¾ to 1 cup sugar
    ⅛ teaspoon salt
    1 teaspoon cinnamon
    ¼ teaspoon nutmeg
    1 recipe Pastry
    2 tablespoons butter

Pare apples and slice. Mix flour, sugar, salt and spices. Sprinkle half the mixture over pastry in pie pan. Add remaining mixture to apples. Fill pastry lined pan. Dot with butter. Adjust top crust. (Do not stretch pastry). Bake in hot oven at 450 degrees for 10 minutes, then in moderate oven at 350 degrees for 40 minutes. If apples do not seem tart add 1 tablespoon lemon juice. Grated lemon rind may also be added. Serve warm or cold. Makes 1 nine inch pie.

Pastry

    2½ cups flour
    1 teaspoon salt
    ¾ cup shortening
    5 to 6 tablespoons water

Sift flour and salt. Cut in shortening with two knives or pastry blender. Add water a little at a time using fork to make stick together. Turn out on waxed paper and press together. Form into two balls. Chill dough. Roll out on floured board and form two circles, one for bottom crust and other for top of pie. Milk may be used instead of water for a slightly browner crust and excellent flavor.

Winchester, Va. South

U.S. 11. Exit #79 on I-81

Hot Apple Pie and Fried Apples are the orders of everyday here. Winchester is the "Apple Capital of the World". You'll be glad you "picked" this Inn—Virginia Country Ham and Steaks are cooked over an open fire in the Open Hearth Restaurant. The Inn overlooks an apple orchard. Visitors from coast to coast attend the Shenandoah Apple Blossom Festival. It's always fun to tour apple orchards. Take time to see apple sauce and apple cider in the making.

SAUTEED MUSHROOMS

    1 pint mushrooms
    ½ cup chopped onion
    ¼ cup butter
    2 teaspoons salt
    1 teaspoon oregano
    1 tablespoon white pepper

Wash mushrooms (do not peel unless the skin is tough). Cut off tough ends of stems. Saute mushrooms and onion in butter, add seasonings. Cook for about 10 minutes, stirring occasionally. Serves 4, or 2 if used as a main dish.

GLAZED WINCHESTER APPLES

    6 Winchester apples
    1 cup granulated sugar
    ½ cup honey
    1 teaspoon clove powder
    1 teaspoon cinnamon
    ½ cup water

Core and slice apples into ½ inch slices. Place in shallow baking pan. Add sugar, honey, clove powder, cinnamon and water. Mix with apples in pan and dot with butter or oleo. Bake in a 400 degree oven until tender. Serves 6.

Bellevue, Wash.

11211 Main Street

You might expect whales carved of ice at The Whale Restaurant here, but a 32-foot whale sculpture, dramatically lighted! It symbolizes the city's whaling heritage. Seafood buffets are superb and diners are always pleased with the chef's specialty, "Tournedo Rossini". Relax and meet at Jonah, the Inn's bar. Try a Boston Whaler or a Harpoon. The Inn's Galley is a great place for breakfast or lunch.

HALIBUT NORWEGIENNE

- 2 pounds halibut, cut in 8 pieces
- 2 tablespoons butter
- ¼ cup flour
- ½ cup diced mushrooms
- ½ cup diced cooked shrimp

Poach halibut in stock of ½ cup white wine, 2 cups water, ½ lemon, 1 bay leaf, 1 whole clove, 5 peppercorns, a small piece celery and ½ teaspoon salt. Poach 5 minutes (do not boil).

While poaching fish, melt butter and mix with flour. Sauté mushrooms and shrimp in additional butter. Place fish in casserole and keep warm. Place 1 pint whipping cream in top of double boiler and thicken with 3 egg yolks (beaten slightly). Add 2 tablespoons cornstarch dissolved in a little water. (Beat egg yolks into cream with wire whisk, then add cornstarch gradually).

Strain fish stock and thicken with flour-butter mixture. Add egg yolk-cream mixture. Last add sautéed mushrooms and shrimp to fish and top with fish sauce. Garnish with chopped parsley. Serve with steamed rice. Serves 6 to 8.

PEAR BELLE HELENE

Scoop 4 large scoops of vanilla ice cream into a serving dish. Place 4 pear halves (peeled and cooked) on top of ice cream. Pour chocolate syrup over pears. Garnish with whipped cream. Serves 4.

Everett, Wash.

I-5 at 128th St. Exit

Everett is the home of Boeing's 747 Superjet, the world's newest and largest jet airliner. Tours of the Boeing Plant may be arranged at the Inn, only 3 miles away. The evergreen vacation region of Puget Sound is a sportsman's paradise. Breathtaking mountains are on two sides of the Inn. There's live entertainment in the Pilot's Room. Enjoy unexcelled Prime Rib beneath vintage oil paintings and wall hangings of airplanes in the dining room.

FISKEN

This is a Nordic favorite with universal appeal . . . poached fillet of sole in sauterne or sherry en casserole on white rice bed with shrimp sauce, accompanied with peas, pearl onions, and tossed salad.

- 2 pounds fillet of sole
- Milk
- 3 ounces sherry or sauterne
- 3 cups rice, cooked
- 3 cups Shrimp Sauce
- 6 sautéed mushroom buttons

Poach fillets of sole in milk 1 inch deep in a frying pan or poaching kettle. Heat milk to just below boiling point, add fillets sprinkled with salt. Reduce heat and cook until tender (try with fork to see if fish flakes easily). Add sherry and simmer last few minutes of cooking. Prepare casserole dish with cooked rice. Gently lift fish on rice and pour a little of milk sauce over it. Then add approximately ½ cup Shrimp Sauce on each fillet. Garnish with parsley and mushroom buttons. Serves 6.

Shrimp Sauce

- 2 tablespoons butter
- 2 tablespoons flour
- 1 cup fish stock
- 1 cup milk
- 1 cup cooked shrimp, in pieces

Melt butter, add flour and then liquids. Stir until thickened. Add shrimp and season to taste. Approx. 3 cups.

Seattle, Wash. South

U.S. 99, Pacific Hwy. S.

Cross Puget Sound by ferry from Seattle to a land of contrasts. Visit Chief Seattle's grave. See old Poulsbo, reminiscent of old Norway with the moored fishing fleet and century old sawmill. Board a ferry southward down Kitsap Peninsula to find quiet inlets and bays. Unusual decor and dining at its best make this Inn a favorite. Do take time to enjoy Seattle and the welcome you'll find at this Holiday Inn.

TOURNEDOS OF BEEF

2 4-ounce beef tenderloins
  Bacon
2 tablespoons butter
  Salt and pepper
1 jigger bourbon

Wrap beef tenderloins with bacon. Sauté in a heavy skillet with butter to desired doneness. Season with salt and pepper. Just before serving, add bourbon to juices. Pour over tournedos when serving. Top each with Baked Tomato Palestine. Serves 2.

Baked Tomato Palestine

2 tomatoes
1 tablespoon pilaf
1 tablespoon minced red sweet pepper
1 tablespoon cooked green peas
1 tablespoon chopped mushrooms
  Buttered bread crumbs

Cut a thin slice from stem end of tomatoes. Remove pulp with spoon and discard seeds. Invert and let drain. Add to the pulp: pilaf (or use cooked rice), minced red sweet pepper, cooked green peas and chopped mushrooms. Stuff tomatoes. Sprinkle tops with buttered bread crumbs. Bake 18-20 minutes at 400 degrees.

Seattle-Tacomo, Wash. International Airport

17338 Pacific Hwy. S.

The Sea-Tac Inn has everything — even singing waiters and waitresses to entertain while you dine. And dining is something else here — in a revolving rooftop restaurant overlooking the nation's busiest Orient orientated airport. The succulent western seafoods please everyone, going and coming. And all entrées include steamy hot 'n hearty soup, served tableside in a tureen. The fritters are not to be missed in the Country Kettle Coffee Shop.

FRITTERS

1 cup fruit
2 eggs
1 cup milk
2 cups flour
3 teaspoons baking powder
¼ teaspoon salt
1 tablespoon sugar
1 tablespoon lemon juice or wine

Prepare fruit — chop apples, slice bananas or measure whole blueberries or whole grain cooked corn, depending on type of fritter desired. Separate eggs and beat yolks slightly. Add milk. Sift dry ingredients and combine with yolk-milk mixture. Add lemon juice or wine (omit in corn fritter). Beat egg whites stiff and fold in last, for delicate textured fritter. Drop batter from spoon for size fritter desired. Fry in hot deep fat until golden and crisp on outside, but light and tender inside, turning once. Drain on absorbent paper. Dust with powdered sugar. Serve hot.

Spokane, Wash.

U.S. 2 & 10 Sunset Hill

A breathtaking view of the city and surrounding mountains is enjoyed by guests at this beautiful Inn high atop Sunset Hill. You'll also enjoy a gourmet view of fine seafoods and traditional dishes in the dining room. There's live entertainment nightly in the Can-Can Room. Bring your golf clubs. A beautiful 18-hole course adjoins the Inn. An Alpine Ski Tournament, Diamond Spur Rodeo and Lilac Festival add to the year round fun in Spokane.

SPRING CHICKEN BREAST WITH POLONAISE NOODLES

    8 whole breasts of spring chicken
    ½ cup butter
    1 quart rich chicken broth
    1 pint half and half
    ½ cup sherry wine
    1 cup bread crumbs
    2 tablespoons butter
    1 pound wide egg noodles, cooked

Remove bones from chicken breasts and dredge in seasoned flour. Sauté in butter (using a heavy skillet) until light golden brown. Remove and arrange in a buttered baking pan. Add chicken broth, cover and bake in a 375 degree oven until half of broth disappears (approx. 30-45 minutes). Blend 2 tablespoons flour in ¼ cup of the cream. Add to juices in sauté pan. Gradually add rest of cream. Thicken over medium heat for cream gravy. Pour sherry over chicken breasts, cover and cook at 300 degrees until fork tender (30-40 minutes).

Gently brown bread crumbs in butter. Toss with cooked noodles. Arrange on a serving platter with chicken. Spoon gravy over each and use sauce bowl for extra gravy. Serves 8.

Tacoma, Wash.

I-5 at Port of Tacoma Exit

Succulent Olympia oysters, freshly caught shrimp, King Salmon baked Indian style, cracked Dungeness crab and more are in store for you here. It's show time six nights a week in the Flagship Room. And sightseeing? Drive beside the blue waters of Puget Sound. See the Narrows Bridge. Explore the Old Fort. Take time to tour the Alpine Mountains.

DESSERT PANCAKES

    1 cup pancake mix
    1¼ cups milk (or less)
    1 large egg
    1 tablespoon salad oil

Combine all ingredients. Cook pancakes on a lightly greased hot griddle. Cook until small bubbles appear, then turn and finish cooking. Place pancakes on paper towels. When serving, spread each pancake with Whipped Orange Butter and roll up. Place rolled side down in a chafing dish. Spoon a small amount of orange juice over pancakes, sprinkle with powdered sugar and heat 10 minutes (or use 350 degree oven). Serve immediately with Cinnamon Syrup. Makes 18-20.

Whipped Orange Butter

    ¼ pound butter
    1 tablespoon grated orange peel
    2 tablespoons orange juice

Whip butter until fluffy, adding grated orange peel and orange juice. Double quantity if desired.

Cinnamon Syrup

    1 cup honey
    ½ teaspoon cinnamon
    Dash nutmeg

Combine and blend all ingredients.

Charleston, W. Va.
No. 1

Downtown at Elk River

The view from this Inn is the junction of the Elk and Kanawha Rivers, near where Daniel Boone lived until 1795. There's fishing in nearby Coonskin Park and snow skiing is only 10 minutes away. The Inn's popular businessmen's Beefeater Cart features Hot Roast Beef and Corned Beef weekdays at noon in the Captain's Lounge. Favorites on the dinner menu are Pompano en Papillote and Red Snapper Amandine.

POMPANO EN PAPILLOTE

Spread 1 tablespoon melted butter in center of sheet of vegetable parchment paper (foil may be used). Make a ball of ¾ cup Papillote Filling. Flatten. Place a 3-ounce pompano fillet on top and add another ¾ cup filling and flatten as before, only smaller. Bring edges of paper together and wrap securely. Bake in 350 degree oven for 20 minutes. One serving.

Pompano Papillote Filling

½ pound butter
1 medium onion, chopped fine
1½ quarts hot milk
1 cup lobster meat, cooked, chopped
1 cup shrimp, chopped
1 cup sea bass or fish fillet, raw

Sauté onion in butter until soft. Add 1 teaspoon salt, pinch nutmeg, ½ teaspoon garlic powder, ½ teaspoon hot sauce and stir. Blend in 1 cup flour and brown 1 minute.

Slowly add hot milk, stirring rapidly to make thick sauce. Add lobster, shrimp and chopped fish. Mix well.

Beat 2 eggs with 1 tablespoon cooking oil and add to sauce. Turn off heat. Let stand 20 minutes. Then cook 1½ hours over low heat, stirring often. Butter will rise to top. Cool before using. Sherry may be added. (Enough for 6-8 servings).

Huntington, W. Va.

29th St. E. Exit from I-64

South Sea island charm and Polynesian specialties await you in the popular Ma-Kiki Club. Try a Pina Party (a double whammy in a pineapple built for 2) before dinner. You'll need time to decide which exotic Polynesian dish to order. The Laredo Room specializes in pleasing the All-American appetite. The only International Nickel Co. plant in the U.S. is located in Huntington. Blenko glass is made within a few miles of the Inn.

HUNGARIAN CHEESE SOUP

2 tablespoons butter
½ large onion, diced fine
2 tablespoons flour
2 cups water
1 #2½ can tomato juice (28-oz.)
1 6-ounce can pimentos, chopped
Salt and pepper to taste
1 green pepper, chopped fine
¾ pound New York sharp cheese, grated

Melt butter in a large saucepan. Add onion and cook until onion is yellow. Stir in flour and add water while stirring. Add tomato juice, pimentos, seasonings and green pepper. Bring to boiling point, then add grated cheese. Stir until cheese melts. Sprinkle paprika on each serving. Serves 6.

CROUTONS

Spread sliced bread (preferably a day old) lightly with butter and cut into cubes. Spread out on a baking sheet. Bake at 350 degrees until brown. Excellent with soup.

Parkersburg, W. Va.

Jct. I-77 & U.S. 50

Mother Nature worked overtime around here. When the great outdoors beckons, check into this Inn. Then spend some time at the nearby North Bend State Park. The huge Wayne National Forest is not far away. This Holiday Inn is 4 miles east of downtown Parkersburg, but local residents think the delicious food served here is worth the trip. You will too. The Inn's Executive Club Lounge is a popular place to compare days at the end of each.

CHICKEN WITH ORANGE SAUCE

10 chicken breasts (6 ounce raw weight, first wing joint on)

Place chicken on greased wire rack of baking pan, skin side up. Season. Brush with melted butter. Add 1 pint chicken stock (⅜ inch deep). Bake in 400 degree oven 25 minutes or until done. Baste with Orange Sauce while baking. Serve with Orange Sauce and a sprinkle of browned almonds. Serves 10.

Orange Sauce

½ cup sliced almonds, blanched
¼ cup shredded fresh coconut
1 pint orange juice
1 pint chicken stock
1 cup fruit juice
1 teaspoon (scant) ginger, ground
¼ cup granulated sugar
¼ cup plus 1 tablespoon Clearjel

Place sliced almonds in very thin layer in large sheet pan. Bake at 350 degrees until golden brown. Follow same procedure with shredded coconut. Bring orange juice, chicken stock, and fruit juice to a boil. Add ginger and sugar, then blend in Clearjel. Add coconut, bring to a boil then remove from heat. Keep warm until ready to serve. 4-5 cups.

Wheeling, W. Va.

(At St. Clairsville, Ohio)

I-70 at Jct. Ohio 214

"Welcome to the Holiday Inn on the Mountain" is the sign you'll see as you drive up to this Inn high on Blaine Hill, overlooking the Ohio River Valley. You'll have a 20 mile view into West Virginia. You'll have a gourmet view in the Inn—when you see a "Bouquetiere" . . . a platter that's a meal with all the trimmings.

BEEF BROCHETTE

1½ pounds tenderloin tips
   (U.S. choice filet in 1-oz. cubes)
   Italian style dressing
8 small, whole white onions
16 green pepper squares
8 cherry tomatoes
   Wooden skewers

Marinate meat in Italian style dressing (enough to cover meat) for about 2 hours. Drain the meat. Then sear on a hot griddle, or in a heavy pan, until the cubes are nicely brown. The cubes must be medium rare only. Alternate meat and vegetables on 5-inch skewers: onion - meat - pepper - meat - pepper - meat - cherry tomato. Glaze with Au Jus Glaze when serving. Serves 8.

Au Jus Glaze

4 cups roast beef gravy or bouillon
¼ cup currant jelly
1 drop red food coloring
¼ cup Clearjel
1 teaspoon beef base

Bring roast beef gravy to a boil. Add currant jelly, food coloring and beef base. Simmer for 3 minutes more. Thicken with Clearjel. Strain and keep hot for serving.

Appleton, Wisc.

U.S. 41

This Inn is a vacation paradise only 5 miles from the Fox River and Lake Winnebago . . . two of Wisconsin's famous sites for fishing, hunting and water skiing. Guests look forward to the Inn's family style Friday Fish Fry and Sunday Chicken Dinner. The Dard Hunter Paper Museum displays how paper has been made from 105 A.D. until today. The largest paper mills in the world are located in the Fox River Valley.

BREAST O' TURKEY WITH HAM AU GRATIN

6 pieces white bread
6 thin slices ham
6 thin slices turkey breast
2 cups Cream Sauce
½ cup Cheddar cheese, shredded
Parmesan cheese
½ cup toasted bread crumbs

Trim the crusts from bread, toast and cut corner to corner. Place these in a long, narrow casserole with point at each end. Place slice of baked ham on each, then slice of turkey on each. Cover with Cream Sauce. Sprinkle Cheddar cheese over all and top with Parmesan cheese and toasted bread crumbs. Place casserole under broiler until crumbs are brown. Garnish with parsley. Serves 6.

Cream Sauce

Melt 3 tablespoons butter, add 4 tablespoons flour and blend. Season with ½ teaspoon salt and a dash of pepper. Add 2 cups scalded milk gradually. Stir and cook over low heat until sauce is smooth and thick. Makes 2 cups.

Eau Claire, Wisc.

I-94 Exit Hwy. 37 North

Visit the Paul Bunyon Logging Camp Museum in nearby Carson Park. The city's Hendrickson Hill Ski Jump hosts a national tournment each winter. This Holiday Inn is famous for its Fish Buffet on Friday nights. (It could be because of the Beer Batter on the fish). Country Style Stew, Sirloin Tips and Mushroom Sauce, and Sausage and German Style Potato Salad always draw a crowd to the daily noon buffets.

SIRLOIN TIPS WITH MUSHROOM SAUCE

2 pounds beef sirloin tips
(cut in strips about 1x2½ inches)
4 tablespoons butter
1 cup sliced mushrooms
2 cloves fresh garlic, minced
½ cup (4 oz.) Burgundy wine
1 quart rich beef stock
Salt, pepper and Accent
2 tablespoons cornstarch

Sauté mushrooms and garlic in 2 tablespoons butter. Add wine and beef stock. Add seasonings. Thicken with cornstarch until right consistency. Brown sirloin tips in remaining butter in a heavy skillet. Add mushroom sauce and bake 1 hour at 350 degrees. Serves 6.

BEER BATTER FOR FISH FRYS

1 cup flour
¼ teaspoon salt
¼ teaspoon Accent
1½ cups beer

Sift flour and seasonings. Blend flour with a small amount of beer, adding rest of beer gradually. Makes 2 cups.

Green Bay, Wisc.

U.S. 41 & Wisc. 32

Everyone knows this is the home of the Green Bay Packers. But everyone should also know what happens at this Inn each Monday night. It's "Beef and Champagne Night" . . . a 70-pound roast prime round of beef is served buffet style with all the champagne you can drink while dining. For sightseers Green Bay offers the Green Bay Packer Hall of Fame, and historical exhibits in the Ft. Howard Museum.

DINNER ROLLS

    1 cup milk
    4 tablespoons melted butter
    4 beaten eggs
    4 tablespoons sugar
    2 teaspoons salt
    2 yeast cakes
    1 cup lukewarm water
      Flour

Scald milk, add butter and mix. When slightly cool, add eggs and mix at a low speed. Dissolve sugar, salt and yeast in water and add to milk mixture. Add flour until right consistency for kneading. Turn out on a floured bread board and knead. Put roll mixture in a buttered bowl, butter top and cover. Let rise approximately 1 hour. Punch down, turn over and butter top. Let rise once more. Then cut to desired size, put in buttered roll pans, butter tops of rolls and let rise. Bake at 400 degrees until brown on top and lightly brown on bottom (12 to 20 minutes). Makes approximately 3 dozen rolls.

Janesville, Wisc.

U.S. 14, Wisc. 26 & I-90

The famous Wisconsin Dells are nearby. Visit the home of Carrie Jacobs Bond, composer of "I Love You Truly". The Lincoln-Tallman Homestead, a nationally known museum of early Indian relics and firearms, is within a few blocks. The Inn's Family Style Chicken Dinners and Top Sirloin Steaks are favorites.

CHICKEN MARENGO

    1 3½- to 4-pound ready-to-cook chicken
    ⅓ cup cooking oil
    1 teaspoon salt
    ¼ teaspoon pepper
    2 teaspoons Lea & Perrins
    12 small white onions, peeled
    12 medium mushrooms
    1 clove garlic, minced
    4 medium tomatoes
    2 cups chicken consomme
    ½ cup white wine

Cut chicken in 8 serving pieces, brown in cooking oil in a large frying pan. Add remaining ingredients except consomme and wine, and bake in a moderate 350 degree oven for about 1 hour, or until chicken is tender. Baste while cooking at least 3 times with consomme. Remove chicken to hot platter. Add dash of Worcestershire and wine. Cook sauce until thickened. Pour over chicken. Serves 6 to 8.

FRUIT SALAD

    6 slices canned pineapple, cut up
    2 cups Queen Anne cherries, pitted
    ½ cup blanched almonds
    ½ pound seedless fresh grapes
    ½ pound marshmallows, cut
    1 cup heavy cream, whipped

Drain fruit and pour Dressing over all. Stir gently. Chill 24 hours. Serves 8-10.

Dressing

Cook in double boiler: 2 beaten egg yolks, ¼ cup sugar, ¼ cup light cream, juice of 1½ lemons and dash salt. Stir until thick. Chill.

La Crosse, Wisc.

U.S. 16, 61 & 14

An inland boat dock and complete marine services for fishing and cruises are right here. This Inn is located on Barron Island, on the west channel of the Mississippi River. It's directly across from Pettibone Park. There's swimming, fishing and boating in the summer, ice fishing, skiing and skating in the winter. International cuisine is superb throughout the year. Saunas and live entertainment too.

ROCK CORNISH HENS STUFFED WITH WILD RICE DRESSING

    5 20-ounce Cornish hens
    ½ teaspoon salt and pepper
    ½ cup rice
    ¼ cup wild rice
    1 cup chicken stock
    ½ cup giblets, ground
    3 tablespoons minced green pepper
    ¼ cup minced celery
    2 tablespoons minced green onion
    ¼ cup butter
    1 egg
    ½ teaspoon poultry seasoning

Rub hens with salt and pepper. Cook rice in chicken stock for 25 minutes. Sauté giblets and vegetables in butter until tender. Combine with cooked rice. Beat egg and spices. Combine mixtures. Stuff the game hens lightly with the dressing. Close the openings with skewers and string. Tie the legs loosely. Place birds, breast side up, on rack in an open roasting pan. Roast approximately 45 minutes to 1 hour in a 350 degree oven until tender. Baste with drippings.

After hens are done, make gravy using pan juices. Blend 1 to 2 tablespoons flour in a little cream. Add to juices. Then add 1 cup light cream or milk. Let heat slowly, stirring until smooth and gravy is thickened. Add sliced mushrooms, if desired, before serving. Serves 5.

Madison, Wisc. - NE

Hwy. 151 North

This Capital City Holiday Inn is a great convention host. You'll find incomparable convention facilities in a resort atmosphere. 3 lakes are in the city. A beautiful indoor pool, sauna baths, putting green and shuffleboard are at the Inn. There's exceptional food too. Do try the Swiss Potato Soup. The University of Wisconsin campus sprawls 9 miles along the scenic shore of Lake Mendota.

SWISS POTATO SOUP

    2 quarts boiling water
    4-6 large potatoes, sliced thin
    2 teaspoons salt
    ½ pound bacon, diced
    2 large onions, sliced
    2 tablespoons flour
    1 teaspoon chives
    1 teaspoon pimento, chopped

Add potatoes and salt to kettle of boiling water. Cook until potatoes are partially done (still firm). Sauté bacon in heavy skillet. Add onions and cook until transparent. Add flour to bacon and onions (use only ½ of bacon fat in skillet). Make a roux. Put this mixture into boiling water and potatoes. Stir until soup is medium thick, add chives and pimento. Add additional seasoning to taste. Cook over low heat 5 to 10 minutes. Serves 8 to 10.

CONFETTI KRAUT SALAD

    1 #2½ can kraut, drained well
    ½ cup raw onion, diced
    ½ cup celery, chopped
    ½ cup pimento, chopped

Make a syrup of ¼ cup vinegar and ¾ cup sugar. Heat to boiling and pour over vegetables. Then refrigerate overnight. Serve either individually or in a dish to pass. Good with all fowl, pork or ham. Serves 8.

Milwaukee, Wisc. Central

1926 W. Wisc. at 19th

Milwaukee's Downtown Convention Center is Holiday Inn Central. (Cars can actually be driven in the exhibit area). But you don't have to come with a crowd to enjoy your stay at this luxurious Inn. It's located in the campus area of Marquette University, near the Civic Center and museum. Drop in the Coach Room for cocktails and entertainment. Order flaming gourmet dishes and pastries, from the Inn's own bakery, in The Carriage Room.

FLEMISH BEEF CARBONNADE

    4 8-ounce fairly thick beef steaks
      (from round or rump)
    2 tablespoons flour
    4 onions, sliced
    2 tablespoons shortening
    1 bottle dark beer
    1 cup light brown stock
    ½ teaspoon thyme
    ½ teaspoon rosemary
    1 bay leaf
    1 clove garlic, crushed
    1 peppercorn, crushed

Score steaks with knife. Season, dip in flour and sauté in greased frying pan. Place in a casserole on a thick layer of thinly sliced onions which have been lightly fried in shortening. Cover with another layer of onions and moisten with 1 bottle of dark beer. Add stock to frying pan and reduce. Then pour over steaks. Add herbs. Cover and cook gently in oven for about 2 hours. Skim fat and serve with boiled potatoes and mixed vegetables. Serves 4.

Milwaukee, Wisc. Midtown

Wisc. Ave. 1 blk. off I-94

Come up in the world—to the Top O' The Inn. Enjoy a panoramic view of Milwaukee's skyline while a Greek toga-clad waitress serves something tall and cool. Sumptuous seafood and many foreign dishes await you in the adjoining Voyager Dining Room. There's a Hot Sandwich Bar Buffet at noon. The Inn will arrange tours through the nearby Schlitz, Millers and Pabst Breweries.

HEUVOS RANCHERO

(Ranch Style Eggs)

    2 tablespoons butter
    1 whole tomato, chopped
    ½ onion, chopped
    3 fresh hot peppers, finely chopped
      Salt and pepper
    2 eggs

Melt butter in frying pan. Place tomato in frying pan, then add onion, hot peppers, salt and pepper to taste. Let simmer for 30 minutes. Spread sauce over 2 braised eggs. 1 portion.

FILLETS OF SOLE

    4 fillets of sole
    1 teaspoon flour
    4 eggs, beaten
    ¼ cup cream
    ¼ pint beer
      Salt to taste

Blend flour in eggs. Add cream, beer and season. Drop fillets in batter to coat. Fry in deep fat at 370 degrees until done. Serves 4.

Milwaukee, Wisc. West

Exit Wisc. 100 N. from I-94

Milwaukee is an important industrial and brewery city: (All of the breweries feature free tours). Foreign ships arrive daily at this inland seaport. Children love the Milwaukee County Zoo—within sight of the Inn. Don't miss the Fish Buffet in the Red Lantern Restaurant—it's worth staying an extra day. The Red Fox Tavern is a favorite unwinding place.

EGGPLANT PARMESAN BAKE

1 large eggplant, peeled
1 beaten egg
1 tablespoon flour
1 tablespoon bread crumbs
2 pounds ground beef
1 onion, finely chopped
1 5-ounce can tomato sauce

Cut eggplant in ¼-inch slices. Bread eggplant in the egg blended with flour and bread crumbs. Fry lightly until golden brown in cooking oil, using a heavy skillet. Sauté ground beef and chopped onion in cooking oil. Season. Add tomato sauce to cooked meat. Alternate layers of eggplant and ground beef mixture. Top with slices of American cheese. Sprinkle grated Parmesan cheese over all. Bake in a 350 degree oven for 30 minutes. 6 servings.

HOLIDAY RICE

2 cups steamed rice
3 green peppers, cut
1 small can pimento, minced

Steam rice until done. Sauté peppers in 2 tablespoons butter, using heavy frying pan. Mix with rice. Add pimento and dash of yellow food coloring. Serves 3-4.

Wausau, Wisc.

201 N. 17th Ave.

You'll never forget the buffet breakfasts or the huge red granite fireplace here. This Holiday Inn could be in Switzerland or Austria—you'd never know from the view of snow clad Rib Mountain from the Inn's ski lounge. Hearty traditional food greets guests from the slopes. Paintings by local artists are on exhibit. The Inn offers a full schedule of summer sports too.

PILAF

¼ pound wild rice
¼ pound white rice
¾ cup drained mushroom pieces, stems
¼ cup green peppers
¼ cup pimento
¼ cup diced onion
Salt and pepper
1 teaspoon salad herbs

Steam rice. Place 2 tablespoons butter or cooking oil in heavy frying pan. Mix all ingredients and grill or fry like hash brown potatoes. Serve with steaks, chops, lobster, etc. 4-5 cups.

BAKED MEAT BALLS

2½ pounds ground beef
3 eggs
Salt and pepper
¾ cup chili sauce
¼ cup onion, diced
¼ cup pepper, diced
1 cup bread crumbs

Mix all ingredients together. Make into small balls and roll in flour. Fry, then place in a deep pan. Cover with mushroom soup and bake for 1 hour slowly. Serves 8 to 10.

Casper, Wyoming

I-25 at N. Platte River

You'll know you are here when you see a sheepherder's camping wagon out front. Come for the old time Western Cookout . . . bar-b-que, turkey and open pit sirloin to enjoy with a western band to entertain. This Inn's Le Baron Dining Room has everything from Beef Wellington to Stuffed Wild Game Roast. Ft. Casper, Indian lore and vast herds of antelope, deer and buffalo are nearby attractions.

STEAK SEASONING

¼ cup salt
1 tablespoon crushed black peppercorns
   Dash garlic
1 teaspoon ground oregano
1 teaspoon M.S.G.

Rub steaks with lemon juice, sprinkle above mixture on steaks and chill. About 1 hour before cooking, remove from refrigerator and let reach room temperature. Broil over hot coals until desired doneness.

CORN ON COB

Keep freshly picked ears of corn in refrigerator until time to cook. Wash well but do not remove corn husks. Place in kettle of unsalted water, cover and bring to boil. Drain well. Remove husks and cover corn with half milk and half water. Cover and boil 5 minutes or until tender. Serve with butter, salt and pepper.

WESTERN BAR-B-QUE SAUCE

1 quart tomato catsup
1 pint tomato purée
1¼ tablespoons mustard
½ lemon (juice)
1 tablespoon brown sugar
1¼ tablespoons beef base
1 tablespoon chili powder
1 tablespoon liquid smoke
½ tablespoon caramel coloring

Mix all ingredients and simmer 1 hour. Stir often and do not let burn. Makes approximately 1 quart.

Cheyenne, Wyo.

I-25 at Central Ave.

When did you last hear a honky tonk piano player in the parlor? Step into the Parlor of this Inn—for delicious food and entertainment. The Coffee Shop is western and wild with wagon wheel lamps and branding irons. Homemade soup is served from a cast iron soup pot at your table. The old wild west is alive all summer at the Hell on Wheels Tent City.

HOMEMADE VEGETABLE SOUP

Place beef shank bone in deep pot and cover with water adding 2 tablespoons salt. Bring water to boil. Simmer 2 hours.

Prepare vegetables, cutting in small pieces:

6 stalks celery
1 large potato
1 large Bermuda onion
6 medium carrots
1 small head cabbage
2 cups canned tomatoes
2 white turnips
2 tablespoons chopped parsley

Add to beef shank, season to taste and simmer 1 hour. Approximately 2 quarts.

BREAD PUDDING

1 quart milk
3 eggs, well beaten
1 cup sugar
1 teaspoon cinnamon
1 teaspoon nutmeg
¾ teaspoon vanilla
4-6 day old sweet rolls
1 cup apples, peaches or pears

Pour milk in bowl adding eggs, sugar, cinnamon, nutmeg, and vanilla. Stir until ingredients are blended. Add chopped rolls and stir until well mixed. Add desired fruit. Cook in buttered flat baking pan for 1 hour at 350 degrees. Serve hot or cold with whipped cream. Serves 6-8.

RECIPE INDEX

RECIPE INDEX

INDEX

INDEX

INDEX

INDEX

INDEX

INDEX

INDEX

INDEX

INDEX

INDEX

INDEX

INDEX

INDEX

INDEX

INDEX

INDEX

INDEX

INDEX

Wine Sauce, 6, 112, 198
    Red, 319
Wine Spaghetti Dinner, 246

Y

Yankee Pot Roast, 176
Yeast Breads and Rolls, see Index·
    Breads, Rolls
Yellow Bird, 157

Yorkshire
    Chicken, 260
    Pudding, 21, 175, 255, 319
Yucatan Sandwich, 238

Z

Zabaglione, 21
Zucchini Casserole, 197
Zwiebel Kuchen, 153

NOTES

NOTES

NOTES

NOTES

NOTES

NOTES